ACTS
LIFE-ON-LIFE DISCIPLE MAKING

The Proclaim Commentary Series

THE PROCLAIM COMMENTARY SERIES

ACTS
LIFE-ON-LIFE DISCIPLE MAKING

NEW TESTAMENT
VOLUME 5

MATTHEW STEVEN BLACK

WENATCHEE, WASHINGTON

Acts: Life-on-Life Disciple Making (The Proclaim Commentary Series)
Copyright © 2022 by Matthew Steven Black
ISBN: 978-1-954858-29-9 (Print Book)
         978-1-954858-30-5 (eBook)

Proclaim Publishers
PO Box 2082, Wenatchee, WA 98807
proclaimpublishers.com

Cover art: *Ancient Road in Old Jerusalem*

Unless otherwise quoted, Scripture quotations are from the ESV® Bible (The Holy Bible, English Standard Version®), copyright © 2001, 2016 by Crossway, a publishing ministry of Good News Publishers. Used by permission. All rights reserved.

Scripture quotations marked NASB are taken from the New American Standard Bible®, Copyright © 1960, 1962, 1963, 1968, 1971, 1972, 1973, 1975, 1977, 1995 by The Lockman Foundation. Used by permission.

Scripture quotations marked NKJV are taken from the New King James Version®. Copyright © 1982 by Thomas Nelson. Used by permission. All rights reserved.

Scripture quotations marked NIV are taken from The Holy Bible New International Version®, NIV® Copyright © 1973, 1978, 1984, 2011 by Biblica, Inc.® Used by permission. All rights reserved worldwide.

Scripture quotations marked CSB are taken from the Christian Standard Bible®, Used by permission. All rights reserved. CSB ©2017 Holman Bible Publishers.

Scripture quotations marked NLT are taken from the Holy Bible, New Living Translation, Copyright ©1996, 2004, 2007 by Tyndale House Foundation. Used by permission of Tyndale House Publishers, Inc., Carol Stream, Illinois 60188. All rights reserved.

Scripture quotations marked KJV are taken from the King James Version of the Bible.

All rights reserved. No part of this publication may be reproduced, stored in a retrieval system or transmitted in any form by any means, electronic, mechanical, photocopy, recording or otherwise, without the prior permission of the publisher, except as provided by USA copyright law.

Notes: (1) Ancient quotations have been at times changed to the ESV as well as some archaic language updated, and additional phrases added for clarification. At times verse references (non-existent until recent times) have been interspersed as well to guide the modern reader. (2) We have done our best to be careful in footnoting. Due to the nature of the sermonic material, various items are quoted freely, and may not have proper footnoting. If any great error is noticed, please contact the publisher, and it will be remedied in whatever way is available to us.

First Printing, September 2022
Manufactured in the United States of America

Dedicated to my dear son-in-law Nathan Ball and his dear wife Kristen. You are great warriors for Christ. May you proclaim the name of Jesus wherever God leads you.

CONTENTS

ABBREVIATIONS **29**

INTRODUCTION **31**

   Date 31
   Author 32
   Message 33
   Timeline of Paul's Life 34
      Conversion 34
      Mission Trips 34
      Paul's Arrest & Death 35
   Outline 35

LIFE-ON-LIFE DISCIPLESHIP ACTS 1-12

1 | ACTS 1:1-11 CLOTHED WITH POWER **39**

      The Great Awakening in Britain 39
      A Great Awakening in Rome 40
   Structure of Acts 41
      A Geographic Outline 41
      A Biographic Outline 42
      Peter's Story 43
   Kingdom Teaching (1:1-3) 44
      The Author and Recipient 45
      40 Days of Kingdom Teaching 46
   Kingdom Power (1:4-8) 46
      The Promise of the Spirit 47
      The Baptism of the Holy Spirit 48
      The Times and Seasons 49
      The Power of the Spirit 50
   Kingdom Authority (1:9-11) 52
      The Authority in Jesus' Ascension 52
      The Authority in Jesus' Return 52
      The Authority in Jesus' Session 53

2 | ACTS 1:12-26 READY FOR REVIVAL **55**

   Ready for God to Work (1:12-14) 56
      The Place of Prayer 56
      The People of Prayer 57
      What Precedes Prayer 58
      The Power of Prayer 60

Ready for World Transformation (1:15-26) 61
   Peter the Brokenhearted 62
   Judas the Betrayer 63
   Matthias the Humble 66

3 | ACTS 2:1-13 PENTECOST 71

Two Meanings of Pentecost 73
   Feast of the First Fruits 74
   Moses Meets God Face to Face 74
The Presence of the Future (2:1) 75
   The Spirit Brings the Future Now 75
   You Have the Future Now 77
The Outpouring of The Spirit (2:2-3) 78
   The Surprise of the Holy Spirit 78
   The Wind of New Creation 78
   The Fire of God's Presence 80
   The Fire and Wind of God's Transcendence 81
The Salvation of the Nations (2:4-13) 82
   The Undoing of Babel 83
   The Filling of the Spirit 84
      A New Culture 85
      A New Amazement 85
      A New Praise 86
      A New Persecution 86

4 | ACTS 2:14-41 A WORLD CHANGING SERMON 89

Empowered by the Spirit (2:14-21) 91
   The Spirit's Moment 91
   The Spirit's Dawning 92
   The Spirit's Sunset 93
Exalting the Savior (2:22-36) 94
   Jesus Lived the Perfect Life 94
   Jesus Died the Perfect Death 97
   Jesus Resurrected from the Dead 99
   Jesus Ascended as God's King 101
Evangelizing the Sinner (2:37-41) 102
   Conviction by the Lord 102
   Conversion to the Lord 103
   Consecration to the Lord 104

5 | ACTS 2:41-47 LIFE-ON-LIFE CHURCH 109

A Church Touched by God (2:41-42) 110
   Touched by Grace 111

Touched for God's Family 112
Touched to Grow 113
   Growing in Teaching *114*
   Growing in Fellowship *115*
   Growing in Communion *116*
   Growing in Prayer *117*

A Church Together for God (2:43-46) 117
Experiencing Purity Together 117
Experiencing Power Together 118
Experiencing Provision Together 118
Experiencing Praise Together 119

A Church Telling the World (2:47) 119
A Favored People 120
A Fruitful People 120

6 | ACTS 3:1-4:4 THE LAME SHALL LEAP! 123

The Miracle (3:1-10) 125
The Lame 126
The Look 127
The Leap 128

The Message (3:11-26) 129
A Personal Message 129
A Powerful Message 130
A Profound Message 130
   Repent *130*
   Refresh & Restore *131*
   Rejoice *132*
   Reflect *132*

The Minefield (4:1-4) 133

7 | ACTS 4:1-22 NO OTHER NAME 135

The Glory of Jesus' Name (4:1-12) 136
Unbelievers Can't See Jesus' Glory 136
   The Rulers' Annoyance *136*
   The Rulers' Theology *136*
   The Rulers' Powerlessness *137*
   The Rulers' Question *138*
Believers Boldly Preach Jesus 139
   The Power of Jesus *139*
   The Name of Jesus *139*
   The Prophecy of Jesus *140*
   The Exclusivity of Jesus *141*

The Greatness of Jesus' Fame (4:13-22) 143
Those Who Promote Jesus' Fame 143
   Uneducated Men *143*

A Healed Man *144*
Those Who Oppose Jesus' Fame 145
Their Decree *146*
The Defiance *146*
Their Dilemma *146*

8 | ACTS 4:23-37 EARTH SHAKING PRAYER 149

The Confidence of Prayer (4:23-28) 150
Confidence in God as Creator of All Things 151
Confidence in God as Controller of All Things 152
Confidence in God as Conqueror of All Things 153

The Commitment of Prayer (4:29-30) 153
To Express God's Word 154
To Extend God's Hand 155
To Exalt God's Son 156

The Consequences of Prayer (4:31-37) 157
The Earth Heaves 157
The Spirit Is Received 158
Unity Is Achieved 159
The Gospel Is Believed 160
The Church Succeeds 160

9 | ACTS 5:1-11 THE DANGER OF SPIRITUAL PRETENSE 163

The Root of Pretense: Pride (5:1-4) 167
The Humility of Barnabas 167
The Harm of Doublemindedness 169

The Source of Pretense: Satan (5:3) 169

The Judgment of Pretense: Discipline (5:5-10) 171
Our Judgment as Sons in This Life 172
Our Judgment as Sinners at the Cross 173
Our Judgment as Servants 173
My Mother's Sin unto Death 174

The Defeat of Pretense: Worship (5:11) 175

10 | ACTS 5:12-42 PRISON BREAK! 177

The Growth of the Church (5:12-16) 178
Growing in Power 179
Growing in Honor 180
Growing in Number 181
Growing in Awe 181

The Grief of the Church (5:17-21a) 182
Heart Break 183
Prison Break 183

No Break!...184
The Goal of the Church (5:21b-32)..185
   A Surprise: Freedom 186
   A Sanction: Obedience 187
   A Sermon: Evangelism 188
The Glory of the Church (5:33-42) 188
   The Glory of Gamaliel's Humility 188
      Be Wary *189*
      Be Wise *190*
   The Glory of the Apostles' Courage... 191
      Glorious Suffering *191*
      Glorious Perseverance *192*
      Glorious Joy *192*
      The Glorious Gospel *193*

11 | ACTS 6:1-7 HOW DEACONS GROW THE CHURCH 195

The Difficulty (6:1-2) 196
   The Difficulty of Growth 196
   The Danger of Division 198
   The Duty of the Deacons 199
   The Dynamic of the Main Thing 200
The Deacons (6:3-6) 201
   Men with Servants' Hearts 202
   Men of a Good Reputation 202
   Men Full of Wisdom.. 203
      Know the Lord *204*
      Know the Bible *204*
      Know People *204*
   Men Who Support the Word.. 205
   Men Full of Faith 206
   Men Full of the Holy Spirit 207
      Nicolaus the Gnostic? *209*
   Men Recognized for Their Gifts 209
The Divine Favor (6:7) 210

12 | ACTS 6:8-7:60 STEPHEN'S SERMON AND MARTYRDOM.....................213

Be Willing to Stand for Christ (6:8-15) 214
   Standing with Power 214
   Standing Amidst Persecution 215
Be Willing to Speak for Christ (7:1-53) 218
   It's Not About the Land! 219
   It's Not About the Law! 222
   It's Not About the Temple! 225
   It's About Jesus (Whom They Murdered) 226

Be Willing to Suffer for Christ (7:54-60) 227
   Suffer with Victory 227
   Suffer with Trust 228
   Suffer with Compassion 229

13 | ACTS 8:1-4 INTRODUCING SAUL OF TARSUS 231

Paul the Persecutor (8:1a) 232
   Saul's Hatred 233
   Saul's History 233
   Saul's Hope 237
The Persecution (8:1b-3) 237
   The Nature of the Persecution 237
   The Nearness of the Persecution 238
   The Noise of the Persecution 239
   The Network of Persecution 239
   The Normalcy of Persecution 241
God's Plan (8:4) 241
   A Plan for the World 241
   A Plan for the Word 242

14 | ACTS 8:5-25 GREAT COMMISSION CHRISTIANS 245

We Leave Our Comfort Zone (8:5-8) 247
   The Gospel Opens New Areas 247
   The Gospel Brings New Attention 248
   The Gospel Brings New Authentication 249
   The Gospel Brings New Animation 250
We are Leery of False Conversions (8:9-13) 250
   A Famous Con Artist 251
   A False Conversion 251
We Look for the Spirit's Confirmation (8:14-24) 252
   The Unity of the Church 253
   The Purity of the Church 254
We Long for Unstoppable Conversions (8:25) 256
   Applications 256
   Evangelism at Work 257
   Evangelism with Friends 257
   Evangelism with Family 258
   Evangelism at Impossible People 258

15 | ACTS 8:26-40 THE GOSPEL TO ETHIOPIA 261

Gospel Preparation (8:25-28) 263
   The Spirit's Work 264
   The Servant's Will 265

The Seeker's Worship 266
The Scriptural Word 267
Gospel Presentation (8:29-35) 268
The Spirit 269
The Surprise 270
The Scriptures 270
The Savior 271
Gospel Transformation (8:36-40) 272
Faith in Christ 272
Confession of Christ 273
Rejoicing in Christ 274
Applications 275

16 | ACTS 9:1-19 PAUL'S CONVERSION 277

The Miracle of Saul's Conversion (9:1-3) 278
His Disgust 279
His Destination 279
His Determination 280
His Deliverance 280
The Manner of Saul's Conversion (9:4-9) 281
The Light 281
The Lord 281
The Leveling 283
The Marks of Saul's Conversion (9:10-19) 284
A Man of Prayer 284
A Man of Power 285
A Man of Purpose 287
A Man of Pain 288
A Man of Perception 289
A Man of Proclamation 289

17 | ACTS 9:17-31 SAUL'S GROWTH IN GRACE 291

A New Family (9:17–19) 292
Family Love 292
The Love of Jesus 292
The Love of the Father 293
Love Poured into Saul by the Spirit 294
Family Loyalty 294
Family Life 295
A New Faith (9:20-22) 295
Preaching the Faith 296
Proving the Faith 296
A New Fight (9:23-25) 297
A Secret Fight 298

A Spoiled Fight 298
A New Friendship (9:26-30) 299
    Rejected Friendship 300
    Redeemed Friendship 300
    Reliable Friendship 301
A New Future (9:31) 301

18 | ACTS 9:32–10:16 MIRACLES, MEALS, & MERCY FOR GENTILES 303

The Miracles (9:32-43) 304
    A Healing 305
        The Person Healed *305*
        The Power of the Healing *305*
        The Purpose of the Healing *305*
    A Resurrection 306
The Meal (10:1-16) 307
    The Meal was about a New People 307
        Cornelius is a Leader *307*
        Cornelius is a Lover of God *308*
        Cornelius is a Learner *308*
    The Meal was about a New Purpose 309
    The Meal was about a New Perspective 310
        Making People Clean *311*
        Making Peter Understand *312*
God's Mercy 312

19 | ACTS 10:17-11:18 THE POWER OF THE GOSPEL 317

Our Seeking God (10:17-23) 318
    God's Heart 318
        He Seeks without Partiality or Prejudice *319*
    God's Holy Spirit 320
    God's Instruments 321
Our Saving God (10:24-48) 322
    The Divine Call 322
        God's Divine Call to Cornelius *322*
        God's Divine Call to Peter *323*
        God's Divine Call to You *324*
    The Doctrine of Jesus 325
        The Preparation *325*
        The Proclamation *326*
        The Promise *326*
    The Display of the Spirit 327
Our Sovereign God (11:1-18) 328
    A Story of God's Sovereignty 329
    The Spirit of God's Sovereignty 330

20 | ACTS 11:19-30 THE ANTIOCH MODEL 333

A Miracle Church (11:19-21) 335
- Miracles in the Midst of Pain 335
- Miracles in the Midst of Proclamation 335
- Miracles in the Midst of a Downpour of Blessing 336

A Moldable Church (11:22-26) 337
- Moldable Through a Human Instrument 337
- Moldable Through Divine Encouragement 338
  - *Encouraged by God's Power* *338*
  - *Encouraging God's People* *338*
  - *Encouraged by God's Presence* *339*
  - *Encouraging the Church's Progress* *340*
- Moldable Through Instruction 340
- Moldable Through Sanctification 340

A Multicultural Church (11:27-30) 341
- Multicultural Mercy Ministry (11:27-30) 341
- Multicultural Membership (13:1) 342
- Multicultural Missions Movement (13:2-3) 342

21 | ACTS 12 GOD IS GOOD WHEN LIFE IS BAD 345

God is in Control Even When We Suffer (12:1-4) 346
- King Herod Agrippa I, Persecutor 346
- James, the First Apostle Martyred 348
- Peter, Fellow Sufferer 349
- The Soldiers 349
- The Application 350
  - *God's Power in Suffering is His Sovereignty* *350*
  - *God's Promise in Suffering is Discipline* *350*
  - *God's Purpose for Suffering is Conformity to Christ* *351*
  - *God's Pathway of Suffering is for Every Christian* *351*

God is in Control Even When it's Midnight (12:5-11) 351
- Midnight is a Good Time to Pray 352
- Midnight is a Good Time to Trust 352
- Midnight is a Good Time to Watch 353
- Midnight is a Good Time to Wonder 354

God's in Control When Our Faith is Weak (12:12-19) 355
- The Fact of Weak Faith 355
- The Fear of Weak Faith 356
- The Feebleness of Faith 357
- The Focus of our Faith 357
- The Forward Movement of our Faith 358

God is in Control When the Wicked Prosper (12:18-25) ... 358
- The Wicked's Power 358
- The Wicked's Peace 358

The Wicked's Praise 359
The Wicked's Punishment 359
The Word of God Prospers 360
The Witness of God Prospers 360

LIFE-ON-LIFE DISCIPLE MAKING ACTS 13-28

22 | ACTS 13:1-12 A PATTERN FOR MISSIONS **365**

The Expansion of the Church (13:1-3) 366
   The Locale of the Antioch Church 366
   The Leaders of the Antioch Church 367
   The Love of the Antioch Church 367
   The Divine Leader of the Antioch Church 368
   The Enlargement of the Antioch Church 369
The Mission of the Church (13:4-5) 369
   The Power of the Mission 370
   The Planning of the Mission 370
   The Proclamation of the Mission 371
   The Personnel of the Mission 372
The Opposition of the Church (13:6-8) 372
   The Devil's Work of Opposition 373
   God's Work in Evangelism 373
The Conquest of the Church (13:9-12) 374
   A Diabolic Conquest 374
   A Dangerous Conquest 375
   A Delightful Conquest 375
   A Dynamic Conquest 376

23 | ACTS 13:13-52 THE MESSAGE OF MISSIONS **379**

The Pathway of the Gospel (13:13) 380
   A Promising Pathway 380
   A Treacherous Pathway 381
   A Familiar Pathway 381
The Proclamation of the Gospel (13:14-41) 382
   A Promising Invitation 383
   A Promised People 383
      Out of Egypt 384
      Out of the Wilderness 384
      Into Canaan 384
      On to the Kingdom 385
   A Promised Savior 385
   A Promised Salvation 386
   A Promised Fulfillment 386
   A Promised Resurrection 387

A Prophecy from Psalm 2 .... *387*
A Prophecy from Isaiah 55 .... *388*
A Prophecy from Psalm 16 .... *388*
A Promised Justification 389
A Powerful Warning 390
The Power of the Gospel (13:42-52) 390
The Gospel Draws People 390
The Gospel Offends People 391
The Gospel Saves People... 392
The Gospel Brings Persecution 394
The Gospel Brings Joy... 394

24 | ACTS 14:1-28 PROGRESS AND PERSECUTION 397

The Gospel Invites Passion (14:1-6) 399
Passionate Rejoicing 399
Passionate Rejection 400
Powerful Revelation 400
Passionate Resolve.. 401
The Gospel Can Bring Pandemonium (14:8-18) 402
The Miracle... 402
The Mayhem... 402
The Message 403
The Gospel Brings Persecution (14:19-23) 404
A Rejection & Resurrection.. 404
A Return.. 405
A Resurgence 406
The Gospel Promises Progress (14:24-28) 408
God's Grace in Progress 408
God's Glory in Progress 408
God's Goal for Progress 409

25 | ACTS 15:1-35 LAW OR GRACE? 411

The Detour from Grace (15:1-5) 412
A Detour Over Doctrine 413
A Detour with Debate 413
A Detour Directed by the Lord 414
A Detour Demanded by False Brothers 414
The Discussion about Grace (15:6-18) 415
A Discussion of the Gospel 415
A Denunciation of Legalism 416
A Declaration of Salvation by Grace 418
A Description of Signs and Wonders 418
A Dependence on the Scriptures.. 419
A Discussion of the Church 419

A Testimony of the Church *420*
A Prophecy of the Church *420*

The Decision for Grace (15:19-29) 422
- The Fellowship of Grace 422
- The Family of Grace 423
- The Freedom of Grace 424

The Delight of Grace (15:30-35) 425
- The Delight of Gracious Leadership 425
- The Delight of Gracious Discipleship 426
- The Delight of Gracious Fellowship 427

26 | ACTS 15:36-16:15 THE MACEDONIAN CALL 429

A New Team Assembled (Acts 15:36-41) 431
- Factions Among the Apostles 431
- Friction on the Team 432
- Friendship on the Team 433
- Expansion Through the Team 433

A New Worker Added (16:1-5) 434
- A Multicultural Man 434
- A Magnanimous Man 435
- A Missions-Minded Man 435
- A Mature Man 436

A New Vision Received (16:6-10) 437
- A Forbidden Direction 437
- A Clear Vision 438
- An Immediate Obedience 438

A New Church Founded (16:11-15) 439
- The Place of the New Church 439
- The People of the New Church 440
- The Profession of the New Church 443

Applications 443

27 | ACTS 16:16-40 JAIL HOUSE CHURCH PLANT 447

The People God Saves (16:12-24) 448
- Lydia the Fashionista 448
- The Slave Girl 449
- The Philippian Jailer 451

The Power of God in Salvation (16:19-34) 451
- Power Despite Persecution 452
- The Power of Praise 453
- The Power of Providence 454
- The Power of Preaching 455
  - *The Preaching of Faith* *455*
  - *The Preaching to Family* *456*

The Power of Provision 457
   The Provision of Relationship *457*
   The Provision of Membership *457*
   The Provision of Discipleship *458*

The Providence of God in Salvation (16:35-40) 458
Rulers in God's Providence 458
Rights in God's Providence 459
Resting in God's Providence 460

28 | ACTS 17:1-15 TURNING THE WORLD UPSIDE DOWN 463

The Preaching of the Word in Thessalonica (17:1-9) 464
Faithfulness to the Gospel 465
   Teaching Hearts *466*
   Opening Eyes *466*
   Proving the Gospel *466*
Faith in the Gospel 467
Factions Because of the Gospel 468
Fruitfulness in the Gospel 470
Falsehood Against the Gospel 470
Fleeing Because of the Gospel 471

The Power of the Word in Berea (17:10-13) 472
Tenderness to God's Word 472
Transformation by God's Word 473
Turmoil Because of God's Word 473

The Preparation for the Word in Athens (17:14-15) 474
The Testimony 474
The Target 475
The Team 475

29 | ACTS 17:16-34 MARS HILL EVANGELISM 477

Defending The Existence of God (17:16-23) 478
The Burden of Evangelism 479
The Places of Evangelism 480
   The Church *480*
   The Marketplace *481*
The Message of Evangelism 481
Responses to Evangelism 482
   Some are Apathetic *482*
   Some are Cynical *482*
   Some are Curious *483*
Methods of Evangelism 485
   Paul was Observant *485*
   Paul was Missional *486*
   Paul was Bold *486*

Describing The Person of God (17:24-29) 487

- God is Creator 488
- God is Ruler 488
- God is Giver 489
- God is Sustainer 490
- God is Advocate 490
- God is Transcendent 491

Declaring The Message of God (17:30-34) 492
- A Message of Repentance... 492
- A Message of Reckoning 493
- A Message of Resurrection 493
- Our Response to the Message 494
  - *The Curious* *494*
  - *The Converted* *494*

30 | ACTS 18:1-17 COURAGE AT CORINTH 497

Gospel Friendships (18:1-5a) 498
- The Problem of Friendlessness 499
- The Privilege of Friendship 499
- The Places of Friendship 500
  - *Friends at Work* *500*
  - *Friends at Worship* *501*
- The Providence of Friendship 502

Gospel Fruit (18:5b-8) 503
- The Instrument of Conversion 503
- The Enemies of Conversion 504
- The Fruit of Conversion 505

Gospel Fellowship (18:9-11) 505
- The Promises of Fellowship 506
  - *A Promise of His Peace* *506*
  - *A Promise of Proclamation* *506*
  - *A Promise of His Presence* *506*
  - *A Promise of His Protection* *507*
  - *A Promise of His People* *507*
- The Productivity of Fellowship 507

Gospel Fire (18:12-17) 508
- The Enemy's Attack Can't Stop Us 508
- The Enemy's Strategy Can't Stop Us 508
- The Enemy is Powerless to Stop Us 509

31 | ACTS 18:18-19:7 THIRD JOURNEY, SAME SPIRIT 511

Set Sail in the Spirit (18:18-22) 513
- His Team 513
- His Thankfulness 514
- His Target 515

His Tenderness 516
His Tribe 517
Strengthen Leaders for the Spirit (18:23-28) 517
   We Need Healthy Churches 517
   We Need Healthy Discipleship 518
      A Cultured Disciple *519*
      A Converted Disciple *519*
      A Committed Disciple *520*
   We Need Healthy Duplication 521
Solidify the Spirit's Work (19:1-7) 521
   The Place of the Spirit's Work 521
   The People of the Spirit's Work 522
   The Proof of the Spirit's Work 523

32 | ACTS 19:8-41 RIOTING AND REJOICING IN EPHESUS 525

The Preparation for Suffering (19:8-12) 526
   Working in the Word 527
      The Message of the Word *527*
      The Persecution of the Word *528*
   Working in the World 528
   Working Wonders 529
The Power of Suffering (19:13-20) 531
   The Power of Oppression 532
      The Devil Leaves You Harassed *532*
      The Devil Leaves You Humiliated *533*
   The Power of Revival 533
   The Price of Revival 534
God's Protection During Suffering (19:21-41) 535
   Trust God's Providence 535
   Trust God's Power 536
   Trust God's Plan 538
   Trust God's Position 539

33 | ACTS 20:1-12 FALLING ASLEEP IN CHURCH 543

Stay Awake (20:1-2) 545
   Be Awake to God's Plan 545
      A Plan of Expansion *546*
      A Plan of Generosity *546*
      A Plan of Expendability *546*
   Be Awake to God's Power 547
Stay Alert (20:3-6) 548
   The Plot 548
   The Pressure 549
   The People 550

Stay Alive (20:7-12) 551
The Midnight Message 551
The Lord's Day 551
The Lord's Supper 552
A Long Sermon 553
The Mishap 553
The Miracle 555

34 | ACTS 20:13-24 A MODEL OF SUPERNATURAL MINISTRY 557

Service to God (20:13-19) 559
Serve with a Heavenly Mindset 560
Serve with a Heart for People 562
Serve with Honorable Men 563
Serve with Humility 564
Serve with Hardship 565
Teaching for the Church (20:20) 566
Our Attitude Toward Teaching 567
The Application of Teaching 568
The Arenas of Teaching 569
Evangelism for the Lost (20:21) 570
The Recipients of Evangelism 570
The Response to Evangelism 571
The Reward of Evangelism 571
Sacrifice of Self (20:22-24) 572
A Spirit-led Sacrifice 572
A Selfless Sacrifice 573
A Satisfying Sacrifice 573

35 | ACTS 20:25-38 A CHARGE TO THE EPHESIAN ELDERS 577

Counsel Yourself (20:25-28a) 578
A Faithful Ministry 579
A Divine Direction 579
A Clean Conscience 580
A Noble Legacy 582
A Personal Care 583
Shepherd the Flock (20:28b) 585
A Word about Membership 585
A Word about Eldership 585
A Word about Discipleship 586
A Word about Headship 587
Protect God's People (20:29-31) 587
Dangers Around Us 587
Dangers Among Us 588
Dangers Within Us 588

Study the Word (20:32) 589
   The Bible Saves Us 589
   The Bible Strengthens Us 590
   The Bible Secures Us 590
   The Bible Sanctifies Us 591
Spurn the World (20:33-38) 591
   Our Christ-centered Hope 591
   Our Christ-centered Hands 592
   Our Christ-centered Heart 593
   Our Christ-centered Harvest 594

36 | ACTS 21:1-16 BOLD STEPS FOR CHRIST 597

Determine to Follow the Lord (21:1-3) 598
   The Price of Following God 598
   The Providence of God 599
   The Promises of God 600
Determine to Fellowship with the Saints (21:4-7) 600
   Fellowship is Essential 601
   Fellowship is Encouraging 601
   Fellowship is Everywhere 602
Determine to Forsake the World (21:8-16) 603
   Through Godly Friendships 603
   Through Godly Family 603
   Through Godly Fellowship 604
   Through Godly Forethought 605
   Through a God-Honoring Future 606

37 | ACTS 21:17-36 PAUL'S ARREST: MAGNIFYING GOD ALONE 609

Magnify God with Community (21:17-20a) 611
   Support Fellowship 611
   Submit to Leadership 611
   Celebrate Partnership 612
Magnify God with Expansion (21:20b-26) 614
   Expect Hostility 614
   Work for Unity 615
   Sacrifice for the Community 616
Magnify God Amidst Opposition (21:27-32) 618
   Look to God in the Face of Defamation 618
   Look to God in the Face of Death 619
   Look to God for Deliverance 619
Magnify God with Evangelism (21:34-36) 620

38 | ACTS 21:37-22:29 WITNESSING FOR JESUS IN JERUSALEM **623**

God's Protection (21:37-22:1) 625
    Protected by an Unlikely Ally 625
    Protected with a Unique Heritage 626
    Protected with an Uncanny Permission 627
    Protected with an Unbelievable Opportunity 627
God's Power (22:2-21) 628
    God's Power to a Lost Sinner 628
    God's Power through a Loving Savior 630
        The Savior's Revelation *630*
        Paul's Repentance *630*
        Paul's Response *631*
    God's Power for a Life-Changing Salvation 631
        Paul's New Friend *631*
        Paul's New Sight *632*
        Paul's New Family *632*
    God's Power for a Lifelong Calling 632
God's Plan (22:22-29) 635
    God's Plan Sometimes Includes Danger 635
    God's Plan Often Brings Deliverance 637
    God's Plan Always Has a Sovereign Purpose 637
    God's Plan is the Only One that Matters 638

39 | ACTS 22:30-23:11 STANDING ALONE: PAUL BEFORE THE SANHEDRIN **641**

Trust God's Plan (22:30) 643
    The Plan of the Romans 643
    The Plan of the Jews 643
    The Plan of God 644
Walk in God's Wisdom (23:1-10) 644
    Wisdom in the Word 644
    Wisdom in the Situation 645
    Wisdom in the Will of God 646
Experience God's Comfort (23:11) 647
    Comfort in God's Presence 647
    Comfort in God's Praise 648
    Comfort in God's Plan 648

40 | ACTS 23:12-35 GOD'S PROTECTION: PAUL AND HIS 40 ASSASSINS **651**

The Design of the Enemy (23:12-15) 652
    The Pledge 653
    The Priests 653

The Plot 653
The Deliverance of God (23:16-30) 654
   God's Agent 655
   God's Army 656
   God's Ambassador 657
The Destination of the Apostle (23:31-35) 658
   Safe Passage 658
   Sound Preaching 659
   Secure Prison 660

41 | ACTS 24:1-27 WAITING ON GOD (FELIX) 663

Distractions with Waiting of God (24:1-9) 664
   Flattery 664
   Falsehoods 665
   False Witnesses 666
Helps for Waiting on God (24:10-21) 666
   An Attitude of Cheerfulness 666
   A Walk of Integrity 667
   A Life of Faith 669
   A Heart of Generosity 670
Opportunities While Waiting on God (24:22-26) 671
   An Opportunity to Enjoy God 671
   An Opportunity to Edify Saints 673
   An Opportunity to Evangelize Sinners 674
      His Audience *674*
      His Message *675*
      His Pattern *676*
The Legacy of Waiting on God (24:27) 676
   A Time to Wait on God 677
   A Purpose for Waiting on God 677

42 | ACTS 25:1-12 FROM BITTERNESS TO BLESSING (FESTUS) 679

The Pain of Injustice (25:1-5) 682
   A Plan to Injure 683
   A Plan Interrupted 684
A Plan for Injustice (25:6-10) 687
   Trust Not in Man 687
      Consider Your Enemies *687*
      Consider Yourself *688*
      Consider Christ's Example *688*
      Follow Christ's Example *689*
      Walk in Your Integrity *689*
   Tell the Truth 689
   Trust in the Lord 690

The Providence of Injustice (25:11-12) 690
   Be Free from Fear 692
   Be Full of Faith 692
      Applications *693*

43 | ACTS 25:13-26:32 ALMOST PERSUADED (AGRIPPA) 697

Those Needing Gospel Persuasion (25:13-27) 698
   The Prince, Agrippa 699
   The Prisoner, Paul 700
   The Proconsul, Festus 703
      The Fancy Meeting *703*
      The Frail Apostle *703*
      The Facts from Festus *704*
      The Fatal Suspicion *705*
The Power of Gospel Persuasion (26:1-23) 705
   Paul's Case 705
      The Magistrate of Paul's Case *706*
      The Motive of Paul's Case *706*
   Paul's Character 707
      The Apostle's Faithfulness *707*
      The Ancient Faith *708*
      The Amazing Fact *709*
   Paul's Commitment 709
   Paul's Conversion 710
   Paul's Commission 712
   Paul's Calling 713
   Paul's Charges 713
The Tragedy of Being "Almost" Persuaded (26:24-32) 714
   Gospel Foolishness 714
   Gospel Boldness 716
   Gospel Persuasion 717
   Gospel Exoneration 718
   Gospel Direction 718

44 | ACTS 27:1-44 GOD'S PROVIDENCE IN OUR SHIPWRECKS 721

The Plan of God's Providence (27:1-8) 724
   The Wonder of God's Plan 724
   The Welfare of God's Plan 725
   The Winds of God's Plan 727
Our Perseverance in God's Providence (27:9-12) 728
   An Important Warning 728
   An Ignored Warning 729
God's Presence in His Providence (27:13-24) 730
   God is Present in Danger 730

God is Present in Despair 731
God is Present to Deliver 732
The Paradox of God's Providence (27:25-44) 733
The Faithfulness of God 734
The Fickleness of Man 734
The Fortitude of Leaders 735
The Fortification of the Lord 736

45 | ACTS 28:1-16 MINISTRY ON CASTAWAY ISLAND 739

The Mess of Ministry (28:1-6) 741
The Kindness 742
The Creature 743
The Confusion 744
The Miracles of Ministry (28:7-10) 745
The Hospitality 745
The Healings 746
The Hand of God 746
The Honor 747
The Meaning of Ministry (28:11-16) 747
Waiting Matures Us 747
God Uses Wandering 749
God Uses Witnessing 749

46 | ACTS 28:17-31 WORTH IT ALL 751

The Hope of Israel (28:17-23) 753
Jesus is Presented 753
Jesus is Pondered 754
Jesus is Preached 754
The Hope of Salvation (28:24-29) 756
The Peril of Rejecting Christ 756
The Prize of Receiving Christ 757
The Hope of the World (28:30-31) 758
A New Ministry 758
An Old Message 759
A Glorious Freedom 759
Paul's Hope and Ours 760
The Outpost of Paul's Hope 760
The Outcome of Paul's Hope 762

SELECTED BIBLIOGRAPHY 765

ABBREVIATIONS

Common

cf – Latin "conferatur", compare, or see, or see also
ff – and following (pages or verses)
i.e. – Latin "id est", that is
e.g. – Latin "exempli gratia", for example
c. — Latin "circa", about

Books of the Bible

OLD TESTAMENT

Genesis	Gen	Nehemiah	Neh
Exodus	Exo	Esther	Est
Leviticus	Lev	Job	Job
Numbers	Num	Psalms	Psa
Deuteronomy	Deut	Proverbs	Pro
Joshua	Josh	Ecclesiastes	Ecc
Judges	Jdg	Song of Solomon	Song
Ruth	Ruth	Isaiah	Isa
1 Samuel	1 Sam	Jeremiah	Jer
2 Samuel	2 Sam	Lamentations	Lam
1 Kings	1 Kgs	Ezekiel	Eze
2 Kings	2 Kgs	Daniel	Dan
1 Chronicles	1 Chr	Hosea	Hos
2 Chronicles	2 Chr	Joel	Joel
Ezra	Ezr	Amos	Amos

Obadiah	Oba	Zephaniah	Zeph
Jonah	Jonah	Haggai	Hag
Micah	Mic	Zechariah	Zech
Nahum	Nah	Malachi	Mal
Habakkuk	Hab		

New Testament

Matthew	Mt	2 Timothy	2 Tim
Mark	Mk	Titus	Titus
Luke	Lk	Philemon	Phm
John	Jn	Hebrews	Heb
Acts	Acts	James	Jas
Romans	Rom	1 Peter	1 Pet
1 Corinthians	1 Cor	2 Peter	2 Pet
2 Corinthians	2 Cor	1 John	1 Jn
Galatians	Gal	2 John	2 Jn
Ephesians	Eph	3 John	3 Jn
Philippians	Phil	Jude	Jud
Colossians	Col	Revelation	Rev
1 Thessalonians	1 Thess		
2 Thessalonians	2 Thess		
1 Timothy	1 Tim		

INTRODUCTION

But you will receive power when the Holy Spirit has come upon you, and you will be my witnesses in Jerusalem and in all Judea and Samaria, and to the end of the earth.
ACTS 1:8

The book of Acts provides a bridge for the writings of the New Testament. As a second volume to Luke's Gospel, it joins what Jesus "began to do and to teach" (1:1) as told in the Gospels with what he continued to do and teach through the apostles' preaching and the establishment of the church. Besides linking the Gospel narratives on the one hand and the apostolic letters on the other, it supplies an account of the life of Paul from which we can learn the setting for his letters. Geographically its story spans the lands between Jerusalem, where the church began, and Rome, the political center of the empire. Historically it recounts the first 30 years of the church. It is also a bridge that ties the church in its beginning with each succeeding age. This book may be studied to gain an understanding of the principles that ought to govern the church of any age.

DATE

The date is not hard to consider, since the recorded events in the book of Acts end around A.D. 63. This date is supported by the silence about later events. While arguments from silence are not conclusive, it is perhaps significant that the book contains no allusion to events that happened after the close of Paul's two-year imprisonment in Rome: e.g., the burning of Rome and the persecution of the Christians there (64 A.D.), the martyrdom of Peter and Paul (possibly 67) and the destruction of Jerusalem (70).

There is also no recorded outcome of Paul's trial. If Luke knew the outcome of the trial Paul was waiting for (*cf* 28:30), why did he not record it at the close of Acts? Perhaps it was because he had brought the history up to date.

AUTHOR

Although the author does not name himself, evidence outside the Scriptures and inferences from the book itself lead to the conclusion that the author was Luke.

The earliest of the external testimonies appears in the Muratorian Canon (c. 170 A.D.), where the explicit statement is made that Luke was the author of both the third Gospel and the "Acts of All the Apostles." Eusebius (c. 325) lists information from numerous sources to identify the author of these books as Luke (Ecclesiastical History, 3.4). Within the writing itself are some clues as to who the author was:

Luke was a companion of Paul. In the description of the happenings in Acts, certain passages make use of the pronoun "we." At these points the author includes himself as a companion of Paul in his travels (16:10–17; 20:5—21:18; 27:1—28:16; see notes on 16:10, 17; 27:1). A historian as careful with details as this author proves to be would have good reason for choosing to use "we" in some places and "they" elsewhere. The author was therefore probably present with Paul at the particular events described in the "we" sections. These "we" passages include the period of Paul's two-year imprisonment at Rome (ch 28). During this time Paul wrote, among other letters, Philemon and Colossians. In them he sends greetings from his companions, and Luke is included among them (*cf* Col 4:9–17; Phm 23–24). In fact, after eliminating those who, for one reason or another, would not fit the requirements for the author of Acts, Luke is left as the most likely candidate.

Luke was a physician. Although it cannot be proved that the author of Acts was a physician simply from his vocabulary, the words he uses and the traits and education reflected in his writings fit well his role as a physician. It is true that the doctor of the first century did not have as specialized a vocabulary as that of doctors today, but there are some usages in Luke-Acts that seem to suggest that a medical man was the author of these books. And it should be remembered that Paul uses the term "doctor" in describing Luke (*cf* Col 4:14; Acts 28:6).

MESSAGE

The message of the book of Acts is an extension of the Lord's great commission. "Go and make disciples of every nation." In the book of Acts we see that when we are doing life-on-life discipleship, we will see the church expand through evangelism and fellowship, enriching each other and growing into the image of Christ.

It was an ordinary procedure for a historian at this time to begin a second volume by summarizing the first volume and indicating the contents anticipated in his second volume. Luke summarized his first volume in 1:1–3; the theme of his second volume is presented in the words of Jesus: "You will be my witnesses in Jerusalem, and in all Judea and Samaria, and to the ends of the earth" (1:8). This is, in effect, an outline of the book of Acts. The main purposes of the book appear to be:

To present a history. The significance of Acts as a historical account of Christian origins cannot be overestimated. It tells of the founding of the church, the spread of the gospel, the beginnings of congregations, and evangelistic efforts in the apostolic pattern. One of the unique aspects of Christianity is its firm historical foundation. The life and teachings of Jesus Christ are established in the four Gospel narratives, and the book of Acts provides a coordinated account of the beginning and spread of the church as the result of the work of the risen Lord and the Holy Spirit through the apostles.

To give a defense. One finds embedded in Acts a record of Christian defenses made to both Jews (e.g., 4:8–12) and Gentiles (e.g., 25:8–11), with the underlying purpose of conversion. It shows how the early church coped with pagan and Jewish thought, the Roman government and Hellenistic society. Luke may have written this work as Paul awaited trial in Rome. If his case came to court, what better court brief could Paul have had than a life of Jesus, a history of the beginnings of the church (including the activity of Paul) and an early collection of Paul's letters?

To provide a guide. Luke had no way of knowing how long the church would continue on this earth, but as long as it pursues its course, the book of Acts will be one of its major guides. In Acts we see basic principles being applied to specific situations in the context of problems and persecutions. These same principles continue to be applicable until Christ returns.

To depict the triumph of Christianity in the face of bitter persecution. The success of the church in carrying the gospel from Jerusalem to Rome and in planting local churches across the Roman empire demonstrated that Christianity was not a merely human work. It triumphed under the rule of the exalted Christ and through the power of the Holy Spirit.

TIMELINE OF PAUL'S LIFE

No timeline of Paul's life can be perfectly accurate, but based on those who have studied Paul's time and circumstances, the following seems to be a faithful, though general, outline of the apostle's life and happenings.

A.D. 6 Born a Roman citizen to Jewish parents in Tarsus (in modern eastern Turkey)

c. 20–30 Studies Torah in Jerusalem with Gamaliel; becomes a Pharisee

c. 30–33 Persecutes followers of Jesus of Nazareth in Jerusalem and Judea

Conversion

c. 33–36 Converted on the way to Damascus; spends three years in Arabia; returns to Damascus to preach Jesus as Messiah

c. 36 Flees Damascus because of persecution; visits Jerusalem and meets with the apostles

36–44 Preaches in Tarsus and surrounding region

44–46 Invited by Barnabas to teach in Antioch

46 With Barnabas visits Jerusalem to bring a famine relief offering

Mission Trips

47–48 First missionary journey with Barnabas, to Cyprus and Galatia

49 At the Council of Jerusalem, Paul argues successfully that Gentile Christians need not follow Jewish law; returns to Antioch; confronts Peter over question of Jewish law

49–52 Second missionary journey with Silas, through Asia Minor and Greece; settles in Corinth; writes letters to **Thessalonians**

52 Visits Jerusalem and Antioch briefly; begins third missionary journey

52–55 Stays in Ephesus; writes the letters to **Galatians** and **Corinthians**

55–57 Travels through Greece and possibly Illyricum (modern Yugoslavia); writes letter to **Romans**

Paul's Arrest & Death

57–59 Returns to Jerusalem and arrested; imprisoned at Caesarea

59–60 Appears before Festus and appeals to Caesar, voyage to Rome

60–62 Under house arrest at Rome; writes letters to **Philippians**, **Ephesians**, **Colossians**, and **Philemon**

62–64 Released, journeys to Spain?, plants church in Crete

64 Writes letters **1 Timothy** and **Titus**

64 Returns to Rome and is arrested again

67 Writes **2 Timothy**

67 A.D. Martyred by beheading, the same day Peter is crucified

OUTLINE

Luke weaves together different interests and emphases as he relates the beginnings and expansion of the church. The design of his book revolves around (1) key persons: Peter and Paul; (2) important topics and events: the role of the Holy Spirit, pioneer missionary outreach to new fields, conversions, the growth of the church, and life in the Christian community; (3) significant problems: conflict between Jews and Gentiles, persecution of the church by some Jewish elements, trials before Jews and Romans, confrontations with Gentiles, and other hardships in the ministry; (4) geographical advances: five significant stages.

Part 1: Peter and the Beginnings of the Church in the Holy Land
Acts 1–12
  A. "Throughout Judea, Galilee and Samaria" Acts 1:1—9:31
    Introduction (1:1–2)
    Christ's resurrection ministry (1:3–11)
    The period of waiting for the Holy Spirit (1:12–26)
    The filling with the Spirit (ch. 2)
    The healing of the lame man and the resultant arrest of Peter and John (3:1—4:31)
    The community of goods (4:32—5:11)

The arrest of the 12 apostles (5:12–42)
The choice of the seven deacons (6:1–7)
Stephen's arrest and martyrdom (6:8—7:60)
The scattering of the Jerusalem believers (8:1–4)
Philip's ministry (8:5–40)
Saul's conversion (9:1–31)

B. "As far as Phoenicia, Cyprus and Antioch" Acts 9:32—12:25
Peter's ministry on the Mediterranean coast (9:32—11:18)
The new Gentile church in Antioch (11:19–30)
Herod's persecution of the church and his subsequent death (12:1-25)

Part 2: Paul and the Expansion of the Church from Antioch to Rome
Acts 13–28
A. "Throughout the region of Phrygia and Galatia" (13:1—15:35)
Paul's first missionary journey (chs. 13–14)
The Jerusalem conference (15:1–35)
B. "Over to Macedonia" (15:36—21:16)
Paul's second missionary journey (15:36—18:22)
Paul's third missionary journey (18:23—21:16)
C. "To Rome" (21:17—28:31)
Paul's imprisonment in Jerusalem (21:17—23:35)
Paul's imprisonment in Caesarea (chs. 24–26)
Voyage to Rome (27:1—28:15)
Two years under house arrest in Rome (28:16–31)

LIFE-ON-LIFE DISCIPLESHIP
ACTS 1-12

1 | ACTS 1:1-11
CLOTHED WITH POWER

> *But you will receive power when the Holy Spirit has come upon you, and you will be my witnesses in Jerusalem and in all Judea and Samaria, and to the end of the earth.*
>
> ACTS 1:8

The entire book of Acts is how the whole world was transformed by a small group of people who were committed to being true disciples of the Lord Jesus Christ. They were empowered to climb out of their pain and sin and live in the resurrection power of Jesus. There was an incredible change that took place in all the disciples in the first two chapters of Acts.

The Roman Empire was slowly falling apart, and there was a small group near the Mediterranean Sea that would turn the world upside down. That's how God always works in history. Infinite power through weak vessels. In Acts it started with 120 gathered in an upper room for prayer. It turned the world upside down. That's how it always begins.

The Great Awakening in Britain

Something similar happened in the middle of the 1700s in France and Britain. Society in Europe was falling apart. The advances in the Industrial Revolution had just begun. The tensions between rich and poor was a powder keg. In France the people turned to civil war, and there was the bloody revolution. So many lives were lost. *Les Misérables* depicts some of that revolution.

In Britain something else happened. Historians now pretty much concede that what happened *instead* of a bloody revolution was something that's called the Great Awakening. In the first few decades of the Great Awakening, millions (nobody knows exactly how many), a fifth to a sixth of the entire population of the British Isles, found themselves converted and swept up into the churches as true believers, born again! It also spread into America under the ministry of Jonathan Edwards.

After that, the next few decades saw a tremendous amount of social healing, and here's why. The power that fell on Pentecost fell on Britain and America. Rich and poor were transformed. The rich became just and generous with their resources. The poor became hard working by the Spirit's power. It turned Britain upside down for good. Meanwhile France languished in secular humanistic darkness. The converts of the Great Awakening abolished the slave trade in the British Empire. Instead of the economy tanking, the economy boomed. There was a reform of the child labor laws. There was a huge increase in literacy. Why? Because the rich and the poor were changed by the Spirit of God. God, through the gospel of Christ, poured out his Spirit on all flesh, once again, just as he had so many times before.

The Spirit of God is in the business of renewing entire societies of people. Most recently, it happened in Britain. It happened several times in America. What preceded these awakenings? Just like Pentecost, small, unknown groups of believers were praying.

A Great Awakening in Rome

The first of all the great awakenings, occurred in the Roman Empire, in the province of Judea, in the city of Jerusalem. It's the prototype of all true awakenings and revivals. Remember that little group that the Spirit fell on? When the first awakening began, the church began! And this little group of people had no political power, no educational power, no cultural power, and no economic power. Yet within two centuries it had swept up millions of people in the Roman Empire. It gave them a joy and peace they'd never known. Christians became the leading force in a Roman society that was falling apart, so that by the third century the emperor had to acknowledge that this was a Christian society, because it was the Christians and the Christians alone who were holding that world together.

There was one, who gathered the eyewitnesses of this first Great Awakening, and wrote about it. It's Dr. Luke, who wrote the book of Acts.[1] I wonder if God's desire in studying the book of Acts for us as a congregation is to bring a new spiritual outpouring upon the families of this nation. Will you pray that this will happen as I preach the word?

The book of Acts is really volume 2 of Luke's first book, called the Gospel of Luke, which bears his name. The book of Acts has traditionally been called 'The Acts of the Apostles', but in truth we should really think of it as 'The Acts of Jesus (II)' since it is the Acts that Jesus began in his life that is being carried out through his church.[2] This is really the acts of Jesus continued through his church, and through you today.

STRUCTURE OF ACTS

How is the world turned upside down in the book of Acts? The structure of Acts tells the story. We could look at it in a couple of ways.

A Geographic Outline

First, you have the promise of Christ, which is a geographic outline of how the Spirit moves on an anointed people. We see the power of the Spirit from a *geographical perspective*.

> **Acts 1:8** | But you will receive power when the Holy Spirit has come upon you, and you will be my witnesses in Jerusalem and in all Judea and Samaria, and to the end of the earth.

So there's the geographic outline. In Acts you see the gospel move in power first in Jerusalem, then in all Israel (Judea and Samaria), and finally to the uttermost parts of the earth. And here's what I want you to understand. If you get ahold of the full orbed discipleship in the Spirit that God has for you, you can expect global reverberations. When you understand the power that you can have in the Holy Spirit, you will not want to live a life less than being "clothed with power". The only way to this abundant life of full discipleship is humility. Disciple means "learner". Without the humility of a child, you cannot be Christ's disciple.

---

[1] Timothy J. Keller. "Many Convincing Proofs," *The Timothy Keller Sermon Archive* (New York City: Redeemer Presbyterian Church, 2013), preached October 12, 2003 on Acts 1:1-11.

[2] Tom Wright, *Acts for Everyone, Part 1: Chapters 1-12* (London: Society for Promoting Christian Knowledge, 2008), 2.

With a tender spirit, and a teachable attitude, you can follow Christ with full power and victory. We can be discipled and disciple each other. We see this in Jerusalem, Judea and Samaria (all Israel), and to the uttermost parts of the earth. Let God do what he wants. Surrender to him completely. *You be the clay; let him be the potter.* And you will see full power through you to the uttermost parts of the world. That's the message of Acts from a *geographical perspective*.

A Biographic Outline

But there is a second outline, a *bibliographical perspective* that people have noticed, and that is one of personalities. You have two primary personalities in the book of Acts: Peter who is the apostle to the Jews, and Paul who is the apostle to the Gentiles.

The first part of Acts deals a lot with Peter's ministry (1-12) and the last part of Acts (13-28) covers Paul's ministry. This is a great study to talk about the world we live in today. So many have asked me questions: what should we do in our current political environment?

John 18:36 | Jesus said, "My kingdom is not of this world."

I like what John MacArthur said recently, commenting on Jesus' words.

> Nothing that happens in our earthly political systems has any effect on the kingdom of God... Even if we had the most ideal human government, it could ultimately do nothing to advance God's kingdom. The kingdom of God is in no way linked to the kingdoms of men. Christ's kingdom is not advanced in the realm of human politics. This is what sets the church apart. Jesus said, "My kingdom is not of this world."[3]

I believe that. It's not what the secular government does that advances the kingdom. It's what you, the church, does that changes the world! And what we are going to see in our study of Acts is that as we live in the Spirit's power for life-on-life discipleship, our lives are going to change. The local church is going to change. Your community is going to change. Then the world will change. That's the idea of the book of Acts, and you have that DNA in verse 8.

---

[3] John MacArthur. Comments at the morning service of Grace Community Church of Sun Valley, California. 17 January 2021. Accessed 23 January 2021, https://www.gracechurch.org/sermons/17225

Acts 1:8 | But you will receive power when the Holy Spirit has come upon you, and you will be my witnesses in Jerusalem and in all Judea and Samaria, and to the end of the earth.

As the Spirit his more hold of us, he will have more hold of the world around us. As Christians grow in Christ and utilize the power of the Spirit in holiness and fellowship and discipleship, the church expands. The Church matures. Acts is a book with a wonderful theme, tracing the work of the Holy Spirit through the birth, infancy, and adolescence of the Church.[4]

Peter's Story

Before we can look at Acts 1, you need to understand the context and background of what's going on. Jesus the Messiah was crucified. In the middle of it all, Peter is just out of control. He's denied the Lord. Of course, we remember the first 13 chapters of Acts revolve a lot around Peter's story. So as we look at Peter's story before Acts, I want you to think about your story. Have you ever thought your life was out of control?

Let's jump into Peter's life and see the mess he's made. Peter's denied his Lord and Savior three times. He's a royal failure. Peter says, basically, "I'm done. I can't do this apostle thing anymore. I'm disqualified." Have you ever felt disqualified? I think Peter really thought what he did was unforgivable. Think about it. The Messiah that he and all Israel had waited for century after century after millennia had finally come to earth, and in his greatest hour of need, Peter fell apart. He was seized with fear. "I don't know him!" "I don't know the man!" "I swear I don't know that Jesus of Nazareth." Three times.

Peter had sworn he would die before he would ever deny him. When they arrested Jesus, he cut off the ear of the high priest's servant, Malchus. But now he'd denied the Lord three times! He was done. He feels unforgivable. "I'm going back to fishing," he says. "I can't be a disciple anymore. I've failed." Have you ever felt that way? But of course, you know who Jesus chooses to preach Pentecost.

Remember what Jesus did? The empathy that flows from Jesus is amazing. He just looks deeply into Peter's eyes and asks him three times: "Do you love me?" Peter basically says, "My actions say I don't

---

[4] R. Kent Hughes, *Acts: The Church Afire*, Preaching the Word (Wheaton, IL: Crossway Books, 1996), 13.

love you, but I cannot lie. I love you!" Three times. "I love you. I love you. I love you." Jesus says: "You are supremely useful to me. Feed my sheep!" (Jn 21:15-17). And he preaches Pentecost.

Maybe you feel like the person in the letter I'm about to read. It's an imaginary letter, but it is similar to questions I receive from time to time.

> Dear Pastor,
>
> I'm confused. No. Not about my salvation. I know I'm saved. I've received Christ's grace by faith. What I'm confused about is life. Not only mine, but the Christians around me. I look around and see saints who struggle just like sinners. Our relationships are not just messy, but often a mess. Our homes are sometimes harsh and cold places. At times we seem to handle suffering little differently than those who do not know Christ. I see Christians who have no sense of who they are in Christ. They seem to sway between self-hatred and self-sufficiency.
>
> What gives? What is the gospel sufficient for? Heaven only? If grace is so sufficient, then why do we seem to be so powerless in our lives and relationships? So, is Christianity all I need or what? If Christ is sufficient, do I really need something more? And if the gospel is sufficient not only for eternal life but for daily life now, then why doesn't it seem sufficient to me and the rest of us? I know you're busy, but if you could find time to reply, I sure would appreciate it.
>
> *Love, Brother Theophilus*[5]

I think Luke was answering questions like this in his accounting of the book of Acts. How is it possible that someone so week could change the world? We all feel like Peter at first. We have to look for that touch and empowerment of the Holy Spirit.

In our study of the book of Acts, we are going to take a journey of discipleship of the Spirit and the word. A disciple is a learner. We are going to hopefully *learn* where and how we get the power to live the Christian life, to be disciples and to be disciple-makers.

KINGDOM TEACHING (1:1-3)

Now one of the most important things about discipleship in the kingdom of God is sound teaching. You have to know who God is. Who

---

[5] Robert Kellemen. *Gospel-Centered Counseling* (Equipping Biblical Counselors) (Grand Rapids, MI: Zondervan, 2014), 25-26.

is this Savior, Messiah? Who is this Spirit being poured out? Do you know your God? Do you know him?

The Author and Recipient

Tradition tells us that Luke, Paul's beloved physician and companion in his missionary journeys, is the author of this book. He's writing to a nobleman named Theophilus.

> **Acts 1:1-2** | In the first book, O Theophilus, I have dealt with all that Jesus began to do and teach, ² until the day when he was taken up, after he had given commands through the Holy Spirit to the apostles whom he had chosen.

Dr. Luke

Saint Luke, also known as Luke the Evangelist, is the author of both the Gospel of Luke and the Book of Acts. Luke wrote more of the New Testament than anyone else—even the Apostle Paul. Luke wasn't an eyewitness to Jesus' ministry, but he lived during the first century, and according to his own writings, he "carefully investigated everything from the beginning" (Lk 1:1–4). Luke is a physician, but he's also an evangelist. He cares about the soul of a certain high-ranking nobleman, it seems, named Theophilus. Luke's careful investigation had him talking to all of the apostles and other eyewitnesses. In total, Luke has a two-volume work. Part 1 is the Gospel of Luke and Part 2 is the book of Acts. Luke's Gospel presents the life of Jesus incarnate *on earth*, and the book of Acts presents the life of Jesus *through his church*.

Theophilus

Who's Theophilus? We know a few things. He might have been wealthy. He might have been a person of nobility, because in Luke 1 he's called, "... most excellent Theophilus ..." which is a title (Lk 1:3). Luke is actually making a case to him about why Christianity is true.[6]

Luke is writing to explain how the God's kingdom is expanding through the people of the kingdom, like you and me. How in the world does something begin so small, with 12 men and a teacher, and it spreads throughout the whole world? What is that powerful? The kingdom with the King at the helm! Jesus is alive and at work!

---

[6] Keller. "Many Convincing Proofs," ibid.

40 Days of Kingdom Teaching

Luke tells us where the apostles got their teaching. They learned a lot during the three years they were with Jesus, but it seems they learned infinitely more during Jesus' post-resurrection teaching! Luke is the only scriptural writer who tells us that Christ's post-resurrection ministry covered forty days. It's truly fascinating.

> **Acts 1:3** | He presented himself alive to them after his suffering by many proofs, appearing to them during forty days and speaking about the kingdom of God.

Evidently Jesus appeared at intervals, coming and going from Heaven at will, showing miraculous signs and instructing his disciples "about the kingdom of God." What was this kingdom teaching like? It was Jesus revealing himself in all the Scriptures so that their hearts burned.

Luke's record of the stunning encounter on the road to Emmaus is a typical example. Christ met the two followers in an altered physical form and "beginning with Moses and all the Prophets, he explained to them what was said in all the Scriptures concerning himself" (Lk 24:27), so that they later said, "Were not our hearts burning within us while he talked with us on the road and opened the Scriptures to us?" (Lk 24:32). The picture of those forty days is one of enraptured excitement, unfolding mystery, suspense, and anticipation.[7] All that God promised in the Old Testament regarding the nations would start to take place. The kingdom of God would be set up on earth, in the hearts of people from every nation under heaven.

Dear saint, Christ is risen from the dead, and he teaches you by his Holy Spirit. Let him teach you about the kingdom and lordship of Christ over all things in your life. Embrace your great God! Do you want to grow in Christ or shrink in selfishness? You can either look to yourself and shrink, or you can embrace our great God, and let him grow your heart. You will never grow in discipleship if you are looking to self.

KINGDOM POWER (1:4-8)

Let's go back to Peter. Remember him? Remember his fear? He denied Christ. Remember his despair? But something radical happened to change the character of Peter and the other disciples. The

---

[7] Hughes. *Acts*, 14.

resurrection and the teaching of Christ was absolutely essential and foundational, but as Christ ascended, they still had no power. They had to wait.

The Promise of the Spirit

> **Acts 1:4-5** | And while staying with them he ordered them not to depart from Jerusalem, but to wait for the promise of the Father, which, he said, "you heard from me; **5** for John baptized with water, but you will be baptized with the Holy Spirit not many days from now."

Luke wants us to get excited. In the days of John the Baptist, he told of Jesus' promise to baptize his people with the Holy Spirit.

> *Matthew 3:11* | I baptize you with water for repentance, but he who is coming after me is mightier than I, whose sandals I am not worthy to carry. He will baptize you with the Holy Spirit and fire.

Jesus had reminded them that something amazing was about to happen during his post-resurrection ministry.

> *Luke 24:49* | And behold, I am sending the promise of my Father upon you. But stay in the city [of Jerusalem] until you are clothed with power from on high.

Now the promised Holy Spirit is about to be sent. Jesus is about to ascend to heaven in a few days, 40 days from Resurrection Sunday. So Jesus is saying here in Acts 1:5, "This is going to happen in just a few days — you will be baptized with the Holy Spirit. John immersed you in water; I am going to immerse you in the Holy Spirit. John drenched you in water; I am going to drench you in the Holy Spirit."[8]

Didn't they have the Spirit already?

The question always comes up, well didn't they have the Spirit of God already? Hadn't Jesus told Nicodemus that he should be "born of the Spirit" (Jn 3:5-6)? Yes! The Spirit was with them. The saints of the Old Testament had to be born of the Spirit, for sure, in order to enter the kingdom of God. That's Jesus' teaching.

---

[8] John Piper. "You Will Be Baptized with the Holy Spirit" Sermon from Acts 1:4-5. (Minneapolis, MN: Bethlehem Baptist Church, September 23, 1990) Accessed 23 January 2021. https://desiringgod.org/messages/you-will-be-baptized-with-the-holy-spirit

John 14:16-17 | I will ask the Father, and he will give you another Helper, to be with you forever, [17] even the Spirit of truth, whom the world cannot receive, because it neither sees him nor knows him. You know him, for he dwells with you and will be in you.

Those disciples knew the Spirit of God *with* them, but he was about to dwell *in* them. So the ministry of the Spirit is increased in a great way at Pentecost. The Spirit lived with the saints of the Old Testament, but he would soon be in them at Pentecost.

The Baptism of the Holy Spirit

So what is this baptism of the Holy Spirit? What is this promise of the Father? Peter explains what is happening in the baptism with the Holy Spirit, he says in verses 16–17:

Acts 2:16-17 | But this is what was uttered through the prophet Joel: [17] "And in the last days it shall be, God declares, that I will pour out my Spirit on all flesh, and your sons and your daughters shall prophesy, and your young men shall see visions, and your old men shall dream dreams."

Jesus said in Acts 1:4, "Wait for the promise of the Father," "Wait for the baptism of the Spirit." What he is saying is, "Wait till the promise of Joel 2 is fulfilled." I say that to help us understand that this baptism is not merely for the Apostles. It is for all flesh. Anyone who believes in Jesus. So what is this baptism? John Piper helps us with his comments.

Being baptized with the Holy Spirit (the way Luke means it) is not the same as being born again or being united to Christ by the work of the Holy Spirit. Well, what then does Jesus mean in Acts 1:5? I think when he says you will be baptized with the Holy Spirit, he means you will receive extraordinary power for Christ-exalting ministry.[9]

Certainly, the Spirit comes to convert and indwell. But the 120 who are waiting for the Spirit are already converted. The Spirit is with them. Of course, the Spirit is going to convert many at Pentecost. But the emphasis of Pentecost is being empowered—clothed with power—for Christ exalting ministry.

---

[9] Ibid.

Wasn't Pentecost Unique?

In some ways the outpouring of the Spirit at Pentecost is a unique event, because it is the birth of the New Testament church. But in another way, it is something that we all have: empowerment. And we need that outpouring over and over and over again, on all flesh, in very generation.

Pentecost was a unique experience, in that it was the inaugural event of the church, but it was not unique in that the power being poured out is the continuing event of the church. The power of Pentecost has not ceased. God intends to clothe all of us in that same power of Pentecost. It was unique in that it was the first time it happened. It was unique in the miracles that occurred, precisely the flaming tongues of fire above their heads and the ability for that moment to reverse the Tower of Babel division of the languages. They could now all understand all nations. Foreign languages were not a barrier on the day of Pentecost. That's all unique. But what is not unique is the power. We are to continue seeking that glorious power, and it's all yours in Christ. We are to live in that power. That's the difference with Peter and all the apostles. That power drove them to the uttermost parts of the earth.

Peter is changed! So let's consider Peter again for a moment. He's waiting and praying. But soon, he's going to stand before the entire crowd and preach with power. What was the difference between him fifty days earlier, and the day of Pentecost? Why the radical change? We know what it was. It was the promise of the Holy Spirit given in Ezekiel and Joel and Isaiah.

We Need This Power

I believe we are in a time when we need this awakening power of the Spirit. It is ours in Christ. It is a power that changes us. It is a power that changes nations. But how?

The Times and Seasons

In the midst of this exciting speculation, Jesus called the eleven together at the crest of the Mount of Olives. The apostolic band was aflame with expectancy.[10] So the apostles, after all this kingdom teaching, and the promise of kingdom power, they still don't get it.

---

[10] Hughes. *Acts*, 15.

Acts 1:6 | So when they had come together, they asked him, "Lord, will you at this time restore the kingdom to Israel?"

What would the pouring out of the Spirit bring? Perhaps, a new theocracy for Israel, or so thought at least some of the apostles. They thought the kingdom of God was going to be established by political, earthly power. Their idea of the Messiah was a soldier like Judas Maccabeus (Judas the Hammer), who was going to be strong enough to drive out the occupying military forces and decimate Rome.[11] They had a different idea of Holy Spirit power than Jesus. They were excited, nonetheless.

Aren't we like that? We are so concerned about God's timing. We get so excited about life, and then a trial comes. We are just like the disciples, aren't we? We want to know how everything is going to turn out. We don't want to wait. We don't want to trust God. But that's precisely what Jesus tells them. Trust God with the times and seasons.

Acts 1:7 | He said to them, "It is not for you to know times or seasons that the Father has fixed by his own authority.

As far as what God does in the sphere of politics and nations, that's up to God. That's not something we direct. It's something the sovereign God directs. Then what's our part? Be a witness where you are. That's what we are called to do. This baptism of the Holy Spirit is for one thing: living out the life of Jesus in witness to the world.

The Power of the Spirit

Acts 1:8 | But you will receive power when the Holy Spirit has come upon you, and you will be my witnesses in Jerusalem and in all Judea and Samaria, and to the end of the earth.

It's essentially, the Spirit changing us. First, we are saved and indwelt. You know you are indwelt, because there is an empowerment. And we are to be witnesses to Christ in our own communities (our Jerusalem). Then the circle grows wider to all Judah and Samaria—all Israel (our nation), and then to the end of the earth (all other nations). There is a concern about my own community, my nation, and the

---

[11] James Montgomery Boice, *Acts: An Expositional Commentary* (Grand Rapids, MI: Baker Books, 1997), 18.

world. If we don't witness for Christ in our own immediate situation, we probably will not be concerned to do so anywhere else.[12]

But practically how did this happen? It was the normal means of grace in life-on-life discipleship. The disciples were meeting daily. They were praying. They were fellowshipping with the word. We learn about that (Acts 2:42-47). We see life-on-life discipleship. Committed to God. Committed to each other.

> *Acts 2:42-43* | And they devoted themselves to the apostles' teaching and the fellowship, to the breaking of bread and the prayers. [43] And awe came upon every soul.

What's the point? It's in the midst of life-on-life discipleship, waiting on God, expecting his empowerment, that the awakening from God comes. It's the awakening that changes individuals and families and churches and nations. It is the enablement of the Spirit that helps us share Jesus with others.

> **Acts 1:8b** | You will be my witnesses in Jerusalem and in all Judea and Samaria, and to the end of the earth.

Jesus' Last Words. These are Jesus' last words on earth. They are his marching orders. The disciples are to wait, and once they have the empowering Holy Spirit, they are to witness. That is what advances the kingdom. Evangelism is not a calling for just some; it is a mandate for every believer. We are to obey Jesus' call to care enough to share Jesus. But it's clear here in Acts, that it's not just words. It's your life. You live out the life of Jesus.

Jesus' with Skin On. God calls us to be Jesus with skin on. We are to be empowered by his presence through the Holy Spirit, and then go be Jesus to each other and to this world. This is in the soil of life-on-life discipleship. Waiting. Prayer. Empowerment. They were living in life-on-life discipleship. That's what we need to be doing. That's when the truly first great awakening came. And thousands have followed.

Not Earthly Politics. We must not be confused as to how we are to spread the kingdom. We are not to do things the world's way. We are not to establish the kingdom politically—by law, by getting Christians into high positions in government, and by imposing our vision of

---

[12] William H. Baker, "Acts," in *Evangelical Commentary on the Bible*, vol. 3, Baker Reference Library (Grand Rapids, MI: Baker Book House, 1995), 886.

society on the world.¹³ No, we are to preach the death and resurrection of Christ, his power to save. That's the only hope for this world. Charles Haddon Spurgeon, one of the greatest preachers who ever lived, said: "I'd rather lead one soul to Jesus than to unpack all the mysteries in the divine word."¹⁴ We believe in the exclusivity of Jesus! He's the only way to the Father.

> Acts 4:12 | There is salvation in no one else, for there is no other name under heaven given among men by which we must be saved.

Go into all the world! Preach the gospel! Be my witnesses. And just as he said that, our Lord Jesus is lifted up on the Mount of Olives and ascends to heaven.

KINGDOM AUTHORITY (1:9-11)

The Authority in Jesus' Ascension

We see the one who gave these marching orders is the King of kings. He's the Messiah of Psalm 2. He's the Ancient of Days from Daniel (Dan 7:9). He ascends to heaven with all power and kingdom authority. Truly, this is the one before whom every knee shall bow and every tongue confess, that he is Lord (Yahweh) and Messiah. Listen to what Luke writes about the ascension.

> **Acts 1:9-11** | And when he had said these things, as they were looking on, he was lifted up, and a cloud took him out of their sight. ¹⁰ And while they were gazing into heaven as he went, behold, two men stood by them in white robes, ¹¹ and said, "Men of Galilee, why do you stand looking into heaven? This Jesus, who was taken up from you into heaven, will come in the same way as you saw him go into heaven."

The Authority in Jesus' Return

With rapt attention the disciples watch as Jesus is taken up from them in a cloud. The two men, probably angelic beings (*cf* Jn 20:12), explain that the ascension is a model for the second advent. Just as you watch him ascend, so you should be watching and waiting for Jesus to

---

¹³ Boice. *Acts*, 19.
¹⁴ Charles Haddon Spurgeon. "Christ in You" Metropolitan Tabernacle Pulpit Volume 29 (London: Passemore & Alabaster, 1873), preached May 13, 1883.

return (*cf* 1 Thess 1:10). ¹⁵ This is the one who's going to judge the living and the dead! Obey him. Listen to him! By the way, if language means anything at all, then Christ's coming will be literal and physical according to the record. The angels said to the disciples:

Acts 1:11b | This Jesus, who was taken up from you into heaven, will come in the same way as you saw him go into heaven.

Nothing could be clearer. And it is important that we stress this physical aspect of Christ's return, for there are those of a liberal persuasion who maintain that it should be interpreted symbolically. They say that Christ came again with the Holy Spirit at Pentecost, or that he is always coming again whenever a person commits his or her life to him in faith.¹⁶ We believe in the personal, physical return of our Lord Jesus Christ in power and glory. I was there on the Mount of Olives where Jesus ascended about three years ago (2018). Just as Jesus ascended into the clouds, he will return in the same way. He's going to split the Mount of Olives.

Zechariah 14:4 | On that day his feet shall stand on the Mount of Olives that lies before Jerusalem on the east, and the Mount of Olives shall be split in two from east to west by a very wide valley, so that one half of the Mount shall move northward, and the other half southward.

We see it has been prophesied that at the moment Jesus' feet touch the ground at the Mount of Olives there will be a great earthquake that will cause the Eastern ("Golden") Gate to open. And he will walk through the Eastern Gate in Jerusalem when he returns to this earth at his Second Coming (*cf* Eze 44:1-2).

The Authority in Jesus' Session

Look at his victorious ascension to the right hand of the Father. What is he doing since he ascended? In heaven today, the Savior is our interceding High Priest, giving us the grace that we need for life and service (Heb 4:14–16). He is also our Advocate before the Father, forgiving us when we confess our sins (1 Jn 1:9–2:2). He ever lives to

---

¹⁵ Baker. *Acts*, ibid.
¹⁶ Peter Williams, *Acts: Church on the Move: An Expositional Commentary on the Acts of the Apostles*, Exploring the Bible Commentary (Leominster: DayOne, 2004), 14.

intercede for us (Heb 7:25). The exalted and glorified Head of the church is now working with his people on earth and helping them accomplish his purposes, to "go into all the world and preach the gospel to every nation" (Mk 16:15–20).[17]

Look at his ascension: he's going up in victory over sin, death, hell and the grave. He sits down in glorious victory at the right hand of the Father. And just as he ascended, he will come again in power and victory. Saints, every eye will see him. You'll see him. The dead will see him. The living will see him. The graves will open, the sea will give up its dead, and the dead in Christ will rise. We will see him when he comes again.

Conclusion

Jesus' ascension means we have the authority and power to change the world. We are Jesus with skin on. We need to remember who God calls to this. It's not the perfect. Remember Peter. We are looking at his life for almost all of the first 13 chapters of Acts. He's a very feeble man. He's weak. But the power of Christ rests upon him. Thousands are saved. This weak man does life-on-life discipleship, and the world is turned upside down. If God could take such a weak vessel as Peter, he can use you.

Are you weak? Are you willing? Are you waiting for the Spirit's empowerment? Seek that empowerment with the Holy Spirit. You are born again. You are indwelt. But are you empowered? It's yours if you want it. Do you want it?

---

[17] Warren W. Wiersbe, *The Bible Exposition Commentary*, vol. 1 (Wheaton, IL: Victor Books, 1996), 404.

2 | ACTS 1:12-26
READY FOR REVIVAL

All these with one accord were devoting themselves to prayer.
ACTS 1:14

Have you ever had a power outage? This past summer in Elgin, we had a microburst come through and rip up trees, tear up yards, and bent my son Will's basketball rim structure in half. We were without power for a bit. Isn't it frustrating to be without power? You've got your fridge, but you can't open it often, or the food will spoil. You're wired for electricity, but no power is surging. We are often powerless in our Christian life. We've got all the equipment, but no power. So the question is: how do I get the power of the Holy Spirit surging in my life?

Where do we start? We need to see what those early disciples did. They met together continually. Satan does his most destructive work when he isolates us. Are you isolated? Are you on your own in your Christian life? Maybe you feel no one cares.

If we want to the world to be interrupted and turned upside down by the gospel, we have to start with coming together. Right after the ascension, the disciples don't disperse, but their grip on each other is tighter; their love is deeper. God had to bring the disciples and apostles together in a unique way: they had seen the Lord risen from the dead. They were taught by him for 40 days. But they are told to wait for the power from the Spirit on high. We learn a lesson from these dear disciples. We dare not go forward in our own power. Without the filling of the Spirit from on high, we are powerless.

We have to be fully committed the idea that God alone must work. We cannot manufacture godliness in our lives. We cannot construct peace and contentment in our own power. Everything we build is a house of sand that only leads to anxiety and anger and despair. Let's not go there but be ready for God alone to work.

READY FOR GOD TO WORK (1:12-14)

Acts 1:12 | Then they returned to Jerusalem from the mount called Olivet, which is near Jerusalem, a Sabbath day's journey away.

I have a vision of excitement in my mind when I picture the disciples returning to Jerusalem from the Mount of Olives to obey the instructions that Jesus had given them. They were ready to obey the Lord together. Many of them had lived life with Jesus for the last three years. Gathered in the upper room were 120 (1:15), the apostles, the family of Jesus, Lazarus, Mary and Martha, and many others. The eleven Apostles that were left after the death of Judas are named in the text, and we are told, these all continued with one accord in prayer and supplication.[18] This is life-on-life discipleship. They were gathering in the Temple and in the upper room near the Temple. They were eating together (1:40-45), having times of fellowship, and talking about the kingdom. But overall, this was a time where they were praying together.

The Place of Prayer

Acts 1:13a | When they had entered, they went up to the upper room, where they were staying.

Though we cannot be perfectly sure, I personally believe this was the same upper room in which our Lord ate the last supper with the disciples. The Greek text says *"the"* upper room (not just any upper room). If this is correct, it is beautifully fitting that the Holy Spirit was given in the very same room in which Jesus promised him.[19]

---

[18] Sproul, *Acts*, 32.
[19] Hughes, *Acts*, 25.

John 14:16–18 | And I will ask the Father, and he will give you another Helper [Counselor], to be with you forever, [17] even the Spirit of truth... [18] I will not leave you as orphans; I will come to you.

The upper room is traditionally thought to be above John Mark's home. He's the youngest apostle, and it's likely that this upper room was the enclosed upper floor above where he lived. There is a good view of the Temple Mount from that the traditional place of the upper room. Oh Holy Spirit, you were promised to us! Meet us where we are. We need you more than we need air. Guide us. Lead us. Let us never go one step in our own human wisdom.

The People of Prayer

We are told in passing that the Apostles were there with the women and Mary the mother of Jesus and with his brothers.

> **Acts 1:13** | And when they had entered, they went up to the upper room, where they were staying, Peter and John and James and Andrew, Philip and Thomas, Bartholomew and Matthew, James the son of Alphaeus and Simon the Zealot and Judas the son of James.

This is the last reference to Mary that we have anywhere in the New Testament, but we see Mary as a member of the first church. She was there with the rest of the disciples as part of the gathered church, praying for and to her own Son. This is the last mention of her in the Scriptures. Along with Mary, the mother of Jesus, were his own half-brothers. We know from the Gospels that Jesus' brothers were skeptics who rejected his claims to be the Messiah. They asked out loud if he had lost his mind and gone crazy. They said, "He is out of his mind" (Mk 3:21). Jesus' brothers had been unbelievers (Jn 7:5) who opposed Jesus' ministry. But here is hope for all of us. They were persuaded and converted by the resurrection of Christ.[20] James and Jude were both half-brothers of the Lord who each wrote a letter in our New Testament. There was also and "the women" who had so faithfully ministered to Jesus during his life on earth (1:14): dear Mary Magdalene, Mary of Clopas, Susanna, Joanna, Mary of Bethany, Martha (in the kitchen no doubt!), and many others.[21] But there were many others: 120 in total in fact (1:15) who

---

[20] Sproul, *Acts*, 34.
[21] Hughes, *Acts*, 25.

were there praying. It's a diverse group, but it's about to get more diverse. So far you have rich and poor. Lazarus is likely there, so you have the formerly dead and the living! You have former prostitutes (like Mary Magdalene), fisherman, probably some Pharisees like Joseph and Nicodemus. It's a motley crew that's about to get "motlier"! Pentecost is coming, and that means, the Spirit is going to be poured out on all flesh.

What Precedes Prayer

We see already two things about how the church behaved in its first week of existence: obedience and fellowship. These things came before the powerful praying they were doing.

> **Acts 1:14** | All these with one accord were devoting themselves to prayer, together with the women and Mary the mother of Jesus, and his brothers.

Radical Obedience

The first thing that characterized the church in the early days was a radical obedience to Christ. This wasn't easy. One thing they might have done was to give up. Jesus didn't drive out the Romans. So they could have given up waiting on the Spirit and gone back to work like it was all a big game or fairy tale.

They could have given up. Peter had given up when Jesus caught him and restored him. They could have went back to their various professions and business obligations. Some had been fishermen. One was a tax collector. During the prior forty days some of them went back to Galilee and began to take up fishing again. The disciples could have said, "Jesus has left us. He said he is going to come back, but we don't know when that's going to be. Right now we have to get on with the business of living."[22]

They could have went straight to evangelizing. But remember, Jesus says, wait for the Spirit. Who, having witnessed Christ, wouldn't be eager to go out and spread the news everywhere? They were biting at the bit, eager to go. Nevertheless, they stayed where they were told to stay. They waited, and they waited obediently. They knew without Christ they could do nothing.

---

[22] Boice, *Exposition of Acts*, 32.

John 15:5 | Without Me, you can do nothing.

We dare not go forward without the power and blessing of the Lord.

Psalm 127:1 | Unless the Lord builds the house, those who build it labor in vain.

Remember what Zechariah the prophet said.

Zechariah 4:6 | Not by might nor by power, but by my Spirit, says the Lord Almighty.

If you aren't radically committed to moving forward in Christ's power alone, then you are depending on another savior. You are worshipping yourself or someone else. All idolatry is rooted in self worship. There is a sweet trust in Christ and a radical abandonment of the world for these who gathered. If you want to see real intimacy in our church, it has to first begin with a radical obedience to Christ.

Deep Fellowship

Second, they needed deep fellowship with each other. We are told that when they came back to the upper room, they came as a group, as a body. People need people. This need is part of what it means to be a human being. One of the worst things that can happen to a person is to be utterly isolated from other people, and the converse of this is that if we are to grow intellectually, socially, and spiritually, we need others. Christians need other Christians. When you become a Christian, you do not become a Christian in isolation.[23] Instead we intertwine our lives with one another. We help each other. We do the hard work of helping each other forward pointing each other to Christ.

White Hot Coal Turned Cold

I heard of a pastor who visited with a parishioner who had been derelict in his duty to participate in the life of the church. The minister asked him, "Why is it that you are never in church? Why aren't you involved in any of the programs? I know you're on our rolls. I remember the day you joined. You've been baptized and you've made a profession of faith, but you're never around."

The fellow replied, "Well, I don't need the church. My faith is private and personal. I don't need the rituals and trappings of religion. I can worship God by myself. I can get by just fine on my own."

---

[23] Boice, *Exposition of Acts,* 32.

They were having a picnic while this discussion was going on, and the minister walked over to a charcoal grill where there was a heap of white burning coals prepared for the cooking of the hamburgers. With the tongs he took one of the coals off the pile and moved it out to the side, away from the center of the fire, and continued to converse with this church member. After a few minutes, he pointed to that coal and said, "Ten minutes ago that coal was white hot, but now it's cold." Once it was removed from the support system of the rest of those burning coals, it lost its heat, its capacity to be productive in the purpose for which it was made.

We cannot stand alone. We need each other. We need the support of fellowship, the mutual encouragement, the strength, and the prayers of the community in which we are involved. I get excited when people join our church and become part of the congregation. There is such a diversity in the Body, and yet there is such a fervency! That is what happened in the early church. The Apostles went back to the upper room. Later 120 gathered there as a group—the very beginning of the church. What did they do? How did they spend their time? "These all continued with one accord in prayer and supplication." They gathered together for prayer.[24]

The Power of Prayer

When the Lord cleansed the temple from its commercialism, he reminded the people that his Father's house was to be a house of prayer (Mt 21:13). The church, during the first week of its existence, was united together in prayer. Don't forget the incredible promises of the power of prayer.

> *Jeremiah 33:3* | Call to me and I will answer you and tell you great and unsearchable things you do not know.

No matter what situation you are in, you can call on God.

> *Psalm 91:15* | When he calls to me, I will answer him; I will be with him in trouble; I will rescue him and honor him.

Luke does not tell us what they were praying about, but there was plenty about which to pray. They could have been offering thanksgiving for what they had witnessed and experienced. They might have spent

---

[24] Sproul, *Acts*, 32.

time in confession as well as praying for the burgeoning expansion of the church that was going to come in the near future. Whatever might have comprised those prayers, they stayed together, praying with one another.

What is prayer but connecting with a God where no idolatry is permitted? You cannot have two masters. You cannot worship God and money, God and sex, God and any way that you want to choose to worship yourself and your way. There is no competition in God's realm. He is God alone. When we enter into eternity, there will be no sin, no confusion, no idolatry. Prayer is turning our hearts to that realm and bringing that realm to earth.

God Alone Can Do What is Needed

Most importantly, prayer teaches us that needs to be done in your life, only God can do. Now we have to come together, as we will see, for God to do it. But the pastor or counselor or fellow believer can't change you. What needs to be done is always done by God, and that is why prayer is so important.

READY FOR WORLD TRANSFORMATION (1:15-26)

When the apostles would one be those who transformed the world. It would later be said of them in Thessalonica:

> Acts 17:6 | These men who have turned the world upside down have come here also.

But at this moment they felt powerless, not world transformers. You may feel powerless today. That's where the disciples were. They had the kingdom teaching from the resurrected Christ. But they lacked power. They dared not go forward without his power. All the men and women listed here are sidelined if you will. They are waiting on God to go forward.

Sidelined Because of Hurt

Maybe you feel sidelined today. Perhaps it's because you've been hurt by the church in the past. The church is an imperfect place. There are sins and scandals sometimes. Jesus had great scandals among his own 12 disciples. Peter had denied him three times.

Discipleship is *messy*. And what about Judas? What greater scandal is there but to have one of Jesus own 12 disciples turn against him and sell him to the highest bidder for 30 pieces of silver? What scandal.

But that's how discipleship is. It's messy. If you don't want messiness, you don't want discipleship. Look at how the disciples were scattered.

Remember Peter had given up completely. And what did Jesus do? He went after him. And what did the apostles do after Judas had betrayed Jesus? They followed the leading of the Spirit. You can't change the world if you are looking at anyone but Jesus. Some of you might be looking at the church, and you're disappointed. You're looking at your spouse, and you're disappointed. You're looking at yourself! And you're disappointed. Stop looking at man and look up to God!

> *Jeremiah 17:5-7* | Cursed is the man who trusts in man... ⁶ He is like a shrub in the desert, and shall not see any good come. ⁷ "Blessed is the man who trusts in the Lord, whose trust is the Lord. ⁸ He is like a tree planted by water.

Every time you look to man, you will be disappointed. God alone can give you the power for joy, satisfaction, and power for the Christian life.

Peter the Brokenhearted

Now we have Peter, in verse 15, standing up and getting them ready as they replace Judas Iscariot. He knows what Christ can do. Here's a man that can testify of the power of Jesus to restore!

> **Acts 1:15** | In those days Peter stood up among the brothers (the company of persons was in all about 120).

Perhaps you are here like Peter, and you are powerless, because you need restoration. You've sinned against the Lord, and you think the Lord is done with you. Can I just encourage you?

> *Psalm 34:18-19* | The Lord is near to the brokenhearted and saves the crushed in spirit. ¹⁹ Many are the afflictions of the righteous, but the Lord delivers him out of them all.

Maybe you're like Peter—afflicted, brokenhearted, crushed in spirit. God will deliver you out of all your afflictions. He loves you. I know you can't imagine a God that would love so deeply, but God is the ultimate standard of what love is. "God is love" (1 Jn 4:8). The story of Peter is a wonderful and thrilling story of the power of God to transform the life of a humble fisherman into that of a mighty leader in the early church.

His prophetic change of name implies that though Peter was weak and impetuous and headstrong, he was going to be a foundation stone with the other Apostles. God can take a weak, cracked vessel of clay, and make him a strong foundation stone. Peter would eventually display that rock-like faith that would enable him to emerge as the leader of God's making.

There is a real sense in which God's grace is doing that all the time. God molds and shapes men and women to make them the kind of people he wants them to be and to fit them for the tasks he wants them to do.[25]

Judas the Betrayer

Here we are dealing with a totally different kind of person as Luke makes clear in his reference to the tragic suicide of Judas.[26] Judas was a very dangerous kind of powerless. He wasn't a believer. He trusted in his own power. That's a scary and frightening thing. He trusted in his education, his family's reputation, and his money. Oh, he had lots of money. He lived the comfortable life, the materialistic life. And Peter stands up among the disciples and tells his story.

> **Acts 1:15-17** | In those days Peter stood up among the brothers (the company of persons was in all about 120) and said, **16** "Brothers, the Scripture had to be fulfilled, which the Holy Spirit spoke beforehand by the mouth of David concerning Judas, who became a guide to those who arrested Jesus. **17** For he was numbered among us and was allotted his share in this ministry."

His Teacher. Judas sat under the greatest Teacher in the history of the world, and yet he remained unconverted. God in human flesh was his Teacher, yet his heart remained hard.

His home. Judas was raised in a believing and devout home. We learn this by his name: "Judas". Judas today is not a good name, but then, it was a name of great honor. With a name Judas, or as it is in Hebrew: "Judah," he was named after the royal line of David, of the tribe of Judah. He would have grown up in a very devout Jewish family.

His education. We learn something from his surname as well. The name "Iscariot" tells us where he lived. Iscariot in Hebrew means "Man

---

[25] Williams, *Acts*, 17.
[26] Ibid., 18-19.

of Carioth" which is a city between Jerusalem and Hebron. Judas was not from Samaria, but a highly educated man of Judah, near Jerusalem.

His deception. Judas was a false convert. He might have fooled the other disciples, but he didn't fool God. He betrayed the Almighty Son of God. But why? From the Scriptures Peter quotes, we see how God sovereignly guided the events. Judas sold the Son of God to be crucified. God is able to use the greatest sins for his greater glory. Through Judas' sin came the greatest redemption. God is not bound by man's sin. James tells us that God is not the author of sin.

> *James 1:13* | God cannot be tempted with evil, and he himself tempts no one.

God is good all the time. Not even this evil man could stop Jesus from pouring out his love to the world. So God guided the events after Judas committed his sin. And Judas was to be replaced. That was what God put in the Scriptures.

His suicide. One other thing. The price Judas received was 30 pieces of silver, but the price he paid in remorse and revulsion was so enormous he could not live with it, and "he went and hanged himself" (Mt 27:5). [27]

> **Acts 1:18-19** | Now this man acquired a field with the reward of his wickedness, and falling headlong he burst open in the middle and all his bowels gushed out. **19** And it became known to all the inhabitants of Jerusalem, so that the field was called in their own language Akeldama, that is, Field of Blood.

Evidently Peter gives a fuller description of the suicide. Judas did hang himself, but the rope snapped, and the traitor fell headlong and was dashed to pieces in the gruesome way Peter describes. Such was the traitor's end: he went "to his own place" (Acts 1:25). He was hurled headlong into a lost eternity. [28]

Judas was remorseful but not repentant. Remorse leads to hopelessness and despair, but repentance leads to restoration and life. [29]

---

[27] Ibid.

[28] John Phillips. *Exploring Acts: An Expository Commentary*, The John Phillips Commentary Series (Grand Rapids, MI: Kregel Publications, 2009), Ac 1:18.

[29] Williams, *Acts*, 18-19.

His destiny. After Jesus ascended, the Apostles went back to the upper room and searched through the Scriptures to see if they could find anything about Judas, and they read David's prophetic writing about the one who would betray the Messiah and how that one would have to be replaced. [30] Peter quotes directly from Psalm 69:25. The second text is Psalm 109:8.

> **Acts 1:20** | "For it is written in the Book of Psalms, "'May his camp become desolate, and let there be no one to dwell in it'; and "'Let another take his office.'"

Judas is called the "son of perdition," or son of *eternal damnation.*

> *John 17:12* | Jesus said, "none of them [his disciples] is lost, but the son of perdition; that the scripture might be fulfilled."

Judas was prophesied by Jesus to be the son of perdition according to Psalm 109:8, "Let another take his office."

His choice. Though all of this was prophesied, we must understand that Judas made all his own free choices. All the great confessions of faith from the Westminster to the Baptist confession all teach that God does not hinder the free agency of man. It was Judas's choice to give himself to the wicked one and try and destroy Jesus. In Luke 22 we read how "Satan entered Judas" (Lk 22:3). That is a dreadfully chilling phrase, since it tells us that Judas, with his eyes wide open, gave our great God incarnate over to death. Judas deliberately sold his soul to the devil. He willingly allowed himself to become the instrument of Satan.

This is a terrifying warning about the hardening power of sin. Judas sinned in the light! He knew better! Judas had shared in the ministry of Christ, had seen his miracles and witnessed his love and compassion. But as time passed instead of growing closer to Christ, he grew away from him. Sin exerted its hardening power until Satan possessed him completely. Don't harden your heart!

So, if you want power, don't be like Judas. He trusted in himself: his education, his money, his ability to deceive people. And don't be discouraged those like Judas in the church. If one out of twelve was a devil in Jesus' congregation, what does that say about his church today? We must not give up on seeking God's power and enablement just

---

[30] Sproul, *Acts*, 36.

because of those like Judas. Even Paul testified of those like Judas among his own friends.

> 2 Timothy 4:10 | Demas, in love with this present world, has deserted me.

Don't get distracted with those who fall away from Christ. It's been my conviction that I will stand, even if I'm the last Christian on earth. Those who we thought were good men have been disqualified from their office, and some have even fallen away from the faith. My constant prayer is God will give me the strength to stand. And in his strength, I will stand for Christ, even if I have to stand alone. Will you? Don't look to those who fall away and get discouraged. Look to those like Peter, who have fallen and been restored!

Matthias the Humble

Now we come to another person who perhaps felt powerless, but he was ready. He wanted the Spirit's. He had been with Jesus from the time of John the Baptist. He was willing to wait as long as he could be used by God. He was faithful. His name is Matthias. We find out he is a man who is willing to replace Judas. He's a man who had intimate personal knowledge of the Lord during his earthly ministry from beginning to end.

Evidently there were a number who were qualified to take Judas' place, which indicates that the number of faithful and consistent followers of Jesus throughout the years of his public ministry was far more than the twelve.[31] We read about Matthias beginning in Acts 1:21.

> **Acts 1:21-23** | So one of the men who have accompanied us during all the time that the Lord Jesus went in and out among us, **22** beginning from the baptism of John until the day when he was taken up from us—one of these men must become with us a witness to his resurrection." **23** And they put forward two, Joseph called Barsabbas, who was also called Justus, and Matthias.

Joseph "Justus" Barsabbas. Now you see these two men: Joseph Barsabbas, whose nick name is "Justus". I kind of get that this is the guy maybe the other disciples were pulling for. They seem to know his father, since he's called Joseph bar (which means "son of") Sabbas.

---

[31] Phillips, *Exploring Acts*, Ac 1:21–22.

Maybe they knew Joseph's father Sabbas. They knew him well enough that they gave him a nickname, "Justus." This is a Latin name, meaning "just" or "righteous", and was probably given him on account of his high character and integrity. In Christian tradition he is numbered among the seventy disciples mentioned in Luke 10, although the Bible mentions no names. It is said that he became the bishop or pastor of a small town church in northern Israel where he died as a martyr under the persecution of the Roman Emperor Vespasian in AD 68.[32] But it's not Justus who is chosen. It's Matthias. God often chooses people who we are not considering.

> *1 Samuel 16:7* | The LORD sees not as man sees: man looks on the outward appearance, but the LORD looks on the heart.

God doesn't call many mighty, but he calls the least among us to be used in the greatest of ways.

> *1 Corinthians 1:26-29, NLT* | Remember, dear brothers and sisters, that few of you were wise in the world's eyes or powerful or wealthy when God called you. ²⁷ Instead, God chose things the world considers foolish in order to shame those who think they are wise. And he chose things that are powerless to shame those who are powerful. ²⁸ God chose things despised by the world, things counted as nothing at all, and used them to bring to nothing what the world considers important. ²⁹ As a result, no one can ever boast in the presence of God.

Criteria for Apostles

If we look carefully at this, we can see three basic criteria for apostleship before Pentecost as they choose Matthias. Matthias had been traveling with Jesus since the beginning. Of course, we know that Jesus personally chose his disciples. He said to them.

> *John 15:16* | You did not choose me, but I chose you.

And this is the first qualification to be an apostle: a candidate had to have been a member of Jesus' disciples from the beginning, for the three years of Jesus' public ministry in order to qualify for selection to the rank of Apostle. Second, he had to have been an eyewitness of the resurrection. The third criterion for apostleship, far and away the most important, is the direct and immediate commissioning to the office by Christ himself. Paul was an exception, but he was commissioned by

---

[32] Josephus. *Wars of the Jews*, Book 4, chapter 8, section 1

Christ directly and went back to Jerusalem for a time to have the full blessing of the twelve there.

Trusting God Alone

The eleven apostles didn't trust themselves to choose the twelfth apostle, so they let God choose by lots. They knew their Bible. The lot was a way of giving God complete control of a decision.

> *Proverbs 16:33* | The lot is cast into the lap, but its every decision is from the Lord.

It's kind of like rolling the dice. In choosing lots, they were following an ancient tradition in the Old Testament involving the use of the Urim and the Thummim. When Old Testament priests were unable to discern the will of God, they prayerfully cast lots, the outcome of which was determined by the providence of God. Here, the lot fell upon Matthias, and we hear no more about him afterward. We have only the record of his selection to apostleship, which completed the Twelve. James was martyred shortly thereafter, but he was not replaced.[33] So Matthias was chosen by lots.

> **Acts 1:24-26**| And they prayed and said, "You, Lord, who know the hearts of all, show which one of these two you have chosen **25** to take the place in this ministry and apostleship from which Judas turned aside to go to his own place." **26** And they cast lots for them, and the lot fell on Matthias, and he was numbered with the eleven apostles.

What a curious practice! Being chosen by lots is not unheard of, even in our modern day. My children's great grandfather (Ira Wenger, *1911-1991*) was a Mennonite deacon and preacher. He was chosen by lots. They brought forth the qualified men there in Wayland, Iowa at Bethel Mennonite Church, where they are still faithfully preaching the gospel today. That's how they did it. They didn't want to choose for themselves. They took three strips of paper—lots, if you will. They let the strips stick out of the Bible, and each man chose a lot. The one with the longest lot was to be the preacher. And that landed on Great Grandpa Ira. I have stacks and stacks of handwritten sermon notes from the late 50s until his death. But he was chosen by lots.

---

[33] Sproul, *Acts*, 36-37.

The apostles had chosen Mathias. They were ready: ready to turn the world upside down. But they had no power. They needed the Spirit to come and clothe them. They dare not venture out in their own power. They were powerless to witness. They could gather in fellowship, they could pray, they could act in unity, they could make decisions regarding the corporate life of the assembly, they could have assurance among themselves that their actions were right, they could talk to each other about Jesus, care for each other's needs. But they were powerless to witness. A hostile world lay beyond the walls of their upper room. They were powerless to impact that world for Christ. For that they needed the Holy Spirit, and for him they had to wait.[34]

Conclusion

Do you feel powerless? Don't be afraid dear child of God. It's true, we have all the equipment: all the Bible learning, all the giftedness and the ability to carry something forward, but we dare not, until we truly have the power. Trust the Lord. Wait on his timing. Surrender all that you are and all that you have to him.

Perhaps you are on the edge, teetering in defeat in your marriage. Maybe you are defeated in some sin of pride and self-will. Don't move forward in your own power. Lean into the Holy Spirit. Be sure you are filled and clothed with the Spirit. Let the gentle dove rest on your marriage. You can't do it alone. You need fellowship. You need brothers and sisters surrounding you with prayer. You might be like Peter, defeated and brokenhearted. Oh, God's got something amazing for you. You see, just when you think it's the end, that's when God steps in.

We dare not go forward in our own power. In C. S. Lewis's novel, *The Chronicles of Narnia*, Aslan, the great lion, is the Christ-figure. The evil White Witch captures him, binds him, and kills him. The four children, Lucy, Edmond, Susan, and Peter, give up all hope. Exhausted weeping over Aslan, they sleep. When they wake up, they're horrified to see mice gnawing on Aslan's dead body.

But upon further, closer, inspection they realize that the mice are actually eating away the ropes that bind the great lion king. Before their eyes, they see him rise. With their own ears they hear him roar. They're ecstatic yet confused. "How? Why? What?" they stammer. Aslan hushes them. And then, Aslan roars a roar that frightens the White

---

[34] Phillips, *Exploring Acts*, Ac 1:26.

Witch, but when the children hear the risen Aslan roar, they are revived go forward in his power, and they conquer the White Witch.

What about you saint? Are you weeping? Do you feel defeated? Powerless? Let's join our Aslan in resurrection power! Let's lean on the power that raised Jesus from the dead. When our peace is interrupted, and our fullness is drained, let us look to the same power that raised Jesus from the dead. This resurrection power is the same power that is at work now within us (Eph 1:18–23).[35] Jesus Christ is alive! He is risen! He is raised to the right hand of the Father in victory! We dare not go forward in our own power, but we go in the power of the Spirit that will transform the world.

---

[35] Robert Kelleman. *Gospel-Centered Counseling* (Grand Rapids: Zondervan, 2014), 90-91.

3 | ACTS 2:1-13
PENTECOST

When the day of Pentecost arrived, they were all together in one place. And suddenly there came from heaven a sound like a mighty rushing wind, and it filled the entire house where they were sitting. And divided tongues as of fire appeared to them and rested on each one of them. And they were all filled with the Holy Spirit.

ACTS 2:1-4

Our passage brings us to the first great outpouring of love from God on the nations. This is not just a promise for the first generation, but every generation till Jesus comes again. I want to experience an outpouring of the love of God. Right now, may the Spirit fill us and cover us with infinite divine love that satisfies every longing, every dream, every desire.

What would it look like to have true visitation from God? When he visited the earth in human flesh, it was in a very humble place: in Bethlehem, which was such a little forgotten town. God visited us in a barn with animals. When God shows up, he shows up for the humble. It's always for the powerless, so that his glory can be displayed.

In the book of Acts, at Pentecost, God came down in his Holy Spirit, and he visited those 120 disciples, who were waiting for that power, to be clothed with power from God. They were powerless and humble and hungry. They knew what needed to be done but had no power to do it. But they knew who had the power. How do we get that special outpouring of the Spirit? Jonathan Edwards, the leader of the Great Awakening some 250 years ago in this country, put it like this:

> From the fall of man to our day, the work of redemption in its effect has mainly been carried on by extraordinary movements of the Spirit of God. Though there is a more constant influence of God's Spirit always in some degree attending his means of grace, yet the way in which the greatest things have been done towards carrying on this work, always have been by remarkable outpourings at special seasons of mercy.[36]

In other words, from time to time, God has moved in extraordinary ways in history through the outpouring of his Spirit on his church to do extraordinary things. God has poured out his Spirit in fresh, new, uncustomary, dramatic ways. These times have been called times of revival or awakening or reformation. These kinds of revivals or reformations often come at times with the moral fabric of a society is ripping apart, and they change the moral fabric of society to reflect Christ. I want to consider how this first happened in Acts 2 to increase your expectation for the Spirit of God for us today.

We desperately need revival in our country. We need personal revival in our own lives. They needed revival at the time of Pentecost. The outpouring of the Spirit was an absolute necessity. The Roman empire was teetering and weak. In the first three centuries, Rome was falling apart, and the gospel's power spread so quickly, that by the third century, the Roman Emperor Constantine, as misguided as he was, recognized that Christians were the only stable fabric of society.

Many awakenings have come since then through men like Peter Waldo (b. 1140), John Wycliffe (b. 1320), and John Hus (b. 1369), but in recent history, we see God breaking forth afresh beginning in 1517 with Martin Luther, and an outpouring of the Holy Spirit followed for fifty years. Over 2000 new congregations of born-again Christians are started throughout Europe through men like Luther, Calvin, John

---

[36] Jonathan Edwards. "A History of Redemption", *Works*, vol. 1 (Carlisle, PA: Banner of Truth Trust, 1974), 539.

Knox, and William Tyndale. The Moravians experienced revivals in the sixteen and seventeen hundreds. Some of the churches during this time in what is today the Czech Republic ministered to around 20,000 people each week in one congregation with various languages. God can do anything!

When God moves, time stops. The Spirit ministers through prayer meetings that seem to have no end. We've seen God pour forth in our own country with many awakenings beginning with Jonathan Edwards in the 1700s and then the second Great Awakening in the 1800s which created the modern mission's movement. After that came the third Great Awakening through D.L. Moody and William Booth in the early 1900s. then most recently, in the 1960s and 70s, God moved again through the Jesus movement where many hundreds of thousands were swept into the kingdom. Some of you here are old enough that you were alive when that happened, and you can remember. Again, I want to emphasize that each of these outpourings have occurred when the country or nation was facing deep unrest. I believe we have come again to a time in our nation when we need to ask the Lord again for his reviving and refreshing presence. My intent is to consider what God has done and can do for us by looking at our text in Acts 2.

In Acts 2, we witness an event that changed human history. A small group of ignorant, uneducated men and women from marginal class in a marginal people group in the Roman Empire, within two centuries became the most powerful force in that Roman Empire. How is that? I understand this is a unique moment, but it is also a moment that carries on to us today. It's a power of the Person of the Holy Spirit that continues to be poured out to all nations, as he promised. Every nation will crumble, but what remains will be the true Christians, anointed with the Holy Spirit. As nations teeter and crumble, God often moves in and does his best work. Pentecost was the first of these great outpourings on the Christian church, and until the task of world evangelization is completed, I believe it is our duty to pray for fresh seasons of the extraordinary outpouring of God's Spirit—to awaken and empower the church and to penetrate the final frontiers of world evangelization.

TWO MEANINGS OF PENTECOST

Let's go back to the first Pentecost of the New Testament church. Let's look at the very first of the Great Awakenings if you will. You ask,

"How did that happen?" You can read the whole book of Acts and you'll see them burning but not burning out, a flame, but not flaming out. Why did Jesus choose Pentecost as the day when he would pour out the Spirit on the disciples? There are two possible reasons.

Feast of the First Fruits

The original meaning of Pentecost was that it was the Feast of the First Fruits. The harvest of first fruits happened about 50 days after Passover. That's where you get the word *Pentecost*. It's a week of weeks: 49 days. It's from our Greek and our Latin word for 50 or 5. Fifty days after Passover was when they were celebrating the harvest. It was the Jewish Thanksgiving of the Old Testament.[37]

Moses Meets God Face to Face

But there's a second meaning of Pentecost. The Jews came to recognize that 50 days after Passover was the first Pentecost, when God came down on Mount Sinai and met with Moses face to face and gave the Law and created the new people of God, created Israel, and constituted them a people of God. So the first Pentecost was Moses meeting God face to face, and his face was so bright, he had to wear a veil (Exo 34:29-35). Remember that? Pentecost is all about meeting with God. The Spirit is poured out on Pentecost so that we might know him in a greater way than even Moses!

> 2 Corinthians 3:12-13, 18 | Since we have such a hope, we are very bold, [13] not like Moses, who would put a veil over his face so that the Israelites might not gaze at the outcome of what was being brought to an end... [18] And we all, with unveiled face, beholding the glory of the Lord, are being transformed into the same image from one degree of glory to another. For this comes from the Lord who is the Spirit.

As a result, the Jews, on Pentecost, celebrated God coming down and meeting Moses face to face and the giving of the Law. What did it mean for God to send down his Spirit on that day? What does it teach us about the Spirit of God? This is what it teaches. God creates a new people on Pentecost. He reconstitutes his people by pouring out his

---

[37] Sproul, *Acts*, 41.

Spirit. We learn that through three things: the presence of the future, the outpouring of the Spirit, the salvation of the nations.[38]

Here's the key thought for this passage: God wants us to experience a fresh outpouring of his love through his Spirit and by his word, that it will shake the nations with the embrace of divine love.

THE PRESENCE OF THE FUTURE (2:1)

Acts 2:1 | When the day of Pentecost arrived, they were all together in one place.

What do we mean when we say that when the day of Pentecost arrived, it's a taste of the future? There's coming a time when we will forever have a perfect view of God's love for us. He will wipe away all tears, and we shall be his people, and he shall be our God. All things will be made new. The lion and lamb and the wolf shall all lie down together. But we have that perfect peace of the new creation right now in our hearts. We have the perfect love of Christ poured out to us right now.

The Spirit Brings the Future Now

Pentecost is the celebration of the *first fruits* of the harvest. Israel's first harvest, the *Feast of First Fruits*, is when you taste something that is to come. It's when you get a small experience of what's going to happen later.

Every year as a child I remember celebrating the first fruits of the strawberry harvest in Ponchatoula, Louisiana. The first ingathering of strawberries was the best. We would have the Strawberry Festival to celebrate. Oh, the strawberries were so big! Some of them were the size of my fist when I was a child. It's a taste of the harvest that's about to come: a taste of the future.

There is a theological word for that future age: *eschatology*, the study of the future eschaton, or the end of the present age.[39] The Spirit of God is eschatological. What will the future be like? That's what the Spirit of God introduces us to at Pentecost. There is coming a day when

---

[38] Timothy J. Keller, *The Timothy Keller Sermon Archive*, "The Spirit of God", sermon preached September 17, 1995 (New York City: Redeemer Presbyterian Church, 2013). Several ideas in this study were adapted from Keller's teaching.

[39] Walter A. Elwell and Barry J. Beitzel, "Eschatology," *Baker Encyclopedia of the Bible* (Grand Rapids, MI: Baker Book House, 1988), 716.

God wipes away all tears and gives perfect joy. The Spirit is sent to deliver that (at least in part) to us.

What was God saying by sending the Spirit of God on the *Feast of First Fruits*? Romans 8 gives us a glimpse. Paul talks about the fact that right now everything in this world is subject to decay. He says, "We groan right now." We groan. Why? Everything is subject to futility and decay (Rom 8:20). So, we are groaning.

> Romans 8:20-23 | For the creation was subjected to futility... in hope [21] that the creation itself will be set free from its bondage to corruption and obtain the freedom of the glory of the children of God. [22] For we know that the whole creation has been groaning together in the pains of childbirth until now. [23] And not only the creation, but we ourselves, who have the firstfruits of the Spirit, groan inwardly as we wait eagerly for adoption as sons, the redemption of our bodies.

Everything is falling apart. It looks like the apostle Paul knows advanced physics. Scientists tell us that since the beginning of time, that the universe has been expanding and running down. Paul knew this because the Creator of the universe had revealed it to him.

There was an enormous expenditure of energy in the beginning, in the creation of the universe, but now it's running down. Everything is falling apart. Every day the universe and everything in the universe expends more energy than it creates, and so it's running down. It will run out. Everything is going to more and more disorder, and that includes you and me. Some of you look great. You will not be able to hold on to that. You're going to fall apart. Some of you feel great. You will not be able to hold onto that. You're going to fall apart. "Everything is falling apart," Paul says. Everything is subject to decay. "But," he says, "someday the full glory of God is coming to earth, and it's going to transform everything." Then he has the audacity to say in 8:23, "We know this because we have the first fruits of the Spirit."[40]

Pentecost is an experience of the future! We get a taste now that makes us groan for more. The Spirit of God that comes down into the Christian when you believe is the first installment of the glory of heaven (*cf* Eph 1:13-14). He's our down payment of heaven. His ministry is a slice, only a slice, but a *real* slice of ultimate reality. It is a taste, only a

---

[40] Keller, ibid.

taste, but a *real* taste of the life and the power and the joy of heaven itself.

You Have the Future Now

What's it going to be like in heaven? In heaven we'll see him face to face. If you have the Spirit of God, you are capable of experiences of his presence that you'll have when you are with him in eternity.

Do you see what Paul is saying here in chapter 8? Remember the place where Ma and Pa Kent at some point had to sit down with little Clark Kent and say, "Let me tell you something about who you really are. Let me tell you what kind of powers you have." This is Paul coming to you and me as Christians and saying, "Little Clark, do you know what you have?" You have the ability to experience heaven on earth and to reflect the perfect image of Christ. That's what we mean when we say the Spirit is eschatological. The Spirit is the very presence of the future. Experience your future now, by being filled and anointed with the poured-out presence of the Spirit. The Spirit is the first fruits of our future glory.

On the one hand, you have to remember that we have the first *fruits* of heaven itself, which means we have inside ourselves and our church the power to stem the tide of decay. We believe, because we have the first fruits of heaven, we have the power of the Spirit to overcome spiritual and psychological and social breakdown. So we should give up our small ambitions and have tremendous hope for ministry.[41] That's what this life-on-life discipleship is all about. We need to be able to talk like John Newton, who expressed our longing so well.

> I'm not what I ought to be. I am not what I hope to be, but I'm not what I used to be. And by the grace of God, I am what I am.[42]

There it is: Pentecost. The Spirit gives us the experience of the future now. Something quite amazing occurs at Pentecost: wind and fire! These are two signs introducing us to the presence of the Lord!

---

[41] Keller, ibid.
[42] John Newton, ed. Joseph Foulkes Winks, *The Christian Pioneer, Volume 10* (London: Simpkin, Marshall, and Co., 1856), 128.

THE OUTPOURING OF THE SPIRIT (2:2-3)

Acts 2:2-3 | And suddenly there came from heaven a sound like a mighty rushing wind, and it filled the entire house where they were sitting. ³ And divided tongues as of fire appeared to them and rested on each one of them.

The Surprise of the Holy Spirit

Suddenly—instantly—something radical happened. In the morning hours of Pentecost, the people suddenly hear the sound of a violent wind blowing from heaven. There's no actual wind, but the sound of the wind, like the sound of a hurricane or tornado.

One important aspect of the coming of the Holy Spirit is the suddenness of his appearance. Although, as they were instructed, the disciples stay in Jerusalem to wait for the outpouring of the Spirit, nonetheless his sudden arrival is surprising.[43] Everywhere in the Old Testament that God actually shows up, every time his presence appears you get wind and fire. When God appears to Job, he appears in a *whirlwind*. When God appears to Abraham, he appears as a *burning torch* passing between the pieces of the animal (Gen 15). With Moses, at the first Pentecost, when God came down on Mount Sinai, he came down in a *windstorm and in fire*. Wind and fire. Acts records the next Pentecost. The coming of the Spirit of God was both audible, like the sound of a mighty rushing wind, and visible, with an observable manifestation of fire. Let's look into these two things. *What is this wind? What is this fire?*

The Wind of New Creation

Acts 2:2 | And suddenly there came from heaven a sound like a mighty rushing wind, and it filled the entire house where they were sitting.

The wind is the wind of the new creation. This sound of a mighty, rushing wind, like a tornado or a hurricane, not only fills the house but is also heard throughout the city.[44] It comes straight from heaven. The

---

[43] Simon J. Kistemaker, *Exposition of the Acts of the Apostles*, vol. 17, New Testament Commentary (Grand Rapids: Baker Book House, 1953–2001), 76.

[44] Chalmer Ernest Faw, *Acts*, Believers Church Bible Commentary (Scottdale, PA: Herald Press, 1993), 42.

word "wind" is also the word for "Spirit" in both the Old and New Testament. The Greek word *pneuma* not only means "spirit," but it also means "wind" and "breath." This wind is associated with the power of creation, as in Genesis 1.[45] It brings us back to the first chapter of the Bible. This rushing wind is the sound of the Spirit that was heard at the first creation.

> *Genesis 1:1-2* | In the beginning, God created the heavens and the earth. ² The earth was without form and void, and darkness was over the face of the deep. And the Spirit of God was hovering over the face of the waters.

The reason for the sound of the rushing wind, is that at Pentecost we have a new creation, a second creation, a creation that is redemptive. This is the Creator God coming to visit us. Just as the Spirit/wind hovered over the face of the waters, here he hovers to bring forth a new creation. It's just like the Valley of the Dry Bones passage in Ezekiel 37, where God summons a new creation from the old.

> *Ezekiel 37:9* | Come from the four winds, O breath, and breathe on these slain, that they may live.

The sound of wind, then, was a reminder of creation, indeed that a *new* creation was beginning. The *old* was giving way to the *new*. As Paul would say,

> *2 Corinthians 5:17* | Therefore, if anyone is in Christ, he is a new creation. The old has passed away; behold, the new has come.

Those who live in this era, post-Pentecost, are living in the power of the new creation now. The new order of existence has broken through into this present space-time continuum. The *breath* of God is being experienced. The life-giving atmosphere of the new creation has arrived.[46] The coming of the Holy Spirit as a violent wind, then, is the coming of the creative power of God to inaugurate a new era in which men and women live in the life-giving, creative power of the Spirit. No longer would he merely be with us, but he would be in us (Jn 14:16-17). This is the beginning of the new creation here at Pentecost.

---

[45] Sproul, *Acts*, 42.
[46] Derek W. H. Thomas, *Acts*, ed. Richard D. Phillips, Philip Graham Ryken, and Daniel M. Doriani, Reformed Expository Commentary (Phillipsburg, NJ: P&R Publishing, 2011), 29.

The Fire of God's Presence

Acts 2:3 | And divided tongues as of fire appeared to them and rested on each one of them.

They heard the wind when the Spirit came: the wind of new creation. Now they see the fire of tongues upon each person. Why tongues of fire? God is reuniting humanity. All the walls of hostility come down when the Spirit comes. The confusion of languages that came at Babel is now removed.

Fire Illuminates

Fire, like wind, was a symbol of the presence of God. A *pillar of fire* led the church through the wilderness (Exo 13:21–22), and it was a *burning bush* that symbolized God's presence to Moses (Exo 3:2–5).[47] These are flames that do not consume but, like the burning bush (Exo 3:2–6), show God's presence.[48] The manifestation of the Spirit as a fire is indicating first, the ministry of the Spirit to guide the believer into all truth. The Spirit is like the fire in the lampstands that gives light to our path. He leads and guides the believer.

Fire Burns

What are these tongues of fire? It is that the presence of God demonstrating that sin had been dealt with. Fire was also a symbol of judgment. Remember the words of John the Baptist in Luke 3 (referring to Jesus).

Luke 3:16 | He will baptize you with the Holy Spirit and with fire.

Jesus would say that he had indeed come to bring "fire" (Lk 12:49–50), but this was a reference to the cross. The lost will spend eternity in a lake of fire.[49] There are the flames of eternal hell fire awaiting those who do not have the Spirit. The burnt offering was a constant fixture in the Temple. And the price had to be paid, the whole burnt offering had to be entirely consumed. The fire of judgment came down *upon Jesus himself!* Glory to God that the presence of the Spirit indicates that sin had been entirely dealt with. The Spirit not only assures the believer

---

[47] Ibid.
[48] Faw, *Acts*, 42.
[49] J. Phillips, *Exploring Acts*, Ac 2:3.

that the judgment has been dealt with, but he also convicts the believer of sin so that we stay far away from it.

Fire Warms

Every believer is a temple of the Holy Spirit (1 Cor 6:19; 1 Pet 4:14). We are warmed by the assurance and comfort of the Spirit. He is our comforter.

Fire Signals

A fire can signal people to come to you. It can point in a certain direction. The fire of God lit up Moses' face and pointed all who knew him to God. He was so luminous that he had to wear a covering over his face.

The Fire and Wind of God's Transcendence

At times the Holy Spirit makes himself known with visible, audible, touchable manifestations. In the Old Testament there was the pillar of cloud and the pillar of fire. At Jesus' baptism there was the dove. In Acts 4 the building shakes. In chapter 6 Stephen's face was like the face of an angel. At times the Spirit stoops to give us visible, audible, touchable demonstrations of his presence and power. Why? To help us understand God's transcendence. That means God transcends everything temporal. Are you worried? Are you angry? Are you bitter? Are you unhappy? Are you bored? Do you know what you need? You need the one true and living God to manifest himself to you. He's not some ho-hum God. When you see him and know him, then you experience the "fear of the Lord."

One of the key passages on God's glorious presence is Exodus 34, where Moses asks to see God's glory. He wants to see God's transcendence, his infinitude, we might say. Moses had already experienced God's immanence, or his nearness. He had spoken to the Lord as a man speaks with his friend, face to face. But there was something beyond that Moses needed to experience. So Moses is hidden in the cleft of the rock, remember? And God's glory, just the backside of his glory, passes by. And God describes his glory as "his goodness." So Moses sees the glory of the transcendent God, but he experiences God's goodness.

In other words, Moses sees the glorious holiness of God, his glory that cannot dwell with sinners. His omnipresence and omniscience that sees all things in all people. And you would think that transcendent glory would absolutely destroy Moses, all the people of Israel, and the entire world. But no. Because God is willing to take that judgment upon himself and absorb our judgment in himself, through his Son, later in redemption history.

Faith in the transcendent God is not just "he loves me just as I am." He does love you, but he's the holy God that can crush you. He's the good God that doesn't allow sinners into heaven. And he's the merciful God that doesn't allow one iota of sin to pass into heaven. He's got to crush sin. And in loving you, he's had to crush his own Son for him to love you. That's the transcendent God worth worshiping. There's no cheap grace, but only costly, painful grace. We are his because of the mighty cost of his own Son.

THE SALVATION OF THE NATIONS (2:4-13)

Now we see God's love outpoured for the nations. Oh, how he loves us. Go to the farthest nation, and you will find God's Spirit pleading with the hearts of men through their conscience and in his word where it is available. You see we forget about the nations, but God never forgets.

> *2 Peter 3:9* | The Lord is... not willing that any should perish, but that all should come to repentance.

> *1 Timothy 2:4* | [God] desires all people to be saved and to come to the knowledge of the truth.

One of the ways you can judge whether a real revival of the Holy Spirit has come is that people are not just praising God for what he's done, but they are coming together in community in an otherwise broken humanity.[50] That's what we read about here. The walls of culture and pride and racism are broken down. It is when we experience the vision of God's glory that these people had seen and experienced that our focus is no longer on ourselves, but on God. That's when the walls of hostility are torn down.

At Pentecost, God prepared 120 people to be seeds to the nations. We know that when Peter stood up to preach on the steps of the Temple, there would have been thirty to sixty thousand people in that area where there are about fifty mikvehs (cleansing pools, i.e. baptistries). God lights these people on fire in order to pour out his Spirit on people from so many diverse nations. Let us receive that same anointing from

---

[50] Keller, ibid.

the Spirit today. We are to be seeds of the gospel to the nations. That's what they were at Pentecost. Let's read about it.

> **Acts 2:4-13** | And they were all filled with the Holy Spirit and began to speak in other tongues as the Spirit gave them utterance. [5] Now there were dwelling in Jerusalem Jews, devout men from every nation under heaven. [6] And at this sound the multitude came together, and they were bewildered, because each one was hearing them speak in his own language. [7] And they were amazed and astonished, saying, "Are not all these who are speaking Galileans? [8] And how is it that we hear, each of us in his own native language? [9] Parthians and Medes and Elamites and residents of Mesopotamia, Judea and Cappadocia, Pontus and Asia, [10] Phrygia and Pamphylia, Egypt and the parts of Libya belonging to Cyrene, and visitors from Rome, [11] both Jews and proselytes, Cretans and Arabians—we hear them telling in our own tongues the mighty works of God." [12] And all were amazed and perplexed, saying to one another, "What does this mean?" [13] But others mocking said, "They are filled with new wine."

The Undoing of Babel

Now we think of the undoing of Babel as the mere unification of the languages. We find out later through Peter that this is a fulfilment of Joel 2.

> *Joel 2:28* | I will pour out my Spirit on all flesh; your sons and your daughters shall prophesy.

But it's more than that. At Pentecost, God had assembled a great multilingual Jewish congregation. During the exile of Israel, Jews emigrated to various nations around the world. They were successful wherever they went, as God through Jeremiah had commanded them.

> *Jeremiah 29:11* | Seek the welfare of the city where I have sent you into exile, and pray to the Lord on its behalf, for in its welfare you will find your welfare.

So there were many successful Israelites from the many nations listed in our passage who would come back for the three main festivals in Israel, the first of which was Passover. Fifty days later you would have Pentecost and then finally Tabernacles. Most of this passage gives you this long table of the nations. Look at all the different nations. Why in the world would Saint Luke, the writer of this passage, make such a long list? Here's why. The last time you see the table of the nations is in Genesis 10. We're told about all the nations of the earth and then in Genesis 11 we're told about the Tower of Babel, that the people of the earth decided to be their own masters and make a name for themselves, and as a result, God divides their languages. They are divided into various nations and people groups through a confusion of their languages.

God came down, we're told on the Tower of Babel, to confuse their languages, which was a way of showing us that when you decide to justify yourself and be your own lord and savior, the result is racial and cultural hostility, and a destruction of human community. We're reminded through the events of Acts 2, that when God came down on Mount Sinai, he created a new people.

So when God comes down at Pentecost, his Spirit creates a new people. Babel is reversed. The first thing that happens is the barriers between cultures come down. The first worship service, the first sermon, was preached in what language? All of them! The first worship service, the first sermon, was preached in what culture? All of them! Why? When God came down he reversed the curse of Babel. [51]

When you find a person that believes in the death, burial and resurrection and knows the power of the Spirit, you say: "I have even more in common with that person than someone from my own culture who doesn't understand this truth." The way you know that a revival has hit is that people get along who could never get along anywhere else.

The Filling of the Spirit

Acts 2:4a | And they were all filled with the Holy Spirit...

Several ministries of the Holy Spirit affect the believer in this age. The baptism of the Holy Spirit places us into the Body of Christ. The indwelling of the Spirit makes us the Temple of the Spirit. The sealing and earnest of the Spirit is the ownership mark of God on the believer. These are all sovereign acts of God bestowed on the believer at the time of salvation. They are unconditional, sovereignly given to every believer in the Lord Jesus. They never need to be repeated, they are never withdrawn, and they guarantee the believer's eternal security and his glorious standing in Christ.

---

[51] Ibid.

But the *filling* of the Holy Spirit is different. It *is* conditional. When Paul speaks of it in Ephesians 5:18 he uses the present continuous tense—literally, "Be being filled"—and he uses as an illustration being filled with wine—a fluctuating state. The filling comes and goes based on how the individual believer surrenders and lives under the Lordship of Christ. He can be filled one moment and, because of some disobedience, empty the next. The purpose of the filling is to change our temperament and make us like Jesus in his nature, person, and personality so that in thought, word, and deed we might show him to a lost world. When we are filled with the Spirit, we are "Jesus with skin on" as one of my seminary professors (Dr. Robert Kelleman) liked to say. The filling is always available to us, but our experience of it depends upon our cooperation with the Holy Spirit. On the day of Pentecost all those present were filled with the Spirit. The filling is available to every believer. There is no exception, and there can be no excuse for not being filled. You should be constantly filled and empowered by the Holy Spirit. Can you see the signs of being filled with the Spirit?

A New Culture

Acts 2:4 | And they were all filled with the Holy Spirit and began to speak in other tongues as the Spirit gave them utterance.

The Spirit's filling brings a new culture. They spoke in other languages as the Spirit gave them utterance. So though we may never see this amazing miracle of people from various countries being able to understand my language without an interpreter, you can see that the filling of the Spirit breaks down cultural boundaries.

Is this happening at your local church? Has this happened to you? Can you see your prejudices and pride coming down? Do you walk into a room and only see the outward, and say, "He's like me. He's not like me." Or do you walk into a room and say, "He needs Christ. She needs Christ. They are like me because they know Christ." Are you creating a new culture, a "Jesus" culture in your family and your church and your neighborhood?

A New Amazement

Acts 2:5-6 | Now there were dwelling in Jerusalem Jews, devout men from every nation under heaven. ⁶And at this sound the multitude came together, and they were bewildered, because each one was hearing them speak in his own language.

When you see something only God can do, that's a miracle. When people have a prayer meeting or a worship service, there should be a sense of amazement if God has showed up. Again, we may not see the miracle of languages again like this, but there are always God size events when the Spirit is working. People see God. Our children see God. They are bewildered, surprised. What is more surprising than seeing the thrice holy God clearly and finding out he loves you.

A New Praise

Acts 2:7-11 | And they were amazed and astonished, saying, "Are not all these who are speaking Galileans? [8] And how is it that we hear, each of us in his own native language? [9] Parthians and Medes and Elamites and residents of Mesopotamia, Judea and Cappadocia, Pontus and Asia, [10] Phrygia and Pamphylia, Egypt and the parts of Libya belonging to Cyrene, and visitors from Rome, [11] both Jews and proselytes, Cretans and Arabians—we hear them telling in our own tongues the mighty works of God."

I mean look at this. People from everywhere shouting the mighty works of God. God breaks through for each one of them. See, one thing we all have in common is the burdens and brokenness of this life. But when the Spirit of God is poured out, the sewers open up. God cleans us out. The mighty works of God are done. And no one can explain it, except to says, "To God be the glory!"

A New Persecution

Acts 2:12-13 | And all were amazed and perplexed, saying to one another, "What does this mean?" [13] But others mocking said, "They are filled with new wine."

People who truly know God and love him are going to live for him no matter what the cost. And you know what happens when you really start serving Jesus? You get a target on your back. This persecution recorded here is mere mockery, but it gets worse from here on out. They are going to begin suffering for Jesus. Remember what Jesus says: "If they hated me, they will also hate you." Be ready to have a wartime posture if you follow Christ in the fullness of the Spirit.

Conclusion

Oh, how we need an outpouring of the Holy Spirit. I know it's winter, but soon we'll get the warmth of summer. In fact, I can think of some summers that it was so scorching that lawns are dead, fruit stands are deserted, and farmers are defeated. I've never seen anything close to a drought, but I'm sure your grandparents could tell you about one of the most famous droughts in the 1930s when it didn't rain for nine years. In the breadbasket of the country, our richest farmlands were turned into a "Dust Bowl." In 1934, thirty-four states experienced severe droughts. On April 14, 1935, a day known as "Black Sunday," the wind whipped across the parched farmland and blew up the dust into an enormous "black blizzard" that whisked away countless acres of topsoil. That's what a drought is like, and most of us have never experienced a real one—not in our countryside at least. But sadly, too often we experience a drought in our spirits. We need the outpouring of the Spirit for our country, for each of us personally. Let's begin expecting and experiencing that downpour.

4 | ACTS 2:14-41
A WORLD CHANGING SERMON

So those who received his word were baptized, and there were added that day about three thousand souls.

ACTS 2:41

We are thinking about what kind of a church God wants our church to be. A New Testament church—a Spirit-filled, Bible-believing, Christ-honoring church—is a mighty weapon in the hands of a holy God. God's pattern is found right here in the book of Acts.

If you want to see the church defeat the devil, you've got to look at this sermon Peter preaches. God will rip the world right out of the hands of the devil if we will do what Peter did: he went in the power of the Spirit, he exalted Christ, and he called sinners to be saved. Three thousand were baptized that day on the front steps of the Temple, where there are still 50 baptistries (mikvehs) there today. There were mikvehs at the Temple and many at every synagogue. There some 800 ancient ritual baths have been discovered in Israel, and 50 of them are near the entrance to the Temple.

Ritual Bath (mikveh) at the South Temple Steps, Jerusalem

God wants us to shine the light of Christ so that we can lift the night of darkness and wickedness from our culture. Oh, as the world gets darker and darker, I'm praying our church gets brighter and brighter. The night is coming when our work will be over. Christ is coming again when we can no longer evangelize. But let us work while it is still day. The night is not here yet. The only way God's going to shake the world one more time, and I believe he will, is if his people go forth empowered. We must speak out and speak boldly. So let me say it here, and let us say it everywhere: Jesus Christ is Lord! *Every knee will bow.* There will be a day when all the Presidents of the United States bow before Christ. They with all people will cry out that "Jesus Christ is Lord." But let's evangelize this world dear saints. Let's not wait.

Fredrich Nietzsche (of whom Hitler was a disciple) was a cynic, an atheist philosopher. He was as ungodly and lascivious as they come. He went insane by the age of 44 and died at the age of 55. He looked at the church of his day. He considered Christianity. Do you know what he said? He said, "If you want me to believe in your Redeemer, you're going to have to look a little more redeemed."[52]

---

[52] Friedrich Nietzsche in Greg Ogden. *Discipleship Essentials: A Guide to Building Your Life in Christ* (Downers Grove, IL: IVP Connect, 2007), 153.

Now, think about it. This world gets their idea of Jesus Christ not from the word of God—because they don't read it; they get that from us. I want to get there, saints. We cannot get there alone. We are learning about life-on-life discipleship. We have to help each other get there.

I'm going to give you a description of a church triumphant, a church that will change the world. Let's be that group of people that is truly forever family. Let's help each other get there. What kind of church do we have to be to be a triumphant church and not a defeated church? We need to be a church that is: empowered by the Spirit, exalting the Savior, and evangelizing sinners! Here's the key thought: Exalt Jesus in the power of the Spirit, and he will grow the church.

EMPOWERED BY THE SPIRIT (2:14-21)

The early church was empowered by the Spirit.[53] The Day of Pentecost had come. All of these signs and wonders had been done. The Spirit has come and been poured out on that group of 120 and far beyond. Thousands from everywhere are experiencing the gift of understanding each other speak the wonderful works of God.

And Peter stands up to preach the gospel so that the Spirit can bring thousands into the kingdom. He relies on the power of the Holy Spirit. If we are to go forward as a church that changes the world, we have to be empowered. But how?

The Spirit's Moment

The Spirit of God was being poured out a specific moment in time. Peter is recognizing that this is the moment we've all been waiting for. The world will never be the same! Recognize this moment as Peter did at Pentecost. Listen to what Peter did. As those who were already saved were filled to the overflow with the Spirit, the ones observing them were mocking them. "They're drunk. So early, but they are stone cold drunk." People who don't understand the Spirit put a target on Peter and the disciples. And you who are Spirit-filled have a target on you! Don't be surprised when the world hates you. But you have an awesome opportunity in that moment of mockery and persecution. Peter didn't walk away like before. Peter saw this as a moment of opportunity. He didn't

---

[53] Adapted from Adrian Rogers, "The Amazing First-Century Church," in *Adrian Rogers Sermon Archive* (Signal Hill, CA: Rogers Family Trust, 2017), Ac 2:22–47.

go into hiding like before. He "stood up"! What a difference the filling of the Spirit makes! Peter stood up with the other eleven apostles and explained this sacred moment to the onlookers.

> **Acts 2:14-16** | But Peter, standing with the eleven, lifted up his voice and addressed them: "Men of Judea and all who dwell in Jerusalem, let this be known to you, and give ear to my words. **15** For these people are not drunk, as you suppose, since it is only the third hour of the day. **16** But this is what was uttered through the prophet Joel.

He says, "We're not drunk!" He doesn't condemn them. He informs them. This is a special moment in history given by the prophet Joel. This outpouring was planned long ago. He doesn't condemn them for their ignorance. He invites them into what the Spirit is doing. How about you? As you get flack for living for Jesus, are you inviting people in? This is a moment for the church at Pentecost. And this week, there are people who are observing your Spirit filled life, and they may think you're crazy. Don't condemn them. Invite them in!

The Spirit's Dawning

Peter said in his sermon that the fulfillment of what Joel had prophesied was what they had just witnessed. The Holy Spirit had been poured out, not on seventy, not on 120, but on hundreds, and soon three thousand. The Spirit falls not just on men, but on women, servants, and everybody in the flock of God. God has poured out his Spirit upon all of us. Peter quotes the book of Joel which describes the Spirit's dawning.

> **Acts 2:17-18** | "'And in the last days it shall be, God declares, that I will pour out my Spirit on all flesh, and your sons and your daughters shall prophesy, and your young men shall see visions, and your old men shall dream dreams; **18** even on my male servants and female servants in those days I will pour out my Spirit, and they shall prophesy.

There is no such thing as a Christian who has not been anointed by the Holy Spirit for ministry. Whatever age, the Spirit falls. "Everyone who calls upon the name of the Lord shall be saved" and gets the Spirit (2:21). Joel is describing the dawning of the age of the Spirit. Little children prophesy. Your sons and daughters are going to prophesy and speak boldly of Christ. When we understand the Spirit, we can put away the myth of teenage rebellion. The greatest revivals are going to happen through our sons and daughters. Young men, like Brother Ahmed will see visions. Others, even old men, will dream dreams. Everyone who is a believer from the heads of households to servants, both male and female receives the outpouring of God's Spirit. If you have believed, you have the Spirit. They saw the Spirit's dawning, and now the Spirit is ready to shine at midday. Is he shining through you dear saint? Paul says,

> 1 Corinthians 12:13 | For by one Spirit we were all baptized into one body.

We do not all have the same gifts, but we have the same Spirit, and let him shine through us! We are all called to be richly involved in the ministry of the kingdom of God: life-on-life discipleship and evangelism.[54] This is the life of the Spirit! With the coming of the Spirit came the Spirit's indwelling, baptizing, sealing, and filling. And believers everywhere started proclaiming Christ, not just in word, but in power. That's what we are to do dear saints: proclaiming Christ, lifting him up in the power of the Spirit. This power of the Spirit was something new—something wonderful and dynamic! Joel's prophecy tells us of the dawn of this wonderful age. The sunset of the age is also described.[55] And it's coming quickly.

The Spirit's Sunset

There's coming a day when the current state of things as we know it will end. What the world has deemed so important will be shown to be worthless. When Jesus comes, people will be hiding under the rocks, but God's people know that day is coming. Let's read about it.

> **Acts 2:19-21** | And I will show wonders in the heavens above and signs on the earth below, blood, and fire, and vapor of smoke; **20** the sun shall be turned to darkness and the moon to blood, before the day of the Lord comes, the great and magnificent day. **21** And it shall come to pass that everyone who calls upon the name of the Lord shall be saved.'

---

[54] Sproul, *Acts*, 50.
[55] Hughes, *Acts*, 39.

There's coming a day, at any moment, when Christ will destroy the earth. Joel tells us this. Peter later talks about this very text and gives us more information.

> 2 Peter 3:10-13 | The day of the Lord will come like a thief, and then the heavens will pass away with a roar, and the heavenly bodies will be burned up and dissolved, and the earth and the works that are done on it will be exposed. [11] Since all these things are thus to be dissolved, what sort of people ought you to be in lives of holiness and godliness, [12] waiting for and hastening the coming of the day of God, because of which the heavens will be set on fire and dissolved, and the heavenly bodies will melt as they burn! [13] But according to his promise we are waiting for new heavens and a new earth in which righteousness dwells.

Peter says, look how we should live, in all holiness and godliness, because of what is soon coming upon the earth. Jesus is coming! Be ready. Preach the gospel today as if Jesus were coming tonight. There's an urgency and love that should be emanating from each of us. The point here is this: we have to be *empowered by the Spirit* for the world to change. And as we are empowered, we need to be *exalting the Savior*.

EXALTING THE SAVIOR (2:22-36)

If we are filled with the Spirit, we will boldly exalt Jesus. That's what Peter did at Pentecost. The church grew because they lifted up Jesus. Jesus said:

> John 12:32 | And I, when I am lifted up from the earth, will draw all people to myself.

No church is going to be a growing, vibrant church that does not exalt the Lord Jesus Christ. Jesus is the attracting power of the church. We are to lift up Jesus in the power of the Spirit so all men will come to him.

Jesus Lived the Perfect Life

Now, notice the message that Peter preached began with Jesus' perfect life. Jesus lived the perfect life that you could not live. He lived in your place so that he could give you his perfect record. And God confirmed that perfect life with miracles. Listen to Peter address the thousands gathered, who are baffled and wondering what this sound of mighty rushing wind is. What is the miraculous fire above the heads of many who are speaking? Peter speaks:

Acts 2:22 | Men of Israel, hear these words: Jesus of Nazareth, a man attested to you by God with mighty works and wonders and signs that God did through him in your midst, as you yourselves know.

Our Lord Jesus Christ was a man attested to by God! The Spirit came down upon him when he began his earthly ministry, and the Father spoke from heaven and said:

Matthew 3:17 | This is my beloved Son in whom I am well pleased.

His Miraculous Birth

Jesus' birth was miraculous. He was raised in Nazareth, but he was born from a virgin in Bethlehem. His birth is unlike any other since he had no earthly father. God was his Father. He was conceived by the Holy Spirit.

Matthew 1:23 | Behold, the virgin shall conceive and bear a son, and they shall call his name Immanuel.

His Perfect Life

Jesus lived in relative obscurity until the age of around 30. Yet Jesus' life was not usual or boring. His life was the most extraordinary life to ever be lived because he never sinned. This is the one who lived a perfect life in my place and in your place. Can you testify with the author of Hebrews?

Hebrews 7:26 | It was indeed fitting that we should have such a high priest, holy, innocent, unstained, separated from sinners, and exalted above the heavens.

The Lord was "tempted in every way like we are, yet without sin" (Heb 4:16, KJV). Jesus lived the one perfect life.

1 John 3:5 | You know that he appeared so that he might take away our sins. And in him is no sin.

He didn't just live a perfect life to be an example. He lived it in place of you and me to exchange our sin for his righteousness (2 Cor 5:21; Zech 3:4). James Allen Francis wrote this about the manner of Jesus' life.

I'm far within the mark when I say that all of the armies that ever marched, and all of the navies that ever were built, and all of the parliaments that ever sat, and all of the kings that ever reigned, put together, have not affected the life of humanity upon this earth as powerfully as that one solitary life, Jesus of Nazareth.[56]

Think about that. And here is another quote from Napoleon himself. I had to look it up and translate it from the French, but here it is:

> I know men and I tell you that Jesus Christ is no mere man. Between him and every other person in the world there is no possible term of comparison. Alexander, Caesar, Charlemagne, and I have founded empires. But on what did we rest the creation of our genius? Upon force. Jesus Christ founded his empire upon love; and at this hour millions of men would die for him.[57]

His Amazing Miracles

His life was also unique because he performed miracles. Jesus' healing miracles got people's attention. Disease and death were vanishing from the countryside of Galilee. Suddenly crippled people are walking around town. Those who were blind can now see. The deaf people could hear. A dead person gets raised to life when Jesus comes to town. Lepers, with gangrene in their limbs are now healed with skin as soft as a baby. That's what happens when Jesus comes to town.

When Jesus arrives in your town, thousands are fed with a little boy's lunch of five loaves and two fishes. It got people's attention. Jesus' miracles were evidence to all that Jesus was who he claimed to be. Everybody there at Pentecost were witnesses of Jesus' perfect life and could testify of mighty signs and wonders. He walked on the sea; he turned water into wine. He banished demons, disease, and death. He healed the sick, cleansed the lepers, and raised the dead. And the miracles recorded are a fraction of those he actually performed. Several times the Gospel writers simply lump miracles together and spoke of almost universal healing.[58]

Matthew 15:30 | And he healed them all.

---

[56] James Allan Francis in Ken Blanchard. *One Solitary Life* (Nashville, TN: J Countryman Books, 2007).

[57] Napoleon Bonaparte in Robert Antoine de Beauterne. *Sentiment de Napoléon Sur Le Christianisme* [*Napoleon's Thoughts on Christianity*] (Paris: Olivier-Fulgence, 1845), xxvi. (Translated into English from French)

[58] J. Phillips, *Exploring Acts,* Ac 2:22.

> *Matthew 9:35* | Jesus went throughout all the cities and villages, teaching in their synagogues and proclaiming the gospel of the kingdom and healing every disease and every affliction.

Every disease! Every affliction! Can you imagine if every one of his miracles were recorded? John ends his gospel narrative by saying that it would be impossible to record all the miracles Jesus did. The world couldn't hold such an infinite record of Jesus' miracles.

> *John 21:25* | Now there are also many other things that Jesus did. Were every one of them to be written, I suppose that the world itself could not contain the books that would be written.

The Miracles at His Death and Resurrection

All those gathered at Pentecost were well aware of Jesus' healings, resurrections, and mighty miracles that Jesus performed, but also the signs and wonders that accompanied his death. The Temple curtain was torn in two. The earth quaked. The sun refused to shine. There were people who were raised from the dead as Jesus himself died on the cross and conquered death. And there were over 500 who were eyewitnesses to his resurrection. And now hear there is this sound, like a mighty windstorm, and everybody in Jerusalem hears it: it's the sound of the Spirit of God arriving and pouring out on all flesh.

The Ultimate Miracle: Salvation

Jesus' miracles in the physical realm pointed to an even greater miracle in the metaphysical realm: the salvation of souls. If Jesus can turn water into wine; if he can raise people from the dead; if he can make blind eyes to see and deaf ears to hear, then he can do an even greater miracle. He can transfer a sinner from earth to heaven. He can change a person's eternal destiny from hell to heaven. What greater miracle can there be than changing your destiny from hell to heaven.

Jesus lived the only perfect, sinless life in your place, to take off your rags of sin and give you a perfect robe of righteousness (Zech 3:4). Not only that, Peter says he died the perfect death. The purpose of the cross, as we learn from this message, is substitution.

Jesus Died the Perfect Death

> *1 Peter 3:18* | Christ also suffered once for sins, the righteous for the unrighteous, that he might bring us to God.

We see as well that Peter preached how Jesus died the perfect death, planned and foreordained by God.

Acts 2:23 | This Jesus, delivered up according to the definite plan and foreknowledge of God, you crucified and killed by the hands of lawless men.

Now, what's Peter saying here? He's saying that Jesus Christ's death was not an accident; it was not an incident; it was planned before the foundation of the earth — "the definite plan and foreknowledge of God." Nothing went wrong. God was not up there in heaven wringing his hands and saying, "Oh, how terrible that this has come to pass!" No God planned for the most glorious and beautiful thing to come out of the greatest sin ever committed: the crucifixion of the Son of God. He did it to give his life for you.

Jesus' death was a divine strategy planned by God. He is called the "Lamb slain from the foundation of the world" (Rev 13:8). The Father planned it. The Son agreed to carry it out and pay for it. And the Spirit of God would apply it beginning at Pentecost, 50 days after the resurrection.

Jesus' death was voluntary. No one took Jesus' life from him. This wasn't an accident, or a plan gone wrong. Jesus said he's the "good shepherd who lays down his life for his sheep" (Jn 10:11). He announced, "No one can take my life from me. I sacrifice it voluntarily. I have authority to lay it down, and I have authority to take it up again" (Jn 10:18). Jesus signed up to be the "Lamb of God that takes away the sin of the world" (Jn 1:29). His life was not taken from him. He voluntarily laid it down for you.

Jesus' death was substitutionary. That is, he exchanged his perfect life for your sinful life. Jesus didn't die for his own sin because he had none. He was the only perfect person who ever lived. He lived a completely sinless life. But he died as a substitute for you and for me.

2 Corinthians 5:21, NKJV | For He made Him who knew no sin to be sin for us, that we might become the righteousness of God in Him.

Christ's death is the propitiation for our sins (1 Jn 2:2). Only the death of Christ could satisfy God holy wrath against sin. Our sin is the obstacle between man and God was removed. Hallelujah! There is therefore now condemnation for those who believe (Rom 8:1).

Jesus Resurrected from the Dead

But not only as the exalted Savior did Peter Christ's perfect life and substitutionary death, but he also spoke of the miracle of his resurrection. There's no way possible that death could keep Jesus in the grave.

The Person of the Resurrection

Acts 2:24 | God raised him up, loosing the pangs of death, because it was not possible for him to be held by it.

God loosed Jesus from the pangs (the horrific powers) of death for himself and for us! Jesus could not be held by death. The One who caused all things to exist cannot be defeated by death. Death cannot hold back the Author of life. So, Christ burst out of the grave that Sunday morning. Nothing can hold Jesus back. The *death of Christ* demonstrated that sin is defeated on our behalf. But the *resurrection* of Christ shows that death itself is defeated on our behalf. Jesus is our champion. He is the champion of heaven, and he is the champion who beat all of hell! Peter opens up to Psalm 16 for his text on Pentecost morning.

The Psalm of the Resurrection

Listen to Peter as he preaches Christ's resurrection. He opens up Psalm 16:8-11 and quotes them as the words of Jesus. He shows that the Holy One who will not see corruption is Jesus, and then Peter proclaims the resurrection of Christ from the dead.

Acts 2:25-28 | For David says concerning him [*Jesus*], "'I saw the Lord always before me, for he is at my right hand that may not be shaken; ²⁶ therefore my heart was glad, and my tongue rejoiced; my flesh also will dwell in hope. ²⁷ For you will not abandon my soul to Hades, or let your Holy One see corruption. ²⁸ You have made known to me the paths of life; you will make me full of gladness with your presence.'

Is this David? No, Peter says that David is talking about Jesus. All the multinational group of people there at Pentecost could not imagine that the Messiah would have to die. But Peter stands up and proclaims from Psalm 16 that he would have to go to his death, but his "heart was glad" and his "tongue rejoiced". Why? How? Because he knew that the Father would not abandon his "soul to Hades." He wouldn't be conquered by death, but he would conquer death. He would pave the "path of life" right out of that tomb. He would be glad in the presence of God!

Psalm 16, Peter says, is a wonderful Psalm about the death and resurrection of Jesus!

The Point of the Resurrection

Listen now as Peter makes the point, first that this Psalm is about how Jesus will live that perfect path of life, and he will die, but he will defeat death. And now he wants to point out that this Psalm couldn't be about David, because David died. David couldn't be the one who defeats death. No, David was a prophet and he foretold how Christ would be the ultimate King and sit on David's throne. That he will sit on the ultimate throne, on the right hand of the Father at his resurrection and ascension.

> **Acts 2:29-31** | "Brothers, I may say to you with confidence about the patriarch David that he both died and was buried, and his tomb is with us to this day. **30** Being therefore a prophet, and knowing that God had sworn with an oath to him that he would set one of his descendants on his throne, **31** he foresaw and spoke about the resurrection of the Christ, that he was not abandoned to Hades, nor did his flesh see corruption.

What is Peter's point? Jesus is the ultimate King. He's David's ultimate descendent. Jesus Christ, who these people had crucified is the Psalm 2 Messiah. They should have worshipped him, but instead they crucified him. But God raised him up, and this was all part of God's plan. His flesh was never going to see corruption, because he came to conquer death.

The Witnesses of the Resurrection

Now Peter gets to the most powerful point. He calls in his witnesses. They are standing right in front of him. Listen to Peter address this crowd of witnesses.

> **Acts 2:32** | This Jesus God raised up, and of that we all are witnesses.

These are the people who crucified the Lord. But they are also the people who were witnesses of his resurrection. And they had just been talking about Jesus and his resurrection in languages that everyone from everywhere could understand. And while you or I haven't seen the very resurrection of Christ, we have seen those who were dead in sin raised to newness of life. We all who know Christ have experienced the power of his resurrection.

Jesus Ascended as God's King

Peter is moving to his ultimate point. This isn't just any king they crucified.

The King's Throne

Acts 2:33a | Being therefore exalted at the right hand of God.

The Person the people of Pentecost crucified is sitting on a throne right now: but it's not merely the throne of Israel. It's an even higher throne. It's at "God's right hand"—the place of omnipotence and divine authority. It's saying this is the highest judge. This is God's very throne. David's descendent would be the eternal king, because he has a throne that is infinite and a life that can never die.

Peter says that the one they crucified is the one who sits on God's throne. He rose again and ascended to God's right hand in power as King of kings. Listen to Peter make this point.

The King's Army of One

Acts 2:33 | Being therefore exalted at the right hand of God, and having received from the Father the promise of the Holy Spirit, he has poured out this that you yourselves are seeing and hearing.

So he sits on God's throne and he sends out God's promise. He doesn't need armies to conquer people. He as King moves his scepter, and the Spirit of God is outpoured. The Spirit of God is greater than a million-man army! He's been sent out to conquer the people of Pentecost. The people who crucified the King. Peter says Christ has "received from the Father the promise of the Holy Spirit" and that this king "has poured out this that you yourselves are seeing and hearing." The King has sent out his army of one: the Holy Spirit.

The King's Deity

I love this. Peter says, if you're looking for David, his body is still in the ground. There was another king who ascended, one who could sit on God's throne.

Acts 2:34-35 | For David did not ascend into the heavens, but he himself says, "'The Lord said to my Lord, "Sit at my right hand, ^{35} until I make your enemies your footstool."'

Peter quotes Psalm 110:1 and begins to preach the glory of the Trinity. Psalm 110 says: The Lord, YHWH, says to my Lord (Adonai): sit at my right hand. I will destroy all your enemies! That's the Father talking to the Son. That's God the Father saying to God the Son: "You are God. You are King of the Universe. You are exalted. You will rule the whole world." It's the same theme as Psalm 2. Jesus is God's Messiah. He's the King of kings and Lord of lords. Peter is saying: if you don't bow and call Jesus YHWH you are going to be destroyed. Paul says I this way in Philippians.

> *Philippians 2:10–11* | Every knee shall bow, and every tongue shall confess that Jesus Christ is Lord, to the glory of God the Father.

You may not be a believer, but I can tell you with all of the authority of the word of God: One day you will confess that Jesus Christ is Lord. I don't care who you are, where you are. That's Peter's message. He exalted Jesus! If we exalt Jesus, the Holy Spirit will begin to work deeply in the hearts of sinners.

Have you experienced the empowering of the Spirit? Are you exalting Jesus? That's what Peter did. That's what any truly born-again Christian does. And we do what Jesus does: we evangelize sinners.

EVANGELIZING THE SINNER (2:37-41)

Now we come to what happens when the power of the Holy Spirit is poured out. Our King's marching orders were:

> *Mark 16:15* | Go into all the world and preach the gospel to every creature.

Let me tell you what true evangelism and true salvation is. Let us look in slow motion as it were how the Holy Spirit converts sinners.

Conviction by the Lord

First of all, people must be convicted by the Spirit. Peter is sweetly bold. He shows them what they've done! They've crucified the Lord of glory.

Conviction of Who the Lord is

> **Acts 2:36** | Let all the house of Israel therefore know for certain that God has made him both Lord and Christ, this Jesus whom you crucified.

Peter says: "The one you hung on a cross was God's Messiah. He is both Lord, YHWH, and Christ." This is good theology. If you don't believe that Jesus Christ is the LORD of Hosts, the God of creation, then you need to go back and read Genesis and John. It was "by Jesus all things were made, and without him was not anything made that was made" (cf Jn 1:1-4).

Yes, he is both Lord (YHWH) and Christ. "God has highly exalted him and bestowed on him the name that is above every name!" (Phil 2:9). Every knee will bow and every tongue confess that Jesus is YHWH. That's a quote referring to YHWH from Isaiah 45:23.

Conviction of Who I Am

They crucified this Lord, the Lord of glory. Now before we get hard on those who crucified the Lord of glory, we have to remember that we joined with them. We need to be convicted that we did it. Martin Luther said, "We all carry about in our pockets his very nails."[59]

That's the realization we will each have if we consider the greatness of our sins. Don't run away from opening up the sewers of your heart. Come to Christ. He will forgive those who crucified him. Of course, this cut the people of Pentecost to heart. They had literally crucified him. They had seen his miracles but let fear and pride overwhelm them. Now they can think of only one thing: How can we be saved? What must we do?

> **Acts 2:37** | Now when they heard this they were cut to the heart, and said to Peter and the rest of the apostles, "Brothers, what shall we do?"

Peter preached and the people were cut to heart. This is what happens when we open up the sewers and we are honest about our sins. This is what made the church so powerful. They came to that place where they saw the greatness of their sins. And they said, "What shall we do?"

Conversion to the Lord

Peter instructs them to throw away their old way of seeing everything. What they have just seen, with Jesus Christ as the Lord of glory,

---

[59] Martin Luther. *Luther's Works. Volume 27: Lectures on Galatians, 1535*, (Saint Louis: Concordia Pub. House, 1964), 407.

the God of the universe, the LORD of all in control of them: that's how the world really is. So repent of how you lived before.

Acts 2:38a | And Peter said to them, "Repent..."

Repent! Be broken. Be sorrowful for how you lived. See how you lived in control of your life, and ignoring God. And repent. To *repent* literally means to "change your mind." Our whole outlook is now changed because we've seen the Lord high and lifted up. That's what Isaiah said. Listen to his testimony of repentance.

Isaiah 6:1 | In the year that King Uzziah died I saw the Lord sitting upon a throne, high and lifted up.

Isaiah says, "I saw the Lord." Then he says, "I saw the angels, and they were shouting one to another.

Isaiah 6:3 | One called to another and said: "Holy, holy, holy is the Lord of hosts; the whole earth is full of his glory!"

What could Isaiah do? He told the truth. His whole world was changed. He was shaken to the core. He confessed and said:

Isaiah 6:5 | "Woe is me! For I am lost; for I am a man of unclean lips, and I dwell in the midst of a people of unclean lips; for my eyes have seen the King, the Lord of hosts!"

This is genuine repentance from Isaiah. The Bible says there can be true and false repentance. False repentance is sorrow over the consequences of sin, but not sorrow over sin itself. Genuine repentance (*cf* 2 Cor 7:10), on the other hand, leads to an inward change of mind toward God, leading to a complete change of life and behavior.[60]

Peter preaches with power, and people's hearts are changing right before him. When we repent, we see the world completely differently now: from God's perspective. We forsake our selfishness and turn in faith to Christ. That's what they did. Then Peter tells them to follow their repentance with a sure sign that they're repentance is real. He says: "Get baptized!"

Consecration to the Lord

Peter tells them to immediately consecrate themselves by identifying with Jesus. Show the evidence of your repentance with baptism!

---

[60] Williams, *Acts*, 29–30.

Acts 2:38b | And Peter said to them, "Repent and be baptized every one of you in the name of Jesus Christ for the forgiveness of your sins.

Identification with Christ

Once people repent, Peter expects true faith to want to identify with Christ. There are at least 50 mikvehs, ritual baths all around the Temple Mount today. They would consecrate themselves this way before they would enter into the Temple. But Peter was telling to consecrate themselves, not for Temple worship, but for Jesus worship, and for forgiveness. Before we talk about baptism, let's talk about the forgiveness offered. The sense of what Peter is saying is: be baptized "because of" the forgiveness of your sins.

Now to the baptism. As I said, there are fifty cleansing baths, baptisteries all around the Temple entrance. There are plenty of places many people at once could be baptized. The word "baptize" here means "to dip" or "immerse."[61] We don't have to guess what it means because you can go to Israel today and find eight hundred of these baptisteries from the time of Jesus scattered around Israel. You could be baptized in many of them today if you wanted to, because several ancient baptisteries are connected to ancient springs and "living water" is flowing in them right now.

Why does he tell them to be baptized? Why a ceremonial cleansing in the name of Jesus? Because it's an identification with Christ. Romans 6 tells us that when we go down into the water, we are identifying with his death and burial into the tomb. When we come out of the water, we identify with Christ in his resurrection. Christ is our Redeemer. We are co-crucified with him and co-resurrected with him.

In the early church until today, baptism is the way we confess Christ as our Lord. Baptism is our wedding ceremony into the church. I loved Jill long before I married her. But she wasn't my wife until I declared my love and lifelong commitment to her publicly. That's baptism.

---

[61] Grant R. Osborne, "Baptism," *Baker Encyclopedia of the Bible* (Grand Rapids, MI: Baker Book House, 1988), 257.

Baptism with the Spirit

And when you repent and believe, what happens? You receive what the 120 had already received, the indwelling Holy Spirit: the promise Spirit that Jesus dispersed when he ascended.

> **Acts 2:38c** | And you will receive the gift of the Holy Spirit.

The Holy Spirit comes into you to control you. The Holy Spirit takes possession now of the person who has been bought with the precious blood of Jesus Christ. *Real salvation is not just to believe something, or to achieve something, but to receive Someone.* The Holy Spirit of God comes into you. He controls you. He overcomes you. He leads and guides you.

Evangelizing Family

With all of Peter's boldness, there is a powerful and genuine response. And he begins to comfort this crowd who crucified the Lord.

> **Acts 2:39** | For the promise is for you and for your children and for all who are far off, everyone whom the Lord our God calls to himself.

He tells them: this promise is for you and your children and your loved ones. Anyone who is far off, come! God is calling! When you come to know Christ, one of the greatest burdens you get is for the salvation of your own family. God can save anyone, near in your family, or those who are far off, scattered in the world and in our lives. God is mighty to save, but we must evangelize.

Separation from the World

Next, as a new believer, you want to separate from the world.

> **Acts 2:40** | And with many other words he bore witness and continued to exhort them, saying, "Save yourselves from this crooked generation."

What a wakeup call to see how crooked this world is. You see that our nation is not progressing. It's falling apart! The foundations are crumbling. They are trampling over truth in the streets. And oh, you see how we need to "save ourselves from this crooked generation."

Continuing with the Church

Finally, we see this great harvest: three thousand souls were added to the church. How did they know who believed? They were baptized.

Acts 2:41 | So those who received his word were baptized, and there were added that day about three thousand souls.

In a sense, only the 3,000 that day heard Peter's great sermon. There are professing Christians who need Christ. They've heard, but they haven't heard. It is possible to be a respectable, well-taught, moral sinner. That is why the Lord said, in the Parable of the Tares, not to pull the tares out of the wheat field, because the roots are tangled together, and we will pull out the wheat too. We cannot tell the difference. Do we *hear* Peter's sermon? If not, the God of grace invites us to come honestly before him who sees all and to allow him to speak to us. [62]

Conclusion

Verse 42 says: "They devoted themselves"—a continuance with the Lord. *Jesus did not call us to make decisions; he called us to make disciples.* I believe we are in a powerful moment in our church to experience the power of the Spirit like never before. But we are going to have to be loving enough to get into each other's lives. We are going to have to invite messy people into our lives and love them and bring them out of this cesspool. Exalt Christ in the power of the Spirit. We must evangelize or we will fossilize. Jesus left his throne on high to bring us to himself. Do you think we could get a little uncomfortable here to love one another? There is no better life to live than one that is empowered by the Spirit, exalting the Savior, and evangelizing sinners. May our merciful God bring it to pass.

---

[62] Hughes, *Acts*, 42–43.

5 | ACTS 2:41-47
LIFE-ON-LIFE CHURCH

And they devoted themselves to the apostles' teaching and the fellowship, to the breaking of bread and the prayers. And awe came upon every soul, and many wonders and signs were being done through the apostles.... And day by day, attending the temple together and breaking bread in their homes, they received their food with glad and generous hearts, praising God and having favor with all the people. And the Lord added to their number day by day those who were being saved.
ACTS 2:42-43, 46-47

How do we do discipleship? [63] The Spirit makes us a family. He binds us together in our souls. We have one Head, and we are his Body. But how do we act like the family that we are? Life-on-life discipleship is really the fruit of God's Spirit. We can preach all we want that Jesus Christ is Lord, but Jesus says we have to live out his love to one another before the world will believe.

John 13:34-35 | A new commandment I give to you, that you love one another: just as I have loved you, you also are to love one another. [35] By

---

[63] Portions of this study are adapted from J. Phillips, *Exploring Acts*, Acts 2:41–47.

this all people will know that you are my disciples, if you have love for one another.

So how do we get there? How can I love my brothers and sisters in Christ the way Christ wants me to. We can't do it in our own power. We can't "white knuckle" it. We need a divine visitation. We need God to touch us. That's exactly what happened at Pentecost. And dear saints, you must believe that Pentecost's power of the Holy Spirit carries on today. The prophecy is that our sons and our daughters will prophesy the word. That's not just some emotional experience. That means they are filled with the Spirit and with joy because they know the truth of God's word, the Bible, deep down in their soul.

Let's see what is necessary, what we need, what we must have, in order to love one another and live out the life-on-life discipleship that we've been reading about in Acts.

> **Acts 2:41-47** | So those who received his word were baptized, and there were added that day about three thousand souls. ⁴² And they devoted themselves to the apostles' teaching and the fellowship, to the breaking of bread and the prayers. ⁴³ And awe came upon every soul, and many wonders and signs were being done through the apostles. ⁴⁴ And all who believed were together and had all things in common. ⁴⁵ And they were selling their possessions and belongings and distributing the proceeds to all, as any had need. ⁴⁶ And day by day, attending the temple together and breaking bread in their homes, they received their food with glad and generous hearts, ⁴⁷ praising God and having favor with all the people. And the Lord added to their number day by day those who were being saved.

The first thing we see, is that the love of God comes from above and touches the heart of otherwise spiritually darkened and selfish people. If we are going to demonstrate Christ's love to one another, we need a touch from God.

A CHURCH TOUCHED BY GOD (2:41-42)

Peter preached the word, and his sermon brought forth instant results. There was a mighty moving of the Holy Spirit on Peter's audience. The word of God attended by the Spirit always brings forth results.

Isaiah 55:11, NKJV | So shall my word be that goes forth from my mouth; it shall not return to me void, but it shall accomplish what I please.

The rest of Acts 2 describes what happened as people chose Christ and stepped out of darkness into life; out of wrath and into grace; out of sin and into freedom; out of religion and into the church. Not all of them sadly, since there were anywhere between thirty to sixty thousand people gathered at any one time on the southern steps of the Temple, but three thousand came to know Christ that day.

If we are going to see this world change, we must know the touch of God personally. At Pentecost, God created a new entity, the church, and it was one that would turn the world upside down. Christ said:

Matthew 16:18 | I will build my church, and the gates of hell shall not prevail against it.

Each of us is a continuation of the church at Pentecost. That was the seedbed of the church throughout the world today. Your DNA is from Pentecost. We must move forward with the same anointed word of God and the same Spirit of God. We need that touch of God or we cannot see the world moved for Christ. At Pentecost you knew who was being touched, because there was immediate obedience. That's the sign of grace in a person's heart. We were once bound in sin, but now we have the freedom to obey the impulse of the Spirit. We don't care what anyone thinks, because we've surrendered! These believers, like us, were touched by grace, transformed forever when God saved them.

Touched by Grace

Acts 2:41, 47| So those who received his word were baptized, and there were added that day about three thousand souls.... And the Lord added to their number day by day those who were being saved.

We believe in a regenerated church membership, because regeneration is God's doing. No one can regenerate themselves. A truly saved person comes to Jesus in repentant faith. That's conversion. That's what we do. That's two sides to the one coin of what God requires. Wherever there is repentance there is faith.

But at the same time, God is doing something only he can do. Theologians call this regeneration. God is creating in us a new heart, giving us new eyes, a new joy, and a new Spirit within us. The wind of the Spirit comes to form a new creation: the church! As a result, those who received Peter's teaching about Jesus were immediately changed and touched by God.

The first thing we see is the Spirit did the work. The transformation and regeneration of the heart is the Spirit's work. We believe. We repent. But it is the Spirit that moves in permanently and indwells us in regeneration. Pentecost created a saved people. Day by day they were being saved. It always happens with the word. But the word has to be accompanied by the Spirit. Salvation is always what happens when the work of conviction is done in a human heart by the Holy Spirit.

Something incredible happened that day. Previously dead sinners had now "received his word" (2:41). The local Jerusalem Church was formed. "There were added that day about three thousand souls" (2:47). No man planned it. The Spirit did the forming. This Jerusalem church is the prototype of our church, and all churches. They were touched by grace! Have you been touched by grace? Have you received the word of the gospel? Is Jesus Christ the very center of your life? If so you are not alone. Look at what they did who received his word. They did something that would demonstrate a new belonging. They joined a new community.

Touched for God's Family

Acts 2:41b | So those who received his word were baptized.

It's such an honor to go to a wedding. You are celebrating a new family. You are rejoicing in the love of a couple that is publicly confessing their love and commitment to each other. They are being joined together in a new entity, a new household. That's what baptism is. It's like a Christian's wedding ceremony to Christ. We are being wedded to one another, with Christ as the Head.

Baptism is an entrance into God's family. People who are born again want to be brought into fellowship and into church membership. When you are born again, you are brought into God's universal church. But when you are baptized, it is an entrance into God's local church. Baptism is an outward ceremony of an inward reality. When I got married, I became responsible for my Bride, to love, cherish, provide and protect her and any children we have. I became accountable to lay my life down for her and treat her right. Baptism is like that. We say publicly: I stand for Christ. I surrender to Christ. Hold me accountable.

Baptism is also a statement. It's saying: I'm co-crucified with Christ. I'm co-buried with Christ. I'm co-resurrected with Christ.

> *Romans 6:3-4* | Do you not know that all of us who have been baptized into Christ Jesus were baptized into his death? [4] We were buried therefore with him by baptism into death, in order that, just as Christ was raised from the dead by the glory of the Father, we too might walk in newness of life.

Baptism doesn't save, but it does make a statement: I'm united with Christ in his death and resurrection. There were various ritual washings used in ancient Judaism, but always on the three pilgrimage festivals (Passover, Pentecost, and Tabernacles) they would immerse themselves. Immersion in a ritual bath (mikveh) is used in Orthodox Judaism during the three festivals, even to this day.[64]

Baptism, Peter tells us, is "the answer of a good conscience toward God" (1 Pet 3:21). Only a true believer in the Lord Jesus can have that.

Baptism is a bold step both today and on the day of Pentecost. For those at Pentecost, it was a bold step to be thus publicly baptized in the name of the Lord Jesus. For many at that time, it meant persecution, to be cut off from family and friends and denied further place in the synagogue and in Jewish society. The price of this first step of obedience remains high in many countries and cultures even today.

You may not be persecuted if you are loosely associated with Christianity, but once you are baptized, and you are totally sold out for Jesus, you may have to pay a price. What else can we do but to join God's forever family in the public ceremony of baptism. Baptism is a beautiful act of obedient faith that pictures Christ's death and resurrection.

Touched to Grow

> **Acts 2:42** | And they devoted themselves to the apostles' teaching and the fellowship, to the breaking of bread and the prayers.

---

[64] Rabbi Maurice Lamm. "The Mikveh's Significance in Traditional Conversion." My Jewish Learning. Accessed 20 February 2021. https://www.myjewishlearning.com/article/why-immerse-in-the-mikveh/

Four pathways of Christian growth marked the infant church. The key word here is "devoted." It means to continually give themselves to four areas of growth: teaching, fellowship, communion, and prayer.

Growing in Teaching

Acts 2:42a | And they devoted themselves to the apostles' teaching.

First, their devotion was marked by *the truth*: "they devoted themselves to the apostles' teaching." The Holy Spirit first gave them a hunger for truth. Do you eat each day? Does someone have to tell you to eat? No. Why? Because you have an internal hunger. So it is for the child of God.

Matthew 4:4 | It is written [*in Deut 8:3*], "Man shall not live by bread alone, but by every word that comes from the mouth of God."

Spirit filling is always connected to a hunger for the word of God. What happens when you are filled with the Spirit? You start speaking and singing God's word.

Ephesians 5:18-19 | And be not drunk with wine, wherein is excess; but be filled with the Spirit; [19] Speaking to yourselves in psalms and hymns and spiritual songs, singing and making melody in your heart to the Lord.

Colossians 3:16 | Let the word of Christ dwell in you richly, teaching and admonishing one another in all wisdom, singing psalms and hymns and spiritual songs, with thankfulness in your hearts to God.

A Christian can no longer live comfortably in sin, and the only way to keep the fire of the Spirit burning in us is by fueling yourself with the word of God.

Psalm 119:11 | I have hidden your word in my heart that I might not sin against you.

Ultimately the written word is so important because by the Spirit we are connected to the incarnate Word, Jesus Christ. It's personal. Jesus said,

John 15:4 | Abide in me, and I in you. As the branch cannot bear fruit by itself, unless it abides in the vine, neither can you, unless you abide in me.

Growing in Fellowship

Acts 2:42b | And they devoted themselves to ... the fellowship.

Second, their devotion was marked by fellowship. New links of love were forged that day, a new community created. The church is God's "forever family." John later wrote:

1 John 3:14 | We know that we have passed from death unto life, because we love the brethren.

The Church is Like a Body

The chu rch is the Body of Christ. Union with our Head means union with the members. What hope does an eye have apart from the body? What hope does an arm or a leg have apart from the body? A hand or foot disconnected from the body is a grotesque thing. So is a Christian disconnected from the Body of Christ. The disconnected Christian is a powerless Christian.

Ephesians 4:15-16 | We are to grow up in every way into him who is the head, into Christ, from whom the whole body, joined and held together by every joint with which it is equipped, when each part is working properly, makes the body grow so that it builds itself up in love.

Dear saints, we need each other. Our bond is forever! We cannot walk the Christian life alone. That's nothing but pride to think you can do this without the help of your brother and sister. We need fellowship.

The Church is Like a Flock

The church is compared to a flock of lambs. Paul instructs the Ephesian shepherds to care for the flock of sheep God's given them.

Acts 20:28 | Pay careful attention to yourselves and to all the flock, in which the Holy Spirit has made you overseers, to care for the church of God, which he obtained with his own blood.

A flock is not a random collection of lambs. Sheep belong to specific flocks. Sheep listen to Jesus' voice, and they listen to those who preach what Jesus taught (Jn 10:27).

The Church is Like a Temple

The church is compared to God's Temple.

Ephesians 2:21 | In whom (Christ) the whole structure, being joined together, grows into a holy temple in the Lord. In him you also are being built together into a dwelling place for God by the Spirit (*cf* 1 Pet 2:4-10).

Notice that we are being built together into God's temple, by the Spirit. The Holy Spirit joins us to one another. I like to think of the individual Christian as a brick in the temple. A brick on its own is missing something vital – it is not fulfilling its purpose.

The Church is Like a Household

The church is compared to a household (family).

Ephesians 2:19 | So then you are no longer strangers and aliens, but you are fellow citizens with the saints and [family] members of the household of God.

We like to say around here that we are God's forever family. Our earthly family will pass away, but God's family endures forever. Often, we have more in common with a brother in Christ than we do with our biological family member if they do not know the Lord.

What's the point? Don't be like a lone cut off member of Christ. To grow, you have to be vitally connected to the Body of Christ, like a flock, a Temple, and a forever family. We have no power in the Christian life as solo, lone ranger Christians.

Growing in Communion

Acts 2:42c | And they devoted themselves …. to the breaking of bread.

The third mark of growth was the Lord's table. Communion is a dramatization of the Lord's death. That's how we grow. We have to die. We have to stretch out our hand and let it be nailed. We die to self. We put on the servant's towel, and out of love we serve. That's what the Lord's table is all about. It's about identification with the death of Christ.

The Lord's last request before he went to the cross was "This do in remembrance of me" (1 Cor 11:24). In *baptism* we enter the church, but in communion we recommit to our place at the Lord's table. We are his forever Bride. We are his friends. You don't have a meal with your enemies. Every communion is a dress rehearsal for the marriage supper of the Lamb.

Growing in Prayer

Acts 2:42 | And they devoted themselves to … the prayers.

And fourth, the devotion of the early church was marked by *constant prayer*. These would often be corporate prayer meetings. Now as believers, our lives are marked by answers to prayer. Some have asked, "If God is sovereign, why pray?" That's a good question. It's because God chooses to use the prayers of his people to do his will. That means: no prayer, no power. Don't expect to grow in Christ or see others grow without prayer. With prayer, we enter into the ministry of Christ, pleading for our loved ones before the throne of grace.

> *Hebrews 4:15-16* | For we do not have a high priest who is unable to sympathize with our weaknesses, but one who in every respect has been tempted as we are, yet without sin. ¹⁶ Let us then with confidence draw near to the throne of grace, that we may receive mercy and find grace to help in time of need.

Let's run to our great High Priest who sits at God's right hand. If you are a Spirit-filled believer, you will see constant answers to prayer.

> *Jeremiah 33:3, NIV* | Call to me and I will answer you and tell you great and unsearchable things you do not know.

A CHURCH TOGETHER FOR GOD (2:43-46)

God created a new entity, the church, and it was one that would turn the world upside down. Christ said,

> *Matthew 16:18* | I will build my church, and the gates of hell shall not prevail against it.

You can't have life-on-life church unless you are wanting to live life together.

Experiencing Purity Together

Acts 2:43a | And awe came upon every soul.

The church does not instill much awe today. The professing church accepts such low standards for its fellowship that lying, immorality, questionable doctrine, deception, and even immorality are allowed. We have forgotten the divine injunction. "Be holy; for I am holy" (1 Pet 1:16). We have forgotten that we are the Temple of the Holy Spirit.

The infant church was holy. It was a fresh, new creation, made by the "wind of the Spirit," so "fear came upon every soul." Those who were within feared the Lord. They knew his presence. When God is moving everybody knows it. There is a holiness, a special sense his working.

Experiencing Power Together

Acts 2:43b | And many wonders and signs were being done through the apostles.

The newly formed church had more than purity; it had power. The gift of the apostles included the power to work miracles. An ungrieved Holy Spirit poured out his power upon those men, and soon Jerusalem rang with stories of miraculous healings.

It was as though Jesus of Nazareth were back, as though he were walking again—giving sight to the blind, making the deaf to hear, the dumb to talk, the dead to live, the lame to walk, cleansing the leper, casting out demons. And so he was. Only now it was his Spirit empowered people that were the vehicle of his miracles.

Don't discount this. I know we see far more miracles in pioneering lands, but God will make himself known to you in doing things that only he can do in your life. Those who discount miracles are blind to the special works of God in our lives. When God does a miracle in our lives, it's like him giving us a hug.

Experiencing Provision Together

Acts 2:44-45 | And all who believed were together and had all things in common. ⁴⁵ And they were selling their possessions and belongings and distributing the proceeds to all, as any had need.

It was a true body, each member caring for and nourishing each other member. Here we see the answer to the Lord's prayer:

John 17:21-23 | That they may all be one, just as you, Father, are in me, and I in you, that they also may be in us, so that the world may believe that you have sent me. ²² The glory that you have given me I have given to them, that they may be one even as we are one, ²³ I in them and you in me, that they may become perfectly one, so that the world may know that you sent me and loved them even as you loved me.

The oneness of the early church was organic oneness, not organized oneness. They were generous and provided for one another. It wasn't that they all lived together in a commune. They were willing to sell extra things they had to meet the needs of any of the brothers or sisters. There was a mutual caring and concern for other believers. There was a spontaneous coming together of like-minded believers in love with the Lord, in love with each other, in love with lost souls.

Experiencing Praise Together

Acts 2:46 | And day by day, attending the temple together and breaking bread in their homes, they received their food with glad and generous hearts.

With life-on-life discipleship, the Spirit of God leads us together. Those who were in love with the Lord found their way to the place of prayer and praise and hospitality together. They went to the Temple because the Temple court was an accommodating and convenient place to meet for worship and for fellowship. The Spirit-filled person will seek out the gathering place of God's people.

Along with participating in the Temple fellowship, this new Christian congregation had the practice of meeting from home to home and sharing meals in a spirit of great joy.[65] God's Spirit always spills over into the mundane aspects of life. We live life together. The Spirit brings his people together in hospitality. When we come to know Christ, we get "refrigerator rights" at each other's homes almost every day. The commonplace things of life, such as eating and drinking, are sanctified into a sacred thing. Life is no longer compartmentalized into the sacred and the secular, but everything becomes an act of worship. When they came together, they met God and had "glad and generous hearts". Glory.

A CHURCH TELLING THE WORLD (2:47)

We worship together. We live life together. And what comes next? The world begins to notice. Your lost family and friends will notice first. They may not understand, but the Lord will often grant you favor with them.

---

[65] Faw, *Acts*, 50.

A Favored People

Acts 2:47a | Praising God and having favor with all the people.

Singing and praise was the pulse of the early church. The people were happy. No wonder their numbers grew. Their joy was infectious. We are worried about coronavirus, but we out to let there be an outbreak of joy and praise; that's the outbreak the world needs. When there is love and praise, we become an attractive company of people, just like the early church. God gave them favor with everyone around them. The joy of the Holy Spirit is noticeable. We have a joy that the world cannot take away.

This praise and joy brought favor among their loved ones, their neighbors, and perhaps complete strangers. And that leads to people coming to know Christ.

A Fruitful People

Acts 2:47b | And the Lord added to their number day by day those who were being saved.

You give the light. You express the joy. You articulate the glorious gospel. But the *Lord* adds to its members those he saves.

Psalm 127:1 | Except the LORD build the house, they labor in vain that build it.

1 Corinthians 3:6 | Some plant, some water, but God gives the increase.

Effective evangelism is the ultimate impact of the first fellowship's worship and growth. Believers faithfully witness; God builds the church.[66] There's nothing wrong with small churches. But, dear saint of God, there's something wrong with a church that's not a growing church, if it's surrounded by lost people.

The early church started out with 12, and the 12 got to be 120 (1:15). Then the 120 added 3000 in one day (2:41). Acts 4:4 tells us that 5000 men (heads of households) were saved, so if you add their families that's likely around 20,000 more. We learn more in Acts 5.

Acts 5:28 | They "filled Jerusalem with [their] teaching" of Jesus.

---

[66] W.H. Baker, *Acts*, 889.

In several places it records that scores of numbers kept coming to know Christ. G. Campbell Morgan estimated it was more like 250,000 members that were added in six months.[67] Let's remember that all the results of our evangelism, if we are at the disposal of the Spirit of God, can never be added up. God will do "exceeding, abundantly above all that you ask or think" (Eph 3:19). Jesus tells us that he wants his heaven full.

> *Luke 14:23* | Go out to the highways and hedges and compel people to come in, that my house may be filled.

He calls us to be "fishers of men" (Mt 4:19). You don't know who God is bringing into the kingdom. But his word never returns void.

Conclusion

The final impression we are left with is of a church that knew the awesome presence of God and the evidence was changed lives and a growth in the church both numerically and spiritually. The gospel hasn't changed. God's power hasn't diminished. People still need rescuing. God used this church because of the Spirit's love they shared together, doing life-on-life church.

How do we get this mentality? It's a total surrender of yourself to love God by loving the Body of Christ.

> *John 13:35* | By this all people will know that you are my disciples, if you have love for one another.

When God originating love that is not dependent on other believers, but is poured out unconditionally on other believers, that's a divine love that no one can stop.

During the Nazi reign, Dietrich Bonhoeffer was cut off from other believers, isolated in a prison cell, and it took a great toll on him. We are told that the pain was more than he could bear. Cut off from the nurturing fellowship of other Christians, he felt a deep hunger for the fellowship that was no longer available to him. Like a hungry man who knows the taste of delicious bread though he can no longer reach and break from the loaf, he knew the power of fellowship when it was painfully absent.

---

[67] G. Campbell Morgan. *The Acts of the Apostles* (New York: Fleming H. Revell Company, 1924), 95.

If you were cut off from the fellowship of the saints, would you miss it? Does it mean to you what Christ intended for you, that you would meet him in a deeper way by living life together? One day Bonhoeffer's reality might be ours. Dear brothers and sisters let's not wait until it is illegal to gather and worship before we long for the fellowship. Don't take this for granted. It's what the Spirit uses to grow us and to expand his kingdom, adding one soul at a time to his church.

6 | ACTS 3:1-4:4
THE LAME SHALL LEAP!

Peter said, "I have no silver and gold, but what I do have I give to you. In the name of Jesus Christ of Nazareth, rise up and walk!" And he took him by the right hand and raised him up, and immediately his feet and ankles were made strong. And leaping up, he stood and began to walk, and entered the temple with them, walking and leaping and praising God
ACTS 3:6-8

Each time a child comes along in our family, there is this feeling of displacement. Sometimes it's the little family dog that's displaced. Maybe you've seen the animated film, Lady and the Tramp. Lady feels so displaced when the baby comes along. A puppy is fine, but wow, a baby!

There is a nervousness and fear about displacement when Jesus comes to earth. All the miracles were drawing the people to Jesus, and away from the religious leaders. As glorious as Herod's Temple was, it was nothing compared to the cosmic power coming from one true Tabernacle of God. Remember when he transfigured himself, and Peter, James, and John witnessed his glory? But his glory was on display in all his miracles. Now with the coming of the Spirit, we all become the Temple of God. God begins to break forth, and the focus from Acts 3 to

Acts 5 is a breaking away from the Jerusalem Temple to the new covenant Temple, which is Christ's Body, the Church.

Something incredible happens in Acts 3 where the leaders and priests who ran the Temple felt threatened that their nervous about being displaced. It had begun in Jesus' ministry. Jesus would do miracle after miracle and send those who were healed to the Temple to be examined by the priests. There are parts of the Old Testament law that tells priests what to do when a leper is healed, or a blind person is healed. The problem was they never had to go to those parts of the law because it never happened. And now they have streams and streams of formerly lame people who are asking for a blessing from the priests. Formerly blind and deaf and crippled people are needing the priestly blessing. And the priests feel threatened.

In the Old Testament, if you wanted to get near the presence of God, you needed to go to the Temple. If you were to go to Gilgal or Shiloh today, you will find so many feet of pottery shards. Why? Because the millions of people who would come three times a year would need to wash their Passover lamb, and break the earthenware vessel, because it was holy. They could never use it again. All the way until the time of Ezekiel, you had the Shekinah glory of God at the Tabernacle and Temple. In the days of Ezekiel, before the exile to Babylon, the presence of the Lord left the Temple, and Ichabod was declared: the glory of God has departed.

But if you wanted to get near God you went to the Tabernacle or Temple. Even in the days of Jesus, if you wanted cleansing, you went to the Temple. If you wanted to offer a sacrifice, you went to the Temple. In Acts 3 something happens where something greater than the Temple is manifested. Something greater than Herod's magnificent Temple is on display. It's the new covenant Temple: the Church.

In Acts chapter 3 through 5 the people of Israel who love the Temple begin to see that the great Temple is being displaced. Yes, it would fall in 70 A.D. But that was just an afterthought. In the first few days of the church, there is a massive Holy Spirit evangelistic outpouring. First 3000 individuals are saved at Pentecost. But just shortly after that, God saves so many people that the apostles are only able to count the men.

> *Acts 4:4* | Many of those who had heard the word believed, and the number of the men came to about five thousand.

People estimate with women and children, the number must have been more like 20,000. What causes all these people to be saved? A miracle by Peter and John and a message by Peter. A miracle is performed by Peter where he heals a lame man that everyone knows well and sees every day. No one can deny it. Not even the priests and leaders of Israel at the Temple can deny it. The Scripture describes this man as "perfectly healed." So many believe. It pales the three thousand of Pentecost. Now it's more like 20,000, since they can only count the men. Can you imagine? People are literally flocking to the apostles: "What must I do?" "Is there mercy for me? Is there mercy for me?"

Here we see the apostles continuing Jesus's ministry in word and deed. The healing of a lame man is a deed that leads to a sermon, where even more people are touched by God than at Pentecost. After hearing that sermon, a multitude of people are converted to faith in Jesus, and the Jewish religious authorities are enraged.[68] The passage breaks down neatly into three parts. This text is about a *miracle* and a *message* and a *minefield* of persecution.

THE MIRACLE (3:1-10)

Acts 3:1-10 | Now Peter and John were going up to the temple at the hour of prayer, the ninth hour. **2** And a man lame from birth was being carried, whom they laid daily at the gate of the temple that is called the Beautiful Gate to ask alms of those entering the temple. **3** Seeing Peter and John about to go into the temple, he asked to receive alms. **4** And Peter directed his gaze at him, as did John, and said, "Look at us." **5** And he fixed his attention on them, expecting to receive something from them. **6** But Peter said, "I have no silver and gold, but what I do have I give to you. In the name of Jesus Christ of Nazareth, rise up and walk!" **7** And he took him by the right hand and raised him up, and immediately his feet and ankles were made strong. **8** And leaping up, he stood and began to walk, and entered the temple with them, walking and leaping and praising God. **9** And all the people saw him walking and praising God, **10** and recognized him as the one who sat at the Beautiful Gate of the temple, asking for alms. And they were filled with wonder and amazement at what had happened to him.

---

[68] Tony Merida. *Exalting Jesus in Acts* (Christ-Centered Exposition Commentary) (Nashville: B&H Publishing Group, 2017), 59-60.

When I read this text, I think about a story I heard about a poor college student attending a church near one of our local Christian colleges. On one occasion a broke college student was so poor he actually put a bacon, egg, and cheese sandwich into the offering bucket with a little note: "Silver and gold have I none, but such as I have, I give unto you!" Poor kid, at least he had a heart to give!

We laugh of course, but this section of Scripture is no joke. This passage begins with an endearing miracle of a lame man and it ends with thousands entering the kingdom. There are *threats* and *arrests*, and a *powerful prayer meeting*. Let's see how all this begins with a great miracle. We are introduced to a dear, forgotten, very poor lame man.

The Lame

> **Acts 3:1-3** | Now Peter and John were going up to the temple at the hour of prayer, the ninth hour. ² And a man lame from birth was being carried, whom they laid daily at the gate of the temple that is called the Beautiful Gate to ask alms of those entering the temple. ³ Seeing Peter and John about to go into the temple, he asked to receive alms.

There were three foundations of Jewish life: the word (Torah), worship at the Temple, and a walk of kindness (giving alms). Every day as the Christians go to the Temple to worship, they pass this man.

He's been carried there almost every day for decades. The man is forty years old. This man had a familiar face to everyone in Jerusalem. They had seen him year after year. Many had given to him over the years.[69] Each day, they carried this dear man "to the gate of the temple," the Gate called "Beautiful." It was called "Beautiful" because it was covered with "Corinthian bronze and far exceeding in value those plated with silver and set in gold."[70] This what we know today as the Eastern Gate, the massive entrance where Pentecost took place. It's where the main entrance and exit are.

Here is this lame man just outside the Eastern Gate, because he cannot enter through it. Levitical law said that a deformed man could

---

[69] Merida. *Acts*, 60.
[70] Flavius Josephus. *The Wars of the Jews or History of the Destruction of Jerusalem* (Salt Lake City, UT: Project Gutenberg, 2009) 5.5.3.

not enter past that gate. He is on the wrong side of a beautiful life. He is just outside the gate, and he's crippled.

> *Leviticus 21:18* | No one who has a blemish shall draw near [to the Temple]: a man blind or lame, disfigured or deformed.

That's where so many people are with God. They feel disfigured. They need healing. They know they are not right with God. The man in view here is not simply broke. He's broken. He's physically crippled. He's humiliated. He's hopeless. And to make things worse, he's more than forty years old (4:22). Presumably, he'd lived this way for decades.[71]

The Look

> **Acts 3:4-5** | And Peter directed his gaze at him, as did John, and said, "Look at us." **5** And he fixed his attention on them, expecting to receive something from them.

The main gate to the temple might have been an excellent place to beg, but with so many people coming by him, lots of people were probably just ignoring him. Apparently, this lame man is sadly looking down. Worn out and tired, he asks Peter and John for money, and Peter tells him to look up (3:4). He makes direct eye contact and sees compassion.[72]

The beggar surely get excited, expecting a gift. But why the look? Peter and John had passed by this man probably hundreds and hundreds of times through the years. Even that week, they were meeting at the Temple "every day." So why now? The answer must be that it was God who put it in the hearts of Peter and John.

One deep, compassionate look at that man, and they were moved by God to perform a miracle. You never know what God's going to do. We have to hear the still, small voice of the Spirit as John and Peter did. Typically, donors would flip a coin in his direction as they hurried into the temple, barely giving the poor man a glance. Peter and John fixed their gaze on him. "Look at me," they said. As if to say, "God's about to do something!" The man responded by giving his total attention to

---

[71] Merida. *Acts*, 60.
[72] Faw, *Acts*, 62.

Peter.[73] There was something God was doing in and through John and Peter. The man fixed his attention to them. I think he was expecting money. But just maybe he knew this was going to be a day that radically changed his life, and the course of the entire world. He didn't know it, but probably around 20,000 people are going to enter the kingdom this day.

The Leap

> **Acts 3:6** | But Peter said, "I have no silver and gold, but what I do have I give to you. In the name of Jesus Christ of Nazareth, rise up and walk!"

The man wanted money, but what he needed was a miracle. It's so good that Peter was out of money! Can you imagine all the good things we all would have missed? It's good when we find ourselves in lack and need. God's got something cooking!

"I have no money, but I do have a miracle," was Peter's sentiment. "In the name of Jesus Christ of Nazareth, rise up and walk!" Hallelujah! This poor, broken man when from lame to leaping! What do you have? Something that we all ought to have is Jesus.

> **Acts 3:7-10** | And he took him by the right hand and raised him up, and immediately his feet and ankles were made strong. **8** And leaping up, he stood and began to walk, and entered the temple with them, walking and leaping and praising God. **9** And all the people saw him walking and praising God, **10** and recognized him as the one who sat at the Beautiful Gate of the temple, asking for alms. And they were filled with wonder and amazement at what had happened to him.

I love this. Peter grabs him by the hand, remembering his weakness, but the man needs no help! The lame man is now leaping up to his feet! He doesn't need Peter's help.

There are a lot of firsts here. For the first time, this man leaped up to his feet. "His feet and ankles were made strong." He stood for the first time. He began to walk for the first time. He began to leap for the first time. He entered the Temple and praised God in the Temple for the first time! And for the first time, people were no longer looking at

---

[73] John B. Polhill, *Acts*, vol. 26, The New American Commentary (Nashville: Broadman & Holman Publishers, 1992), 127.

him in pity, but with wonder and amazement and joy! All the people who once pitied him were now envying him. What a miracle. We see something amazing. The man didn't need the Temple anymore. He's glad to be there, but the man is the Temple. The Spirit made this man strong. Surely he comes to faith soon enough.

THE MESSAGE (3:11-26)

A Personal Message

The great crowd of people in the thousands, see this lame man leaping, and everybody knows him, and they are astounded. This would be like seeing John Soen running around leaping and so happy. They are all caught up in the wonder and the joy.

> **Acts 3:11** | While he clung to Peter and John, all the people, utterly astounded, ran together to them in the portico called Solomon's.

Peter takes the opportunity to deliver a very personal message to the people.

> **Acts 3:12-15** | And when Peter saw it he addressed the people: "Men of Israel, why do you wonder at this, or why do you stare at us, as though by our own power or piety we have made him walk? **13** The God of Abraham, the God of Isaac, and the God of Jacob, the God of our fathers, glorified his servant Jesus, whom you delivered over and denied in the presence of Pilate, when he had decided to release him. **14** But you denied the Holy and Righteous One, and asked for a murderer to be granted to you, **15** and you killed the Author of life, whom God raised from the dead. To this we are witnesses.

It's your God who sent Jesus. It's the God of the Old Testament who sent him. Jesus is not only called "God's servant" (like the Servant of Isaiah's Servant Songs), but Peter calls him the Author of life. He says something so profound, "You killed the Author of Life, but God raised him from the dead." The simple gospel. He exposes the depth of their sin. He makes it so personal. Your God sent Jesus. The God of Abraham, Isaac, Jacob. This is the God of your fathers. You crucified him, but God raised him. We all are witnesses.

A Powerful Message

Acts 3:16 | And his name—by faith in his name—has made this man strong whom you see and know, and the faith that is through Jesus has given the man this perfect health in the presence of you all.

Peter makes clear first of all, that there's nothing in himself that brought about this miracle. It's all by the glorious name of Jesus. Peter is able to do the kind of thing that Jesus did by acting in the name and power of Jesus. We see there is a continuing link between the ministry of Jesus and the power of the church.[74] So who had faith in Christ's name? The emphasis is on Peter. God is drawing the cripple man to salvation for sure, but it is not the faith of the lame that God used. It's the faith of Peter. Where's your faith for the lost? Peter begins his message with a miracle. People are asking, how did God do that for the lame man? Is there mercy for me?

A Profound Message

Peter preached Pentecost not long before and now he tells another group of thousands how to enter the kingdom.

Repent

Acts 3:17-19 | And now, brothers, I know that you acted in ignorance, as did also your rulers. **18** But what God foretold by the mouth of all the prophets, that his Christ would suffer, he thus fulfilled. **19** Repent therefore, and turn back, that your sins may be blotted out.

They knew that Christ would suffer. The prophets were clear.

Isaiah 53:6 | All we like sheep have gone astray; we have turned—every one—to his own way; and the Lord has laid on him the iniquity of us all.

Daniel 9:26, NIV | The Anointed One will be put to death.

Psalm 22:16 | They pierced my hands and feet.

---

[74] I. Howard Marshall, *Acts: An Introduction and Commentary*, vol. 5, Tyndale New Testament Commentaries (Downers Grove, IL: InterVarsity Press, 1980), 93.

Your sins killed Jesus. These people had actually put to death the Author of life. So Peter tells them, and all of us: "Repent."

Acts 3:19 | Repent therefore, and turn back, that your sins may be blotted out.

Acts 17:30 | God commands all people everywhere to repent.

What does it mean to repent? Peter gave the call to repentance with two expressions: "repent" (*metanoeō*) which means to "change your mind and position."[75] Peter also says to "turn back to God" (*epistrephō*).[76] Stop rejecting Christ. Stop keeping him on the outskirts of your life and thinking. Bring him into the center of your heart and mind and worship him. Love him. Change your mind. Stop running from God and turn to God. Repent so that all "your sins may be blotted out." What's the worst sin ever committed? How about putting to death the Author of life (3:15)? What happens when you believe in Jesus? All your sins are taken away! "Whom the Son sets free will be free indeed" (Jn 8:36). Remember what Isaiah said:

Isaiah 1:18 | Come now, let us reason together, says the Lord: though your sins are like scarlet, they shall be as white as snow; though they are red like crimson, they shall become like wool.

How great is the love of Christ? The Puritan Richard Sibbes famously said, "There is more mercy in Christ than sin in us." [77]

Refresh & Restore

But here is a massive application here that Peter gives to the crowd.

Acts 3:20-21 | That times of refreshing may come from the presence of the Lord, and that he may send the Christ appointed for you, Jesus. ²¹ Whom heaven must receive until the time for restoring all the things about which God spoke by the mouth of his holy prophets long ago.

He says, basically, there's a coming restoration of all things. Heaven and earth will one day be restored and come together as one.

---

[75] John F. MacArthur Jr., *Acts*, vol. 1, MacArthur New Testament Commentary (Chicago: Moody Press, 1994), 114.
[76] Polhill, *Acts*, 134.
[77] Richard Sibbes, *The Bruised Reed and Smoking Flax* (London: Gooch Booksellers, 1630), 16.

"The lion and the wolf shall lay down together" (Isa 11:6). When you repent and turn to Jesus, you get a taste of that. That's what God wants you to live in. Are you living in that refreshment saint? That's what this sermon is all about. It's all about the refreshment that the lame man who is now leaping feels. Are you experiencing that in your life? Can you say that you are living in the "fullness of joy" that is found in God's presence (Psa 16:11)?

Are you feeling lame in your walk with God? Leap up in the name of Jesus! Holy Spirit, pour over me right now. No longer can we be lame. The Spirit is bidding us to get up and walk and leap for him in the name of Jesus.

Rejoice

Acts 3:21b | God spoke by the mouth of his holy prophets long ago.

The time is here! Let's rejoice! The prophets talked about it. Every prophet pointed to the refreshing times of Jesus, but now they are here! Dive into the ocean of God's mercy! The time has finally come! It's time. Dive into God's love!

Reflect

Acts 3:22-26 | Moses said, 'The Lord God will raise up for you a prophet like me from your brothers. You shall listen to him in whatever he tells you. ²³ And it shall be that every soul who does not listen to that prophet shall be destroyed from the people.' ²⁴ And all the prophets who have spoken, from Samuel and those who came after him, also proclaimed these days. ²⁵ You are the sons of the prophets and of the covenant that God made with your fathers, saying to Abraham, 'And in your offspring shall all the families of the earth be blessed.' ²⁶ God, having raised up his servant, sent him to you first, to bless you by turning every one of you from your wickedness."

So Peter closes his message and says, "This is the ultimate Promised Son of Abraham." "This is the ultimate Prophet that is greater than Moses." "This is the Servant of Isaiah, the Messiah who would suffer." I love this. Peter says, "Turn to him who wants to bless you." Jesus wants to bless you. Turn to him now. Thousands flock to Jesus, running to hear Peter's message and see the lame man leaping (4:4). That's what we should be seeing when Jesus is manifested. People want the refreshing from Jesus. They want a taste of the full restoration that is coming in the new heaven and new earth.

THE MINEFIELD (4:1-4)

> **Acts 4:1-4** | And as they were speaking to the people, the priests and the captain of the temple and the Sadducees came upon them, ² greatly annoyed because they were teaching the people and proclaiming in Jesus the resurrection from the dead. ³ And they arrested them and put them in custody until the next day, for it was already evening. ⁴ But many of those who had heard the word believed, and the number of the men came to about five thousand.

People were running from every place to see this man. He was leaping who was once lame. The Temple leaders didn't like it. So they arrested Peter and John. The people didn't care. They were amazed at the leaping man who was once lame. But now they are so much more amazed at Jesus. They want this refreshment for their soul. So the people are flocking so much to be saved, that they had to stop counting men and women and children. Now they were only counting the men: heads of households. That means likely more than 20,000 people came to Christ that day.

What a minefield it is to come to know Christ. What a train wreck! But what are we afraid of? Being refreshed by Jesus is far better than any of the silver and gold this world offers.

Conclusion

Why were so many flocking to Christ? Was it just the miracle? No. It was Peter's message. He says: come to Christ and repent, and you will have times of refreshing that will give you a taste of the final restoration. And the people believed and experienced something greater than the Temple. They literally became the Temple of the Holy Spirit. People were so relieved and happy, that multitudes just kept flocking to the Lord. Family after family. They couldn't count everyone, so they counted heads of households.

7 | ACTS 4:1-22
NO OTHER NAME

Now when they saw the boldness of Peter and John, and perceived that they were uneducated, common men, they were astonished. And they recognized that they had been with Jesus.... But in order that it may spread no further among the people, let us warn them to speak no more to anyone in this name." So they called them and charged them not to speak or teach at all in the name of Jesus. But Peter and John answered them, "Whether it is right in the sight of God to listen to you rather than to God, you must judge, for we cannot but speak of what we have seen and heard."

ACTS 4:13, 17-20

I am deeply desirous that our church exalt the name of Jesus. There is no other name under heaven by which people are saved. There is no greater joy than for the Spirit to fill us.

So why do we stay in the deadness and coldness of the world? Some of it is that there are lost people among us. That's shocking, but it's something we need to face. If you do not have the Spirit moving in your life, it could be that you are knowledgeable but lost. So many that are so on fire today would confess to you that for years they were lost church members. So please know if you do not have the Spirit of God, then you do not have eternal life.

As a believer, the only reason that you would not be filled with the Spirit is that you've given place to the devil through anger or anxiety or worldliness. Is your heart cold? How can your heart be cold? Let the love of Jesus warm your heart. His arms are open. His name is exalted. His love is infinite. Let us all listen to his call to come to him. There were many in the time of the book of Acts who neglected their heart, and they were hardened and cold.

THE GLORY OF JESUS' NAME (4:1-12)

The name of Jesus can melt hearts, amen? That's why we must lift up the name of Jesus always. But in the events of the story in Acts 4, we are going to see Satan blinding the eyes of people in high places. But these uneducated, poor apostles are humble and unafraid. They lift up the name of Jesus. Before we look at the glory of Jesus' name, I want us to look with pity at the blindness that people who know the Bible are in.

Unbelievers Can't See Jesus' Glory

My heart is first moved with astonishment at the cold hearts of the leaders of Israel.

The Rulers' Annoyance

Acts 4:1-2a | And as they were speaking to the people, the priests and the captain of the temple and the Sadducees came upon them, ² greatly annoyed.

They see the greatest miracles, and their response is annoyance? How cold and hard they are. They witnessed the life and miracles of the Lord of glory, and they crucified him. But he rose again. They even witness the miracle of a lame man that they were very familiar with. They had seen him day after day, but yet they can still have a cold, unmoved heart. That's terrible frightening that a human heart can be so hard. How can a heart be so hard that you could see the love of God poured out in front of you, and be annoyed and angry like these Jewish rulers?

The Rulers' Theology

Acts 4:2 | Greatly annoyed because they were teaching the people and proclaiming in Jesus the resurrection from the dead.

Why are they so annoyed? Because they have bad theology. The Sadducees were the main rulers in the Temple. Most of the priests are Sadducees. Most of the teachers of the law in the synagogues are Pharisees. The Sadducees administrate the Temple. Most of the high priests are Sadducees. They are annoyed at the apostles because they are teaching the resurrection of Jesus. The Sadducees are "sad you see" because they deny the resurrection.

The Sadducees were people who believed in morality, but once you die, that's it. They do not believe in any other part of the Bible or religion. They did not believe in the supernatural. They didn't believe in miracles. They didn't believe in resurrection. They didn't believe in afterlife. They didn't believe in a spiritual world at all. They're what we today would call secular people, moral rationalists. Religious liberals, you might call them.[78] There were about 5000 Sadducees at the time of Jesus, slightly less than the 7000 Pharisees.

Just consider that you have Temple that God gave to his people to bless them with his presence through the Spirit. And here they are so blind and coldhearted that they forbid the miracles and message of Jesus. Realize that these are leaders that study the Bible for a living. You can read the Bible and be cold and hard if you don't give up your life to Jesus. Just take this as a warning and beware. Don't think just because a person is using the Bible that they are safe. Many wolves use the Bible. Be careful saints.

The Rulers' Powerlessness

Acts 4:3-4 | And they arrested them and put them in custody until the next day, for it was already evening. ⁴ But many of those who had heard the word believed, and the number of the men came to about five thousand.

Because it was getting late, the authorities locked up the two apostles for the night. All that night news would be coming in of rejoicing among the thousands who had been born again that day. The whole city must have been humming with the news. The story of the healing, excerpts from Peter's sermon, the joy of those who had been so deeply convicted but who were now in the family of God rang through the city.

---

[78] Timothy J. Keller, *The Timothy Keller Sermon Archive*, "Unbelief" from the series on The Book of Acts—October 22, 1995, *Acts 4:1–20* (New York City: Redeemer Presbyterian Church, 2013).

What a stir there must have been.[79] Ultimately, the Jewish rulers could arrest Peter and John, but they could not stop the power of Jesus through the Holy Spirit from changing and transforming lives.

God wants his heaven full, and no one will stop him. Five thousand men, likely heads of households, came to know Jesus that day. If you count the wives and children, it's more like twenty thousand! Give yourself to Christ. Yield to the mighty Spirit of God.

This growth of the church is something we have every right to wish to see occur again in our time. Then, as now, it must be viewed as a sovereign outpouring of the Spirit.[80] The only thing stopping the church from growing is you grieving the Holy Spirit. Start yielding to the Spirit and see him touch hearts and change lives.

The Rulers' Question

Acts 4:5-6 | On the next day their rulers and elders and scribes gathered together in Jerusalem, **6** with Annas the high priest and Caiaphas and John and Alexander, and all who were of the high-priestly family.

Now all the powerful people are gathered. This was a gathering of the Sanhedrin. What an impressive crowd it was that gathered there that day to intimidate two Galilean fishermen. The Sanhedrin was composed of seventy-two members—the high priest being the president of the court. The liberal Sadducees, who dominated it, didn't want to hear anything of a resurrection. A powerful minority was made up of Pharisees, a party to which most of the scribes (the professional expositors and preachers of the Bible) belonged.

Annas was the previous high priest, who had great power. Five of his sons, a grandson, and son-in-law (Caiaphas) occupied the office after him. Caiaphas was the son-in-law of Annas. Remember, he's the one who tried Jesus in his kangaroo court.[81] How bad can this go? But Peter and John have no fear. They listen to the question given by these powerful people.

Acts 4:7 | And when they had set them in the midst, they inquired, "By what power or by what name did you do this?"

---

[79] J. Phillips, *Exploring Acts,* Ac 4:3–4.
[80] Thomas, *Acts*, 95.
[81] J. Phillips, Ac 4:5–6.

What power, what authority, what name is giving you this miraculous power? They all knew the man that had been healed. He was around forty years old, so he had been there likely since he was small. He was crippled. All were taught to give generously to the crippled and poor. God's people were the "government assistance."

And there it was, out in the open, the crux of everything: the question of the *name*. Peter could not have been asked a better leading question. Unwittingly they handed him his text on a silver platter. Thus, God makes the wrath of man to praise him. The anger of Jesus' foes is used to introduce the glory of his name.[82] Isn't it amazing that in persecution, we don't have to over think things? God has promised to give us the words we need at the time we need it.

Believers Boldly Preach Jesus

Peter, fresh from Pentecost and now fresh from a miracle is filled with the Holy Spirit. He's ready to proclaim the Name of Jesus!

The Power of Jesus

Acts 4:8-9 | Then Peter, filled with the Holy Spirit, said to them, Rulers of the people and elders, ⁹ if we are being examined today concerning a good deed done to a crippled man, by what means this man has been healed.

What have we done? Is it a sin to demonstrate the power of Jesus? Is it wrong to bring the power of the new creation to this crippled man that we all know? Peter asks, "Are we on trial for doing a good deed for a lame man?" They all know this man. Peter is bold. Peter is ready to answer the question. By what power was this man healed? Peter answers.

The Name of Jesus

Acts 4:10 | Let it be known to all of you and to all the people of Israel that by the name of Jesus Christ of Nazareth, whom you crucified, whom God raised from the dead—by him this man is standing before you well.

Salvation has always been by grace through faith in Jesus. Some have said, "In the Old Testament they came to God through the Law."

---

[82] Ibid., Ac 4:7.

This is false. No one can draw near to God in his own works. David is clear about this.

Psalm 130:3 | If you, O LORD, should mark iniquities, O Lord, who could stand?

Isaiah preached Christ when he said:

Isaiah 53:6 | All we like sheep have gone astray; we have turned—every one—to his own way; and the Lord has laid on him the iniquity of us all.

The One who healed this lame man who is now leaping? His name is Jesus! Jesus! Jesus! What a name! The name above all names! Peter says, "You know this Jesus well, because not long ago, you crucified him. But now he is risen from the dead. You couldn't' keep him dead." Look at the boldness that comes when we are filled with the Spirit.

This is the same Peter who a couple of months before had trembled before a slip of a girl and denied his Lord with cursing, frightened since he, too, could be arrested and crucified. This new boldness was the result of the resurrection and the filling of the Holy Spirit.[83] Saints, this is the boldness we need to live in.

The Prophecy of Jesus

Acts 4:11 | This Jesus is the stone that was rejected by you, the builders, which has become the cornerstone.

Peter quotes a wonderful prophecy which we love to sing about.[84] Jesus is the Architect of our salvation. They knew the quote well. It was from Psalm 118:22, a recognized prophecy that God's King would come into the world and be rejected. Peter made it personal. "Jesus is the stone that was rejected *by you*, the builders." For the leaders of Israel, it was not a wonderful prophecy. They were to build the true temple in Christ, but they rejected the main foundation stone. It spoke of how they rejected their Lord and Savior. They crucified the One who is the only way of salvation.

How shocking that God the Son offers himself as the foundation of these leaders' lives. They study the Bible for a living. But they reject him over and over again: in his life (they put him to death), after his

---

[83] Ibid., Ac 4:8–10.
[84] "Christ is Made the Sure Foundation", "Cornerstone", "In Christ Alone".

resurrection, and after he is exalted in healing. Unbelief is shocking. Peter gets to the point of why this rejection is so tragic.

The Exclusivity of Jesus

> **Acts 4:12** | And there is salvation in no one else, for there is no other name under heaven given among men by which we must be saved.

Jesus is the exclusive way to heaven. He said, "I am the way, and the truth, and the life. No one comes to the Father except through me" (Jn 14:6). The name of Jesus, by which the lame man had been healed; the name they hated, was the only name by which they could be saved. They could be saved. They must be saved. But first they must turn to the very Jesus they had crucified and slain. God would save even them on those terms. Is there grace greater than that? Saints, let's proclaim everywhere to everyone that Jesus is the only way of salvation. Jesus said, "I am the door" (Jn 10:9), insisting that "he who does not enter the sheepfold by the door, the same is a thief and a robber" (Jn 10:1).

Consider this belief in the Roman world. In the Roman world, you would've believed certain things. First, everybody believed that there were many gods, many religions. Secondly, every god had limited sovereignty. It meant you had a god of Ephesus, but the god of Ephesus wasn't the god of Sparta. There were gods of agriculture or love or war. Finally, in Roman society, there was no one god who was *the one true God* over all the rest.[85] That makes sense, because that's how the demonic world is. Demons are regional rulers. They are limited created beings, and all the false gods of this world are actually just demons.

> *1 Corinthians 10:18, NIV* | People who do not know God bring gifts of animals in worship. But they have given them to demons, not to God.

Now in the Jewish world, to say Jesus is the only way, that salvation is by grace through faith in Jesus, is offensive to both the Pharisees and the Sadducees. The Pharisees were deceived thinking salvation was through keeping the Law of Moses. And Sadducees were deceived because they just denied that there was an afterlife or that anyone had to meet God. They were like Deists who thought God put the world into

---

[85] Keller, sermon on "Unbelief" from Acts 4.

motion and just walked away from it. The god of the Sadducees was completely impersonal.

Our God is the one true and living God revealing himself as the Triune God of the Scriptures: Father, Son, and Holy Spirit. If you want to come to the Father, you have to go through the Son of God. There is no other way. And Jesus paid it all. It's by grace we are saved through faith in Christ. In Christ alone our hope is found! We can't say it better than the bold words of Peter:

> **Acts 4:12** | And there is salvation in no one else, for there is no other name under heaven given among men by which we must be saved.

Praise the Lord for the glory of Jesus' name! There is no one like him: King of kings, Lord of lords! He's the second Person of the Trinity! He is the Alpha and Omega, the First and the Last, the Beginning and the End. He's the Architect of our salvation, the Foundation and Cornerstone of the Church. He's my great High Priest. He's the Way, the Truth, and the Life! He's my Prophet, Priest, and King. Unto Jesus be all glory, honor and praise!

He's the Lamb of God that takes away the sin of the world. He's the Lion of the tribe of Judah that judges the world. He's the only Mediator between God and man, the man Christ Jesus. He's my good Shepherd. He's the Door for the sheep. He's my Living Water. He's my Bread of Life.

And there is salvation in no other. Mr. Good Works won't get you there. Good intentions won't get you there. Your parents' faith won't get you there. Denying the existence of God won't get you there. Can I try to fix myself or save myself? Can I do penance and punish myself enough? Well, what can wash away my sins? What can make me whole again? Nothing. Nothing. Nothing. Nothing. Nothing but the blood of Jesus! Jesus is the only way. Never forget it. Spurgeon says, Christianity must be a very narrow, negative religion, for there is clearly no other way.

> A thousand errors may live in peace with one another, but truth is the hammer that breaks them all in pieces. A hundred lying religions may sleep peaceably in one bed, but wherever the gospel of Christ goes as the truth, it is like a firebrand, and it abides nothing that is not more substantial than the wood, the hay, and the stubble of carnal error. All the gods of the heathen, and all other religions are born of hell, and

therefore, they are children of the same father, the devil. ...But God, who is the author of all truth, says that whoever rejects the loving Christ shall perish without mercy.... We are not the intolerant ones, for we are but echoing the words of him that speaks from heaven, and who declares, that cursed is the man who rejects this religion of Christ, seeing that there is no salvation out of him.[86]

God would have his heaven full. We are not intolerant ones! "God is not willing that any should perish" (2 Pet 3:9). He "desires all people to be saved and to come to the knowledge of the truth" (1 Tim 2:4). "The grace of God has appeared, bringing salvation for all people" (Titus 2:11). "Christ Jesus came into the world to save sinners" (1 Tim 1:15). Jesus stretches out his hands to sinners everywhere and says:

> *Matthew 11:28-30* | Come to me, all who labor and are heavy laden, and I will give you rest. [29] Take my yoke upon you, and learn from me, for I am gentle and lowly in heart, and you will find rest for your souls. [30] For my yoke is easy, and my burden is light.

Come to Jesus. He paid the price. There is no other Savior. No one else lived the perfect life for you. No one else satisfies God's justice perfectly for your sins. Come! The door is open wide but come to Jesus while you can! There will be a day when the door is closed. Death is coming. Christ is returning. Run to Jesus while you can!

THE GREATNESS OF JESUS' FAME (4:13-22)

Now who is it that makes Jesus famous?

Those Who Promote Jesus' Fame

Jesus' followers are nobodies. Jesus gets all the glory from his people, because he resists the proud and only calls the humble to speak for him.

Uneducated Men

> **Acts 4:13** | Now when they [the Jewish rulers] saw the boldness of Peter and John, and perceived that they were uneducated, common men, they were astonished. And they recognized that they had been with Jesus.

---

[86] Charles Haddon Spurgeon. "The Way of Salvation" Metropolitan Tabernacle Pulpit Volume 4 (London: Passemore & Alabaster, 1858), preached August 15, 1858.

The rulers of Israel are astonished. The apostles' only qualification was "that they had been with Jesus." These men were bold. Why were they bold? They had been with Jesus. They had seen Christ alive, resurrected, and now Christ lives in them. And all of the forces of hell could not intimidate them. They could not shut them up, and they could not hold them back. The apostles refused to let up, shut up, or back up, because they were filled with the Spirit of God and the presence of Jesus.

The ignorant rulers of Israel notice that Peter and John are not sophisticated. They have no education. The only glory any of us have is that we boast in the Cross of Jesus Christ. Education is nothing. Sophistication is nothing. All our achievements are dung compared to the excellency of the knowledge of Christ. The rulers perceived that these men "had been with Jesus." That's the recognition I want!

Don't get me wrong: I'm glad we have education. I'm glad we have all the wonderful opportunities we have in this country that is free for now. But what does education matter if you don't know Jesus? Our greatest achievement will not be what we accomplished on this earth, but what Jesus accomplished in and through us! He saved me! Hallelujah! And as we follow him, we are pointing others to Christ. Our greatest honor is to spread the fame of Jesus' name! So who is it that God uses to spread Jesus' fame? The nobodies. Those who do not trust in education, though we may be educated. We do not trust in riches, though God may have blessed us with financial gain. Our only boast is the One who saved me, died for me, rose from the dead for me. We really are nobodies. The Jewish rulers were shocked at who God was using! Now here's someone else God uses: a cripple—a lame man who is now leaping!

A Healed Man

Acts 4:14-16 | But seeing the man who was healed standing beside them, they had nothing to say in opposition. **15** But when they had commanded them to leave the council, they conferred with one another, **16** saying, "What shall we do with these men? For that a notable sign has been performed through them is evident to all the inhabitants of Jerusalem, and we cannot deny it.

Peter and John were not trained interpreters of Scripture from the rabbinic tradition. They didn't have theological book training. Their training was from the Lord himself. Forbidding lay Christians in handling and interpreting the Bible has been a frequent issue in church history. Central to the Reformation was the urgency to translate the Bible into the common language of the people. That means today, Christians with little or no formal training, using the "ordinary means" of reading the Scriptures themselves, listening to sermons, reading daily devotional guides, attending Bible studies and faithful online Web sites, may come to know God and walk with him, without the assistance of professionals. As the Westminster Confession of Faith puts it:

> All things in Scripture are not alike plain in themselves, nor alike clear unto all; yet those things which are necessary to be known, believed, and observed for salvation, are so clearly propounded, and opened in some place of Scripture or other, that not only the learned, but *the unlearned*, in a due use of the ordinary means, may attain unto a sufficient understanding of them.[87]

What did these men know? Well, they knew Jesus. And because of knowing Jesus, they knew the Scriptures better than the Sadducees and Pharisees. Peter and John knew the prophecy of Jesus being the chief Cornerstone and Architect of our salvation who was rejected (*cf* 4:11). God doesn't choose many mighty or many wise.

> *1 Corinthians 1:26-31* | For or you see your calling, brethren, how that not many wise men after the flesh, not many mighty, not many noble, are called: [27] But God has chosen the foolish things of the world to confound the wise; and God has chosen the weak things of the world to confound the things which are mighty; [28] And base things of the world, and things which are despised, has God chosen, yea, and things which are not, to bring to nothing things that are: [29] That no flesh should glory in his presence... [31] That, according as it is written, "He that glories, let him glory in the Lord."

Those Who Oppose Jesus' Fame

In the midst of the power of Jesus being demonstrated in the lame man, and the power of the prophecy of Scripture being displayed in the humility of Peter and John, it's an amazing display of God: his power and his word! But the blind can't see. The deaf can't hear. The truly crippled ones were not the ones lying outside the temple, but it was the

---

[87] Westminster Assembly, *The Westminster Confession of Faith: Edinburgh Edition* (Philadelphia: William S. Young, 1851), 19.

ones running the temple and the leaders who were supposed to be teaching the word of God. But they were deaf and blind. That's why they warn the apostles to stop preaching Jesus.

Their Decree

Acts 4:17-18 | But in order that it may spread no further among the people, let us warn them to speak no more to anyone in this name." **18** So they called them and charged them not to speak or teach at all in the name of Jesus.

Astonishing! They see the power of God in the leaping man who was once lame. This is the name, that likely 20,000 people in the Temple were flocking to. And they think they can stop the spread of Jesus' fame with a mere warning?

The Defiance

Acts 4:19-20 | But Peter and John answered them, "Whether it is right in the sight of God to listen to you rather than to God, you must judge, **20** for we cannot but speak of what we have seen and heard."

Peter and John want to be respectful. They are not there to rebel against their authorities. But what do Christians do when our authorities are asking us to sin? What do we do when the government tells us to stop talking about Jesus? I love what R.C. Sproul says about this.

> Only a few weeks had gone by since the Apostles had heard the words of Jesus that we call the Great Commission: "Go therefore and make disciples of all the nations, baptizing them in the name of the Father and of the Son and of the Holy Spirit" (Mt 28:19). Jesus gave to Peter and to John and to the entire church of the first century a mandate. It is our mandate too. If any authority under heaven comes to the Christian and tells him he may not pray, or preach, or gather for worship, or tithe, or do any of the things God commands, that Christian not only may disobey, but he must disobey.[88]

Their Dilemma

At the end of the day, the dilemma and great difficulty was not on Peter and John and the now more than 23,000 followers of Jesus. The

---

[88] R. C. Sproul, *Acts*, St. Andrew's Expositional Commentary (Wheaton, IL: Crossway, 2010), 100–101.

dilemma is on the unbelieving religious leaders at the Temple. They are lost in their sin. The power of God is breaking out through the Spirit and the word. Revival is happening. And the leaders can't disprove it. God is working. Everyone is praising God. How sad and so ironic are the leaders actions.

> **Acts 4:21-22** | And when they had further threatened them, they let them go, finding no way to punish them, because of the people, for all were praising God for what had happened. ²² For the man on whom this sign of healing was performed was more than forty years old.

The leaders threatened the Christians. That's all they could do because it's not a crime to praise God, Amen! At least it wasn't at that moment. The man who was healed was more than forty years old. Imagine the one who they saw all those years. They knew him. He's leaping and jumping and praising God. Why won't these leaders join and rejoice in God for what he has done. That's the frightening thing about hardness of heart. It ignores the great work of God.

Conclusion

So my conclusion today is: don't harden your heart. No matter what you are going through, it's not to fix your job of fix your marriage. The answer is to fix your eyes on Jesus. The "baseball" evangelist Billy Sunday, who was saved at Pacific Garden Mission in Chicago said:

> There are two hundred and fifty-six names given in the Bible for the Lord Jesus Christ, and I suppose this was because he was infinitely beyond all that any one name could express.[89]

Great names come and go, but the name of Jesus remains. The devil still hates it, the world still opposes it, but God still blesses it, and we can still claim it! It is "at the Name of Jesus" that every knee will bow, and every tongue confess the Lordship and Deity of Jesus Christ. If God is your Abba, Father, then you know that his Son Jesus is the only way, the truth and the life. There's no other way to know God the Father. There's no one like Jesus. Drop everything and come to him.

---

[89] Billy Sunday in Elijah P. Brown. *The Real Billy Sunday: The Life and Work of Rev. William Ashley Sunday, The Baseball Evangelist* (Dayton, OH: Otterbein Press, 1914), 272.

Follow him. His arms are open. There is no other name under heaven whereby people can be saved.

8 | ACTS 4:23-37
EARTH SHAKING PRAYER

And when they had prayed, the place in which they were gathered together was shaken, and they were all filled with the Holy Spirit and continued to speak the word of God with boldness.

ACTS 4:31

True prayer is the most beautiful expression in the universe. It is to say man is powerless and God is omnipotent. It is to recognize our true state. Man has no self-sustaining power in and of himself. It is in the Lord that we "live and move and have our being" (Acts 17:28). We should have no confidence in ourselves, but only in the Lord. If anything is done, he must do it. That does not mean we are fatalists. We are not passive do-nothings waiting around for God to do something. No. God calls us to cooperate with him in the movement and orchestration of salvation. We are his great symphony. We carry out his plans. He is the director, and we are the orchestra. We ask for him to carry out what he has promised, and he answers. God will answer when we pray! He may even bring an earthquake as he did in Acts 4:23-32. We believe in the power of prayer!

Acts 4:23-32 | When they were released, they went to their friends and reported what the chief priests and the elders had said to them. ²⁴ And when they heard it, they lifted their voices together to God and said, "Sovereign Lord, who made the heaven and the earth and the sea and everything in them, [25] who through the mouth of our father David, your servant, said by the Holy Spirit, "'Why did the Gentiles rage, and the peoples plot in vain? [26] The kings of the earth set themselves, and the rulers were gathered together, against the Lord and against his Anointed'— [27] for truly in this city there were gathered together against your holy servant Jesus, whom you anointed, both Herod and Pontius Pilate, along with the Gentiles and the peoples of Israel, [28] to do whatever your hand and your plan had predestined to take place. [29] And now, Lord, look upon their threats and grant to your servants to continue to speak your word with all boldness, [30] while you stretch out your hand to heal, and signs and wonders are performed through the name of your holy servant Jesus." [31] And when they had prayed, the place in which they were gathered together was shaken, and they were all filled with the Holy Spirit and continued to speak the word of God with boldness. [32] Now the full number of those who believed were of one heart and soul, and no one said that any of the things that belonged to him was his own, but they had everything in common.

We need to pray in a way that we meet God in a life changing way. We need to have those "wrestle with God" moments, like Jacob, and he was never the same. Here's the key thought for this study: We need to know the presence of God in a way that shakes us to the core! If that happens, we will be changed, and God will change the world.

The prayer we read in Acts 4 not only shook the people that prayed, it shook the entire Roman empire. Within the first six months of the church, people estimate that between 50 to 200 thousand people were born again. How did it happen? What was the fuel that ran that engine? It was simple, total surrender to God in prayer.

THE CONFIDENCE OF PRAYER (4:23-28)

I want you to see that it was trouble that brought the church to prayer. The gospel of our Lord and Savior Jesus Christ was being opposed. Christians were being threatened. And this was the catalyst for this great prayer meeting. Someone has said: Christians are like tea—their real strength comes out when they're in hot water. The church of the Lord Jesus Christ today ought to always be praying because we are always in the hot water of warfare.

I look around and I see militant, marching secular humanism. I see an emotionalist false Christianity that is spreading like wildfire. I see the communist menace that once circled the globe making its home in the deepest places of power in America. I look inside of this beloved nation of ours and I see moral corruption and utter degradation in the movies and television. I see the slaughter of the unborn innocent babies. I see a drug epidemic, alcoholism, and sexual perversion. I see a mockery of marriage among homosexuals. I see gender blenders in our public schools, turning our children against God. I see a people that do not know God; millions and billions of people—who have heard the name of Jesus, but either reject him or remake him into their own image. And I am convinced that only prayer can hold back the floodtide of sin and deliver millions who are living in sin's dark night. Only divinely empowered prayer can send revival.

Now it is not just any prayer that we need, but it is prayer with power. It is not the rhetoric of our prayer—how eloquent our prayers are; it is not the sound of our prayer—how beautiful our prayers are; it is not the logic of our prayer—how intellectual our prayers are; it is not the method of our prayer—how carefully detailed our prayers are; but it is the power of our prayer that counts.

We are only God to experience the power of God if we meet with God himself. He's got to shake us. Power with God begins with total trust and faith. That faith brings a recognition of our own powerlessness. And it comes when we recognize God's power and walk in it. When these disciples prayed like that, the place was shaken. There was divine power that literally shook the place. God said amen to their prayers with an earthquake.

Confidence in God as Creator of All Things

> **Acts 4:23-24** | When they were released, they went to their friends and reported what the chief priests and the elders had said to them. ²⁴ And when they heard it, they lifted their voices together to God and said, "Sovereign Lord, who made the heaven and the earth and the sea and everything in them."

We hear a prayer that sees God as the Creator of all things. He is the sovereign, omnipotent God. He is the Almighty God. Now this Jewish high court has told them not to preach or teach in the name of Jesus. But they were not taken back with fear, but with divine comfort under the "shadow of the Almighty." They recognized that God is the Creator and the rulers who oppose Christ are the created. And they prayed, basically, "Lord, because you are the Sovereign Creator of heaven and earth, we don't have to be intimidated by them, because all of the forces of the universe are at your fingertips." God had a plan for all their pain and persecution. Corrie Ten Boom said it this way: "There is no panic in heaven, only plans."[90]

The Holy Trinity never meets in an emergency session. Dear saint, it's necessary that when we're opposed, and when trouble comes, we go back and put things into perspective, look beyond the visible to the invisible, and look beyond the creature to the Creator, to bring whatever difficult situation you are facing into focus so that you can pray with confidence.

Confidence in God as Controller of All Things

Now they saw God, in verse 24, as the Creator of all things; and so it follows, as night follows day, that they saw God as the Controller of all things. If he is Creator God, then he has perfect control of every detail of every event that occurs. In fact, they begin quoting Scripture about God's control, Psalm 2 to be exact. They go on in their prayer speaking of the Creator God.

> **Acts 4:25-28** | Who through the mouth of our father David, your servant, said by the Holy Spirit, "'Why did the Gentiles rage, and the peoples plot in vain? [26] The kings of the earth set themselves, and the rulers were gathered together, against the Lord and against his Anointed'— [27] for truly in this city there were gathered together against your holy servant Jesus, whom you anointed, both Herod and Pontius Pilate, along with the Gentiles and the peoples of Israel, [28] to do whatever your hand and your plan had predestined to take place.

Now these disciples were facing a difficult situation. But then they looked back to the darkest day that they had ever known, when all of their hopes, aspirations, and dreams were nailed to a hellish Roman cross; when the Son of God was ganged up on by the high court, by Herod, by Pontius Pilate, and when all of these people nailed the Son

---

[90] Corrie Ten Boom in Adrian Rogers, "How to Put Power in Your Prayer," in *Adrian Rogers Sermon Archive* (Signal Hill, CA: Rogers Family Trust, 2017), Ac 4:23–33.

of God to the cross. But they said this: "Nothing has gotten out of control, because according to the Scriptures, God is in control." They quoted from Psalm 2 and they understood that David had said seven hundred years before Jesus Christ was born in Psalm 2 that this was exactly, precisely, what was going to happen. I want you to pay close attention in verse 28. Those rulers who crucified Christ gathered together "to do whatever God's hand and God's plan had predestined to take place."

Now what God showed these people is that he controls all things. Nothing was out of the control of Almighty God, that God not only foresaw it all, but he predestined all things, even to do good things through the actions of bad men, to carry out his plan of redemption. We get all bent out of shape. We think, "Somehow the devil has taken over, and things are not going to turn out as the Bible says they are going to turn out." But, dear saint, that's impossible. The word of God is unbreakable. God will guide all events to completion for your good and his glory. He is in absolute control of all events, so do not be afraid.

Confidence in God as Conqueror of All Things

If God is the Creator and Controller of all things, then it follows that he is the Conqueror of all things—because if you read Psalm 2, it tells about how earth's rulers would crucify the Lord Jesus Christ, and then in Psalm 2 it says:

Psalm 2:6 | As for me, I have set my King on Zion, my holy hill.

David speaks of how the Lord Jesus Christ is going to rule, how he is going to conquer, and how he must prevail. It tells us that God is on the throne, that sin cannot win, that faith cannot fail, and that our God is the conquering God.

We know the last chapter, and Jesus wins. The devil will one day be cast into a Lake of Fire, which burns with fire and brimstone day and night forever (Rev 20:10). Jesus is King of kings and Lord of lords, and he will reign forever and ever (Rev 19:6, 16). Christ has conquered! Christ has won!

THE COMMITMENT OF PRAYER (4:29-30)

Prayer is a sign of our total commitment and dependence on God. We are God's servants.

Acts 4:29 | And now, Lord, look upon their threats and grant to your servants to continue to speak your word with all boldness.

Underscore, please, the word *servants*. That speaks of the commitment of mighty prayer. That word is a translation of a Greek word that literally means "bond slaves." Now, saints, the reason that many of our prayers are not answered is that we have not made that commitment to the Lord.

Every now and then I'll come behind a car, and it will have a bumper sticker on it that says, "God is my co-pilot." No, he's not. Some businessman says, "Well, I'm going to open a business, and I want God as my partner." He doesn't want to be your partner; dear saint, he is your Lord. He is not your partner. He is not your co-pilot. You are his slave, and he is your sovereign Lord. The only way God wants to partner with you is not you giving him your plans, but God giving you his plans. You've got to commit yourself completely to your Sovereign Lord.

Often, we come to prayer meetings, and our prayers are focused on temporal things. That ought not be. Look at the requests these early disciples had. The first was that they would be bold to express God's word.

To Express God's Word

Acts 4:29 | And now, Lord, look upon their threats and grant to your servants to continue to speak your word with all boldness.

They prayed that they might speak God's word with boldness. Is that the desire of your heart: to spread the gospel of Jesus Christ, to obey the Great Commission? Grant, Lord, that we can "speak your word with all boldness."

Now I remind you, it was the expression of God's word and it was the preaching of God's word that got them into trouble to begin with. They didn't say, "Lord, move us to more favorable circumstances." They didn't say, "Lord, keep us safe." Do you know what they prayed? They prayed, "Lord, give us more of what got us into trouble in the first place." Now, you think about that: "Lord, we're in trouble for preaching your word. Now, God, give us boldness to preach it some more." Amen? "We want to express your word." Dear saints, Jesus Christ did not come to get you out of trouble; he came to get into trouble with you. And that is exciting. These disciples, if you read the book of Acts, they just stayed in trouble. They said, "Lord, give us boldness." When you preach Christ, you are going against the current of this world. You ought not be concerned if you are being persecuted. You should be very concerned if you are not being persecuted. If you are not being persecuted, it might mean you are being silent about God's word. Are you living a comfortable life? Is that your goal? If you live godly in Christ Jesus, you will suffer persecution (2 Tim 3:12). If you are not being persecuted, you might be sinning by omission. It's not just evil to do things God tells you not to do. It's also evil to refuse or neglect the things God has told you to do. Preach the name of Jesus everywhere you go. That's a command. To not do so is a sin. So, they prayed for boldness to lift up the name of Jesus. That's a good prayer! "Oh, Lord, please let your people at your church be bold witnesses for you. Amen!"

To Extend God's Hand

Acts 4:30a | While you stretch out your hand to heal, and signs and wonders are performed...

How was Jesus going to stretch forth his hand? After all, Jesus had ascended to heaven and is ruling and reigning at the right hand of the Father. How was our exalted Lord going to stretch forth his hand? The answer is simple: Jesus uses our hands. He calls all his people to be "Jesus with skin on." We are his Body, his Temple. We pray that we will be Jesus with skin on. The apostles did "signs and wonders are performed through the name of... Jesus." If Jesus is in heaven, then the disciples' hands were to become Jesus' hands. What they were saying is, "Lord, take our hands and do through our hands what you would do if you were here in the flesh." Do signs. Do wonders. Reveal Jesus. Let us love like Jesus. Let us serve like Jesus. Let the presence of Jesus be known to all who are in our lives. We are going to be touched and empowered to do Jesus' work in this earth through prayer! We need to pray, "Lord, stretch forth your hand through me. Touch someone's life through me."

I read about a cathedral in Europe that was bombed in World War II. Some of the Americans were there and they wanted to rebuild the cathedral, and so they did. In that cathedral was a magnificent statue of Christ with his arms outstretched, and underneath it the scripture, *"Come to me, all who labor and are heavy laden, and I will give you rest"* (Mt 11:28). The statue had been broken to pieces. They searched through the rubble. They found all of the parts of that statue of Christ and they assembled them back together. But when they came to the hands, they could not find the hands. The hands had been destroyed, and they couldn't find them. They didn't know what to do, until somebody had an idea, and he wrote beneath that statue with those arms without hands stretched out, "He has no hands but our hands." That is so true.[91]

To Exalt God's Son

> **Acts 4:30b** | Signs and wonders are performed through the name of your holy servant Jesus.

The apostles prayed for miracles to be performed to exalt the name of Jesus. A miracle is God intersecting into our lives in a supernatural way. They wanted to demonstrate that the name of Jesus is powerful, supernatural, miraculous. That's how we all ought to live, so that Jesus' name is exalted! People ought to see Jesus living and moving in and through us. His humility. His love. His gentleness. His kindness. His truth. And he gets all the glory.

The apostles weren't in ministry to "brand" their own names or to make a name for their church. They did miracles to exalt the name of Jesus. Someone's name stands for the character of the person. When it is done, it will be obvious that Jesus Christ is doing it, and Jesus Christ will get the glory, and Jesus Christ will get the praise. They were committed to prayer so they could have the power to continue to lift up the person of Christ in the midst of terrible persecution. Remember what Jesus said:

> *John 12:32* | And I, when I am lifted up from the earth, will draw all people to myself.

Jesus said that we are to pray in his name (Jn 14:13–14; 15:16; 16:23–24, 26). That is what they're talking about. Praying in the name of Jesus is not just something at the end of your prayer, tacking on a little phrase, "In Jesus' name, amen." It means, "Jesus, with your authority, and in your power, and for your glory, Lord, do this. We want you, Lord Jesus, to be exalted." The power of all prayer is that it the purpose and motive is exalt the name of Jesus Christ.

---

[91] Ibid.

God's people had very powerful, Bible-based prayer requests: to express God's word, to extend God's hand, and to exalt God's Son. If you pray that way, God will answer!

THE CONSEQUENCES OF PRAYER (4:31-37)

When you pray with no confidence in yourself and all your trust is in God, you will get an answer.

> *Jeremiah 33:3* | Call to me and I will answer you, and will tell you great and hidden things that you have not known.

And what an answer these persecuted believers got! The earth began to heave. The place began to shake. The Lord had heard, and the signs of Pentecost continued. There was no more the sound of a rushing mighty wind, no tongues of fire. But the place began to quake and shake and heave.

The Earth Heaves

> **Acts 4:31a** | And when they had prayed, the place in which they were gathered together was shaken.

The answer to their prayer was instantaneous. The Holy Spirit was present in power, and the whole meeting place shook. The shaking of that house was symbolic of the shaking now taking place in the house of Israel. The whole nation trembled on the brink of a major transformation. The Old Covenant was being uncovered to reveal the New Covenant. All the old systems, ceremonies, and power structures in Israel are being shaken to the very foundations by the proclamation of the name of Jesus.[92] No longer were God's people experiencing symbol and ceremony, but they were experiencing the real, living presence of God himself.

They were stepping into the Holy of holies by the blood of Christ. There's now no condemnation. There's no wrath to fear any longer! Many were rushing to God's new house, the church as a result. So powerful is God's entrance that the place is shaking with an earthquake. The prayer of Isaiah 64 is answered.

> *Isaiah 64:1, 3* | Oh that you would rend the heavens and come down, that the mountains might quake at your presence—³When you did

---

[92] J. Phillips, *Exploring Acts,* Ac 4:31a.

awesome things that we did not look for, you came down, the mountains quaked at your presence.

When God attends a prayer meeting, something ought to happen! If there is not a quaking in the ground, there ought to at least be a quaking in your heart. When we pray like this, wanting the Lord's presence more than we need air or water, we will see him come down.

The Spirit Is Received

Acts 4:31b | And they were all filled with the Holy Spirit and continued to speak the word of God with boldness.

Now they had already been filled with the Holy Spirit in Acts 2, but now they are filled with the Holy Spirit again. And that teaches us a lesson: that we cannot operate on yesterday's experience. There must be a fresh filling of God's Holy Spirit. And there must be this time when day after day in powerful prayer we are filled with the Spirit. Yesterday's power is not sufficient for this hour.

Ephesians 5:19 | And do not get drunk with wine, for that is debauchery, but be filled with the Spirit.

The idea is to "be being constantly filled" with the Holy Spirit. We need filling and refilling and refilling. And the filling is not merely to capacity, but more like a thimble trying to contain an ocean.

There is also another lesson here. We read:

Acts 4:31b | And they were all filled with the Holy Spirit and continued to speak the word of God with boldness.

Remember they prayed earlier that they would "continue to speak God's word with all boldness"? Well here is their answer. A big part of that answer is the filling of the Holy Spirit. When the Spirit fills, the mouth speaks with boldness. We cannot separate the fullness of the Spirit from our bold witness for Christ. If you are a bond slave of Jesus, you want the whole world to know him. The Spirit is going to fill you so that you will lift Jesus up. The Holy Spirit of God will fill you when you're committed to be a witness for Jesus with holy boldness.

Unity Is Achieved

Acts 4:32 | Now the full number of those who believed were of one heart and soul, and no one said that any of the things that belonged to him was his own, but they had everything in common.

When the church prayed together, they became fused together. They became one. Prayer, more than anything else, unites the church. We are not to be wired together by organization. We are not to be frozen together by formalism. We are not to be rusted together by tradition. But we are to be fused and melted together by prayer. When the church prays, that Spirit is received, and that unity is achieved.

Psalm 133:1 | Behold, how good and pleasant it is when brothers dwell in unity.

How is this unity achieved? Through prayer—as we pray and seek the face of God. And, by the way, if you have ever had a prayer partner, or been in a prayer group, then you will know that those people that you've prayed with have become friends for life because of the divine unity God grants through prayer. If we want our church to stay unified and be greatly unified, then indeed we must practice this kind of prayer. Whenever a prayer meeting is called, it ought to be highly attended. You ought to have a feeling of sorrow if you can't make the prayer meeting. There ought to be a hunger like you haven't had lunch or dinner, and you are starving for prayer. That's how the church is revived, and the world is changed.

When I was in college, I had the honor of praying with men every night who understood this. From 10 to 10:30pm each evening we groaned for revival. When the 10:30 bell rang, we were so sad that it had to end, and we couldn't wait for it to start again the next night. It wasn't because we couldn't wait to be with each other mainly. It was because *God* met us in a special way. That ought to be our attitude toward corporate prayer. We may not be there yet saints, but you can only get there if you want it.

Now something else happens when we pray. The gospel is believed! When the Spirit is received, when unity is achieved, then the gospel is believed.

The Gospel Is Believed

Acts 4:33 | And with great power the apostles were giving their testimony to the resurrection of the Lord Jesus, and great grace was upon them all.

This is the kind of fellowship that attracts lost people. We want to be the kind of fellowship that the Spirit is attracting people of every family, culture, language and country. Far from silencing the apostles, the action of the Sanhedrin put the power of God on display. You put a tea bag in hot water, and you find out what's inside. You cannot hurt the church, because the more you persecute Christians, the more Christ is displayed. The more Christ is lifted up. The more the resurrection is preached, and great grace pours out!

Persecution drove the early church to their knees, and the Holy Spirit drove them to their feet. Grace and power flowed through them. No enemy or council could intimidate them; no fear could paralyze them. And it was the resurrection they preached.[93] When we pray, we don't have to "white knuckle" our evangelism. Grace is upon us. It is the grace of God working in the heart that saves a lost sinner. They can have their intellect exercised all day long. No one was ever saved by losing an argument. People are saved when the grace of God first humbles them, and then gives them hope in the death and resurrection of Jesus.

The Church Succeeds

Acts 4:34-37 | There was not a needy person among them, for as many as were owners of lands or houses sold them and brought the proceeds of what was sold ³⁵ and laid it at the apostles' feet, and it was distributed to each as any had need. ³⁶ Thus Joseph, who was also called by the apostles Barnabas (which means son of encouragement), a Levite, a native of Cyprus, ³⁷ sold a field that belonged to him and brought the money and laid it at the apostles' feet.

We meet a man named Barnabas, which means "son of encouragement." He's the kind of brother who walks beside you and just constantly encourages you. He's a man of great faith. He's the brother who lovingly picks you up when you are down. I want to be that brother.

---

[93] J. Phillips, *Exploring Acts*, Ac 4:33.

When you pray together, *you become family*. Like Barnabas, you show *real agape sacrifice*. Barnabas was willing to make a real sacrifice to help the spread of the gospel. Barnabas and others didn't mind selling and bringing proceeds to the apostles. It wasn't communism. They met house to house. They kept owning land a property. The Bible teaches we should voluntarily sacrifice for each other. That's a beautiful mark of a church's success.

When you pray together, *you want to comfort and encourage the Body of Christ*. You don't mind giving away things that are earthly. Barnabas is singled as an example even though others in the church also were generous to the Jerusalem church. Why? I think it's because he truly loved the church and wanted to encourage his brothers and sisters. His birth name is Joseph, but his fellow-believers gave him the nickname of Barnabas which means "son of encouragement."[94] Prayer will do that. When someone is filled with the Spirit, you will become a person of comfort and encouragement for the Body. When we pray, we all become those sons and daughters of encouragement. We take someone by the hand and teach them to pray. We don't just wish them well, but, like Barnabas, we walk side by side with them, in prayer, in gospel living.

Conclusion

You might say, "What does this message on prayer have to do with my life?" I'll tell you what it has to do with your life. The time will come—if it has not already come—when God is going to teach you to pray. He'll often teach us by bringing us through trouble. Now are you going to pray for boldness or are you going to simply pray for the trouble to go away?

We need to pray in a way that we meet God in a life changing way. We need to have those "wrestle with God" moments, like Jacob, and he was never the same. We need to know the presence of God in a way that shakes us to the core!

One more thing: The point of this study means that your life, your home, your family, this church, this community, America, and our world, will never see the power of God as they ought until God's people learn how to pray with power. The need of the hour is prayer with power. Will you commit to regular, earnest, corporate prayer?

---

[94] Williams, *Acts*, 50.

9 | ACTS 5:1-11
THE DANGER OF SPIRITUAL PRETENSE

But a man named Ananias, with his wife Sapphira, sold a piece of property, and with his wife's knowledge he kept back for himself some of the proceeds and brought only a part of it and laid it at the apostles' feet. But Peter said, "Ananias, why has Satan filled your heart to lie to the Holy Spirit and to keep back for yourself part of the proceeds of the land? While it remained unsold, did it not remain your own? And after it was sold, was it not at your disposal? Why is it that you have contrived this deed in your heart? You have not lied to man but to God." When Ananias heard these words, he fell down and breathed his last. And great fear came upon all who heard of it. The young men rose and wrapped him up and carried him out and buried him.

ACTS 5:1-6

Some of the most miserable times in our lives are when we start focusing on ourselves. We were not made to think about ourselves as the center of the universe. We are called to behold the glory of God and be amazed. Behold our God! The story of Ananias and Saphira is really a story of selfishness. It might seem a bit over the top to us, but God acts in certain ways when he wants to do a great work. This is a very special time of the church's growth, and these two believers' selfishness was getting in the way. God would not have a lukewarm church. In the previous chapter (Acts 4), we learn about an earth-shaking prayer meeting. In Acts 5, we find the story of two believers who are chastened by God and brought home far too early. The point of today is simple: This life is not about you. When you focus on yourself you get misery, chastening, and at times, even death. Self-focus for the Christian is like drinking poison. It's dangerous.

We must respect Luke as a historian. He doesn't ignore the faults of the early church. This is a reminder that even in the most Spirit-filled congregations, the evil one is at work. Every gospel-preaching church will face opposition from the outside (4:1-31), and this story teaches how sinful actions create opposition on the inside, too (5:1-11). [95]

Here is a story that is similar to other frightening stories in the Bible where God strikes people dead. We read about the story of Achan and his family, when he broke the command of God, and stole the Babylonian garment, the silver and the gold (Josh 7). He had hidden these things in his tent, and he brought his family in on it. What did God do? Before we answer that, I want to consider that Achan was likely a believer. He glorified God with his confession of faith before he was put to death. But God still allowed the ground to swallow up Achan, his dear wife, and precious children, and all their property.

Another story comes to mind: that of Uzzah (1 Chr 13:9-12). Here he is, carefully transporting the ark of the covenant, and the cart shakes, the ark begins to topple, and Uzzah steadies the cart just in time. And for that, God takes Uzzah home.

God had decreed that if a Kohathite priest—the only ones permitted to transport the ark—merely glanced at the ark in the Holy of Holies for an instant that he would die. Not only was Uzzah forbidden to touch the ark, but he was also forbidden even to look at it. He touched it anyway. He stretched out his hand and placed it squarely on the ark, steadying it in place lest it fall to the ground. An act of holy heroism? No! It was an act of arrogance, a sin of presumption. R.C. Sproul give an enlightening conclusion: "Uzzah assumed that his hand was less polluted than the earth."[96] God took this dear brother home.

---

[95] Merida. *Acts*, 87.
[96] Sproul, *Acts*, 160–164.

And then in Acts 5, Luke records the sad story of Ananias, and his wife Sapphira, also committed acts worthy for God to take them home. They were willingly hypocritical. I believe they were saved people. They knew the Lord. But after having such light and knowledge of the Lord, witnessing miracles, possibly having been taught by the Lord in his life and in his resurrection ministry, they had a greater standard of accountability. "To whom much is given, much is required" (Lk 12:48).

They lie about their church offering. Christians have lied before. We believe in 1 John 1:9, that if we confess and forsake our sin, we will be restored to fellowship with the Lord.

We see these three stories together and point out, that so far as we can tell, each of these individuals was "a believer." That is, they were not in the same category as the heathen, who are ignorant of God, or kings or philosophers, who in the arrogance of their unbelief set themselves against God. These people were in the fellowship of God's family and were all engaged in Christian worship or service. Moreover, they were struck dead for what, to us at least, seem to be—what are not, but what we might see as—*trivial* offenses. We must conclude that God will discipline those he loves (Heb 12:6). We also conclude that when we see God's judgment in a believer's life, it is the judgment of correction for that believer and the church at large, as the apostle Peter told us.

> *1 Peter 4:7* | For it is time for judgment to begin at the household of God; and if it begins with us, what will be the outcome for those who do not obey the gospel of God?

Another thing we notice is that when we put these stories together, we discover that in each instance, it was a time of important new beginnings for God's people. This may explain some of the severity of the correction. Something new was being inaugurated; a new era was about to come in. It would seem that God established himself as the center of glory and honor at the beginning of these special times of revealing himself.[97] So as we read this text, I want you to get used to saying something to yourself: "It's not about me! It's about Jesus!" Ananias and Sapphira made their gift to the church not about Jesus, but about themselves, and as we are going to see that's a dangerous thing.

> **Acts 5:1-11** | But a man named Ananias, with his wife Sapphira, sold a piece of property, ² and with his wife's knowledge he kept back

---

[97] Boice, *Exposition of Acts*, 95.

for himself some of the proceeds and brought only a part of it and laid it at the apostles' feet. **³** But Peter said, "Ananias, why has Satan filled your heart to lie to the Holy Spirit and to keep back for yourself part of the proceeds of the land? **⁴** While it remained unsold, did it not remain your own? And after it was sold, was it not at your disposal? Why is it that you have contrived this deed in your heart? You have not lied to man but to God." **⁵** When Ananias heard these words, he fell down and breathed his last. And great fear came upon all who heard of it. **⁶** The young men rose and wrapped him up and carried him out and buried him. **⁷** After an interval of about three hours his wife came in, not knowing what had happened. **⁸** And Peter said to her, "Tell me whether you sold the land for so much." And she said, "Yes, for so much." **⁹** But Peter said to her, "How is it that you have agreed together to test the Spirit of the Lord? Behold, the feet of those who have buried your husband are at the door, and they will carry you out." **¹⁰** Immediately she fell down at his feet and breathed her last. When the young men came in they found her dead, and they carried her out and buried her beside her husband. **¹¹** And great fear came upon the whole church and upon all who heard of these things.

The devil had tried intimidation through persecution. Intimidation only drove the church to her knees and caused them to have greater power. And so now, the devil decides, "Well, if I cannot bombard the church from the outside, I will infiltrate, and I will work from the inside. If I cannot conquer the church, I will corrupt the church, and thereby I will conquer the church." All the devil has to do to weaken and paralyze the church is to get your eyes off Jesus.

Now, the church of the Lord Jesus Christ has always been hurt far more her own corruption and loss of focus than by persecution. Persecution only causes the church to grow. Inward corruption causes the church to disintegrate. At the dawn of this new era of grace for the world, the Holy Spirit brings great warning to his people. He did it when his people crossed the Jordan, and Achan died. He did it in the time of David, where not long after David's son Solomon would build the Temple in Jerusalem, and Uzzah touched the ark and died. Now he does it again when the church is born. What does Satan use to destroy us? Our own pride. He wants to make us think that everything, even the Christian life, is about us, and not about Jesus. The enemy wants to misdirect our focus to ourselves and breed anger, anxiety, despair, and foolish thinking, which all come from the pride of self-focus.

THE ROOT OF PRETENSE: PRIDE (5:1-4)

> **Acts 5:1-4** | But a man named Ananias, with his wife Sapphira, sold a piece of property, ² and with his wife's knowledge he kept back for himself some of the proceeds and brought only a part of it and laid it at the apostles' feet. ³ But Peter said, "Ananias, why has Satan filled your heart to lie to the Holy Spirit and to keep back for yourself part of the proceeds of the land? ⁴ While it remained unsold, did it not remain your own? And after it was sold, was it not at your disposal? Why is it that you have contrived this deed in your heart? You have not lied to man but to God."

Pride says, "It's all about me." That's why we give ourselves to anger or anxiety or despair. That's why sometimes we don't listen. We can even deceive ourselves in our prideful blindness as these two believers did. Be afraid of your own pride. Be very afraid. This didn't have to happen.

The Humility of Barnabas

We see how the focus got off of Jesus. It was the pride of jealousy that welled up in the hearts of Ananias and Sapphira. There was a man named Barnabas who made a great gift to the church, and he didn't do it to show off, but he did it because God touched his heart. Ananias and Sapphira saw how praise was given to them, and Ananias and Sapphira were jealous. They wanted the attention. Just imagine, they got their focus off of Jesus and onto themselves. We are all too good at that. When start feeling upset because we are not getting our way, or we really want something, even a good thing, and we turn it into something we must have, then pride enters in. Anything you are willing to sin to get is an idol. Examine your life. Is there anything you are anxious about? Fear and anxiety are atheism. You've gone too far. You want something too much. Idolatry always brings misery.

Ananias and Sapphira sold their property, thinking that nobody knew how much they got for it, and brought the money to the church, and pretended that they were giving every cent that they received for that property to the treasurer of the church. And of course, they were pretending. They were seeking happiness in something outside the glory of God. They had not given it all; they had kept back part of it secretly. They were living a life of pretense, and they were lying to the Holy Spirit.

Ananias and Sapphira appeared to be Christians, and I believe they were, as did St. Augustine and Alexander Maclaren and others. We ourselves are terribly susceptible to their sin, a spiritual error to which believers still fall. Their correction was a "sanctifying discipline" for the church, to use Puritan Jeremy Taylor's words.[98] What was so horrible that the Holy Spirit had to take the lives of two of his children? The gravity was a warning about the root of their sin, which was pride. Ananias and Sapphira wanted to bask in the glow of Barnabas, instead of Jesus. They were jealous to be treated like Barnabas instead of jealous for their relationship with the Holy Spirit. Pride made them a sitting duck for the devil, and pride will do the same thing to you or to me. Peter says:

> *1 Peter 5:5* | Clothe yourselves, all of you, with humility toward one another, for "God opposes the proud but gives grace to the humble."

The reason that you need to be clothed with humility is:

> *1 Peter 5:8-9* | Your adversary the devil prowls around like a roaring lion, seeking someone to devour. ⁹Resist him, firm in your faith.

The devil is after you. Jonathan Edwards said many years ago, "Nothing will put you further out of the devil's reach than genuine humility."[99] But when you become proud, you are ripe for Satan's attack. So, the root of the sin of Ananias and Sapphira was pride. The fruit of their sin was pretense. What is pretense? It's when you act like the Spirit is moving you when he's not. It's trying to live the life of the Spirit in the flesh. We can't put on the Spirit's power in the strength of the flesh. Don't pretend to be Spirit-filled if you are not.

What should we do then? If you are not Spirit-filled, let people know so they can pray for you. Humble yourself by letting elders and others know and ask for prayer that you might filled with the fullness of the Spirit. It may be that there is some sin hidden from your understanding that is holding you back. Or it may be a stronghold you have

---

[98] Hughes, *Acts*, 76. Jeremy Taylor lived from 1613-1667.

[99] Jonathan Edwards. *Works, Volume 1* (London: Childs & Son Publishers, 1839), 399.

tried to defeat, but it is still holding you back. God wants to unite the church behind you so Satan will flee from you. We can't do this alone. We must humble ourselves so the Lord will exalt and use us.

Now, I want to make something very clear. Their sin was not refusing to give. They gave. Their sin was making it about themselves. Nor was their sin refusing to give all of it. God had not commanded nor demanded that they give all of it. Their sin was the sin of pretense, saying that they had given all, when they had given all. That's where the sin was. It's very clear.

The Harm of Doublemindedness

By way of application, let me say that all believers who get their focus on themselves are immature and doubleminded. James tells us about doublemindedness. James says the one with half-way faith "is like a wave of the sea that is driven and tossed by the wind" (Jas 1:6). He goes on to say:

> *James 1:8* | A double-minded man is unstable in all his ways.

Doublemindedness is a sign of serious immaturity. One day you love Jesus, the next you love the world. You can't have one foot in the world and one foot with Jesus. You've got to keep your eyes on Jesus. The moment you start thinking everything is about you, then anger and anxiety and foolishness open the door to Satan to take a foothold.

THE SOURCE OF PRETENSE: SATAN (5:3)

What was the source of this sin? It was Satan.

> **Acts 5:3** | But Peter said, "Ananias, why has Satan filled your heart to lie to the Holy Spirit and to keep back for yourself part of the proceeds of the land?"

Satan is the father of lies and the author of pride. It was Satan who put it into their heart. It was the devil who whispered, "Tell them you're giving it all. Tell them you're giving everything." Whenever we give way to sin of any kind in our lives, Satan takes a seat at your heart to counsel you. Ephesians

> *Ephesians 4:26-27* | Be angry and do not sin; do not let the sun go down on your anger, [27] and give no opportunity to the devil.

Jesus said,

John 8:44 | [Satan] is a liar and the father of lies.

The devil wants you to think that everything is all about you. He knows all about you and how to push your buttons.

Ephesians 6:12-13 | For we do not wrestle against flesh and blood, but against the rulers, against the authorities, against the cosmic powers over this present darkness, against the spiritual forces of evil in the heavenly places. [13] Therefore take up the whole armor of God, that you may be able to withstand in the evil day, and having done all, to stand firm.

When you tell a lie—big lie, little lie, white lie, technicolor lie, makes no difference—when you tell a lie, you are acting like the devil. That's the reason Satan gets a seat at our hearts: we give him authority over us, even though Christ has purchased our freedom. We end up going back to Doubting Castle or to Prideful Palace or to Escape Island. We are no match for Satan, but I do know this:

1 John 4:4, KJV | Greater is he that is in you, than he that is in the world.

But if you give in to pride, anxiety or anger, then you will be acting in pretense and doublemindedness. Don't let Satan tempt you to play act. You can't act holy if you are really focused on yourself. Be humble if you are sinning. Let people know if you are caught in sin. You want revival? Don't play act.

Satan filled the hearts of Ananias and Sapphira. He didn't possess them. That's impossible for a Christian. But they gave him a seat at the table of their hearts to counsel them. He came in through the door of pride. But Satan can counsel a Christian through the door of anger or fear and anxiety. Satan comes through despair. Satan comes through fleshly pleasure. He comes through worldly thinking. How do you stop Satan from tempting you? Close all those doors. He comes through your emotions and your worldly desires. Die to material things. Die to the entertainment of media. Die to fear. Die to love for comfort and your reputation, and pleasing people. Live for God. You cannot have two masters. Don't let Satan fill your heart. Resist him. I have to keep my heart with all diligence, for out of my heart are the issues of life. Don't lie to yourself and the Holy Spirit and try to paint yourself more spiritual or more generous than you are. The Spirit knows your heart. Don't lie to him.

THE JUDGMENT OF PRETENSE: DISCIPLINE (5:5-10)

Now we all understand the reality of our guilt. That without Christ we deserve eternal hell.

> *Romans 6:23* | The wages of sin is death, and the gift of God is eternal life through Jesus Christ our Lord.

But there is a judgment that has nothing to do with condemnation, because for the Christian, our guilt is completely removed.

> *Romans 8:1* | There is therefore now no condemnation for those who are in Christ Jesus.

How could there be? Jesus paid it all! But there is a judgment of discipline. There is correction. As we said before, God will discipline those he loves (Heb 12:6). When we see God's judgment in a believer's life, it is the judgment of correction for that believer and the church at large, as the apostle Peter told us.

> *1 Peter 4:7* | For it is time for judgment to begin at the household of God; and if it begins with us, what will be the outcome for those who do not obey the gospel of God?

That is, God says, my child that's enough, and he may send sickness or trials. Not that everyone who is sick or in trials is sinning. Remember Job. You may be living righteously and still in terrible sickness. But there is a sickness for the erring saint. There is even death for the erring saint that won't repent. Remember what Paul told the Corinthians.

> *1 Corinthians 11:29-30* | Anyone who eats and drinks without discerning the body eats and drinks judgment on himself. ^{30} That is why many of you are weak and ill, and some have died.

God's people weren't taking the Lord's communion table seriously, so God made some of them sick, and some died as a result and went home early. If you decide you're going to just slide along, and you don't care if you are in the Lord's active use for his kingdom, he could make you sick, or you could die, like Ananias and Sapphira. God wants us all to know that it's dangerous to think the Christian life is all about you. To pretend you are more spiritual than you are when you are not is dangerous for the Christian. It was dangerous for Ananias.

> **Acts 5:5-6** | When Ananias heard these words, he fell down and breathed his last. And great fear came upon all who heard of

it. **⁶** The young men rose and wrapped him up and carried him out and buried him.

Ananias was stricken dead. It was a severe judgment. God took him home. Ananias falls down, and the Bible says that the young men came in, and bound him up, and carried him out, and buried him. Later on, the same thing happened to Sapphira.

> **Acts 5:7-10** | After an interval of about three hours his wife came in, not knowing what had happened. **⁸** And Peter said to her, "Tell me whether you sold the land for so much." And she said, "Yes, for so much." **⁹** But Peter said to her, "How is it that you have agreed together to test the Spirit of the Lord? Behold, the feet of those who have buried your husband are at the door, and they will carry you out." **¹⁰** Immediately she fell down at his feet and breathed her last. When the young men came in they found her dead, and they carried her out and buried her beside her husband.

We read here that Sapphira came in about three hours later. I wonder why? I wonder if it was to make a grand entrance, so everybody could see her as she came forward. The same thing happened to Sapphira that had happened to her husband. God immediately took her life and took her home. We wonder, were Ananias and Sapphira really Christians? As I said, I think they were. One of the reasons I think they were is because of this judgment. You see, God does not judge the unsaved this way; they get their judgment at the Great White Throne—but God does deal sometimes very seriously with his own children during their lives.

Our Judgment as Sons in This Life

There is a judgment that is not condemnation but correction that we all go through in this life. Remember what the Lord said in John 15.

> *John 15:2* | Every branch in me that does not bear fruit he takes away, and every branch that does bear fruit he prunes, that it may bear more fruit.

Hebrews 12 says that whom the Father loves he chastens and disciplines every son whom he may receive—whom he may receive. And I believe that this was the Father's judgment, the scourging upon Ananias and Sapphira.

Hebrews 12:6-8 | My son, do not regard lightly the discipline of the Lord, nor be weary when reproved by him. ⁶ For the Lord disciplines the one he loves, and chastises every son whom he receives. ⁷ It is for discipline that you have to endure. God is treating you as sons. For what son is there whom his father does not discipline? ⁸ If you are left without discipline, in which all have participated, then you are illegitimate children and not sons.

God does correct his children. That kind of loving judgment of correction has to begin at the house of God. Remember the judgment of our sins took place at the cross.

Our Judgment as Sinners at the Cross

There's the judgment that we receive as a sinner that comes at the cross. Jesus took our judgment for us as sinners—that's the cross.

1 Peter 2:24 | He himself bore our sins in his body on the tree, that we might die to sin and live to righteousness. By his wounds you have been healed.

Our Judgment as Servants

There's another judgment we should consider, and that is a judgment as servants. It's not a judgment of condemnation, but a judgment of commendation. That's at the judgment seat of Christ. And we're going to receive a reward for the things that we've done or suffer loss for the way that we've failed. We're not saved by works, but we will be rewarded for our fruit.

2 Corinthians 5:10 | For we must all appear before the judgment seat of Christ, so that each one may receive what is due for what he has done in the body, whether good or evil.

The Bible says at the judgment seat of Christ, we as Christians will never be judged for our sin, but we will be judged for the quality of our fruit.

1 Corinthians 3:11-15 | For no one can lay a foundation other than that which is laid, which is Jesus Christ. ¹² Now if anyone builds on the foundation with gold, silver, precious stones, wood, hay, straw— ¹³ each one's work will become manifest, for the Day will disclose it, because it will be revealed by fire, and the fire will test what sort of work each one has done. ¹⁴ If the work that anyone has built on the foundation survives, he will receive a reward. ¹⁵ If anyone's work is burned up, he will suffer loss, though he himself will be saved, but only as through fire.

I want my fruit and my rewards to be great at the tribunal of Christ. Whatever crown I get, I want to cast it before his feet. He is worthy!

A Severe Judgment

Ananias and Sapphira were children of God, but they had committed the sin of pretense, and there was a very severe judgment. But, you say, "Can it be that severe?" Yes. We already saw how God judged the Corinthian believers when they were irreverent with the Lord's table. Some of them got sick. Others died. God's discipline can be so severe that God will call you home early. We also read 1 Corinthians 5, talking about a man who was in the church, and the context makes it clear that he was a brother, but he was committing a sin of sexual immorality, and Paul said:

> *1 Corinthians 5:5* | Deliver such a one to Satan for the destruction of the flesh, that the spirit may be saved in the day of the Lord Jesus.

If a believer decides to go on sinning and not listen to the brothers and sisters and the elders in the church, we are to give that one over to Satan for the destruction of the flesh. That's Job like trials in order for that person to get so desperate, that as a true believer he or she turns back to God. Whom the Lord loves, he chastens. I believe the Lord loved Ananias and Sapphira, and I believe that Ananias and Sapphira, like many in this building, loved the Lord, but what they committed the sin of pretending a devotion for Jesus that they really did not have, and God brought a very severe judgment. I believe I have seen it happen.

> *1 John 5:16* | There is a sin unto death.

One likely interpretation of this is that the sin leading to death refers to a Christian's sin that is so serious that God takes the life of the one committing it.[100]

My Mother's Sin unto Death

My own mother made a profession of faith in her last couple of years on earth. I believe she came to know the Lord. I have two of her Bibles and they are scrawled through with notes on repentance and

---

[100] John MacArthur, *1, 2, 3 John*, MacArthur New Testament Commentary (Chicago, IL: Moody Publishers, 2007), 205.

faith in Christ. I believe my mother, who was not a good mother to me, came to know Christ. I remember going to church with her for several months. And I think my mom, misguided, wanted to please the Lord, but she married an unsaved man. She didn't want to live in sin with men. But she got marriage on her mind. She stopped attending church. I came to know the Lord around that time, and I remember she was now dating a man and was thinking about marriage. I think the Lord said to my mom, "Barbara, I've saved you. You'd better wait for the right man, a man who knows and loves me." And the man she married was a good man, but he wasn't a saved man. Two weeks after my mother married this man, my mother died of a massive heart attack. God called her home. She was 49 years old. Now why would God do something like that? The wicked he allows to go on, but the righteous, he will call home if they want to go against the Holy Spirit in their lives. Why?

This kind of judgment is a saving judgment. It's merciful. As Paul said, we are to: "Deliver such a one to Satan for the destruction of the flesh, that the spirit may be saved in the day of the Lord Jesus" (1 Cor 5:5). Now what happens when we see God really working on his church and disciplining us? There is a cleansing, a purifying, a worship, indeed a revival!

THE DEFEAT OF PRETENSE: WORSHIP (5:11)

> **Acts 5:11** | And great fear came upon the whole church and upon all who heard of these things.

Why would the Lord take any believer home ahead of time? Because there is something more dangerous than physical disease and plague. There is the dryness waywardness of his people. There is the waywardness of professing Christians who have no effect on the culture. Instead, the culture is having an effect on his church. And the Spirit will not have it. We are called to pray that God will do as he promised and send the reviving Holy Spirit. Who will pray for the fullness of the Spirit?

> *Isaiah 44:3-5* | I will pour water on the thirsty land, and streams on the dry ground; I will pour my Spirit upon your offspring, and my blessing on your descendants. ⁴ They shall spring up among the grass like willows by flowing streams. ⁵ This one will say, 'I am the Lord's,'

another will call on the name of Jacob, and another will write on his hand, 'The Lord's,' and name himself by the name of Israel.

God wants his people to worship him. That's why he'd take his children home early. He loves them too much to leave them in dryness. And when he is ready to do a new work, he may bring hardship and sickness, and even death.

Conclusion

God would much rather pour out the effect of his presence from the heavens. When we ask God to rend the heavens and come down (Isa 64:1), we are not saying God is less than omnipresent. We are asking for the interaction of his presence to be felt among men and women. We are asking him to personally deal with his people. That's what we want more than we want breath. May it be so, in the name of Jesus!

10 | ACTS 5:12-42
PRISON BREAK!

They arrested the apostles and put them in the public prison. But during the night an angel of the Lord opened the prison doors and brought them out, and said, "Go and stand in the temple and speak to the people all the words of this Life." And when they heard this, they entered the temple at daybreak and began to teach.
ACTS 5:18-21

The passage before us really is about the unstoppable joy of the gospel. You can come against it; you can lock people up; you can (as is happening today) take away people's church buildings. But you cannot take away the joy of Jesus in the heart of the believer. The joy of Christ is unstoppable in the heart of the believer.

Here in Acts 5, we find that the church's growth comes as a result of intense persecution. Despite the persecution, the joy of Jesus cannot be abated. The apostles are sent to prison, and there is an unusual prison break. An angel escort delivers the apostles from the prison. Not sure exactly how it happened, but under threat of death, they went right back preaching. Then they are flogged with 39 lashes, and rejoice, and again, go right back lifting up the name of Jesus. This is unstoppable joy. Whatever prison you are in today, if you are paralyzed by the idols of your heart, living in anger or fear or despair, let me give you hope today. If you will put your trust in Christ, and get help from other believers, you can be a Holy Spirit filled, joy filled Christian.

Jesus said that he will build his church, and the gates of hell will not prevail against it. That means the church is on the offensive, going right up to the gates of hell and yanking people out of eternal destruction. The church will prevail. The government can take away our freedoms, take away our buildings, put pastors in jail, tell us we cannot gather, but we will never stop lifting high the name of Jesus. You see there is a more dangerous disease than any of the diseases afflicting people. That is the disease of sin. And there is a one hundred percent mortality rate. Ten out of ten people die because the soul that sins will die. The only anecdote to sin is Jesus Christ. That is why we must gather. That is why churches ought to be open. That is why we must constantly be preaching the gospel. They can ban us from social media, but the gospel will never be silenced. No one can defeat Jesus. He is the unconquerable King. He is our victorious Lion. Persecution will always come against the church. Remember what Paul said to Timothy.

> 2 Timothy 3:12 | Indeed, all who desire to live a godly life in Christ Jesus will be persecuted.

John Calvin speaks about this. He says, "We must realize that God is longing to shower blessings on his church, but that he still allows it to be harassed by the ungodly. So, we must always be ready for the battle."[101] And despite the raging battle, there is unstoppable, unquenchable joy in Christ! This is why the church grows in the midst of fierce persecution.

THE GROWTH OF THE CHURCH (5:12-16)

Despite what happened with Ananias and Sapphira, the church described here completely triumphed over the attacks of Satan! The Lord dealt with the duplicity of this couple so that the church in Jerusalem could continue to multiply. The people were still growing in power (5:12), in honor (5:13), in number (5:14), and in awe (5:15-16). Multitudes were added to the Lord. These are the signs of a very healthy church.

We see in Acts 5, while the church is growing at an incomprehensible rate, the devil is still on the prowl. A church that is constantly

---

[101] John Calvin, *Acts* (Wheaton, IL: Crossway, 1995), 76.

growing in all the ways it should grow: spiritually, influentially, and numerically. But the growing church will also face the constant attack and harassment of the unseen realm. With fantastic growth comes the furious attack of Satan. Know it. Be ready for it. Maturing Christians always have to be ready to trust in the Lord, fight with the word, and persevere. How do we persevere? First there should be a growth and manifestation of supernatural power.

Growing in Power

> **Acts 5:12** | Now many signs and wonders were regularly done among the people by the hands of the apostles. And they were all together in Solomon's Portico.

I want you to see how power is linked together with fellowship. They gathered together, and they saw the miraculous performed. Do not discount the power of our common fellowship in the word and prayer together.

Seeing God move is what unites a congregation. It's never enough that a church is sound in doctrine. We must be sound in doctrine, but we could be the frozen chosen; we want to be the fiery chosen. We should preach with what D. Martin Lloyd-Jones called "doctrine on fire."[102] God is never impressed with mere sound doctrine. Think of the Pharisees. Their doctrine was correct, but their hearts were far from God. We need to see God moving in our congregation in both usual and unusual ways.

What a place Solomon's porch must have been in those days! What enormous crowds must have congregated there! Miracles were being done. This is the place where Jesus himself ministered (Jn 10:23). Many signs and wonders were regularly done by the apostles. Wow. I can't even imagine. More lame people were leaping. Those shut off in the darkness of mental illness were surely healed. That means not just limbs were healed, but families and communities were healed.

We should be seeing this kind of thing in our local churches. Though we cannot do all the miracles that the apostles did, we should be seeing constant lives being touched and changed by the gospel. We

---

[102] David Martin Lloyd-Jones in Jason C. Meyer, *Lloyd-Jones on the Christian Life* (Carol Stream, IL: Crossway, 2018), 15.

should also see signs and wonders, which we will describe in more detail in just a moment (*cf* 5:15-16).

Growing in Honor

Acts 5:13 | None of the rest dared join them, but the people held them in high esteem.

Now understand, with all the miracles there was also a new note of caution. Those who were simply curious or wanted the fringe benefits of Christianity, kept their distance. There was great power, and there were wonderful miracles. With the power of God displayed, there was a reverence even from those who were not fully invested. They didn't want to pay the price of persecution, so they dared not join the apostles and believers. But all the people honored the early Christians.

We see that a pure church is an honorable church. When we enact church discipline and take the gospel, and our conduct, and our doctrine seriously, then the Lord blesses. The people will once again hold the church in great honor and high esteem. That means, we need to pray for God to open up the sewers, like with Ananias and Sapphira. We need to ask God to display any gross misconduct in our congregation. If you are living in sin, you are holding back the power of God, and the best thing for you to do is to confess it before God has to deal with you.

Hebrews 10:31 | It's a fearful thing to fall into the hands of the living God.

We must live as a pure church. We want to deal with sin in our congregation. It's not that honorable churches don't have sin. Then we would have to leave the earth. But we confess our sins one to another. And for those who will not repent, we exercise church discipline. Let's be open and honest about any coldness, worldliness, idolatry or spiritual adultery among us. Let us repent and be restored. Let us run to the arms of our Abba Father who waits for his prodigals with eagerness and love with a ring, and a robe, and a banquet. Then we will be held in "high esteem". People will want to know this incredible love of Jesus. So you can imagine, there was a constant rate of multiplication in the church. That's what we want to see.

Growing in Number

Acts 5:14 | And more than ever believers were added to the Lord, multitudes of both men and women.

When an ungrieved Holy Spirit does his work unhindered and unhampered, souls will be saved. Don't be afraid for the sewers to open. They have to open. Sin must be exposed. Forgiveness and love must be experienced. God is on the move. God would have his heaven full. He says:

Luke 14:23 | Go out to the highways and hedges and compel people to come in, that my house may be filled.

Indeed, we hear of God's own command from the apostle Paul.

Acts 17:30 | God... commands all people everywhere to repent.

Everywhere at all times, the Spirit is moving, convicting, and drawing lost souls to a saving knowledge of Christ. Every day the Spirit adds new souls to the church. Sinners repent, and heaven rejoices! Let us cooperate with the Spirit of God and do his work in his way, and he will add souls to the church.

The church that doesn't evangelize will fossilize. A church that is ok with being dry will soon die. Dear saints, we need the rivers of living water flowing through us. We need the Spirit's streams to flow in the desert wilderness. There are lives that need to be touched and changed through you. The Holy Spirit is always at work. If he is not working powerfully in our midst, perhaps there is sin somewhere that is choking the channel.

One quick note: the text says that "multitudes of both men and women" were added. That's important because in chapter 4:4 we saw that five thousand men were added. There were so many they stopped counting the women and possibly children. But now there is a clarification that it is actually both men and women being added. Praise God.

Growing in Awe

Now we see that the power that is being poured out by the Spirit is truly awe inspiring.

Acts 5:15-16 | So that they even carried out the sick into the streets and laid them on cots and mats, that as Peter came by at least his shadow might fall on some of them. **16** The people also gathered from the towns around Jerusalem, bringing the sick and those afflicted with unclean spirits, and they were all healed.

People wanted just Peter's shadow to be cast upon them, and here is the absolutely thrilling note: "they were all healed." All of them! Not one exception. Now obviously there is a power among the apostles that was foundational for the church. If anyone on earth had this power today, all the hospitals would be empty. There would be no need for doctors.

And yet, we cannot discount God's miracle working power in all times, generations and seasons. It will not be on this scale for very important reasons. You don't need to pour the foundation of a building more than once. Yet and still, structure and good engineering need to be depended on, so God's miraculous power still flows through his temple. In what ways? We have solid records of how God pours out his Spirit and what miracles have been done in the various awakenings of the church.

For instance, we are told that were only about 500 Iranian Christians from a Muslim background forty years ago, but over the past forty years, more Muslims have come to Christ than in the past 1,300 years. Now, through visions and dreams, the population of born-again believers in Iran is over 1 million. Thousands of believers are being added to the church across the Islamic curtain on monthly basis. We are hearing reports of miracles, healings, and more dreams and visions in the Muslim world. God would have his heaven full.

Now whenever there is unprecedented growth, there will be great persecution and grief. Get ready for it.

THE GRIEF OF THE CHURCH (5:17-21A)

A growing church is going to face grief and persecution. Listen to the important warning of Jesus.

> *John 15:18-19* | If the world hates you, know that it has hated me before it hated you. [19] If you were of the world, the world would love you as its own; but because you are not of the world, but I chose you out of the world, therefore the world hates you.

Dear saint, if you live for God, you will be persecuted. If you are not persecuted at some time, you are not living for God. There will be great heartbreak for you, as there was for the early Christians. It was the high priest himself that Satan used to harass these dear believers at the

Jerusalem church. Look at this high priest. The one who should protect God's people is persecuting them.

Heart Break

Acts 5:17-18 | But the high priest rose up, and all who were with him (that is, the party of the Sadducees), and filled with jealousy **18** they arrested the apostles and put them in the public prison.

Apparently, the high priest was jealous of all the attention the miracles of the apostles was bringing. There was a neediness for attention by the high priest who was a Sadducee. They didn't believe in the possibility of the supernatural. They lived for carnal recognition. Sad.

If Christ lives in you, you will attract the hatred of the world. That means you may not be accepted by friends and family. You may lose a job one day because of your Christian faith. You certainly won't be popular in the political sphere of this world. You will suffer persecution. It's inevitable. The devil hates when the church multiplies. So, what do the Sadducees do? They think iron bars can keep God's work from going forward, just like some Roman soldiers thought a tomb could keep Jesus imprisoned. God's work is unstoppable.

What we read next is the most incredible prison break you could ever imagine. If what we see later in Philippi is any indication, there were likely songs in the night, with Peter perhaps singing bass! The Jerusalem city jail had never seen anything like this, nor had the guards witnessed anything like what was about to happen.[103] The apostles go from heart break to prison break! An angel steps out of the darkness of the jail to set them free.

Prison Break

Acts 5:19 | But during the night an angel of the Lord opened the prison doors and brought them out...

The gates of hell will not prevail, and that sometimes means even physical bars of iron. Iron bars cannot hold back the gospel. Persecution ought never take away our true joy. The apostles got a special visitation from an angel.

---

[103] Hughes, *Acts*, 85.

Can you just imagine? They were divinely delivered. Either God lulled the guards into sleep, or the apostles were made temporarily invisible. Whatever happened, it must have been great fun to be out on the streets while the prison lay locked behind them. There is some divine humor here, too, because the Sadducees did not believe in angels. And yet here, right in their own city, were some close encounters of the spiritual kind.

Why the angelic intervention? God was teaching the twelve apostles that he can deliver his servants from the world's oppression anytime he sees fit. He delivers in a similar way two other times in Acts—once with Peter (12:6–11) and once with Paul and Silas (16:26ff.), though in the latter case God did not want his apostles to escape but to stay in the jail despite the doors being opened—perhaps for an even greater witness.

Not only were the apostles divinely delivered—they were divinely commissioned.

> **Acts 5:20** | An angel ... said, [20] "Go and stand in the temple and speak to the people all the words of this Life."

So that's what they did: they taught in the Temple. The guards were still under the belief that they were incarcerated, but they were in fact free and back at it in the Temple: preaching and speaking the gospel to all the people. So they got no break. They went from jail break to breaking down the gates of hell again. Look what happened after they heard what the angel said.

No Break!

> **Acts 5:21a** | And when they heard this, they entered the temple at daybreak and began to teach.

In other words, Peter and John were granted a prison break, but they got *no break* from teaching in the Temple. Right at sunrise they walked back into the Temple, and they began teaching the hungry crowds.

Perseverance is the sign of real spiritual growth in the Christian life. Here were the apostles: one moment in prison, the next set free. Did they take a break? No. There is no break in war time. We are at war. We must get up and persevere in the Christian life. We must continue moving forward, teaching and making disciples no matter what comes against us.

THE GOAL OF THE CHURCH (5:21B-32)

The goal of the church is always to carry out Jesus' great commission, to preach the gospel to all people everywhere, beginning at Jerusalem and going to the uttermost parts of the earth. No prison bars can keep the Holy Spirit from filling men and women everywhere from preaching the good news of Christ to every person on earth.

Just a note, I saw an interview recently with one of the most intelligent men on earth, Jordan Peterson. He's not a believer, but when asked about repenting and believing on Jesus Christ, he said, "It becomes something with a power that transcends your ability to resist it." He's thinking through the gospel on a deep level, really on every level, psychologically, biologically, and morally, considering if the good news makes sense. And he describes the call to follow "irresistible" in its beauty and logic. He said he is shocked that he considers that the gospel and claims of Christ "seem to be oddly plausible."

Christ is drawing him right now. He ended the interview, still unconverted, but said, "I still don't know what to make of it, partly because it's too terrifying a reality to fully believe. I don't even know what would happen to you if you fully believed it."[104] It's incredible to see one of the world's greatest intellects become humble and childlike when he considers the weight and plausibility of the claims of Christ. The Spirit is working on him.

This is why we preach the gospel to every creature, because God can save anyone in any situation with any background. Nothing is too hard for the Lord. He can save the Jordan Petersons just like he could save the C.S. Lewises and the Sauls of Tarsus. God can draw an individual in a quiet room with no one looking on, or his Spirit can fall on an entire town, and hundreds are swept into the kingdom in one hour, as in the Welsh Revivals of 1904 and 1905.

---

[104] Adam Ford. "God is working on Jordan Peterson." (Jordan B. Peterson Podcast, March 8, 2021), Retrieved March 9, 2021, from https://notthebee.com/article/watch-jordan-peterson-tear-up-while-talking-about-following-jesus

A Surprise: Freedom

So, God is doing a great work in Jerusalem, and bars of iron cannot stop the work of God. The high priest then is in for a big surprise. He has no idea of the prison break and how the angel (who he doesn't believe in because he's a Sadducee) has released Peter and John from prison. So there is a fantastic surprise.

> **Acts 5:21b-25** | Now when the high priest came, and those who were with him, they called together the council, all the senate of the people of Israel, and sent to the prison to have them brought. ²² But when the officers came, they did not find them in the prison, so they returned and reported, ²³ "We found the prison securely locked and the guards standing at the doors, but when we opened them we found no one inside." ²⁴ Now when the captain of the temple and the chief priests heard these words, they were greatly perplexed about them, wondering what this would come to. ²⁵ And someone came and told them, "Look! The men whom you put in prison are standing in the temple and teaching the people."

Isn't it fantastic to see the power of God in all of this? These Sadducees with all their power and prisons cannot stop the gospel from going forth. That's the boldness we need in every generation. Go do what God has called you to do, and do not worry about the powers the align against you. God, who raised Jesus from the dead and busted Peter and John out of prison is on your side.

> *Romans 8:37* | We are more than conquerors through him who loved us.

What a great surprise for these unbelieving, lost religious leaders. They found a gospel more powerful than soldiers and prison bars.

You ought to expect many surprises in the Christian life. Often the devil wants to make us negative in our outlook, but people of faith are hopeful. We should never live in doubting castle for any length of time. We don't have to live in despair. We have the power and hope of a God who loves to surprise us. God can open doors you thought were shut, even a prison door.

A Sanction: Obedience

The apostles are now confronted with obedience. They are to obey the sanction of the Sanhedrin. The officers were forced to treat the apostles with respect because the sentiment of the people, who had been so changed and helped by the apostles was sympathetic toward the apostles. But Peter has to give a reason why they are setting aside the law of man in order to obey the law of God.

> **Acts 5:26-29** | The captain with the officers went and brought them, but not by force, for they were afraid of being stoned by the people. ²⁷ And when they had brought them, they set them before the council. And the high priest questioned them, ²⁸ saying, "We strictly charged you not to teach in this name, yet here you have filled Jerusalem with your teaching, and you intend to bring this man's blood upon us." ²⁹ But Peter and the apostles answered, "We must obey God rather than men."

We are at a place in our country when the laws of man oppose the law of God. We will not recognize any law of man that opposes the law of God. There is one greater than Caesar, and his name is the Lord Jesus Christ. And when we read in the book of Daniel that there is a kingdom, a stone that dashes to pieces all other kingdoms (Dan 2:44-45), we know that that stone is the kingdom of Jesus. All the great nations and governments that exist are metaphorically called "Babylon" in the book of Revelation, and there will be a day when we will say "Babylon has fallen" (Rev 18:2). But let it be known that we as Christians will never submit to the ungodly laws of men—not because we are against men who lie with men or women who lie with women. We are not against them, but against their behavior. We are not against abortionists or fornicators, but against their behavior. And it is love for them that compels us to confront the laws that protect that behavior. Let us not be afraid to confront ungodly laws but remember that all cowards shall have their part in the lake of fire (Rev 21:8). Let us never submit to the ungodly laws that promote the lifestyles of Sodom and Gomorrah. Peter and the apostles could no more obey the law to stop preaching about Jesus than any Spirit filled Christian could. Christians do not recognize laws that oppose the law of God. If we should support ungodly laws, we would be denying our faith, and repudiating the Lord who bought us, which we could never do. This was Peter's point.

A Sermon: Evangelism

Now that Peter has clearly set the reason why they will disobey human law, he preaches the gospel to his audience of the Jewish senate, the Sanhedrin. Listen to Peter's proclamation of Christ.

> **Acts 5:30-32** | "The God of our fathers raised Jesus, whom you killed by hanging him on a tree. ³¹ God exalted him at his right hand as Leader and Savior, to give repentance to Israel and forgiveness of sins. ³² And we are witnesses to these things, and so is the Holy Spirit, whom God has given to those who obey him."

Wow! What a sermon. So simple. Again, we see the boldness of Peter explaining the gospel clearly. "You killed him. You hanged him on a tree. God highly exalted him." You can just hear Peter calling for repentance for Israel and forgiveness for their sins of rejecting Christ.

Now you don't see the leaders of Israel repenting, but you do see them persecuting Peter and John. They hate the bright light of the gospel. It's like waking a person who is sleeping with the brightest flashlight in their face. The leaders and the Sanhedrin are angry. When the gospel is preached correctly, there is always either rioting or rejoicing. No one can be truly neutral.

So we saw the *growth* of the church as they multiplied. We saw the *grief* of the church as they were persecuted. We saw the *goal* of the church which is to give glory to God by teaching the gospel so God can move in people's lives. But now look at the *glory* of the church.

THE GLORY OF THE CHURCH (5:33-42)

Now Peter and John are about to get stoned by the Sadducees. But thankfully a very beloved Pharisee named Gamaliel stands up and calls for a private meeting of the Sanhedrin. He's going to call for everyone to leave the followers of Jesus alone. Let it play out. And the apostles end up glorying in the persecution and suffering they have to endure. They are so grateful to glory in the name of Jesus and suffer for him. What an honor!

The Glory of Gamaliel's Humility

> **Acts 5:33-34** | When they heard this, they were enraged and wanted to kill them. ³⁴ But a Pharisee in the council named Gamaliel, a teacher of the law held in honor by all the people, stood up and gave orders to put the men outside for a little while.

Gamaliel jumps to no conclusions. He's weighing the incredible evidence of Jesus. He's seen the miracles. He had certainly heard Peter and John had been released from prison by an angel. He invites Peter and John to have a private council meeting with the rest of the Sanhedrin. Of course, as the text says, Gamaliel is beloved and honored by all in Jerusalem. His best student at the time was Saul of Tarsus (Acts 22:3). But Gamaliel is not hostile toward John and Peter. It really seems he's curious and humble.

With the death penalty looming over Peter and John, the great Rabbi Gamaliel is showing kindness to the apostles. Gamaliel according to Jewish tradition was not only a legendary teacher and grandson of the great Rabbi Hillel, but he was also the co-chair of the Sanhedrin with the high priest. Look at the case Gamaliel makes.

The Pharisees were known as being lenient with sentencing, and so Gamaliel makes a case to get the death sentence reduced to a mere flogging.

Be Wary

Acts 5:35 | And he said to them, "Men of Israel, take care what you are about to do with these men."

Gamaliel's case was first, to be careful. He saw that God could be in this. The wise of this world are usually much more dismissive of the things of God, but Gamaliel saw the need to act carefully and slowly.

He had spoken with those who saw the resurrected Lord. And the miracles! Who could tell what the next miracle might be? Who could predict the reaction of the great crowds in Jerusalem? Persecuting the Christians could bring an even greater awakening. Gamaliel could see what was happening with his own eyes. Gamaliel goes on. He names a couple manmade movements that came to nothing. He says,

Acts 5:35-37 | For before these days Theudas rose up, claiming to be somebody, and a number of men, about four hundred, joined him. He was killed, and all who followed him were dispersed and came to nothing. [37] After him Judas the Galilean rose up in the days of the census and drew away some of the people after him. He too perished, and all who followed him were scattered.

Nothing is known for certain about the first of these insurrectionists, Theudas. We do know that when the detested Herod the Great died in 4 B.C. numerous would-be liberators surfaced in Palestine, and Theudas might have been one of them.

More is known about Judas of Galilee, who led a revolt against Rome that was crushed. The rallying call of Judas was that, because God was Israel's King, it was high treason to pay tribute to Caesar. Although the Romans crushed the revolt, the movement lived on through the Zealot political party. Gamaliel seems to have played down the whole thing in this speech.

The point is, manmade movements die. If this is a manmade movement, it will destroy itself. So, he says, be very careful before you try to destroy it. Move slowly and carefully, and you will be wise. Gamaliel now makes his main point. He says, be wise!

Be Wise

Acts 5:39 | So in the present case I tell you, keep away from these men and let them alone, for if this plan or this undertaking is of man, it will fail; **39** but if it is of God, you will not be able to overthrow them. You might even be found opposing God!" So they took his advice.

Perhaps the most important realization Gamaliel had was that this could be coming directly from God. You don't want to oppose God. Gamaliel was humble enough to consider the claims of the apostles, the power of the miracles, and the extraordinary things that had been happening in Jerusalem at the time. Remember all the miracles that had already happened.

At the time of the crucifixion, the thick veil of the Temple was torn in two (Mk 15:38; Lk 23:44-45). There was an earthquake (Mt 27:51). And probably most extraordinarily of all, some of the Old Testament saints were resurrected from their graves and were walking around Jerusalem (Mt 27:52-53). Perhaps Gamaliel might have even spoken to some of these resurrected saints. He was a Pharisee, so he would have taken the Bible seriously, believed in the supernatural, and believed the Bible's teaching, even though he was not a believer in Christ. So, Gamaliel rests his case and pleads for the council to "leave them alone" because they very well may be working for God and his kingdom.

The more I consider the argument of this great Rabbi, the more it makes sense. Gamaliel won because he was right. Jesus was the leader who had been put to death, but now they were faced with an empty tomb and with followers who were performing signs and wonders, who were preaching with great power, so that the church was rapidly growing. All the evidence pointed to the fact that God was on the move in this, and they had better be careful not to oppose God in their zeal to protect their interests. I am reminded of the words of our Lord,

Mark 12:34 | You are not far from the kingdom of God.

After Gamaliel's case is made, the Bible says, the council of the Sanhedrin took Gamaliel's advice. Then the apostles were given a reduced punishment: flogging.

The Glory of the Apostles' Courage

Now Gamaliel had their charges reduced to flogging but consider the glory of the church of Jesus Christ that they are willing to die or be flogged. They count their lives as nothing, as long as the glory of Christ can be displayed.

Glorious Suffering

Acts 5:40a | And when they had called in the apostles, they beat them.

Evidently, because of Gamaliel's plea for leniency, a compromise was reached, and the apostles were let off easy—easy, that is, if we think thirty-nine stripes is easy. This was the Jewish punishment of 'forty lashes less one' which could be inflicted by the Sanhedrin or the officials of a synagogue for offences against the Jewish law (22:19; *cf* Deut 25:2-3, 2 Cor 11:24; Mk 13:9). Giving more than 40 lashes was considered degrading, and it could lead to death. So, it was no soft option. It was meant to be a serious lesson to offenders.[105]

But let's consider what Dr. Luke is getting at. No beating can stop the gospel. No amount of threatenings can intimidate Holy Spirit filled people. Death and flogging is nothing when you consider that all Christians, through Christ, have sidestepped hell by the powerful blood of Jesus. Death and suffering is nothing compared to the penalty for our sins being erased!

---

[105] Marshall, *Acts*, 130.

Glorious Perseverance

Acts 5:40 | And when they had called in the apostles, they beat them and charged them not to speak in the name of Jesus, and let them go.

They were told "not to speak in the name of Jesus". It doesn't say they agreed to it. The apostles have already made it clear that they will obey God rather than men (Acts 5:29). How glorious it is that nothing can stop the courage of those filled with the Holy Spirit to preach the gospel.

Of course, the Sanhedrin was serious; so much so that the charge not to preach the gospel was emphasized by a terrible flogging. But this was something the apostles had already explained they could not obey. They had told the Sanhedrin that they had to listen to God over the Jewish rulers. They said, "we cannot but speak of what we have seen and heard" (4:19-20). The courage of the apostles is glorious. All of us must be courageous. The Bible gives severe warnings to cowards.

Revelation 21:8 | But as for the cowardly, the faithless, the detestable, as for murderers, the sexually immoral, sorcerers, idolaters, and all liars, their portion will be in the lake that burns with fire and sulfur, which is the second death.

The glory of the church is that no beating, no iron bars, no laws against Jesus Christ can keep his people silent. No human power or authority can harness or harass or halt the forward movement of the Holy Spirit. The gospel will prevail and go forth regardless of the opposition.

Glorious Joy

Now notice, when persecution comes, the apostles' joy is glorious!

Acts 5:41 | Then they left the presence of the council, rejoicing that they were counted worthy to suffer dishonor for the name.

One by one they were whipped until the flesh parted. And one by one they experienced supernatural joy. They were glad to be counted among the persecuted. Nothing could stop their joy: not a prison, not persecution, not panic. They were unafraid. They wanted to worship the Lord and live life on life discipleship literally more than they wanted to breath. Instead of being intimidated, they began to rejoice because they knew Christ. Peter would later encourage all of us.

1 Peter 1:8 | Though you do not now see him, you believe in him and rejoice with joy that is inexpressible and filled with glory.

It is a privilege to suffer for the name of Christ. Let us rejoice with glorious joy that when all is stripped away, all we have is Christ, and that's all we could ever need or hope for! Glorious joy in Christ!

The Glorious Gospel

Acts 5:42 | And every day, in the temple and from house to house, they did not cease teaching and preaching that the Christ is Jesus.

Not only did the punishment not discourage the Christians, but they had so much joy they could not stop proclaiming the glorious power and joy that is found in Jesus. gospel means good news, and knowing Jesus personally is the best news ever. We are reconciled with the Father. We are filled with the Spirit. And it's all because of the sacrifice of Jesus, the Lamb of God who takes away the sin of the world.

The apostles proclaimed Christ *every day*, the text says. Whether they were threatened or left to teach peacefully, they lifted up Christ every day. And he was drawing all people to himself.

They proclaimed Christ *everywhere*. They kept teaching publicly (in the Temple) and privately (house to house). Apparently, there was nothing the Sanhedrin could do now. They had warned them and flogged them. But these Spirit-filled believers kept obeying God.

They proclaimed Christ at *every opportunity*. Wherever they were in private or in public, in whatever situation, it says:

Acts 5:42b | They did not cease teaching and preaching that the Christ is Jesus.

Glory and hallelujah. They were doing life on life discipleship at every moment, in every situation, to every people group that they encountered.

Conclusion

What a prison break these apostles experienced. They were undeterred from teaching about Jesus no matter what the threats and sufferings they had to endure. They found so much joy in Jesus they were willing to lose their own lives.

You may not meet an angelic messenger to break you out of the prisons of life, but you do have the blessed Holy Spirit. He is with you, and if you feel stuck in your life, it can feel like a prison. Let the Spirit break you out of whatever cage you are stuck in.

Are you stuck in an unhappy marriage? Are you looking for greener grass? Water your own grass. Let the Spirit bring you joy that cannot be taken away. If you are joyless because of your circumstances, it's because you are an idol worshipper instead of a Christ worshipper. If your happiness can be threatened so easily by another human being or an amount of money or because of a health scare, then you're hoping in the wrong thing! Another thing that shows that we might be loving the world is a spirit of ingratitude. Look at the apostles when they suffered. They were grateful. Are you grateful for all things?

I want to ask you—do you need a prison break today? I can't promise a visitation by an angel. But if you are stuck in fear or loneliness or frustration with your life, Jesus will be with you. You can be set free. The apostles were fearless and unafraid. God is calling us to be a generation of men and women who are unafraid. Look at the apostles. They were threatened, imprisoned, beaten, but they kept returning to preach the gospel. This is Christianity. Christ calls us to bear a cross in this life. We have to be bold and courageous. We will suffer, but we have to get up over and over and over again and persevere. Never give up. Never give in. Isn't the Lamb of God worthy of the reward for his suffering? He wants you—your life, your heart. Give it all to him now.

11 | ACTS 6:1-7
HOW DEACONS GROW THE CHURCH

Therefore, brothers, pick out from among you seven men of good repute, full of the Spirit and of wisdom, whom we will appoint to this duty. But we will devote ourselves to prayer and to the ministry of the word.... And the word of God continued to increase, and the number of the disciples multiplied greatly in Jerusalem, and a great many of the priests became obedient to the faith.

ACTS 6:3-4, 7

I don't know whether you've ever experienced growing pains. When I was a kid, the growing pains were so bad at times that they woke me up out of my sleep. My mom would tell me, "It'll be ok, you just have growing pains." When I got to be a teenager, I can remember some emotional growing pains, as I was trying to adjust to the awkwardness of teenage life.

Those of us who are on the road of spiritual maturity, we know something about growing pains as well, because, just as you grow physically through pain, you grow spiritually through pain. We hear it in the Psalms. It's only when God enlarges our heart, that we have the power to be faithful in trials.

Psalm 4:1, KJV | Thou hast enlarged me when I was in distress.

When you're being stretched, you know you are growing. Not only do individuals have growing pains physically, emotionally, and spiritually, but churches have growing pains. With growth comes pain. It was true of the early church. It is true of any church that grows. The church in Acts had a difficulty as they were growing in great numbers. Here's the key thought: The normal Christian life is one of exemplary power and Spirit-filling with much fruit.

In the early days of the church, as the church grew at an incredible rate, there were problems that could only be solved by Spirit-filled servants of God, who helped the apostles so they could preach and pray. All of us need to be those Spirit filled examples of the believer, because difficulties and problems will come. We can't just ignore it. We have to step up when difficulties come. Listen to Dr. Luke describe the difficulty.

THE DIFFICULTY (6:1-2)

Acts 6:1-2 | Now in these days when the disciples were increasing in number, a complaint by the Hellenists arose against the Hebrews because their widows were being neglected in the daily distribution. ² And the twelve summoned the full number of the disciples and said, "It is not right that we should give up preaching the word of God to serve tables."

The Difficulty of Growth

Acts 6:1a | Now in these days ... the disciples were increasing in number.

It's hard to be a growing church. There has to be a mentality of victory and faith, or the church will isolate and insulate itself from problems. We must not have an insulated view of the Christian life. We are called to pierce the darkness, not run away from it.

The church in Jerusalem was not running away from evangelism because they were being persecuted, they were lifting up Christ in the midst of severe persecution. The apostles had just been jailed, released by an angel, and then beaten with 39 lashes. They don't get out of jail and out of their beating and say, "You know what, things are less tyrannical in Syria or North Africa. Let's move." I understand our freedoms are being taken away in this state of Illinois where we live. But the apostles didn't make a march out of town. They stayed, were imprisoned, beaten, and they kept preaching in that tyrannical city of Jerusalem. They were told to stop preaching Christ, but they stayed and preached Christ.

Because they had this mindset of evangelism in the face of tyranny, the church in Jerusalem is no longer growing by addition. It was addition in Acts 2. Now it is multiplication. There's something terribly wrong with any church, small or large, that is not growing. We don't run away from tyrants. We confront them with the claims of Jesus Christ.

We ought to be interested in growing right where we are in this dark time in history. I know there is a great temptation to want to run away from the expansion of tyrannical government powers in our state. We all want to live peaceably and enjoy the Christian life. But we really on a rescue mission. We are on the offense; we are going right up to the gates of hell and snatching people out. Christ will build his church and the gates of hell will not prevail. Those gates cannot keep people bound. The Son will set them free. I love the quote from the missionary to Africa, C.T. Studd. It's one of my favorite quotes of all time. He said, "Some wish to live within the sound of a chapel bell; I wish to run a rescue mission within a yard of hell."[106]

If we all have this mentality, we are going to grow. But growing is not automatic, nor is growing easy. These early disciples prayed that they might grow. They planned that they might grow. They cultivated, and they watered, but it was God that gave the increase (1 Cor 3:6). But, in the last analysis, their growth was there because of their spiritual vitality—their walk with God. Numerical growth is the result of spiritual growth.

We know three thousand joined the one hundred and twenty on the day of Pentecost. Then five thousand heads of households came to Christ, likely twenty thousand if you include women and children. So that's around twenty-three thousand. But now there is multiplication. The disciples are "increasing in number." Some have estimated that up to a hundred thousand would join the church in the first six months. That's a revival of historic proportions, especially since the world's population at the time was only 300 million at the time of the book of Acts.

---

[106] C.T. Studd in Norman Percy Grubb, *C.T. Studd Cricketer and Pioneer* (Cambridge, England, UK: Lutterworth, 2014), 55.

There are a number of ways the church increases in number. We pray. We preach. God draws people, but the church has to be bold and preach the gospel. Without the word, no amount of prayers will bring anyone to Christ. A person cannot be converted without the word of God. That's where we come in. We must always be "ready to give an answer" as Peter says (1 Pet 3:15).

> *Romans 10:14* | How are they to believe in him of whom they have never heard? And how are they to hear without someone preaching?

If we give the word, the Spirit will convert the hearts, and numbers of people will be added to the church. But with growth comes problems.

The Danger of Division

> **Acts 6:1** | Now in these days when the disciples were increasing in number, a complaint by the Hellenists arose against the Hebrews because their widows were being neglected in the daily distribution.

As the church was growing at an incredible rate, the early church in Jerusalem had a specific difficulty. What happened is this: There were two types of Jews in the early church. There were the Hellenistic Jews, and there were the Hebrew Jews. The Hellenistic Jews were adapted to Greek and Roman culture. They spoke Greek. The Hebrew Jews were separate from the culture and lived an exclusively Jewish life. They spoke Aramaic and Hebrew. At this time, there was a division between the two. Some of those who were of the Hellenistic group felt that they were being overlooked, even discriminated against. And to see how wrong it was, Luke mentions that these were widows. Widows, in that day, had no other means of support. There was no Social Security. These widows had to be taken care of by the church, if they were to survive. They were being overlooked, and the apostles saw this and began meeting their needs, but it took them away from the preaching of the word.

The natural response to problems in those days and in ours is complaining. The Scripture says, "a complaint" arose and there was a division between the Hebrews and the Hellenist Christians. People's mothers and grandmothers were involved. This is Satan's scheme when the church is growing. He's going to tempt us with division, with complaining. When new people come into the church there can be jealousy.

There can be a shuffling of duties and gifts. There also can be neglect, which was happening in Jerusalem. Ephesians warns us.

> *Ephesians 4:2-3* | Walk... worthy... with all humility and gentleness, with patience, bearing with one another in love, ³ eager to maintain the unity of the Spirit in the bond of peace.

We must not divide, which means we find our identity in Christ. Unity, not complaining, is the way of the Spirit of God. It's fine to bring a legitimate need, but there ought to be no murmuring as the church grows. Murmuring is the devil's way to divide when God wants to multiply. Paul said,

> *Philippians 2:14* | Do all things without grumbling or disputing.

I want every Christian, every believer in this church, to hear that. Do all things without grumbling or complaining. Why? Because when you have people, and you progress together, you are going to have problems. And the problem in the Jerusalem church was not doctrinal; it was functional. It was not primary; it was secondary. Now, it was necessary that it be addressed; but it's generally not the big things that divide churches today. It is the small things, the functional matters, the petty matters.

"They moved our classroom. They divided our class. We were not notified. Our opinion is not important." Well, no one should do things carelessly, but anybody can make mistakes. And, dear saint, one of the most dangerous things that you can do to the fellowship of the church is to murmur. Remember this: that anything that grows must adjust, and anything that moves generally makes friction. And there's always more opportunity for problems in a growing church than in a church that's not growing. But I'd rather be in a growing church than a dead church. The apostles guarded the growth of the church by bring a solution to the problem.

The Duty of the Deacons

The apostles as we see were faced with a natural fault line that threatened to fracture the very unity Christ died to achieve. The gospel insists, after all, that our unity in Christ supersedes any worldly difference. So, make no mistake: the apostles did not delegate the problem to others because it wasn't important, but because it was. They could have imposed a swift, superficial solution and moved on. Instead, they laid groundwork for an ongoing solution and a permanent church office.

Given the root problem of disunity facing the seven, we can conclude that deacons should be those who muffle shock waves, not make them reverberate further. Contentious persons make poor deacons, for they only compound the kind of headaches deacons are meant to relieve. The best deacons, therefore, are far more than business managers or handymen. They are persons with fine-tuned "conflict radars." They love solutions more than drama, and rise to respond, in creatively constructive ways, to promote the harmony of the whole church.[107]

The Dynamic of the Main Thing

> **Acts 6:2** | And the twelve summoned the full number of the disciples and said, "It is not right that we should give up preaching the word of God to serve tables.

What was the solution? They have to keep the main thing the main thing. No matter what, the preaching has to go forward. Let's keep first things first. The word of God and prayer have to be first. The teachers and elders cannot be serving tables as their main job. Their job is the word and prayer. So they need to set apart for ministry those who will be flexible and take on these duties. We ought not be overcome by problems. Be flexible. Be a servant. It's not ok to complain. But be communicative. When problems arise, it's an opportunity to serve.

Notice that the main thing has to remain the main thing. The word of God has to be primary. The word of God and prayer are the primary means for the congregation to be filled with the Holy Spirit. It is the primary way to grow the church. If measures are not taken to lift up the Jesus through the word and prayer, in evangelism and discipleship, then the church will die. It was vital for the early church to set apart qualified men to be what would become the office of deacon in the church. Now as we look at these first deacons (though they are not called deacons, but they function as deacons), we are going to see that they are exemplary men.

---

[107] Matt Smethurst, "5 Questions About Deacons" (Wheaton, IL: Crossway, 2021, April 18). Retrieved May 03, 2021, from https://www.crossway.org/articles/5-questions-about-deacons.

THE DEACONS (6:3-6)

Acts 6:3-6 | Therefore, brothers, pick out from among you seven men of good repute, full of the Spirit and of wisdom, whom we will appoint to this duty. [4] But we will devote ourselves to prayer and to the ministry of the word." [5] And what they said pleased the whole gathering, and they chose Stephen, a man full of faith and of the Holy Spirit, and Philip, and Prochorus, and Nicanor, and Timon, and Parmenas, and Nicolaus, a proselyte of Antioch. [6] These they set before the apostles, and they prayed and laid their hands on them.

Now, the solution here was a very simple, wonderful solution. You're going to find out that the Bible is a very practical book. Any person who walks with God is going to be deeply spiritual and intensely practical at the same time. God is a God of order. And so, God had an orderly way to deal with this problem. You're going to find that when the Holy Spirit moves, he always brings an orderly cosmos out of chaos.

He moved upon the darkness there in the early chapters of Genesis, and he took that chaos, and he made a cosmos out of it. And, if things are out of order, God will make order. Disorder is generally a mark of carnality. I confess that my desk, is sometimes very carnal. The Bible says, "Let all things be done decently and in order." And so, the church organization is engineered by God, and the machinery is oiled by the Holy Spirit of God.

Now, learn this about this church, or any church. Any church that is growing is going to have to adjust, but there are no problems too big to solve; only people too small to solve them. They looked among them, likely around 23,000 people, and at least 6000 or so heads of households. They set apart servants for the church. These are not called deacons, but they were definitely a model for the first deacons.

And what we find as we see them described, is that they are each an example for the believer. Remember we are all to lead exemplary lives as believers.

1 Timothy 4:12 | Be an example to all believers in what you say, in the way you live, in your love, your faith, and your purity.

These men, as we will see, set an excellent example for the believer. We are all called to be like these deacons. First, we are called to have the heart of a servant. The officer in the church must be willing to serve, to stretch, to lay his life down for the church. That's the life of a slave of Jesus. We must have a servant's heart, like these first prototypes for the deacons.

Men with Servants' Hearts

> **Acts 6:2** | And the twelve summoned the full number of the disciples and said, "It is not right that we should give up preaching the word of God to serve tables."

These were superior men. It takes a superior man to serve. In this passage, there are a cluster of Greek words that have the word *deacon* or *diakonos* in them, which means "deacon" or "servant." These seven men may have been the very first deacons. Not just anyone was chosen. They had to search for these men. These were not inferior men.

> *Matthew 10:28* | Even as the Son of man came not to be ministered unto, but to minister, and to give his life a ransom for many.

Jesus said he came to be a deacon. He also said we all should be ministers or "servants." The apostles themselves were not averse to waiting tables. They were glad to serve. They would have been glad to serve, but they needed the deacons to help them so they could serve in a different way, by preaching the word and leading prayer meetings. But indeed, all of us is called to serve. This is the mark of greatness in the Christian life.

> *Mark 10:43* | But whosoever will be great among you shall be your minister.

The word here "minister" (Mk 10:43) literally means your "servant." There are two principles in serving the Body of Christ: expendability and flexibility. All parts of Christ's body are expendable. None of us is needed. We can give way to others. But on the other hand, we need to each be flexible, and when we are needed, we should be willing to step up. We should all be willing to do anything for the Lord Jesus Christ.

Men of a Good Reputation

Now, what qualities does it take for a man to be a deacon in any New Testament church? These were men of a good reputation. They were clearly living out the Christian life with joy and consistency.

Acts 6:3a | Therefore, brothers, pick out from among you seven men of good repute.

Out of the 23,000 souls converted thus far, most of them were Aramaic speaking, Hebrew cultured Jews. Yet every one of the men they choose are Greek-speaking Jews. They are cultured in Rome and Greece. But notice that culture doesn't matter. It just makes things more interesting. What matters is character. It doesn't matter what culture you are from. There is so much diversity and culture here at Living Hope, and we celebrate that. That ought never divide us. Just as a body has many parts, so the body of Christ has many cultures. We celebrate the diversity, because God gave you your culture to do your part of his kingdom work. Our society would have you focus on culture as something that divides us. The media would have you consider how much racism and vitriol people have toward one another. That may be true about the world, but the church is all about replacing racism with "gracism." In Christ culture is not divisive; it is celebrated. Christ's body is made up of every culture. God wants his churches to look like heaven.

> *Revelation 7:9* | I looked, and behold, a great multitude that no one could number, from every nation, from all tribes and peoples and languages, standing before the throne and before the Lamb, clothed in white robes.

What matters in the kingdom is not so much culture but character. Each of these deacons had Greek names and could speak Greek. They had experienced areas of culture that the Hebrew Jews didn't. But that's not the most important thing. Character and a good reputation is what matters. I constantly have told my children, you may get a great education, be very talented, be popular, and gain the whole world, but if you don't have Christ you are a total failure. What we need is children and parents who want to be conformed to the image of Christ. We need that kind of reputation: constantly growing and changing to be like Christ.

Men Full of Wisdom

Acts 6:3 | Men ... full of ... wisdom, whom we will appoint to this duty.

Deacons are to an example of the believer, and that means they are to be wise and understanding in the congregation. In this passage, there are a cluster of Greek words that have the word *deacon* or *diakonos* in them, which means "deacon" or "servant." These seven men were the first deacon prototypes. Not just anyone was chosen.

Know the Lord

They were men who were full of wisdom. That means they didn't just know the word and doctrine, but they knew how to walk with the Lord and walk in the word, applying it to their lives. The greatest step forward in wisdom is the fear of the Lord, or what we might call "practicing the presence of God". Until you realize that the word is not the end but a means to an end, that of knowing God in Christ, then you cannot say you are wise.

> *Proverbs 9:10* | The fear of the LORD is the beginning of wisdom, and the knowledge of the Holy One is insight.

So wisdom is really knowing how to walk with God. Think of Enoch. He was walking with God so closely, and then God just took him to heaven without dying.

> *Genesis 5:24* | Enoch walked with God, and he was not, for God took him.

Know the Bible

> *Psalm 119:105* | Your word is a lamp to my feet and a light to my path.

It's not just the pastors that need to know the Bible. And of course, deacons should know the Scriptures, but not just them. Each Christian should be "wise unto salvation" (2 Tim 3:15). Every Christian should be competent to counsel and instruct each other. We are to build each other up in Christ our head (Eph 4:11-16).

Know People

Not only does wisdom mean we know God, but we have compassion on our brothers and sisters. Deacons are to know what is going on in the lives of the people. At this time, these men were to get to know what was happening in the lives of these widows. This means deacons are peacemakers and problem solvers. What Paul says of the Romans, should be true of all of us. He says:

Romans 15:14 | I myself am satisfied about you, my brothers, that you yourselves are full of goodness, filled with all knowledge and able to instruct one another.

Are you full of wisdom? If you are a new Christian, you can at least start giving the gospel to those around you. If you came to know Christ, then you have the ability to share how you were saved. But don't stay there. You are your brother's and your sister's keeper (Gen 4:9). Gain the wisdom of not just knowing the word but walking in the word (Jas 1:22-25). Don't just be a "forgetful hearer" but be a "doer" of the work. You'd better not wait until you get a Ph.D. to start helping your brothers and sisters grow. It's just like a family. Wisdom is gained by doing. Go and learn how to apply the word of God to your life. Help others do the same. That's wisdom.

Men Who Support the Word

In some functional ways, the apostles are the counterpart of the pastors and the preachers and missionaries today. They had to continue the ministry of the word of God. Look, if you will, in verse 2. They said,

Acts 6:2 | "It is not right that we should give up preaching the word of God to serve tables."

Now, it's not that they were too good to do it. It just did not make sense. Look in verse 4:

Acts 6:4 | "But we will devote ourselves to prayer and to the ministry of the word."

The apostles are not saying that they are not willing to serve. Of course they are. Every Christian is called to serve in the most menial ways! It's our honor to imitate the servant's heart of Jesus. The apostles are just called to serve in a different way. They're saying, "We can be more effective if we do that which God has called us to do, and that is to pray and minister the word of God." The early deacons were not there to free the pastor from work, but to free the pastor to work. It's not that the apostles were too good or too dignified to serve. They had a different assignment. They were getting behind with their prayer, with their sermon preparation, with their soul winning, and with their preaching and the ministry of the word of God. And they said, "This doesn't make sense." In other words, the pastors and elders who stayed long term after the apostles' work, knew that if they didn't evangelize and disciple those who were coming to Christ, the church would die.

Many in the ministry today have left the emphasis on prayer and the word of God. They are so involved in the administrative details of their church that they have little time left for intercession and study of the word. Yet pastors and elders are given to the church "for the equipping of the saints for the work of service, to the building up of the body of Christ" (Eph 4:12). Their calling is to mature the saints so they can do the work of the ministry. By neglecting that calling, they doom their congregations to languish in spiritual infancy. Programs are no substitute for the power of God and his word. Those whom God has called to the ministry of prayer and the word must make it their priority.[108]

I've learned a long time ago that a preacher who's always available isn't worth a whole lot when he is available. He needs to be alone with God. He needs to be in the word of God. And the best time that I can spend on your behalf is not when I am before you, talking to you about God, but when I am before God, talking to him about you, and filling my heart with the word of God, and preparing to preach, and then ministering the word of God, and serving, and equipping you to serve.

So, the early apostles said, "Now, it doesn't make sense that our ministry be cancelled out by doing these things." And so, they need to continue to do what God had called them to do. So, there was the *spiritual ministry*—that is, for spiritual food.

Men Full of Faith

> **Acts 6:5a** | And what they said pleased the whole gathering, and they chose Stephen, a man full of faith.

Stephen was an exceptional man of faith. We see that by his confrontation of the Sanhedrin in the next chapter. Deacons are to be those who are well grounded in the faith. This is not only doctrinal, which we will find out is absolutely necessary, but also, these men are not just financial men. They are that. They help with the distribution of the funds to the needy. But they are to be full of faith.

Deacons are to be an example of the normal believer who is not only supposed to be a good steward, a person of ethics, but also a

---

[108] MacArthur., *Acts*, 179.

person of vision and faith. God works in ways that go "exceeding abundantly above all that we ask or think" (Eph 3:20, KJV).

Men Full of the Holy Spirit

> **Acts 6:5** | And what they said pleased the whole gathering, and they chose Stephen, a man full of faith and of the Holy Spirit, and Philip, and Prochorus, and Nicanor, and Timon, and Parmenas, and Nicolaus, a proselyte of Antioch.

Now all these men have Green names because they were all Hellenists. They all spoke Greek. But Stephen is singled out here. We know why. Gamaliel is training someone very important who is also a Hellenist: Saul of Tarsus. Saul of Tarsus is going to take over where Stephen leaves off. Stephen in the next chapter will boldly proclaim Christ at the cost of his own life. But God saves that other Hellenist Jew, Saul of Tarsus, and Saul, also known as Paul (his Hellenist name) will take the gospel not only to Samaria, but to the ends of the earth.

Not only was Stephen filled with faith, but he was also filled with the Spirit. This is the prototype not only for a deacon but for any believer. Officers of the church are to be those who are examples of the Spirit-filled life. To be Spirit-filled means that these men are not characterized by anger, anxiety, despair or worldliness, but by the presence of God in their lives. What's a Spirit-filled life look like? It looks like a heart filled with the word, with worship, and with the wonder of gratitude.

> *Ephesians 5:18-21* | And do not get drunk with wine, for that is debauchery, but be filled with the Spirit, [19] addressing one another in psalms and hymns and spiritual songs, singing and making melody to the Lord with your heart, [20] giving thanks always and for everything to God the Father in the name of our Lord Jesus Christ, [21] submitting to one another out of reverence for Christ.

Remember, if your heart is not filled with the word of God, with worship, and with wonder, then you are withering away. The flesh will wither you. Be filled with the Spirit! The Spirit-filled life is the opposite of the anger and anxiety of the flesh. It's not the fleshly life that is never satisfied. G. Campbell Morgan said that the Spirit-filled life is the normal Christian life.

A man full of the Spirit is one who is living a normal Christian life. Fulness of the Spirit is not a state of the spiritual elite, to which few can attain. Anything less than the fulness of the Spirit for the Christian man is disease of the spiritual life, a low ebb of vitality. Fullness of the Spirit is not abnormal, but the normal Christian life.[109]

There is zero room for fear and faithlessness. Stop being paralyzed by your anger and anxiety. Stop drinking from the broken cisterns of the world. Put on the Lord Jesus. Rest in him. Look at how Paul describes this powerful Spirit-filled life. Look at what it is not and then what it is.

Galatians 5:19-24 | Now the works of the flesh are evident: sexual immorality, impurity, sensuality, [20] idolatry, sorcery, enmity, strife, jealousy, fits of anger, rivalries, dissensions, divisions, [21] envy, drunkenness, orgies, and things like these. I warn you, as I warned you before, that those who do such things will not inherit the kingdom of God. [22] But the fruit of the Spirit is love, joy, peace, patience, kindness, goodness, faithfulness, [23] gentleness, self-control; against such things there is no law. [24] And those who belong to Christ Jesus have crucified the flesh with its passions and desires.

There is a sense of unrest and doublemindedness in the fleshly heart. You are tossed about by your emotions and paralyzed by the devil. But the Spirit wants to bring you emotional maturity. Some of you think you are Spirit-filled because you have sound doctrine. The Spirit promotes sound doctrine, for sure, but you can have sound doctrine and be filled with the works of the flesh. The evidence of the Spirit is the heart at perfect peace and love and joy in God. There is this wonderful rest and faith and sweet character that proceeds from the child of God, one of gentleness and not of frustration or fear, one of self-control, and not sexual promiscuity, but purity.

Is your heart pure? Are you at peace? Are you Spirit-filled? There's only one way to the Spirit-filled life. It's a life of total trust and surrender to the Spirit. Your flesh will lie to you, so you must insist on believing the word of God despite what you feel. Trust in God. Stop striving. Rest in Jesus, and God's peace will come to you.

---

[109] G. Campbell Morgan, *The Acts of the Apostles* (Westwood, NJ: Revell, 1924), 174.

Nicolaus the Gnostic?

It is interesting that even the apostles do not have infallible discernment. Nicolaus, the proselyte of Antioch, is said later to have gone astray, and some believe he is one of the major proponents and founders of the Gnostic heresy, which taught that the body was worthless and only the Spirit mattered. This brought about a great lawless kind of living and great immorality in some who called themselves Christians. The book of 1 John is a polemic against this false teaching.

Later Paul had a companion named Demas. Remember Paul's report about this man who had traveled with the great apostle? "Demas, in love with this present world, has deserted me" (2 Tim 4:10). Jesus chose twelve apostles, but one of them was a devil. We must do our best to choose godly, Spirit-filled men. We don't want a Demas or a Judas. We want the faithful, Spirit-filled men, like Stephen. God have mercy on us that we might all be examples of the Spirit-filled life.

Men Recognized for Their Gifts

Acts 6:6 | These they set before the apostles, and they prayed and laid their hands on them.

These men are recognized by the apostles for their gifts and their servant's heart. The apostles set these men apart and ordain them. The apostles pray and look to God for the church to be cared for through the gifting of set apart men. They laid hands on them. What does that mean? It means they recognized their gifts. That's how it is in every healthy congregation. The elders and pastors will recognize those who are living an exemplary Christian life with servants hearts and set them apart for service to the church. These men, though humble, are recognized here by the apostles for their gifts and their ability to serve.

We also recognize something else: though each of these men is a Greek speaking Jew, they serve the majority who are Aramaic speaking Jews. What a beautiful display of unity—especially considering that all those chosen had Greek names. The Greek cultured people were serving the Jewish cultured people. The Holy Spirit was reigning. The result?[110] God's blessing and favor was manifestly upon them.

---

[110] Hughes, *Acts*, 98.

THE DIVINE FAVOR (6:7)

Acts 6:7 | And the word of God continued to increase, and the number of the disciples multiplied greatly in Jerusalem, and a great many of the priests became obedient to the faith.

The organization of the church freed the apostles to devote themselves to prayer and the word. It also avoided a church split. Luke closes this section, as he has before, by noting the development of the church. The word of God kept on spreading from the church as a direct result of the freeing of the apostles to carry out their primary ministry, and also of the church's unity.[111]

What was the result? The blessing of God continued and increased! The church was still unified (Acts 6:5), multiplied (Acts 6:7), and magnified (Acts 6:8). In Acts 6:7, Dr. Luke describes the climax of the ministry in Jerusalem, for the persecution following Stephen's death will take the gospel to the Samaritans and then to the Gentiles. It has been estimated that there were 8,000 Jewish priests attached to the temple ministry in Jerusalem, and "a great company" of them trusted Jesus Christ as Savior![112]

Conclusion

I want to leave you with this thought: what if you were the prototype for the local church? What would the church look like if everyone were following your example? Deacons are those who live exemplary lives who are entrusted to serve the needs of the saints, to be buffers of division, and are worthy to be followed. We should all be like Jesus, the ultimate deacon who did not come to be served, but to serve by giving his life.

I wonder, are you living an exemplary Christian life? Are you serving the way you want to serve? Are you filled with faith and the Holy Spirit? If not, I know that if you are a Christian, you are miserable. We Christians can only be happy if we are humble and holy. We must have the fullness of the Spirit, or we are miserable. The world no longer satisfies us. As you live the Spirit-filled life, you will go beyond "hoop jumping" of good behavior. You will have a heart rich with God's

---

[111] MacArthur., *Acts*, 184.
[112] Wiersbe, *The Bible Exposition Commentary*, 430.

presence, and your happiness will flow out of you. You will bear fruit, not only joy and peace, but souls. That is the normal Christian life.

We as a church must be committed to lifting up the word. That means we all need to be serving where God puts us. Pastors teaching, equipping, leading the congregation in prayer. Deacons, Spirit-filled examples of service. And the entire congregation building itself up in love, being fitly formed together under Christ. Service is not another program of works. Seek first the kingdom. Let God show up and show out. You yield your life to him, and he will be seen in and through you!

12 | ACTS 6:8-7:60
STEPHEN'S SERMON AND MARTYRDOM

Lord Jesus, receive my spirit.
ACTS 7:59

There's coming a time, dear saint, when you are going to have to be one against the crowd, and you're going to be all by yourself against great odds. The night I came to the Lord, the evangelist said, "If you don't stand for something, you'll fall for everything." When we come to know Christ, we have to be willing to stand alone.

It might be in school for you students. It may even be here at church. Some of you are in your career and may have to stand alone. Your co-workers may talk about fornication; or there may be obscenity; there will be dishonesty; and there will be materialism. And you as a Christian, in the name of Jesus, will have to stand alone. Some of you in your social life will have to stand alone. Everyone is out dating, but there is not a suitable person who loves Jesus, and God calls you to singleness rather than date someone who doesn't know the Lord.

I heard of two couples who were out double-dating, and one of them suggested that they stop and go into a kind of seedy dance club. They're about to go in there, but the young lady in the back seat with her date says, "No, I don't want to go in there. I have someone with me who would not enjoy that place." And the boy who was with her said,

"Oh, I don't mind going in there at all." She said, "I wasn't talking about you. I was talking about the Holy Spirit of God that lives in my heart."

There are times when we are going to have to stand alone, because we are twice-born people in a world of once-born people, and we're going to find ourselves going against the tide. And as we get closer to the coming of the Lord Jesus Christ, we're going to find that the opposition is sharpening, and the hostility is emerging more fierce and furious than ever, and we will have to stand alone.

BE WILLING TO STAND FOR CHRIST (6:8-15)

Stephen was one of the first deacons, and he was a man who was willing to stand alone for Christ. He was also a Hellenist, that is, he was a Greek speaking Jew who had taken on a more Western culture. He was a passionate believer in Jesus Christ who belonged to a Jewish synagogue, as all the Jews did, but in a foreign land. He, along with all the rest of the deacons, were chosen to care for the widows. God chose Stephen and the other deacons to be take the first step beyond the Jews in the direction of the Gentiles.

Standing with Power

The mantle of Stephen falls strangely on Saul, one of Stephen's most bitter enemies. Saul, also called Paul, is a member of the Sanhedrin. It may be that the apostle Paul owes much of his exposure to the gospel to the sermon that Stephen is about to preach. Stephen was a noble personality. He was essential to God's plan for world evangelization. It was his martyrdom that launches the church into the world. We see something quite important. He wasn't intimidated by the earthly power of the Sadducees and Pharisees who made up the Sanhedrin. He is described as "full of grace and power" working miracles.

> **Acts 6:8** | And Stephen, full of grace and power, was doing great wonders and signs among the people.

Stephen is filled with the supernatural power of the Holy Spirit, performing miracles and signs among the people. Nothing more is said here about the nature of these miracles, but we need to understand that miracles are more common in places where the word of God is either not present or outlawed. We read about some of the miracles later in Acts, especially healings. But there are dreams and visions. There are miraculous escapes from prisons, like with Peter in Jerusalem and Paul in Philippi. There are earthquakes that result from prayer meetings. There was an incredible demonstration of power from the apostles and their co-workers. The new covenant had begun, and the powers of the new creation were on display.

Standing Amidst Persecution

Stephen is about to find out that there is a plot, a scheme to take his life. A certain synagogue with a very prominent member leads the way.

Stephen's Conspirators

Acts 6:9 | Then some of those who belonged to the synagogue of the Freedmen (as it was called), and of the Cyrenians, and of the Alexandrians, and of those from Cilicia and Asia, rose up and disputed with Stephen.

Who were this group of men from various synagogues? Synagogue worship seems to have had its roots in the Babylonian Exile. Jews congregated in synagogues to hear the Scriptures read and expounded. They became common gathering centers of the Jews, especially in the lands of their dispersion. Any sizable town with a Jewish population had its synagogue, sometimes several.

The "synagogue of the Freedmen" in Jerusalem seems to have been attended by Jews from various parts of the Dispersion. The mention of Jews from Cilicia suggests that this was the synagogue attended by Saul of Tarsus when he was in Jerusalem. Tarsus is located in Cilicia, the birthplace of Saul, the persecutor of the church, and later an apostle. Since Paul's hometown of Tarsus was located in Cilicia (Acts 21:39; 22:3), he likely attended their synagogue in Jerusalem. That he was present for the events surrounding Stephen's trial and execution is evident from 7:58 and 8:1. It is possible that, as a student of the great Rabbi Gamaliel, he even participated in the debate with Stephen.[113] Jews from this synagogue of the Freedmen engaged Stephen in hot debate over the question of whether Jesus is really the Messiah, and if he is, is the Temple necessary anymore?

---

[113] MacArthur, *Acts*, 193.

Stephen's Controversy

Acts 6:10-11 | But they could not withstand the wisdom and the Spirit with which he was speaking. [11] Then they secretly instigated men who said, "We have heard him speak blasphemous words against Moses and God."

Stephen's able handling of the Scriptures was such that not even the most knowledgeable Jewish apologists could defeat him. They could not withstand the wisdom of the Spirit of God within him. He was right, and they knew it. But they kept lying to themselves. They privately convinced people to say that Stephen hated the Temple and the Bible. But truly Stephen loved them more than all of them. He knew the real meaning of the Temple. It was to point to Jesus. He knew the meaning of the Bible: it was to celebrate Jesus. But sometimes people can love the reflection of a thing more than the thing itself.

Then they persuaded people to lie, who said they had heard him speak blasphemous words against Moses and against God. Hired informers were now engaged to distort Stephen's words in the most damaging way possible. He was accused of blasphemy against Moses, because he was telling them the beautiful story of how Jesus fulfilled all the law and the prophets.

It's kind of like they were all looking at a black and white photo of Jesus. They were in love with the photo, but Stephen was telling them that the actual person had come! They didn't want to hear about it. The Temple and customs that pointed to Jesus were more important to the people than Jesus himself.

The Court

Acts 6:12-14 | And they stirred up the people and the elders and the scribes, and they came upon him and seized him and brought him before the council, [13] and they set up false witnesses who said, "This man never ceases to speak words against this holy place and the law, [14] for we have heard him say that this Jesus of Nazareth will destroy this place and will change the customs that Moses delivered to us."

They arrest Stephen and drag him before the Sanhedrin. The Sanhedrin is made up of the elders (the Sadducees who were the politicians and theological liberals) and the scribes (the Pharisees who were the teachers of the law and theologically conservative). Again, this is the Jewish senate who had crucified Jesus and had already told the apostles never to preach in the name of Jesus. They had jailed the apostles and beaten them. They charged Stephen with the same charges they trumped up for our Lord. But Stephen stood, even if he stood alone. He did not waver. Stephen's ministry, though brief, was essential to God's plan for world evangelism. He showed that the efforts of one courageous person, though of short duration, can have far-reaching effects.[114]

He was charged with blasphemy and destroying the law and the customs of the Temple. Stephen was being treated in the same way as his Lord. Jesus does not destroy the law or the Temple, but he does fulfill them. The religious leaders loved these gifts of God for all the wrong reasons. They loved the law because it gave power to them over the people. They loved the Temple because it gave the leaders prestige. Power and prestige had replaced the humble faith they should have had for the Lord, so they missed the Messiah when God sent him. Not only did they miss him—they crucified him.

Stephen's Countenance

They wanted to debate Stephen, but Stephen had an anointing on him. The leaders of the Sanhedrin could clearly see the manifestation of the Spirit of God on him.

> **Acts 6:15** | And gazing at him, all who sat in the council saw that his face was like the face of an angel.

Stephen's address opens with "the God of glory" and closes with the glory of God (Acts 7:55); and all the time he spoke, his face radiated that same glory! Why? Because Israel was the only nation privileged to have the glory of God as a part of its inheritance (Rom 9:4). Alas, the glory of God had departed, first from the tabernacle (1 Sam 4:19–22) and then from the temple (Eze 10:4, 18). God's glory had come in his Son (Jn 1:14), but the nation had rejected him.[115]

This scene presents a striking contrast. Stephen stood before the Sanhedrin accused of being an evil blasphemer of God, the temple, and the law. Yet when the members of that council fixed their gaze on him, they saw his face like the face of an angel. Far from being evil, Stephen

---

[114] MacArthur, *Acts volume 1*, 188.
[115] Wiersbe, *The Bible Exposition Commentary*, 430–431.

radiated the holiness and glory of God. God himself answered their false charges by putting his glory on Stephen's face—something Moses experienced (Exo 34:27–35). He thus showed his approval of Stephen's teaching in exactly the same way he did that of Moses.[116] Stephen had the filling of the Spirit and you could see it on his face. In fact, we who know Christ have a great glory than Moses! Moses had to veil his face because of God's glory radiating from his face. Paul tells us:

> *2 Corinthians 4:18* | We all, with unveiled face, beholding the glory of the Lord, are being transformed into the same image from one degree of glory to another. For this comes from the Lord who is the Spirit.

Stephen demonstrates that you can stand for Christ without being angry or rude. Like God who loved the world and wants to see his heaven full, so Stephen's motive was to see many in the Sanhedrin come to Christ. That's why he was willing to stand alone for Christ.

But remember it's not our faces that will bring people to Christ. We must open our mouths with the message of the gospel. And Stephen gives a demonstration of how we can all preach the gospel even to a hostile crowd.

BE WILLING TO SPEAK FOR CHRIST (7:1-53)

Stephen is then asked a question about the accusations about him.

Acts 7:1 | And the high priest said, "Are these things so?"

Stephen was ready to give an answer, and speak up, and so should we.

> *1 Peter 3:15* | In your hearts honor Christ the Lord as holy, always being prepared to make a defense to anyone who asks you for a reason for the hope that is in you; yet do it with gentleness and respect.

Stephen is asked, "Is it true that you Stephen are setting aside the land, the law and the temple?" That would be blasphemous in the minds of the Sanhedrin! Stephen had a choice to make then and there. Will he speak for Christ? Will he try to defend himself, or will he simply give the gospel? Stephen's choice is very helpful for all of us. He chooses not to answer the charges or defend himself. Like his Lord, Stephen was like a sheep before her shearers is silent, and he did not open his

---

[116] MacArthur, 195–196.

mouth to defend himself. Instead, he lifted up Jesus from the Old Testament.

What Stephen did do was kick out the false pillars they were staking their lives and eternity on: the land, the law, and the temple. These were good things, but they were means to an end, not an end in and of themselves. You see the religious leaders had loved the photograph of Jesus: the land, the law, and the Temple—more than they loved the real thing. Jesus comes as the fulfillment of these things, and they crucify him. It's like they're crying out, "We don't want the real thing! We want the picture." You see they gained some things through those pictures that they would lose if they followed Jesus. They gained worldly power and prestige. Intoxicated with power, and unwilling to let it go, they crucified their Messiah.

You see whatever controls you is your Lord. Whatever makes you angry and anxious is your little "g" god. That might as well be the title of Stephen's sermon. The gist of his message is stop worshipping the photograph—the real Messiah is here. Don't worship the wrapping paper when God wants you to worship the gift.

It's Not About the Land!

One thing the leaders of Israel were in love with was the land. They felt they were uniquely blessed by God because they lived in the Promised Land. They had come back from exile. The inheritance of the land proved that the Jews have the blessing of God.

Abraham and the Land

Stephen says, God's is not the inheritance of the land, but the inheritance of knowing Jesus. Stephen starts where we should all start: the Abrahamic covenant. Abraham is justified by grace through faith. It wasn't the land that was special. It was his faith in the Lord! His inheritance in Christ was what made the difference, not the land.

> **Acts 7:2-8** | And Stephen said: "Brothers and fathers, hear me. The God of glory appeared to our father Abraham when he was in Mesopotamia, before he lived in Haran, **3** and said to him, 'Go out from your land and from your kindred and go into the land that I will show you.' **4** Then he went out from the land of the Chaldeans and lived in Haran. And after his father died, God removed him from there into this land in which you are now living. **5** Yet he gave him no inheritance in it, not even a foot's length, but promised to

give it to him as a possession and to his offspring after him, though he had no child. ⁶And God spoke to this effect—that his offspring would be sojourners in a land belonging to others, who would enslave them and afflict them four hundred years. ⁷'But I will judge the nation that they serve,' said God, 'and after that they shall come out and worship me in this place.' ⁸And he gave him the covenant of circumcision. And so Abraham became the father of Isaac, and circumcised him on the eighth day, and Isaac became the father of Jacob, and Jacob of the twelve patriarchs.

The popular opinion of the time was that God gave special spiritual privileges to those living on the real estate of Palestine. The resulting veneration of the land and the status that went with it left little room for the ultimate inheritance we have in Jesus the Messiah. Stephen argued that God's blessing on Abraham had nothing to do with the land, but came because of his faith in the coming Messiah. Abraham spent considerable time in the land but did not own any part of it. Stephen is emphatic. [117]

> **Acts 7:5** | God gave Abraham no inheritance in the land, not even a foot's length, but promised to give it to him as a possession and to his offspring after him, though he had no child.

Abraham who was promised the land and a people to inhabit it never owned even a "foot's length" in the Promised Land. You see, Stephen's point is, the land is the wrapping paper. It's certainly not the ultimate inheritance. Christ is the gift inside the wrapping paper. He is our eternal inheritance. That's Stephen's point. The Sanhedrin, including Saul of Tarsus, are so enthralled with the wrapping paper that they not only hate the gift of Jesus, they crucify him.

Joseph and the Land

Again, if the land is so important, why is it, Stephen says, that the none of the twelve patriarchs owned land was a burial plot.

> **Acts 7:9-16** | "And the patriarchs, jealous of Joseph, sold him into Egypt; but God was with him ¹⁰ and rescued him out of all his afflictions and gave him favor and wisdom before Pharaoh, king of Egypt, who made him ruler over Egypt and over all his

---

[117] Hughes, *Acts*, 104.

household. **11** Now there came a famine throughout all Egypt and Canaan, and great affliction, and our fathers could find no food. **12** But when Jacob heard that there was grain in Egypt, he sent out our fathers on their first visit. **13** And on the second visit Joseph made himself known to his brothers, and Joseph's family became known to Pharaoh. **14** And Joseph sent and summoned Jacob his father and all his kindred, seventy-five persons in all. **15** And Jacob went down into Egypt, and he died, he and our fathers, **16** and they were carried back to Shechem and laid in the tomb that Abraham had bought for a sum of silver from the sons of Hamor in Shechem.

God blessed them through Joseph in Egypt even though the only part of the Holy Land they possessed was the family tomb.[118]

Moses and the Land

Again, if the land is so important, why is it, Stephen says, that the none of the twelve patriarchs owned land was Abraham's burial plot?

Acts 7:17-36 | "But as the time of the promise drew near, which God had granted to Abraham, the people increased and multiplied in Egypt **18** until there arose over Egypt another king who did not know Joseph. **19** He dealt shrewdly with our race and forced our fathers to expose their infants, so that they would not be kept alive. **20** At this time Moses was born; and he was beautiful in God's sight. And he was brought up for three months in his father's house, **21** and when he was exposed, Pharaoh's daughter adopted him and brought him up as her own son. **22** And Moses was instructed in all the wisdom of the Egyptians, and he was mighty in his words and deeds. **23** "When he was forty years old, it came into his heart to visit his brothers, the children of Israel. **24** And seeing one of them being wronged, he defended the oppressed man and avenged him by striking down the Egyptian. **25** He supposed that his brothers would understand that God was giving them salvation by his hand, but they did not understand. **26** And on the following day he appeared to them as they were quarreling and tried to reconcile them, saying, 'Men, you are brothers. Why do you wrong each other?' **27** But the man who was wronging his neighbor thrust him aside, saying, 'Who made you a ruler and a judge over us? **28** Do you want to kill me as you killed

---

[118] Ibid., 105.

the Egyptian yesterday?' **29** At this retort Moses fled and became an exile in the land of Midian, where he became the father of two sons. **30** "Now when forty years had passed, an angel appeared to him in the wilderness of Mount Sinai, in a flame of fire in a bush. **31** When Moses saw it, he was amazed at the sight, and as he drew near to look, there came the voice of the Lord: **32** 'I am the God of your fathers, the God of Abraham and of Isaac and of Jacob.' And Moses trembled and did not dare to look. **33** Then the Lord said to him, 'Take off the sandals from your feet, for the place where you are standing is holy ground. **34** I have surely seen the affliction of my people who are in Egypt, and have heard their groaning, and I have come down to deliver them. And now come, I will send you to Egypt.' **35** "This Moses, whom they rejected, saying, 'Who made you a ruler and a judge?'—this man God sent as both ruler and redeemer by the hand of the angel who appeared to him in the bush. **36** This man led them out, performing wonders and signs in Egypt and at the Red Sea and in the wilderness for forty years.

Stephen's clinching example was Moses, described in verses 17–36. God met and took care of Moses and his people *outside* the Holy Land. Moses was raised in Egypt (vv. 17–22). He matured in Midian (v. 29). He was commissioned near Mt. Sinai, and God called the area "holy ground" (vv. 30–34). "Holy ground" is wherever God meets his people, and not just inside the borders of Palestine. The greatest miracles of Israel happened in Egypt, at the Red Sea, and in the desert—not in the Promised Land.[119]

It's Not About the Law!

Stephen's basic argument (7:37) is built on Moses' words from Deuteronomy 18:15, when Moses predicted that God would raise up for the Jews "a prophet like me from your own people."

Moses and the Law

Acts 7:37-41 | This is the Moses who said to the Israelites, 'God will raise up for you a prophet like me from your brothers.' **38** This is the one who was in the congregation in the wilderness with the angel who spoke to him at Mount Sinai, and with our fathers. He received living oracles to give to us. **39** Our fathers refused to obey

---

[119] Ibid.

him, but thrust him aside, and in their hearts they turned to Egypt, **40** saying to Aaron, 'Make for us gods who will go before us. As for this Moses who led us out from the land of Egypt, we do not know what has become of him.' **41** And they made a calf in those days, and offered a sacrifice to the idol and were rejoicing in the works of their hands.

The Jews' hope of redemption should never have been the law of Moses. The law of Moses didn't die for them, but Jesus did. There is a Prophet that is infinitely greater than Moses, because he is God and because he as the God-man substituted his life's blood for their sin.

Of course, the Jews in Moses' day rejected both Moses and the law anyway.[120] The people of Jesus' day lost the whole purpose of the law when they rejected Jesus, who kept the law perfectly for them. If they would only believe, his righteousness could be applied to them (2 Cor 5:21).

Stephen's opponents had accused him of speaking against the sacred law of Moses, but the history of Israel revealed that the nation had repeatedly *broken* that Law. God gave the law to his church in the wilderness at Mount Sinai, his living word through the mediation of angels (*cf* Acts 7:53; Gal 3:19). No sooner had the people received the law than they disobeyed it by asking Aaron to make them an idol (Exo 32), and thereby broke the first two of the Ten Commandments (Exo 20:1–6).[121]

When Stephen quoted Amos 5:25–27, he revealed what the Jews had really been doing all those years: in outward form, they were worshiping Yahweh; but in their hearts, they were worshiping foreign gods!

> **Acts 7:42-43** | But God turned away and gave them over to worship the host of heaven, as it is written in the book of the prophets [*Amos 5:25-27*]: "'Did you bring to me slain beasts and sacrifices, during the forty years in the wilderness, O house of Israel? **43** You took up the tent of Moloch and the star of your god Rephan, the images that you made to worship; and I will send you into exile beyond Babylon.'

The form of the question in Acts 7:42 demands a negative reply: "No, you were not offering those sacrifices to the Lord!" In our day of "pluralism" of religions and an emphasis on "toleration," we must

---

[120] Ibid.
[121] Wiersbe, *The Bible Exposition Commentary*, 432.

understand why God hated the pagan religions and instructed Israel to destroy them. To begin with, these religions were unspeakably obscene in their worship of sex and their use of religious prostitutes. Their practices were also brutal, even to the point of offering children as sacrifices to their gods. It was basically demon worship, and it opened the way for all kinds of godless living on the part of the Jews. Had the nation turned from the true God and succumbed to idolatry, it could have meant the end of the godly remnant and the fulfillment of the promise of the Redeemer.[122]

This brings up an important point: idols will eventually make you miserable. Idols are like a delicious cake laced with poison. It tastes so good, but the poison of self-worship and self-focus will afflict your soul with worry: what do people think of me? Your anger or frustration or despair will rise anytime your reputation is tarnished because you care too much of the opinion of others. The poison of self-comfort will have you will eat you up with worry about your health and a million other things as you try to protect your life, which is already in God's hands. Worry and despair will take hold of you as you try to guard your wealth and comfort from money. The problem with idols is they are never, never enough. You look to relationships as an idol, and you become a needy person. Or perhaps you become jaded and give up on people all together. Whichever end of the spectrum, it's poisonous idolatry. Trust in God. Forgive people. Don't look to idols because they will always be tormentors adding to your misery. Replace idols with the worship of the forever satisfying God who made you. Find your identity in Christ, not in other people's expectations or even your own expectations.

God's law was given to the Jews to protect them from the pagan influence around them, and to enable them to enjoy the blessings of the land. It was God's law that made them a holy people, different from the other nations.[123] The law was never meant to take the place of Christ. The law was meant as a grace to guide them to a Person. The law was the means and never the goal. The Jews made the law the goal. Keeping the law was their "chief end." They failed at terribly. When Stephen points out as Paul did to the Galatians that "The law is our schoolmaster that leads us to Christ" (Gal 3:24), they want to kill him.

---

[122] Ibid.
[123] Ibid., 432.

Galatians 3:24, KJV | The law was our schoolmaster to bring us unto Christ, that we might be justified by faith.

The Sanhedrin of Stephen's day had already crucified the one who kept the law perfectly. And they are about to stone Stephen who was a blameless, godly brother. Why? Because the Sanhedrin idolizes the law. Idolatry will make you a terrorist and a tyrant. Mess with the idol and you get punished!

It's Not About the Temple!

Now Stephen turns his attention to the Temple. The Jews thought they were untouchable. They had the Temple. Stephen delineates the folly of building a house for the Creator-God who has all heaven and earth for his dwelling place (vv. 49–50).[124]

Moses, Joshua and the Tabernacle

The Tabernacle is not to be admired. It's the wrapping paper. Look at the very presence of God himself. He is the gift to Israel.

> **Acts 7:44-45a** | "Our fathers had the tent of witness in the wilderness, just as he who spoke to Moses directed him to make it, according to the pattern that he had seen. **45** Our fathers in turn brought it in with Joshua when they dispossessed the nations that God drove out before our fathers.

The Tabernacle and Temple are pictures of our relationship with God. From the Menorah to the Table of Showbread, we see Jesus. The Menorah or lamp stand was a symbol of Jesus who is the light of the world. As we see in Revelation, the lampstand is a beautiful picture of the Spirit of God burning in the churches where Jesus is the head. Remember the table of showbread with twelve loaves. Of course, Jesus called himself the bread of life (Jn 6:48). The altar of incense that was constantly burning day and night represents our prayers. Just as the sweet smells of incense filled the room, so our prayers are sweet to God! Oh, how he loves us to spend time with him in prayer. At the front of the courtyard was the Bronze Altar. This is where animal sacrifices were offered. The alter reminds us that Jesus is, as John the Baptist said, "the lamb of God who takes away the sin of the world" (Jn 1:29).

---

[124] Polhill, *Acts*, 203.

David, Solomon and the Temple

Stephen makes his point. When it comes to the Temple and the Tabernacle, these were nothing more than wrapping paper.

> **Acts 7:45b-50** | So it was until the days of David, [46] who found favor in the sight of God and asked to find a dwelling place for the God of Jacob. [47] But it was Solomon who built a house for him. [48] Yet the Most High does not dwell in houses made by hands, as the prophet says, [49] "'Heaven is my throne, and the earth is my footstool. What kind of house will you build for me, says the Lord, or what is the place of my rest? [50] Did not my hand make all these things?'

This magnificent provision for true worship nevertheless is not to be revered, Stephen implies, for "the Most High does not dwell in houses made by hands" (7:48). God is far too great for that.[125] Stephen was clinging to the God who was made flesh. Jesus reveals the Father for us (Jn 1:18). If you don't come to God through Jesus who the land, the law and the Temple point to, then you cannot come to God. As God the Son, Jesus is the exclusive way to the Father (Jn 14:6).

What does all this have to do with us today? *The land.* It is possible to imagine that since we live in a privileged nation where so much good has been done and so many godly people reared, we will surely inherit God's blessing. *The law.* Sometimes we, like the Jews of old, make a fetish out of God's word. We carry it with us, mark it appropriately, thumb it piously, but fail to let it take root in our hearts. *The temple.* It is easy to suppose that since we go to the place where God has chosen to meet his people, we will receive special blessings. Three times, not necessarily so! It is possible to have all these things and yet be pitifully and utterly damned or saved but defeated and disobedient.[126]

It's About Jesus (Whom They Murdered)

The Sanhedrin didn't get it. They were mainly made up of Sadducees who rejected the supernatural. For sure there were many Pharisees as well who did believe in the supernatural, one of whom was Saul of Tarsus. Though they accepted the supernatural, they rejected Jesus of Nazareth as Messiah. Yet look at Stephen, he does not wilt in the face

---

[125] Baker, *Acts*, 894.
[126] Hughes, *Acts*, 105–106.

of unbelief. He speaks the truth in love. Remember when they looked at him, he had the "face of an angel." He proclaims the gospel to the most important religious body in Israel. What he says is not rudeness but truth. He's loving their souls. He wants them to come out of their unbelief.

> **Acts 7:51-53** | "You stiff-necked people, uncircumcised in heart and ears, you always resist the Holy Spirit. As your fathers did, so do you. **52** Which of the prophets did your fathers not persecute? And they killed those who announced beforehand the coming of the Righteous One, whom you have now betrayed and murdered, **53** you who received the law as delivered by angels and did not keep it."

He holds nothing back, even though it would cost him his life. Stephen says, "The land, the law and the Temple point to Jesus, and you murdered him. In your idolatry you killed what all this pointed to." How sad. They were given the law through angels, but they refused to keep the law they so revere.

BE WILLING TO SUFFER FOR CHRIST (7:54-60)

The Sanhedrin had turned these wonderful pictures of Christ into idols. And we are about to see that idolatry turns a person into a tyrant. The Jews who crucified Jesus are now wanting more blood: Stephen's blood to be exact.

Everyone who loves Jesus will suffer for him in this world. Stephen put aside their love for the land, the law, and the Temple because they loved these gifts of God that pointed to Christ more than they loved God. They loved God's gifts so much that when the true gift came, they crucified him.

Suffer with Victory

Incredibly, Steven was not at all worried about the angry mob of the Sanhedrim preparing to execute him. He was too busy gazing at the victorious Christ.

> **Acts 7:54-56** | Now when they heard these things they were enraged, and they ground their teeth at him. **55** But he, full of the Holy Spirit, gazed into heaven and saw the glory of God, and Jesus standing at the right hand of God. **56** And he said, "Behold, I

see the heavens opened, and the Son of Man standing at the right hand of God."

"There he is," Stephen must have thought, "My prophet, priest and king! The Son of Man." He's not sitting though; he is standing at the right hand of God. How easy it is for us to let fear take hold of us, and when that happens, we cannot see Jesus. But Stephen, filled with faith, got to see Jesus, and he wasn't sitting on his throne, but standing, cheering Stephen on from heaven. In that moment, I think Stephen's face was still glowing like an angel, because even though the men began shouting and stopping their ears at Stephen's words, he kept gazing into heaven, amazed at the sight of Jesus welcoming him.

Suffer with Trust

In that moment, I think Stephen's face was still glowing like an angel, because even though the men began shouting and stopping their ears at Stephen's words, he kept gazing into heaven, amazed at the sight of Jesus welcoming him.

> **Acts 7:57-58** | But they cried out with a loud voice and stopped their ears and rushed together at him. **58** Then they cast him out of the city and stoned him. And the witnesses laid down their garments at the feet of a young man named Saul.

These respected, dignified aristocrats descended on young, innocent Stephen and executed him! Their action was illegal, brutal, immoral, but they did not care. They probably took him outside the city where the witnesses repeated their charges, threw him down an embankment (it was the witnesses' privilege to do so), and cast great stones on him, followed by more stones from the crowd.[127] Frederick Buechner describes it this way:

> Stoning somebody to death, even somebody as young and healthy as Stephen, is not easy. You do not get the job done with the first few rocks and broken bottles, and even after you get the man down, it is a long, hot business. To prepare themselves for the work-out, they stripped to the waist and got somebody to keep an eye on their things till they were through. The man they got was a fire-breathing young

---

[127] Hughes, *Acts*, 106–107.

arch-conservative Jew named Saul, who was there because he thoroughly approved of what they were doing.[128]

There is Saul of Tarsus who would write thirteen books in our New Testament. Even though Stephen's life was being taken away from him, God was filling Stephen's Greek-speaking, Hellenistic shoes with the greatest persecutor of Christians among the Jews. No one could have known that the chief instigator of hate toward the Christians would became their greatest friend and proponent. He would soon become the famed Apostle to the Gentiles.

Suffer with Compassion

Finally, we have another way to suffer. We need to suffer with compassion. We cannot hold bitterness against those who persecute us. Look at Stephen's amazing example.

> **Acts 7:59-60** | And as they were stoning Stephen, he called out, "Lord Jesus, receive my spirit." **60** And falling to his knees he cried out with a loud voice, "Lord, do not hold this sin against them." And when he had said this, he fell asleep.

Like Jesus, he prayed for his executioners. This was an overflow of grace—God's unmerited, unconditional favor.[129] Jesus who crushed the serpent's head at the cross, is now going to crush the serpent's plans in a different way. He's going to use the prayer of Stephen, which is answered in the next chapter. Do you think God is stopped by the most devious plans of men? Think again! He can take your greatest failures and turn them into great gains for the kingdom of God. All we have to do is look beyond the suffering and persecution.

Conclusion

Saul of Tarsus was so offended by Stephen's message that he gathered a crowd to stone him, and as a member of the Sanhedrin, gave his approval for executing him. Was Stephen's death worth it? The Apostle Paul would say so because it was the memory of Stephen that tormented him and refused to let go.

---

[128] Frederick Buechner, *Peculiar Treasures* (San Francisco: Harper & Row, 1979), 162.

[129] Hughes, *Acts,* 106–107.

1 Corinthians 13:9 | For I am the least of the apostles, unworthy to be called an apostle, because I persecuted the church of God.

Galatians 1:13 | For you have heard of my former life in Judaism, how I persecuted the church of God violently and tried to destroy it.

Philippians 3:4-6 | If anyone else thinks he has reason for confidence in the flesh, I have more: ⁵ circumcised on the eighth day, of the people of Israel, of the tribe of Benjamin, a Hebrew of Hebrews; as to the law, a Pharisee; ⁶ as to zeal, a persecutor of the church.

1 Timothy 1:13 | Though formerly I was a blasphemer, persecutor, and insolent opponent. But I received mercy because I had acted ignorantly in unbelief.

1 Timothy 1:15 | The saying is trustworthy and deserving of full acceptance, that Christ Jesus came into the world to save sinners, of whom I am the foremost.

Conclusion

Stephen's death kept goading the persecutor Saul, nudging him toward the throne of grace.[130] Paul would be won by that angel-faced deacon. Paul would carry on the work that Stephen started. Stephen and Paul had something in common: they were both Hellenized Jews. They were Greek speaking Jews who had adapted to the Greek culture. And now Saul (his Jewish name) would find his Hellenized name, Paul, to be very helpful. It would be Paul's desire to see all men everywhere repent and find hope in Jesus.

That's my hope for you today. Perhaps you are zealous about religion and doctrine, like Saul of Tarsus, but you don't know the Lord. You are zealous about the wrapping paper, but you haven't yet received the gift. Come home and receive the welcome of Jesus. He loves you. Come you weak who are burdened down by the law and find the one who kept the law for you. He alone satisfies. Come home today!

---

[130] Hughes, 108.

13 | ACTS 8:1-4
INTRODUCING SAUL OF TARSUS

Saul was ravaging the church, and entering house after house, he dragged off men and women and committed them to prison.

ACTS 8:3

God has an amazing way of choosing his servants. We find in this chapter a zealous Pharisee named Saul of Tarsus, one of the most prominent members of the Sanhedrin, violently persecuting the church of Jesus Christ. In Acts 9, this same persecutor is converted on the Damascus Road and is turned apostle. He becomes one of the great giants of the faith to this very day. Isn't God good? Could you have imagined that he would have chosen you? God is so gracious! He doesn't choose many wise, and if he does, he has to humble them to the dust, which he does with Saul of Tarsus (*cf* 1 Cor 1:26-31).

The stoning of Stephen was the signal for a campaign of persecution against the church in Jerusalem, in which somehow the apostles seem to have enjoyed immunity for the most part. The public respected pious men who were devoted to the Temple services, and they evidently distinguished them from people like Stephen who denounced the Temple. Reading between the lines, we may infer that the Hellenists (to whom Stephen belonged) were the main targets of attack. In the accounts of the dispersal of believers from Jerusalem it is only Hellenists who are mentioned (Philip in verse 5 and others unnamed in Acts 11:19).[131]

At the very center of the persecution in Jerusalem, is this key figure, Saul of Tarsus. Who is the greatest baseball player that ever lived? Who is the best running back in the NFL? People argue the answers to such questions endlessly. We are always arguing about who is the best. The answer is clear, however, when we ask the identity of the greatest theologian who has ever lived—the Apostle Paul. He was also the greatest missionary and evangelist and pastor. What God wrought in and through the life of that man whom he gifted so graciously, and who performed so valiantly and gallantly on behalf of the gospel, staggers the imagination.[132] Much of the rest of Acts is about Saul of Tarsus, who we know by his Greek name, Paul. Before he was an apostle, he was the rising star of Israel, a rabbi who was trained under Gamaliel. His zeal was misguided. He believed it was God's will to eradicate Christianity from the earth. So he planned and approved of the execution of Stephen.

I want us to consider the key thought for these verses, and it is this: Whatever difficult circumstances you are in, embrace them as your mission field, and lift up the name of Jesus! You may find yourself with some horrible illness, and you are seeing a lot of doctors and nurses. I dare say that your service to them in preaching Christ to them is far greater than their earthly service to you in healing your body. Wherever you are. Whatever you are doing, remember your mission: lift up the name of Jesus. The goal cannot be to change your circumstances. The goal is that every person on earth will be touched by Jesus through you and all God's people.

PAUL THE PERSECUTOR (8:1A)

Acts 8:1a | And Saul approved of his execution.

Saul looked with approval on the murder of Stephen. He did not see it as murder. Religion blinded his eyes. "I obtained mercy," he wrote in later years, "because I did it ignorantly," (1 Tim 1:13). Saul was too

---

[131] F. F. Bruce, *Acts: Bible Study Commentary* (Nashville, TN; Bath, England: Kingsley Books, 2017), Ac 8:1b–8.
[132] Sproul, *Acts*, 137.

refined to stand there throwing stones, but not too refined to hold the coats of those who did.[133]

These verses serve as a transition from one major section of Acts to another as the story of Stephen ends, launching the spread of the gospel according to Jesus' plan in 1:8. They also further introduce Saul, who will become the main character for much of the rest of Acts.

Saul's Hatred

Saul goes from looking after coats at Stephen's murder to "ravaging the church," forcing his way into Christian homes and taking people off to prison (8:3; *cf* 9:13). In our day we would say he was "radicalized": he hated the followers of Jesus and wanted to see the movement wiped out. As an apostle, Paul himself never forgot his past, mentioning it in his speeches in Acts and in his letters (22:4–5; 26:10; 1 Cor 15:9; Gal 1:13, 23; Phil 3:6; 1 Tim 1:13). It is important not to conceive of Paul as faithful according to the old covenant. Before his conversion, Paul was *not a faithful Jew*. One cannot be faithful while rejecting the fulfillment of God's promise to Abraham. Yet he sincerely thought he was faithful.

However, Paul does highlight the unexpected nature of God's way of carrying out his plan for the world. From choosing an idol worshiper (Abraham) in Ur for the fulfillment of his ultimate promises and an Egyptian-educated man in Pharaoh's court to save Israel from slavery (Moses), to raising up a boy who kills a giant with a slingshot and becomes king (David)—not to mention coming as a carpenter from Nazareth who tells people the greatest thing they can become is a servant and who dies, cursed, on a cross—no one but God would write this script.[134] So, let me introduce to you the most unlikely of converts, Saul of Tarsus.

Saul's History

Born the same year as Jesus. Paul was born, according to tradition, in the same year that Jesus was born.

Born of the tribe of Benjamin. He was born of the Tribe of Benjamin in Asia Minor, in the city of Tarsus. He describes himself as a

---

[133] J. Phillips, *Exploring Acts,* Ac 8:1a.
[134] James M. Hamilton Jr. and Brian J. Vickers, *John–Acts*, ed. Iain M. Duguid, James M. Hamilton Jr., and Jay Sklar, vol. IX, ESV Expository Commentary (Wheaton, IL: Crossway, 2019), 406.

"Hebrew of the Hebrews" (*cf* 2 Cor 11:22; Phil 3:5) and the "son of a Pharisee" (Acts 23:6).

His Hebrew and Greek names. In Jewish circles he was known by his name's sake, the most famous Benjaminite of Israel: King Saul, so he was called Saul among his family and Jewish friends. Roman citizenship meant that the apostle also had a full Latin name: Paulus, which is the name he used in Gentile circles.[135]

A Roman citizen. His father was a Roman citizen, and it seems he must have been a well-respected merchant, as Tarsus is a merchant city on a major trade route. The fact that Saul's father was a Roman citizen meant Saul was born a free man, and he inherited that citizenship from his father.

His languages. Though Paul from infancy could speak Greek, the common language of the Roman Empire, he of course spoke Aramaic at home, read the Hebrew Scriptures, and would have had a working knowledge of Latin. The school attached to the Tarsus synagogue taught nothing but the Hebrew text of the sacred Law. Each boy repeated its phrases in chorus after the hazzan, or synagogue keeper, until vowels, accent, and rhythm were precisely correct. Paul learned to write the Hebrew characters accurately on papyrus, thus gradually forming his own rolls of the Scriptures.[136]

Tarsus, a famous trade city. It's helpful that Saul is from the trade city of Tarsus. Tarsus was at the extreme southeastern tip of Asia Minor, close to Antioch, just a little bit north of Jerusalem. Tarsus was on the trade routes, where all merchandise moved from Europe and Asia south through the Middle East, down into Africa, and back. In antiquity Tarsus was one of the wealthiest cities of that region. Paul would have had such a great exposure to the Gentile world that would later melt his heart with compassion, where he could say:

> 1 Timothy 2:4 | God desires all people to be saved and to come to the knowledge of the truth.

Tarsus University. Saul was further exposed to the highest level of education in the city where he lived. *Tarsus University* was the largest university in the world at that time, bigger than the universities in

---

[135] John Pollock, *The Apostle: The Life of Paul* (John Pollock Series) (Colorado Springs, CO: David C Cook, 2012), 17.

[136] Pollock, *The Apostle,* 18.

Athens and Alexandria.¹³⁷ Tarsus was a cosmopolitan city, a city in which merchants, scholars, intellectuals, and travelers from all over the world mingled.¹³⁸

Taught by Rabbi Gamaliel. At the age of thirteen, because of the prowess and brilliance that he had already displayed, he would have been sent away from Tarsus to Jerusalem to go to a kind of seminary, as it were, to study under the tutorship of the leading theologian in the world of that time, Gamaliel. (We were introduced to Gamaliel in Acts 5; *cf* 22:3). Saul studied under Gamaliel for seven years and received the equivalent of two PhDs in theology. It has been said that by the age of twenty-one Saul of Tarsus was the most educated Jew in Palestine. He had mastered the Old Testament and all the rabbinic interpretations of it, and his star had risen in meteoric fashion.¹³⁹ He may have later possibly for a time studied at the University of Tarsus as well. Between the cosmopolitan education that he received in Tarsus and the elite religious education he received "at the feet of Gamaliel," Saul of Tarsus was a brilliant mind and a religious renaissance man, if you will. Listen to his testimony:

> *Acts 22:3* | I am a Jew, born in Tarsus in Cilicia, but brought up in this city [Jerusalem], educated at the feet of Gamaliel according to the strict manner of the law of our fathers, being zealous for God as all of you are this day.

Saul the tentmaker. The young Saul grew up in that environment. Initially he followed a commonplace tradition of the time, which was learning a trade through apprenticeship. One of the most lucrative trades in that day and region was tentmaking. As a young lad, Saul would have learned the trade of making tents, which served him well throughout his life.

Member of the Sanhedrin. By the age of 30, Saul of Tarsus was a prominent member of the Sanhedrin. The Sanhedrin was the Jewish senate based on the seventy elders who aided Moses (Num 11:16-17). There were seventy members plus the high priest.

Possible marriage. Paul may have at one time been married. When listing the rights of an apostle and arguing on behalf of himself

---

¹³⁷ Howard Clark Kee & Franklin W. Young. *Understanding The New Testament* (Englewood Cliffs, New Jersey: Prentice Hall, Inc. 1958), 208.
¹³⁸ Sproul, *Acts*, 138.
¹³⁹ Ibid.

and Barnabas, he said, "Don't we have the right to take a believing wife along with us, as do the other apostles and the Lord's brothers and Cephas?" (1 Cor 9:5). In interpreting this statement, some scholars say Paul's question, taken with his statement that he was unmarried, suggests he was a widower who had at least occasionally traveled with his wife before she died.

As a member of the Sanhedrin and a prominent rabbi and Pharisee, marriage was strongly encouraged. It would have been unheard of to be an unmarried rabbi. It seems, looking at the wording of 1 Corinthians 7, that Paul was most likely a widower. It seems he was likely married for a short time but sometime before his conversion, he became a widower. Sometime after his conversion he was given the gift of celibacy ("a genuine gift of freedom from sexual need").[140] Paul desires for everyone with this gift to use it as he has for the sake of the kingdom.

Directed Stephen's execution. As a revered rabbi, Paul would have been well known in and around the academic circles of Jerusalem by the time of the stoning of Stephen, where we find him present, directing the people who are executing the church's first martyr.

> **Acts 7:58** | They cast him out of the city and stoned him. And the witnesses laid down their clothes at the feet of a young man named Saul.

Stephen's execution is the first thing for which Paul is known in biblical history. The Bible does not tell us why the witnesses laid their clothes at the feet of Saul, but it is not hard to guess. Not only was his scholarship known to everyone in the crowd, but his profound hostility to Christianity was also well known. No one present would have doubted that Saul, at very least, would acquiesce to the act.[141] Two verses later Luke tells us:

> **Acts 8:1a** | And Saul approved of his execution.

What does that tell us? It tells us that our God is a merciful God.

---

[140] Gordon D. Fee. *The First Epistle to the Corinthians* (The New International Commentary on the New Testament) (Grand Rapids, MI: Wm. B. Eerdmans Publishing Co., 1987), 288.

[141] Sproul, *Acts*, 139.

Saul's Hope

With all of Saul's hardness and hatred and self-righteous pride, we might be tempted to think Saul and people like him are without home. We would be wrong. God is not like us. He sees all of us. He knows our sins. We may try to weigh the character of certain people. But God chooses the most unworthy people. None of us would have chosen Saul of Tarsus to be the premier apostle. And that's where God differs from us. He is infinitely more merciful than any one of us. Paul would later testify to this infinite mercy he received from God.

> *1 Timothy 1:12-17* | I thank him who has given me strength, Christ Jesus our Lord, because he judged me faithful, appointing me to his service, [13] though formerly I was a blasphemer, persecutor, and insolent opponent. But I received mercy because I had acted ignorantly in unbelief, [14] and the grace of our Lord overflowed for me with the faith and love that are in Christ Jesus. [15] The saying is trustworthy and deserving of full acceptance, that Christ Jesus came into the world to save sinners, of whom I am the foremost. [16] But I received mercy for this reason, that in me, as the foremost, Jesus Christ might display his perfect patience as an example to those who were to believe in him for eternal life. [17] To the King of the ages, immortal, invisible, the only God, be honor and glory forever and ever. Amen.

All of Saul's brilliance was being used against the church, specifically Stephen. This zealous Pharisee Saul was there approving of Stephen's execution. But God is able to radically transform the heart. And he's about to do that for Saul, but not before he continues his rampage against the church.

THE PERSECUTION (8:1B-3)

> **Acts 8:1b-3** | …And there arose on that day a great persecution against the church in Jerusalem, and they were all scattered throughout the regions of Judea and Samaria, except the apostles. [2] Devout men buried Stephen and made great lamentation over him. [3] But Saul was ravaging the church, and entering house after house, he dragged off men and women and committed them to prison.

The Nature of the Persecution

> **Acts 8:1b** | …And there arose on that day a great persecution…

It was a fierce persecution. It was a great, or fierce persecution laser focused against followers of Jesus Christ. Saul's zeal for the Law was displayed most vividly in his persecution of the church (Gal 1:13–14; Phil 3:6). He really thought that persecuting the believers was one way of serving God, so he did it with a clear conscience (2 Tim 1:3). He obeyed the light that he had and, when God gave him more light, he obeyed that and became a Christian!

The Nearness of the Persecution

Acts 8:1c | ... a great persecution against the church in Jerusalem, and they were all scattered throughout the regions of Judea and Samaria, except the apostles.

The persecution was in Jerusalem where most of the believers were. It was near. They had to leave their homes. They were scattered, running for their lives. There are different words for "scattered" in Greek. One means dispersed so that the item is gone from that point on, like scattering a person's ashes on the ocean's waves. That is not the word used here in verses 1 and 4. The word used here means scattered in order to be planted. When God scatters his people, it brings great hardship, but he does it for a purpose. Difficulty and trials all fit into God's perfect kingdom plan for his people. We may feel scattered, but God is planting his people to bring the lost to Christ. Is that true of you? Wherever you find yourself—whether scattered by work or family or education or some other means—have you considered yourself planted in that place? Have you put down roots and born fruit for Jesus Christ? That is what these early Christians did.[142]

Acts 8:1d | ... all scattered throughout the regions of Judea and Samaria, except the apostles.

The apostles stayed in Jerusalem. It seems that the Hellenized believers were scattered, but the Hebrew believers were left alone. That the Jerusalem church continued to exist is clear from Acts 9:26; 11:2, 22; 15:4; and 21:17. What it does mean is that the church was broken up, and many of its members forced to flee.[143] From this time onward the Jerusalem church appears to have consisted almost entirely of

---

[142] Boice, *Exposition of Acts*, 133.
[143] MacArthur. *Acts*, 230–231.

"Hebrews."[144] It was only natural that the Hellenists of which Stephen was likely one would bear the brunt of the persecution. The apostles saw it as their duty to remain and not abandon their posts as shepherds and protectors of those who remained in Jerusalem.[145] The persecution was so near, and the church was broken in pieces, but remember that Christ's church cannot be ultimately broken. He scatters us to plant us. We must always remember the words of our Lord:

> *Matthew 16:18* | I will build my church, and the gates of hell shall not prevail against it.

The Noise of the Persecution

> **Acts 8:2** | Devout men buried Stephen and made great lamentation over him.

The devout men here, may not even be referring to believers, but-people from Stephen's synagogue. So, proper funeral honors are given Stephen. It's interesting that according to the oral law, the Mishnah, you were not allowed to mourn a person who was executed (Mishnah Sanhedrin 6.6). Here we see the love of believers as well as perhaps the honor from devout men who may not have known the Lord.[146] They protested the death of Stephen. This was not right! Saul didn't care. He thought he was doing a service for God. Jesus said this would happen.

> *John 16:2* | They will put you out of the synagogues. Indeed, the hour is coming when whoever kills you will think he is offering service to God.

The Network of Persecution

Saul thought he was serving God. He knew how to exterminate the Christians. He was very connected. He went everywhere driving out the Christians. He was ruthless and showed no mercy. He would later say that "as to zeal," he was "a persecutor of the church" (Phil 3:6). We see this recorded in Acts 8:3.

---

[144] Bruce. *The Book of the Acts*, 174
[145] Thomas, *Acts*, 218.
[146] Faw, *Acts*, 102.

Acts 8:3 | But Saul was ravaging the church, and entering house after house, he dragged off men and women and committed them to prison.

In what ways did Saul persecute the church? He "was ravaging the church," and the verb here describes a wild animal mangling its prey. The expression is used of the ravages of a wild boar. He had his hit list. He entered every house where a believer lived. There was hardly a home where his cruelty was not felt. The prisons overflowed.[147] The stoning of Stephen, which Saul approved, shows the lengths to which he would go to achieve his purpose. He persecuted Christians, both men and women, "unto the death." Paul testifies:

Acts 22:4 | I persecuted this Way to the death, binding and delivering to prison both men and women.

He not only chased them down in houses, but he went to their places of worship, in the synagogues.

Acts 22:19 | In one synagogue after another I imprisoned and beat those who believed in you.

He had the believers imprisoned and beaten. Paul testified to King Agrippa.

Acts 26:9-11 | I myself was convinced that I ought to do many things in opposing the name of Jesus of Nazareth. [10] And I did so in Jerusalem. I not only locked up many of the saints in prison after receiving authority from the chief priests, but when they were put to death I cast my vote against them. [11] And I punished them often in all the synagogues and tried to make them blaspheme, and in raging fury against them I persecuted them even to foreign cities.

If they renounced their faith in Jesus Christ ("compelling them to blaspheme"—Acts 26:11), they were set free; if they did not recant, they could be killed.[148]

After Stephen's death, the Jewish authorities, with Paul as their chief agent, embarked on systematic persecution of Jesus' followers.[149]

The persecution was such that it was both civil and religious. Church and state in Israel were united. We saw this in the death of

---

[147] J. Phillips. *Acts*, Ac 8:3.
[148] Wiersbe, *The Bible Exposition Commentary*, 434.
[149] Pollock, *The Apostle*, 28.

Christ. Jewish and Roman authorities put him to death. Saul made sure he used all his authority to "ravage" the people of God.

It's interesting that Saul would drag Christians away and commit them to prison. Remember the same fate would befall Saul, later in life, as an apostle, Paul would write several of the New Testament letters from prison.

The Normalcy of Persecution

Every Christian who lives godly is going to suffer persecution.

> *2 Timothy 3:12* | Yea, and all that will live godly in Christ Jesus shall suffer persecution.

The interesting thing in Acts is that it is clear that when one of God's recruits goes down, God raises another up. And here we find that Stephen's replacement is Saul of Tarsus. Saul has a similar upbringing as Stephen, but he's even more brilliant. He will suffer so much more than what he inflicted on the church. Remember the words that the Lord gave to Ananias.

> *Acts 9:15-16* | But the Lord said to him, "Go, for he is a chosen instrument of mine to carry my name before the Gentiles and kings and the children of Israel. ¹⁶ For I will show him how much he must suffer for the sake of my name."

GOD'S PLAN (8:4)

> **Acts 8:4** | Now those who were scattered went about preaching the word.

A Plan for the World

God loves the world and wants to see people everywhere saved. And you are part of that. If you don't obey the great commission and go, God will scatter his church so that we do bring the gospel to every nation and every people group.

Sometimes God brings us what we might see as bad or difficult circumstances. It looks like a wall or a pit to us. But whenever we think there is a wall in front of us, God makes a door. God always turns our stumbling blocks into stepping-stones.

We must come to the realization as God's dearly loved children, that changing our circumstances can sometimes be a way of fighting against God. God has you right where he wants you to complete his perfect plan. God wants us to bring the riches of Christ to the whole world. That plan is spoken of in many places, for instance in Ephesians.

> *Ephesians 3:8-9* | To preach to the Gentiles the unsearchable riches of Christ, [9] and to bring to light for everyone what is the plan of the mystery hidden for ages in God.

Jesus made this plan clear in Acts 1.

> *Acts 1:8* | You will receive power when the Holy Spirit has come upon you, and you will be my witnesses in Jerusalem and in all Judea and Samaria, and to the end of the earth.

Go! Jesus says. But sometimes we get distracted. We don't want to go. We like our comfort zone. Jesus will make sure we go. Whether it be through normal circumstance or through devastating circumstances, Jesus will put us where we need to be to lift up his name and bring people into his kingdom.

A Plan for the Word

> **Acts 8:4** | Now those who were scattered went about preaching the word.

Wherever these dear disciples went, they preached the word. They didn't hold on too tightly to earthly things. They refused to get distracted. They preached Jesus to everyone they saw.

You can see God's plan to display the glory of Jesus. God puts us in places that we never could have imagined being. Some of you would never choose Chicagoland to live, but God has placed you here.

God wants the word of God to seep out of you. Are you in the word "day and night" (Psa 1:1) loving the God of the word as you meditate on the word of God? Are you meeting with God and his Spirit in his word? Are you saturated in the word? When you get poked or discouraged or find yourself in a trial, are you going to the word? Are you around people who love the word?

Are you preaching the word with humility and brokenness wherever you are? Are you lifting up the name of Jesus in your home? If you are married, are you lifting up the name of Jesus to your spouse? If you have children, are you displaying the glory of Jesus to your kids? Are you ready to preach Christ and give an answer for the hope that is in you in your workplace? Are you praying right now for those in your life who are lost? Name them in your mind right now. Pray for them right now.

Are you willing to be scattered? Are you willing to go if God calls you? We are called to the ends of the earth! Some of you would much rather be somewhere other than Chicago. Perhaps God has scattered you here. Maybe I should be asking, are you willing to stay in this rebellious city of Chicago? Are you willing to stay and preach and lift up the name of Jesus?

Conclusion

As you consider the persecution that came through Saul of Tarsus, remember, he becomes the Apostle Paul. Are there people in your life, and you just cannot imagine them as believers? I pray this study is helping you to put away the idea that anyone is beyond saving. God can bring the hardest sinner or the most self-righteous Pharisee to himself. Just look at your own conversion if you doubt! God is able to save to the uttermost.

Perhaps you yourself find yourself beyond saving. I remember when my twin sister came to the Lord at age 25, she was in a tiny Reformed Baptist church in the bayou of Louisiana. There weren't more than thirty people there. She heard a clear gospel message, and there was a little twelve-year-old girl sitting next to her, the pastor's daughter. My sister said to the little girl, "I'm too great a sinner for Jesus to save me." The little girl said, "No, that's just who Jesus saves. He came to save sinners." My sister came to know Jesus that day. What a radical change occurred because of her simple faith in the infinite saving power of Jesus. Today my dear sister is a pastor's wife near New Orleans. Truly, no one is beyond saving!

Come to Christ today. You don't have to have perfect faith. Jesus said to come with the faith of a mustard seed. It's not about your faith, it's about Jesus' faithfulness. Come to Jesus today, and he will save you to the uttermost! Amen and amen!

14 | ACTS 8:5-25
GREAT COMMISSION CHRISTIANS

> *Philip went down to the city of Samaria and proclaimed to them the Christ. And crowds with one accord paid attention to what was being said by Philip when they heard him and saw the signs that he did.*
> ACTS 8:5-6

All growing Christians want to bear fruit for Jesus. We want to see people embrace Jesus and follow him faithfully. Discipleship is not just learning to walk with Christ, it is to introduce others to him. Jesus told us to go and evangelize all nations. Are you a great commission Christian? Do you have a heart for the lost? From what we can tell from this passage, bearing the fruit of souls and conversions is not as hard as people might make it. When the Spirit of God is moving, he can do in five seconds what people cannot do in five years of all the best planning. Jesus said:

> John 15:5 | I am the vine; you are the branches. Whoever abides in me and I in him, he it is that bears much fruit, for apart from me you can do nothing.

Remember Jesus' command was that the gospel was to spread to Judea and Samaria, and then to the uttermost parts of the world. Jesus' last words before he ascended to heaven were clear.

> *Acts 1:8* | You will receive power when the Holy Spirit has come upon you, and you will be my witnesses in Jerusalem and in all Judea and Samaria, and to the end of the earth.

We see this incredible fruit in Acts chapter 8 with the expansion of the gospel to Samaria. For years the Jewish people hated the Samaritans. They felt they were lower than the dogs, even lower than the Gentiles. There was a real prejudice and even racism. But the gospel changes that. The gospel brings us together as one body and one forever family. God wants his family to be from every tribe, family, and nation.

Remember Jesus' command to go into all the world and preach the gospel first to Judea and Samaria and to the farthest reaches of the world. Here we witness the gospel's power expanding to a new people group. The main point we learn is that if you have God's heart, you will tell the lost of Jesus. We see here that the gospel takes us out of our comfort zone, since God doesn't just want us to reach people who look like us. He wants us to reach people of every tribe, culture, and nation. This study is not a guilt trip. Evangelism ought not to be done because your arm is being twisted. Instead, evangelism is the love letter we send to the world when we realize we ourselves have been forgiven of so much. We want to have the longing heart of God for people to be saved. God did more than say, "I love you." He sent his only Son to die for the sins of an unworthy world.

When I came to know Christ, I thought, "If this is true, why hasn't someone told me this before?" Of course, many had told me, but I didn't have ears to hear at the time. The point is, now that I knew, I wanted every single person in the world to know of God's love. This was Philip's motive. A deep desire to evangelize is a major evidence of the Spirit's good work in you, and that you are a Christian. When God's love in Christ truly gets ahold of us, like Philip, we want to preach the gospel to the lost. From what we can tell from this passage, it's not as hard as people might make it. When the Spirit of God is moving, he can do in five seconds what people cannot do in five years of all the best planning.

We see this in Acts chapter 8 with the expansion of the gospel to Samaria. Remember Jesus' command to go into all the world and preach the gospel first to Judea and Samaria and to the farthest reaches of the world. Here we witness the gospel's power expanding to a new people group when Philip and others are willing to leave their comfort zone.

WE LEAVE OUR COMFORT ZONE (8:5-8)

Acts 8:5 | Philip went down to the city of Samaria and proclaimed to them the Christ.

Philip went down to Samaria to preach. "Down" doesn't refer to going south, because Samaria is north—it refers to going downhill. Remember that Jerusalem is built upon Mount Moriah, the high point in the area. Everyone who goes to Jerusalem, goes "up" to Jerusalem. When you leave Jerusalem, no matter where you go, you are going "down."

So Philip when down from Jerusalem north to Samaria. Remember Philip is one of the seven deacon prototypes. One preacher, Stephen, had already been executed by Saul of Tarsus. Philip continued his ministry despite the intense persecution going on. As we think about Philip, ask yourself, "Am I an evangelist?" Not all have the gift of evangelism, but all have the command to evangelize. Jesus said, "Go therefore and make disciples of all nations" (Mt 28:19a). Are you bearing fruit through evangelism? You ought to preach the gospel to every person since God promises to bless it and bring a harvest of souls (Isa 55:11; Mk 16:15). We see this in Philip's example.

The Gospel Opens New Areas

We read that Philip goes to the Samaritans. This was a despised group. It was a hated group. But remember the gospel brings the walls of hostility down (Eph 2:14). Philip was willing to venture to Samaria to reach a new people group. Normally if a Samaritan wanted to follow the Lord, they would have to leave their culture and become Jewish. Philip, obeying the Lord's command to break down cultural barriers and redeem the culture for Christ, brings the gospel to those who were once formerly despised in Israel: the Samaritans.

Acts 8:5 | Philip went down to the city of Samaria and proclaimed to them the Christ.

In Judea tens of thousands were being saved, but there was also a great persecution taking place. Philip, led by the Spirit, goes to

Samaria to preach. Samaria was different than Judea. There was a long-standing animosity between Jews and Samaritans. However, that did not deter Philip, one of Stephen's colleagues on the board of appointed alms givers (Acts 6:5), from going to "a city of Samaria" (8:5) and preaching the gospel there. Which city it was is not stated; perhaps it was Gitta, which Justin Martyr (himself a native of Samaria) tells us was the home of Simon Magus (8:9). It would be interesting if the city were proved to be in the vicinity of Sychar where Jesus had met the woman at the well. That Philip's preaching found such joyful acceptance would be easy to understand if he found himself among the people with whom Jesus had once spent two days (Jn 4:40). In that case, others had labored (notably the Lord himself) and Philip was now entering into their labors and reaping where they had sown (Jn 4:38).[150]

The Gospel Brings New Attention

Philip's preaching brought a new interest. No longer was it the droning and speculation of the teachers. Here was a kind of preaching that brought rapt attention when they heard Philip.

> **Acts 8:6a** | And the crowds with one accord paid attention to what was being said by Philip, when they heard him...

Philip's message was one of hope and forgiveness of sin through Jesus Christ. Philip's message was the same as Stephen's before and Paul after him. The law never delivered anyone. The law points us to Jesus. Gospel preaching encourages Christians. We hear that Jesus paid it all. The same way we are saved is the same way we are sanctified. Many Christians are bored with moralistic preaching. "Do better. Work harder." That's not the Christian message. Christ says, "Come to me and I will give you rest" (Mt 11:28). Rest in Christ. Stop your works. Just experience his love, and you will gladly work for him. "Whoever is forgiven much, loves much" (Lk 7:47). When you experience the gospel of the majestic God of heaven coming down to rescue lowly, wretched sinners like us, suddenly the love of God gets ahold of you and your heart is alive with joy. This is the draw of the gospel. People pay attention to a gospel that is actually good news. "Do better" is not good news. It's actually devastating and despairing. There's no end to "doing

---

[150] Bruce. *The Book of the Acts*, Ac 8:1b–8.

better." The difference between the gospel and every other religion is six letters. Religion says, DO. Christ says DONE. Christ has done it all! It is finished. Rest in the finished work of Christ. Receive his love and watch the love of God swell in your heart. That gets people's attention.

The Gospel Brings New Authentication

It wasn't just the word of God that was proclaimed. There was a credibility that was apparent by the signs and wonders. People's lives were dramatically changed. There was a new credibility.

> **Acts 8:6b-7** | They ...saw the signs that he did. ⁷ For unclean spirits, crying out with a loud voice, came out of many who had them, and many who were paralyzed or lame were healed.

As the gospel is preached, lives will be radically changed. Here Philip was casting out demons, and they were crying out in a loud voice. Demons often cried out when they were cast out of an individual (*cf* Mk 1:23, 26; 3:11; 5:7; Lk 4:33, 41), perhaps in rage and protest.[151] Paralyzed people and people who had deformed limbs were healed. It would be like a crippled person getting out of his wheelchair. Just imagine!

Sometimes God does this through healings. We have seen this in our congregation. One brother not too many years ago was given two weeks to live. We prayed for healing. He needed a liver transplant, or he was going to die. Suddenly we found he had moved up to the top of the list and a liver came in. He's walking around like Lazarus today. We've heard of visions and dreams where lost people were introduced to Jesus, were pointed to a church where they came to hear the gospel and be saved. We know that God does miracles today, but we see them most where the word of God and the gospel are being authenticated. During the times of the apostles, there was a great authentication with the word through signs and miracles.

> *Hebrews 2:3-4* | How shall we escape if we neglect such a great salvation? It was declared at first by the Lord, and it was attested to us by those who heard, ⁴ while God also bore witness by signs and wonders and various miracles and by gifts of the Holy Spirit distributed according to his will.

Remember though that the sure word of prophecy we have in the word of God is infinitely greater than any miracle.

---

[151] MacArthur, *Acts*, 234.

2 Peter 1:18-19, KJV | This voice which came from heaven we heard, when we were with him in the holy mount. ¹⁹ We have also a more sure word of prophecy; whereunto ye do well that ye take heed.

One thing we can agree on is that the greatest miracle of all is the transformation of lives by the gospel and the joy that comes as a result.

The Gospel Brings New Animation

When a person comes to know Jesus, there is joy. That's why a Christian doesn't have to change his circumstances. Knowing Jesus replaces all other ambitions. That's where true and meaningful joy comes from. This happened with the preaching of the gospel in Samaria.

Acts 8:8 | So there was much joy in that city.

As your life begins to change in Jesus, there is much joy, and that's what happened in the Samaritan city where Philip preached. When people are converted to Christ, there is great joy.

There's always joy when Jesus is present. There's always joy when there is real revival, joy unspeakable and full of glory. The Christian life is one that always leads to joy, not in the improvement of our circumstances, but the joy that comes from knowing Jesus alone. This is what evangelism is all about.

WE ARE LEERY OF FALSE CONVERSIONS (8:9-13)

One great distraction in evangelism is what we might call false conversions. How can you know if someone is truly following Christ? How do you know if a person is converted? There is a difference between calling and conversion. "Many are called, but few are chosen" (Mt 22:14). The gospel call goes out to every creature. But only those who come by faith and show the fruit of faith demonstrate they are chosen. There is an external call that goes out to everyone. But have come to grips with the internal call of God that has changed your heart?

So many have professed faith in Christ with no change in their life. That's what we find here in Acts 8:9 when Philip meets a man by the name of Simon the Great. He's a con artist and a faker. Philip is going to see great fruit, but also great distractions, especially from Simon. You know, when God opens the windows of heavens to bless us, the devil opens the doors of hell to blast us.

Acts 8:9 | But there was a man named Simon, who had previously practiced magic in the city and amazed the people of Samaria, saying that he himself was somebody great.

When the power of the Spirit is poured out and the borders of God's kingdom expand, expect satanic attack. This time it comes in the form of this con artist.

A Famous Con Artist

Simon Magus is a famous magician from Samaria. He's a true con artist. He's convinced people that he's someone important. He's even learned to do great magic to impress people with miracles. By the say, you know that Satan can do wonders as he tries to imitate the power of God. There was force in what this man was doing, and the people were all dazzled by it. Listen to how Satan had used this satanic power to bring attention to Simon.

Acts 8:9-11 | But there was a man named Simon, who had previously practiced magic in the city and amazed the people of Samaria, saying that he himself was somebody great. [10] They all paid attention to him, from the least to the greatest, saying, "This man is the power of God that is called Great." [11] And they paid attention to him because for a long time he had amazed them with his magic.

Here Simon is doing magic. This is not just illusion; it is witchcraft. The power of Satan is alive and well in America today. Witchcraft is alive and well in your town or city today. There are new age, satanic philosophies that are alive and well in many churches. I'm telling you the truth. Many people are dazzled by this. They fail to understand that there is a power from the unseen world that is not from God. What Simon was doing was not just a bag of cheap tricks. It's not just that he was an illusionist—he was in league with the devil. Whenever there is revival, you can expect satanic opposition. The opposition here comes from a false conversion.

A False Conversion

Just because people profess faith in Christ does not make them truly born again. Faith does not come from mere words but must come from the heart. The words can say one thing, and the heart can believe another. True believers love Jesus from the heart. The new birth is a mystery, and only God knows the heart. The only way we can truly test a true convert is by the good fruit that comes from good soil throughout their life. "By their fruit you shall know them," Jesus said (Mt 7:16).

> **Acts 8:12-13** | When they believed Philip as he preached good news about the kingdom of God and the name of Jesus Christ, they were baptized, both men and women. **13** Even Simon himself believed, and after being baptized he continued with Philip. And seeing signs and great miracles performed, he was amazed.

The devil is a counterfeiter, and he loves creating a false imitation. Rather than to deny the faith, he counterfeits the faith, and that is doubly dangerous.

In the book of Matthew, chapter 13, Jesus tells the parable of the soils. He gives four soils, symbolizing different heart attitudes toward the gospel. Only one of the soils is good. Three are hard hearts. One is hardened by the world (pathway). Another is hardened by worries (thorns). Another is hardened by weariness (rocky). There's only one good, truly believing heart in the parable. How many times do we see people profess faith in Christ, but then they quickly fall away! Look for the fruit. Jesus said,

> *Matthew 7:16* | By their fruit you shall know them.

The powerful miracles and preaching of Philip resulted, as it had in Jerusalem, in the salvation of many Samaritans. But as true biblical preaching inevitably does, it produced another vastly different response. Some accepted the gospel, believing and reacting with much rejoicing. Others were superficial hearers, false converts who were nothing but the tares and weeds.[152] They were pretenders and fakes. But there is a confirming seal that all believers are given: the Holy Spirit.

WE LOOK FOR THE SPIRIT'S CONFIRMATION (8:14-24)

When people are born again, the Spirit will confirm them with his filling and his spiritual fruit. That's true for every believer, even though it was a bit of a delay for the Samaritans, but for good reason.

---

[152] MacArthur, *Acts*, 234–235.

We get to see the Spirit of God being poured out onto the Samaritans. But there is a delay.

The Unity of the Church

> **Acts 8:14-17** | Now when the apostles at Jerusalem heard that Samaria had received the word of God, they sent to them Peter and John, ¹⁵ who came down and prayed for them that they might receive the Holy Spirit, ¹⁶ for he had not yet fallen on any of them, but they had only been baptized in the name of the Lord Jesus. ¹⁷ Then they laid their hands on them and they received the Holy Spirit.

One Multicultural, Universal Church. Why did the Samaritans (and later the Gentiles) have to wait for the apostles before receiving the Spirit? For centuries, the Samaritans and the Jews had been bitter rivals. If the Samaritans had received the Spirit independent of the Jerusalem church, that rift would have been perpetuated. There could well have been two separate churches, a Jewish church and a Samaritan church. But God has designed one church that is united by Christ alone. The church is not solely Jewish, but is from "every tribe, tongue, people, and language." As Paul says:

> *Galatians 3:28-29* | There is neither Jew nor Greek, there is neither slave nor free, there is no male and female, for you are all one in Christ Jesus. ²⁹ And if you are Christ's, then you are Abraham's offspring, heirs according to promise.

By delaying the Spirit's coming until Peter and John arrived, God preserved the unity of the church. The apostles needed to see for themselves, and give firsthand testimony to the Jerusalem church, that the Spirit came upon the Samaritans. The Samaritans also needed to learn that they were subject to apostolic authority. The Jewish believers and the Samaritans were thus linked together into one body.[153]

The Spirit Confirms. Remember that the Holy Spirit is God's seal of ownership. All true Christians have the imprint of the Spirit on their hearts. This is what unifies us.

> *Ephesians 1:13-14* | In him you also, when you heard the word of truth, the gospel of your salvation, and believed in him, were sealed with

---

[153] MacArthur, Acts, vol 1, 245.

the promised Holy Spirit, [14] who is the guarantee of our inheritance until we acquire possession of it, to the praise of his glory.

The Church Unifies. The doctrine of the church's unity is what we need for this day and time. At a time when our culture is looking to divide us through the media, the church stands with the only solution for a divided society. The culture lifts up the problems but gives no real solutions. They want us divided. It is only in Christ that people come together as one, and it is only by the Spirit that indwells all true believers.

The Purity of the Church

Unity is not the only difficulty of the church. Martin Luther's slogan was "Peace if possible; truth at all costs." Elders and pastors admit people into the church. We are called to bring people into the church. People are baptized and become members of God's local churches. We want a pure, regenerated church membership. We want all to be born again. But it's impossible to know the true motives of everyone who makes a profession of faith in Christ. There will be some who falsely come into the church. We see that with Simon Magnus.

> **Acts 8:18-24** | Now when Simon saw that the Spirit was given through the laying on of the apostles' hands, he offered them money, [19] saying, "Give me this power also, so that anyone on whom I lay my hands may receive the Holy Spirit." [20] But Peter said to him, "May your silver perish with you, because you thought you could obtain the gift of God with money! [21] You have neither part nor lot in this matter, for your heart is not right before God. [22] Repent, therefore, of this wickedness of yours, and pray to the Lord that, if possible, the intent of your heart may be forgiven you. [23] For I see that you are in the gall of bitterness and in the bond of iniquity." [24] And Simon answered, "Pray for me to the Lord, that nothing of what you have said may come upon me."

Simon shows his true colors. When Peter and John arrived, they began laying their hands on the Samaritan believers, and they were receiving the Holy Spirit. That was too much for Simon. When he saw that the Spirit was bestowed through the laying on of the apostles' hands, he offered them money. Philip had impressed him with his preaching, but Peter and John overwhelmed him with the manifestation of the Spirit upon these Samaritan believers. Perhaps they began speaking in tongues like at Pentecost. Regardless, they were manifestly filled with the Spirit.

Simon asked them brashly and excitedly, "Give this authority to me as well, so that everyone on whom I lay my hands may receive the Holy Spirit." He treated the Spirit like the magic he practiced. He attempted to negotiate the price to buy the secret of the Spirit's power. In Simon's world everything had a price. The Spirit of God had a market value to him. He set a cash value on spiritual things and offered the apostles money. By this act, Simon gave his name to the term "simony," which through history has referred to the buying and selling of ecclesiastical offices. [154]

God's Salvation is Free. Nothing God has, however, is for sale—certainly not the Holy Spirit! Indeed, there is nothing sinful men have to offer him. Salvation and spiritual blessing are free gifts God loves to pour out. In Isaiah God cries out,

> *Isaiah 55:1* | Come, everyone who thirsts, come to the waters; and he who has no money, come, buy and eat! Come, buy wine and milk without money and without price.

Simon the Pliable. Simon wasn't really the "great" one. He was the pliable one. Simon Magnus was a false convert. He liked magic when he was around his witchcraft people. He liked God and the Bible and the Spirit when he was around Christians. He was like "Pliable" in the story of Pilgrim's progress. Whoever Pliable is around, he's like them. But no Pliable is a true Christian. They're a flimsy imitation. We remember Demas who was a companion to the Apostle Paul. He had been faithful. But in 2 Timothy Paul writes of his apostasy.

> *2 Timothy 4:2* | Demas has forsaken me, having loved this present world.

False converts are actors. They are in it for themselves. Don't be discouraged by the false converts that may arise. We've seen men, even preachers, who seemed to handle the word wisely fall into great sin and even walk away from the faith. Don't be surprised, for Jesus said this would happen.

> *Matthew 7:21-23, NKJV* | Not everyone who says to Me, "Lord, Lord," shall enter the kingdom of heaven, but he who does the will of My

---

[154] MacArthur, *Acts*, vol 1, ibid.

Father in heaven. ²² Many will say to Me in that day, "Lord, Lord, have we not prophesied in Your name, cast out demons in Your name, and done many wonders in Your name?" ²³ And then I will declare to them, "I never knew you; depart from Me, you who practice lawlessness!"

We as elders are diligent as much as is possible in keeping our church pure. But we cannot see into anyone's heart. We do warn those who give bad fruit of their peril, just like the apostles warned Simon Magnus.

WE LONG FOR UNSTOPPABLE CONVERSIONS (8:25)

Despite satanic distractions and false converts, Christ will build his church, and the gates of hell will not prevail against it.

Acts 8:25 | Now when they had testified and spoken the word of the Lord, they returned to Jerusalem, preaching the gospel to many villages of the Samaritans.

The story concludes with a note of how the apostles themselves, on their way back to Jerusalem, preached to the people and evangelized many Samaritan villages. The despised Samaritans were being saved and brought into the kingdom![155]

On the way back, the apostles stopped in village after village, testifying of God's grace and love through Jesus. They saturated the province of Samaria with the gospel. Thus, the next phase of world evangelism was accomplished. Jerusalem, Judaea, and Samaria had heard the gospel. Now the state is set to evangelize "the uttermost parts of the earth."[156] What about you? Are you leaving your comfort zone and reaching the people God put around you?

Applications

1. *Share the gospel.* What are some ways we can share the gospel? A good question to begin with is: "If you God were to ask you, why should I let you into my heaven," what would you say? This reveals where the person's heart is. Most people will say, I'm a good person. You can show them from the law how greatly they need Christ. "Have you ever told a lie? You're a liar. 'All liars have their part in the lake of fire,' the Bible says (Rev 21:8). Have you ever looked with lust? Jesus says, you are an adulterer in your heart. It's not enough to not murder.

---

[155] Marshall, *Acts*, 169.
[156] J. Phillips, *Exploring Acts*, Ac 8:25.

Jesus says if you have anger toward someone, you've committed murder in your heart. If you've stole, you're a thief. Does it concern you that you are a lying, thieving, adulterous murderer, and you have to face a holy God on judgment day? From that moment you can give the solution to that person. You can tell them, "Christ doesn't want you to perish. He's paid the debt you could not pay. He died for your sins on the cross. He takes your rags of sin and gives you his robe of righteousness (2 Cor 5:21)." Then you urge them to put their faith in Christ. So share the gospel. You may not be able to give an articulate gospel presentation, but you can give people a gospel tract. You can share your testimony of how you came to know Christ.

2. *Search your heart.* Can you really say you are a growing Christian if you are not sharing the gospel, not obeying our Lord's last word to us (Acts 1:8)?

3. *Pray for the lost.* Would you think of 3 people right now that you can pray for and witness to? Would you be willing to take some gospel tracts and hand them out? Would you be willing to invite at least one person to church in the next few weeks?

Conclusion

I want to bear fruit as I am connected to the vine. If I am to bear fruit, I must be willing to preach to all people. Is there someone in your life that you are praying for right now? Are you willing to share Jesus Christ with them?

Evangelism at Work

Do you have stories of conversions? You ought to. I started evangelizing as a sixteen-year-old kid. I worked at Ponderosa and on my breaks, I would sit down with an open Bible and go through the Romans Road with anyone who would listen. If all you know is John 3:16, you can evangelize.

Evangelism with Friends

Are you praying for people to come to Christ? My best friend growing up was Ralph Jr. I remember praying for Ralph's father, Ralph Sr., who was dying of cancer. I prayed every day for his salvation. I was sixteen years old and had no way to give the gospel to him. I remember him coming over to our house, and he was so swollen from the radiation therapy for his leukemia, he looked like a large plum. After many months, I heard he passed away, and I was broken with sorrow. I had prayed so earnestly, but it seemed God had not answered. As far as I knew he died without Christ and was suffering in hell. I went to his funeral distraught when my best friend Ralph Jr. introduced me to his Uncle Lee who was a Christian wrestler who worked with Athletes in Action. Uncle Lee exploded with some great news: three months before Ralph Sr. died, he had come to a saving knowledge of Christ and was excited to grow and change in his final three months. Ralph Sr. was born again and in heaven. I began jumping up and down in the funeral parlor, praising God for answered prayer. Sometimes you cannot even give the gospel to someone, but you can pray for them. Pray! God will answer. It may not be through you.

Evangelism with Family

Are you praying and witnessing to your family? I witnessed to my twin sister Tammie for ten years, from the time we were fifteen to age twenty-five. During that time, I also fasted and prayed constantly for her soul. For so many years she rejected the gospel. One day I heard about a church that was near our childhood home in Louisiana, and I asked her to visit there. It was such a tiny church in the backwoods bayou of Louisiana, a mile into the woods. After the service Tammie called me.

She burst out: "I'm saved!"

"What? What do you mean, you're 'saved'?" I asked.

She told me how the preacher had told her how Jesus died for a world of sinners and that Christ had died for her. After the service a little girl of twelve years, the pastor's daughter, who was sitting next to her, spoke to her about the message.

Tammie said, "I'm too big a sinner for God to save me."

The little girl replied, "Well that's just who God saves. He didn't come to call the righteous, but sinners to repentance."

She told me how the pastor came over and pointed her to Christ and she was saved.

I said, "Are you sure? Did you do it right?" I was so nervous and completely amazed. God had answered my prayers!

Evangelism at Impossible People

Are you praying and witnessing to people you think would never come to Christ? One of the most profound illustrations of this is the story of my dearest friends, Cedric and Nicole. I'll never forget sitting at their kitchen table on October 31, 2011. Cedric was a five-time felon, and Nicole was an Italian girl who grew up Catholic. Both were into the drug scene. They were desperate. They had gotten married in Las Vegas in a fly-by-night wedding. Nicole was desperate and showed up at church one Sunday.

"Can you talk to us? Is there any hope?" she said. I assured here there was hope in Jesus.

I visited their home and we started studying through Ephesians for several weeks. One evening, we got to that place in Ephesians 2, where it says we were "dead in our trespasses and sins" – and then it says, "But God who is rich in mercy raised us up with Christ..."

I'll never forget, Cedric interrupted and said, "Pastor, I got to pray!"

Nicole at that time being a proper Italian Catholic, said, "Cedric, don't interrupt the priest! We're here to learn from 'Father Matt'."

I chuckled at her calling me "Father Matt," but I told her – "The Spirit is giving birth to Cedric. He is about to be a new creation. Just as when you gave birth to your children, you couldn't hold it back, so the Spirit is birthing Cedric into the kingdom."

With that Cedric prayed with such an intensity and fervency, it was as if it was just him and God in the room, and he was swept into the glorious kingdom of God by faith in Jesus. And then Nicole followed right after and was born again! Cedric has grown so much and is now a preacher of God's word. Nicole is our church secretary. Don't ever think there are any impossible conversions. God can save anyone! God can do great things if you would just make yourself available. Are you available?

15 | ACTS 8:26-40
THE GOSPEL TO ETHIOPIA

The Spirit said to Philip, "Go over and join this chariot." So Philip ran to him and heard him reading Isaiah the prophet and asked, "Do you understand what you are reading?" And he said, "How can I, unless someone guides me?" And he invited Philip to come up and sit with him.

ACTS 8:29-31

God can do the unimaginable. Nothing is impossible for him. Jesus said that the gospel message of his death and resurrection was to go into all the world. We see this in the Old Testament. Isaiah says the gospel will go forth to all the known world: Egypt and Africa. We read in Isaiah:

Isaiah 19:25 | Blessed be Egypt my people, and Assyria the work of my hands, and Israel my inheritance.

At the time Isaiah is writing, it is the twenty-fifth dynasty in Egypt when Ethiopia from Africa had taken over the throne. So in referring to Egypt, God is including Africa as well. God loves the world. This is one of the bedrock truths of the gospel.

Throughout redemptive history, God has poured out his blessings to mankind through the channel of his covenant people. God never intended Israel to be a reservoir, storing up divine blessings for themselves. Instead, they were to be a funnel through which those blessings could be dispersed to a lost world. In Isaiah 42, God identified them as a lamp lighting the darkness around them. He said to Israel:

> *Isaiah 42:6* | I am the LORD, I have called you in righteousness, I will also hold you by the hand and watch over you, and I will appoint you as a covenant to the people, as a light to the nations.

Of course, Israel was a great failure in her mission. Israel seemed to go to two extremes: first to try and be like the nations in their idolatry and worshipping pagan gods. Then when they returned from captivity, they were separatistic, despising the Gentiles and wanting nothing to do with the outside nations. Israel failed. But with the coming of the Holy Spirit at Pentecost, God would cut a new channel through born again believers to reach the world for Jesus Christ.

In our last study, we looked at how the gospel began to be preached among the "half-breed" Samaritans. They were more despised than the Gentiles.

> **Acts 8:25** | Now when they had testified and spoken the word of the Lord, they returned to Jerusalem, preaching the gospel to many villages of the Samaritans.

There was much joy where Philip preached in among the Samaritans (8:8). But now it was time to begin to reach the final group of people Jesus promised to save: the Gentiles. Philip is called away from the great Samaritan revival to go to one man: an Ethiopian eunuch in the middle of nowhere! Through this one man, God will set the tone for the great warriors of the faith in the early church. Many of the greatest and most enduring leaders of the early church were from Africa. So God takes Philip away from a booming revival to reach just one man. God knows what he is doing! Don't ever doubt his ways. Remember, God's ways are not our ways (Isa 55:8-9). He can use you to save one soul or one million.

This was a time of unusual blessing on the church. To judge from the story, it would even seem that the incredible revival in Samaria was still growing. Philip was an important part of this, being the primary evangelist. Peter and John had been sent to inspect the work, but they had then gone back to Jerusalem to report. Philip was the front-line man. He seemed to be utterly indispensable. Yet it was at precisely this moment when God called him to leave the area.[157] God will build his church in Samaria and everywhere else with or without you. We are all expendable. God sends an angel to Philip and says: leave the great Samaritan revival and go to the desert to reach just one man! I'm glad Philip obeyed. He reaches the first Gentile with the gospel.

Interestingly, before we hear of Paul and Barnabas going out as missionaries from the Antioch church, we find that the mission field has come to the church. There are people from all nations in Jerusalem for the three main festivals they have each year, and proselytes from everywhere come to worship the Lord with all the faithful.

In this passage we meet the Ethiopian eunuch who is a very high official in the royal court of Candace, queen of the Ethiopians. He's in charge of all her treasure. Here is someone from the continent of Africa who is about to place his faith in the Lord Jesus Christ as the first Gentile convert in the church. We are going to see that genuine faith requires three elements: the proper preparation, the proper presentation, and the proper response.

GOSPEL PREPARATION (8:25-28)

Genuine saving faith demands the proper preparation. We all know that God must do the work.

> 1 Corinthians 3:6 | I planted, Apollos watered, but God gave the growth.

God has to give the growth, but here in Acts 8, there are four features that prepared the soil of the Eunuch's heart, and we see this in all conversions.

> **Acts 8:26-28** | Now an angel of the Lord said to Philip, "Rise and go toward the south to the road that goes down from Jerusalem to Gaza." This is a desert place. ²⁷ And he rose and went. And there was an Ethiopian, a eunuch, a court official of Candace, queen of the Ethiopians, who was in charge of all her treasure. He had come to Jerusalem to worship ²⁸ and was returning, seated in his chariot, and he was reading the prophet Isaiah.

There must be preparation of the human heart if anyone is going to come to Christ. We are dead in our trespasses and sins, so the human

---

[157] Boice, *Exposition of Acts,* 140.

will is free to do what it wants, but it wants to "drink iniquity like water" (Job 15:16). If we are to come to Christ, the human heart must be drawn by the Spirit of God. Listen to Jesus' words.

> *John 6:44* | No one can come to me unless the Father who sent me draws him. And I will raise him up on the last day.

Man's heart must be moved upon if he will come. This is vital to remember as we see the first Gentile convert. We can see God's fingerprints all over this conversion. Remember Philip was in Samaria, headed back to Jerusalem. God wanted him in a remote desert place in Gaza where a certain Ethiopian eunuch was reading from the Prophet Isaiah. Even to own a scroll, this man must have been wealthy. And we find out he's in charge of the Ethiopian queen's treasury. But God had to make a divine appointment between Philip and the Ethiopian.

The Spirit's Work

The Spirit began his preparatory work by maneuvering Philip into a strategic position. Philip and the apostles John and Peter solemnly testified and spoke the word of the Lord to the Samaritan villages. (8:25). But God sovereignly interrupted Philip and gave him direction. Until this time there have been records of great revivals totaling a number exceeding 25,000 people. But now we come to our first one-on-one gospel presentation. And it is quite unusual.

> **Acts 8:26** | Now an angel of the Lord said to Philip, "Rise and go toward the south to the road that goes down from Jerusalem to Gaza." This is a desert place.

The circumstances that were to lead to the eunuch's salvation were sovereignly and specifically arranged by the Spirit of God. Salvation, both in its eternal planning and its temporal outworking, is totally God's work. Salvation originates in the sovereign will of God (Acts 13:48; Rom 8:29ff.; Eph 1:3–7) and is implemented by his grace (Eph 2:8–9; 2 Thess 2:13; 2 Tim 2:10; Titus 1:1; 1 Pet 1:1).

The city of Gaza, one of five important Philistine cities, had been destroyed by Alexander the Great. A new city was built as well as a new road. The old desert road that Philip is commanded to take would have been out of use for quite some time. Luke's mention of the old Gaza road in the desert underscores the strangeness of the Spirit's command to Philip. Nobody went on the old Gaza road anymore, so it was almost as if God were directing Philip into the middle of the desert for no apparent reason. But Philip obeyed the commandment of the Lord and went down from Samaria past Jerusalem and made his way along the road.[158] God had a divine appointment, though the command to go to this deserted road would have sounded very strange to Philip. Yet Philip obeyed! And praise God he did. He was a vessel of the Holy Spirit who was drawing this Ethiopian eunuch to salvation.

Two insurmountable barriers keep man from grasping God's salvation by his own efforts: spiritual death and satanic control. First, men are spiritually dead and therefore unable to respond to God. Ephesians 2:1 says simply and directly, "You were dead in your trespasses and sins."[159] The second is that all lost people are under satanic control. Paul says that the god of this world (Satan) has blinded the minds of those who do not believe (2 Cor 4:4). Listen, if the Spirit doesn't work, man will remain dead in sin. The Spirit must draw and enliven the heart (Eph 2:1-4; Eze 26:25-27).

The Servant's Will

A huge part of evangelism is the obedience of God's people. Praise God, Philip obeyed the Spirit.

Acts 8:27a | And he rose and went.

Are you being used of God for evangelism? Paul tells us there is a qualification. You've got to be holy and set apart to God.

> *2 Timothy 2:20-21* | Now in a great house there are not only vessels of gold and silver but also of wood and clay, some for honorable use, some for dishonorable. ²¹ Therefore, if anyone cleanses himself from what is dishonorable, he will be a vessel for honorable use, set apart as holy, useful to the master of the house, ready for every good work.

Philip was such an instrument. He was in deep communion with God and heard the voice of God directing him. It seemed irrational to go to that deserted road toward Gaza. Who would be there? Just one man that God wanted in his kingdom. As we obey the Lord, he will give us those wonderful divine appointments where we can share Christ.

Philip obeyed *the subjective inner voice of the Holy Spirit*. He remained open as to how God would lead him. When we are in touch with

---

[158] Sproul, *Acts*, 148.
[159] MacArthur, *Acts*, 252.

the Holy Spirit, we will be sensitive to his guidance—sometimes through difficulties, sometimes through an inner voice, maybe even through angels—and thus we will be the touch of God to others.[160] Let me be clear that the word of God was Philip's authority. But God guides us in his providence. If you think the Spirit is leading you in a certain way, you must subject all things to the word of God. Those who claim to be led by the Spirit when it contradicts the word of God are deceived. Praise God that Philip, a man filled with the Spirit and the word, obeyed the Spirit to go and preach in that deserted place.

The Seeker's Worship

God had prepared the way for Philip. The eunuch's heart had already been touched by the Spirit of God. We read more about him in verse 27.

> **Acts 8:27b** | And there was an Ethiopian, a eunuch, a court official of Candace, queen of the Ethiopians, who was in charge of all her treasure. He had come to Jerusalem to worship.

This eunuch was a proselyte or God-fearer and had come from his own country in order to worship at the temple in Jerusalem.[161] We now witness the first of three remarkable conversions. In chapter 8 we have the conversion of an Ethiopian, a representative of the family of *Ham*; in chapter 9 we have the conversion of Saul of Tarsus, a Jew, a representative of the family of *Shem*; in chapter 10 we have the conversion of Cornelius, a Roman centurion, from the family of *Japheth*. The families of the earth that were separated at Babel are now made one in the family of God. The curse of Babel, which enforced God's deliberate division of mankind, is reversed in the church.[162] The walls of hostility are torn down (Eph 2:14).

In ancient Ethiopia, the king was considered divine incarnations of the sun god, and the everyday affairs of government were held to be beneath them. Real power lay with the queen mothers, known by the official title Candace (which is not a proper name, but an official title, like Pharaoh or Caesar). So Queen Candace was the true ruler of the country. Her son, the king, was the "divine" figurehead. This Ethiopian

---

[160] Hughes, *Acts,* 118–119.
[161] P Williams, *Acts,* 93.
[162] J. Phillips, *Exploring Acts,* Ac 8:27.

Eunuch was in charge of all her treasure. In modern terms, he was the Minister of Finance, or Secretary of the Treasury.[163]

Note that this man was a eunuch. In antiquity a eunuch was someone who had been surgically made a eunuch in order to be trusted, and it this case he was the companion of the queen mother. The king could trust a man who was unable to be sexually tempted.[164]

Despite his power and prestige, the Ethiopian eunuch had a vast emptiness in his soul. He made a long, arduous journey from his homeland to Jerusalem, searching for the true God. Unfortunately, given the state of contemporary Judaism, he probably went away still empty. But the Spirit was drawing him, whetting his appetite for worship of the true God. God's sovereignty in salvation does not obviate man's responsibility. That God rewards the seeking heart is the clear teaching of Scripture. In Jeremiah, God said,

Jeremiah 29:13 | You will seek me and find me, when you search for me with all your heart.

The eunuch is a classic example of one who lived up to the light he had. God then gave him the full revelation of Jesus Christ through Philip's ministry.[165]

The Scriptural Word

With all the preparation of the eunuch's heart, he would be helpless without the all sufficient word of God.

Acts 8:27b-28 | He had come to Jerusalem to worship [28] and was returning, seated in his chariot, and he was reading the prophet Isaiah.

He had just begun his journey back to return to Ethiopia. He was reading the prophet Isaiah. Good things happen when we read the Bible. The Spirit does his work. Can we all agree that God's word is powerful? He was one of the few people in the ancient word that could afford a copy of God's word, likely in a scroll. Each copy of God's word had to be handwritten until the invention of the printing press in 1450. So he would have been reading a handwritten copy of the word of God.

---

[163] MacArthur, *Acts*, 254.
[164] Sproul, *Acts*, 149.
[165] MacArthur, *Acts*, 254–255.

It's good that he had that copy of the word. We all need the word of God to know God in a saving way. God's existence, and attributes, can be discerned from creation (Rom 1:20). That's why you'll never meet a true atheist. Paul says all men know who God is in their hearts, even though they are running from him. But creation is a general revelation of who God is. It cannot reveal the person and work of Christ to us. For that we need the written word of God, his special revelation. Indeed, a true, personal, saving knowledge of God comes only through the Scriptures. Jesus said the Bible is all about him.

John 5:39 | You search the Scriptures, because you think that in them you have eternal life; and it is these that bear witness of me.

In verse 46 he added,

John 5:46 | If you believed Moses, you would believe me; for he wrote of me.

After the resurrection, Christ met two disciples on the road to Emmaus and gave them the true way of understanding the word.

Luke 24:27 | Beginning with Moses and with all the prophets, He explained to them the things concerning Himself in all the Scriptures.

You must be confronted with the word of God in order to know Christ, because the message of the Bible centers on the Person and work of Jesus Christ.

All the essentials were in place; the Spirit's work of preparation was complete. Philip had obeyed the Spirit's call and was in place to meet the man. The eunuch's heart was seeking, prepared by reading the Scriptures. All was set for the next step.

GOSPEL PRESENTATION (8:29-35)

Why was this Ethiopian finance minister there in Jerusalem, hundreds of miles from home? It might be that this Ethiopian man remembered the Queen of Sheba, a thousand years before, who had heard of the true and living God from Solomon. Perhaps all these years God preserved a remnant there in north Africa where Candace and her treasurer were from. This Ethiopian man had traveled hundreds of miles with the queen mother Candace to worship the true God.

Acts 8:29-35 | And the Spirit said to Philip, "Go over and join this chariot." **30** So Philip ran to him and heard him reading Isaiah the prophet and asked, "Do you understand what you are reading?" **31** And he said, "How can I, unless someone guides me?" And he invited Philip to come up and sit with him. **32** Now the passage of the Scripture that he was reading was this: "Like a sheep he was led to the slaughter and like a lamb before its shearer is silent, so he opens not his mouth. **33** In his humiliation justice was denied him. Who can describe his generation? For his life is taken away from the earth." **34** And the eunuch said to Philip, "About whom, I ask you, does the prophet say this, about himself or about someone else?" **35** Then Philip opened his mouth, and beginning with this Scripture he told him the good news about Jesus.

The Spirit

The Spirit spoke to Philip's heart. The Spirit is constantly talking to the Christian's heart. The question is, are you listening?

Acts 8:29-30a | And the Spirit said to Philip, "Go over and join this chariot." **30** So Philip ran to him and heard him reading Isaiah the prophet...

The Spirit speaks, and Philip obeys and *runs* up to the chariot. He would have noticed that the chariot is decked out with rich furnishings. Philip is just a poor evangelist, but the Spirit gives boldness to all who are Spirit filled. He would have seen a driver in the front seat and the distinguished Ethiopian finance minister seated comfortably behind, busily reading the biblical scroll of Isaiah (8:28). The *Spirit*, now directing Philip (8:29) after the angel's initial command (8:26), tells the evangelist to join the carriage. To do so, he actually runs up alongside it, close enough to hear the man reading aloud (8:30).[166] What a sight! But we are called to do what the Spirit tells us to do.

How vital it is to have a tender heart so we can hear the Spirit's voice. There is a providential leading of the Spirit. He promises to direct our steps. There are so many distractions today. People are on their cell phones and media, and there is a cost to all that. We drown out the voice of the Spirit. God promises to lead us by his Spirit through his word to do his will. That includes evangelism opportunities. Your lost friends and neighbors and even strangers need you to be walking in step with the Spirit so you can hear his voice.

---

[166] Faw, *Acts*, 106.

The Surprise

What a surprise that there's an evangelist in a remote desert. What are the chances of a man like this, burdened by his sin and searching for answers to some of the greatest questions a man can ask, finding someone like Philip on a lonely desert road? Slim to none! However, this type of temporal perspective fails to reckon with the overruling providence of God. *Nothing* is impossible when God has determined a certain course of action.[167] So here, in the middle of nowhere, you have a miscellaneous Jewish evangelist running by the chariot of this Ethiopian official just as he is reading aloud the Scriptures. This miraculous providence is a major theme here, because just as suddenly as Philip is running beside the chariot, at the end of this scene, he is miraculously taken away and transported by the Spirit to a destination twenty miles away.

The ancient custom of reading aloud provided an opening for Philip, who, though a complete stranger, boldly asked, "Do you understand what you are reading?" What a surprise! Perhaps the finance minister was praying just then for help in the Scriptures. We don't know, but God can do anything.

> **Acts 8:30-31** | So Philip ran to him and heard him reading Isaiah the prophet and asked, "Do you understand what you are reading?" **31** And he said, "How can I, unless someone guides me?" And he invited Philip to come up and sit with him.

The man was so perplexed by the passage he had been reading that he seems not to have cared who Philip was or why he was in his presence. The eunuch just exclaimed, "Well, how could I understand, unless someone guides me?" Amazingly, he then invited Philip to come up and sit with him. Philip's heart must have been rejoicing at how God had so prepared this man. When you are walking in submission to the Spirit and the word, there are plenty of surprises in the Christ life.

The Scriptures

An effective presentation of the gospel must be based solidly on Scripture. The use of personal testimony, stories, tracts, and other tools is no substitute. The gospel message in the Scripture alone is "the power of God for salvation to everyone who believes, to the Jew first

---

[167] Thomas, *Acts*, 240.

and also to the Greek" (Rom. 1:16). The power is in the word.[168] God uses his word to transform hearts of stone into hearts of flesh. The passage this man was reading is found in Isaiah 53:7-8.

> **Acts 8:32-34** | Now the passage of the Scripture that he was reading was this: "Like a sheep he was led to the slaughter and like a lamb before its shearer is silent, so he opens not his mouth. **33** In his humiliation justice was denied him. Who can describe his generation? For his life is taken away from the earth." **34** And the eunuch said to Philip, "About whom, I ask you, does the prophet say this, about himself or about someone else?"

Here is perhaps the clearest presentation of Jesus Christ in the Old Testament, and yet this very educated man is confused. "Is this about the prophet or someone else?" he asks. Satan has blinded the eyes of all those who do not believe in Christ (2 Cor 4:4). And we have the responsibility to restore sight to the blind as evangelists. That's exactly what Philip did.

The Savior

How exciting it must have been for Philip to explain this passage to this distinguished Ethiopian man.

> **Acts 8:35** | Then Philip opened his mouth, and beginning with this Scripture he told him the good news about Jesus.

Jesus is the Lamb of God who takes away the sin of the world (Jn 1:29). He is the substitute for all the world. Though he is God in human flesh, absolutely perfect in his humanity, he was led to the slaughter. He chose to be silent like a lamb, gladly suffering for the sins of his people. He didn't get justice for himself, but he received the full justice and wrath of God for the sins of all who will believe (Jn 3:16; 36).

Dear saints, lets preach the gospel! So many people, even pastors, cannot give a clear gospel presentation. There are many verses that simply present the gospel.

> *1 Peter 3:18* | Christ also suffered once for sins, the righteous for the unrighteous, that he might bring us to God.

---

[168] MacArthur, *Acts*, 257.

John 3:16 | For God so loved the world, that he gave his only Son, that whoever believes in him should not perish but have eternal life.

2 Corinthians 5:21, NASB | He made Him who knew no sin to be sin in our behalf, so that we might become the righteousness of God in Him.

Jesus said, "I, when I am lifted up from the earth, will draw all people to myself" (Jn 12:32). Lift him up! And when you lift him up, the Spirit can transform the heart, and Jesus becomes irresistible.

GOSPEL TRANSFORMATION (8:36-40)

When we lift Christ up, and a person comes in faith to Christ, there is true salvation.

Faith in Christ

It seems as the Ethiopian official understood the gospel, he must have expressed his faith in Christ to Philip, and Philip likely explained to the him about baptism.

Acts 8:36 | And as they were going along the road they came to some water, and the eunuch said, "See, here is water! What prevents me from being baptized?"

Salvation is by grace alone through faith alone in Christ alone to the glory of God alone. Anyone who believes the simple gospel should not be refused baptism.

Some manuscripts (and therefore some translations) omit Acts 8:37. In the New King James Version it reads,

Acts 8:37 (NKJV) | Then Philip said, "If you believe with all your heart, you may." And he answered and said, "I believe that Jesus Christ is the Son of God."

These words are very similar to what Paul said to the Philippian jailer in Acts 16.

Acts 16:31 | Believe on the Lord Jesus Christ, and you will be saved.

The Greek is not just "believe *in*," but "believe *on*" or better yet "believe *into*" Jesus Christ, suggesting that our faith must lodge in the most intimate of ways with Jesus Christ.[169] It is not enough to believe the right things about Jesus Christ, for James tells us:

---

[169] Thomas, *Acts*, 240–241.

James 2:19 | The devils believe and tremble.

We must trust on Jesus. That means founding our whole life up our Lord Jesus who is our chief Cornerstone. Often the language of "asking Jesus into your heart" can be confusing. The main place we hear that in Scripture is in Ephesians.

Ephesians 3:17 | That Christ may dwell in your hearts through faith.

This is fine if by it you mean Christ is coming into your control your inner being. He is Lord! Sadly, often when people "ask Jesus into their heart" they are just adding him to a thousand other idols. Let's work to be clearer as to what true Christianity is. It is absolute conversion. It is the miracle of regeneration that transforms the heart of stone into a heart of flesh (Eze 36:26). It's when the old passes away, and the new comes, and you become a new creation (2 Cor 5:17). It is God making our inner man alive and raising us from death to life (Eph 2:4). This is not attainable through human effort or manipulation. It is a miracle of God (Eph 2:7-8).

Confession of Christ

Acts 8:38 | And he commanded the chariot to stop, and they both went down into the water, Philip and the eunuch, and he baptized him.

Philip had surely talked about the Great Commission—the call to go into all the world preaching and teaching Christ and baptizing all nations in the name of the Father, the Son, and the Holy Spirit—and about the fact that baptism is the sign of the new covenant.[170]

They came across a pool or stream in the desert at just the appropriate moment for the man to publicly testify to his saving faith by being obedient to the ordinance of immersion. That is yet another example of the sovereign Spirit's control of events.[171] Baptism is an outward sign of an inward reality. The Greek word is *baptizo*, which means to immerse or to dip. Philip immersed him. There's a symbolic reason for immersion. Baptism is a picture of our union with Christ in what he did in his death and resurrection. When we go down into the water, we show that we are united with Christ's death and burial. When we come

---

[170] Sproul, *Acts*, 151.
[171] MacArthur, *Acts*, 259.

out of the water, we show that we are united with Christ in his resurrection. It's a beautiful picture of our faith in Christ.

Baptism is like a wedding ring. It's symbolic, but it is the willingness to come before all and make vows before the whole church, that you are his Body and Bride. Why did he do that? As we said, he was demonstrating the death, burial, and resurrection of Jesus Christ. We are buried with Him by baptism, like as Christ was raised from the dead by the glory of the Father, even so we all should walk in newness of life. But also, he was going public with his faith. He demonstrated his faith to all his entourage. He's not traveling alone. This man is a government official, so there's a great entourage. Can you imagine what it meant to them to see this high ranking official humble himself? He got out of the chariot and went down into the water there, and he let this Jewish evangelist plunge him beneath the water. It was a testimony that something radical had happened in his heart, and it was a testimony to others. When he went under the water, he's saying, the old life is dead and buried, and when he comes up out of the water, it pictures a new person raised to walk in newness of life.

Are you here today as an unbaptized believer in Christ? You've seen several baptized here today at Living Hope. Baptism is the first step of obedience as a believer. If you've believed but not been baptized, there ought to be an excitement about obeying the Lord. I remember when I realized that I was attending a church, but I was unbaptized. I was seventeen years old. The Spirit of God moved in my heart. I had been a believer for two years. But suddenly I couldn't wait to get baptized. I told the pastor and was baptized the next Sunday. Baptism is a first step of expressing your faith in Christ and making yourself accountable to a local church. It's saying, "I'm part of the Body and Bride of Christ, and I'm unashamed."

Rejoicing in Christ

> **Acts 8:39-40** | And when they came up out of the water, the Spirit of the Lord carried Philip away, and the eunuch saw him no more, and went on his way rejoicing. ⁴⁰ But Philip found himself at Azotus, and as he passed through he preached the gospel to all the towns until he came to Caesarea.

Philip was suddenly taken away. I'm sure he was rejoicing at the faith of this Ethiopian diplomat. But the eunuch was also rejoicing. He was so grateful for his salvation. And so Philip was transported twenty miles away to Azotus, or as the ancient name is Ashdod. What an incredible privilege to preach the good news. As he made his way north toward Caesarea Maritime, where he and his family apparently made their home (Acts 21:9), he preached in the cities (such as Joppa and Lydda, which Peter would shortly visit) as he traveled.[172] There is so much to rejoice for when you are spreading the gospel seed everywhere.

And if Philip only knew the great things that would happen in and through the Ethiopian eunuch, he would have been rejoicing even more. The conversion of this one man from Africa would impact the church for centuries to come. We need only remember that some of the most important names in early church history were Africans—Cyprian, Tertullian, and Augustine, to name but three.[173]

Conclusion

We have a privilege that angels don't have—bringing souls to Jesus Christ. And we have an opportunity that we will not have in the world to come—that is, to bring souls to Jesus Christ. Now, God is calling you to be an evangelist. Every member of Jesus' church is to be an evangelist.

Applications

Come to Christ. God brought Philip out of Samaria down to the desert, why? He brought him there because there was somebody there that needed the gospel. I am bold enough to say that you're not here by accident today. God put this message on my heart, and God brought you here. You know why? He loves you. He wants you to be saved. You may be here without Christ. The same Savior who saved this Ethiopian official desires to save you. God's been preparing you to know him. He has no desire for you to go to a Christless eternity in the Lake of fire without any hope. There is hope today, but there may not be hope tomorrow. You may die at any moment, and the Bible says that after death is the judgment. If you're not ready for that judgement day, let me give you hope. You can be ready. It's not by making yourself better. You cannot heal yourself. But if you put your faith in Christ, God will heal you.

---

[172] MacArthur, *Acts*, 260.
[173] Thomas, *Acts*, 236.

Confess Christ in baptism. If you are here today as an unbaptized believer, I want you to consider something. Do you have the Spirit? If baptism is the first step of obedience, won't you obey the Lord? Come and tell an elder or a pastor that you need baptism. It's one of the most joyous things you can do to tell the world about Christ.

Tell of Christ. Are you sharing this gospel everywhere you go? Or are you a slave of what people think of you? Break free. You cannot be a true disciple if you are not evangelizing. If you have no heart for the lost, you are not growing and maturing like you ought. So many need to hear. The most sobering reality in the world today is that people are dying and going to hell today.

Will you tell the lost? Think of children in your family or other family members. You need to give Christ to. They need you to explain it to them. Think of your co-workers who need Christ. Who are you praying for today to be saved? When is the last time you shared your faith?

16 | ACTS 9:1-19
PAUL'S CONVERSION

Now as he went on his way, he approached Damascus, and suddenly a light from heaven shone around him. And falling to the ground, he heard a voice saying to him, "Saul, Saul, why are you persecuting me?" And he said, "Who are you, Lord?" And he said, "I am Jesus, whom you are persecuting."

ACTS 9:3-5

Do you remember when God saved you? Salvation is a miracle, isn't it? One of the most dramatic conversions was John Newton. He was raised by a godly Christian mother and knew the truth well. Sadly, his mother died when he was seven years old, and he went learned the art of seafaring from his ungodly father. Like most sailors of his day, he lived a life of sin and rebellion. For several years, he worked on slave ships, capturing slaves for sale to the plantations of the New World. So low did he sink that at one point he became a slave himself, captive of another slave trader. Eventually, he became the captain of his own slave ship. He would later record that he had kidnapped twenty thousand African people into slavery, about half of which died on the way over because of sickness and malnutrition. John Newton was one of the vilest persons on the planet. But there was mercy even for such a filthy sinner. God was calling John Newton to salvation.

One night there was a frightening storm at sea, and John Newton picked up Thomas á Kempis's classic book *Imitation of Christ*. He called that moment his "day of great awakening" because it was in that storm that God planted the seeds that resulted in his conversion. He went on to become a leader in the evangelical movement in England. Along with William Wilberforce, this slave ship captain helped to end the slave trade in Britain. On his tombstone is inscribed the following epitaph, written by Newton himself:

> John Newton, clerk, once an infidel and Libertine, a servant of slavers in Africa, was, by the rich mercy of our Lord and Savior Jesus Christ, preserved, restored, pardoned, and appointed to preach the Faith he had long labored to destroy.

When he penned the beloved hymn "Amazing Grace," he knew firsthand the truths it proclaimed. [174]

Church history is abounding with glorious accounts such as these, which demonstrate the marvelous power of the gospel to transform sinners. But perhaps no transformation is as remarkable, or has had such far-reaching implications for church history, as the conversion of Saul of Tarsus. So significant an event was his conversion that Scripture records it no less than three times (*cf* Acts 22:1–16; 26:4–18).[175] The great Reformer from Geneva, John Calvin says, "Luke records the story of Paul's conversion. He tells how the Lord not only brought him under his control when he was like a wild animal but also made him a new person."[176] There is no one that is too far off from God's grace. There is no one who is too great a sinner for God to save. Truly we say with Jonah:

> Jonah 2:9 | Salvation belongs to the Lord.

THE MIRACLE OF SAUL'S CONVERSION (9:1-3)

Saul, even as a lost Pharisee, was an intellectual giant. He knew that there could be no peaceful coexistence between militant Judaism and on-fire Christianity. Revival was spreading from Jerusalem to Judea and now to Samaria. Saul was determined to stop it. Everything in

---

[174] Kenneth W. Osbeck, *101 Hymn Stories* (Grand Rapids: Kregel, 1982), 28
[175] MacArthur, *Acts*, 264.
[176] Calvin, *Acts*, 149.

Saul drove him into a head-on battle royal with the Christians.[177] Saul is so furious about Christianity, he is described like a wild animal looking for prey.

His Disgust

> **Acts 9:1** | But Saul, still breathing threats and murder against the disciples of the Lord, went to the high priest.

Paul (his Greek name), or Saul (his Hebrew name) is described in some translations as "one breathing out fire," taking on the attributes of Satan who is like a dragon and a lion that seeks whom he may devour (cf Rev 12:9; 1 Pet 5:8). Breathing in threats of murder and destruction may sound strange, but the idea is that Saul was so passionately determined to carry on his persecution against the growing Christian community that he was like a wild beast that snorts before it attacks. Saul was unhinged in his disgust for Jesus Christ. He fiercely and viciously persecuted any followers of Christ he could find. And he had a mission in Damascus.

His Destination

> **Acts 9:1b-2a** | But Saul... went to the high priest ² and asked him for letters to the synagogues at Damascus, so that if he found any belonging to the Way, men or women, he might bring them bound to Jerusalem.

Damascus is one of the oldest cities in the history of the world. Damascus was known even to Abraham. The Damascus road from Jerusalem stretched for about two hundred miles. Saul was a frightening, violent enemy. He must have heard of the great revivals in Samaria and saw that it was now reaching Damascus, where tens of thousands of Jews lived. He violently opposed them converting to Jesus. Saul was determined to snuff out Christianity. It's a miracle that it is at this moment he retires from persecuting the church. He travels to Damascus to hurt Christians, but he will leave Damascus a transformed man.

---

[177] J. Phillips, *Exploring Acts*, Ac 9:1a.

His Determination

Acts 9:2b | ...if he found any belonging to the Way, men or women, he might bring them bound to Jerusalem.

Saul of Tarsus was determined to stop whatever revival had begun over there. Little did he know, he was going to be one of the main people that not only carries the revival through Samaria, but to the uttermost parts of the world. Saul didn't believe Jesus was the way to eternal life, but that's what Christianity was called back then: "The Way." The description of Christianity as the Way appears several times in Acts (19:9, 23; 22:4; 24:14, 22). It apparently derives from Jesus' description of himself as "the way, and the truth, and the life" (Jn 14:6).

Saul, hearing of the revivals in Samaria and realizing the next frontier for Christianity was the large population of Jews in Damascus wanted to head off these followers of Jesus. He got the necessary papers to go to each synagogue and place any Christians under arrest and bring them back to Jerusalem for further punishment, perhaps even execution. [178] Saul was doing all he could to stop this revival from spreading. The city of Dan, on the northern most edge of Israel stands high, elevated above the Damascus road in the valley there, just outside of Israel. Little did he know the Son of God would be standing in his way on that road.

His Deliverance

Acts 9:3 | Now as he went on his way, he approached Damascus, and suddenly a light from heaven shone around him.

Saul is near Damascus when a strange and glorious *light from heaven* blazes forth, and he falls to the ground (9:3). God could have destroyed this persecutor of the church, but instead the heavenly light is a light of grace. Jesus came to call this great enemy to join his team and called this hater of Jesus to become a lover of Jesus. God loves to transform the most stubborn, tough customers.

Salvation and sanctification are all of God's grace. We cannot save ourselves and we cannot fix ourselves. The reason Saul of Tarsus was radically changed was he got his eyes off of himself and onto Christ. That's the only way to truly repent is not to over-focus on our sin, but

---

[178] Sproul, *Acts*, 156.

to focus on Christ, the one who "while we were still sinners died for us" (Rom 5:8).

THE MANNER OF SAUL'S CONVERSION (9:4-9)

The Light

Acts 9:3b | Suddenly a light from heaven shone around him.

The light was not just a flash but a sustained flood of light, terrifying and inexplicable.[179] The light demonstrates God's divine power. The light that Jesus displays is the shekinah glory of God, as was seen in the Glory Cloud from the Old Testament. God displayed himself aa glory cloud: a pillar of cloud by day and pillar of fire by night. This also reminds us of the glory that Isaiah witnessed, which was so bright that the seraphim covered their eyes, and Isaiah called out, "Woe is me!" When the shepherds saw this glory, the "glory of the Lord" shone all around the shepherds, and they too were struck down with fear (Lk 2:9).

Christ's glory was usually veiled during his earthly ministry, but during the transfiguration we see his glory for a few brief moments (Mt 17:1–8).[180] As Saul looked at Christ, it was as if he were looking at God face to face. As a result, we find out later that he becomes blinded!

The Lord

Suddenly, Saul hears a voice from the Lord, and he clearly recognizes him as divine. In conversion, a person comes to understand the person and work of Jesus Christ. Christ is the Messiah from Psalm 2, the one God promised and that everyone would need to bow before in total allegiance. Jesus is God's king, and he is extending his mercy to this great persecutor of the church.

The Lord's Majesty

Acts 9:4a | And falling to the ground, he heard a voice.

We do not know whether Paul had ever met Jesus when he lived on earth. It's possible, but if so Paul never mentions it. Paul's first

---

[179] Pollock, *The Apostle*, 33.
[180] W.H. Baker, *Acts*, 897.

encounter with Jesus seems to have been here and now on the Damascus road.[181]

This is not a revelation of Christ incarnate on earth in a merely human body, but something infinitely more majestic. Think of the revelation of Christ in the first chapter of Revelation. Here is Jesus being revealed after he's ascended to heaven. He's being revealed to Saul of Tarsus as a glorious figure. His voice and appearance is so great that he falls to the ground. I am reminded of what Paul later says in Philippians 2.

> *Philippians 2:10-11* | At the name of Jesus every knee should bow... [11] and every tongue confess that Jesus Christ is Lord, to the glory of God the Father.

Saul of Tarsus is now on his knees in a meeting with the King of kings and Lord of lords. He meets the Messiah. An interesting dialogue ensues. He hears a voice, at once calm and authoritative, speak in Aramaic.

The Lord's Family

Acts 9:4-5 | And falling to the ground, he heard a voice saying to him, "Saul, Saul, why are you persecuting me?" [5] And he said, "Who are you, Lord?" And he said, "I am Jesus, whom you are persecuting."

Suddenly, Paul knew. In a second that seemed an eternity he saw the wounds in Jesus' hands and feet, saw the face, and knew he had seen the Lord, that Jesus of Nazareth was the Messiah, and he was alive.[182]

Saul now realizes that he's on the wrong team. What a shock to hear the exalted Messiah in all his glory tell Saul that when he persecuted Christians, he was actually persecuting Jesus himself. Saul has been messing with Jesus' very family.

Now, instantaneously, Saul of Tarsus was shattering aware that he had been fighting Jesus—and fighting himself, his conscience, his powerlessness, the darkness and chaos in his own soul. God hovered over this chaos and brought him to the moment of new creation.[183]

---

[181] J. Phillips, *Exploring Acts*, Ac 9:4–5.
[182] Pollock, *The Apostle*, 34.
[183] Ibid.

Anytime you suffer for Christ, the Lord's got a purpose for it. It may be that the way God gets your loved ones to stop rejecting your and persecuting you is to convert them and saved them and bring them to love Jesus. When any Christian suffers for Christ, Jesus takes it personally. He will vindicate you. He may do it in judgment, but he'd rather do it in salvation.

The Lord's Mercy

> **Acts 9:6** | "But rise and enter the city, and you will be told what you are to do."

Jesus commands Saul to go to a certain city, and Saul humbly obeys. He's a changed man. Acts 9:6 has a textual variant. It's insightful. Look at how the New King James translates it.

> *Acts 9:6, NKJV* | So he, trembling and astonished, said, "Lord, what do You want me to do?" Then the Lord said to him, "Arise and go into the city, and you will be told what you must do."

There is a tenderness in Saul. He realizes he's a recipient of the Lord's mercy. He calls Jesus Lord. That's a title in this context that means Yahweh. He understands this is the Messiah. His eyes are opened. He's trembling. He should be dead. He deserves death, but strangely he's alive. He's bowing under the authority and mercy of Jesus.

The Leveling

> **Acts 9:7-9** | The men who were traveling with him stood speechless, hearing the voice but seeing no one. [8] Saul rose from the ground, and although his eyes were opened, he saw nothing. So they led him by the hand and brought him into Damascus. [9] And for three days he was without sight, and neither ate nor drank.

Saul does not realize the full effect of the bright light until he gets up and tries to walk. Then he discovers that he is totally blind and must have someone lead him by the hand (9:8). Luke paints a dramatic picture of this fiery persecutor now rendered so helpless that he must depend on others like a child! When we come to Christ, he humbles us to the dust. Not many wise and not many strong are called (1 Cor 1:26). But some wise and strong are called, though they be few. And when they are called, they must be humbled, often in dramatic and overwhelming ways.

It is a short distance into Damascus, and Saul's companions take him to a place only revealed later (9:11), the house of Ananias. He is so in awe of what has happened that for three days he can neither eat nor drink (9:9). [184]

THE MARKS OF SAUL'S CONVERSION (9:10-19)

The marks we are about to witness demonstrate a radical change in Paul. We see several marks of conversion.

A Man of Prayer

The first mark of conversion shows Saul's immediate fellowship with God. He is praying. Saul's been blinded by the light of Christ's glory, and now God has to send a man to restore Saul's sight. We are introduced to a humble believer named Ananias who receives a vision from the Lord about Saul, the great persecutor. He's told Saul has been blinded by Christ's glory, and Ananias is to lay hands on him so that he might see again.

> **Acts 9:10-12** | Now there was a disciple at Damascus named Ananias. The Lord said to him in a vision, "Ananias." And he said, "Here I am, Lord." **11** And the Lord said to him, "Rise and go to the street called Straight, and at the house of Judas look for a man of Tarsus named Saul, for behold, he is praying, **12** and he has seen in a vision a man named Ananias come in and lay his hands on him so that he might regain his sight."

Note a very important detail in verse 11, "Behold, he is praying." Fellowship with God is the first sign of conversion. Martin Luther said when a person is born again, prayer flows out of the believer like breath and cries flow out of a newborn baby. He said, "To be a Christian without prayer is no more possible than to be alive without breathing."[185] Charles Spurgeon had saw that prayer has such an exalted, vital role in the Christian life and in heaven.

> Our tears in prayer are the diamonds of heaven; sighs are a part of the music of Jehovah's court and are numbered with "the sublimest

---

[184] Faw, *Acts*, 111.
[185] Martin Luther in Warren W. Wiersbe, *Be Determined (Nehemiah): Standing Firm in the Face of Opposition* (Colorado Springs, CO: David C. Cook, 2010), 168.

strains that reach the majesty on high." Think not that your prayer, however weak or trembling, will be unregarded. Jacob's ladder is lofty, but our prayers shall lean upon the Angel of the covenant and so climb its starry rounds. Our God not only hears prayer but also loves to hear it.[186]

Saul had been intrinsically changed. That's what' conversion does. The old heart of stone is replaced by a tender heart of flesh (Eze 36:26). Everybody has a nature change when they meet the Lord Jesus. Repentant faith means we have repudiated trust in all idols, and we have now put our entire trust in Christ.

We are changed forever: radically, dramatically, eternally, visibly, spiritually, emotionally changed, when we are born again. There is an intrinsic change. We're not talking about a tadpole becoming a frog. We're talking about a frog becoming a prince by the kiss of grace. We're talking about a miracle—a change that is supernatural, radical. Paul began to pray because he had been united with the living God. He was forever transformed.

A Man of Power

Another mark of conversion is the divine power of conversion. Saul of Tarsus was at one moment killing Christian, but the next moment he is worshipping Christ. Every Christian has that same divine power.

Ananias is told in the vision to go to a certain house of a man named Judas. The Lord tells him exactly where to go. Go to the street called Straight, and you'll find Saul of Tarsus. You can imagine Ananias' thoughts. "What? Wait! *The* Saul of Tarsus? The persecutor? Ananias has an objection.

> **Acts 9:13-14** | But Ananias answered, "Lord, I have heard from many about this man, how much evil he has done to your saints at Jerusalem. [14] And here he has authority from the chief priests to bind all who call on your name."

You see Saul of Tarsus was a man of position and authority. He had permission to bring great suffering and even death to the saints at Jerusalem and throughout Israel.

Given Saul's recent ravaging of the church, the first Christians would not trust Saul's call to a position of church leadership. His

---

[186] C. H. Spurgeon, *Morning and Evening* (Fearn, Ross-shire, UK: Christian Focus, 1994), reading for November 3.

reputation preceded him. No one trusted the newly converted Saul. R.C. Sproul said it well. Saul's conversion would have seemed to the fledgling New Testament church much as it would seem to us if Osama Bin Laden were to come to America claiming to be a convert to U.S. patriotism.[187] Saul had the power to destroy more Christians, but the Lord took the most infamous persecutor and made him a promoter of Christianity. No matter how great a man's power and position is, it's nothing compared to God's position. From his infinite and exalted position God loves to call the hardest, most impossible, hard-hearted people, and melt them.

God can save anyone, anywhere in the very worst of circumstances. He doesn't have to ask our permission. God sometimes calls people we don't want to be saved. God's heart is infinitely more compassionate than our heart. We are all so much like the Prophet Jonah who ran away from God when he was called to preach repentance to the dreaded and vile Ninevites of ancient Assyria. God loves to save those most unlikely candidates, like Saul of Tarsus. "Is there anything too hard for the Lord?" (Gen 18:14). I love the words of Jeremiah.

> *Jeremiah 32:17* | Ah, Lord God! It is you who have made the heavens and the earth by your great power and by your outstretched arm! Nothing is too hard for you.

What is impossible for man is possible for God (Lk 18:27). God can save anyone! Remember whatever power and position Paul had when he was lost is really nothing. Paul later concludes that all his earthly attainments were like "dung" compared to the "excellency of knowing Christ" (Phil 3:8).

Now that Paul was in Christ, he had true power and authority, seated in the highest place, united with the King of all the earth. Through Christ, all Christians have an exalted position.

> *Ephesians 2:6* | God raised us up with him and seated us with him in the heavenly places in Christ Jesus.

Whatever Saul's greatness and position was before he knew Christ, it was limited and earthly. In coming to know Christ, he would have that limitless and eternal position in Christ.

---

[187] Sproul, *Acts*, 156–157.

What could change a man of such position and power to reverse course and go the opposite direction? What could change such a man? Only the power of God.

A Man of Purpose

Another mark of conversion is purpose. Everyone in the Body of Christ is given a place to serve Christ. For Paul, he is here called to be an apostle. Now we see that this man of great power and authority is called by God to be an apostle. Saul the persecutor becomes Paul the great apostle. He becomes God's "chosen instrument" for bringing the gospel to the Gentiles.

> **Acts 9:15** | But the Lord said to him, "Go, for he is a chosen instrument of mine to carry my name before the Gentiles and kings and the children of Israel."

Christ had gotten hold of Saul of Tarsus and would make of him the greatest apostle, a writer of thirteen books in our New Testament. God chose Saul, and because of the choosing, he would gladly proclaim Christ for the rest of his life. He marveled at the splendors of God's grace, and so do we. Paul knew that not only he, but all Christians are chosen.

> *Ephesians 1:4–5* | He chose us in him before the foundation of the world, that we should be holy and blameless before him. In love [5] he predestined us for adoption to himself as sons.

Paul testifies: God "set me apart before I was born" (Gal 1:15). And in time, God grabbed hold of Paul. Paul would later say he wanted to take hold of Christ the way Christ took hold of him.

> *Philippians 3:12* | I press on to take hold of that for which Christ Jesus took hold of me.

Saul of Tarsus had been hunting down Christians until he met Jesus. Now his purpose has changed. Jesus told him he was now "to carry my name before the Gentiles and kings and the children of Israel" (9:15).

Saul was a chosen vessel. God had determined the course of his life. All Saul's previous life had been a preparation for this moment: his birth into a family enjoying Roman citizenship and his city noted for its seafaring commerce and its world-famous university. Saul's Hellenistic culture made him familiar with the Greek language, learning, and logic. His birth into a Hebrew home where he was brought up in the synagogue, gave him an intimate knowledge of the Scriptures. He was acquainted from childhood days with the knowledge of God and the Hebrew Bible. Even his hatred of Christ and the church and his savage persecutions would be turned to good, showing God is willing and able to save the most impossible people.

Saul was a chosen vessel. So are we all. Each of us has special training, talents, temperament, a unique background and upbringing, and a specific culture and characteristics that he wants to use to expand his kingdom. God makes no two people alike.[188]

A Man of Pain

Another mark of conversion is pain and suffering. This world is a warzone for the Christian. Every Christian will experience a measure of suffering of some sort if they live a godly life. Paul is told how very much he must suffer now that he is a follower of the Messiah. The man who inflicted so much pain to believers would now be on the receiving end for his newfound faith. This might have been a shock to him, and it is often a shock to most new believers.

> **Acts 9:16** | For I will show him how much he must suffer for the sake of my name."

Years later Paul gave the Corinthians a partial catalog of his sufferings.

> *2 Corinthians 11:23b–28* | ... imprisonments, ... countless beatings, and often near death. [24] Five times I received at the hands of the Jews the forty lashes less one. [25] Three times I was beaten with rods. Once I was stoned. Three times I was shipwrecked; a night and a day I was adrift at sea; [26] on frequent journeys, in danger from rivers, danger from robbers, danger from my own people, danger from Gentiles, danger in the city, danger in the wilderness, danger at sea, danger from false brothers; [27] in toil and hardship, through many a sleepless night, in hunger and thirst, often without food, in cold and exposure. [28] And, apart from other things, there is the daily pressure on me of my anxiety for all the churches.

---

[188] J. Phillips, *Exploring Acts,* Ac 9:15.

Ananias had no need to worry about Saul's making the saints to suffer. From now on Saul would do the suffering. The Christian is called to be bold and courageous and Saul who was now appointed to be an apostle, would be an amazing example in suffering.

A Man of Perception

> **Acts 9:17-18a** | So Ananias departed and entered the house. And laying his hands on him he said, "Brother Saul, the Lord Jesus who appeared to you on the road by which you came has sent me so that you may regain your sight and be filled with the Holy Spirit." **18** And immediately something like scales fell from his eyes, and he regained his sight.

Spiritual perception is another mark of conversion. Saul was granted his sight through the touch of Ananias. What a joy to see Ananias willingness to be used of the Lord. God used this unknown man Ananias to encourage Saul of Tarsus to follow Christ. We never hear of him again, though he did a great work. Who remembers who led D. L. Moody to Christ? Who knows the name of the person who pointed Jim Elliot to the Way? How many know the name of the one who led Charles Spurgeon to the Lord?[189]

The fact that "Brother Saul" received the Holy Spirit and his sight at the same time indicates the beautiful order of salvation. Paul was "drawn by the Father" and he began praying. He was likely praying to God about his newfound faith in Christ. Having done so, Ananias lays hands on him, and he receives the Holy Spirit, and suddenly he can see! God here emphasizes how faith gives Saul new eyes to see by literally giving him physical sight! And there was a real physical aspect to this, since scales fell from Saul's eyes.

Saul used to have power from the authorities to put Christians to death, but now he has the true and glorious power of the Holy Spirit to repair broken men and women and to bring them to spiritual life again. That's the power we need!

A Man of Proclamation

> **Acts 9:18b-19** | Then he rose and was baptized; **19** and taking food, he was strengthened.

---

[189] Hughes, *Acts*, 131.

Proclamation of Christ is a major mark of conversion. Those who are truly saved first begin proclaiming Christ through baptism. The Ethiopian eunuch wanted baptism in the previous chapter. Now Saul the persecutor turned pastor is baptized. Saul is so weak at this moment, having gone without food for three days, but he wants to be baptized even before he eats.

Baptism is the first step of obedience in the life of a Christian. When a person professes faith in Christ, but their life doesn't change, I doubt that profession. A person who is truly born again wants to obey the Lord. Jesus said, "If you love me, keep my commandments" (Jn 14:15). But God's commands are a delight to every child of God. When the inner life is changed and empowered, the outer life will change as well!

> *2 Corinthians 5:17* | Therefore, if anyone is in Christ, he is a new creation. The old has passed away; behold, the new has come.

Conclusion

What a transformation that took place in Saul of Tarsus. Who could have imagined he would become the Apostle Paul? We must never underestimate the value of one person brought to Christ. The great apostle Peter was ministering to thousands in Jerusalem, and Philip the evangelist had seen a great harvest among the Samaritan people, but obscure Ananias was sent to only one man.

Who are you reaching for Christ? Are you praying for the hard cases? Are you praying for those impossible conversions? Remember what is impossible with man is possible with God!

17 | ACTS 9:17-31
SAUL'S GROWTH IN GRACE

For some days he was with the disciples at Damascus. And immediately he proclaimed Jesus in the synagogues, saying, "He is the Son of God." And all who heard him were amazed and said, "Is not this the man who made havoc in Jerusalem of those who called upon this name?
ACTS 9:20-21

God has called every Christian everywhere to grow in Christ. Christians are predestined to be "conformed to the image of Christ" (Rom 8:28-30). Repentant faith in Christ produces a renewal of the mind. We are united to Christ by the Holy Spirit of God. That union makes us uncomfortable with sin, hungry for the truth, and loving the fellowship of fellow believers. All these things are like the sun and water that enrich the soil of our hearts and help us grow. We see this in the conversion of Paul. In this passage, we are going to see five pillars of growth for every Christian. If you want to grow as a Christian, you have to start here, where the apostle Paul started.

The first pillar we see is that Saul of Tarsus has a new family, a forever family in Christ. I have a very hard time with anyone who calls themselves a Christian who has isolated themselves from the Body of Christ. A Christian who isolates themselves is either very sick spiritually or is just pretending to be a Christian. A robust, growing Christian has a deep desire to be with their forever family in Christ in a local church.

A NEW FAMILY (9:17–19)

Christian growth takes place in a family that is diverse, from every tribe, tongue, people, and nation. We have unity because of our union with Christ, through the Father and by the Spirit.

Just like we don't choose our children, but each is given to us as a gift, so we don't get to choose who is in the Body of Christ. So it was with Saul of Tarsus. He was a terrorizer of the church. We are introduced to a previously unknown believer named Ananias who is sent to welcome this terrorizer of God's church and invite him to come into the kingdom of God and receive him into God's family. Ananias welcomes Saul and calls him "brother."

Family Love

The Father, Son and Holy Spirit are all involved in salvation. We see this as Saul is welcomed into the family of God by a believer that until now is completely unknown.

The Love of Jesus

We see here the love of Jesus. Saul had put his faith and trust in the true Messiah on the Damascus Road. Though Ananias was surely terrified that Saul could be putting on a ruse in order to trap him, he believed Saul's faith was real. God had said that this man had not only come to Christ through faith, but he was a "chosen instrument"—an apostle to the Gentiles (9:15).

> **Acts 9:17a** | So Ananias departed and entered the house. And laying his hands on him…

Those who put their faith in Jesus are now believers. Salvation is not by works, but by faith in the righteousness of Christ. God told Ananias to seek out Saul because he had now put his faith in Christ. Ananias was to lay hands on Saul, indicating God's authenticating of Saul's faith. Do you think this might have been hard for Ananias? He had heard about Saul laying hands on countless believers to destroy them. Now Ananias was to lay hands on Saul to confirm him?

We must learn to love those whom God loves. They have come to Christ from afar off. God's conversions are often surprising to us. We may be surprised at who God saves, but God is not. He only saves sinner. Jesus said, "I came not to call the righteous, but sinners to repentance" (Lk 5:32). Paul later said, "Jesus came into the world to save sinners, of whom I am the foremost" (1 Tim 1:15). Ananias laying hands on Saul indicated that Saul's faith in Jesus was genuine.

Ananias believed in the reality of Saul's conversion. What a delightful greeting he gave him—"Brother Saul." The man who had been his enemy was now a brother in Christ. Only the power of God through the Holy Spirit can bring about a change like that.

Ananias was no great pillar of the faith, yet he was the first to greet the one who would become the great apostle, Paul. Ananias would demonstrate the forever family love and acceptance that we should have for all believers. Remember, Ananias had argued with the Lord. "This man has terrorized the church." Nonetheless, he obeyed the Lord.

The Love of the Father

Acts 9:17b | Ananias ... entered the house. And laying his hands on him he said, "Brother Saul..."

It was like the Father in heaven was saying, "This one is mine. Go lay your hands on him. Claim him for my kingdom!" Saul was now an adopted child of our heavenly Father, a brother in Christ. The first contact the saved terrorist had with the church was the kindly touch of a fellow believer's hand. The first words he heard from another believer's lips was the lovely word "Brother." "Brother Saul." It must have gone straight to his heart. This was Saul's introduction to his new family.

From the Christian perspective, and especially within the fellowship of the church, we must be prepared to accept a new believer as they are, and not concentrate on what they were before Christ saved them. What are you now saint? You have the stamp of the Father's love on you. You are a brother or sister in God's forever family. All believers have had their past wiped out. If God accepts that person, let us accept him, or her, as a brother or sister in Christ.

Love Poured into Saul by the Spirit

Acts 9:17c | "Brother Saul, the Lord Jesus who appeared to you on the road by which you came has sent me so that you may regain your sight and be filled with the Holy Spirit."

The Spirit was about to put his stamp of approval onto Saul's faith. Saul was now to be filled with the Holy Spirit. Spirit baptism is the sign of our union with Christ. The Spirit pours God's love into our hearts.

Romans 5:5 | God's love has been poured into our hearts through the Holy Spirit who has been given to us.

All who are born again are the Temple of God's Spirit.

1 Corinthians 6:19 | Do you not know that your body is a temple of the Holy Spirit within you, whom you have from God?

The Agent of salvation is the blessed Holy Spirit, but the Spirit uses human agents to fill up and pour out. Don't tell me you are filled with the Spirit if you won't give the gospel to the lost. "How shall they hear without a preacher?" (Rom 10:14). You are a human agent of the Holy Spirit. The part Ananias played in the conversion experience of Saul illustrates what a great privilege it is to be used of God in bringing someone to know Christ as their Lord and Savior. Ananias was God's instrument, not only to restore Saul's physical sight, but also to give him spiritual sight into the truth of salvation. Saul was 'filled with the Holy Spirit' (Acts 9:17). From the human standpoint we can say that Ananias was the man who gave Paul to the church, and to the Gentile world. [190]

The great mark of salvation is the fellowship and togetherness that the Spirit brings to every believer by uniting them to the Body of Christ. Ananias rightly called Saul "brother." Saul was not part of God's forever family. Every Christian longs to gather with God's family. Saul knew he was not alone. Dear saint, you are not alone. You are part of God's family.

Family Loyalty

Acts 9:18 | And immediately something like scales fell from his eyes, and he regained his sight. Then he rose and was baptized.

---

[190] Williams, *Acts*, 101-102.

There is a loyalty in every believer that we show to Christ and to our forever family through baptism. Something like literal scales fell from Saul's eyes, and his blindness is removed, and his eyes opened. The first thing he saw was the face of a Christian brother. He knew enough of Christian life to know that he had an obligation to identify himself with Christ and the family of God's people by being baptized.

Outside of the baptism of Jesus in the Jordan, the baptism of Saul of Tarsus in Damascus was, perhaps, the most remarkable and startling single baptism in the whole course of Christian history. His baptism was like God raising the flag of victory over the one man most zealously opposed to Christ on the earth at the time.

Baptism publicly proclaimed him a member of the new and noble family of twice-born children of the living God.[191] That wouldn't have been at all popular or accepted among his closest friends and family. Baptism is not just an immersion into the family of God. Sometimes it means losing the love and acceptance of your own family and friends. But our true family is our forever family in Christ.

Family Life

Acts 9:19 | And taking food, he was strengthened. For some days he was with the disciples at Damascus.

This fellowship with believers in Damascus is a wonderful evidence of genuine conversion. John says,

1 John 3:14 | We know that we have passed from death unto life, because we love the brothers.

Love and fellowship with Christ's body is a sure sign of conversion and growth in a true child of God. Those who make excuses for missing the gathering of the saints are either woefully immature or sadly deceived about their salvation.

A NEW FAITH (9:20-22)

Christian growth takes place by preaching the faith of Christ to ourselves and to others.

Real discipleship takes place as we immediately evangelize others. We can simply give our own testimony like Paul did, proclaiming Jesus

---

[191] J. Phillips, *Exploring Acts*, Ac 9:18.

as the true Messiah, King of kings, the Son of God. When we preach to others, we are also preaching to ourselves.

Preaching the Faith

> **Acts 9:20** | And immediately he proclaimed Jesus in the synagogues, saying, "He is the Son of God."

Saul was a trained theologian, but he had no heart of compassion for others, until now. He had been driving by the Law, and all the Law can do is crush. The grace of Christ had now captured his heart. Grace enlivens and does ten times what the Law could hope to do. Grace brings life. Now that Paul was born again, he wanted "every creature" to know that Jesus is the Son of God. Saul was no man to sit still even though he had just been introduced to Jesus. He seems to have wasted no time in making his way into the synagogues. "Jesus is King!"

The term "Son of God" does refer to his deity, but it mainly refers to his position as Messiah, God's ultimate King: a reference to Psalm 2. The Messiah in Scripture is the figure who is "King of kings and Lord of lords." There in Psalm 2 we are told to "Kiss the Son" or pay homage to him. The best way to do that is to proclaim him to the lost. Every child of God has a clear view of who Jesus Christ is. He is Lord of all.

Proving the Faith

It wasn't Paul's preaching that was challenged, but his reputation. Can God really save someone who was so vicious toward the church? The answer is a very loud, "Yes!"

> **Acts 9:21-22** | And all who heard him were amazed and said, "Is not this the man who made havoc in Jerusalem of those who called upon this name? And has he not come here for this purpose, to bring them bound before the chief priests?" **22** But Saul increased all the more in strength, and confounded the Jews who lived in Damascus by proving that Jesus was the Christ.

The text says that Saul not only "increased in strength" but also that he "confounded the Jews... proving that Jesus was the Christ." We can picture what happened. News of his arrival would cause an immediate stir. Here was the greatest teacher of the Sanhedrin, armed with documents demanding full cooperation of the faithful in the task entrusted to him of rooting out heresy. The ruler of the synagogue would be deferential and certainly be honored for him to teach. It was not every day an accredited agent of the Sanhedrin crossed the threshold of the Damascus synagogue. Saul would be given the chief seat. Every eye would be on him. Some would gaze at him with approval, others with apprehension. In due course Saul would beckon for the Scriptures to be handed to him. He would stand and read a passage, hand back the scroll, and face the congregation. A hush would fall. Now it was coming—a denunciation of the new sect. But instead, taking the reading of the day as his text, Paul preached Christ to the people, proving that Jesus is the Son of God. Their astonishment must have known no bounds.[192] The term Son of God gives us a clue what text he might have preached from Psalm 2.

> *Psalm 2:7-12* | I will tell of the decree: The Lord said to me, "You are my Son; today I have begotten you. ⁸ Ask of me, and I will make the nations your heritage, and the ends of the earth your possession. ⁹ You shall break them with a rod of iron and dash them in pieces like a potter's vessel." ¹⁰ Now therefore, O kings, be wise; be warned, O rulers of the earth. ¹¹ Serve the Lord with fear, and rejoice with trembling. ¹² Kiss the Son, lest he be angry, and you perish in the way, for his wrath is quickly kindled. Blessed are all who take refuge in him.

This is one of those "every knee shall bow and every tongue confess" kind of texts. Bow before Christ. Kiss the Son. Worship him. Pay homage to him. That's what we need to preach. A vital sign of real growth in the Christian life is when you see everyone as a soul that needs Christ. Do you have a heart that breaks for the lost?

A NEW FIGHT (9:23-25)

Christian growth takes place as we persevere through daily spiritual warfare.

If you aren't facing satanic harassment or persecution, then you are not growing. When a tree grows, it has to persevere through the elements, the rain and snow, the hot and cold weather. It has to be able to take the howling winds. But it grows. We move forward in growth as Christians, not by looking to ourselves and "white knuckling" it. We look to Christ, and we persevere in spiritual warfare.

---

[192] J. Phillips, *Exploring Acts,* Ac 9:20.

A Secret Fight

Acts 9:23 | When many days had passed, the Jews plotted to kill him.

Of course, the Jewish leaders plotted to kill Saul, just like they had plotted and succeeded in murdering our Lord Jesus. The battle is real. We wrestle not against flesh and blood. Our real enemy is even more secret and unseen than the Jews who wanted to kill Saul. We face the same enemy. The devil is on the prowl. If you don't face spiritual warfare against the battle, that might say something about the side you're on. All true Christians suffer persecution. Sometimes it's persecution from people. But there is constant persecution from the demonic world. The only way around it is to look to the cross of Jesus in faith. Put on the whole armor of God.

> *Ephesians 6:11-13* | Put on the whole armor of God, that you may be able to stand against the schemes of the devil. [12] For we do not wrestle against flesh and blood, but against the rulers, against the authorities, against the cosmic powers over this present darkness, against the spiritual forces of evil in the heavenly places. [13] Therefore take up the whole armor of God.

We are the church militant on earth. We are in a warzone. Prayer is your walkie talkie. The word of God is your sword. It's not enough to know the word, you have to walk in the word. Wielding the word of God is the only way to make the enemy flee so you can win the fight.

A Spoiled Fight

Of course, we already know we have the victory. Saul realized this. The enemies of Christ plotted to kill Saul, but Saul is spared. Let's read about it.

> **Acts 9:24-25** | Their plot became known to Saul. They were watching the gates day and night in order to kill him, [25] but his disciples took him by night and let him down through an opening in the wall, lowering him in a basket.

God allowed this plot to be known by Saul, even though many were waiting to execute him by the main city gates. So Saul decided to go out a different way with help from fellow believers, who lowered him down through an opening in the wall. He descended in a basket through the wall.

The Bible encourages us that "the battle is the Lord's" (2 Chron 20:15) and "greater is he who is in you than he who is in the world" (1 Jn 4:4). The Lord has already won.

Expect to fight constant daily spiritual battles as you grow in Christ. The only "big deal" in life is knowing Christ and walking with him. Everything else when it comes to us, our personal comfort or reputation, we can sacrifice. His unrelenting love is better than anything this life can offer (Psa 63:3).

Saul escaped with his life through the wall in a basket. No matter what we lose, even if it is our life, we must always remember that nothing can separate us from the love of Christ. That's where true happiness and joy is found.

We don't read about it here, but upon escaping Damascus, Paul spends about three years learning from the Lord personally in the desert of Arabia. According to Galatians 1:15-18, he left Damascus and went into Arabia, which may mean the surrounding desert countryside. We have no idea how far south into the Arabian Peninsula Paul may have wandered, but we know he later returned to Damascus. Galatians 1:17-18 says that "after three years" he went to Jerusalem. Saul wanted new friendships in Jerusalem, but he didn't find them there.

> **Acts 9:26a** | And when he had come to Jerusalem, he attempted to join the disciples. And they were all afraid of him...

A NEW FRIENDSHIP (9:26-30)

Christian growth takes place in the midst of real friends, not all of whom are accepting of us. We are all growing. We all are porcupines. Growth takes place when we are humble enough to love all those who are born again, even when they are hard to love.

The book of Acts is all about life-on-life discipleship. A huge part of discipleship is real friendship. At times people will say, "Pastor Matt I really want discipleship." What you are asking for is someone to come and speak into your life, and you speak into their life. You have to pursue that. The pastors and elders will do their best at pursuing people, but we will fail, just based on the sheer magnitude of trying to shepherd every person in the congregation. It is every believer's responsibility to seek out discipleship, and that means friendship. Often, we find when we follow Christ, we lose our friends in the world and even our family.

When Saul was saved, most in the church wanted nothing to do with him.

Rejected Friendship

> **Acts 9:26** | And when he had come to Jerusalem, he attempted to join the disciples. And they were all afraid of him, for they did not believe that he was a disciple.

It's true that the saints opposed Saul when he became a believer because, as verse 26 says, "They were all afraid of him, for they did not believe that he was a disciple." I get that. The same thing happened in our own church. God saved a man from Saudi Arabia and made him an evangelist and had him be a member of our church. At first there was great resistance to him. There was fear. There may still be fear. But that is a greatly immature faith. We are called to receive a brother, no matter what his previous sins were. So, yes, God wants to save jihadist Muslims and make them followers of Christ. We have to have open arms for all who come.

> *1 Corinthians 6:11* | Such were some of you. But you were washed, you were sanctified, you were justified in the name of the Lord Jesus Christ and by the Spirit of our God.

Redeemed Friendship

I understand that some in the church will reject the harder cases when they come to Christ. That's just immaturity. But we need to have those mature believers, like Barnabas, who will teach us how to love through their actions.

> **Acts 9:27** | But Barnabas took him and brought him to the apostles and declared to them how on the road he had seen the Lord, who spoke to him, and how at Damascus he had preached boldly in the name of Jesus.

When all rejected Saul, Barnabas was there as the "son of encouragement" to really comfort him and support him and speak up for Paul. Barnabas had witnessed Paul's strong preaching in the name of Jesus when they were in Damascus.

We all need a Barnabas in our lives that can encourage us and walk alongside us. All of us need a Paul that can pull us up when we are weak, hold us accountable, and be firm with us. And we all need a Timothy in our lives that we can pull up and encourage. When you teach others, you are also teaching yourself. That's redeemed friendship. Barnabas, "the son of encouragement," threw caution to the wind, sought Saul, heard him out, and was convinced of the genuineness of his faith. This was the beginning of a lifelong friendship.[193]

Reliable Friendship

Friendship in the Lord is forever. It's the most reliable friendship we can have. The place where Paul had once bound Christians and stoned them, he is now preaching Christ.

> **Acts 9:28-30** | So he went in and out among them at Jerusalem, preaching boldly in the name of the Lord. [29] And he spoke and disputed against the Hellenists. But they were seeking to kill him. [30] And when the brothers learned this, they brought him down to Caesarea and sent him off to Tarsus.

We can imagine the heightened emotion when those who had received floggings at Paul's orders gave him the kiss of peace and then, they shared bread and wine affirming their union with each other and the Lord.[194] Christ can do that! That's our forever family and the forever friendship we have in Christ.

And when the Hellenistic Jews wanted to kill Paul, the brothers in Christ protected him. He goes from preaching to persecution. How unusual the Christian life is. There is so many ups and downs in the Christian life that we need friends. We can't do this alone. During Paul's ministry years, sometimes there were successes, sometimes there were failures, and sometimes there were quiet times. We do not hear from Saul again for ten years—until Barnabas comes to Tarsus to ask him to help with the work in Antioch.[195]

Are you experiencing the ups and downs of the Christian life? You need the brothers. You need fellowship. You need the Body of Christ.

A NEW FUTURE (9:31)

When real Christian growth takes place, the entire church grows and multiplies.

---

[193] Hughes, *Acts*, 139.
[194] Pollock, *The Apostle*, 42.
[195] Hughes, *Acts*, 139–140.

Acts 9:31 | So the church throughout all Judea and Galilee and Samaria had peace and was being built up. And walking in the fear of the Lord and in the comfort of the Holy Spirit, it multiplied.

Paul now goes off stage until he reappears in 11:25f. But an important point has now been achieved in Luke's story. All the preparations have been made for the decisive step forward in the mission of the church which took it to the Gentiles. So Luke pauses to give a general summary of the situation.[196]

Saul was moved out of harm's way. He went off to his home city of Tarsus. God multiplied the peace of the church. There were many signs of true growth for God's people: peace in the church, the fear of the Lord, the comfort of the church, and a multiplication of new believers. I want to see that. That's the sign of real growth and maturity in the church.

Conclusion

Are you growing into the image of Christ? Is there fruit? The answer is not to get self-focused and try to turn the Christian life into a self-help program. The answer is to look to Christ alone.

---

[196] Marshall, *Acts*, 186.

18 | ACTS 9:32–10:16
MIRACLES, MEALS, & MERCY FOR GENTILES

> *At Caesarea there was a man named Cornelius, a centurion of what was known as the Italian Cohort, a devout man who feared God with all his household, gave alms generously to the people, and prayed continually to God.*
>
> ACTS 10:1-2

I don't know about you, but I deeply desire to see God working in our lives personally, and in our congregation. I believe he is at work. We are studying in the book of Acts about life-on-life discipleship, and one thing that is apparent is that if you are growing as a disciple, you are going to see God working, expanding the boundaries of his kingdom. We see the second Gentile convert. The first one was the Ethiopian eunuch. So the first New Testament Gentile convert was from Africa. The second one is a Roman named Cornelius.

Are you seeing God move in your life? What is holding you back? It might be culture. People say, "Well, if the music was better at church, I'd really follow Jesus. I'd really serve him. I'd really reach souls." Or perhaps it's, "If my marriage was better, I'd see God move." Or it could be, "I'm so sick and suffering, and if I wasn't suffering so much, I'd see

God move." Can I say the obvious? The only thing holding you back from God moving in your life is you. It's not your circumstances or your culture or your church or your marriage or your singleness. It's your unbelief.

So many of us are living in our caskets of fear and frustration. Yes, anger and anxiety tempt us and haunt us throughout each day, but what do you do? We try to change our circumstances. That's the most useless thing we can do. God is more interested in changing your heart than changing your circumstances. Indeed, when we suffer, we tend to be humbled and more willing to draw near to God. So who here will get out of the casket? Who will live in the power of the resurrection and insist that if God works anywhere, he works here and now in your life, in your church? Who will call on God for that?

That was the attitude of the apostles and disciples in Acts 9 and 10. God was on the move, and they had been used to seeing God work. Isn't that amazing to get to that point. No longer are we in unbelief, but we are just expecting God to work every time we get together for prayer, for the word, for singing, for fellowship. God is on the move. If you believe that say, "Amen!"

Key Thought: When God is working, God will use you to bring people to Christ, even if they have little in common with you.

In Acts 10, we are going to learn that when God is working, we see three things: miracles, meals, and man's conversion. People will start coming to Christ, and it's not merely because of your friendship with them, or that you work together, or your charm. But God is calling them, and he will use you to transform their heart from a heart of fear to a heart of faith.

THE MIRACLES (9:32-43)

Here we see two miracles by Peter, and it is remarkable. One is a dramatic healing. The other is a glorious resurrection. Peter is carrying on the ministry of Jesus.

God can do anything. We often don't believe God can do anything. But he can. Often God, when he is getting ready to do something impactful through a saint, he will stretch their faith with an impossible situation. Do you need a faith-stretching miracle? We see two in the last part of Acts 9.

A Healing

First, we learn of a man who was bedridden for eight years, and Peter heals him. It's an impossible situation, but Peter does not flinch. You can see he's done this before. Remember Acts 3 when Peter and John healed the lame man, and he began leaping around, and Peter's message about the Christ who heals led to a revival? He's seen many miracles done by his Lord Jesus Christ, as well as each of the apostles. He just commands this paralyzed man to walk.

The Person Healed

Acts 9:32-33 | Now as Peter went here and there among them all, he came down also to the saints who lived at Lydda. ³³ There he found a man named Aeneas, bedridden for eight years, who was paralyzed.

Eight years is a long time to be sick in bed, day after day, week after week, month after month, year after year, and no end in sight. The doctors had long since given up the case of Aeneas as hopeless. There was not only the pain and suffering, the sense of uselessness, of being a constant burden to others; there was the nagging and unanswerable question, why me?[197] If we will turn to God, he will either heal us or show us the purpose for our suffering as we trust in him.

The Power of the Healing

Peter had the gift of healing, one of the authenticating gifts of the early church. He instantly healed this man in the name of Jesus. Though we don't necessarily have apostolic gifts, this physical healing is not the greatest kind of healing. Salvation is the greatest healing. All those who are divinely healed will face a just God on judgement day. We need to have something more than physical healing. We need to experience the power of the resurrection. We need the healing of our sins being forgiven, our minds being renewed, and our hearts being cleansed of idols and filled with love and worship for Jesus.

The Purpose of the Healing

Acts 9:35 | And all the residents of Lydda and Sharon saw him, and they turned to the Lord.

---

[197] J. Phillips, *Exploring Acts*, Ac 9:33.

Long story short, the man is completely healed, and when the town people see him, they glorify God. Luke said the people of the region turned to the Lord as a result of Aeneas's healing. One recalls how the news of Jesus' miracles also spread to the surrounding neighborhood and attracted crowds to him. As we have seen before, the miracles in Acts are signs of the power of Jesus and often serve as the initial basis that leads to ultimate commitment. They are never, however, a substitute for faith.[198] Conversions of Jews are taking place all over the region because of this. As much as this did for the inhabitants of Lydda, this is really about Peter's faith being built up and stretched.

A Resurrection

If healing wasn't enough, Peter goes to another place, not far away to Joppa, and he finds a girl named Tabitha (her Aramaic name), also known as Dorcas (her Greek name. She became ill and died, and Peter raises her from the dead.

> **Acts 9:36-43** | Now there was in Joppa a disciple named Tabitha, which, translated, means Dorcas. She was full of good works and acts of charity. **37** In those days she became ill and died, and when they had washed her, they laid her in an upper room. **38** Since Lydda was near Joppa, the disciples, hearing that Peter was there, sent two men to him, urging him, "Please come to us without delay." **39** So Peter rose and went with them. And when he arrived, they took him to the upper room. All the widows stood beside him weeping and showing tunics and other garments that Dorcas made while she was with them. **40** But Peter put them all outside, and knelt down and prayed; and turning to the body he said, "Tabitha, arise." And she opened her eyes, and when she saw Peter she sat up. **41** And he gave her his hand and raised her up. Then, calling the saints and widows, he presented her alive. **42** And it became known throughout all Joppa, and many believed in the Lord. **43** And he stayed in Joppa for many days with one Simon, a tanner.

What do we say to this? God is a miracle working God. This is a miracle so similar to the raising of Jairus' daughter, Talitha (Mk 5:21-43). You get the idea. These are the acts of Jesus through the apostles.

---

[198] Polhill, *Acts*, 246.

Though we are not apostles, you must know that God is working through you in a similar way. Jesus is going to expand his kingdom, not just through the pastors and teachers and preachers, but through you. Do you get that? Take hold of that. If you are not evangelizing people, you are stuck in your growth. You are Jesus with skin on.

THE MEAL (10:1-16)

Now we see the reason for these miracles for Peter. God is about to turn Peter's world upside down. Peter has never seen a Gentile come to faith outside of Jerusalem. You see there is a ritual for Gentile converts, and what is about to happen is going to stretch Peter's faith beyond the borders of Israel. God is about to save a Roman centurion named Cornelius.

The Meal was about a New People

Here we have a divine appointment for a Gentile named Cornelius. He lived in Caesarea which was the capital of the Roman occupation of Israel. It was a military town. It's right on the coast, thirty-one miles north of Joppa. It's important to know that the Jews hated Caesarea. They called it the daughter of Edom, a place of ungodliness. It was a symbolic name for Rome.

Cornelius is a Leader

Cornelius is a captain of the occupying Roman army. As a centurion, he would have commanded about a hundred Roman soldiers posted in Caesarea, and he would have been paid as much as five times more than an ordinary soldier. So he's a wealthy and influential man. Jews, however, surely resented him.[199]

> **Acts 10:1** | At Caesarea there was a man named Cornelius, a centurion of what was known as the Italian Cohort.

A normal Roman cohort, consisting of 600 men, was the tenth part of a legion. Each company of 100 men was commanded by a centurion, a tough-minded, iron-disciplined, well-trained, brave-hearted man. The Italian cohort would have been a cohort levied in Italy.[200]

---

[199] Merida, *Exalting Jesus in Acts*, 164.
[200] J. Phillips, *Exploring Acts*, Ac 10:1–2.

Cornelius is a Lover of God

Acts 10:2 | A devout man who feared God with all his household, gave alms generously to the people, and prayed continually to God.

Luke doesn't want us to miss Cornelius's religious devotion (10:2). The man "feared God." He is a Gentile openly seeking after God. He's not "all in", but he is a seeker. The term "God fearer" was applied to Gentiles who adhered to Judaism's faith in one God as they obeyed the Ten Commandments.[201] Many of them attended the synagogue and were instructed in the Scriptures and even observed the Sabbath and, to some extent, the Jewish dietary laws. They drew the line, however, at becoming full proselytes by circumcision, baptism, and sacrifice.

The Holy Spirit underlines three things about this very fine person, Cornelius. He mentions *his faith*. He was "a devout man, and one that feared God." Cornelius lived up to the light that he had. He mentions his *family*. He feared God with all in his household. He knew the Lord. This man had thick skin as a Roman soldier, but he had a big heart for God and for his family. Then we learn about his *fervor* for the Lord. He was generous with his giving to the poor, and he had a fellowship with God, praying continually.

Cornelius is a Learner

More than anything, Cornelius is a learner. That's what "disciple" means. He goes to synagogue. But he's not circumcised or baptized, so he can't offer sacrifices in Jerusalem. Yet it seems he's born again. God sends an angel to let him know that his prayers are answered. That's amazing! But he's not yet received the indwelling of the Holy Spirit.

Acts 10:3-8 | About the ninth hour of the day he saw clearly in a vision an angel of God come in and say to him, "Cornelius." **4** And he stared at him in terror and said, "What is it, Lord?" And he said to him, "Your prayers and your alms have ascended as a memorial before God. **5** And now send men to Joppa and bring one Simon who is called Peter. **6** He is lodging with one Simon, a tanner, whose house is by the sea." **7** When the angel who spoke to him had departed, he called two of his servants and a devout soldier from among those who attended him, **8** and having related everything to them, he sent them to Joppa.

---

[201] Johnson, *Let's Study Acts*, 124.

Cornelius was a seasoned, rugged Roman soldier, but the appearance of the angel brought him great terror. When God interacts with us, we are often surprised. But the angel tells him that his prayers are answered. I don't know the content of his prayers, but as a God-fearer, he wasn't circumcised, and he wouldn't have been welcomed by the Jews. He must have been lonely. But he's following the one true God.

Peter is sent to tell him the gospel more clearly, specifically that Jesus died for his sins, that the Messiah has come. So now, without true fellowship for his whole life, Cornelius is now sent the Apostle Peter of all people! He was to call on the great Apostle and invite him to his own house. To be a true disciple of Jesus Christ, we must be learners. A disciple means "learner". That means we are tender to God, and we are going to be taught and equipped by those all around us.

When we celebrate the Lord's supper, it reflects God's heart. All the prejudice and pride in the corrupt hearts of men is cleansed by the blood of Christ. We come together as one loaf, participating with Christ. We are his body. All the walls of our pride and sin between all the ethnicities of the earth are torn down by the atonement of Christ. He brings us into one body, and he calls all people everywhere to repent and take part in his kingdom where we are all part of God's forever family. You are my family in you belong to Jesus.

The Meal was about a New Purpose

Peter falls into a trance, where he is awake, but he's seeing a vision. He is shown a strange meal in this vision. God says to him: Rise and eat some unclean food, Peter. "No" says Peter, "Never! I'm a faithful Jew, and I've never eaten anything unclean." Isn't it funny that he's getting a revelation from God, but he thinks he knows better? Let's read about this vision.

> **Acts 10:9-13** | The next day, as they were on their journey and approaching the city, Peter went up on the housetop about the sixth hour [*12 noon*] to pray. [10] And he became hungry and wanted something to eat, but while they were preparing it, he fell into a trance [11] and saw the heavens opened and something like a great sheet descending, being let down by its four corners upon the earth. [12] In it were all kinds of animals and reptiles and birds of the air. [13] And there came a voice to him: "Rise, Peter; kill and eat."

Here was this blanket of birds and animals. He had been hungry, but he's not hungry anymore. This sheet has also been translated "sail" which would also be an appropriate symbol for the gospel on the move.

Above him the sun shone down and over yonder he could see the Great Sea (so much bigger than his little Sea of Galilee), its horizons stretching farther and farther away to the west and to the Gentile nations of the mighty Roman world. Down below could be heard the sounds of the tanner and his men busy at their dubious trade. And up from the kitchen wafted the provocative smell of food sizzling in the pan.[202] Peter saw so many different animals in the vision: clean and unclean.

The point of the meal (and actually the point of the entire Old Testament sacrificial system of clean and unclean animals) was that though we are to be separate from the world because of a life of holiness, the church is to be made up of every tribe, language, ethnicity, and nation. When it comes to people, what makes us unclean is our sin. We are born sinners. But God is willing to make all people clean in Christ. In other words, it's not about race, it's about grace.

The purpose of the vision was to illustrate the inclusion of Gentiles into the covenant with Israel. Anyone who comes by faith can be saved. No longer do we have to come by ceremonies and rituals. It was always God's plan to pour his Spirit out on the whole world. God is drawing all kinds of people to himself, weather you realize it or not. Let's expand our vision to match God's heart.

The Meal was about a New Perspective

Acts 10:13-14 | And there came a voice to him: "Rise, Peter; kill and eat." **14** But Peter said, "By no means, Lord; for I have never eaten anything that is common or unclean."

Peter was shocked by what God had asked. Never before had he eaten anything that was unclean. Never before had he reached out to a Gentile to give him the gospel. This is for the Jews. Peter was being asked by the Lord to "kill and eat." This wasn't about food but about people. He needed to go and meet Cornelius and give him the gospel.

Instead, Peter started arguing with the Lord's messenger. "Never! By no means!" You will remember that Peter has a habit of standing

---

[202] J. Phillips, *Exploring Acts*, Ac 10:17a.

against the Lord's plans. Once when the Lord told Peter and the disciples that he was going to die at Jerusalem, Peter rebuked him.

> *Matthew 16:21-23* | From that time Jesus began to show his disciples that he must go to Jerusalem and suffer many things from the elders and chief priests and scribes, and be killed, and on the third day be raised. [22] And Peter took him aside and began to rebuke him, saying, "Far be it from you, Lord! This shall never happen to you." [23] But he turned and said to Peter, "Get behind me, Satan! You are a hindrance to me. For you are not setting your mind on the things of God, but on the things of man."

Jesus gave Peter a nickname for the way he was acting. Do you see what it was? He called Peter "Satan". Sometimes God's people do Satan's work better than the evil one himself. We don't mean to. We mean well. Peter meant well. But he got his eyes on "the things of man" and not on the "things of God". And this is how it goes for us as Christians. The moment we start thinking about the kingdom of self, we start doing Satan's work.

Making People Clean

Now after Peter's arguing, the Lord gave a new perspective to Peter. He says, don't call unclean, what God makes clean. God can make people clean.

> **Acts 10:15** | And the voice came to him again a second time, "What God has made clean, do not call common."

Jesus was calling Peter through this angel to reach the Gentiles. Jews hated Gentiles, and the feelings were mutual. The ancient world was filled with race riots, racial slaughters, and long-standing bitterness. But God always loved the Gentiles. He had commanded Israel to reach them (Isa 2:2-5; 26:5-8; 56:3-8; 60:3-5). Instead, they either joined into their pagan worship of false gods, or they isolated themselves from them altogether, like the Pharisees. The Jews looked at the Gentiles, because of their pagan worship and customs, as "unclean" and common.

God's heart for the nations is seen in Jesus' marching orders before he ascends to heaven. He said, "Go therefore and make disciples of all nations." The word "nations" happens also to be the Greek word for "Gentile", *ethnos*, which correlates to the Hebrew word, *goyim* (Mt 28:19; *cf* Acts 1:8; 11:18). A "Jew" was anyone who belonged to one of the twelve tribes of Israel, and a "Gentile" was everyone else. As typically used in the New Testament, "Gentile" simply means "non-Jewish". God makes people whether Jew or Gentile, religious or non-religious, clean by the blood of Jesus Christ.

Making Peter Understand

Was Peter getting it? Maybe not at first. There is an indication that he needed more convincing. Notice the vision was seen by Peter three times.

> **Acts 10:16** | This happened three times, and the thing was taken up at once to heaven.

Why three times? It could have been God's way of telling Peter, "Hey, It's really me. Remember when you denied me three times and three times you said you loved me? Well, here's another three times. It really is me, so take this seriously!" Still on the roof, trying to understand the vision and what the voice of God told him, three Gentiles arrived at the house where Peter was staying to invite him to meet a Gentile that God wants to save.

What about you? God wants you to get out of your comfort zone and be willing to reach people that are not like you. Peter was uncomfortable with non-Jewish culture. He wasn't like Paul who was immersed in the Greek culture all around him. Peter was offended by Gentile culture. But God was calling him to wake up to the world that was dying and going to hell. They need a preacher to tell them about Jesus. The same is true for you and I. We are Jesus with skin on. We are called to reach the unclean and the untouchables. We are called to reach those who it might be uncomfortable to reach.

GOD'S MERCY

Do you see God's mercy of this vision? Whether a person was raised religious or atheist, we all need Christ. There is hope for all of us. We all need a Savior.

Our world today is in shambles because of racial divisions in our culture, but our world is not much different than how the world has always been. The talking heads and sociologists today are telling us there is no remedy for racial divisions in our society. And to a point, in ourselves, they are right. The best the world can offer is a new kind of segregation. It truly is shocking to me how people today want to move backwards to allow for even greater divisions and animosity.

When I look out and see the problems of our culture, the world has no answers. There are deep divisions in our society and throughout the world that are centuries old. But it's nothing new. The world is always tearing itself apart. Jesus came to give us life and life more abundantly. Jesus has the answer for division. He's torn the walls down through his blood on the cross. When we get a glimpse of the new heaven and the new earth, it is composed of "people from every tribe, tongue, people, and nation" (Rev 7:9). The DNA for Jesus' church is found in Acts 9 and 10. It cannot be a church of just one culture. We will have a diversity of cultures if we preach the gospel of Christ's love to all people. What is happening to heal division in the world today occurs because of what we are going to see in this study before us.

Jesus is the only one who has the solution for racial division in any culture and in any time period. The only answer to racism is "gracism". We have to realize that there are sinful tendencies in every culture. We need to repent of what is sinful in our culture and celebrate everything else. We are all different. Praise God! How boring would life be if we were all the same!

So let me make the point: the solution to racism is see our great and merciful God exalted over every tribe, tongue, people, and nation. We have to be humble enough to say to those who are different than us: welcome. We have to be humble enough to confess the sins of our culture and our family. Our fathers and mothers have not done everything right. There are sins that are passed down from generation to generation, and we need to put aside the sins of past generations and say: no more! And then we need to adopt what I like to call the "Jesus culture" of loving one another, celebrating the diversity and ingenuity of God in the Body of Christ. Isn't God amazing?

I was thinking even on a sociological level, God has a way of communicating to us. I heard about a couple of different ethnicities who had a set of twins; one girl was white, and the other was black. I love that! That's God. There are really not different races. There is the human race. The Bible says we are all of "one blood." We are all brothers and sisters, and we need to treat each other with love, respect, kindness, and compassion. God "made of one blood all nations of men for to dwell on all the face of the earth" (Acts 17:26, KJV). We are all "one blood"! That means if I need blood, and you are my blood type, I need your blood no matter what kind of superficial differences there might be in your looks than mine. We are all different. Even in my own family, there was a running joke between my older brothers about my twin sister and I being adopted. You see my four brothers were all dark and hairy. My father had jet black hair and my mom's hair and skin were darker. And here were these twin babies, and we were "towheads" with platinum blonde hair, and pail, white skin. Of course, we weren't adopted. We were just different. And like a symphony having different instruments or a body with different parts, our differences should be celebrated, harmonized, and utilized for God's glory and kingdom. That was something that Peter was just being introduced to, and it offended him at first. But as a Christian, we had all better get used to it, because God wants his heaven full. He wants you to go outside of your comfort zone and reach those different from you.

Conclusion

Let me encourage you if you are uncomfortable with reaching out to those who are different than you. Jesus touched the untouchables. He hugged the lepers. Peter was uncomfortable as well. But it was the Holy Spirit who showed him the love of God for all people (10:28).

Here's where I think we are as a congregation. I believe we are like a fully fuel and sophisticated rocket ship. We have all the power and fuel of sound doctrine and the joy of the Holy Spirit, but I think we've got to get off the launching pad. I believe we are like Peter, content with doing healings and resurrections (both amazing things), but we need to get out of the borders of our comfort zone and go to the Corneliuses of this world. God wants to pour out his mercy and reach so many people that are so different than you, so don't get in his way. He's going to use you. Yes you! Christians (and that means you) are the only representatives of Christ on the earth. We need to reach out. So I want to close with a prayer challenge. And be careful what you ask for because God answers prayer. Will you pray for that person or those persons in your life that you are not reaching out to, but you know you should? Pray that God by his Holy Spirit will show you how dear they are to him, even if you are uncomfortable. If you pray that prayer, God will answer it.

God calls sinners to repentance and gives them new life. But who will be the rescuers? God sets before us as it were a burning building.

People are crying out in their terror and misery. And God has made you the fireman. Will you just pass up the burning building? You have the equipment to put out the fire and save the people. But will you just sit in your fire engine and turn the music up as people burn up?

In the days of World War II in Germany there were Jews being transported to their death, where six million died for the crime of just being Jewish. And these railroad cars, filled with Jews on their way to extermination, passed by behind the churches. The people could sometimes hear the screams of the people from the railroad cars, but they chose to sing a little louder to drown out their cries from their conscience. Let me implore you. Don't just sing a little louder. Reach out to the lost and dying. Rescue the perishing Jesus has sent you! Amen.

19 | ACTS 10:17-11:18
THE POWER OF THE GOSPEL

The believers from among the circumcised who had come with Peter were amazed, because the gift of the Holy Spirit was poured out even on the Gentiles.
Acts 11:45

I am amazed at the power of the gospel. God alone is able to save people. Our sophisticated presentations and lights and wonderful programs are all fine and good, but no power of man ever brought a soul into the kingdom. We are just instruments in the Redeemers hands. God uses the power of his message that Jesus died for sinners and applies it by the Holy Spirit to transform sinners into saints. The gospel of Jesus Christ is powerful to save! Paul testified of the gospel's power.

Romans 1:16a | For I am not ashamed of the gospel, for it is the power of God for salvation to everyone who believes.

I wonder if we all realize here today how powerful the gospel is. When you believed that Jesus was your only substitute for sin, and that he was your righteousness before a holy God, you were saved. We have no other plea.

Key Thought: The gospel is powerful to save. It doesn't need editing. It needs proclaiming.

It is the Holy Spirit alone that unites us in that gospel power. He humbles us and shows us our great sin, and our incredible forgiveness. We see this in the amazing story of Cornelius the Roman centurion commander. He had charge over 600 men. He's a rough, tough Gentile—a military commander. You would think he's a most unlikely candidate for salvation. This is not the man you or I would choose to start a worldwide revival with Jesus reaching all the nations of the world. But God's ways are not our ways. His thoughts are so much higher than our thoughts. Our God is a seeking God!

OUR SEEKING GOD (10:17-23)

God's heart for the lost is infinitely bigger than ours. God is right now drawing people to come to him in your sphere of influence.

God stops Peter in his tracks with a vision. It's like Peter is sleeping on the Gentile world. They need Christ. Peter needs a wakeup call.

God's Heart

The vision Peter receives displays a blanket that comes down from the sky, and on it are all different kinds of animals.

> **Acts 10:9-12** | The next day, as they were on their journey and approaching the city, Peter went up on the housetop about the sixth hour [*12 noon*] to pray. [10] And he became hungry and wanted something to eat, but while they were preparing it, he fell into a trance [11] and saw the heavens opened and something like a great sheet descending, being let down by its four corners upon the earth. [12] In it were all kinds of animals and reptiles and birds of the air.

While Peter is waiting for his noon meal, and he can smell the food being prepared (vs 10), a vision in the sky opens up. He has a trance, a vision. God is just like that. He reveals his heart to us at the most unexpected times. Peter is hungry, so God uses a vision of food!

Of course, the vision is about people, not food. The Jews despised the Gentiles and their pagan ways. So Israel isolated themselves from the nations they were supposed to reach. They thought they were doing God's will, but they were actually breaking God's heart.

God is seeking people from all nations. He first called the Jews, but they rejected him. Jesus "came to his own, and his own people did not receive him" (Jn 1:11). This vision is about God's heart of love being poured out to all the nations.

Jesus' last command before he ascended to heaven was to "Go into all the world." He wants people in his kingdom from every nation. God wants his heaven full! Remember, Jesus said "Go out to the highways and hedges and compel people to come in, that my house may be filled" (Lk 14:23). God calls "all people everywhere to repent" (Acts 17:30). He is "not wishing that any should perish, but that all should reach repentance" (2 Pet 3:9). He takes "no pleasure in the death of the wicked, but rather that they turn from their ways and live" (Eze 33:11). "He is the propitiation for our sins, and not for ours only but also for the sins of the whole world" (1 Jn 2:2). Do you see God's heart? God is a seeking God. He calls all people groups to himself.

He Seeks without Partiality or Prejudice

It doesn't matter if you were born in a Christian home or raised as a pagan, God calls all men to repentance. Jew or Gentile, rich or poor, people from every culture and family, Jesus says, "Come to me, and I will give you rest" (Mt 11:28). This is the new revelation Peter gets. It's time to share God's love with the entire world, beginning with that Roman soldier, Cornelius.

Peter falls into a trance, where he is awake, but he's seeing a vision. He is shown a strange meal in this vision. God says to him: Rise and eat some unclean food, Peter. "No" says Peter, "Never! I'm a faithful Jew, and I've never eaten anything unclean." Isn't it funny that he's getting a revelation from God, but he thinks he knows better?

> **Acts 10:13-16** | And there came a voice to him: "Rise, Peter; kill and eat." [14] But Peter said, "By no means, Lord; for I have never eaten anything that is common or unclean." [15] And the voice came to him again a second time, "What God has made clean, do not call common." [16] This happened three times, and the thing was taken up at once to heaven.

Here was this blanket of birds and animals. He had been hungry, but he's not hungry anymore. Actually, this sheet has also been translated "sail" which would also be an appropriate symbol for the gospel on the move. Again, this vision is not about animals, but about a diversity of nations filled with people.

Above Peter the sun was shining down and just above the buildings of Joppa, he could see the great Mediterranean Sea (so much bigger than his little Sea of Galilee). The horizon stretched to the Gentile nations of the mighty Roman world. He could hear the sounds of his friend, Simon the tanner and his men busy at their trade, making leather items. And up from the kitchen wafted the delightful smell of food sizzling in the pan, probably reminding Peter of his hunger.[203] Peter saw so many different animals in the vision: clean and unclean.

When it comes to people, what makes us unclean is our sin. We are born sinners. But God is willing to make all people clean in Christ. In other words, it's not about race, it's about grace.

Perhaps you are here today, and God is drawing you. It doesn't matter what your background is. God has no favorites. The ground is level at the cross. We all need the blood of Christ to save us. Do you see the point of this vision? Whether you were raised religious or atheist, you need Christ. There is hope for all of us. We all need a Savior.

God's Holy Spirit

The vision was not about food, but about precious souls that the Holy Spirit is drawing to himself. Jesus said people will not come to him unless they are first drawn by the Father by the power of the Spirit.

> *John 6:44* | No one can come to me unless the Father who sent me draws him.

Just as the vision was concluding, the three men that Cornelius sent to fetch Peter arrived. God will stop at no lengths to draw sinners to himself. He appeared to Cornelius in a dream, and now they were on their way to invite Peter to preach the gospel to Cornelius at Caesarea. The mover in this story is not Peter but the Holy Spirit.

Peter was not thinking at all about reaching the Gentiles, but the Holy Spirit was already working in some Gentiles hearts. Imagine his surprise when he looks out and sees two slaves and an armed Roman soldier there shouting his name![204] Peter is staying at Simon the tanner's home in Joppa (modern Tel Aviv), 35 miles south of Caesarea Maritima on the coast of the Mediterranean Sea, so the men had come a long way.

---

[203] J. Phillips, *Exploring Acts*, Ac 10:17a.
[204] Faw, *Acts*, 126.

Acts 10:17-18 | Now while Peter was inwardly perplexed as to what the vision that he had seen might mean, behold, the men who were sent by Cornelius, having made inquiry for Simon's house, stood at the gate [18] and called out to ask whether Simon who was called Peter was lodging there.

It's starting to dawn on Peter what this meal is all about. He's still not eaten, and he's probably no longer hungry!

God's Instruments

Now the Spirit begins to speak to Peter. Peter listens and obeys! See how gentle the Spirit is with Peter. Peter's like us, a bit hardheaded. He saw this vision of clean and unclean animals, and now he has people who were considered ceremonially unclean, and he a ceremonial clean Jew was to meet with them. The Spirit says, go and rush to them. Join them, fellowship with them "without hesitation." And Peter obeyed the Lord!

Acts 10:19-23 | And while Peter was pondering the vision, the Spirit said to him, "Behold, three men are looking for you. [20] Rise and go down and accompany them without hesitation, for I have sent them." [21] And Peter went down to the men and said, "I am the one you are looking for. What is the reason for your coming?" [22] And they said, "Cornelius, a centurion, an upright and God-fearing man, who is well spoken of by the whole Jewish nation, was directed by a holy angel to send for you to come to his house and to hear what you have to say." [23] So he invited them in to be his guests.

Cornelius was a well-known example of faith as a God-fearer. He was not initiated with circumcision. He was not offering sacrifices. He would not have been permitted. This tells us that salvation is by faith, not by our rituals. With salvation comes a personal relationship, a deep personal fellowship with Christ.

Peter recognized this man who seemed to be drawn by God but he wasn't yet indwelt by the Spirit. Peter, showing God's favor to this man, sat down to eat with him, as a guest of this Roman warrior and soldier.

OUR SAVING GOD (10:24-48)

God is able to transform the most hopeless cases. All of us are a case study in God's amazing power to do the impossible and save the unsavable.

The purpose for the miracles and the meal is to see the expansion of the gospel through this Gentile named Cornelius. A Gentile is a non-Jewish person. We have a group of them. Peter has just entered a Gentile home which was unheard of for a Jew.

What Cornelius needs is what we call in the New Testament: conversion. He's been drawn by God, but he's not yet been indwelt by God. He doesn't yet have the Spirit. Something new is happening here.

How can a person be converted? We see it clearly here in the following verses.

The Divine Call

Peter is still pondering the dream, and he has been summoned to Cornelius's home. The Spirit is going to teach him why, but initially, this is new revelation that Peter must grasp.

God's Divine Call to Cornelius

The Gentiles are the next wave of people God is calling into his church. God is calling all people everywhere to come to him. So God calls Peter to go and visit Cornelius. God has opened the way of salvation to the Gentiles.

> **Acts 10:24-29a** | The next day he [*Peter*] rose and went away with them [*Cornelius' servants*], and some of the brothers from Joppa accompanied him. ²⁴ And on the following day they entered Caesarea. Cornelius was expecting them and had called together his relatives and close friends. ²⁵ When Peter entered, Cornelius met him and fell down at his feet and worshiped him. ²⁶ But Peter lifted him up, saying, "Stand up; I too am a man." ²⁷ And as he talked with him, he went in and found many persons gathered. ²⁸ And he said to them, "You yourselves know how unlawful it is for a Jew to associate with or to visit anyone of another nation, but God has shown me that I should not call any person common or unclean. ²⁹ So when I was sent for, I came without objection.

Cornelius is so overwhelmed at meeting Peter he falls down to worship him, and Peter rebukes him (10:25-26).

Notice he "had called together his relatives and close friends" (10:24). Before he's even Spirit-filled, he's evangelizing his family and friends.

Peter now gets it! God has shown him. He understands that the ground is level at the cross. Peter is nothing special to be worshipped but a horrible and wretched sinner that has been introduced to the love of God. Remember Peter had denied the Lord three times. He was forgiven, and he knew the forgiveness of God so well, that God chose him to preach Pentecost.

Peter truly gets it. There's no difference between a faithful Jew like Peter and a rough centurion military leader from Rome. Both are wretched sinners and need the mercy of Christ. We are all equally in need of Christ. No one gets in because they are religious. And no one is kept out because they are a notorious sinner. We are all given the same opportunity. God has no favorites.

Acts 17:30 | God calls all men everywhere to repent.

God is calling every person to himself. All people everywhere are called. Some are called and actually come. Anyone who comes must come by faith and trust in Christ. That means you stop trusting in yourself, your ways, and your ability to change your circumstances. And instead you turn to Christ, trusting him as the Leader of your life. He has control of every detail, and that makes your life sweet even if your circumstances are terrible.

God's Divine Call to Peter

Peter asks, "Why have you sent for me Cornelius?" The answer is because whenever God calls individuals to come to him, he uses people like you and I to preach and teach the free gift of salvation. People can't hear unless they have a preacher. We are called to preach the gospel. In other words, God uses human instruments to sound his call to sinners. So in our text, Peter asks an important question.

Acts 10:29b-33 | I ask then why you sent for me." [30] And Cornelius said, "Four days ago, about this hour, I was praying in my house at the ninth hour, and behold, a man stood before me in bright clothing [31] and said, 'Cornelius, your prayer has been heard and your alms have been remembered before God. **32** Send therefore to Joppa and ask for Simon who is called Peter. He is lodging in the house of Simon, a tanner, by the sea.' **33** So I sent for you at once, and you have been kind enough to come. Now therefore we are all here in the presence of God to hear all that you have been commanded by the Lord."

Cornelius basically says, I need you to preach the gospel to me. The Lord has commanded you to preach a message to the nations, and you need to tell me. We are commanded to tell people about how their sins can be forgiven through Jesus.

God's Divine Call to You

What about you? Is God calling you? Are you born again? It's not enough to be called. Many are called but few are chosen. Few are actually converted to Christ. Let me tell you a story about how God calls us to himself.

When I was a child, I used to play out in the bayou in the trails by the Tickfaw River by my house in Louisiana. Sometimes we'd go way out into the blackberry fields, quite a ways from our home. But I could always hear my mom's voice. "Matthew, it's suppertime." You know there's a difference between hearing the call for dinner and actually eating dinner. Many are called to come to God's feast. God says, "It's dinner time. I'm here to call you my own child and invite you to my table." God is calling many of you. Some of you young people have come to Christ recently. But some of you are resisting the Holy Spirit. Don't resist him. You come. God calls so many to his banquet table, but they ignore the call. Just like ignoring mama's call for dinner. Jesus tells a parable about it in Luke 14.

> *Luke 14:21-23* | The Master... said to his servant, 'Go out quickly to the streets and lanes of the city, and bring in the poor and crippled and blind and lame.' **22** And the servant said, 'Sir, what you commanded has been done, and still there is room.' **23** And the master said to the servant, 'Go out to the highways and hedges and compel people to come in, that my house may be filled.

You may be called, but are you converted? Have you humbled yourself and surrendered your whole life to Jesus? You don't have to do anything, but simply trust in what Jesus has done for you.

Cornelius knows all about the one true living God. But he doesn't yet know about how God sent his Son Jesus to save us. So now Peter explains this to this Gentile military leader, this Roman centurion. It's just as we read in Romans 10.

> *Romans 10:14* | How are they to believe in him of whom they have never heard? And how are they to hear without someone preaching?

Are you willing as a Christian to share the good news with your lost loved ones? If not you, who will do it. If you are honest with yourself, you will realize that God is calling you personally to do it. Young person, do you have siblings? You know the good news that Jesus died for you, but do your siblings know? We all need to share Christ to everyone around us.

The Doctrine of Jesus

We saw the divine call, but now we see the doctrine of Jesus. This is Peter preaching the way of eternal life. Peter is about to do what we all should do in any situation where you're not sure if the person is born again: preach the gospel.

The Preparation

> **Acts 10:34-35** | I So Peter opened his mouth and said: "Truly I understand that God shows no partiality, **35** but in every nation anyone who fears him and does what is right is acceptable to him.

Commenting on this verse, Everett Harrison remarks,

> The meaning is not that such persons are thereby saved (*cf* Acts 11:14) but rather that they are suitable candidates for salvation. Such preparation promises a spiritual earnestness that will result in faith as the gospel is heard and received.[205]

Cornelius responded to the work of God in his soul, yet it must not be thought that he did that on his own, apart from the grace of God. The truth is that no one, whether Gentile (*cf* Rom 1:18ff) or Jew (*cf* Rom 2:1ff) does that (Rom 3:10–18). God had worked in Cornelius's heart so that he sought to know and obey God, and when he heard the saving truth of the gospel, he eagerly responded.[206]

---

[205] Everett Harrison, *Interpreting Acts: The Expanding Church* (Grand Rapids: Zondervan, 1986), 182

[206] MacArthur, *Acts*, 301.

The Proclamation

Peter now presents the story of Christ and the good news of real peace and reconciliation with God. This is the Apostle Peter preaching the gospel message that saves.

> **Acts 10:36-42** | As for the word that he sent to Israel, preaching good news of peace through Jesus Christ (he is Lord of all), **37** you yourselves know what happened throughout all Judea, beginning from Galilee after the baptism that John proclaimed: **38** how God anointed Jesus of Nazareth with the Holy Spirit and with power. He went about doing good and healing all who were oppressed by the devil, for God was with him. **39** And we are witnesses of all that he did both in the country of the Jews and in Jerusalem. They put him to death by hanging him on a tree, **40** but God raised him on the third day and made him to appear, **41** not to all the people but to us who had been chosen by God as witnesses, who ate and drank with him after he rose from the dead. **42** And he commanded us to preach to the people and to testify that he is the one appointed by God to be judge of the living and the dead.

Listen to the message preached by Peter. Believe that Christ lived and died for you. He is God Almighty, the Judge of the living and the dead. Jesus is either your deliverer or your judge.

Believe that God the Son became human and died for you. Believe that he defeated death and hell. Believe that his death was a substitution for your death. God gave the perfect one in your place as a wicked sinner, so you could be made perfect. Believe that, and you will have eternal life.

The Promise

Forgiveness! That's what God promises. An erasing of all our sins.

> **Acts 10:43** | To him all the prophets bear witness that everyone who believes in him receives forgiveness of sins through his name."

The prophets of the Old Testament had much to say about the forgiveness Messiah would bring.

> *Isaiah 53:6* | All we like sheep have gone astray; we have turned—every one—to his own way; and the Lord has laid on him the iniquity of us all.

Jeremiah 31:34 | I will forgive their iniquity, and I will remember their sin no more.

Zechariah 13:1 | On that day there shall be a fountain opened... to cleanse them from sin and uncleanness.

Psalm 103:12 | As far as the east is from the west, so far does he remove our transgressions from us.

You are offered forgiveness of all your sins: past, present and future. Christ takes your record of sin and wretchedness and failure. He cleanses you from all your filth. He takes on your filth and gives you his robe of righteousness. That's good news. This is not just the promise of the New Testament but the Old Covenant as well. Cornelius believed this good news, and something amazing happens.

The Display of the Spirit

Suddenly as Peter is preaching, his sermon is dramatically interrupted by the Holy Spirit! No altar call! No invitation! They simply believed and were born again on the spot![207] This is the kind of interruption we long for! As soon as the Roman centurion Cornelius and his Gentile companions believed, the Spirit took residence inside of them, and they began praising God!

> **Acts 10:44-48** | While Peter was still saying these things, the Holy Spirit fell on all who heard the word. **45** And the believers from among the circumcised who had come with Peter were amazed, because the gift of the Holy Spirit was poured out even on the Gentiles. **46** For they were hearing them speaking in tongues and extolling God. Then Peter declared, **47** "Can anyone withhold water for baptizing these people, who have received the Holy Spirit just as we have?" **48** And he commanded them to be baptized in the name of Jesus Christ. Then they asked him to remain for some days.

By the manifestation of the Spirit, we see that God had welcomed Gentile believers into his family on equal terms with believing Jews. The right conclusion was immediately made: since God had given the same gift of the Spirit to Gentiles and Jews, the church must give them

---

[207] Hughes, *Acts*, 152.

an equal welcome. If God had given them Spirit baptism, the church must not deny them water baptism. "God does not show favoritism."[208]

Peter doesn't say they need to go through any Jewish ritual, like circumcision. He doesn't give them a Jewish dietary list. He simply says: go public with your faith and be baptized.

How about you? Do you believe? Do you have the evidence of the Spirit? These Gentiles got the gift of tongues immediately, as an immediate confirmation that they were born again. Not everyone would get the gift of tongues as some wrongly teach. This was the Gentile Pentecost. We had the Jewish Pentecost in Acts 2. Now in Acts 10 you had the Gentile Pentecost.[209]

The greater sign of salvation for all believers is that "they were extolling God" (11:46). That's the mark of the Spirit in your life. When Christ becomes the blazing center of your life, and you are infinitely more grateful for the work of Jesus on the cross for you than for anything, by far, you start extolling and worshipping God. That is one of the first signs of salvation.

What about you? Are you in Christ? Have you surrendered? Then you are clean. God has removed your impurities from his sight and given you access into his presence. He knows the sin that remains in you, but if you have put yourself at the feet of Christ, he cleansed you completely, embraced you, and adopted you into his family. Others may call you unclean, but remember that God said to Peter, "What God has cleansed you must not call common."[210]

OUR SOVEREIGN GOD (11:1-18)

God is calling a people for himself and will save them. He saved you not just to sit and soak, but to be his instrument to bring the gospel to everyone around you.

Of course, God is the only one that can save people. So God has indwelt you by his Holy Spirit. He is the great physician that is guiding your hands, your heart, and your words as he brings people to salvation.

---

[208] John Stott, *Through the Bible: Through the Year* (Grand Rapids: Baker, 2006), 328.

[209] Adrian Rogers, "Who Is the Man Jesus Christ?," in *Adrian Rogers Sermon Archive* (Signal Hill, CA: Rogers Family Trust, 2017), Ac 10:34–43.

[210] Sproul, *Acts*, 183.

Peter, though reluctantly, has experienced the love of this sovereign God saving the most unlikely of sinners. Now Peter goes back to the apostles and Christians throughout Judea who at this time were all Jewish, and some of them criticize Peter for preaching the gospel to these unclean Gentiles.

A Story of God's Sovereignty

Peter says basically, "I was just a passenger on something God has done. The sovereign God wants to save the Gentiles." Peter recounts the story of what God commanded him to do.

> **Acts 11:1-15** | Now the apostles and the brothers who were throughout Judea heard that the Gentiles also had received the word of God. ² So when Peter went up to Jerusalem, the circumcision party criticized him, saying, ³ "You went to uncircumcised men and ate with them." ⁴ But Peter began and explained it to them in order: ⁵ "I was in the city of Joppa praying, and in a trance I saw a vision, something like a great sheet descending, being let down from heaven by its four corners, and it came down to me. ⁶ Looking at it closely, I observed animals and beasts of prey and reptiles and birds of the air. ⁷ And I heard a voice saying to me, 'Rise, Peter; kill and eat.' ⁸ But I said, 'By no means, Lord; for nothing common or unclean has ever entered my mouth.' ⁹ But the voice answered a second time from heaven, 'What God has made clean, do not call common.' ¹⁰ This happened three times, and all was drawn up again into heaven. ¹¹ And behold, at that very moment three men arrived at the house in which we were, sent to me from Caesarea. ¹² And the Spirit told me to go with them, making no distinction. These six brothers also accompanied me, and we entered the man's house. ¹³ And he told us how he had seen the angel stand in his house and say, 'Send to Joppa and bring Simon who is called Peter; ¹⁴ he will declare to you a message by which you will be saved, you and all your household.' ¹⁵ As I began to speak, the Holy Spirit fell on them just as on us at the beginning.

So Peter, says, basically, "This was an act of God. The Spirit himself was poured out on these Gentiles. I am just a human instrument."

The Spirit of God's Sovereignty

I want you to notice that Peter calls attention, that this salvation of the Gentiles is a sovereign act of God. Peter basically says, I couldn't have stopped it if I wanted to. The Spirit of God is sovereign. He called and converted Gentiles. When God works, it is an omnipotent occurrence from our great God.

> **Acts 11:16-18** | And I remembered the word of the Lord, how he said, 'John baptized with water, but you will be baptized with the Holy Spirit.' [17] If then God gave the same gift to them as he gave to us when we believed in the Lord Jesus Christ, who was I that I could stand in God's way?" [18] When they heard these things they fell silent. And they glorified God, saying, "Then to the Gentiles also God has granted repentance that leads to life."

I love Peter's words, "who was I that I could stand in God's way?" (10:17). I would ask you the same question. God wants to do some great things in the days to come. We are asking you to actively invite your friends and family every Sunday. We are asking if you are visiting with us and you don't have a church home, to commit to God and to this congregation as a member. We are asking you to get busy for God. Will it be uncomfortable? Peter would tell you, yes! It will be a bit uncomfortable. You may not be as popular when you preach the gospel as when you keep your mouth shut. But I'm asking you to not remain silent. More importantly, God is commanding you to open your mouth and preach the gospel, like Peter does with Cornelius, and leave the results up to God.

Conclusion

D.L. Moody once pondered the question of an evangelist he heard make the challenge to full consecration. He said, "The world has yet to see what God can do with a man fully consecrated to him. By God's help, I aim to be that man."[211]

We see the sovereign, saving, seeking God who is here calling the most unlikely people for salvation. But Paul asked, "How shall they hear without a preacher?" Look at our great God who sovereignly saves sinners. It's glorious. But we are his conduits. We are his instruments. Let's put aside our prejudices and reach the people around us.

---

[211] D.L. Moody in Roberts Liardon. *God's Generals Dwight L. Moody* (New Kensington, PA: Whitaker House, 2008), 4.

Do you know that God can call prejudiced people and fill their heart with love instead of hatred? He can take those who take advantage of women and make them good husbands. He can take homosexuals and transform their desires. Jesus is the answer for the transgendered people of this world in all their dysphoria and confusion. God can give us a new mind and a new heart. God calls and cleanses those who abuse alcohol, who try to self-medicate.

The church is a spiritual hospital, and you are the emergency room doctors. The ambulances are piled one in front of the other at your door. But for some of you, the ER doors are locked, and you won't open the doors to treat the patients. Whatever your excuses are, you must answer them with this fact: people are dying and going to hell today. Unlike an ER doctor, the greatest danger is not the physical life of your patient, but the spiritual life. If you allow people around you to perish without Christ, where do they go for eternity? Do you have a heart like God's? He can't just tune out and forget about the dying. He sent his Son for them to be saved. God is calling sinners. He's awakening them from their sleep of death. Will you rescue them or leave them to perish? Our sovereign God is a saving and seeking God. Will you seek souls in cooperation with the Father?

Lift up the cross of Christ! Anyone can do this. Yesterday morning, I had two young men, aged 17 and 12 ring my doorbell and give me the gospel. I told them I was a pastor and how I was so grateful that at such a young age they were going door to door sharing the love of Christ here in Elgin. They said it was part of their youth group activity. Now that's what I call a youth activity! Dear saints, children are doing this in Elgin. What a wonderful example of Spirit-filled living. Let's open up the ER doors and see how God brings in sinners that he is sovereignly calling. How?

Pray for God to lead you to sinner he is drawing. Learn how to clearly present the gospel. Know the gospel from God's word (Rom 6:23; Jn 3:16; 2 Cor 5:21, etc.). Open your mouth and give the gospel everywhere: give out gospel tracts when you are in the drive-thru, when you are with your neighbors. If you have children, give the gospel to your children regularly. Let's end where we began. The message of the gospel saves. We don't have to edit it. We just have to proclaim it.

Romans 1:16a | For I am not ashamed of the gospel, for it is the power of God for salvation to everyone who believes.

20 | ACTS 11:19-30
THE ANTIOCH MODEL

In Antioch the disciples were first called Christians.
ACTS 11:26

The expansion of God's kingdom on earth is always the result of the mighty hand of God.

Psalm 121:1 | Unless the Lord build the house, they labor in vain that build it.

I love this example of the Antioch church in Acts 11, because they teach us how to have a congregation that looks and acts like heaven. God would have his heaven full of people from all tribes, tongues, and nations. We cannot manufacture this unity amidst great diversity through human programs or mechanical rules. We've got to get out of the way and let God do his good work. In Antioch we see God building his church. He says,

Matthew 16:18 | I will build my church and the gates of hell shall not prevail against it.

Antioch was one of the earliest centers of Christianity; it was there that the followers of Christ were first called Christians, and the city was the headquarters of the missionary the Apostle Paul about 47–55 A.D. It's the first Jewish-Gentile church of the New Testament era. Antioch was the third largest city in the Greco-Roman world, behind

Rome and Alexandria. It boasted some five hundred thousand people at the time.[212] The city bore the nickname "the queen of the Eastern cities." It was cosmopolitan and commercial. It was the capitol city of Syria, and it was also a base for the Roman military.

The city was incredibly diverse and served as a crossroads, having major highways going to the north, south, and east with the Mediterranean Sea to the west. Greeks, Romans, Syrians, Phoenicians, Jews, Arabs, Egyptians, Africans, Indians, and Asians all populated Antioch, making it remarkably diverse.

Government leaders in Antioch led a kind of sophisticated hedonism. On one side they were sophisticated and well established, providing police protection, stability, and order. All of that is impressive, especially for the ancient world. But then they would plan public events of pagan hedonism with appetites for lavish indulgences in gambling, chariot races, brothels, exotic banquets, and the like.[213] All of this made Antioch a great place for a church. John Stott notes, "No more appropriate place could be imagined, either as the venue for the first international church, or as the springboard for the worldwide Christian mission."[214] We could say that about the location of our church here in Chicagoland. There is no better place for a church to reach the world than where we are at right now.

The church in Antioch—not the mother church in Jerusalem—changed the world. The Jerusalem church was wonderful, and it should be appreciated for its uniqueness and power, but it had its challenges when it came to evangelizing non-Jews. Antioch, by contrast, was an international church. What made the church in Antioch so powerful? What are the ingredients of a church with the New Testament mission? Luke describes at least five marks of a mission-oriented church. They are simple to understand but difficult to apply. We need to pray for "the grace of God" (11:23) as we seek to imitate the Antioch Christians.[215] It was a miracle church, a moldable church, and a multicultural missions church.

---

[212] Walter A. Elwell and Barry J. Beitzel, "Antioch of Syria," *Baker Encyclopedia of the Bible* (Grand Rapids, MI: Baker Book House, 1988), 120.
[213] Ibid.
[214] Stott, *The Message of Acts*, 203.
[215] Merida, *Exalting Jesus in Acts*, 174.

A MIRACLE CHURCH (11:19-21)

Notice that with all the persecution against this church, it really shouldn't even exist.

Miracles in the Midst of Pain

There is persecution. The church is scattered. They don't close down or give up. These Jewish believers are pushed by persecution to Antioch, and they plant the first non-Jewish church. Here you have the missions bastion of the New Testament. Paul is sent out of this church on each of his three missionary journeys. The church of Antioch was birthed by its intentional outreach to unbelievers. This is a miracle church that shouldn't exist.

> **Acts 11:19-21** | Now those who were scattered because of the persecution that arose over Stephen traveled as far as Phoenicia and Cyprus and Antioch, speaking the word to no one except Jews. [20] But there were some of them, men of Cyprus and Cyrene, who on coming to Antioch spoke to the Hellenists also, preaching the Lord Jesus. [21] And the hand of the Lord was with them, and a great number who believed turned to the Lord.

All these believers from Jerusalem are persecuted during the time of Stephen's martyrdom. They are refugees—on the run. They are running for their lives and end up as far as Phoenicia, which is way north of Israel in modern day Lebanon. Others flee way west to the island of Cyprus. Still others go south to Africa in Cyrene. Some of these believers return to Antioch and preach the gospel there.

Antioch is located three hundred miles north of Jerusalem. It is the third largest city, at half a million people, as Luke is writing the book of Acts. That's a mega-city at the time when the population of the earth was so much smaller. The church at Antioch was built on the foundation of evangelism from people who were focused on the gospel in several ways.

Miracles in the Midst of Proclamation

Now notice, it is in Antioch, that instead of just preaching the gospel to Jewish people, they begin reaching out to Gentiles. There was a cultural boldness. They were crossing the lines of their comfort zone.

> **Acts 11:19-20** | Now those who were scattered [were] speaking the word to no one except Jews. [20] But there were some of them, men

of Cyprus and Cyrene, who on coming to Antioch spoke to the
Hellenists also, preaching the Lord Jesus.

A Hellenist is simply a Greek speaking person. Sometimes, like Paul and Stephen and Philip, it refers to a Greek speaking Jew. But there is a contrast in verse 19. It says normally, they would preach the gospel to "no one except Jews." But there were some who were preaching to Gentile Greek speakers there in Antioch.

As believers, we can't be afraid to engage people of vastly different cultures. There are mosques going up around us. Be ready to share the love of Jesus with Muslims. There are people who no longer no what sin is. They no longer have any moral barriers. We are called to engage and teach the good news about Jesus, not retreat into escapism.

Acts 11:20b | ...preaching the Lord Jesus.

Notice these bold men and women were able to engage with Hellenist Gentiles, preaching the Lord Jesus Christ. They didn't come in with some gimmick. They didn't survey the soccer moms to see how they would like to do religion. They preached the unedited gospel. There was a commitment of each of the believers there to preach the gospel, spreading the good news through their various relationships.

Miracles in the Midst of a Downpour of Blessing

Acts 11:21 | And the hand of the Lord was with them, and a great number who believed turned to the Lord.

The hand of the Lord was with them! Can we say that as a church? This is the answer if we want great gospel fruit. We need God's hand upon us. As a result, there was a great influx of Gentile and Jewish sinners that turned to the Lord Jesus Christ. The result was a wonderful Christ centered church that was neither mainly Jewish nor mainly Gentile. It was a "Jesus-cultured" church. The church in Antioch was birthed by effective evangelism, and as a result, "in Antioch we have the first church that is made up of Jewish and Gentile believers together."[216]

---

[216] David G. Peterson, *Acts of the Apostles*, 351.

A MOLDABLE CHURCH (11:22-26)

They weren't trying to be Jewish or Gentile. They were being molded into the image of Jesus. I love the reminder from the book of Isaiah. He says:

> *Isaiah 64:8* | But now, O Lord, you are our Father; we are the clay, and you are our potter; we are all the work of your hand.

God is our potter; we are the clay! Here in Antioch was the first local church made up of various tribes and cultures. The goal couldn't be about one culture or another culture, but about "Jesus" culture. We all want to be like Jesus.

Even though Peter had a vision about a church like this with the different kinds of people mixed together, this kind of church had never existed before.

The news of what was happening at Antioch must have caused a considerable stir in Jerusalem. Though Peter had officially opened the door of the church to the Gentiles it never occurred to anyone, apparently not even Peter, to take the next logical step and begin evangelizing the Gentile population of Jerusalem and Judea.[217] The Jerusalem church wanted to verify what God was doing in Antioch, so they send Barnabas.

Moldable Through a Human Instrument

> **Acts 11:22** | The report of this came to the ears of the church in Jerusalem, and they sent Barnabas to Antioch

In Antioch, we have the first account of a truly new covenant church plant. We have Jews and Gentiles together, praising the Lord, reading the word. The hand of the Lord is upon them. But they needed oversite and shepherding and love.

By sending Barnabas, the Antioch church gets a sweet and encouraging teacher as well as a good example of life-on-life discipleship. We learn in Ephesians that the DNA of the church has to be rich with teachers who model and teach the Christian life. Pastors and teachers are called to "equip the saints for the work of ministry, for building up the body of Christ" (Eph 4:12). That is the role that Barnabas was fulfilling. It begins with a commitment of a godly man (as in Barnabas) and other

---

[217] J. Phillips, *Exploring Acts*, Ac 11:22.

godly men (as with Paul later, 11:25 and other godly men, 13:1). It's a huge commitment to be a teacher in the Lord's church.

Moldable Through Divine Encouragement

God sends a true encourager from Jerusalem: Barnabas. Barnabas is the encourager, but he himself was encouraged.

Encouraged by God's Power

Acts 11:23a | When he came and saw the grace of God, he was glad.

What kind of a man was Barnabas? He was an encourager. He was born with the name Joseph, and he's from the island of Cyprus. He has the nickname of Barnabas, which means in Hebrew, "the son of encouragement). He was Jewish but he had a great love and affinity for spreading the gospel to the non-Jewish people of the nations. He was drawn to help those who were different. Remember, we are first introduced to him when he defends the great Saul of Tarsus when he becomes a Christian. His encourager is sent to Antioch. Remember, a disciple is a learner. To learn, we need teachers who will mentor us, show us how to live the Christian life, and hold us accountable with nurture, love, and truth.

Encouraging God's People

Acts 11:23b | And he exhorted them all to remain faithful to the Lord with steadfast purpose.

The Scripture says he exhorted the saints at Antioch to remain faithful. Exhort (*parakaléō*) is a powerful discipleship word which means "to come along side of, to encourage." [218] Specifically, Barnabas encouraged them to be faithful to the Lord with an unrelenting purpose. Paul presents this purpose as being "conformed to the image" of Christ (Rom 8:28-30).

Barnabas exhorted them, that is, he came alongside them in that purpose of knowing Christ and becoming like him. But how? This word, parakaléō, gives us a clue. It is a title for the Holy Spirit, the Comforter. The Spirit is our *Paraclete*, or, our ultimate "Helper, Counselor, and

---

[218] Timothy Friberg, Barbara Friberg, and Neva F. Miller, *Analytical Lexicon of the Greek New Testament*, Baker's Greek New Testament Library, "παρακαλέω" (Grand Rapids, MI: Baker Books, 2000), 296.

Comforter". So the essence of discipleship is to be an instrument of the Holy Spirit.

Parakaléō is one of the oldest and richest words in the Greek language. This word brought to mind at least five vivid pictures to the Greek imagination. Each is an application to how we are to come along side in discipleship.

To rekindle a flame. This pictures someone gently, patiently blowing on dying embers to bring a fire to life again.

To call forth comfort. This pictures the cries of a frightened child in the night calling for the comfort and reassurance of his father.

To call a physician. This pictures someone who was injured calling for a physician to set his broken bone or bind his wound.

To stabilize the troops. This pictures the military officer who, in the heat of battle, could calmly encourage, exhort, and steady the frightened soldiers in his ranks.

To plead one's case. This pictures the counsel for the defense, making an appeal for his client before a judge.

This is the ministry of the Holy Spirit, and it is our ministry as we come along side one another to stir up the flame of Christ!

Encouraged by God's Presence

This was Barnabas's ministry as a man whose life bore visible fruit. Luke described it this way,

Acts 11:24a | For he was a good man, full of the Holy Spirit and of faith.

Luke knew Barnabas and accompanied him on several missionary tours. He had witnessed firsthand his godliness and friendly disposition. It seems that Luke was saying that Barnabas was "glad" at what he saw because of his godly character. This was the kind of man he was. He was utterly genuine and sincere, and he loved the Lord with all his heart.[219]

It is worth pondering what might have happened to the shape of the New Testament church had someone less supportive been sent to Antioch, someone whose policy was to suffocate all enthusiasm and add significant restrictive policies to Gentiles contemplating conversion. Without doubt, the church would have taken a very different shape had this been the case. We might ask ourselves whether we are

---

[219] Thomas, *Acts*, 321.

encouragers by temperament. Are we the ones carping at the sidelines or are we earnestly seeking the growth of the church? It is easy to be the former, but it takes determination and discernment to do the latter.[220]

Encouraging the Church's Progress

Acts 11:24 | And a great many people were added to the Lord.

This shows that Barnabas's discipleship efforts apparently involved helping to equip and encourage lay evangelists to share the gospel with their friends. And while Barnabas must have been thrilled with God's grace in Antioch, he needed help to keep up the work of discipling all the new believers. This, in fact, is a common problem leaders face when their churches grow. They are concerned about how best to disciple everyone, and it's not a job that can be done without help. In the case of Barnabas and his work among the Antioch believers, another disciple maker is needed. Wisely, Barnabas enlists Saul's help.[221]

Moldable Through Instruction

Acts 11:25-26a | So Barnabas went to Tarsus to look for Saul, **26** and when he had found him, he brought him to Antioch. For a whole year they met with the church and taught a great many people.

Barnabas goes to find Saul, with whom he had spent time previously (9:27). He knew of Saul's calling to be an apostle to the Gentiles (9:15-16). He knows of Saul's bridge-building capacity; the man could communicate to diverse groups and was well informed about Scripture. Barnabas knows Saul is just the man to instruct this world-reaching congregation.[222] Luke tells us that Barnabas and Paul were a great team at Antioch where they "taught a great many people." This was megachurch but it was 300 miles north of Jerusalem.

Moldable Through Sanctification

Acts 11:26b | And in Antioch the disciples were first called Christians.

All believers are called to grow and change into the image of Jesus Christ. At Antioch, people from outside the church started calling them

---

[220] Ibid.
[221] Merida, *Exalting Jesus in Acts*, 179.
[222] Ibid. 179-180.

"Christians" or "little Christs". The Jews and Gentiles became one here and looked more like Christ than either their Hebrew or Gentile cultures. That's what we want: the Jesus culture! That's sanctification.

A MULTICULTURAL CHURCH (11:27-30)

This new multicultural church now expands greatly in three ways: mercy ministry, multicultural leadership and membership, and a missions movement from the church.

Multicultural Mercy Ministry (11:27-30)

In an event recorded in chapter 21, Agabus prophesies that a famine will impact the entire empire. This famine would be the result of the flooding of the Nile River in AD 45. The harvest of Egypt, breadbasket of the region, was damaged greatly by the flood. This sent grain prices skyrocketing throughout the Roman world for years, including in Judea.[223] The prophetic word spoken by Agabus gave the Christians an opportunity to show support for those in Jerusalem. In Acts 11 the Antioch Christians give, according to each person's ability, and they send the gift with Barnabas and Saul.

> **Acts 11:27-30** | Now in these days prophets came down from Jerusalem to Antioch. **28** And one of them named Agabus stood up and foretold by the Spirit that there would be a great famine over all the world (this took place in the days of Claudius). **29** So the disciples determined, every one according to his ability, to send relief to the brothers living in Judea. **30** And they did so, sending it to the elders by the hand of Barnabas and Saul.

Their giving was selfless. The famine hasn't taken place yet when the disciples determine to send relief. They are living by faith. They are selfless. They know the famine is coming, but they don't think about themselves, hoarding their resources for selfish security, but they give it away to the saints at Jerusalem.

Their giving was generous. They "gave according to their ability" (11:29). The church doesn't ask, How much will it cost? They simply give as much as they can.

Their giving was corporate, from one church to another. The church corporately took up the offering and sent it to the Jerusalem church's elders "by the hand of Barnabas and Saul."

---

[223] Witherington III, *Acts of the Apostles*, 368.

I've seen this at living hope. When we heard about a young believer in the Dominican Republic, you gave over $5000 to help him have a special surgery. I'm so grateful for your incredible generosity in so many mercy ministries, including Vacation Bible School last week. We had over 40 volunteers and over 50 kids registered. That's amazing!

Multicultural Membership (13:1)

Jesus will build his church from every nation around the earth, and the gates of hell shall not prevail. We see this in the Antioch church.

> **Acts 13:1** | Now there were in the church at Antioch prophets and teachers, Barnabas, Simeon who was called Niger, Lucius of Cyrene, Manaen a lifelong friend of Herod the tetrarch, and Saul.

You had *Barnabas*, a Jew and a native of Cyprus. Then there was *Simeon* who was likely from north Africa, and some think he may have been the one who carried the Lord's cross. There was *Lucius of Cyrene* (which is in Libya today), so he is also an African brother in Christ. *Manaen* is a member of the court of Herod the tetrarch: very likely an Idumean and Jewish mix. Many believe he was actually raised in the same household with Herod as a brother. He would have been considered to be a Gentile by the Jews. And then you had the great teacher and *Rabbi Saul of Tarsus*, who we know as the Apostle Paul. What a multicultural leadership team!

So you had two Jews and three Gentiles and two Jewish men on the leadership team. They were very diverse in their ethnicity. They were a multi-cultural ministry. They were an ethnically integrated church.

Do you know what else this church is? This will become the sending church of the Apostle Paul and Barnabas on their missionary journeys! A miracle has taken place and the church that becomes the very cradle of where Gentile Christianity is born and raised! The Antioch church was divinely planted. It was a miracle church.

There were Jewish believers from Cyrene, which is northern Africa—as well as the Island of Cyprus, about a hundred miles off the coast of Israel. And they come together and start evangelizing Gentiles, and a church is born!

Multicultural Missions Movement (13:2-3)

Here we have the start of the New Testament missions movement!

Acts 13:2-3 | While they were worshiping the Lord and fasting, the Holy Spirit said, "Set apart for me Barnabas and Saul for the work to which I have called them." **³** Then after fasting and praying they laid their hands on them and sent them off.

You can't just go to seminary or Bible college and become a missionary or a pastor. Training is vital, but the call of the gospel minister is from the Holy Spirit. The Spirit said, "Set apart" my servants. The local church at Antioch obeyed the voice of the Holy Spirit. They were moldable. They were teachable. They were humble. They weren't brilliant in their plans, but they followed the plan of God!

And so began the greatest miracle in the history of missions! The first of Paul's three great missionary journeys commenced. Soon, because of the efforts of this church, people would be saying, "Those people who have turned the world upside down have now come to us!"

Conclusion

As you consider the possibilities of what God might have us do as a church, let us be ready to listen to his voice. Let us look out beyond these four walls and think of the lost people that need to hear the name of Jesus from your lips. Let us be moved to diligently seek the face of God in prayer. Let us wait on God and see him use us in ways we never imagined!

21 | ACTS 12
GOD IS GOOD WHEN LIFE IS BAD

So Peter was kept in prison, but earnest prayer for him was made to God by the church.
ACTS 12:5

God is in control. Do you believe that? It doesn't matter what happens to you. It doesn't matter the pain and suffering you experience. You must never think that God has fallen asleep or that he's uninterested. He is in control, and he is good. He is directing all events in your life for your good and his glory. Now some of you are suffering incredibly. But it is our suffering that humbles all of us so that we can know God. Here's what I want us to understand. If we truly understood the goodness of God, that he is love, and that his love is fixed on doing good to unworthy people like us, it would transform us.

God is supremely good. And he is in control of all things. He's in control even when you can't see it or understand it. The theological concept is the God is sovereign. Many understand the theological term, but don't have the reality of God's peace in their life. When you know that God is good and that he's in control, directing all things for your good, then you can truly have peace. Do you have peace in your heart? So here is the key truth: God is good even when life is bad.

Let me put it another way: there is nothing that happens to me that can ultimately hurt me if I am in Christ. He will use it for his glory and for my good, to conform me to the image of Jesus (Rom 8:29). He will ultimately prove to me that he is wise and righteous for bringing that event into my life. This is what it means for God to be in control.

Now there is something in your life that has shaken you. And you were trusting God, trusting God, trusting God, and then it happened. And something shook you so bad, that you said, "I was on your program God until this happened. This is too hard. How can you use this for good?" When these life changing tragedies occur in your life, you have one of two choices: trust God or doubt God.

My mother died when I was 15 years old, just three months after I came to know Christ. She was only 49 years old. At that moment I put my full trust in God for that tragedy. I told my twin sister at the time, "I don't know what God is doing, but I know he is good, and I will follow him wherever he leads me." But had I doubted the next years of my life, instead of being the best years (which they were) would have been the worst years. What if instead of giving myself to prayer and to the arms of my good heavenly Father, I would have given myself to drugs and drink and sinful living? Where would my life be today? So let me say it again: God is good all the time. And all the time God is good! I want us to trust God today. We need to trust that God is good when life is bad. And there are four situations we can see the goodness of God.[224]

GOD IS IN CONTROL EVEN WHEN WE SUFFER (12:1-4)

First, we need to remember that God is good and is guiding our lives even when we suffer unjustly. Wherever there is violence or abuse, we are prone to say, "Where is God in this situation?" "How can God just stand by and let this happen?" Sometimes God allows hateful people or circumstances into our lives to bring us suffering. God controls kings and nations and events. God sometimes allows bad things to happen to his people.

King Herod Agrippa I, Persecutor

We find a very bad man inflicting violence on the church in verse 1. God is in control even when I'm suffering under wicked government rulers. Look at this wicked ruler. His name is Herod.

---

[224] The main points for this message is taken from *Walk in the Word ministries*.

Herod Agrippa's Background

Acts 12:1 | About that time Herod the king laid violent hands on some who belonged to the church.

Who is Herod? This is Herod Agrippa. The name Herod means "hero." It's kind of a surname for four brothers who were all rulers in Israel during the early church. Their grandfather is "Herod the Great". Herod the Great was like the Donald Trump when it came to the architecture of the ancient world, but on steroids. He owned everything and was one of the greatest builders in the ancient world.

Herod the Great's four grandsons had something in common with the grandfather. They were all tyrants. We find out that Herod Agrippa wants to make the Jews happy, and what makes them happy is to kill Christians. Herod Agrippa had control over Jerusalem and the surround area, and he was happy to oblige.

Herod Agrippa's Evil Deeds

Acts 12:1 | About that time Herod [Agrippa I] the king laid violent hands on some who belonged to the church.

King Herod Agrippa targets believers and rips them away from their churches and families. He "laid violent hands on them". That means he made a public display of some of them. He likely had soldiers enter their meeting place and beat them violently. That's going on today in places around the world. North Korea, Afghanistan. In a one year period there were 791 deaths that happened in Nigeria alone. So this is not just book of Acts stuff. It's happening now even more than back then.

God is in Control of Evil Government

There are many people who say, "We need to get back to the early church. I wish we could live in the days of the early church." Have you read the book of Acts? Yet and still God is in control of evil government rulers. Listen to the words of Daniel.

Daniel 2:20-21 | Blessed be the name of God forever and ever, to whom belong wisdom and might. [21] He changes times and seasons; he removes kings and sets up kings.

That was true back then, and it is still true today. It was true when the evil Herod Agrippa was in charge. And it is true today. God is in control, even when we suffer due to evil government policies. Christ will build his church and the gates of hell will not prevail against it. Think about what was happening in the book of Acts. The people's families were being ripped apart by persecution. But it gets worse. Agrippa flat out kills James, the brother of the Apostle John.

James, the First Apostle Martyred

Acts 12:2 | He [Herod Agrippa] killed James the brother of John with the sword.

This is not the "book of James" author. That's a different guy. This is the James from the "Peter, James, and John inner circle of Jesus." So this is a major loss for the church. The Apostle James is the first of the apostles that is martyred. Verse 2 says that Herod Agrippa "killed James the brother of John with the sword." So James, one of the inner three disciples was beheaded. He is the first apostle martyred. Imagine the shock to the church. James is suffering and is put to death. The church is suffering.

Bad things happen to God's people. It is God's will at times that his dear, precious children suffer and even die. James wasn't just a Christian. He wasn't just a chief leader in the church. He wasn't even just an apostle. He was in the *top three* of the apostles. He is one of the greatest leaders of the early church worldwide! And he was put to death. Perhaps he had a wife and children. He was dragged in, a sword was taken out, and his head was cut off. Never again does the book of Acts refer to the apostles as "the twelve". Now they are only eleven. Interesting Fact: James is the first of the apostles to die. John, his brother, is the last of the apostles to die.

The point is: God is good even when life is bad. We are going to see how good God is when we suffer. God has a design for our pain. God is in control. God is working out his purposes. When I can see it he's in control, and when I can't see it, he's still in control. When I feel God's presence, he's in control, and even when I can't feel his presence he's still in control, working out his good purposes for me.

Peter, Fellow Sufferer

Could it get any worse? The church is suffering violent persecution. Families are being ripped apart. The great apostle James is put to death with the sword, and now we see that Peter wasn't exempt from suffering either. Peter gets arrested. They want to kill Peter now.

> **Acts 12:3** | And when he [Agrippa] saw that it pleased the Jews, he proceeded to arrest Peter also. This was during the days of Unleavened Bread [Passover].

The Jews loved it when they took out James, "number 3" in the church, so now Herod wants to take out "Number 1". This is the third time in jail for Peter. He was arrested for healing the lame man in Acts 4, and they lectured him, and beat him, and let him and John go. He was in jail again in Acts 5:18, and an angel freed him and the other apostles during the night.

The Soldiers

So now we are introduced to the soldiers, and they are a helpless group compared to the omnipotent, almighty God. But they station a very large number of soldiers to guard Peter. I mean Peter might as well be superman. Last time he was imprisoned by Herod (Acts 5), he was released by an angel. They can definitely stop an angel with 16 soldiers, right? Let's read about it.

> **Acts 12:4** | And when he [Herod Agrippa] had seized him, he put him in prison, delivering him over to four squads of soldiers to guard him, intending after the Passover to bring him out to the people.

Why does Agrippa want to bring peter out to the people? Remember what he did with James? A public execution by the sword. And since Peter had already been imprisoned and released by an angel once already, they put 16 soldiers all around him day and night to guard Peter. A squad is a group of 4 soldiers each, and 4 squads equals 16 soldiers total guarding Peter. They only had a few soldiers last time (Acts 5), and Peter was released by an angel. So now they had to be incredibly paranoid about this, and they put 16 soldiers on him. How many of you believe that even 1600 soldiers could not stop God? Amen!

Peter is imprisoned with four squads of soldiers, but if you know this story, you know Peter is at peace and goes to sleep. He's not worried. And Peter is later is freed from prison. But did James get out? No.

How do you explain that? Does God love James less? No. Let me make this point loud and clear. God never promised you a life of ease, but instead a life of suffering.

God's best for you is not defined by your lack of suffering. It is defined by your conformity to Jesus Christ. Are you looking more like Christ? Then God's plan is succeeding. You must understand that God has perfect control over every detail of every situation. His purposes are not always seen or known. But there is one overarching purpose we can count on. It is that all our suffering will conform us to Christ. Saints, do you want to be conformed to Christ?

The Application

What shall we say to these things? How is God in control of our suffering?

God's Power in Suffering is His Sovereignty

God is in control when we are suffering. He is absolutely sovereign. God has never been like, "Oh I can't believe this happened." God is never like that. God is in complete control. Even when James is killed, and Peter is arrested. As far as he can see, it looks like Peter is going to die. We know from the book of Mark, that Peter has a wife. Despite all the pressure of being imprisoned, we know that God is in complete control. Peter believed that because later we see him sleeping. He's at peace and at rest even on what should be his last night alive. God is in complete control when I am suffering. That should bring every child of God peace.

God's Promise in Suffering is Discipline

God promises in Hebrews 12 that whoever he loves he bring discipline into their life. If you're not getting discipline in your life, you are not one of God's kids. If you find yourself on easy street, and suffering is not leading you to become more like Christ, you are not one of God's kids. God knows that true happiness comes through holiness. Holiness is conformity to Christ. If your suffering makes you like Christ, your happiness in Christ will far exceed suffering you have in this world. Holiness is so satisfying that if you get a drink of it, you'll be like a man in a desert drinking a cold glass of water. Holiness is what you were made for. It's when you heart and God's heart are united. That's what God is doing through your suffering and pain.

God's Purpose for Suffering is Conformity to Christ

God never promised we'd understand everything in this life, but he did promise he's working out his purposes in your life in your suffering. God's best for you is never defined by your lack of suffering or how good things go in your life. God's best is defined by your conformity to Jesus Christ (Rom 8:28-30).

God's Pathway of Suffering is for Every Christian

Let me reiterate that there is no exemption from suffering. We are all going to suffer in the Christian life. Jesus said this life will be filled with tribulation. Remember the words of Jesus.

> *John 16:33* | In the world you will have tribulation. But take heart; I have overcome the world.

Your faithfulness is not an exemption from suffering. Think about Job. He was such a faithful and righteous man but remember what he said.

> *Job 23:10* | He knows the way that I take; when he has tried me, I shall come out as gold.

If we are to follow Christ, we also ought to expect suffering. God has a wonderful purpose for pain in your life. C.S. Lewis said that "pain is God's megaphone to rouse a deaf world."[225] Suffering is one of the primary tools in God's toolbox for refining our character to be like Jesus. God uses pain in our lives to awaken us to areas of our life that are not conformed to Christ. He wants you to come forth as gold.

GOD IS IN CONTROL EVEN WHEN IT'S MIDNIGHT (12:5-11)

Second, God is good and is in control even when we have to wait. Even when it's midnight, and down to the wire, and there's no time left on the clock, then God is in control. You think there's no time for God to do something, and I'm telling you God can do anything. There's nothing too hard for the Lord. God is not limited to time and space.

Now let's see how the early church is not all that different from us. They had to wait too. We see in verse 5, that God is making the church wait until the very last minute to answer their prayers.

---

[225] C. S. Lewis, *The Problem of Pain* (New York: Simon & Schuster, 1996), 83.

Midnight is a Good Time to Pray

Notice that when the worst has happened, the church always has recourse with God.

> **Acts 12:5** | So Peter was kept in prison, but earnest prayer for him was made to God by the church.

When you think your life couldn't get any worse, when you feel there's no more light at the end of the tunnel, and you have nowhere else to turn, that's always when God shows up. That's why it's a good time to pray. When the church, God's people are most vulnerable, they are at their best! We surrender our fears to God, and let him answer as he will. When we are completely weak, and we have nowhere to turn, that's when we are at our best. We are going to pray. Bring your greatest and most difficult problems to him. What does he say?

> *Jeremiah 32:27* | I am the LORD, the God of all the peoples of the world. Is anything too hard for me?

Listen, if you are not a believer in Christ today, God is using your greatest brokenness to bring you to faith in Christ. If you are not a believer, then God is using your situation to grow you. Either way, God is in control even when it's midnight. Midnight is a good time to pray.

Midnight is a Good Time to Trust

Consider Peter's attitude when he is chained to two of the Roman soldiers.

> **Acts 12:6a** | Now when Herod was about to bring him out [*to execute him*], on that very night, Peter was sleeping between two soldiers, bound with two chains, and sentries before the door were guarding the prison.

So you had fourteen sentries guarding the door, two soldiers chained to Peter, and Peter is sleeping. How far away is Peter from death? It's not hours. He's minutes away from death. The king has already dropped his scepter and said, "Bring him out." The soldiers' feet are just beginning to make their way down the hallway. The keys are rattling. And what is Peter doing? Peter is sleeping! Peter is in the most stressful situation humanly imaginable. What was his secret?

> *Isaiah 26:3* | You keep him in perfect peace whose mind is fixed on you, because he trusts in you.

Why is Peter sleeping? Because he has so much peace. This is his third imprisonment. This is a mature faith. This is more than a dozen years after Pentecost, and for Peter, this is imprisonment number three! The secret to peace is to magnify the Lord as bigger than your circumstances.

Psalm 34:3 | O magnify the Lord with me, and let us exalt his name together.

God is in control, even when it's midnight. God is the God who dwells outside of time and space because he's bigger than time or space. He never sweats. He never slumbers. He's a thousand percent interested in your situation. Trust him!

The church is praying earnestly (12:5). What does earnest mean? Urgent, sincere prayer. The church has no idea what God is up to! But Peter is resting. It's midnight. If it's up to Herod, Peter's going to die in the morning. But Peter is not afraid of death. Christ has conquered death. Death has no sting for Peter, so he is sleeping. But he's about to get a wakeup call.

Midnight is a Good Time to Watch

The plot thickens. The saints are praying. Peter is sleeping. The soldiers are marching toward the cell. Where's God? He's up to something. He may not change your circumstance, but he's going to wake you up, just like he did Peter.

Acts 12:7a | And behold, an angel of the Lord stood next to him, and a light shone in the cell. He struck Peter on the side and woke him, saying, "Get up quickly."

Sometimes we think angels are feminine creatures with wings of down and soft hair. Listen, angels are warriors! Yahweh is called the LORD of the hosts of the angel armies! So the angel strikes Peter. Peter had to be sleeping hard! He wacked him. You've heard of getting touched by an angel. What about getting wacked by an angel?!

Acts 12:7 | And behold, an angel of the Lord stood next to him, and a light shone in the cell. He struck Peter on the side and woke him, saying, "Get up quickly." And the chains fell off his hands.

That's God. They didn't take the chains off. They just fell off. That's God. God can do that. Whatever chains you have in your life, God is the chain breaker!

> **Acts 12:8** | And the angel said to him, "Dress yourself and put on your sandals." And he did so. And he said to him, "Wrap your cloak around you and follow me."

Peter was totally out of it. He had to be told what to do. "Get dressed! Put your sandals on." He did whatever the angel said. "Get your coat on!" "Come on let's go!" Peter seems to have really enjoyed his rest. It's almost like Peter was having such a good rest he had trouble following the angel's orders.

> **Acts 12:9** | And he went out and followed him. He did not know that what was being done by the angel was real, but thought he was seeing a vision.

Peter has no clue whether this is real life or a dream! But he's about to get real-life delivered from the situation. Listen, midnight in your life is a good time to watch for God to do something beyond your imagination. Remember God's promises to us. God wants to do so much more than we are asking.

> *1 Corinthians 2:9* | No eye has seen, no ear has heard, and no mind has imagined what God has prepared for those who love him.

> *Ephesians 3:20-21* | Now to him who is able to do far more abundantly than all that we ask or think, according to the power at work within us, [21] to him be glory in the church.

Midnight is a Good Time to Wonder

When there is nothing we can do, and we are in the midnight of a situation, then this is the time to see God's miracle power.

> **Acts 12:10a** | When they had passed the first and the second guard, they came to the iron gate leading into the city. It opened for them of its own accord...

So Peter and the angel are running toward the iron gate leading to the city. It's night. There are watchmen. You can't just get in. But God opens that too. So far two locked gates have opened. God, at any moment, can open any door for us. God can do anything! Peter was minutes away from execution, and now he's running as fast as he can toward a locked gate, and it supernaturally opens!

> **Acts 12:10b** | And they went out and went along one street, and immediately the angel left him.

So he's running with an angel, and then suddenly, he's all alone.

> **Acts 12:11** | When Peter came to himself, he said, "Now I am sure that the Lord has sent his angel and rescued me from the hand of Herod and from all that the Jewish people were expecting."

These are the first words recorded out of Peter's mouth. "I am sure that the Lord sent his angel." The sovereign Lord is in control. Peter had to wait until the last minute, but he got an answer.

God is good even when it is midnight! It's not that God is not able to answer. He wants you to learn to trust him. Peter learned that! "Now I am sure!" "It was the Lord!! Herod couldn't touch me! The blood thirsty Jewish leaders couldn't touch me!" What are you facing? What is your midnight situation? Remember to pray. Trust the Lord. Watch the Lord work. And wonder at his miracles when he answers.

GOD'S IN CONTROL WHEN OUR FAITH IS WEAK (12:12-19)

God is in control even when my faith is weak. The early Christians believed in the power of prayer, but their faith was weak. They prayed earnestly, sincerely, urgently for Peter (12:5), but we find that the last person they were expecting at their prayer meeting was Peter!

The Fact of Weak Faith

> **Acts 12:12** | When he [*Peter*] realized this [*that he was free*], he went to the house of Mary, the mother of John whose other name was Mark, where many were gathered together and were praying.

So who is this Mark? He's a new guy. This is John Mark, the author of the Gospel of Mark. This is the cousin of Barnabas who twenty years later is going to see first see Peter put to death by Nero, and then Paul. He's going to become Peter and Paul's right-hand man in their golden years. The saints were at John Mark's house under lock and key because of the awful persecution. This is also likely the house where the disciples met for the Passover in the upper room. The upper room is likely located in the upper part of John Mark's house. I've been to this location. You can see the southern steps of the Temple where Pentecost took place from this room. Peter's just been released from prison, and he goes to this strategic house. He joins the prayer meeting where they are already praying for him. Can you imagine? They are praying for a miracle—something impossible. In fact, some are probably by this time asking God to help Peter's family in their grief since he's probably *dead* by now.

The Fear of Weak Faith

These were people that had weak and wavering faith like us. And there was a gateway, so it was a big house with a gateway and a courtyard and a fence surrounding it. They were in a secure place.

> **Acts 12:13a** | And when he knocked at the door of the gateway...

Peter's just been released from prison, and he's knocking at the door of this rich house. He was supposed to be put to death the next morning. Do you see the irony? Peter's just been let out of the prison by an angel, but he's locked out of the prayer meeting where they are praying for him! Peter knocks and meets a servant girl.

> **Acts 12:13b** | A servant girl named Rhoda came to answer.

Rhoda, the little servant girl is praying. This tells us that our children should at times be in our prayer services. She hears someone knocking at the gateway in the courtyard. She gets up. The gate is obviously locked, or Peter would have come right in. Why is the gate locked? It's clear why the gate was locked. Because Christians are being killed! It's against the law to be a Christ follower! They were all scared!

Peter shows up and Rhoda doesn't even let him in!

> **Acts 12:14** | Recognizing Peter's voice, in her joy she did not open the gate but ran in and reported that Peter was standing at the gate.

Poor Peter. He is left outside the locked gate. Angels opened gates for him in the prison, but he's locked out of the prayer meeting. Have you ever been praying about things, and you halfway don't expect an answer? Now we are supposed to pray in faith. But there are often times when our faith wavers. The early believers struggled in the same way.

The Feebleness of Faith

Rhoda rushes into the believers with Peter standing outside and it says she "reported that Peter was standing at the gate" (12:14). What was their response?

Acts 12:15a | They said to her, "You are out of your mind."

They thought she was certifiably insane! Why were they praying if they didn't think that God could do it? Look at this great faith they had! No their faith was feeble and frail. They had the faith of a mustard seed. The Christians had such weak faith, they thought Peter was dead and this was either and angel or Peter's ghost.

Acts 12:15b | But she kept insisting that it was so, and they kept saying, "It is his angel!"

Wouldn't you still go and see if it was an angel?! "Just an angel?!" "We'll pass!" "Only if it's Peter!" The point is, they thought that Peter was *dead*.

The Focus of our Faith

Acts 12:16a | But Peter continued knocking...

Rhoda's back in the house. And Peter's on the wrong side of a locked door, and it says he "continued knocking" and was locked out of the prayer meeting. Why do you think he kept knocking? He just escaped from prison! You can almost hear the dogs barking in the street, and Peter kept knocking. He's a fugitive! But God wants to bring their faith to a new level. Look at the weak faith of these Christians. They finally open the gate for him. You see that God is growing their faith.

Acts 12:16b | And when they opened, they saw him and were amazed.

What were they? They were *amazed*! They were astonished! That doesn't sound like expectant faith! But their faith is growing. God looks at us as his dear children. We are weak and feeble, but we are his. You can imagine them shouting and rejoicing and utterly shocked! But Peter quiets them.

Acts 12:17a | But motioning to them with his hand to be silent, he described to them how the Lord had brought him out of the prison. And he said, "Tell these things to James and to the brothers."

He's telling them about how he was surrounded by 16 soldiers, sound asleep! He told them "how the Lord had brought him out of the prison." He's verifying the amazing account that Luke later writes. It's all true.

The Forward Movement of our Faith

Acts 12:17b | Then he departed and went to another place.

Peter went on to many more adventures of faith. He didn't take time off to recover. He's at ease. He's at rest. I love this example of faith.

Did the early Christians at times have very weak faith? Is God good despite our weak and wavering faith? Can God work even though our faith is small? Absolutely! Be encouraged!

GOD IS IN CONTROL WHEN THE WICKED PROSPER (12:18-25)

Now this is the end of the story, and it is a bit surprising. We see that there is a great stir when Peter is not found in the prison. He's disappeared again. He's been "touched by an angel" again. This is becoming common place for Peter. It is here we are introduced to the unmitigated power of a tyrant.

The Wicked's Power

Acts 12:18-19 | Now when day came, there was no little disturbance among the soldiers over what had become of Peter. [19] And after Herod searched for him and did not find him, he examined the sentries and ordered that they should be put to death. Then he went down from Judea to Caesarea and spent time there.

Herod Agrippa finds the 16 soldiers and puts them to death. He's so disturbed that he needs a vacation, and he heads to his grandfather's magnificent palace and campus there in Caesarea Maritima by the Mediterranean Sea. It's marvelous collection of architecture. The remains of the buildings are still intact today. I've walked among them myself. The point is, this king looks like he has no accountability. It seems he can do whatever he wants, but we find it's not so.

The Wicked's Peace

Here we have a mirage of peace that King Herod Agrippa seems to enjoy with the people.

Acts 12:20 | Now Herod was angry with the people of Tyre and Sidon, and they came to him with one accord, and having persuaded Blastus, the king's chamberlain, they asked for peace, because their country depended on the king's country for food.

Herod Agrippa was not a good man. He wasn't even a great man like his grandfather. He was really just paying off the population to like him. It's like all the buying of votes with empty promises that politicians make today. And this made Herod Agrippa popular at least with some people.

The Wicked's Praise

It seems that there are always a contingent of people who will say anything as long as the government is giving them what they want.

Acts 12:21-22 | On an appointed day Herod put on his royal robes, took his seat upon the throne, and delivered an oration to them. [22] And the people were shouting, "The voice of a god, and not of a man!"

It's dangerous for a fallen human being to be a glory thief and receive the praise that only belongs to the Lord. But they praised Herod, and he thought he could be worshipped without accountability.

The Wicked's Punishment

Acts 12:23 | Immediately an angel of the Lord struck him down, because he did not give God the glory, and he was eaten by worms and breathed his last.

Can you see that God is in control? He will punish wicked tyrants, if not now, when he returns. Remember that "every knee will bow"!

Philippians 2:10-11 | At the name of Jesus every knee should bow..."[11] and every tongue confess that Jesus Christ is Lord.

Herod was given the fate of all those who do not know Christ. You see, God is not willing that anyone should perish and go to hell, but that all should come to repentance (1 Pet 3:9). But if you bypass the mercy of God, you will have to pay for your own sins yourself, forever and ever in the lake of fire. Notice Herod Agrippa was "eaten by worms." Why? "Because he did not give God the glory." And let me tell you, the physical destruction of Herod's body by worms was just a foreshadowing of the eternal torment that is coming for anyone who does not know

Christ. The Bible says that hell's lake of fire is a place where "the worms [maggots] never die, and the fire is never quenched" (Mk 9:28). You don't want to go there. The torment goes on forever because people there never stop sinning against God. God doesn't want anyone to go there.

Learn from this king who would not turn to God. He perished, but it's not too late for you. Bow your knee. Give God the glory. All those great and small on this earth who insist on living as if God is a low priority, judgment is coming. "Seek first the kingdom of God" (Mt 6:33). Let's give Christ the preeminence and give him all the glory! God dealt with that wicked king. And what was the result? God's word prospered and spread.

Notice also God's control of Peter's circumstances. Peter was right to rest even though he was sentenced to death that night. Instead of Peter dying, all of the Roman soldiers guarding him were put to death as well as King Herod Agrippa. If that doesn't demonstrate God's sovereignty to us, nothing will. He is in control, and we can trust him fully.

The Word of God Prospers

Acts 12:24 | But the word of God increased and multiplied.

You see God is in control, even when the wicked prosper. And despite the wicked, the word of God prospers. God will take care of the wicked. There are tyrants in the government, but they cannot overrule God. We have to live with courage and faith and take a stand against tyrants. What that mostly means is that we never stop preaching and giving the hope of Christ. The government of this world can never stop us from evangelizing and discipleship.

The Witness of God Prospers

Acts 12:25 | And Barnabas and Saul returned from Jerusalem when they had completed their service, bringing with them John, whose other name was Mark.

What we find out now is that Barnabas and Saul and John Mark get together and start planning for the first missionary journey that will be launched in the next chapter. We have to trust that God is in control when the government is trying to control our lives and divide the church. This is a time of great satanic power in our country, but don't be discouraged—God is still on the throne. The gospel will go forth. Tyrants try to disrupt the power of God from building his church but is impossible. God has control over the tyrants. The church will be built, and the gates of hell shall not prevail!

Conclusion

You may be suffering today, and you can't make sense of it. You know God is in control, but you can't see through the shadows and darkness of your circumstances. When you can't see the hand of God, trust his heart. He wants to do the ultimate good for you, which is to rescue you from ultimate death.

Think about life like a beautiful tapestry. When you look at the backside, all you see is loose strings and knots and messes. But turn it over and it is a beautiful work of art. That's our life. All the suffering is like the knots that form in us the beautiful heart of Christ. God's making a truly beautiful tapestry out of your life.

If you are without Christ, you are in a greater dilemma than Peter. Peter got out of prison, not because he needed to be rescued from death. Death was already conquered for Peter. He had trusted in Christ. But he needed to be released so he could rescue others from death. There was a lot of missionary work he needed to do, and he would ultimate live another twenty plus years and die preaching the gospel in Rome where he would be crucified. We learn that he didn't feel worthy to die the same way our Lord died, so he asked to be crucified upside down. Was that a defeat for Peter? No! Death is just the beginning for the believer. All who know Christ will live forever with him. Soon Christ will return and renew the earth, and we will live forever here in a renewed earth with a renewed body. Death is defeated. God is in total control, and he is working all things for our good and his glory.

LIFE-ON-LIFE DISCIPLE MAKING
ACTS 13-28

FIRST MISSIONARY JOURNEY

22 | ACTS 13:1-12
A PATTERN FOR MISSIONS

While they were worshiping the Lord and fasting, the Holy Spirit said, "Set apart for me Barnabas and Saul for the work to which I have called them." Then after fasting and praying they laid their hands on them and sent them off.
ACTS 13:2-3

I have learned to love adventure in my life. Sometimes that adventure has come through sad and unfortunate circumstances. I was nine years old when my family broke up and I moved with my mom and twin sister from Chicago to Louisiana. Many adventures were had, like jumping into the Tickfaw River out of the top of a sixty-foot cypress tree. Or eating strange but tantalizing food like crawfish, jambalaya, and gumbo. And then there was the greatest adventure. I had no idea that the Holy Spirit had plans for me. At age fifteen, the eyes of my heart were opened, I wase born again at an Assemblies of God meeting and then discipled in a little Southern Baptist church. God had plans for me. I was in darkness, and suddenly I was part of God's worldwide adventure for his church. He will indeed build his church, and the gates of hell will not prevail against it. God's plans for me had been made before the foundation of the world.

What we find out in Acts 13 is that the Holy Spirit has plans for a whole lot of unlikely people. He loves to take those who are in darkness and bring them into the light of Christ. The Spirit was on the move then, and he is on the move today. We read about the pattern of expansion for the church in this text in Acts 13.

Our key thought for today is that God wants you to be personally involved in evangelism and discipleship. It may not be your specific gifting to teach or evangelize, but every believer ought to be pointing people to Christ, inviting people to know Jesus and making disciples.

THE EXPANSION OF THE CHURCH (13:1-3)

What we are going to see is that a healthy church is a growing church, expanding in its influence.

> **Acts 13:1-3** | Now there were in the church at Antioch prophets and teachers, Barnabas, Simeon who was called Niger, Lucius of Cyrene, Manaen a lifelong friend of Herod the tetrarch, and Saul. ² While they were worshiping the Lord and fasting, the Holy Spirit said, "Set apart for me Barnabas and Saul for the work to which I have called them." ³ Then after fasting and praying they laid their hands on them and sent them off.

In these first three verses we see the DNA for any New Testament church that is healthy and growing.

The Locale of the Antioch Church

> **Acts 13:1a** | Now there were in the church at Antioch prophets and teachers.

It was local, "at Antioch." Antioch was at a cultural crossroads for travelers and had a diverse population. Every congregation is somewhere in time and space. It is a church: because it was a congregation. The local church is the prized venue of God's work.

What is a church? John Owen said, "The church is a society of people called by the word to the obedience of the faith of Christ, and joint performance of the worship of God in the same individual ordinances, according to the order by Christ prescribed." Mark Dever describes a church as "united by God and committed to one another." The apostle Paul says it's a place of truth. It is the "pillar and ground of the truth."

As geographically accessible and strategically located for worldwide evangelism as Antioch was in it is day almost any city in modern

USA is far more so. We have no excuse. The burden of the Great Commission is just as much ours as it was theirs.

The Leaders of the Antioch Church

Acts 13:1 | Now there were in the church at Antioch prophets and teachers, Barnabas, Simeon who was called Niger, Lucius of Cyrene, Manaen a lifelong friend of Herod the tetrarch, and Saul.

There were many leaders at Antioch: prophets and teachers, apostles, some of the seven deacons (Acts 6). This was a church filled with leaders! They had a diversity on their leadership team (Acts 13:1). The leadership team and the church reflected the church triumphant in heaven! Consider their leadership team. *Barnabas* is a Jew and a native of Cyprus. *Simeon* was likely an African, and some think he may have been the one who carried the Lord's cross. *Lucius of Cyrene* is also an African brother in Christ. *Manaen* is a member of the court of Herod the tetrarch—very likely an Idumean and Jewish mix. Many believe he was actually raised in the same household with Herod as a brother. He would have been considered a Gentile by the Jews. *Rabbi Saul*, a once very decorated Pharisee is also a Jew.

You had two Jews and three Gentiles on the leadership team. They were very diverse in their ethnicity, but they were of one heart in preaching the gospel and building up the church. They were a multicultural ministry. They were an ethnically integrated church.

The Love of the Antioch Church

Acts 13:2a | While they were worshiping the Lord and fasting, the Holy Spirit said...

There was Christ-centered service. "They were worshipping the Lord." There was consensual self-denial—they fasted. The Spirit spoke to them. They prayed! The utter dependence of the early church on prayer is unmistakable in Acts. As a result, there was a commission by setting-apart "they set apart Paul and Barnabas." A praying church is always going to be a sending church. If you love God, you are going to love the nations.

Consider what the great men in the movements of God had in common. These were not great men. They were small men with a great God. These were men who spent hours each day in prayer. And many of them led congregations that knew what it was to pray! Consider Pentecost. They prayed. They sought God. They waited. They waited on God and sought him until they were endued with power from on high! That's what we need!

The Divine Leader of the Antioch Church

> **Acts 13:2** | While they were worshiping the Lord and fasting, the Holy Spirit said, "Set apart for me Barnabas and Saul for the work to which I have called them."

How the Holy Spirit communicated to the church is not revealed. Presumably he spoke through one of the prophets. However, the message was communicated, the church's response was instant obedience. There was no grumbling or resentment; the Holy Spirit demanded the church's best, and Antioch joyously provided Saul and Barnabas.[226]

Who is the leader of the Antioch church and our church? It is the Holy Spirit. There is objective determination of God's will. There is also subjective determination of God's will. influence by the word of God, the personality of leaders, divine providence, the gifts of believers, and the location of church.

The Spirit of God is the one who burdens the prayerful heart with direction. It is the Spirit that has people he wants to save in China or Africa or Japan. A returned missionary might say, "Why don't you come to Brazil?" or, "We could use you in Germany." But the call must come from the Holy Spirit, not from a man, a mission board, or a church. No one has the right to deny the clear leading of the Holy Spirit in a person's life just because that person is not the right age or not sufficiently educated.

George Müller became a missionary at the age of seventy. He had been turned down as a missionary five times in the first eight years of his new life in Christ! What a prospective missionary the shortsighted mission boards lost in George Müller—one of the greatest giants of faith of all time![227] We need a church filled with people who are ready to follow the leading of the Holy Spirit and say, "Here I am Lord, send me" (Isa 6:8).

---

[226] John F. MacArthur Jr., *Acts*, vol. 2, MacArthur New Testament Commentary (Chicago: Moody Press, 1994), 6.

[227] J. Phillips, *Exploring Acts,* Ac 13:2b.

The Enlargement of the Antioch Church

Acts 13:2-3 | While they were worshiping the Lord and fasting, the Holy Spirit said, "Set apart for me Barnabas and Saul for the work to which I have called them." ³ Then after fasting and praying they laid their hands on them and sent them off.

They were set apart by the Holy Spirit and sent off by the church. They didn't have ten books on how to plant a church. They had the word of God and the power of the Holy Spirit. Remember Jesus' words.

Matthew 16:18 | I will build my church, and the gates of hell shall not prevail against it.

The Antioch church has a heart for the nations. Their location was suitable for Western expansion. Their attitude toward outsiders was warm and embracing. They sent their own leaders to do the work. We see some of this in our own church. We needed a pastor for our Hispanic ministry, and God allowed us to raise up a pastor from our midst. He was already a faithful member of our church, serving the Lord as an assistant in preaching. That should not be a rare thing, but it sometimes is.

Antioch was a city of around 200,000 people during the time of the book of Acts. Within a ten-mile radius of Living Hope, there well over half a million people (635,000), and that is a conservative estimate.

As geographically accessible and strategically located for worldwide evangelism as Antioch was in its day almost any city in modern USA is far more so. We have no excuse. The burden of the Great Commission is just as much ours as it was theirs.

THE MISSION OF THE CHURCH (13:4-5)

The importance of the present narrative is that it describes the first piece of planned overseas mission carried out by representatives of a particular church, rather than by solitary individuals, and begun by a deliberate church decision, inspired by the Spirit, rather than somewhat more casually as a result of persecution.[228] This is a crucial event in the life of the church of Jesus Christ. The mission is to proclaim the gospel in the power of the Holy Spirit and see people turn to Christ.

---

[228] E. Best, 'Acts 13:1–3', *The Journal of Biblical Studies* 11, 1960, 344–348.

Acts 13:4-5 | So, being sent out by the Holy Spirit, they went down to Seleucia, and from there they sailed to Cyprus. ⁵ When they arrived at Salamis, they proclaimed the word of God in the synagogues of the Jews. And they had John to assist them.

The Power of the Mission

Acts 13:4a | So, being sent out by the Holy Spirit.

These were sent out by the Holy Spirit. We can commission people, but we have no power. We can license, ordain, and send people on sacred tasks, but unless the Holy Spirit anoints them, their labors will be in vain.[229] Remember the promise of the Holy Spirit for every one of us.

Acts 1:8 | You will receive power when the Holy Spirit has come upon you, and you will be my witnesses in Jerusalem and in all Judea and Samaria, and to the end of the earth.

We have no power in ourselves, but we have infinite power in the Spirit. Zechariah told us as much.

Zechariah 4:6 | Not by might, nor by power, but by my Spirit, says the Lord of hosts.

The Planning of the Mission

Acts 13:4b | They went down to Seleucia, and from there they sailed to Cyprus.

Saul and Barnabas no doubt chose to begin their missionary outreach on Cyprus for several reasons. According to Acts 4:36, it was Barnabas's home and thus it would have been familiar territory. Also, it was close to Antioch, probably two days' journey at most. Further, Cyprus had a large Jewish population. All those reasons made it an ideal starting point for outreach to the Gentile world.[230]

In leaving their comfort zone in Antioch, there is a great act of faith that changes the world as we know it. We find the beginning of the most significant missionary movement in the entire history of the church, indeed of the world. It begins with some geographical details. They had been at Antioch on the Orontes River, and from there they went first to Seleucia, the harbor that served that part of Syria, and they boarded a

---

[229] Sproul, *Acts*, 221–222.
[230] MacArthur, *Acts*, 7.

ship. We are told, even by geographers today, that on a clear day, if you stand on the coast of Syria in what was once Seleucia and look out into the Mediterranean—130 miles in the distance on a clear day—you can still see the shape and outline of that large island of Cyprus. That was in the vision of Paul and Barnabas as they set sail.[231]

Paul and Barnabas are sent out by the Spirit (13:4a). It's not our plan. It's God's plan from the foundation of the world. Yet being filled with the Spirit gives us big, broken hearts for the lost. Christ died for lost souls, and he would have them saved. There is an urgency. The most sobering reality in the world today is that people are dying and going to hell today. We see a blueprint for Paul's first missionary journey. He evangelized the great population centers of his day, the centers of culture, commerce, and government. He sought to plant his pioneer churches in the cities; those churches could then evangelize the surrounding area.[232] Ephesus, for example was planted by Paul, and then Ephesus evangelized Asia Minor, and hence we have the seven churches named in Revelation.

The Proclamation of the Mission

Acts 13:5a | When they arrived at Salamis, they proclaimed the word of God in the synagogues of the Jews.

Paul and Barnabas went first to the Jewish population to preach Jesus. These were those who were already familiar with the word of God. Later they would branch out to the Gentiles. Paul would later explain his strategy.

Romans 1:16 | For I am not ashamed of the gospel, for it is the power of God for salvation to everyone who believes, to the Jew first and also to the Greek.

At the end of the day all the planning in the world will not get the job done. The power comes from the word of God itself. We must proclaim the message of the gospel. We dare not tame the gospel or edit it or dumb it down. The fact that we are dead in our sins, worthy of hell must be stated. It is not until we see how desperate our state is that we can truly see our need for Christ. Oh, the wonder of Jesus' love! He, as God the Son took on a human body and lived a perfect life on our

---

[231] Sproul, *Acts*, 222.
[232] Phillips, *Acts*, Ac 13:4.

behalf. He was then crucified as a sacrifice for our sin. We give him our rags of sin, and he gives us his robe of righteousness. After Christ died on the cross, he was risen from the dead by the same Spirit that raises us from the dead when we believe. We can be filled and guided and directed now by the Spirit. Our hearts are Christ's throne. This is the good news! Proclaim it far and wide, that the whole world will know that Jesus Christ is Lord!

The Personnel of the Mission

Acts 13:5b | And they had John to assist them.

This is John Mark, the cousin to Barnabas, and the author of the Gospel of Mark, which is really the work of the apostle Peter. John Mark and Barnabas would soon part ways from Paul, due to the harshness of the work as we read a few verses later in Acts 13:13, "Paul and his companions set sail from Paphos and came to Perga in Pamphylia. And John left them and returned to Jerusalem" (*cf* Acts 15:36-41). This caused no small controversy between Paul and Barnabas. Nonetheless, John Mark would later author the Gospel of Mark with most of the work coming from Peter.

Listen, God's got his people right where he wants them. John Mark might not have been as mature as Paul, but he was willing, and he was growing. He had a setback, but he kept going. The early church father John Chrysostom said that John Mark likely had a fit of homesickness. Whatever the reason he retreated. Paul would eventually forgive him, and he would become a strategic partner for both the apostles, Peter and Paul, in their time imprisonment in Rome. We all have to start somewhere. At least John Mark was willing to go with the great Paul and Barnabas! Also, John Mark teaches us that it's more important how you end than how you finish.

THE OPPOSITION OF THE CHURCH (13:6-8)

Whenever God opens the door of the gospel to someone, there will always be satanic attack. Expect it. Here we are introduced to a certain magician named Elymas Bar-Jesus. We find out that as Paul and Barnabas explain the faith to a high ranking official, the governor proconsul of Cyprus, named Sergius Paulus, this false teacher seeks to turn him away from the faith of Christ.

Acts 13:6-8 | When they had gone through the whole island as far as Paphos, they came upon a certain magician, a Jewish false prophet named Bar-Jesus. ⁷ He was with the proconsul, Sergius Paulus, a man of intelligence, who summoned Barnabas and Saul and sought to hear the word of God. ⁸ But Elymas the magician (for that is the meaning of his name) opposed them, seeking to turn the proconsul away from the faith.

The Devil's Work of Opposition

We find out in church history that Barnabas is later martyred by Elymas Bar-Jesus. We find out that as Paul and Barnabas explain the faith to a high ranking official, the governor proconsul of Cyprus, named Sergius Paulus, and he is being drawn to the word of God to believe. All the while, this wicked false teacher Elymas seeks to turn him away from the faith of Christ.

Be ready to face opposition when you live for Christ. Everyone who lives out the holiness of the Christian life will face persecution. So the question today is are you facing any enemies? If you have no enemies then you should wonder which side you are on. If you are not garnering persecution that should tell you something about the dimness of your life and light. Are you shining the light of Christ, or do you have your light hidden under a basket? Don't be afraid of the devil's work. Consider it an honor to be opposed. It says something about the power and influence of your testimony.

God's Work in Evangelism

God is working through Paul and Barnabas. The Spirit has targeted a governor, proconsul named Sergius Paulus. Think of it! In Cyprus, two hundred miles away from Antioch in Syria, on an island in the middle of the Mediterranean Sea, was a man whom God wanted in the kingdom of God. God was saying in effect, "I want this man! I am going to make a straight path between Sergius Paulus and the two men in the church in Antioch, Barnabas and Saul. I will bring them together, and I will ensure that as they walk in my ways in obedience to my calling and equipping, a glorious conversion will take place. No matter what Satan may try to do to oppose it, 'the gates of hell will not prevail.' I will prevail," says the Spirit.

We might be tempted to think that what had attracted the proconsul was the scholarship and charismatic personalities of the two ambassadors of Christ from Antioch, but while it may well be true that he had heard something of their reputation, it is not what Luke wants us to understand as the fundamental emphasis. It was first and foremost a work of God. The word of God was doing its work (13:7).

God is at work. It is as though he had been drawing a straight line from Antioch to Sergius Paulus (there is Paphos, Cyprus) saying, "I will build a highway from this city to that city." It is a display of the sovereignty of God in missionary work and evangelism. When God is at work, nothing can stand in his way.[233]

Be always about the mission of pointing to Christ, and God will put you in situations to share God's word and bring people to Christ. No opposition can stop you since God is omnipotent.

THE CONQUEST OF THE CHURCH (13:9-12)

Paul was not afraid but confronted the opposition and called him out for what he was, a "son of the devil." So really we see two people being conquered by the word of God, one in a negative way and the other in a positive way. The false teacher-magician, Elymas is conquered in a very bad way. He is rendered blind. And then you have the proconsul-governor of Cyprus who is conquered by the word of God in a very positive way. He believes and is converted.

A Diabolic Conquest

Paul knew he wasn't just up against some unknown magician named Elymas, but that Elymas was a pawn of the devil to try and oppose God. Paul told Elymas the gig was up.

> **Acts 13:9-10** | But Saul, who was also called Paul, filled with the Holy Spirit, looked intently at him **10** and said, "You son of the devil, you enemy of all righteousness, full of all deceit and villainy, will you not stop making crooked the straight paths of the Lord?

We have to realize that when we evangelize, we are not wrestling against flesh and blood, but against demonic powers in the unseen realm (Eph 6:11-12). Paul merely reiterates this to Elymas' face. Paul is not insulting Elymas but warning him. That's what we are to do with the enemies of the Lord.

---

[233] Thomas, *Acts*, 360–361.

A Dangerous Conquest

Acts 13:11 | And now, behold, the hand of the Lord is upon you, and you will be blind and unable to see the sun for a time." Immediately mist and darkness fell upon him, and he went about seeking people to lead him by the hand.

When we warn those who oppose the gospel, it is up to the Lord what do to with them. For Elymas, Paul was given a prophecy and a miracle. This isn't the kind of miracle you want and pray for. Elymas would not relent or repent so God granted him temporary blindness to humble him. While it did keep him from harassing Sergius Paulus, it did not stop him for long. Church history records, as I mentioned already, that Elymas is the one who later on martyrs Barnabas.

Don't worry about the enemies of God. They will come and harass you, but like their father the devil, they have no power to bring you meaningful harm. They can roar but they cannot harm. God will restrain the enemy anytime he needs to. Do you have a fear of evangelism because of the enemy? Don't be afraid of him. Satan is already a defeated foe.

1 John 4:4 | Greater is he that is in you, than he that is in the world.

Romans 8:37 | We are more than conquerors through him who loved us.

A Delightful Conquest

Paul and Barnabas had no idea what was about to happen with Sergius Paulus, but they kept plowing forward no matter the difficulties that were launched by the enemy. The greatest and most delightful conquest took place: Sergius Paulus became a follower of Jesus Christ!

Acts 13:12a | Then the proconsul believed, when he saw what had occurred.

The great proconsul of Cyprus believed the gospel after he had seen the miracle blindness upon that wicked Elymas the sorcerer. The greater miracle was not the blindness of Elymas but the spiritual sight of Sergius Paulus. Don't be surprised what God can do in bringing someone to salvation. We must not be bound up by fear and worry when it comes to the salvation of souls. We are merely instruments in the Redeemer's hands. He does the work of opening the blind eyes. He raises the spiritually dead. Be careful of fear and worry because it can drive you to two extremes: one is to avoid evangelism all together. The other is to try and create false conversions through manipulation. We must wait on the Lord to do his work. Notice how God did the work in the heart of the great governor of Cyprus, Sergius Paulus.

A Dynamic Conquest

Acts 13:12b | For he was astonished at the teaching of the Lord.

The word of God did all the work. God's word is powerful. It is what transforms the soul. I love this. It wasn't the personalities or even the emotional or moving words of Paul and Barnabas. It was the teaching of the word of the Lord that astonished this powerful man and converted his heart.

> *Hebrews 4:12* | For the word of God is living and active, sharper than any two-edged sword, piercing to the division of soul and of spirit, of joints and of marrow, and discerning the thoughts and intentions of the heart.

Remember in the book of Ezekiel (chapter 37) there was a valley of dry bones, a cemetery of sorts containing the bones of the army of Israel. What did Ezekiel do in order to bring the army of God's people to life? He prophesied and preached the word of God. He preached and the wind of God's Spirit made the cemetery of people alive.

Applications

God wants you to become personally involved in evangelism and discipleship. God is in the business of saving souls. How can you be a part of God's great work of building his church?

Be conformed to Christ personally. Paul and Barnabas were men who walked with Christ on a personal level. They were worshipping when the Spirit of God set them apart. When they spoke the word of God, they did so from personal experience. The Spirit was moving them with the word every day. If you want to be personally involved in the expansion of the church, you've got to surround yourself with God's word, the Spirit's work through the word in your own heart, and with God's people. Sin has to be confronted in your life by the word, by the Spirit and by the church. Constant repentance and humility ought to the be experience of your life. Constant joy in Jesus and satisfaction in the word will keep you happy and holy.

Pray for lost souls. Begin in your family. You have to believe that God can save anyone. Perhaps that is hardest when it comes to your own family. You have a lost son or daughter. Pray and believe that God will save them! You have a lost parent. Pray and believe. Have you given up? Pray for opportunities. God will open doors. There is a prayer meeting each day this week where we can do this on a corporate level. Come a couple of days this week for corporate prayer.

Do personal evangelism. Be preaching Christ wherever you are. In a restaurant you can ask the server if you can pray for them. They'll often join with you. There is a world of people who are hurting and broken, and we are so afraid, we lose our boldness. Be loving but be bold. People need you to be courageous to give them the gospel. "How are they to believe in him of whom they have never heard? And how are they to hear without someone preaching?" (Rom 10:14). Who else is going to tell the world about Christ? If you are growing in Christ, you will evangelize.

Encourage discipleship. Are you doing your part in discipleship? Discipleship begins with faithful walking with God yourself. You have to be committed to the body of Christ. Be here when the doors are open. Be here for Sunday School. Join God's people for Sunday evening service the first Sunday of each month. Be texting the saints during the day. Get in the habit of sharing your burdens and carrying the burdens of those in this body. Be sharing what you are learning with others in the body.

Conclusion

When I was a child, we used to camp out on the weekends on my friend's land. There were plenty of pine trees down there in the outskirts of New Orleans. One of our favorite things was to make a gigantic bonfire. We would clear the land of branches and dead trees and just set it on fire. As big as it was, it would start to die down and someone would gather new firewood to keep it aflame. The key is to spread the flame to new material.

It's like than in evangelism. Any fire that does not spread will eventually go out. A church that is not on fire with the Holy Spirit and holiness will not evangelize. Don't be discouraged if you are struggling with evangelism. Start small. Share a Bible verse with a co-worker or family member. It can be as simple as sharing Romans 6:23, "For the wages of sin is death, but the free gift of God is eternal life in Christ Jesus our

Lord." I know we have another twelve months until the next Christmas, but Jesus is a gift you can give all year round!

23 | ACTS 13:13-52
THE MESSAGE OF MISSIONS

Brothers, sons of the family of Abraham, and those among you who fear God, to us has been sent the message of this salvation.
ACTS 13:26

When I was just a toddler, my brother David, 12 years older than me, found a maple tree seed—what we call helicopters or whirly birds. David decided to plant one of those half-grown silver maples growing from that whirly bird. My dad did his best to mow it over, but he only mowed once a week, and that little tree grew even when my dad was sleeping. Eventually autumn would come, and that little tree won. Today you can see that tree from the Satellite photos it's so big! My dad saw just a tiny seed, but my brother saw a mighty maple. The gospel is a lot like that seed my brother planted. Some plant the gospel message, and some water, but God makes it grow. He gives the increase in the human heart.

In our text, we learned how the proconsul Sergius Paulus came to know Christ. After this great Roman governor became a Christian, Saul took the name Paul, and this event increased the number of conversions in Cyprus. Even many years later, while the vast majority of Jews living on the island were hostile to the Christians, the Gentiles were filling the churches.[234]

Their activity seriously disturbed the Jewish community. Initially, the apostles taught the Jews only, but when they rejected them, they began to preach the good news to the Gentiles. The tradition of Cyprus maintains that under the pressure of outraged Jewish community, Paul was captured in Paphos and, after being tied to the whipping post, punished with 39 strokes of the whip.[235] While in Cyprus, according to tradition, many others, mainly Gentiles, were converted, including Herakleidios, who became one of the first pastors there in Cyprus scattered in various cities throughout the island.[236]

THE PATHWAY OF THE GOSPEL (13:13)

Though it was such a fruitful time, it was intense, and at points likely vicious, so John Mark deserts his friends and makes his way back to Jerusalem while "Paul and his companions" continued to plant the first churches in Asia.

A Promising Pathway

Paul, Barnabas, and others set sail to evangelize a whole new part of the world: Asia, what is modern-day Turkey. They felt the direction of the Holy Spirit leading them to stay in the east and evangelize.

> **Acts 13:13a** | Now Paul and his companions set sail from Paphos and came to Perga in Pamphylia.

There were many Roman colonies in Asia, and Paul knew this was the way the gospel could get to the whole world. These were the worlds crossroads at the time. If God had led them to Cyprus in order to save Sergius Paulus, the governor there, then what else did he have in mind for Asia?

When we look out at the harvest fields, it's easy to become jaded and critical, but how vital it is to remember the Lord's promises to save our loved ones and to see God's heaven full. We must always have an attitude as wide as God's love and power. He can and will save

---

[234] Mariusz Misztal, *Historia Cypru* (Kraków, Poland: Issue 628 of Praca Monograficzne, Commission of National Education in Kraków, 2013), 86.
[235] Ibid., 85.
[236] F. Halkin, *Les actes apocryphes de Saint Héraclide de Chypre, disciple de l'apôtre Barnabé,* (Analecta Bollandiana, vol. 82, 1964), 133–169.

multitudes for his kingdom. He has promised to do so. Go into the highways and hedges and compel them to come (*cf* Lk 14:23)! Of all people the Lord's saints should be the most hopeful on the planet. God saved you, didn't he? He can save anyone.

A Treacherous Pathway

Sadly, not everyone seemed to have that hope. John Mark seems to have been discouraged if not intimidated by the journey.

Acts 13:13b | And John left them and returned to Jerusalem.

John Mark knew that to plant churches in Asia, you had to go through the Taurus mountain range, and that would be treacherous. It extends across the coast and inland of what is today the country of Turkey. Paul had grown up in the highlands of the Taurus mountain range. This may have been too hard a task for John Mark, so he departed back home to Jerusalem. Paul and Barnabas on the other hand, plowed forward. Nothing it seemed could stop them from spreading the good news to the cities of Asia.

John Mark may have retreated because there was an obvious management change, from Barnabas to Paul. Barnabas was very familiar with Cyprus, and there had been an amazing response. But here in Acts, it is very clear, if we look at the text closely, this from this moment on Paul is the one in charge of the missionary journey, not Barnabas. Paul is the one so familiar with Asia Minor, not Barnabas. Paul is clearly leading the way. It may be that John Mark did not appreciate that Paul had been given the leadership position over his Uncle Barnabas. We hear no complaint from Barnabas about his loss in status, but obviously there was a complaint from John Mark.[237]

A Familiar Pathway

From Cyprus, Paul and Barnabas and other companions head to evangelize Asia. They landed in Perga, a small port city on the coast of the Mediterranean, just north of Cyprus. This is Paul's stomping grounds. He's from Tarsus.

Acts 21:39 | Paul replied, "I am a Jew, from Tarsus in Cilicia, a citizen of no obscure city."

---

[237] Sproul, *Acts*, 229.

Perga is not that far from Tarsus. Paul had arrived in a neighborhood familiar to him since boyhood days. His birthplace was in these parts.[238] Paul would have already travelled these pathways before. Paul knew the treacherous pathways throughout the Taurus Mountains. He knew how to get through these roads safely. He would have had contacts that would assist them in their travels. As familiar as they were, they were treacherous, that along with the intense persecution, John Mark headed back home to Jerusalem. Barnabas and Paul continued on to Perga and on to Antioch beyond the Taurus Mountains, into the land of Galatia.

It is during this trip to Asia, we learn later, in Lystra and Derbe that a young man named Timothy hears the gospel and is converted to Christ. He's from a very faithful family with a Jewish mom, and grandmother, but an unbelieving Greek father.

THE PROCLAMATION OF THE GOSPEL (13:14-41)

Acts 13:14 | But they went on from Perga and came to Antioch in Pisidia. And on the Sabbath day they went into the synagogue and sat down.

The first stop in preaching the gospel in Asia is in Antioch of Pisidia, also known as Caesarea Antioch. It's a treacherous journey to get there, being 3,600 feet above sea level. This is to be the location of the first church plant in Galatia. This is the launching point for the churches of Galatia, to which Paul later writes his letter. The four Galatian churches are Antioch of Pisidia, Iconium, Lystra and Derbe.

Paul's master plan for Gentile evangelism almost always included a witness for Christ in the local synagogue. Because he was a trained rabbi, a graduate of the famous school of Gamaliel in Jerusalem, he could be sure of an initial hearing in any synagogue. If he could reap a quick harvest for Christ in the local synagogue, he would have a nucleus for organizing a church.[239] They go to the Jews in the synagogue on the Sabbath day and Paul is invited, as a guest rabbi, to teach the people there.

---

[238] J. Phillips, *Exploring Acts*, Ac 13:13a.
[239] Ibid., Ac 13:14a.

A Promising Invitation

Acts 13:15-16 | After the reading from the Law and the Prophets, the rulers of the synagogue sent a message to them, saying, "Brothers, if you have any word of encouragement for the people, say it." **16** So Paul stood up, and motioning with his hand said: "Men of Israel and you who fear God, listen.

The order of service proceeded with the usual prayers and Scripture readings, Paul and Barnabas making the responses as ordinary members of the congregation. When Paul and Barnabas had first come in, the presiding elders of the synagogue no doubt met them. It would not take them long to recognize that these men had recently been in Jerusalem, were well-traveled, well-informed, and well-taught. What would be more natural than to turn the podium over to them? In a place like Pisidian Antioch, somewhat off the beaten track and certainly remote and isolated from Jerusalem, visitors of their caliber must have been rare. There would be a natural curiosity about the men as well as a hunger for news from Jerusalem.

Paul's procedure was to wait until opportunity came and then to seize it firmly with both hands. He had not gone to the synagogue that Sabbath hoping someone would invite him home for a meal, or to expound the theories of Hillel, or to relate news from here and there. He had gone there looking for an opportunity to preach Christ, and now it had come. Decisions as to his movements had been right. The platform was now his.[240]

Don't be worried about how God will open up the door for you to preach the gospel. Paul and Barnabas had no idea what God was going to do in this strategic city, but they were led by the Spirit. They went not knowing if they would be able to share Jesus with these people. But God opened the door and gave the words.

A Promised People

The text before us now contains the first recorded sermon of the Apostle Paul. The content seems to be taken both from Stephen's sermon and the Apostle Peter's at Pentecost. He uses the same outline as Stephen and the same texts as Peter. It's astounding that the prayer of

---

[240] Phillips, *Acts*, Ac 13:14b–15.

Stephen to save his hearers was answered in the life and message of the great Apostle Paul.

Out of Egypt

God calls a people out of Egypt. Helpless people are the only kind that God calls. He resists the proud, but he gives grace to the humble.

> **Acts 13:17** | The God of this people Israel chose our fathers and made the people great during their stay in the land of Egypt, and with uplifted arm he led them out of it.

We find that Paul reminds his hearers of the helplessness of all who do not know Christ. Israel was like that. They were in slavery, and it was truly an impossible situation. "With uplifted arm" he brought them out of the land of Egypt. Remember Egypt was called "the iron furnace" (Deut 4:20). It was a place where they were told what to do by their taskmasters. Isn't that what our old life was like? We were all in our own Egypt. We had the taskmasters of the idols of our heart. We were blinded by our sin and in a completely impossible situation. We were all dead in our sin and headed to a sinner's hell. But God led us out of Egypt!

Out of the Wilderness

Paul then told them of how God calls his people out of the wilderness. He provides for us there. Shoes don't wear out there. Manna rains from heaven. We see the goodness of God in the wilderness.

> **Acts 13:18** | And for about forty years he put up with them in the wilderness.

It is interesting Paul says that God "put up with them." Glory to God he sometimes puts up with us and our sin. He loves us. He will never leave us or forsake us. He wants us to come out of the wilderness and into his Canaan land.

Into Canaan

> **Acts 13:19** | And after destroying seven nations in the land of Canaan, he gave them their land as an inheritance.

Then he continues the history of Israel about the conquests of Canaan, even seven nations under the command of General Joshua. In one day, God made the sun stand still so that Israel could keep conquering the nations. They had such a victory they couldn't do it all in one day (*cf* Josh 10-11; Deut 7:1). Dear saints, we have our own General Joshua. His name is Yeshua, and he will make the sun stand still for you as well. He will conquer all your enemies.

On to the Kingdom

Now Paul turns to an exciting time where God brings Israel to a kingdom under David.

> **Acts 13:20-22** | All this took about 450 years. And after that he gave them judges until Samuel the prophet. [21] Then they asked for a king, and God gave them Saul the son of Kish, a man of the tribe of Benjamin, for forty years. [22] And when he had removed him, he raised up David to be their king, of whom he testified and said, 'I have found in David the son of Jesse a man after my heart, who will do all my will.'

How promising the history of Israel is to bring Israel to a king, yet this king is terribly imperfect. As great as any of the kings were, each was marred by sin and selfishness. They did not completely fulfill God's promises to his people.

A Promised Savior

All the kings of Israel left God's people disappointed. They kept waiting for the true king, the Messiah. And finally, he came! The prophecies are fulfilled. "When the fullness of time had come, God sent forth his Son, born of woman, born under the law, [5] to redeem those who were under the law" (Gal 4:4-5). Paul announces that the Messiah has come to save their souls.

> **Acts 13:23** | Of this man's [*David's*] offspring God has brought to Israel a Savior, Jesus, as he promised.

Hallelujah, Paul gets to the heart of the message. The blazing center of the Bible's message is Jesus, Jesus, Jesus. He's our promised prophet, priest, and king.

Paul's message was about Jesus as the fulfillment of all the Old Testament promises. Jesus is *the* Messiah, the *only* Messiah, and the *Jewish* Messiah. Jesus came from the seed "as he promised" (13:23). Paul was establishing an important principle in the interpretation of the Old Testament Scriptures: they pointed to and culminated in Jesus

Christ.[241] When the resurrected Christ taught the Scriptures, he did the same thing.

> Luke 24:27 | Beginning with Moses and all the Prophets, he interpreted to them in all the Scriptures the things concerning himself.

A Promised Salvation

Now Paul recounts how Christ came into history, announced by John the Baptist, who may have been more famous than Jesus at this time. They had surely heard of John, but had they considered John's message about the coming Messiah?

> **Acts 13:24-26** | Before his coming, John had proclaimed a baptism of repentance to all the people of Israel. **25** And as John was finishing his course, he said, 'What do you suppose that I am? I am not he. No, but behold, after me one is coming, the sandals of whose feet I am not worthy to untie.' **26** "Brothers, sons of the family of Abraham, and those among you who fear God, to us has been sent the message of this salvation.

The message of salvation through Jesus came first through John the Baptist. Remember he said, "Behold the Lamb of God who takes away the sin of the world" (Jn 1:29)? Now Paul was telling those in the synagogue at Caesarea Antioch in the rugged Taurus mountains that Jesus had to suffer and die for our sins. He's the Messiah for all nations. He speaks not only to the Jews—"sons of the family of Abraham," but also to those "who fear God," that is Gentiles that had become proselytes of Judaism. Paul is announcing that the salvation through Messiah promised by the prophets had finally come.

A Promised Fulfillment

Not only had the Messiah come, but specific prophecies have been fulfilled. Paul goes through several prophecies here.

> **Acts 13:27-31** | For those who live in Jerusalem and their rulers, because they did not recognize him nor understand the utterances of the prophets, which are read every Sabbath, fulfilled them by condemning him. **28** And though they found in him no guilt worthy of death, they asked Pilate to have him executed. **29** And when they had carried out all that was written of him, they took

---

[241] Thomas, *Acts*, 369.

him down from the tree and laid him in a tomb. ³⁰ But God raised him from the dead, ³¹ and for many days he appeared to those who had come up with him from Galilee to Jerusalem, who are now his witnesses to the people.

All that "was written of him" was fulfilled through the rulers of Israel. He was put to death, executed by Pontius Pilate. Paul's about to tell them that his death was a substitutionary death, that through his death the could be justified, their sins forgiven. But right now, Paul is going through the historic fulfillment of the prophecies. Just as the prophets wrote of Jesus, he not only died, but he was buried, and then he rose again on the third day. The prophet Hosea had promised that Messiah would rise on the third day (Hos 6:2). Then Paul, as he often does, calls eyewitnesses to account. He tells them there is evidence that can be submitted for the resurrection: you can talk to those who witnessed it. We know there were over 500 who were scattered from Galilee to Jerusalem, and likely throughout Asia and Europe by this time. They went forth from Pentecost to every nation under heaven. Perhaps some in this synagogue in Antioch of Pisidia had already heard one of the witnesses testify of Jesus.

A Promised Resurrection

Now Paul is going to start quoting Scripture and calling God as his witness, that the Messiah would die and rise again, since this might have been a very strange teaching at first. To establish that Messiah would need to rise from the dead, Paul quotes three passages: Psalm 2, Isaiah 55:3, and Psalm 16.

A Prophecy from Psalm 2

Paul begins in Psalm 2, which is the main coronation Psalm for the kings of Israel.

> **Acts 13:32-33** | And we bring you the good news that what God promised to the fathers, ³³ this he has fulfilled to us their children by raising Jesus, as also it is written in the second Psalm, "'You are my Son, today I have begotten you.'

When Paul made this appeal to Psalm 2, he was not talking about a moment when Jesus was begotten, since Jesus is eternal. On an earthly level, the kings of Israel were said to have been "begotten" on the day of their coronation.[242] Jesus' coronation as King of kings, when he was "highly exalted" was on the day of his resurrection (cf Phil 2:9). He is begotten, coronated, so that "every knee shall bow, and every tongue confess that he is Lord" and king (Phil 2:10; cf Isa 45:23). Jesus is not only the son of David, his offspring, God's "Savior" of Israel, he is God's Son who is coronated at his resurrection.[243]

A Prophecy from Isaiah 55

Now Paul moves to Isaiah the prophet. He quotes Isaiah 55:3, which promises that God will not forget his covenant to David to bring an eternal king from his loins. The underlying text is the promise to David that he would always have a descendant on the throne (cf 2 Sam 7:12–13).[244]

> **Acts 13:34** | And as for the fact that he raised him from the dead, no more to return to corruption, he has spoken in this way, "'I will give you the holy and sure blessings of David.'

The point is that God raised Jesus from the dead, because he promised in Isaiah 55 the sure blessings of an eternal covenant with David, and there has to be an eternal inhabitant on the throne.

Indeed, God fulfills this in the human birth of the eternal Son of God, but according to prophecy, Messiah is put to death. How does this coincide with prophecy? There must be a resurrection. Paul gives a final Scripture, proving the resurrection from Psalm 16.

A Prophecy from Psalm 16

> **Acts 13:35-37** | Therefore he says also in another psalm, "'You will not let your Holy One see corruption.' **36** For David, after he had served the purpose of God in his own generation, fell asleep and was laid with his fathers and saw corruption, **37** but he whom God raised up did not see corruption.

King David could never fulfill God's eternal covenant, Paul says, because he died, and his body is still in the tomb. Of course, Messiah would also die, but according to Psalm 16:10, his body would not see

---

[242] Sproul, *Acts*, 239.
[243] Hamilton, *John–Acts*, 463.
[244] Ibid.

corruption, and he would rise again from the dead. The one who would die, but not see corruption is God's Holy One, the eternal Son of God.

Christ's body must escape not merely from corruption and decay but from death itself. And so it did. He not only saw no corruption. Hallelujah, he conquered death itself![245]

A Promised Justification

Now Paul begins to apply the gospel. This is important. Why did Messiah have to come and die and be buried and rise again. Paul gives us the answer. Jesus' death is substitutionary. It's for the forgiveness of sins. From Jesus' work on the cross comes our justification before God.

> **Acts 13:38-39** | Let it be known to you therefore, brothers, that through this man forgiveness of sins is proclaimed to you, **39** and by him everyone who believes is freed from everything from which you could not be freed by the law of Moses.

Forgiveness can be granted to anyone who believes. When belief is exercised on Christ, the person is "freed" or literally, "justified." Paul employed the important term "to justify" (*dikaioo*, twice) in verse 39, where the ESV translates it "freed"[246] Paul was teaching, in his first recorded sermon, the doctrine of justification by faith alone. He repeats this theme over and over again.

> *Galatians 2:16* | By the works of the law no flesh shall be justified.

> *Romans 5:1* | Since we have been justified by faith, we have peace with God through our Lord Jesus Christ.

> *Philippians 3:9* | And be found in him, not having a righteousness of my own that comes from the law, but that which comes through faith in Christ, the righteousness from God that depends on faith.

Indeed, at the cross, there is a glorious exchange, my rags of sin for Jesus' robe of righteousness. Because of this, the moment we believe, we are positionally perfect and righteous in the sight of God. We are as holy and perfect as Jesus is, because God sees us through the righteousness of Christ. What amazing news.

---

[245] J. Phillips, *Exploring Acts*, Ac 13:37.
[246] Thomas, *Acts*, 371.

A Powerful Warning

Paul ends on a warning. He says to beware of the gospel. If you accept it, your heart is softened, but if you reject it your heart will get hard. God's doing a great work, so don't reject him. Paul quotes the warning from Habakkuk 1:5.

> **Acts 13:40-41** | Beware, therefore, lest what is said in the Prophets should come about: **41** "'Look, you scoffers, be astounded and perish; for I am doing a work in your days, a work that you will not believe, even if one tells it to you.'"

The choice with which Paul left his audience is the choice every person faces. Accepting the salvation offered in Jesus Christ brings forgiveness of sin and eternal bliss. Rejecting it brings judgment and eternal damnation. God's grace and love do not cancel His justice and holy hatred of sin.[247]

From the patriarchs all the way to the prophets, the Old Testament Scriptures have spoken about God's revealed intention to rescue and redeem humanity. The unfolding story of the Old Testament reached its climax in the birth, life, death, and resurrection of Jesus of Nazareth. Paul gave them a way of understanding their own Scriptures. In effect, he was saying to them that unless they acknowledged Jesus as the Messiah, they had utterly failed to understand the Scriptures.[248]

THE POWER OF THE GOSPEL (13:42-52)

What were the results of Paul's preaching? It was a powerful result. God's word always does its work.

> *Isaiah 55:11* | My word ... shall not return to me void, but it shall accomplish what I please.

> *Romans 1:16* | I am not ashamed of the gospel, for it is the power of God for salvation to everyone who believes, to the Jew first and also to the Greek.

The Gospel Draws People

Look how God's word does the work! The word had such an effect that people were begging to hear more.

---

[247] MacArthur, *Acts*, vol. 2, 27.
[248] Thomas, *Acts*, 370.

Acts 13:42-43 | As they went out, the people begged that these things might be told them the next Sabbath. ⁴³ And after the meeting of the synagogue broke up, many Jews and devout converts to Judaism followed Paul and Barnabas, who, as they spoke with them, urged them to continue in the grace of God.

We see what happened in Antioch of Pisidia. The word was preached, and the people begged to hear more. Theologically, we learn that God is drawing people to salvation. God has to do the drawing. He has to open the sinner's eyes and give him a new heart.

John 6:37, 44 | All that the Father gives me will come to me, and whoever comes to me I will never cast out. ⁴⁴ No one can come to me unless the Father who sent me draws him.

We see what happened in Antioch of Pisidia. The word was preached, and the people begged to hear more. Theologically, we learn that God is drawing people to salvation. God has to do the drawing. He has to open the sinner's eyes and give him a new heart.

We are drawn in love and drawn in grace, but it is an irresistible drawing. The word can actually be translated "dragged" (21:30, where people are dragged before magistrates). The idea is that God is sovereignly working in the heart of man to bring him to salvation. Without that drawing no one would come to Christ. The gospel is drawing people.

What can you do? We must understand the means of grace. God uses your prayers, your fasting, your evangelism in powerful ways to open up the eyes of the blind. We cannot neglect that people will never hear without a preacher. You have to pray and fast and tell others if they are going to be added to the kingdom.

The Gospel Offends People

A week later the synagogue is filled to capacity. Thousands are gathered, both Jews and Gentiles to hear Paul teach the Bible.

Acts 13:44 | The next Sabbath almost the whole city gathered to hear the word of the Lord.

The Apostle Paul had a deep desire that his own kinsmen should be saved. He said in Romans 9 that he was willing to be damned if that would bring them to Christ. Yet the Jews here rejected the gospel.

> **Acts 13:45** | But when the Jews saw the crowds, they were filled with jealousy and began to contradict what was spoken by Paul, reviling him.

A door was slammed in Paul's face. He had hoped to be able to evangelize his own people. This was always his burning desire (Rom 9:1–3; 10:1). We don't know what he said that second Sabbath in Antioch of Pisidian, but the Jews were jealous and didn't want to hear it.

The Spirit of God must have brought such conviction on people that instead of rejoicing, they were angry that their own teaching didn't bring such joy and conviction. It was so powerful that the place was standing room only. People must have kept inviting more people. This kind of jealousy moved the leaders of Israel to crucify the Lord. Jesus told us that if they hated him, they will hate his followers as well. So Paul came unto his own, the Jews, and his own received him not, just as they did not receive the Lord. What does the Lord's servant do when confronted with the obvious fact of a closed door? He looks for one that is open.[249]

> **Acts 13:46-47** | And Paul and Barnabas spoke out boldly, saying, "It was necessary that the word of God be spoken first to you. Since you thrust it aside and judge yourselves unworthy of eternal life, behold, we are turning to the Gentiles. **⁴⁷** For so the Lord has commanded us, saying, "'I have made you a light for the Gentiles, that you may bring salvation to the ends of the earth.'"

Paul quotes Isaiah 49, a prophecy of Christ being a light to the Gentiles. Paul and Barnabas now take a decided turn away from the Jews and the synagogues and begin intentionally seeking the Gentiles for salvation.

The Gospel Saves People

Even in the midst of the Jews being offended, the Gentiles were being brought into the kingdom. Whenever there is opposition, that means you are preaching the gospel rightly. The gospel normally produces rejoicing or rioting. If it is hear rightly, people will have a fierce response to it, either positive or negative. So after the negative response, we see a resounding positive response, where there is great joy and celebration for the Gentiles gladly receive the truth of Christ.

---

[249] J. Phillips, *Exploring Acts,* Ac 13:45.

Acts 13:48 | And when the Gentiles heard this, they began rejoicing and glorifying the word of the Lord, and as many as were appointed to eternal life believed.

Those appointed to eternal life will believe. You would think it would be the other way around, that those who believe will be appointed, but it is the opposite. This points to the glorious doctrine of election and predestination: that God has already written our names in the book of life and appointed us. When the word comes to us, our eyes are opened, and the word transforms our heart from stone to flesh. We believe and are granted the eternal life we were appointed for. So we see two vital truths in understanding the gospel: the sovereignty of God in opening the eyes of dead sinners, and the responsibility of man to choose Christ. Both are truth. Both must be taught. One does not cancel out the other.

Then we hear this wonderful verse of how the word was doing the work not only in the hearts of the Gentiles in southern Galatia in Antioch of Pisidian, but "throughout the whole region."

Acts 13:49 | And the word of the Lord was spreading throughout the whole region.

I love this quote from Martin Luther that explains how thousands of churches were planted throughout Europe during his day. People were starting to call Christians "Lutherans" in Germany, and Luther was horrified. He wanted to give proper honor to the word of God that does the work.

> What is Luther? The teaching is not mine. Nor was I crucified for anyone ... How did I, poor stinking bag of maggots that I am, come to the point where people call the children of Christ by my evil name? [i.e., "*Lutherans*"] ... I simply taught, preached, wrote God's word; otherwise, I did nothing. And while I slept or drank Wittenberg beer with my friends Philip and Amsdorf, the word so greatly weakened the papacy that no prince or emperor ever inflicted such losses upon it. I did nothing; the word did everything.[250]

---

[250] Martin Luther in Timothy George, *Theology of the Reformers* (Nashville, TN: B&H Publishing Group, 2013), 54.

The Gospel Brings Persecution

Now we find out that after seeing such an fantastic reaction from the Gentiles, they Jews have the opposite reaction.

Acts 13:50 | But the Jews incited the devout women of high standing and the leading men of the city, stirred up persecution against Paul and Barnabas, and drove them out of their district.

Paul and Barnabas were forced to leave the city when a riot was stirred up against them, but the Holy Spirit could not be driven out. He remained with the converts as the source of their new life, power and joy.[251] Being driven out from one place means an open door for another.

Acts 13:51 | But they shook off the dust from their feet against them.

Like Jesus taught the 70 when they went out, Paul and his missionary team "shook off the dust from their feet against them." The Jews of Paul's day were scrupulous not to bring Gentile dust back into Israel. By their act, Paul and Barnabas were saying in effect that they considered the Jews at Antioch no better than pagans. There could be no stronger condemnation. Those Jews were left in their obstinate unbelief.[252]

The Gospel Brings Joy

There was no room for doom and gloom or disappointment. Paul, Barnabas, and their friends went to the next open door.

Acts 13:52 | And went to Iconium. And the disciples were filled with joy and with the Holy Spirit.

Joy? I thought they had just suffered rejection at this place where they labored. The Christian's joy is not based on our circumstances. They were filled with joy for several reasons: first, God did a great work in Antioch of Pisidia among the Gentiles—the first church in Asia is planted. Moreover, they leave behind them freshly converted disciples who, like all new Christians, are *filled with joy and with the Holy Spirit* (13:52; *cf* 2:44–47; 8:8, 39b).[253] Second, they also believed God would do a great work in the next cities, beginning with Iconium. Third, God is in charge of granting eternal life. He appoints those who believe. The

---

[251] Bruce, *Acts: Bible Study Commentary*, Ac 13:42–52.
[252] MacArthur, *Acts*, vol. 2, 40.
[253] Faw, *Acts*, 155.

burden is not for us to convert, but merely to preach God's word and his gospel faithfully.

Are you filled with joy right now? You should be! You have Christ. Is Jesus the center of your life? Or are you down in the dumps because your eyes are on this broken world? Get your eyes off yourself. Turn your eyes upon Jesus.

Conclusion

God can do the impossible. He can change the heart of the most stubborn sinner and make him humble. The average cost of a physical heart transplant including the immunosuppressant drugs after the surgery is close to a million dollars. Yet, the best heart transplant a man can receive is a spiritual heart transplant. It costs him nothing and the new heart will never fail. We can't give that spiritual heart transplant, but God can and will.

We are called to plant the seeds of the gospel wherever we go. We cannot make it grow. God has to do that. We plant, and we water, but God gives the increase.

24 | ACTS 14:1-28
PROGRESS AND PERSECUTION

Jews came from Antioch and Iconium, and having persuaded the crowds, they stoned Paul and dragged him out of the city, supposing that he was dead. But when the disciples gathered about him, he rose up and entered the city, and on the next day he went on with Barnabas to Derbe. When they had preached the gospel to that city and had made many disciples, they returned to Lystra and to Iconium and to Antioch, strengthening the souls of the disciples, encouraging them to continue in the faith, and saying that through many tribulations we must enter the kingdom of God.

ACTS 14:19-22

Have you ever added salt to your coffee? I teased my daughter Ava the other day. She grabbed the glass sugar container and put a sprinkle on her bran flakes. I told her: what if I put salt in there? She said, "You didn't!" I said playfully, "You'll just have to try it and see." She tried it and found out I was just playing. Of course, we know that just because salt looks like sugar doesn't mean it is. Once a friend of my sisters who had just learned to drive actually put diesel in her car.

Cars that run on gasoline don't go very far on diesel. There are certain things in life that are irreplicable. I've been trying to eat better with a low carb diet. My dear wife tries to buy me different kinds of low carb pizza. I've tried pizza crust made of cauliflower. I've tried it made of an egg base. Finally, my dear daughter Katie declared the obvious. She said, "Dad, there is no substitute for pizza!" So true! Pizza is pizza! There are some things you cannot substitute. Now food is superficial, but our souls are not. How true it is that the gospel cannot be substituted! Whenever the gospel goes forth, if it is preached rightly, you can tell by its effect whether or not it was preached clearly and fully. The gospel is the gospel. It cannot be substituted. How do you know if the gospel is being preached rightly? One way is that it invites persecution.

> **Key Thought**: Wherever there is progress in the gospel, you should expect persecution.

As you make progress in your growth in Christ, expect hardship, tests, and persecution. If you start having a passion for evangelism, you need to expect problems that are unique since Satan hates you sharing the gospel. As you begin a new ministry endeavor for Christ, you will also be tested severely. Satan will try to get you to stop. Get you somewhere else where "the grass is greener." Don't take the bait. Persevere.

Paul and his team leave Antioch of Pisidia and take a seventy-eight-mile journey southeast to the pristine city of Iconium. Its name is proper, since it truly is an iconic city located on a vast plain known for its beauty and agricultural fertility (13:51). The population was prospering as a proud, sophisticated, and glorious Greek city. Highways from Syria to Ephesus pass through the city, and it buzzed with traders and merchants from distant lands. It was a bit of a melting pot with people from everywhere living there, and there was a large, thriving Jewish population with a fair-sized synagogue. It is here the apostles begin a new work.[254] Acts 14 depicts Paul and Barnabas completing their first missionary journey, traveling through Iconium, Lystra, and Derbe, and returning to home base in Antioch in Syria.[255] The gospel is having great success. As we see the gospel spread to Jews and Gentiles here in Iconium, there are four indications of the gospel's success in the hearts of people.

---

[254] Faw, *Acts*, 155.
[255] Hughes, *Acts: The Church Afire*, 182.

THE GOSPEL INVITES PASSION (14:1-6)

The first mark we see of gospel advancement is passion, both positive and negative. There is both joy and hatred when the gospel is preached. There is both rejoicing and rioting. When the gospel is preached properly, people aren't able to hide on some neutral ground. One must choose sides. There is this great distinction of responses when the gospel is preached rightly.

Often when the gospel is preached, there is at first rejoicing. It's what excites us about evangelism. That's exactly what happens in Iconium. People were coming to know Christ, both Jews and Gentiles.

Passionate Rejoicing

Acts 14:1 | Now at Iconium they entered together into the Jewish synagogue and spoke in such a way that a great number of both Jews and Greeks believed.

A Great Message. They "spoke in such a way that a great number of both Jews and Greeks believed." What way was that? As Paul and Barnabas preached, the Holy Spirit energized their words and melted the hearts of the hearers. The apostles did not persuade with the eloquent "words which man's wisdom teaches" but in words "which the Holy Spirit teaches" (1 Cor 2:13).

The Spirit cuts right to the heart. What made the message great was nothing in the messengers. Some plant and some water, but "God gives the increase" (1 Cor 3:6). The increase comes by the power of the Holy Spirit applying the message of salvation. Like he brooded over creation and turned chaos into order, so he creates a new heart and transforms the heart of stone into a living heart by the word preached.

A Great Response. "A great number believed." When God's word is proclaimed with courage and love and boldness, God will open people's eyes so that there is great rejoicing. God can put a passion for the gospel in the hearts of sinners.

A Great Number. It wasn't just a few who believed, but there was such rejoicing that "a great number" of Jews and Gentiles believed. Perhaps you remember Paul and Barnabas had declared, "We are turning to the Gentiles" (13:46), but that did not mean they were abandoning the Jews. After all, Paul will later write that he would perish eternally if that would bring the Jews in.

> *Romans 9:3* | I could wish that I myself were accursed and cut off from Christ for the sake of my brothers, my kinsmen according to the flesh.

Paul is the apostle to the Gentiles, but not to the exclusion of the Jews.[256]

A Great Unity. "Both Jews and Greeks believed." Paul and Barnabas know that God is "not wishing that any should perish, but that all should come to repentance" (2 Pet 3:9). Their pattern in most new cities will continue in the same manner: to the Jew first, and then to the Gentile (Rom 1:16). What is glorious here is that when the gospel is preached it brings people together who were before perhaps opposed to each other. When the gospel unites people, we become part of God's forever family.

Passionate Rejection

While some rejoice in Iconium, so many others resisted the gospel.

> **Acts 14:2** | But the unbelieving Jews stirred up the Gentiles and poisoned their minds against the brothers.

While we preach the truth, Satan will be busy working in the hearts and minds of unbelievers, and the wicked one never plays fair. He is the father of lies, and he will bring opposition against you when you are faithful to preach the good news of Jesus. Expect satanic attack.

Powerful Revelation

We should be passionate about preaching the gospel. If we are, God will open the eyes of the blind. He will even bring miracles to vindicate your message amidst persecution.

God is passionate about your preaching of the gospel, and he will give glorious revelation in the face of opposition. He will open the eyes of the blind and if necessary, he can give signs and wonders. Missionary Paul and Barnabas and their team stayed on and witnessed boldly for Christ, and God gave signs and wonders.[257]

> **Acts 14:3** | So they remained for a long time, speaking boldly for the Lord, who bore witness to the word of his grace, granting signs and wonders to be done by their hands.

---

[256] Hamilton, *John–Acts*, 468.
[257] Wiersbe, *The Bible Exposition Commentary*, vol. 1, 459.

Now whenever you are attacked for Jesus' sake, you must remain courageous and bold. God will vindicate you. People will recognize that you are from the Lord. They may not like it, but if you stand in your integrity, God will defend you. Great signs and wonders accompanied the preaching of the apostles.

Most importantly, notice the content of the message Paul preached—it was "the word of his grace." Salvation, both Old and New Testament, had always been by grace through faith. Eternal life is always given not by human merit, but by the merit of another. This was the content of Paul's message. There was no New Testament at the time, so Paul was preaching the gospel of God's grace from the Old Testament.

Notice they spoke boldly! That is the mark of the filling of the Holy Spirit. Bold proclamation of the truth of the gospel is urgently needed in our time. We need preaching of the caliber of the Puritan Richard Baxter. We should all adopt his mindset of boldness and urgency.

> I preached as never sure to preach again, And as a dying man to dying men![258]

Passionate Resolve

After preaching and teaching the people for a long time, the effects of the gospel began dividing the city, and great persecution came, so that the apostles' lives were in danger.

> **Acts 14:4-7** | But the people of the city were divided; some sided with the Jews and some with the apostles. ⁵ When an attempt was made by both Gentiles and Jews, with their rulers, to mistreat them and to stone them, ⁶ they learned of it and fled to Lystra and Derbe, cities of Lycaonia, and to the surrounding country, ⁷ and there they continued to preach the gospel.

Notice that the apostles didn't give up. Their lives were threatened, but they kept on preaching. It looks like they attempted to stone Paul and Barnabas (14:5). That's a big deal. They wanted to carry out the death penalty on them, but they were able to escape.

They could no longer preach in Iconium, so they fled to the twin cities of Lystra and Derbe. They could have gone home, but instead they

---

[258] Richard Baxter, *Poetical Fragments* (London, 1821), 39–40, quoted in John Stott, *I Believe in Preaching* (London: Hodder & Stoughton, 1982), 277.

carried on. They came, first, to Lystra (eighteen miles east) and then Derbe (a further fifty-five miles away), and to the surrounding area.[259] What passion they had for the word.

THE GOSPEL CAN BRING PANDEMONIUM (14:8-18)

Whenever the gospel has great success, you can expect the wicked one to try and bring chaos and pandemonium, which is exactly what happened. Yet they started out with a very promising meeting with a healing.

Don't think that just because everything starts well, that you can avoid persecution and pandemonium. This meeting starts so good. It's almost like you can forget about all the suffering and persecution when things go well.

The Miracle

Paul, Barnabas, and their missionary team were at Lystra for quite a while (*cf* 14:20, there were already many "disciples" by this time), and one day this incredible miracle was performed.

> **Acts 14:8-10** | Now at Lystra there was a man sitting who could not use his feet. He was crippled from birth and had never walked. ⁹ He listened to Paul speaking. And Paul, looking intently at him and seeing that he had faith to be made well, ¹⁰ said in a loud voice, "Stand upright on your feet." And he sprang up and began walking.

This sounds a lot like many miracles in the book of Acts. Normally from these miracles there is great revival and an outbreak of conversions. Not this time. This time there is great mayhem because of the significance of the place Paul is. They are in Lystra, the place of the great visitation of Zeus and Hermes, the Greek gods.

The Mayhem

Paul and Barnabas may well have known the story of the author Ovid, titled *Metamorphoses*, written half a century or so earlier about the Greek gods' visitation to the area of Lystra. The story told of two Greek gods, Zeus and Hermes.[260] During the gods' visit, they were turned away from a thousand homes until they reached an elderly

---

[259] Thomas, *Acts*, 383.
[260] Thomas, ibid.

couple's home, where they were given lodging. Zeus and Hermes destroyed those who had turned them away and gave special honor to the elderly couple, making them priests in the pagan temples. The people who saw what Paul and Barnabas had done must have been very familiar with this story, and they mistook the apostles for two famous Greek gods.

> **Acts 14:11-13** | And when the crowds saw what Paul had done, they lifted up their voices, saying in Lycaonian, "The gods have come down to us in the likeness of men!" ¹² Barnabas they called Zeus, and Paul, Hermes, because he was the chief speaker. ¹³ And the priest of Zeus, whose temple was at the entrance to the city, brought oxen and garlands to the gates and wanted to offer sacrifice with the crowds.

They thought Paul was Hermes because Hermes was the messenger of Zeus. The apostles are merely preaching the gospel, and now all mayhem and confusion break loose. You never know what's going to happen when you preach the gospel, but I'm sure the apostles were not expecting to be worshipped as gods!

The Message

They quickly responded with a strong message: we are not gods. Don't worship us, instead worship the one true and living God! Listen to what happened.

> **Acts 14:14-18** | But when the apostles Barnabas and Paul heard of it, they tore their garments and rushed out into the crowd, crying out, ¹⁵ "Men, why are you doing these things? We also are men, of like nature with you, and we bring you good news, that you should turn from these vain things to a living God, who made the heaven and the earth and the sea and all that is in them. ¹⁶ In past generations he allowed all the nations to walk in their own ways. ¹⁷ Yet he did not leave himself without witness, for he did good by giving you rains from heaven and fruitful seasons, satisfying your hearts with food and gladness." ¹⁸ Even with these words they scarcely restrained the people from offering sacrifice to them.

One of the first things you have to do with those of a pagan mindset is to help them gain a true understanding of the one true God. There are not many gods, but only one. He created us. He gives us rain and harvest. So far so good, but instead of repenting and believing the gospel, they go from worshipping Paul to stoning him!

This is a reminder that we are not responsible for the outcome and response of the gospel. We are just the messenger (the mailman), but in Paul's case, they decided to stone the messenger.

THE GOSPEL BRINGS PERSECUTION (14:19-23)

Now we see that when the gospel is preached there will inevitably be persecution. It is unavoidable. Paul says to Timothy who is from the Lystra area, "Indeed, all who desire to live a godly life in Christ Jesus will be persecuted" (2 Tim 3:2).

A Rejection & Resurrection

Little did Paul know that Jews from Antioch and Iconium followed him eventually to Lystra, and there they carried out the death penalty. After they killed him there at Lystra, they dragged him out of the city where the believers there gathered around him.

> **Acts 14:19-20** | But Jews came from Antioch and Iconium, and having persuaded the crowds, they stoned Paul and dragged him out of the city [*of Lystra*], supposing that he was dead. **20** But when the disciples gathered about him, he rose up and entered the city, and on the next day he went on with Barnabas to Derbe.

Rocks hit Paul all over his body, tearing his flesh until he was knocked unconscious to the ground. Supposing that he was dead, the people opposed to him grabbed him by the feet and dragged him outside the city.[261] This is the occasion which he recalls several years later in 2 Corinthians 11:25: "once I was stoned." The scars received at Lystra were among the "marks of Jesus" which he bore to his dying day (Gal 6:17).[262]

Can you believe it? After being stoned, Paul is resurrected and goes right back into the city, probably to recover at a disciple's home. But it was just for one day! Paul wastes no time, even though this might have been the fiercest persecution of all his journeys. Paul writes later about these fierce persecutions.

---

[261] Sproul, *Acts*, 258.
[262] Bruce, *Acts: Bible Study Commentary*, Ac 14:19–28.

2 Timothy 3:10-11 | You, however, have followed my teaching, my conduct, my aim in life, my faith, my patience, my love, my steadfastness, ¹¹ my persecutions and sufferings that happened to me at Antioch, at Iconium, and at Lystra—which persecutions I endured; yet from them all the Lord rescued me.

The Lord rescued Paul, even through what was probably a resurrection. Notice the people at Lystra go from worshipping Paul and Barnabas to murdering them. They go from adoration to assassination so quickly. We cannot depend on the whims of our audience to understand the success of ministry. We must depend on God to give the increase no matter what we see with our eyes.

It's very likely that the rescue that Paul speaks of was indeed a resurrection. Paul at another time speaks of how he actually visited God in the third heaven. In 2 Corinthians 12, he says he wasn't even allowed to talk about the things he saw in the third heaven. He "heard things that cannot be told, which man may not utter" (2 Cor 12:3). It's very likely that Paul is referring to his own death at Lystra, and that he was raised from the dead.

After recovering for a day at Lystra, we read "the next day he went on with Barnabas to Derbe" (14:20b). From there it was a fairly short walk back to Tarsus and Paul likely would have returned home were it not for the positive response to the gospel he found in Derbe and the surrounding region (14:19–21). Encouraged, he decided instead to retrace his steps back through Lystra, Iconium and Pisidian Antioch.[263] Not even death by stoning could stop the Apostle Paul from going to the next city and preaching the gospel. He truly believed that he was immortal until God was finished with him.

A Return

We need to see the pattern in Acts is not just evangelism but also discipleship. Paul and Barnabas had seen many be converted to Christ, but they didn't leave these as babes without guidance. They returned and encouraged those who trusted in Christ under their ministry.

> **Acts 14:21-22** | When they had preached the gospel to that city and had made many disciples, they returned to Lystra and to Iconium and to Antioch, ²² strengthening the souls of the disciples,

---

[263] Paul H. Wright, *Rose Then and Now Bible Map Atlas with Biblical Background and Culture* (Torrance, CA: Rose Publishing, 2012), 240–241.

> encouraging them to continue in the faith, and saying that through many tribulations we must enter the kingdom of God.

A major part of the apostles' ongoing discipleship was to teach about suffering and perseverance in trials and tribulations. How different from so much preaching today, which promises to those who trust Christ material prosperity, good health, and a sunny path through life, and which declares that lack of those things is evidence of lack of faith. Apostolic preaching took it for granted that tribulation and affliction would be the lot in life of those who love the Lord.[264]

In the midst of one of Paul's greatest trials (being put to death by stoning) a great number of converts were made at Lystra whom they strengthened (14:22); among them, apparently, was one who would render Paul quite special service in days to come—Timothy (*cf* Acts 16:1–3).[265]

A Resurgence

They had been persecuted, driven out, even Paul was killed. But what do the apostles do? They establish the churches. They resurged where they were rejected. They *never* gave up!

> **Acts 14:23** | And when they had appointed elders for them in every church, with prayer and fasting they committed them to the Lord in whom they had believed.

Here for the first time in the Book of Acts we find the appointing of elders (14:23), which we learn later was to become Paul's natural pattern of church organization. I do not know how "elderly" these elders were, but I know they had not been Christians very long, since the gospel itself had not been known to them very long. Was that any way to establish a church?[266] Certainly these were men who were Scripturally qualified, men of good reputation, men who were blameless, and men who were mature in the Scriptures. Probably they had studied the Scriptures for years but had just recently come to understand who Christ was. Here we have the first council of elders established outside Jerusalem and Antioch.

---

[264] J. Phillips, *Exploring Acts,* Ac 14:22.
[265] Bruce, *Acts: Bible Study Commentary,* Ac 14:19–28.
[266] Boice, *Acts: An Expositional Commentary,* 257.

A plurality of elders is absolutely vital for the health of the local church. Paul and Barnabas were able to appoint the mature men who had believed in Christ to be elders. They did this in each of the cities they had preached in. Everywhere Paul would go, he would follow the pattern at Jerusalem and Antioch of a plurality of elders. Elders were leaders, elsewhere called "shepherds" (i.e., "pastors," Eph 4:11) and "overseers" (*episkopoi*, or "bishops," Acts 20:17, 28; Titus 1:5, 7; 1 Pet 5:1–2). This pattern of leadership grew directly out of the Old Testament, where God is the shepherd of Israel (Psa 80:1).[267] The synagogue in the time of Jesus would elect elders from the community who had authority to bring people in as members of the synagogue community or dismiss them as members (*cf* Mt 18). The consistent pattern in the New Testament is that every church had a plurality of elders (Acts 14:23; 15:2; 20:17, 28; Phil 1:1; 1 Thess 5:12; 1 Tim 31:7; Titus 1:5-9; Heb 13:7, 17).

Why a plurality of elders? What does a plurality of elders mean for the church? A plurality provides:

- *Accountability.* Mutual accountability is necessary to avoid falling into sin or making unwise decisions. Because there is always more than one elder, authority never resides with just one person.
- *Encouragement.* The teaching pastor(s) is one among several elders. The teaching pastor does not have ultimate authority over the other elders nor is he seen as an employee of the elders.
- *Authority.* Authority belongs collectively to the entire group of elders. The teaching elder is not to take all the heat if someone doesn't like a change. At the same time, he doesn't get all the credit either!
- *Submission.* The teaching pastor himself is subject to the authority of the elder board as a whole. This goes for all the associate pastors as well.
- *Unity.* No major decisions are made without a unanimous vote of the eldership.

The churches established on Paul's first missionary journey were healthy and multiplied under the leadership of these elders. Paul later

---

[267] Thomas, *Acts*, 396.

writes the epistle to the Galatians to these churches (Antioch of Pisidia, Iconium, Lystra, and Derbe). Pastors are just people, no different than you. They need encouragement. Pray for your pastors and elders. Encourage them. Call and text them and let them know you love them.

THE GOSPEL PROMISES PROGRESS (14:24-28)

Now Paul concludes his first missionary journey. Jesus said, "I will build my church, and the gates of hell shall not prevail against it" (Mt 16:18). That's the progress Jesus promised.

God's Grace in Progress

> **Acts 14:24-26** | Then they passed through Pisidia and came to Pamphylia. ²⁵ And when they had spoken the word in Perga, they went down to Attalia, ²⁶ and from there they sailed to Antioch, where they had been commended to the grace of God for the work that they had fulfilled.

Paul and Barnabas had been commended to the grace of God for the work God did through them. At the end of the day, the forward movement of the gospel is because of the grace and power of God. None of us can take credit. We are just the mailmen. God is the one who transforms hearts by his grace.

God's Glory in Progress

When Paul and Barnabas got back to Antioch, they had a praise service. "To God be the glory, great things he has done!"

> **Acts 14:27** | And when they arrived and gathered the church together, they declared all that God had done with them, and how he had opened a door of faith to the Gentiles.

God gets all the glory for open doors. Man is dead in sin and unable to respond to the gospel in his own power. It is the gospel itself that opens the door to our heart so that we can place our faith in Christ.

> *James 1:18a* | Of his own will he brought us forth by the word of truth.

We didn't find God. God wasn't lost. We were lost, and God found us and saved us. He called us with the word of truth and transformed our hearts by the preaching of the gospel. Truly, we confess with the Psalmist:

Psalm 127:1 | Unless the Lord builds the house, those who build it labor in vain.

God's Goal for Progress

How do we measure the progress of missions? We have to remember the goal. It is the great commission. There is no time to waste. There is no sabbatical of rest.

Acts 14:28 | And they remained no little time with the disciples.

Until every tribe, language, people, and nation are reached, then we have not reached the goal. What we see next is just as soon as the first missionary journey is concluded, they are off to another mission. The apostles are committed to the great commission. It's not the great suggestion. We are commissioned by the Lord.

Mark 16:15, NKJV | Go into all the world and preach the gospel to every creature.

We find out that Paul and Barnabas need to get to Jerusalem to discuss how to do church membership for the Gentiles. What are the requirements for bringing the Gentiles into the church? They didn't have much time before the next challenge is before them.

That's a healthy New Testament church. The church at Antioch is constantly facing difficulties and challenges because that's the territory of Christian growth. If you want to grow God's forever family, you have to change a lot of diapers and feed a lot of little ones. It's our highest privilege to do so. We can't be stopped by the problems that come with evangelism. Persecution will indeed come, but we must persevere in God's unstoppable grace.

Conclusion

What if you were a fireman and instead of running into the burning building, knocking down walls, and doing whatever it takes to rescue people, you simply sat in the fire truck, put on your headphones, and ignored the screams of the perishing? What if you stayed comfortable? What would happen to a fireman like that? He'd be disqualified. Dear saint, you are not disqualified. You are filled with the Spirit. Don't let anything stop you from sharing Christ with your loved ones, friends, and strangers. They need Christ, and you are the vessel God is going to use to bring them into the kingdom.

Someone said, "The test of your character is what it takes to stop you." What is it that will stop you from sharing Christ with others? Are you afraid of rejection from friends and family and even strangers? Don't be afraid of rejection. Be more concerned that your family and friends who are without Christ are on their way to hell. Don't let anything stop you.

25 | ACTS 15:1-35
LAW OR GRACE?

> *We believe that we will be saved through the grace of the Lord Jesus, just as they will.*
> ACTS 15:11

As Paul comes back from his first missionary journey, there is a great battle between love and legalism in the newly planted churches of Galatia. Things were going incredibly well—too well for the enemy's taste, and the inevitable satanic counterattack soon came.[268] Many people were coming to Christ in the Gentile world, but false teachers soon came and were teaching that grace is not enough to be saved. They said you need Jesus plus the law.

The major theological controversy in the early church is over the core issue of the faith: What is required for salvation? In fact, this is the major theological issue for all times and eras: What does it mean for a person to become a Christian and part of God's people? Is it works or grace?[269] Is it performance or promise?

False teachers have plagued the church throughout its history. They are emissaries of Satan, sent to destroy the church's power and

---

[268] Hughes, *Acts: The Church Afire*, 190.
[269] Hamilton, *John–Acts*, 475.

corrupt its proclamation.[270] Paul warned the leaders at Ephesus to be on the lookout for wolves that will destroy the flock.

> *Acts 20:29–30* | I know that after my departure fierce wolves will come in among you, not sparing the flock; ³⁰ and from among your own selves will arise men speaking twisted things, to draw away the disciples after them.

Peter said the same thing.

> *2 Peter 2:1* | There will also be false teachers among you, who will secretly introduce destructive heresies, even denying the Master who bought them.

The teaching of legalism for salvation or sanctification is dangerous. We are saved and sanctified by the Spirit, the same power that raised Jesus from the dead.

Key Thought: We must guard ourselves against coming to God with a works-based, performance mindset. We've been set free in Christ. Grace alone saves and empowers us! Legalism can only condemn!

Christ's life and death satisfies the law and brings us to God, perfect and unblemished before his throne! His resurrection gives us the power for holiness that far exceeds any written law.

THE DETOUR FROM GRACE (15:1-5)

The most destructive of the "destructive heresies," since it damns men, is the teaching that salvation is by human works, which Peter warned against.[271] We get a taste of this in Acts 15. Paul and Barnabas are back from their first missionary journey, and the greatest threat to the gospel is a false gospel of works righteousness. With all the grace of salvation that was advancing, Satan sent his minions against the gospel, false teachers that put God's grace into question.

We are not saved by works, neither are we sanctified by works. That's legalism. Legalism is not obedience. They are two completely different things. Legalism is concerned with keeping the law while ignoring the lawgiver. It's Christless law keeping. Grace is looking to Jesus and being conformed to him in your heart, walking after him in righteousness in a way that supersedes the law. The sacrifice of love far exceeds the demands of legalism.

---

[270] MacArthur, *Acts*, vol. 2, 62.
[271] Ibid.

In our passage there was a group of people who were zealous to keep the law. Grace teaches Jesus plus nothing. They were teaching Jesus plus the law. That's a false gospel.

A Detour Over Doctrine

> **Acts 15:1** | But some men came down from Judea and were teaching the brothers, "Unless you are circumcised according to the custom of Moses, you cannot be saved."

Good-bye, free grace! Good-bye, joy! These men—Judaizers—did not deny salvation by grace per se. They simply said salvation came by "grace plus..."—specifically "grace plus circumcision"[272] and "grace plus law keeping." Most people don't deny God's grace. They are much more deceptive. They add to it. The apostles are going to teach us here that we are saved by grace alone, plus nothing. No law keeping or ceremonies or sacrifices required.

A Detour with Debate

And so the argument began. There were Judaizers, professing believers who believed after salvation you needed to be circumcised and keep the law of Moses. Paul and Barnabas argued with them. It was so intense they decided to settle it with the twelve apostles in Jerusalem. After Paul's first missionary journey to Galatia, he has to settle an argument in Jerusalem before venturing forth on his second missionary journey to Europe.

> **Acts 15:2** | And after Paul and Barnabas had no small dissension and debate with them, Paul and Barnabas and some of the others were appointed to go up to Jerusalem to the apostles and the elders about this question.

Paul and Barnabas knew what the apostles would say. They heard Peter preach faith alone in Christ alone at Pentecost, but they needed the verification of the apostles in Jerusalem.

So they departed for the holy city Jerusalem to get an audience with the twelve. This passage is the first reference in Acts to the legalists who dogged the steps of Paul wherever he went and were dealt with specifically in his letter to the Galatians.[273] The four Galatian churches are

---

[272] Hughes, *Acts: The Church Afire*, 190.
[273] Baker, "Acts," in *Evangelical Commentary*, 906.

those that Paul and Barnabas just planted: Antioch of Pisidia, Iconium, Lystra and Derbe. The debate and dissension were over the question of grace versus law. Is salvation completely and forever free, or must I do certain things to keep it?

A Detour Directed by the Lord

God is not up in heaven ringing his hands when these detours come. In fact, God has good plans even though bad people and bad circumstances try to interrupt the expansion of Christ's kingdom. Therefore, because Paul and Barnabas know that God is sovereign, they don't stop their joy. They don't stop rejoicing and praising God for all the good things he is doing.

> **Acts 15:3-4** | So, being sent on their way by the church, they passed through both Phoenicia and Samaria, describing in detail the conversion of the Gentiles, and brought great joy to all the brothers. [4] When they came to Jerusalem, they were welcomed by the church and the apostles and the elders, and they declared all that God had done with them.

Even though they had to make a detour before Paul's second missionary journey, they see that God wanted them to use this detour to encourage the brothers in Phoenicia and Samaria. Often what we think is a detour is really God's direction. We must always understand that we are not under the tyranny of our circumstances but under the sovereignty of our loving God.

It's easy to get our eyes off Jesus when problems and distractions arise. No matter what is trying to detour your faith, you keep your eyes on the prize. Keep your eyes on Jesus. That's what the Paul and Barnabas did when coming to the twelve. They encouraged each other and the apostles and elders at Jerusalem with all that God had done. They weren't panicking or wondering if the wheels were going to come off Christ's kingdom. God is fully in charge, and they know it.

A Detour Demanded by False Brothers

Are there those in the church that claim to be brothers but are not? Yes. We see that at least they are confused. Look at their claims before the twelve apostles. They demand that after faith, the believers need to add the law in order to be true Christians.

Acts 15:5 | But some believers who belonged to the party of the Pharisees rose up and said, "It is necessary to circumcise them and to order them to keep the law of Moses."

They are presenting a false gospel. You are going to have that in the church. Many immature believers might propose wrong things. We have to be patient with them and teach them and bring them around to sound doctrine. There may even be false brothers, who are not brothers at all, wolves in sheep's clothing. We have to let the elders take the time to examine false doctrine. Realize that shepherds are here to protect the church from being torn to pieces by the wolves.

THE DISCUSSION ABOUT GRACE (15:6-18)

The twelve apostles meet with the first missionaries and the elders of Jerusalem, led by James, the brother of our Lord, the pastor at the church of Jerusalem. They discuss the essence of the true gospel, that it is by grace through faith, and that there are no works or keeping of the law that is required to merit salvation.

A Discussion of the Gospel

Here is the great Jerusalem council with Peter. The spokesman for the twelve leads the way.

Acts 15:6-9 | The apostles and the elders were gathered together to consider this matter. **7** And after there had been much debate, Peter stood up and said to them, "Brothers, you know that in the early days God made a choice among you, that by my mouth the Gentiles should hear the word of the gospel and believe. **8** And God, who knows the heart, bore witness to them, by giving them the Holy Spirit just as he did to us, **9** and he made no distinction between us and them, having cleansed their hearts by faith."

Peter says, basically that this is a matter that's already been settled (back in Acts 11 with Cornelius's conversion). Peter's witness is that the people were saved by grace alone through faith, and they were given the Holy Spirit. Justification is by faith alone in Christ alone. Peter preached the word of the gospel of grace that was to be accepted by faith alone. The apostles preached this same gospel that they were commissioned to preach by Jesus. Consider Paul's custom in Acts 17.

Acts 17:2-3 | According to Paul's custom, he went to them, and for three Sabbaths reasoned with them from the Scriptures, explaining and giving evidence that the Christ had to suffer and rise again from the dead, and saying, "This Jesus whom I am proclaiming to you is the Christ."

God makes no distinction between those who keep the Jewish customs and those who do not. All who come to know by Jesus Christ "have cleansed their hearts by faith" (15:9). The implication is that salvation is by God's grace through faith alone in Christ alone. And it's to the glory of God alone. God does it from beginning to end. The five solas of the Reformation are a summary of the Jerusalem council.

- Sola scriptura: "Scripture alone"
- Sola fide: "faith alone"
- Sola gratia: "grace alone"
- Solus Christus: "Christ alone"
- Soli Deo gloria: "to the glory of God alone"

This is the same gospel we believe today. Jesus is still "the way, the truth, and the life. No one comes to the Father" except through him (Jn 14:6).

A Denunciation of Legalism

Peter continues on. Remember he's the one who preached Pentecost after denying Christ three times. If there is anyone who knows about grace and needs grace, it's Peter. You can see from his words here that he's righteously indignant at the idea of any legalistic, performance-based way of coming to God. Hear his words. Peter says:

> **Acts 15:10** | "Now, therefore, why are you putting God to the test by placing a yoke on the neck of the disciples that neither our fathers nor we have been able to bear?"

The Pharisees who claimed to be believers had said in verse 5, "It is necessary to circumcise them and to order them to keep the law of Moses." Peter basically says, "No! This is false. Legalism kills, and our forefathers can testify to it." Legalism cannot save, Peter says.

The law is good, Paul tells us later. The law is the reflection of the character of Christ in us. We serve something greater than the law of Moses, dear saints. We have the law of the Spirit of Christ in us, which far exceeds the written law. The Spirit himself has circumcised and tenderized our hearts to surrender to him in all things (Deut 19:16; 30:6).

The apostles will later tell us that the law was never given to make us righteous. That's a yoke that no one can carry. Remember the words of David.

> *Psalm 130:3-4* | If you, O Lord, should mark iniquities, O Lord, who could stand? ⁴But with you there is forgiveness, that you may be feared.

Salvation was never, ever by works or performance. The law was not given to save anybody. The law was given to "increase the transgression" so that the abundance of grace could be experienced.

> *Romans 5:20* | Now the law came in to increase the trespass, but where sin increased, grace abounded all the more.

People in the Old Testament saw their sin because of the mirror of the law. Like a mirror showing our flaws, the law increased the awareness of our trespasses, and God's grace abounded. He could have destroyed his people, but in grace he forgave them and preserved them, and pointed them to Christ.

> *Galatians 3:24, KJV* | The law was our schoolmaster to bring us unto Christ, that we might be justified by faith.

People needed to see the reality of their sins so they could experience the actuality of salvation by grace. The law is our schoolmaster that points us to Christ. Why did God give the law to the Old Testament saints if it doesn't save anyone? Paul tells us another reason in Galatians.

> *Galatians 3:19* | Why then the law? It was added because of transgressions, until the offspring should come to whom the promise had been made.

God had to preserve his people. Without the law, they would have destroyed each other. God has always been a God of grace. Remember that's how he revealed himself to Moses.

> *Exodus 34:6* | The Lord passed before him and proclaimed, "The Lord, the Lord, a God merciful and gracious, slow to anger, and abounding in steadfast love and faithfulness, ⁷keeping steadfast love for thousands, forgiving iniquity and transgression and sin...

Legalism had to be denounced at the Jerusalem council. It never saved anyone. Anyone who has ever been saved has been saved by grace.

A Declaration of Salvation by Grace

Rejecting legalism, Peter's plea for the gospel is clear. He reiterates what we still believe today: that the gospel of God's grace is through faith alone in Christ alone. That can never change.

> **Acts 15:11** | "But we believe that we will be saved through the grace of the Lord Jesus, just as they will."

Peter, who had denied the Lord three times, understood that the gospel had to be a gospel of pure grace, requiring nothing but our sincere trust. Peter was a forgiven sinner. If salvation were by works, he was of all people most condemned. The gospel he preached was salvation by grace alone, through faith alone, in Jesus Christ alone. This is what he tells the apostles. Peter tells them straight up: salvation is by the grace of the Lord Jesus Christ for them and us and everybody. Paul later summed it up well when he spoke to the church at Ephesus.

> *Ephesians 2:8-9* | For by grace you have been saved through faith. And this is not your own doing; it is the gift of God, ⁹not a result of works, so that no one may boast.

A Description of Signs and Wonders

The assembly there was so moved by Peter, that the Jerusalem council fell silent.

> **Acts 15:12** | And all the assembly fell silent, and they listened to Barnabas and Paul as they related what signs and wonders God had done through them among the Gentiles.

As the silence blanketed the great council, Barnabas and Paul spoke about how the Spirit confirmed their testimony with signs and wonders as they preached the glorious gospel of God's grace through faith in Christ alone to the Gentiles. Remember how Hebrews 2 talks about why the signs and wonders were done. They were there to confirm the gospel.

> *Hebrews 2:3-4* | How shall we escape if we neglect such a great salvation? It was declared at first by the Lord, and it was attested to us by those who heard, ⁴while God also bore witness by signs and wonders

and various miracles and by gifts of the Holy Spirit distributed according to his will.

Let us never compromise the gospel. It may be confirmed by signs and wonders, but our faith doesn't stand on any miracle. The modern prosperity gospel is heretical for many reasons, one of which is, they have turned their worship away from Christ to the experience of miracles. We don't worship miracles, we worship Christ. The gospel does not stand on any miracle, but on its own authority. The gospel is always by faith alone, through grace alone in Christ alone, to the glory of God alone. Christ plus nothing. A person who believers the gospel will worship Christ alone. Here we stand. We can do no other.

A Dependence on the Scriptures

James begins to discuss how the gospel of grace results in the birth of the New Testament church. He's going to let us know that there is agreement from Scripture that the church, the rebuilt Israel ("tent of David") is made up of both Jews and Gentiles. Notice, they defend the gospel of grace to the nations by what we call "sola Scriptura," the doctrine of "Scripture alone." That is they didn't defend the gospel from the authority of their own experience, but they turn to the Scriptures.

> **Acts 15:13-15a** | After they finished speaking, James replied, "Brothers, listen to me. [14] Simeon has related how God first visited the Gentiles, to take from them a people for his name. [15] And with this the words of the prophets agree."

Peter had told them, "When we preached the gospel, God confirmed their faith with signs and miracles." Paul and Barnabas said the same thing. Both Peter and James and Paul are always appealing to the Scriptures as their final authority. Remember Peter had before appealed to this from Joel 2, which tells us that signs and wonders would accompany the Spirit's anointing on all humanity, from the youngest to the eldest, from the poorest to the richest. Little ones would prophesy, people from various nations would dream dreams. That was happening in the ministry of Peter as well as Paul and Barnabas, and it continues today.

A Discussion of the Church

Now James begins to discuss how the gospel of grace results in the birth of the New Testament church. He's going to let us know that there is agreement from Scripture that the church, the rebuilt tent of Israel ("tent of David") is made up of both Jews *and* Gentiles.

A Testimony of the Church

James now reflects on Peter's testimony of how God is bringing Gentiles in among his people.

> **Acts 15:13-15a** | After they finished speaking, James replied, "Brothers, listen to me. **14** Simeon has related how God first visited the Gentiles, to take from them a people for his name. **15** And with this the words of the prophets agree."

All the Old Testament predicted that the Gentiles would come into Israel and worship the Messiah. For example, Isaiah says that in the "latter days"—that the time of Jesus crucifixion until the second coming, the Lord is going to establish his house, his forever family, and all the nations will flow into it.

> *Isaiah 2:2* | It shall come to pass in the latter days that the mountain of the house of the Lord shall be established as the highest of the mountains, and shall be lifted up above the hills; and all the nations shall flow to it.

A Prophecy of the Church

James could have quoted literally hundreds of prophecies like this, but he chooses to quote Amos 9:11-12.

> **Acts 15:15b-18** | Just as it is written, **16** "'After this I will return, and I will rebuild the tent of David that has fallen; I will rebuild its ruins, and I will restore it, **17** that the remnant of mankind may seek the Lord, and all the Gentiles who are called by my name, says the Lord, who makes these things **18** known from of old.'

Notice, James and the apostles defend the gospel of grace to the nations by what we call "sola Scriptura," the doctrine of "Scripture alone." That is, they didn't defend the gospel from the authority of their own experience, but they turn to the Scriptures.

James agrees with Peter that the New Testament church is a continuation of the old covenant people. He calls the church the "rebuilt tent of David."

James is quoting a passage in the prophet Amos, where he promises Israel to be raised up, possessing Edom, a neighboring nation, as well as "all the nations who are called by my name" (Amos 9:11-12). The prophecy of Amos was fulfilled when Jesus himself, Yahweh in the flesh returned and he rebuilt the "tent of David." He rebuilt Israel that had fallen so that, as Amos says, "the remnant of mankind may seek the Lord" including "all the Gentiles who are called by my name." The church is the rebuilt Israel. The people of national Israel are the "picture" of what is coming. God's ultimate plan is not just for Israel, but for Israel to expand to all the nations, which is what has happened! The church not only of Israel, but of all nations, with Christ as her head, is the ultimate Israel. Glory to God!

This is very similar to the concept that Paul teaches us in the book of Romans that the church is the result of the Gentiles who believe being "grafted in" to Israel. Paul gives the illustration of a wild olive tree (outside the olive garden of the Lord) being grafted into the olive tree in the garden of the Lord (*cf* Rom 11:17-24).

> *Romans 11:17* | But if some of the branches [*of Israel*] were broken off, and you [*Gentiles*], although a wild olive shoot, were grafted in among the others and now share in the nourishing root of the olive tree [*Israel*].

As Israel is called the Lord's garden of olive trees, so are we in the New Testament church because we've been grafted into Israel. Jesus uses metaphor of the grape vine.

> *John 15:5* | I am the vine; you are the branches. Whoever abides in me and I in him, he it is that bears much fruit, for apart from me you can do nothing.

Not only that, but because we are grafted into Israel, Paul later tells us that all the promises of Abraham our ours by faith.

> *Galatians 3:29* | If you are Christ's, then you are Abraham's offspring, heirs according to promise

James sums up the council's conclusions. The Old Testament prophets foretold a time when the Gentiles would be called by God's name and grafted into Israel (15:17). The true remnant of believing Israel now had to accept these Gentile brothers and sisters in this new covenant.[274] Jews and Gentiles abide together in the church under a new covenant.

THE DECISION FOR GRACE (15:19-29)

The great concern of the apostles now becomes very pastoral. They don't want the sheep to feel burdened by having to keep the law. They want the believers to walk in the grace and love of Christ. There are a few things they need to separate from for the sake of holiness, but the great desire of the apostles is for the saints to be free from the burdens of legalism.

The Fellowship of Grace

Sometimes in order to have fellowship, we have to do away with some parts of our culture. For the Gentiles there were several elements of pagan Roman culture that had to be left behind so they could fellowship with the Jews. Here the apostles outline a simple way of living in grace for sake of the Jews. The way of grace is always so much simpler that legalism.

> **Acts 15:19-20** | Therefore my judgment is that we should not trouble those of the Gentiles who turn to God, **20** but should write to them to abstain from the things polluted by idols, and from sexual immorality, and from what has been strangled, and from blood.

Four things are prohibited by the apostles. These things have to do with Christian holiness and Christian love.

First, the new Gentiles believers were to have nothing to do with the idol worship of their culture ("things polluted by idols"). Those coming out of pagan idolatry were to have nothing to do with "things polluted by idols" such as sacrifices sold at the market, since, while is not directly sin to eat meat in this way, it could defile the conscience of someone coming from that life.

Avoiding sexual immorality may sound like a "no-brainer," but that was not the case for people coming from centuries of pagan practice.[275] Temple prostitution was also very much connected to Gentile worship, such as the worship of Diana. Illicit sex was an integral part of the pagan Gentile worship. Temple priestesses were often little more than

---

[274] Lawrence O. Richards, *The Teacher's Commentary* (Wheaton, IL: Victor Books, 1987), 782.

[275] Hamilton, *John–Acts*, 479.

prostitutes.[276] And while divorce was not very common among the Roman elite, sexual relations with mistresses and slaves for both genders was commonplace and somewhat accepted. First-century Gentiles could not have been expected to come by biblical, sexual morality naturally; it would have represented an entirely new way of living for the Gentile believers.[277] This was a major cultural mindset that had to change in coming to Christ.

The walk of the Christian is to be one of holiness and separation from the world. We don't worship idols or live for pleasure. Our pleasure is in the Lord, and we enjoy everything by enjoying him first. Why were the apostles concerned about these things? Because they were all connected with the idolatry of the temple cults of Roman polytheism. Each town had different gods, but they almost always moved toward the sacrificing of animals to demons and temple prostitution.

The next two prohibitions also had to do with Christian love. They were to give up unbutchered meat or "things strangled" (where the blood was not drained). This was not only part of the pagan rituals, but it also was something tremendously offensive to the Jew, which could have made it very hard for a Jew to have fellowship with a Gentile brother (*cf* Lev 17:10–14; Deut 12:16, 23–25).

The last thing was they were to abstain from was "blood" which they were not to drink (*cf* Lev 7:26; 17:12).

Morality was not the issue at the Jerusalem Conference. Fellowship was, and the decrees were a way for Gentile and Jewish Christians to respect each other's culture so they could fellowship together.[278] All of these things would have not only made fellowship with the Jews impossible, but they were commonly connected to idol worship. These four activities made it immediately possible to build the new Jewish-Gentile churches. This would allow the Gentiles to live out the grace of the Lord Jesus Christ.

The Family of Grace

The law of Moses is read in every synagogue everywhere; so these requirements should come as no shock to the Gentiles.

---

[276] MacArthur, *Acts*, vol. 2, 71.
[277] Hamilton, *John-Acts*, 479–480.
[278] Polhill, *Acts*, 332.

Acts 15:21 | For from ancient generations Moses has had in every city those who proclaim him, for he is read every Sabbath in the synagogues.

Gentiles should have a heart for Jews who need Jesus. At this point, the new covenant church was growing out of the old covenant people. Gentile Christians should be sensitive to their scruples and not give them offense in these ritual matters, for they too may be reached with the gospel.[279] The gospel of grace is growing, and if you want to reach Jews, it's best not to be offensive in hanging on to these pagan habits and holdovers.

The Freedom of Grace

The church is God's forever family, and shepherds need to be gentle with the sheep. It is vital that we treat the sheep with love and meekness. This is why the apostles went out of their way to send the best men to the Gentiles as well as to inform them with a personal letter.

Acts 15:22-29 | Then it seemed good to the apostles and the elders, with the whole church, to choose men from among them and send them to Antioch with Paul and Barnabas. They sent Judas called Barsabbas, and Silas, leading men among the brothers, **23** with the following letter: "The brothers, both the apostles and the elders, to the brothers who are of the Gentiles in Antioch and Syria and Cilicia, greetings. **24** Since we have heard that some persons have gone out from us and troubled you with words, unsettling your minds, although we gave them no instructions, **25** it has seemed good to us, having come to one accord, to choose men and send them to you with our beloved Barnabas and Paul, **26** men who have risked their lives for the name of our Lord Jesus Christ. **27** We have therefore sent Judas and Silas, who themselves will tell you the same things by word of mouth. **28** For it has seemed good to the Holy Spirit and to us to lay on you no greater burden than these requirements: **29** that you abstain from what has been sacrificed to idols, and from blood, and from what has been strangled, and from sexual immorality. If you keep yourselves from these, you will do well. Farewell."

They were to stay away from sexual immorality and from things sacrificed to idols. They were to live a life free from the slavery to idols

---

[279] Polhill, ibid.

and immorality. They did not say, "Keep the law of Moses" or "Become Jewish." So much of the Mosaic law was symbolic and ceremonial. Christ has come. Now they needed to keep their eyes and on Christ and live for him and live a life of simple devotion to Christ. Leave behind those things that enslave or distract.

The legalists among Paul wanted to treat these practices with heavy burdens of legalism, but the apostles were simply telling them live a life separate from the old practices of the world.

Living a life out of grace instead of legalism is absolutely essential to living in the power of the Spirit and living out of the fruit of the Spirit (love, joy, peace, etc.). We are called to walk in the freedom of the Spirit, not the burden of legalism and rule keeping.

The difference between love and legalism can be illustrated with marriage. This year my wife and I celebrate 25 years of marriage. On that day, if I give my wife 25 roses, and she says, "Thank you!" If I reply, "Oh honey, don't worry about it. I'm your husband. I'm required to give these to you. It's the right thing to do." She would be crushed. What she ought to hear is, "Oh honey, I'm madly in love with you after 25 years. It's my greatest joy to be married to you." That's the difference between love and legalism. In the same way, we ought to love Christ, not because of legalistic rules, but out of a heart of love, a heart filled with the Holy Spirit. Paul will later tell the Romans that the law of the Spirit and love far exceeds the written law of Moses.

> Romans 8:2-4 | For the law of the Spirit of life has set you free in Christ Jesus from the law of sin and death. [3] For God has done what the law, weakened by the flesh, could not do. By sending his own Son in the likeness of sinful flesh and for sin, he condemned sin in the flesh, [4] in order that the righteous requirement of the law might be fulfilled in us, who walk not according to the flesh but according to the Spirit.

Having written this sweet and simple letter to the Gentiles where the gospel was advancing, they were ready to deliver it.

THE DELIGHT OF GRACE (15:30-35)

Living in the grace of God is what brings true happiness.

The Delight of Gracious Leadership

The Paul and Barnabas bring the letter from the apostles in Jerusalem, and the church at Antioch is overwhelmed with gratitude.

Acts 15:30-31 | So when they were sent off, they went down to Antioch, and having gathered the congregation together, they delivered the letter. ³¹ And when they had read it, they rejoiced because of its encouragement.

The formalism of the law never made anyone happy. Can you imagine all the laws: circumcision laws, clothing laws, food laws, the need to bring sacrifices to Jerusalem? All of that is done away with, say the apostles. It's now all about grace and your walk with the Lord! Now that's something to rejoice in. It's all about grace, God's free gift.

What was it that made the believers at Antioch of Syria rejoice? The missionaries, Paul, and Barnabas let the congregation know about their freedom in Christ. They rejoiced.

This is what they had preached in Antioch and everywhere. We new covenant believers have a new relationship with the law.

There are many difficult things we have to address as pastors and elders. We have to be courageous and instruct the church in difficult issues. Saying the hard things that need to be said is an act of grace that protects the church. This may not seem difficult to us today, but remember the church is in a great transition. They are moving from mainly Jewish in Jerusalem to predominantly Gentile in the various nations they are reaching. The message of grace made the believers rejoice!

The letter to this Gentile church at Antioch was a letter of instruction. They are told, basically, to live in the grace of Christ and not under the burden of the law. The believers in Antioch, which includes both Jews and plenty of Gentiles were grateful that they received this message of grace from the apostles. How encouraged they were to hear it.

The Old Testament law with all its ceremonies and types is such a beautiful picture of Jesus. But since Christ has come, and we have received him, why would we have to go back to all those ceremonies and types? Now that Christ has come, we need to keep our eyes on Christ. That's where true happiness can be found.

The Delight of Gracious Discipleship

Judas and Silas were engaged in Christian discipleship. We might call it "biblical counseling" in today's language.

Acts 15:32-33 | And Judas and Silas, who were themselves prophets, encouraged and strengthened the brothers with many words. **³³** And after they had spent some time, they were sent off in peace by the brothers to those who had sent them.

Judas and Silas were prophets, very well educated in the Scriptures, and they took what was in the Scriptures and personally applied it to the believers' lives. They "encouraged and strengthened the brothers with many words" from the Scriptures. They did this for some time.

Discipleship occurs when we share from God's word how to walk in the word with another believer. It's that simple. If we are only contributing information, we are not doing discipleship. Real life-on-life discipleship occurs when we apply God's word and walk in it.

We don't see Acts 15:34 in the ESV as it is a textual variant not found in the earlier Greek manuscripts, but here it is in the NKJV.

Acts 15:34, NKJV | However, it seemed good to Silas to remain there.

The substance of this detail does not affect the story of the text either way. Whether Silas stayed in Antioch or went back to Jerusalem is inconsequential. He will eventually join Paul on another missionary journey, but this does not happen right away as is clear from the text.

Regardless, it would be appropriate that Silas would participate in the delight of Christian discipleship as well. If he did indeed stay there, that would be a fantastic reason to stay.

The Delight of Gracious Fellowship

Paul later tells us that the church is the "pillar and ground" of the truth (1 Tim 3:15). The truth is most obviously established through the preaching of the word in the local church. That's exactly what they did.

Acts 15:35 | But Paul and Barnabas remained in Antioch, teaching and preaching the word of the Lord, with many others also.

Paul and Barnabas didn't want to leave. They loved the fellowship of their home church. They "remained in Antioch." Fellowship is necessary for Christian growth. Sunday church is not just about digesting a message, but it's about getting to know the family of God.

Fellowship includes the teaching and preaching of God's word. We learn about grace from the Scriptures, which Paul and Barnabas were faithful to teach. But the fact that they remained there with their "forever family" in Antioch made all the difference. It's through our fellowship and example that we can really have an impact on people on how to live out the word. They didn't just deliver this letter. They lived it out, life-on-life with their brothers and sisters in Christ.

The theology of the gospel of grace comes directly from the Old Testament. We are all called to preach the word. We as pastors and elders don't get to edit the word or replace it with popular psychology or with health and wealth, syrupy sweet self-help nonsense. We are called to teach and preach the truth of God from the word of God: line upon line, precept upon precept, chapter by chapter, book by book through the entire Bible.

Why is this vital? It's the "word of the Lord"—it's the story of the grace of Jesus from Genesis to Revelation. Do you want to know him? Read and listen to his word. Meditate on his word day and night (Psa 1:2) Walk in his word (Jas 1:22-25). Live out his word. And demand nothing less from your pastors and elders that they preach and teach the word of God. The word points to the grace of Jesus on every page.

Conclusion

The famous evangelist, D. L. Moody, helps us understand the difference between law and grace. "The Law tells me how crooked I am. Grace comes along and straightens me out."[280] Our salvation from beginning to end is a free gift of God. Only God can change the human heart.

Dear saint, you cannot be happy trying to fulfill the law. The law only points you to your own failures. A lady cannot wash her face with the mirror. The law is a mirror that shows you where you fall short. Trying to be saved or sanctified by the law is an endeavor in despair and misery. For cleansing, you need the water of grace! It is the free grace of God through the sacrifice of our Savior that washes away your sin. Wash yourself in the water of the grace of Christ. Turn your eyes on Jesus, and you will live above even the high standard of the law. You will live in the perfection and righteousness of Jesus Christ.

---

[280] D.L. Moody. *The Overcoming Life and Other Sermons* (Chicago: Bible Institute Colportage Association, 1896), 42-43.

SECOND MISSIONARY JOURNEY

26 | ACTS 15:36-16:15
THE MACEDONIAN CALL

A vision appeared to Paul in the night: a man of Macedonia was standing there, urging him and saying, "Come over to Macedonia and help us." And when Paul had seen the vision, immediately we sought to go on into Macedonia, concluding that God had called us to preach the gospel to them.
ACTS 16:9-10

Sometimes the best laid plans are not the best plans at all. God has promised to build his church. "Unless the Lord builds the house, those who build it labor in vain" (Psa 127:1). As believers, we have to be willing to throw out our plans and follow the Lord in obedience. Can we all agree that God's plans are better than our plans?

> *Isaiah 55:8-9* | My thoughts are not your thoughts, neither are your ways my ways, declares the Lord. ⁹ For as the heavens are higher than the earth, so are my ways higher than your ways and my thoughts than your thoughts.

God knows better than us. I'm so glad he promises to lead us, because we all have strange ideas of what we want in life.

Do you remember people asking you when you were young: what do you want to be when you grow up? At times I had different answers.

I wanted to be a doctor, but I found out I'm not smart enough. I wanted to be a lawyer, but that too slipped from my imagination. Then when I was a teenager, I saw the movie top gun, and I had the opportunity to go up in a restored World War II fighter plane. We even did a roll, upside down in the sky! I was so pumped. From then on I wanted to be a pilot. When I went to enlist, I found out my eyes are terrible, and I could never go into aviation. I got into music, and then I wanted to be in a rock band. Then I came to know Christ, and I thought, I'll be a Christian musician. All of that is fine and good, but I'm so glad God is the one who leads us, not our own hearts. Eventually, God led Jill and I to do church planting missionary work in Spain. Finally, he called us back here to Chicagoland, where we couldn't be happier serving him! You never know what God's plans are for you! God has some things in store for you that you could never dream of or imagine yourself. He's a much better planner for our lives than we could ever be.

Paul knew God had plans for him too. For the apostle Paul, his home church at Antioch was not a parking lot: it was a launching pad. He could never settle down to a "comfortable ministry" anywhere as long as there were open doors for the preaching of the gospel.[281] The church helped him greatly, and he needed to let them send him off on his second missionary journey.

He first begins by strengthening the brothers in the provinces of Syria and Cilicia. Of course, God's plan is to expand the gospel to Europe. Paul starts in Syria where his home church of Antioch is. Cilicia is where Tarsus is, Paul's hometown. Now with every gospel expansion there is always testing, trials, and tribulation, and this moment was no different. There are several levels of disagreement and dissention before the great expansion into Europe. The first is between Paul and Peter, over the essence of the gospel, and then between Paul, and Barnabas over the suitableness of John Mark. Yet, amidst all the distractions and commotion of dissension, we are going to see how God expands the church planning efforts even through these difficulties.

The greater our weakness is, the greater God's power will be displayed through us! In fact, the greater the obstacle, the greater our God's power is displayed. There is no difficulty too great for God. Nothing is impossible for him.

---

[281] Wiersbe, *The Bible Exposition Commentary*, vol. 1, 465.

There are a couple of obstacles that occur during this time. First, Paul gets into it with Peter who almost causes a church split at Antioch (*cf* Gal 2:11-14). Then Paul writes the letter to Galatians, which is quite polemic. This all precedes the Jerusalem council earlier in Acts 15. It looks like things could be on very shaky ground for the second missionary journey, and if you think that, then you don't understand how God loves to display his power in our weakness!

A NEW TEAM ASSEMBLED (ACTS 15:36-41)

Just when it looks like something exciting is about to happen for the kingdom of God, there is a great big problem, and sometimes several. Often when the church is expanding, there is not only persecution, but there can also be infighting in the church. We see that in the highest ranks, first with Peter, and then amidst the great missionary team of Paul and Barnabas.

There were several new elements in this second journey that indicated that God was still at work, despite the seeming obstacles and personal serious public and personal difficulties that arose.

Factions Among the Apostles

Before Paul had gone down to Jerusalem to settle the issue of law or grace, he had to first do battle with the apostle Peter himself. Just after this sharp rebuke of Peter, he writes a letter to the Galatian churches and mentions the confrontation in the letter.

> *Galatians 2:11-14* | But when Cephas [*Peter*] came to Antioch, I opposed him to his face, because he stood condemned. [12] For before certain men came from James, he was eating with the Gentiles; but when they came he drew back and separated himself, fearing the circumcision party. [13] And the rest of the Jews acted hypocritically along with him, so that even Barnabas was led astray by their hypocrisy. [14] But when I saw that their conduct was not in step with the truth of the gospel, I said to Cephas before them all, "If you, though a Jew, live like a Gentile and not like a Jew, how can you force the Gentiles to live like Jews?"

Peter had been eating together with the Gentiles, not observing Jewish food laws, and incorporating himself into the church of many nations at Antioch. What a joy to see the gospel on display! But once certain professing Christian Pharisees came from Jerusalem, Peter (here called Cephas) started showing preference to the Pharisee

Christians and even influenced Barnabas. Paul told Peter that this was blatant hypocrisy. Peter had sinned publicly, and so Paul gave him public rebuke. The beauty of godly leadership is that there is humility. Peter most certainly demonstrated godly repentance, for when the issue came up later at the Jerusalem council, the apostle who was first to stand at Pentecost, was the first to stand and speak a witness to grace alone at the Jerusalem council. Praise God that even factions in humble, godly leadership can be handled with humility, grace, and repentance.

Friction on the Team

What we read about to begin Paul's second missionary journey is a massive, impactful disagreement. It all began when Paul suggested to Barnabas that they revisit the churches in Galatia "to see how they are" (15:36). Some time had passed; "after some days" in verse 36 may suggest that the winter of A.D. 48 had given way to the spring of A.D. 49, and travel was once again feasible.[282] Paul had likely written the letter to the Galatians even before the Jerusalem council. So he wants to go back to the churches of Galatia (Antioch of Pisidia, Iconium, Lystra, and Derbe) on a second missionary journey and encourage them. It's likely that with communication limited, Paul was wondering how his letter had been received by the churches of Galatia.

> **Acts 15:36-39** | And after some days Paul said to Barnabas, "Let us return and visit the brothers in every city where we proclaimed the word of the Lord, and see how they are." **37** Now Barnabas wanted to take with them John called Mark. **38** But Paul thought best not to take with them one who had withdrawn from them in Pamphylia and had not gone with them to the work. **39** And there arose a sharp disagreement, so that they separated from each other. Barnabas took Mark with him and sailed away to Cyprus.

Paul and Barnabas agreed on the importance of the trip, but they could not agree on the composition of the "team." Here were two dedicated men who had just helped bring unity to the church, and yet they could not settle their own disagreements! Disturbing and painful as these conflicts are, they are often found in church history; and yet God is able to overrule them and accomplish his purposes.

---

[282] Thomas, *Acts*, 436.

Friendship on the Team

Paul and Barnabas wanted this second missionary journey to take place, but they chose different teams. Barnabas took Mark back to Cyprus. And Paul chose another team member: Silas.

> **Acts 15:40** | But Paul chose Silas and departed, having been commended by the brothers to the grace of the Lord.

At times, God may allow the breakup of a ministry team or even a congregation in order to multiply the manpower going forward. Barnabas and John Mark went to Cyprus, and church history tells us they continued the work there. Barnabas would be soon martyred in Cyprus around A.D. 60. John Mark would go on to be a vital help encouragement both to Paul and especially Peter. John Mark is the author of the second gospel that bears his name. His main source was the apostle Peter.

So John Mark is not lost by Paul as much as he is gained by Barnabas. Paul chooses Silas to create a new missionary team for his second missionary journey, beginning in Galatia and trekking forward into the expanse of Europe.

Paul's new partner, Silas, had been one of the leaders of the Jerusalem church. "Silas" is probably a Greek version of the name *Saul*. He was coauthor with Paul of the Thessalonian epistles, and he was the secretary for Peter's first epistle (1 Pet 5:12).[283] He was in every respect a suitable man for missionary work. As a prophet (15:32), he was adept at proclaiming and teaching the word. As a Jew, he had entrance into the synagogues. As a Roman citizen (16:37), he enjoyed the same protection and benefits as did Paul. And his status as a respected leader of both the Jerusalem and the Antioch churches uniquely prepared him for the multicultural ministry that they were about to embark on.[284]

Expansion Through the Team

You would think with all the disagreement and dissension that the gospel would be hindered, but that did not happen in the least. Paul went with Silas and ventured out on his second missionary journey.

---

[283] Wiersbe, *The Bible Exposition Commentary*, vol. 1, 466.
[284] MacArthur, *Acts*, vol. 2, 82–83.

Acts 15:41 | And he went through Syria and Cilicia, strengthening the churches.

God changes his workmen, but his work goes right on. Now there were *two* missionary teams instead of one! If God had to depend on perfect people to accomplish his work, he would never ever get anything done. Our limitations and imperfections are good reasons for us to depend on the grace of God, for our sufficiency is from him alone (2 Cor 3:5).[285]

Little do they know that a great companion to Paul is about to be added to the missionary team. Let me introduce Paul's son in the faith: Timothy!

A NEW WORKER ADDED (16:1-5)

At Lystra, the missionaries are joined by a certain disciple named Timothy. This is going to change the entire trajectory of Paul's missionary labors. He says to the Philippians that Timothy is indispensable to his ministry.

> *Philippians 2:20, 22* | I have no one like him, who will be genuinely concerned for your welfare... ²² But you know Timothy's proven worth, how as a son with a father he has served with me in the gospel.

A Multicultural Man

Paul goes back to Derbe and all the way back to Lystra (sixty miles west of Derbe). It's an important visit, because it is in Lystra that Paul is introduced to Timothy. Just as Silas had replaced Barnabas, so Timothy replaced John Mark. Timothy was to play a key role in Paul's life, eventually becoming his right-hand man (1 Cor 4:17; 1 Thess 3:2; Phil 2:19). Timothy was also Paul's "true child in the faith" (1 Tim 1:2; *cf* 1 Cor 4:17; 2 Tim 1:2).[286]

Acts 16:1 | Paul came also to Derbe and to Lystra. A disciple was there, named Timothy, the son of a Jewish woman who was a believer, but his father was a Greek.

Like Paul and even Stephen before him, Timothy was a multi-cultural man. As a Hellenized Jew, he knew the worldly culture of Rome as well as the more separated culture of Israel. He would have spoken

---

[285] Wiersbe, *The Bible Exposition Commentary*, vol. 1, 466.
[286] MacArthur, *Acts*, vol. 2, 83.

Hebrew as well as Greek, and probably Latin as well. Because of the conquests of Alexander the Great almost 400 years earlier, the language of the diverse peoples had a unifying language (koine Greek). Knowing Hebrew, Timothy would know the Hebrew Scriptures as well as the Greek translation, called the Septuagint.

A Magnanimous Man

Timothy wasn't the strongest in his physical stature. He had a weak stomach, and at times could struggle with introversion and timidness. Yet he was well spoken of by his brothers and sisters in the churches.

> **Acts 16:2** | He was well spoken of by the brothers at Lystra and Iconium.

Timothy and his mother had been converted when Paul and Barnabas pioneered the work in the area. During the time that Paul had been away, young Timothy had made considerable progress. Indeed, he was considered a promising young man by the other believers.[287]

Why was Timothy so trusted among the brothers? Timothy's value was not based on his physical strength or personality, both which were somewhat weak. His value was based on the fact that he was a F.A.T. Christian. God wants us to be F.A.T. and happy! Faithful. Available. Teachable. When we are present and committed to our local congregation, available for service and ministry, and growing in the grace and knowledge of Christ, applying the word and walking faithfully with Christ, then the Lord will bind our hearts together for greater ministry.

A Missions-Minded Man

To have had a member of his entourage be of Jewish lineage and yet uncircumcised would have hampered his effectiveness among the Jews. It was at the very least a matter of missionary strategy to circumcise Timothy.

> **Acts 16:3** | Paul wanted Timothy to accompany him, and he took him and circumcised him because of the Jews who were in those places, for they all knew that his father was a Greek.

Many scholars have argued that Paul would never have asked Timothy to be circumcised, since he objected so strenuously to that rite in Galatians (*cf* 6:12ff; 5:11). That, however, is to overlook the fact that

---

[287] J. Phillips, *Exploring Acts,* Ac 16:1b.

Galatians was written to Gentiles and Timothy was considered a Jew. There was no question of circumcising Gentiles. The Jerusalem Conference agreed on that. Gentiles would not be required to become Jews in order to be Christians. The converse was also true: Jews would not be required to abandon their Jewishness in order to become Christians.[288]

Paul's strategy as a Jew was to begin with evangelizing the Jewish synagogues. He expresses this to the Corinthians.

> *1 Corinthians 9:20* | To the Jews I became as a Jew, in order to win Jews. To those under the law I became as one under the law (though not being myself under the law) that I might win those under the law.

Circumcision, though not at all required for salvation, was an effective expression of Jewishness that would have endeared Timothy to the synagogue ministry.

A Mature Man

Timothy had grown up in Lystra. He likely saw Paul get executed by stoning and put to death. He likely saw Paul's lifeless body dragged out of the city. Yet, Timothy doesn't give up, even though he might be prone to that in his personality. He wasn't the biggest kid on the football team if you know what I mean. But his faith was a thousand times bigger than his gifts or abilities. He was like Captain America before he became Captain America. So, Timothy accompanied Paul back to the places where there was so much persecution.

> **Acts 16:4-5** | As they went on their way through the cities, they delivered to them for observance the decisions that had been reached by the apostles and elders who were in Jerusalem. ⁵ So the churches were strengthened in the faith, and they increased in numbers daily.

Paul and Silas and Timothy began with the churches of Galatia that they had reached on Paul's first missionary journey. There was much suffering and persecution from these cities, but this is what Jesus had promised.

> *John 15:18* | If the world hates you, know that it has hated me before it hated you.

---

[288] Polhill, *Acts*, 342–343.

Maturity and selflessness go hand-and-hand. Mature people don't make excuses. They don't cop out because it's hard. They do the hard thing. Their heart's desire is not ease and comfort, but whatever it takes to honor the Lord and expand his kingdom.

A NEW VISION RECEIVED (16:6-10)

Every congregation has a beginning. The church at Jerusalem began on Pentecost with the coming of the Holy Spirit and the preaching of the apostles (Acts 2). The church in Samaria began with Philip's preaching the word (Acts 8). The church at Philippi began with Paul hearing the Macedonian call (16:9). Paul and his team of missionaries were going to circle Asia and head back East, but the Holy Spirit forbid them to preach in Asia (south) and Bithynia (north). The Spirit gave Paul a vision of a man saying, "Come over into Macedonia, and help us" (16:9).

A Forbidden Direction

After visiting the churches he had founded, Paul tried to enter new territory for the Lord by traveling east into Asia Minor and Bithynia, but the Lord closed the door.[289]

> **Acts 16:6-7** | And they went through the region of Phrygia and Galatia, having been forbidden by the Holy Spirit to speak the word in Asia. ⁷ And when they had come up to Mysia, they attempted to go into Bithynia, but the Spirit of Jesus did not allow them.

Paul was forbidden by the Holy Spirit at this time to go to Bithynia, further north in Asia (now Turkey), but this doesn't mean the Spirit doesn't want these people to be saved. Peter later writes his first epistle "to those who are elect exiles of the Dispersion in Pontus, Galatia, Cappadocia, Asia, and Bithynia" (1 Pet 1:1). Since Peter names Silas and John Mark in his letter to Bithynia, et al (1 Pet 5:12-13), it seems they all may have been involved in planting and discipling those churches. Many churches are planted and flourish in this region, but Paul was forbidden to go there. God had others go there and do the work. The Spirit forbid Paul to go into northern Asia because at this time he wanted him to go to Europe and plant the first European church in the city of Philippi, there in Macedonia.

---

[289] Wiersbe, *The Bible Exposition Commentary*, vol. 1, 467.

To hear that the Spirit is closing a door on ministry must have been discouraging to the apostle Paul. It is, however, comforting to know that even apostles are not always clear on God's direction for ministry. We all have to rely on our walk with the Holy Spirit as he opens doors.

A Clear Vision

As a result of the closed doors to northern Asia, they head to western Asia, over to the port of Troas on the Aegean Sea. They knew God would eventually reveal where he wanted them to go if they kept moving. At last, in dramatic fashion, he did so through a vision of a man from Macedonia in Europe.[290]

> **Acts 16:8-9** | So, passing by Mysia, they went down to Troas. **9** And a vision appeared to Paul in the night: a man of Macedonia was standing there, urging him and saying, "Come over to Macedonia and help us."

Who is this "man of Macedonia"? Some have speculated that it might very well be Luke the physician, since he says, "Come over to… help *us*." In the next verse (16:10), Luke, the author of Acts, incorporates himself into the story. Though we don't know the identity of this man, it seems that there is a Gentile Christian working in Macedonia that gives an invitation through a vision to Paul and his team. The physician Luke joins the team at Troas. They immediately seek to make their journey into the Roman Province of Macedonia (which is today is Europe).

An Immediate Obedience

After Paul received the vision, he must have shared it with his traveling companions, for the result was they all immediately got ready and crossed over the sea to Macedonia. It was the official opening of Europe to Christianity, and with it the gospel began the long westward march that eventually brought it to us.[291]

> **Acts 16:10** | And when Paul had seen the vision, immediately we sought to go on into Macedonia, concluding that God had called us to preach the gospel to them.

---

[290] MacArthur, *Acts*, vol. 2, 86.
[291] Boice, *Acts: An Expositional Commentary*, 275.

In obedience Paul, Silas, Timothy, and Luke went straight through Asia to Macedonia (modern day Greece, Macedonia, and Bulgaria). It seems the Lord wanted the gospel to impact Philippi, an important port city. For the first time the gospel would be preached in Europe. Paul would share a special friendship with the Christians at Philippi. That friendship started in a strange way, which is described in the 16th chapter of Acts. Paul and his companions were on a missionary journey. Paul had his idea to go to Asia, but the Holy Spirit had other plans, so Paul and his companions caught the next ship to Macedonia, and proceeded to Philippi, its leading city.

What about you? Are you open to God changing your plans? This happens a lot in the Christian life. Are you walking with God in such a way that he is leading you? The Christian should strive for nothing less than God's perfect peace in his leading. That comes from a constant diet of the word while being led by the Holy Spirit.

A NEW CHURCH FOUNDED (16:11-15)

The Holy Spirit assembled the team even in the midst of dissention and disagreement. They have plans to go to Asia, but the Holy Spirit directs them to Europe. They have to throw their plans out the window, and they obey the Spirit and get on a boat for Greece.

The Place of the New Church

None of the team know exactly where they are going in Greece, but they end up in a major port city of Philippi.

> **Acts 16:11-12** | So, setting sail from Troas, we made a direct voyage to Samothrace, and the following day to Neapolis, **12** and from there to Philippi, which is a leading city of the district of Macedonia and a Roman colony. We remained in this city some days.

Philippi, named after Philip of Macedon, father of Alexander the Great, had become a Roman colony and was a bustling center of military activity, the leading city of eastern Macedonia. It was self-governing city, a "little Rome."[292] The total population of Philippi at the time

---

[292] Pollock, *The Apostle*, 123.

of time of Paul's visit was nearly 10,000 with slaves making up about 20% of the population.[293]

Philippi became established because it was considered a port city, right off the Aegean Sea. It also was supplied with gold mines nearby. Most importantly, as a port city, people could be evangelized here and then like seeds, go to their own cities far away and bring the gospel they learned in Philippi. It's a wonderful strategy.

The People of the New Church

Now we come to the direct providence of God where we learn we can trust God to introduce us to the people he is drawing to himself. It is here we first learn of the great Gentile fashionista businesswoman named Lydia. Lydia is from Thyatira, but she has a vacation home in Philippi. She's having a Bible study, minding her own business, when she runs into the apostle Paul.

> **Acts 16:13-14a** | And on the Sabbath day we went outside the gate to the riverside, where we supposed there was a place of prayer, and we sat down and spoke to the women who had come together. **14** One who heard us was a woman named Lydia, from the city of Thyatira, a seller of purple goods, who was a worshiper of God. The Lord opened her heart to pay attention to what was said by Paul.

It is at the place of prayer that they meet Lydia. What was this place of prayer? In sources from the Second Temple period "place of prayer" (*proseuchē*) is the most common word used to describe a synagogue building whereas the word for synagogue (*synagōgē*) may indicate a congregation, an assembly, as well as a building or a place of assembly. It is not clear why authors prefer one word to the other or use the two words alternately.[294] The Jewish women of Philippi weren't meeting out in the open on a riverbank. They had their own building, a *proseuchē*. This kind of building is common in the Second Temple period of the Jewish dispersion. It is in this building that they first heard the gospel message from another Jew, the apostle Paul. Many synagogues

---

[293] Eduard Verhoef, *Philippi: How Christianity Began in Europe: The Epistle to the Philippians and the Excavations at Philippi* (New York: T&T Clark, 2013), 9, 12.

[294] Pieter W. van der Horst, *Japheth in the Tents of Shem: Studies on Jewish Hellenism in Antiquity* (Peeters: Leuven, 2002), 59.

(including the prayer-house in Philippi) were built near sources of water, such as rivers, to facilitate ritual washings and baptisms. This is significant for the woman they meet there named Lydia.

Who is Lydia according to the passage? Lydia is a rich woman with at least two homes. It's probably July or August of A.D. 49. She's studying the Bible on the shores of the Aegean Sea. Her house and position in life demonstrate that she is extremely wealthy for a woman of her day. She has a booming business in selling purple fabric for clothing. A "seller of purple" (16:14) meant Lydia sold purple clothes or cloth. At the time, such clothes were so expensive they were only worn by royalty and the rich.

Thyatira and Philippi are cities with booming economies. Lydia then is basically a Greek fashionista, CEO, on top of the fashion empire. Today we might say she has a house in Chicago and in Paris. She's a serious mover in her world. Isn't it wonderful that God can humble someone like Lydia? She's what the Bible calls a "God-fearer." Here's what that means. She's rejected paganism and polytheism. She does not believe that there are dozens of gods: god of the wind, the rain, the purple cloth; god of the sea, god of the fashion world. She's come to believe there is only one God ruling the universe. So a God-fearer is that she is a monotheist. She's in the synagogue. She's listening to the teaching of the Jews. She's trying to live a moral life. I want you to see how God goes after her. She is an intellect. She is a seeker. She understands the law, if she knows the Torah. She knows she needs forgiveness. She knows she needs a blood sacrifice. She needs atonement. She needs to be justified before God. But she's confused. Enter Paul.

> **Acts 16:14b** | The Lord opened her heart to pay attention to what was said by Paul.

Paul enters into what is basically a women's Bible study and pauses Nancy Leigh DeMoss app and begins to teach them. Paul basically connects the dots for them. God opens her eyes. Lydia is a thinker. She's an intellect. She's a God fearer. She is listening to the word of God, and she experiences the wisdom of God when God opens her eyes. After her conversion, she "constrained" the missionaries to use this house as a base of operations, so it must have been much larger than needed. Later, we find out that her home in Philippi became the place where the new church met (16:40).

How and why did Lydia come to faith in Christ? "The Lord opened her heart to pay attention to what was said by Paul." The Spirit alone draws people to God and opens their eyes so they can see. God opened the eyes of Lydia. God can do this. I want you to hear the testimony of a guy named Becket Cook.[295] He was a gay fashion designer in Hollywood.

He's out at a coffee shop in Hollywood, and he looks over and sees a group of young people talking about the Lord with Bibles open on the table. They are talking about Jesus, and finally he turns around and says, "Are you guys Christians?" And they said yes, and they then explained to him the gospel. Now remember this is a guy who's designed sets for Oprah and Katy Perry, and Paris Hilton. So, he asks this group of young Christians, "What does your church in Hollywood believe about homosexuality?" And they said, "Well, you know, we believe it's a sin." So, this gay fashion designer really appreciated how frank and honest they were. They leave him by inviting him to church that Sunday. Sunday comes around, and he knows he needs to go this Bible preaching church in Hollywood, where he'd been invited. Listen to his testimony once he arrived.

> The pastor comes out and he starts preaching on Romans chapter 7, and something strange started happening. Everything he was saying, every word he was saying, every sentence he was saying started to resonate this truth in my mind, in my heart, and I didn't know why. I was on the edge of my seat, literally on the edge of my seat. It was the first time I had really heard the gospel and understood it. And before he left, he invited people to get prayed with on the side of the church.[296]

He goes forward for prayer, and the prayer is so loving and clear. Listen how he explains his conversion during the prayer time.

> Suddenly, the Holy Spirit just floods me, and God revealed himself to me in that moment. And he's like, "You're now adopted into my kingdom. Welcome." And I was like, "Whoa!" I just like started bawling, hysterically balling. And in that moment, I knew in the core of my

---

[295] Becket Cook from Nathaniel Banister, "'Being Gay Was No Longer Who I Was': The Supernatural Moment This Hollywood Designer Met Jesus Christ," CBN News, February 18, 2022, https://www1.cbn.com/cbnnews/us/2022/february/being-gay-was-no-longer-who-i-was-the-supernatural-moment-this-hollywood-designer-met-jesus-christ.

[296] Ibid.

being that being gay was no longer who I was. And I didn't care because I had just met Jesus Christ. I now no longer live for a happiness from the world. It's a joy that comes from Christ. With God, I feel this unconditional love from him that will never leave. He'll never leave or forsake me. I'm happy to leave that dead man and dead life behind because Jesus Christ is worth it.[297]

This is the kind of movement in people's lives we ought to expect as the Spirit moves. This is not just for the time of the book of Acts. This is for now. It's not just for Hollywood types, but for us. We are all testimonies to the Becket Cooks and the Lydias and the Philippian jailers. We all need the eyes of our heart opened by the Holy Spirit.

The Profession of the New Church

There is no church, no elders, no new members' class. It's just Paul and his companions. Lydia comes to true faith in the Lord, and the fruit of her new life is immediately obvious. She wants to be baptized!

Acts 16:15 | And after she was baptized, and her household as well, she urged us, saying, "If you have judged me to be faithful to the Lord, come to my house and stay." And she prevailed upon us.

Lydia and her whole household chose to follow the Lord in believers' baptism. She also started the church of Philippi in her living room. Lydia's reputation changed with her baptism. She wasn't just the fashionista of Philippi. Now her main identity could not be the style maven of Macedonia. Now she is first and foremost a follower of Jesus Christ.

APPLICATIONS

1. Are you in a place of joyful obedience in your life? Are you fulfilling your spiritual calling? Are you fanning into flame the spiritual gifts that God has given you? You don't have to be an evangelist missionary to be used of God. Remember those young people in the coffee shop who pointed Becket Cook to Christ. How many people are like that all around you? Are you in a place of joyful obedience in your life? Because if you are the Lydias and the Beckets of this world will be led to you by the Holy Spirit.

2. Are you ready to throw out your best laid plans? Plan A, B, C, and D didn't work. Are you ready to scrap your plans and come to a place of total surrender to God? Sometimes the greatest obstacles to

---

[297] Ibid.

God's will in our life is our own plans. We were saved by the Spirit of God. Do you think we can be perfected now by the flesh? Stop trying to live the Christian life in your own power. Find rest and surrender in Christ. Stop trying to change your marriage and start serving your spouse. Stop complaining about your job and start serving the lost at your workplace. Stop looking at the greener grass in everyone else's life, and water your own grass.

3. Are you ready to launch out into a new ministry? Spring is coming. So many opportunities are going to be opening up here at Living Hope. We are planning on evangelism teams once the weather gets nicer. It may include door to door evangelism and street preaching. It will also include a lot of praying for the lost. We want to reach them at the murder mill abortion centers. We have plans to go into the city of Chicago, and partner with a church there, sharing the gospel on the street corners. We want to reach people wherever they are: in the streets and in their own homes. Are you ready? You don't have to preach. You can sing and bring people around to hear good gospel singing. You can pray. Every one of us can go to these places as a team and pray. We are all qualified for that. But are you willing to get uncomfortable and launch out into new evangelistic ministry?

Conclusion

Whatever your plans are, you need to submit them to God. You need to surrender your life and your plans to Jesus Christ. All your best programs and ideas cannot draw people to Christ. But we need to be in a place where God can use us, stirring up the flames of our lives in service to Christ.

There is a common saying, "If you want to make God laugh, tell him your plans!" Years ago, I met a young former Muslim man named Ahmed. My friend had introduced us. I told them, "Don't trust him just because he says he's a Christian. Muslims are allowed to lie. He probably wants to blow our church up!" How little faith I had. I had never ever thought about ministry to Muslim peoples. Most that I knew who wanted to reach Muslims sold all they had and started a business of sorts to be among them and reach them. Little did I know that God was going to open up an entirely new ministry of church planting, and this young man, Dr. Ahmed, would be like an Arabian Saul of Tarsus. Now there are seven church plants among Arabic speaking peoples that our church supports!

You never know what God is going to do. There are so many Lydias and Ahmeds out there that he wants to send you way. The best thing you can do is be tender to the voice of the Holy Spirit and be ready to throw out any of your best plans for the plans of the God who is building his church.

27 | ACTS 16:16-40
JAIL HOUSE CHURCH PLANT

Then he brought them out and said, "Sirs, what must I do to be saved?" And they said, "Believe in the Lord Jesus, and you will be saved, you and your household." And they spoke the word of the Lord to him and to all who were in his house.
ACTS 16:30-32

As a child, my wife was very much into aviation. She still has books all about planes and jets. She knows a lot about planes. She told me that you can really feel powerless in an airplane when an engine stalls. You feel like you want to climb higher, but actually what you have to do in that moment of powerlessness when your engine has failed is you have to plunge downward. That's counterintuitive. It's frightening. It feels like you are going to crash. But what happens when you get low with your plane is it catches the wind that reboots the engine. That's how God works. When we feel powerless and low, the wind of the Spirit is able to lift us up to heights unimaginable.

Imagine the apostle Paul as he's had a vision of the first church plant in Europe. God tells him and his team to go! They obey. And bam! They're in jail. How do you plant a church when you are in jail? That's an interesting question that we are going to answer in our passage where we learn of Paul and Silas in jail, planting the church of the Philippians. Philippi is the first church plant of Europe. It's Paul's second missionary journey. Remember his first missionary journey is to Galatia primarily. His second is to Eastern Europe. The first church that is planted by the new missionary team is in Philippi. Their initial headquarters is a jail cell.

THE PEOPLE GOD SAVES (16:12-24)

In the Jewish Mishnah (collection of Jewish history and traditions) it is said that a Jewish man would thank God daily for three things: that he was not a woman, a slave, or a Gentile. That's interesting because that was the founding group for the Philippian church.

Lydia the Fashionista

If we look to Acts 16, Lydia we find is from Thyatira, but has a home in Philippi. She's a rich woman. She has a booming business in selling purple fabric for clothing. A "seller of purple" (Acts 16:14) meant Lydia sold purple clothes or cloth. At the time, such clothes were so expensive they were only worn by royalty and the rich. Let's read about her. They came to a city, it says in Acts 16:12, named...

> **Acts 16:12-15** | Philippi, which is a leading city of the district of Macedonia and a Roman colony. We remained in this city some days. [13] And on the Sabbath day we went outside the gate to the riverside, where we supposed there was a place of prayer, and we sat down and spoke to the women who had come together. [14] One who heard us was a woman named Lydia, from the city of Thyatira, a seller of purple goods, who was a worshiper of God. The Lord opened her heart to pay attention to what was said by Paul. [15] And after she was baptized, and her household as well, she urged us, saying, "If you have judged me to be faithful to the Lord, come to my house and stay." And she prevailed upon us.

Thyatira and Philippi are cities with booming economies. Lydia then is basically a Greek fashionista, CEO, on top of some fashion empire. Today we might say she has a house in Chicago and in Paris. She's a serious mover in her world. Isn't it wonderful that God can humble someone like Lydia? She's what the Bible calls a "God-fearer." Here's what that means. She's rejected paganism and polytheism. She does not believe that there are dozens of gods: god of the wind, the rain, the purple cloth; god of the sea, god of the fashion world... She's come to believe there is only one God ruling the universe. So a God-fearer is that she is a monotheist. She's in the synagogue. She's listening to the teaching of the Jews. She's trying to live a moral life. I want you to see how God goes after her. She is an intellect. She is a seeker. She understands the law, and she knows the Torah. She knows she needs forgiveness. She knows she needs a blood sacrifice. She needs atonement. She needs to be justified before God. But she's confused.

Enter Paul. He enters into what is basically a women's Bible study and pauses the Nancy Leigh DeMoss app and begins to teach them. Paul basically connects the dots for them. God opens her eyes. Lydia is a thinker. She's an intellect. She's a God fearer. She is listening to the word of God, and she experiences the wisdom of God when God opens her eyes. After her conversion, she "constrained" the missionaries to use this house as a base of operations, so it must have been much larger than needed. Her home in Philippi became the place where the new church met (16:40).

The Slave Girl

Here in Acts 16, we are also introduced to a slave girl. She's manic. She's mental. She's possessed by a demon. She's making tons of money for her handlers. She's following Paul and Silas and Luke around, causing trouble. She's interrupting and screaming speaking of Paul and his Savior Jesus. That sounds good, but it's not. She's screaming and causing a scene for them. This is an evil spirit that has her tongue. Let's read about her.

> **Acts 16:16-18** | As we were going to the place of prayer, we were met by a slave girl who had a spirit of divination and brought her owners much gain by fortune-telling. **17** She followed Paul and us, crying out, "These men are servants of the Most High God, who proclaim to you the way of salvation." **18** And this she kept doing for many days. Paul, having become greatly annoyed, turned and said to the spirit, "I command you in the name of Jesus Christ to come out of her." And it came out that very hour.

Here we have one of many "we" passages in the book of Acts. Luke says, "we" went to "the place of prayer." Silas and Paul—Timothy and Luke—all went to the synagogue. Suddenly the author of the book includes himself in the narrative; he is no longer just a recorder of what was taking place but is himself one who participates. Luke enters into the entourage at this point.

The slave girl had the spirit of divination. That is, she was involved in sorcery and fortune-telling. She was so good at it that she made them a lot of money. Anytime you see this, understand this is driven by demons. She's not merely a huckster, but she is dealing with the demonic, giving shockingly accurate predictions of the future, and this slave girl would sell her predictions.[298]

So popular was this slave girl would have been consulted by statesmen and ambassadors alike. Controlled by whatever strange force of evil, she was in much demand by men and women wanting to peer into the future.[299]

It's interesting how the Scripture says that Paul was "greatly annoyed" (16:18). He had a holy annoyance. Don't misunderstand. Paul is a man filled with the Holy Spirit. He knows what this girl needs. He is annoyed that this girl is under the power of the wicked one. She needs to experience the power of the gospel not merely through wisdom, which she knew and had been spouting off about. Mere knowledge was not enough to convert this girl. She needed to experience Christ as the power of God. So, Paul commands the demon to come out of her. There's an implication in the text that the gospel is being preached. This girl was beyond just assessing the facts of the gospel. She was demonized. Preaching the gospel is the greatest way to relieve the lost of demonization and demon harassment. There's convert number two. The slave girl is converted through the power of God, just like Lydia.

This conversion eventually causes a riot, because the gospel has major economic consequences for the city of Philippi. Even though Paul is a Roman citizen, he is thrown into prison with Silas. It seems Luke and Timothy are in Philippi, but they are not arrested.

> **Acts 16:19-22** | But when her owners saw that their hope of gain was gone, they seized Paul and Silas and dragged them into the marketplace before the rulers. **20** And when they had brought them to the magistrates, they said, "These men are Jews, and they are disturbing our city. **21** They advocate customs that are not lawful for us as Romans to accept or practice." **22** The crowd joined in

---

[298] Sproul, *Acts*, 294.
[299] Pollock, *The Apostle*, 127.

attacking them, and the magistrates tore the garments off them and gave orders to beat them with rods.

Now it looks like their ministry in Philippi was over. This is about the time that we would write home and let everyone know that we are done with missionary work. We are done with ministry. I mean we can only take so much, right? No, it is here that God says, now that you are in chains Paul and Silas, now that you can do nothing, I'm going to really build this church in Philippi. You see that jailer? He's convert number 3.

The Philippian Jailer

Acts 16:23-24 | And when they had inflicted many blows upon them, they threw them into prison, ordering the jailer to keep them safely. ²⁴ Having received this order, he put them into the inner prison and fastened their feet in the stocks.

So here we have an introduction to our ex-Roman military Philippian jailer. He's likely a GI, a Roman soldier that is now a warden. He's a tough guy. We know that because he's supposed to keep Paul and Silas safe, but he tortures them.

Not only does he beat them, but he puts them in stocks. Now when we modern people think of stocks, we think of the 1700s when a person would have their hands and their head restrained by stocks. The Roman practice of stocks was not nearly as kind. Stocks in Roman practice was a form of torture in the prisoners would be shackled to the wall in painful positions.

This jailer is not just keeping them safe. He's torturing them. He's going above and beyond in making sure they never want to cause a problem in Philippi again. But something happens. The Philippian jailer comes to know the Lord. God delivers them, and the Philippians jailer and his whole family come to know the Lord.

THE POWER OF GOD IN SALVATION (16:19-34)

Let's slow down for a moment and look at all this in slow motion. I want us to see how and when God works salvation here. He saves the Philippian jailer when Paul and Silas are chained up. Paul and Silas are absolutely powerless. This is when God does his most glorious work!

Power Despite Persecution

When we have our church planting classes in Seminary, there is not usually a section on persecution. Usually, you need a good location and a lot of good advertisement. Paul and Silas had none of these advantages. Instead, their second convert in Philippi, the slave girl, caused them to be arrested, since the girl's owners had lost a major source of income when she came to know the Lord Jesus Christ. In turn, they took their anger out on Paul and Silas. They charged them with disrupting the peace.

> **Acts 16:19-24** | But when her owners saw that their hope of gain was gone, they seized Paul and Silas and dragged them into the marketplace before the rulers. [20] And when they had brought them to the magistrates, they said, "These men are Jews, and they are disturbing our city. [21] They advocate customs that are not lawful for us as Romans to accept or practice." [22] The crowd joined in attacking them, and the magistrates tore the garments off them and gave orders to beat them with rods. [23] And when they had inflicted many blows upon them, they threw them into prison, ordering the jailer to keep them safely. [24] Having received this order, he put them into the inner prison and fastened their feet in the stocks.

After "many blows" had been inflicted on them, Paul and Silas were thrown into prison where their feet were secured in stocks. Roman stocks had several holes so that, if desired, the legs could be widely separated, adding to the torture. These were "a horrible instrument," explains Gustav Stählin, "in which the prisoners' legs could be divaricated as widely as desired, in such a way as to prevent sleeping."[300]

Philippi was an excruciating trial for Paul. We look at him as if he's superhuman. Paul has the same nerve endings as you do. It was hard! He writes about these difficulties later to the Thessalonians.

> *1 Thessalonians 2:1-2* | For you yourselves know, brothers, that our coming to you was not in vain. [2] But though we had already suffered and been shamefully treated at Philippi, as you know, we had

---

[300] Gustav Stählin, ed. Otto Böcher and Klaus Haacker. "Haustafel" in *Verborum Veritas: Festschrift for Gustav Stählin's 70th Birthday* (Wuppertal: Brockhaus, 1970), 239-240.

boldness in our God to declare to you the gospel of God in the midst of much conflict.

Not only were such floggings dreadful punishments, pushing human endurance to the limit but, in the case of Paul and Silas, they were also against the law in their case. Why? Roman laws established that no Roman citizen could be beaten. Both Paul and Silas had Roman citizenship.

The torture and beatings he endured at Philippi were hard for Paul, but it didn't stop him. You see persecution doesn't hold back the power of God. God's power was seen in Paul's boldness to the Philippians.

So, in the middle of the night, prevented from sleeping because of the painful stocks, and their backs no doubt covered with painful wounds, Paul and Silas began praying and singing hymns to God.

The Power of Praise

Notice they did not give up. They were not trusting in human acumen and their well laid plans to convert the Philippian people. God could do just as much work or more when they were imprisoned and tortured as when they were free.

Paul and Silas were not complaining and fussing about all they had to endure for the Lord's work. They counted it a privilege to suffer for Christ. They were so honored, they began singing. And this is when God's most glorious work is done!

> **Acts 16:25-26** | About midnight Paul and Silas were praying and singing hymns to God, and the prisoners were listening to them, **26** and suddenly there was a great earthquake, so that the foundations of the prison were shaken. And immediately all the doors were opened, and everyone's bonds were unfastened.

This is what we call revival! Their singing causes a natural disaster that breaks everyone free. When you are in pain, the midnight hour is not the easiest time for a sacred concert, but God gives "songs in the night" (Job 35:10; *cf* Psa 42:8).[301] Notice the other prisoners were listening to them pray and praise God (16:25). Most importantly, God was listening, and he sends an earthquake to shake the foundations of the prison, so much so that all the doors of the prison were opened!

---

[301] Wiersbe, *The Bible Exposition Commentary*, vol. 1, 468.

Saints, if this teaches us nothing else, there is power in praise. No matter what your situation, you can praise the Lord. If you are hurting and in pain, praise the Lord. We have something that no one else has. We have a God that works all things together for our good to those who love him! Praise him! Love him! See the walls come down!

Have you ever felt powerless? I can remember as I watched my daughter Kristen, then 16 years old, slipping away from this world. I didn't know it, but she had an allergic reaction, and her tongue was swelling; her throat was closing. I called 9-1-1. No matter what I said to the operator, she couldn't make the paramedics get to my house fast enough. I tried to demonstrate hope to my daughter, but there was a moment when I began to say goodbye. Forever. There are no words to describe what it is like to say goodbye to your 16-year-old daughter. I could do nothing but watch her slip away. Then the paramedics arrived. They used an EpiPen and measured her vitals. They saved the day. I did what I could, which was just about nothing.

When we are powerless, that's when God comes in and saves the day. When we are powerless, he works his greatest wonders. When we have no strength or ability to change our situation, he comes and changes our hearts. That's our great God!

The Power of Providence

The earthquake of praise brings a wonderful gospel preaching opportunity to Paul and Silas. As we are faithful, God will put people in his providential circumstances, so that they see their need for Christ. If you are faithful, he will send them to you! Here comes the jailer, ready to kill himself, and Paul is given an opportunity to preach the gospel.

> **Acts 16:27-28** | When the jailer woke and saw that the prison doors were open, he drew his sword and was about to kill himself, supposing that the prisoners had escaped. **28** But Paul cried with a loud voice, "Do not harm yourself, for we are all here."

Prayer and praise are powerful weapons (2 Chron 20:1–22; Acts 4:23–37). God responds by shaking the foundations of the prison, opening all the doors, and loosening the prisoners' chains. Jesus is the ultimate chain breaker! The prisoners could have fled to freedom, but instead they remained right where they were. For one thing, Paul immediately took command; and, no doubt, the fear of God was on these pagan men. The prisoners must have realized that there was something very special about those two Jewish preachers!

Paul's attention was fixed on the jailer, the man he really wanted to win to Christ. It was a Roman law that if a guard lost a prisoner, he was given the same punishment the prisoner would have received; so there must have been some men in the prison who had committed capital crimes. The jailer would rather commit suicide than face shame and execution. Paul had been in stocks and imprisoned, but now he was free. Truly, it was the jailer who was the prisoner, not Paul; and Paul not only saved the man's life but pointed him to eternal life in Christ.[302]

The man was by now thoroughly under conviction. He had been brought into contact with a quality of life superior to anything he had known. The jailer's first reaction was to bring Paul and Barnabas out where he could get a better look at them. His second reaction was to ask them how he could be saved. A sense of his own personal sinfulness weighed upon him.[303]

The Power of Preaching

No doubt having first made sure the other prisoners were secure, the jailer brought Paul and Silas out into the courtyard. There he asked the question that was burning in his heart.[304]

> **Acts 16:29-30** | And the jailer called for lights and rushed in, and trembling with fear he fell down before Paul and Silas. **30** Then he brought them out and said, "Sirs, what must I do to be saved?"

When people see the power of God on display in your life, they will respond with the beautiful question, "What must I do to be saved?" (16:30). When that question is asked, you had better have the right answer. Paul and Silas definitely had the right answer!

The Preaching of Faith

> **Acts 16:31** | And they said, "Believe in the Lord Jesus, and you will be saved, you and your household."

Do? Why all the doing has been done. Done by Jesus in his immaculate life and atoning death. "Believe!" That was the word now. Stop

---

[302] Wiersbe, ibid.
[303] Phillips, *Exploring Acts*, Ac 16:30–31.
[304] MacArthur, *Acts*, vol. 2, 108.

doing and start trusting! Hallelujah, salvation is by grace alone, through faith alone, in Christ alone! "Believe in the Lord Jesus." What does that mean? It means to trust him. *Believe*: not in a creed but in the Christ, not in a statement of faith, not in baptism, not in good works, not in a ritual—but believe in the Lord Jesus Christ, in that glorious living, dynamic person who is alive for evermore and is mighty to save. He's the Lord: he's our Master, the Lord God Almighty. His name is Jesus: he became man. He went from the highest position to the lowest, born in a manger as an infant in Bethlehem. He is the Christ: that is, he is the Messiah—the King of kings and Lord of lords. Believe and trust in his lordship and guidance over your entire life. He calls you to come to him, and he will be your God and you will be his child.

What about the other prisoners? Luke doesn't give us the details, but it is possible that some of them were also born again through the witness of Paul and Silas and the jailer. Some of these prisoners may have been waiting for execution, so imagine their joy at hearing a message of salvation![305]

The Preaching to Family

Acts 16:31-32 | And they said, "Believe in the Lord Jesus, and you will be saved, you and your household." **32** And they spoke the word of the Lord to him and to all who were in his house.

Luke records that Paul's words were not just for the Philippian jailer, but for his entire household: his wife, his children, and his servants. Sometimes this is a passage that dear brothers will use to teach infant baptism, that we should baptize our children. Now all Christians believe we should dedicate our children and that children born in believing families have a much greater responsibility to believe, since they are born and raised in the light. But notice the command here is not to baptize, but to believe first, and then there would be salvation.

The emphasis here is found verse 32, that Paul and Silas "spoke the word of the Lord" to the whole family. We don't baptize anyone until they have a sound understanding of salvation. They must entrust their lives to Christ as Lord and Savior first, and then be baptized.

The weight of this passage has to do with believing. We have hope if our children have faith in Christ. The gospel is not just for fathers and

---

[305] Wiersbe, *The Bible Exposition Commentary*, vol. 1, 469.

mothers, but for children and all we come into contact with. The greatest missionaries in the world are missionary mom and dad.

The Power of Provision

Now that they believed, they showed immediate fruit.

The Provision of Relationship

Acts 16:33a | And he took them the same hour of the night and washed their wounds.

It is touching to see the radical change in the attitude of the jailer as he washed the wounds of these two prisoners who were now his brothers in Christ. The walls of hostility come down when we come in faith to Christ. Those who were once enemies are now part of God's forever family, and as family we treat one another with tenderness and love.

The Provision of Membership

Acts 16:33b | And he was baptized at once, he and all his family.

What a joy that with baptism they are added to the new church at Philippi. We later find out that they will be meeting in Lydia's living room for church. When they believed they realized that they were members of God's forever family. They wanted to go public with their faith in Jesus Christ. So they went and found a baptistry. It wouldn't have been hard.

You may ask, where would they have been baptized? Remember earlier Paul and his missionary team had gone to the "place of prayer," that is, the synagogue. Outside most synagogues would be a *mikveh*, or what we would call a baptistry. A mikveh would have "living" or running water coming from a spring below. There were usually a number of mikvehs outside of each synagogue. Even today, if you visit an ancient synagogue or even the Temple itself in Jerusalem, there are mikvehs with running water from natural springs below. When I visited the synagogue at Magdala in Galilee they found dozens of mikvehs which had been buried for almost 2000 years from a mudslide that occurred in A.D. 70. When they uncovered them, because they are connected to underground springs, they started running again. In fact, they are still running to this very day. We don't know exactly where Lydia would have been baptized, but it could have been a mikveh. Another place would be the rivers that ran around Philippi (Strymon and Nestos Rivers). Today there is a memorial site near a river attributed to Lydia's baptism, though we cannot be sure.

So they went over and baptized the whole family, the Philippian jailer and his wife, the kids, and the servants. They all put their faith in the Lord Jesus Christ. Wow!

The Provision of Discipleship

> **Acts 16:34** | Then he brought them up into his house and set food before them. And he rejoiced along with his entire household that he had believed in God.

Then they went back to the jailer's home, surely a very nice home as a retired Roman soldier, and they had a nice meal, all rejoicing that the Philippian jailer had the courage to put his faith in Christ and lead his whole family to Jesus Christ.

Discipleship begins immediately with fellowship. They start praising God and edifying each other. The home is the best place for discipleship.

THE PROVIDENCE OF GOD IN SALVATION (16:35-40)

Now that all of this has happened, how do you build the church of Philippi when you were already charged with disturbing the peace and the day before you had caused a riot in the city center of Philippi? What's going to happen? Remember no matter what is happening, God is in control. We see his providence in every circumstance. God is sovereignly guiding all things for his glory and your good.

Rulers in God's Providence

What happens with the rulers and magistrates that arrested Paul and Silas? It looks like, in God's providence, that night they had a change of heart, and in the morning, they decide to drop all charges against Paul and his missionary companion Silas.

> **Acts 16:35-36** | But when it was day, the magistrates sent the police, saying, "Let those men go." **36** And the jailer reported these words to Paul, saying, "The magistrates have sent to let you go. Therefore come out now and go in peace."

The city officials knew that they had no convincing case against Paul and Silas, so they sent word to the jailer to release them.

Rights in God's Providence

Not everyone was a Roman citizen, but Paul and Silas were. Not everyone is a U.S. citizen today, but you likely are. And so Paul and Silas used their rights as Roman citizens to protect the new fledgling church.

> **Acts 16:37-39** | But Paul said to them, "They have beaten us publicly, uncondemned, men who are Roman citizens, and have thrown us into prison; and do they now throw us out secretly? No! Let them come themselves and take us out." **38** The police reported these words to the magistrates, and they were afraid when they heard that they were Roman citizens. **39** So they came and apologized to them. And they took them out and asked them to leave the city.

Paul was free to go, but he was unwilling to "sneak out of town," for that kind of exit would have left the new church under a cloud of suspicion. People would have asked, "Why did they leave so quickly? What do their followers believe?" Paul and his associates wanted to leave behind a strong witness of their own integrity as well as a good testimony for the infant church in Philippi. It was then that Paul made use of his Roman citizenship and boldly challenged the officials on the legality of their treatment. This was not personal revenge but a desire to give protection and respect for the church.[306]

The only ones actually guilty of breaking the laws of the state are the people and authorities in Philippi. By law, a Roman citizen had a right to trial before being condemned. Here we see Paul acting according to his views concerning civil government (*cf* Rom 13:1–7). He respects governing officials but also calls them to perform their God-given responsibility of doing what is right for those under their rule, reserving punishment for only those who do wrong (Rom 13:4).

Upon hearing of their mistake, the magistrates come personally—as demanded by Paul—to let the prisoners go. They offer apologies and ask them kindly to leave Philippi. Paul declines to take his rights a step further and see the magistrates punished for their injustice to him and Silas.[307] Paul uses his rights as a Roman citizen to protect the church.

We are called to honor our authorities, but we are also called to hold them accountable as citizens of the land. There is a separation of

---

[306] Wiersbe, *The Bible Exposition Commentary*, vol. 1, 469.
[307] Hamilton, *John–Acts*, 496.

church and state. We, as Christ's church, are called in civil matters to submit to government as long as it does not violate God's law, but when it comes to our worship, the state has no authority over the church. The church is the realm where Jesus Christ is our King. There is no competition with his rule.

Resting in God's Providence

All the terrible persecution in Philippi only served to expand the church. Before leaving town, Paul visited his new beloved forever family there in Philippi.

> **Acts 16:40** | So they went out of the prison and visited Lydia. And when they had seen the brothers, they encouraged them and departed.

What a ragtag group: Lydia, the slave girl, and the Philippian jailer and his family. Maybe there were some of the other former prisoners as well. It's not a large church, but we see that they are meeting at Lydia's home. They had to learn what we all must learn. We cannot rest in our circumstances, but we can rest in Christ.

Conclusion

What can we say about this new church plant in Europe? It was all God's doing. The more things went wrong, the more they went right! God sits in the heavens and laughs at man's attempt to stop the gospel from going forth. When they beat Paul and Silas, they sing. When they are imprisoned, God sends an earthquake and opens the door. When they have no power to bring the gospel to anyone since they are chained and shackled, God sets them free and adds the jailer of the prison to the member roll of the saints and gives him and his whole family a new heart and life in Christ. The more things go wrong, the more God works. God's power is perfected in our weakness!

My first car was a 1989 Oldsmobile Cutlass Supreme. It was a diesel. I didn't own it very long. I knew the engine was gone when nothing, but pure white smoke was coming out of the tailpipe. It was dead. Good for nothing. A friend of mine bought the car from me for a few hundred bucks. In a few weeks he had put a new engine in it, and it ran like new. Regeneration is like that new engine. I know nothing about putting in a new engine, but my mechanic friend did. God is the great mechanic. When we were dead, but God put new life into us! God is the great mechanic. When we can do nothing, God can do it all.

God's the only one that can take the dead and make dead sinners alive. We can be bound in a prison like Paul, or we can have all the bells and whistles of modern society. We are equally powerless to bring about the work of God. God has to do it. All we can do is be ready and surrendered. If you are weak and sense your inability to do anything for the Lord, you are in a good place. The more weak we are, the more obvious God's power is. Rest in him. Surrender to him, and he will lift you up as his instrument.

28 | ACTS 17:1-15
TURNING THE WORLD UPSIDE DOWN

> *They dragged Jason and some of the brothers before the city authorities, shouting, "These men who have turned the world upside down have come here also."*
> ACTS 17:6

The General Secretary of the Bible Society in Zimbabwe, tried to give a New Testament to a very belligerent man. The man insisted he would roll the pages and use them to make cigarettes. Mr. Kambarami, the General Secretary said, "I understand that, but at least promise to read the page of the New Testament before you smoke it." The man agreed, and the two went their separate ways.

Fifteen years later, the two men met at a convention in Zimbabwe. The Scripture-smoking pagan had given his life to Christ and was now a full-time evangelist. He told the audience, "I smoked Matthew, and I smoked Mark, and I smoked Luke. But when I got to John 3:16, I couldn't smoke anymore. My life was changed from that moment." Aren't you glad God's word is more than just words on paper? It's the living, breathing, life-transforming, powerful word of God.

Hebrews 4:12 | For the word of God is living and active, sharper than any two-edged sword, piercing to the division of soul and of spirit, of joints and of marrow, and discerning the thoughts and intentions of the heart.

The expansion of God's kingdom comes through the power of the word of God. Sometimes as Christians, we dream of our church growing and expanding, not just in our character and in our hearts and lives, but also numerically in evangelism and influence in our culture. I've seen some really crazy ideas that churches have adopted that make them look more like a circus than a house of worship. Indeed, so many pastors are entertaining the goats instead of feeding the sheep. We are called to feed the sheep with God's word.

We have been learning that God will build his church (Mt 16:18; Psa 127:1). Paul was in a jail cell when the foundation of the church of Philippi was put in place. What you could not stop Paul from doing was expositing the word of God and demonstrating who Jesus was. It is the word of God by the Spirit of God that draws and transfers people from the kingdom of darkness to the kingdom of God's Son.

In Paul's day, people of many cultures would examine these things, and the Holy Spirit would open the eyes of people to expand and advance Christ's kingdom one soul at a time. As simple as that may sound, that's what turns the world upside down. It's what radically ripped the fabric out of paganism in Paul's day, and it what has expanded God's kingdom every day since.

> Key thought: God's word is sufficient! Let us be done with the pragmatism of manufacturing false converts but instead boldly preach God's word, drawing hell bound sinners to be heaven transformed saints.

THE PREACHING OF THE WORD IN THESSALONICA (17:1-9)

We start Acts 17 with Paul leaving Philippi after an apology from the government officials for beating and imprisoning Paul and Silas who were both Roman citizens. They see the church of Philippi established in Lydia's living room. It continues to grow year after year so that by the third and fourth centuries there were many churches in Philippi. Paul later writes of how impoverished the churches of Macedonia were. Lydia's help only went so far, but even though they were the poorest of all the churches, they were the most generous. How does a little tiny church grow with such amazing influence over a pagan culture? They were faithful to exposit the word and preach the gospel.

Faithfulness to the Gospel

Paul moved on from Philippi and went to a beautiful and influential port city with a large population of Jews. Remember, though a number of Jews are coming to know Christ, many other Jews are opposing the gospel ministry of Paul. Thessalonica is going to cause Paul a lot of trouble, but he's not afraid. He knows God's word is powerful to save.

> **Acts 17:1** | Now when they had passed through Amphipolis and Apollonia, they came to Thessalonica, where there was a synagogue of the Jews.

This was at least a three-day journey of about 100 miles from Philippi. When they arrived, they found a thriving city of about 20,000.[308] Thessalonica was the capital city of Macedonia. It is to this day a beautiful port city set on the Aegean Sea with a direct view of the famous Mount Olympus. They were a self-governing city which retained their Greek culture. There was also a significant Jewish population that thrived in that city until the time of World War II, when they were sadly shipped to Germany and put to death. But when Paul arrived at Thessalonica, the Jewish population was strong.

Despite the treatment Paul and his companions receive, we know that the gospel takes a firm hold in the city, based on Paul's writings in 1 Thessalonians. This epistle also reveals that the majority of believers in Thessalonica were Gentiles. Paul commends how they "turned to God from idols to serve the living and true God" (1 Thess 1:9). Luke does record that some Jews and many God-fearers believed as well (17:4).[309] We find out that they start their church planting effort in the synagogue in Thessalonica during three Sabbath days.

> **Acts 17:2-3** | And Paul went in, as was his custom, and on three Sabbath days he reasoned with them from the Scriptures, ³ explaining and proving that it was necessary for the Christ to suffer and to rise from the dead, and saying, "This Jesus, whom I proclaim to you, is the Christ."

Paul would take the Scriptures of the Old Testament, since that's mainly what they had at the time, and he would preach Jesus.

---

[308] Hughes, *Acts: The Church Afire*, 222.
[309] Hamilton, *John–Acts*, 498.

Remember Jesus did this in Luke 24. How did Paul preach? Paul's public ministry was three-pronged in Thessalonica.

Teaching Hearts

Acts 17:2 | And Paul went in, as was his custom, and on three Sabbath days he reasoned with them from the Scriptures.

First, he "reasoned with them from the Scriptures." The word translated "reasoned" is the root for our English word dialogue. Paul talked through the Scriptures regarding Jesus. There was exchange, questions, and answers. He dialogued with them "from the Scriptures." They would together take up the vellum and parchment copies of the popular Greek Septuagint, and Paul would select a passage and read through it, opening the floor for a give and take.

Opening Eyes

Acts 17:3a | And Paul went in... explaining...

Further, there was "explaining. This word literally means "opening." This is a very strong word, Luke used it to describe the opening of the womb in Luke 2:23 and in the 24th chapter for the opening of spiritual eyes on the road to Emmaus.[310]

> *Luke 24:31-32* | And their eyes were **opened**, and they recognized him. And he vanished from their sight. ³² They said to each other, "Did not our hearts burn within us while he talked to us on the road, while he **opened** to us the Scriptures?"

Paul was very simple and plain when it came to dialoging about the Scriptures. He read it, talked about it, and answered questions from the Scriptures, letting the Holy Spirit open the eyes of the blind. No flourishes or scams were needed.

Proving the Gospel

Acts 17:3 | And Paul went in... explaining and proving that it was necessary for the Christ to suffer and to rise from the dead, and saying, "This Jesus, whom I proclaim to you, is the Christ."

The third prong of his method is stated as proving, or literally "giving evidence" from the Scriptures that Christ needed to die and rise

---

[310] Hughes, *Acts*, 222.

again. It means he gave Scriptural evidence from throughout the Old Testament. Paul would prove his case, leading his hearers to a particular verdict. The message was that the Messiah had to suffer. No doubt Paul took them to many Scriptures, including Psalm 22 and Isaiah 53.[311]

> *Isaiah 53:5* | But he was pierced for our transgressions, he was crushed for our iniquities; the punishment that brought us peace was upon him, and by his wounds we are healed.

He proved Christ's resurrection to them as well. He gave them Scriptural evidence. I can hear Paul in Hosea 6:2 telling them, "After two days he will revive Christ, the true Israel, and on the third day he will raise him up." To be able to do this, Paul had to be committed to the word of God. Remember, Paul didn't just study his Bible all day. He often had to work at tentmaking and whatever else just to make ends meet. But he studied the word of God. If you want to see the gospel expanding, you need to be a studier of God's word. You've got to spend time in the word diligently, day and night (Psa 1:2).

Are you faithful to the gospel, seeing Christ on every page of the Bible, walking with him in your own personal life on a daily basis? Are you coming to the gatherings and listening to the truth proclaimed as often as is humanly possible? Are you faithful? Remember the words of Dwight L. Moody, founder of the Moody Bible Institute.

> Either the word of God is going to keep you from sin, or sin will keep you from the word.—D.L. Moody

Faith in the Gospel

Luke reports that Paul's scriptural arguments with the Spirit's influence were enough to win over many of his hearers. There was a healthy response to the faithful teaching of God's word.

> **Acts 17:4** | And some of them were persuaded and joined Paul and Silas, as did a great many of the devout Greeks and not a few of the leading women.

The devout Greeks were the men and women who had not been circumcised but they were faithful to the synagogue. They are born again. It's inferred here that the persuasion that occurs is brought

---

[311] Hughes, ibid, 223.

about by the Spirit of God applying the word of God. Faith is engendered by the word of God.

> *Romans 10:17* | Faith comes from hearing, and hearing through the word of Christ.

> *James 1:18* | Of his own will he brought us forth by the word of truth.

There is no other way to bring a person to faith in Christ but by the powerful word of God. You must tell them the truth from God's word about themselves, that they are sinners—about God, that he is holy and demands justice—and about God's mercy, that he sent his only Son to die for our sins and rise again for our justification. Paul said, "I am not ashamed of the gospel, for it is the power of God for salvation to everyone who believes" (Rom 1:16). God can open the eyes of an individual like Lydia, or he can open the eyes of a great number as here in Thessalonica.

As a result of the faithful preaching of the gospel, a few Jews believed, along with an impressive number of God-seeking Greeks, including a number of prominent women. A spiritual foundation was beginning to form in Thessalonica.[312] But these results did not bring joy to everybody. The unbelieving Jews envied Paul's success and were grieved to see the Gentiles and the influential women leaving the synagogue. Paul hoped that the salvation of the Gentiles would "provoke" the Jews into studying the Scriptures and discovering their promised Messiah (Rom 11:13–14), but in this case, it only provoked them into persecuting the infant church.[313]

Factions Because of the Gospel

What we see now are the lengths that Satan is willing to go to in order to discourage and hold back the gospel. The religious people go and recruit a mob of what one translator renders "bums" or as the ESV says, "rabble." Whatever you call this mob, it looks like it's getting interesting in Thessalonica.

> **Acts 17:5** | But the Jews were jealous, and taking some wicked men of the rabble, they formed a mob, set the city in an uproar, and

---

[312] Hughes, *Acts: The Church Afire*, 224.
[313] Wiersbe, *The Bible Exposition Commentary*, vol. 1, 470.

attacked the house of Jason, seeking to bring them out to the crowd.

This was "rent-a-mob" justice.[314] Since Thessalonica was a free city, it had a popular tribunal (17:6), a panel of judges before whom charges could be laid. The Jews attempted to bring Paul and Silas before this panel of city authorities.[315] They did this by causing a riot so that their charges of "disturbing the peace" would stick to Paul and Silas. It's likely that Jason gave Paul and Silas work and housing while they were in Thessalonica and was eventually converted by the missionaries. In any event, the crowd did not find the missionaries at Jason's. Possibly they had learned of the riot and had fled elsewhere.[316] The house of Jason was attacked. Mob justice is always unpredictable, emotionally charged and filled with all manner of prejudices expressed in violent outbursts.

A similar incident comes from the Great Awakening, in the preaching of John and Charles Wesley in early summer 1743. John Wesley was making his way from Walsall to Wednesbury, and his biographer gives the following account. It begins with a graphic description of Wesley's physical suffering:

> Some tried to seize him by the collar and pull him down. A big, lusty fellow just behind him struck at him several times with an oaken club. If one of these blows had taken effect, as Wesley says, "it would have saved all further trouble. But every time the blow was turned aside, I know not how, for I could not move to the right hand or left." Another, rushing through the crowd, lifted his arm to strike, but on a sudden let it drop and only stroked Wesley's head, saying, "What soft hair he has!" One man struck him on the breast, and another on the mouth with such force that the blood gushed out; but he felt no more pain, he affirms, from either than if they had touched him with a straw; not, certainly, because he was over excited or alarmed, for he assures us that from the beginning to the end he was enabled to maintain as much presence of mind as if he had been sitting in his study, but his

---

[314] Thomas, *Acts*, 482.
[315] Marshall, *Acts*, 294.
[316] Polhill, *Acts*, 361.

thoughts were entirely absorbed in watching the movements of the rioters.[317] —from the book, "John Wesley, Evangelist"

What Wesley experienced is an example of what the early apostles encountered when they preached the gospel. There is no guarantee that such scenes will not be witnessed in our own time as, indeed, they are in some parts of the world today. There is a cost to being faithful to Jesus Christ.[318]

Fruitfulness in the Gospel

What was the accusation that was leveled against Paul and his missionary team? They were guilty of "turning the world upside down."

> **Acts 17:6** | And when they could not find them, they dragged Jason and some of the brothers before the city authorities, shouting, "These men who have turned the world upside down have come here also."

Paul and Silas were accused of changing the culture and way of life for the ancient world. They couldn't find Paul and Silas, so they arrested Jason and dragged him before the city magistrates in Thessalonica. They charged the Christian missionaries with preaching political rebellion. They knew their charge to be a lie, and yet it is expressed in terms that were full of significance. They said, "Those who are upsetting the civilized world have arrived here."[319] The gospel was not just turning Thessalonica upside down, but the entire world, and so it is even today. That's the fruitfulness of the gospel. Man tries to do what he can to stop it: creating mobs, instigating persecution, making up lies about God's people—but no one and nothing can stop the advance **of the gospel**. It is and will turn the world upside down.

Falsehood Against the Gospel

The Jewish leaders followed the script of those who crucified Jesus. They got the mob stirred up and then leveled the charges they thought would really get the magistrates irritated: treason. They are setting up another kingdom!

---

[317] Rev. Richard Green, *John Wesley—Evangelist* (London: Religious Tract Society, 1905; Nampa, ID: Northwest Nazarene University, 1999), http://wesley.nnu.edu/john_wesley/methodist/ch12.htm

[318] Thomas, *Acts*, 482-483.

[319] Barclay, *The Acts of the Apostles*, 150.

Acts 17:7 | "And Jason has received them, and they are all acting against the decrees of Caesar, saying that there is another king, Jesus."

The charges were simple enough: disrupting the peace and treason. They had acted contrary to the decree of the Roman emperor by saying that there was another King, named Jesus. The charge of treason, of course, was far more serious and, if substantiated, carried with it the penalty of death.

Paul had urged people to turn away from idols, including the plethora of Roman gods (1 Thess 1:9). Paul's preaching about the second coming (a major feature of his first and second letters to Thessalonica) may well have been construed as suggesting a coming overthrow of the Roman emperor. It would not be difficult for pagans to hear sedition in Christians' talk about Jesus, especially when they heard Christians refer to him as "Lord."[320]

Fleeing Because of the Gospel

Acts 17:8-9 | And the people and the city authorities were disturbed when they heard these things. ⁹ And when they had taken money as security from Jason and the rest, they let them go.

Jason and the others had been forced to post bond for the good behavior of the apostles, and there really was nothing for it but to leave Thessalonica as quickly as possible, lest they be the cause of harm coming to others.

The city is thrown into such confusion that Paul and Silas are forced to leave and go on to Berea (17:10–15). Their departure is so premature, so far as Paul is concerned, that he worries a great deal about the Thessalonian converts until Timothy goes to investigate and returns with a favorable report (1 Thess 2:17–3:10).

1 Thessalonians 2:17 | Since we were torn away from you, brothers, for a short time, in person not in heart, we endeavored the more eagerly and with great desire to see you face to face.

Paul had to flee, but he described it as being "torn away" from the believers there who were so precious to him. In response to this Paul

---

[320] Thomas, *Acts*, 483.

writes the two Thessalonian letters from Corinth.[321] Even though persecution came, the believers there in Thessalonica were examples to all the believers in Europe.

> *1 Thessalonians 1:7-9* | You became an example to all the believers in Macedonia and in Achaia. ⁸For not only has the word of the Lord sounded forth from you in Macedonia and Achaia, but your faith in God has gone forth everywhere, so that we need not say anything. ⁹For they themselves report concerning us the kind of reception we had among you, and how you turned to God from idols to serve the living and true God.

Note very clearly how a church is established. It is founded upon the expository preaching of God's word. This is how we evangelize and disciple people, through the word of God, going through every part of Scripture verse by verse, chapter by chapter, precept by precept.

THE POWER OF THE WORD IN BEREA (17:10-13)

We see a similar trend in Berea as in Thessalonica with the difference being the response of the Jews was not to throw Paul and Silas out. The Berean Jews took to studying God's word in earnest. In this way they were "more noble than those in Thessalonica" (17:11).

Tenderness to God's Word

Being tender to God's word makes all the difference.

> **Acts 17:10-11** | The brothers immediately sent Paul and Silas away by night to Berea, and when they arrived they went into the Jewish synagogue. ¹¹Now these Jews were more noble than those in Thessalonica; they received the word with all eagerness, examining the Scriptures daily to see if these things were so.

The Bereans are called "more noble" mainly because of how their attitude "eagerness" is connected to their practice of daily searching the Scriptures. Their "eagerness" carries the idea of rushing forward. They could not wait to receive God's message! Eagerness makes all the difference in the flavor, quality, and nobility of our Christian lives.[322]

The word of God should be exposited, and hopefully it is in any church you are a part of. But it's not enough for God's people just to

---

[321] Baker, "Acts," in *Evangelical Commentary*, 910.
[322] Hughes, *Acts: The Church Afire*, 226.

listen to the sermons. That wasn't enough for the Bereans. They earnestly studied during the week what Paul had taught them. They examined the word to see if it was really there.

Notice it was their "daily" practice to search the word. They didn't just want a superficial reading, but they wanted to actually walk in the word. In order to change, a believer must have both internal and external influences. We must adopt the thinking of the word in our heart internally, having different thoughts and emotions about hard situations. We must reject the slavery of fear and frustration and adopt the attitude of the Spirit. Externally, the Bereans also came together in the synagogue to talk about what they were learning. They held each other accountable externally for what the Spirit was teaching them internally. It ended with them coming to faith in Christ.

Transformation by God's Word

The word was exposited. The message was earnestly examined and studied daily. God blesses that and grants them faith.

> **Acts 17:12** | Many of them therefore believed, with not a few Greek women of high standing as well as men.

The Jews' response in the Berean synagogue was more encouraging than that in Thessalonica. They were willing to give Paul a ready hearing and to see for themselves if his message was supported by scripture.[323] God's word engenders faith! Preach the word, and people will be converted.

> *1 Peter 1:23* | You have been born again, not of perishable seed but of imperishable, through the living and abiding word of God.

The bottom line is you are powerless to change people's hearts. Only God's word can transform the heart. Like Ezekiel of old, we can only preach to the valley of dry bones. We must prophesy to the wind of deadness, and the wind of God's Spirit will raise the dry bones from the dead and bring his army of regenerate soldiers to life.

Turmoil Because of God's Word

Mark this: whenever you move mountains into the sea, you will face satanic agitation. As fruit increases you will face the foes of hell. So it was in Berea.

---

[323] Bruce, *Acts: Bible Study Commentary*, Ac 17:10–15.

Acts 17:13 | But when the Jews from Thessalonica learned that the word of God was proclaimed by Paul at Berea also, they came there too, agitating and stirring up the crowds.

Evidently this time the main attack was on Paul, the primary preacher of the word (17:13), since Silas and Timothy did not have to leave town with him (17:14).[324] Understand that this turmoil and persecution sets up Paul for another missionary venture, this time to Athens! Silas and Timothy are slated to hold down the fort in Berea, helping the believers there to grow and change.

Don't be worried about the consequences of faithfulness. It usually sets you up for more fruitfulness, even though you will have to suffer some. God will use the suffering to prune you and bring forth more fruit.

THE PREPARATION FOR THE WORD IN ATHENS (17:14-15)

Once more, Paul had to leave a place of rich ministry and break away from dear people he had come to love.[325] But this is just preparation for the next ministry, now to the center of Greek culture: Athens. Never forget that in all your trials and turmoil, God has a perfect plan to expand his kingdom through you.

Just as Jesus taught the 12 and the 70, we are to preach the gospel and leave the results up to the Lord. Each person is responsible to respond. God's word will do the work. The fruit comes from God, so Paul is not paralyzed over the persecution. He's not stewing over the shunning he's getting from the Jews. Paul is the apostle to the Gentiles, and so he ventures to one of the greatest Gentile cities after Rome: the glorious city of Athens. This is where God wants the gospel to expand and advance.

As we see fruit, we will also see foes. But the gospel preaching must always be expanding to more and more people. The Spirit of God uses difficulties in our lives to direct us to the fruit he is preparing.

The Testimony

The new mission field of Athens needed a preacher, and the preacher God chose was the apostle, Paul.

---

[324] Polhill, *Acts*, 364.
[325] Wiersbe, *The Bible Exposition Commentary*, vol. 1, 471.

Acts 17:14 | Then the brothers immediately sent Paul off on his way to the sea, but Silas and Timothy remained there.

Silas and Timothy stayed in Berea but would later join Paul in Athens. This was certainly not Paul's initial plan. He certainly would like to have stayed in Berea longer, but God sends him to a new mission field: Athens.

The Target

Paul didn't know exactly where he was going as he fled from Berea, but the Holy Spirit did.

Acts 17:15a | Those who conducted Paul brought him as far as Athens.

The Spirit was preparing Paul to preach the gospel at Athens. How would he do it? Usually he would find a synagogue, but Athens would be completely different. He went to the city first and later to the synagogue. This in some ways is a new frontier.

The Team

A little after Paul's arrival to Athens, Silas and Timothy join him.

Acts 17:15b | And after receiving a command for Silas and Timothy to come to him as soon as possible, they departed.

How grateful we are that we are not called to be alone in the Christian life. There ought not to often be a solo pastor, but a council of elders. There should always be a plurality of leadership since we are not made to lead the church alone. God will provide the companions of ministry that we need. All these leaders are unsurpassed in their commitment to the word of God. What a team! That's how we operate at our church: word centered. You cannot be God-centered unless you are relentlessly word-centered.

Conclusion

A park ranger at Yellowstone National Park was leading a group of hikers to a fire lookout. The ranger was so intent on telling the hikers about the flowers and animals that he considered the messages on his two-way radio distracting, so he switched it off. As the group neared the tower, the ranger was met by a nearly breathless lookout, who asked why he hadn't responded to the messages on his radio. A grizzly bear had been seen stalking the group, and the authorities were trying to warn them of the danger.

We cannot lead this generation out of danger and into God's salvation without the word of God. You are not going to grow by trying to figure out your problems on your own. You need the word to change you first before it can change the world. The moment we switch off the power of the word in our lives and ministries, we turn off any meaningful ability to help people. May the Lord give us the grace to proclaim the word and see his kingdom expand.

29 | ACTS 17:16-34
MARS HILL EVANGELISM

As I passed along and observed the objects of your worship, I found also an altar with this inscription: 'To the unknown god.' What therefore you worship as unknown, this I proclaim to you. The God who made the world and everything in it, being Lord of heaven and earth, does not live in temples made by man.

ACTS 17:23-24

Salvation is of the Lord. It's all of grace. I've never been able to win anyone to Christ through my charm or good looks. It is true that I do not have beautiful hair. I have a few hairs that are turning grey and some that are turning loose. Nor do I have beautiful teeth, for several of them are really not mine; they were made by the dentist. I do not have a beautiful face, nor can I afford to wear beautiful clothes. Almost everything I am wearing, including my shoes were either given to me or purchased at the secondhand clothing store. But this I know: I have beautiful feet!

> *Isaiah 52:7* | How beautiful upon the mountains are the feet of him that brings good tidings, that publishes peace.

Do you have beautiful feet? When God saved you, he saved you entirely, and that includes your feet. Jesus tells us to "Go into all the world and preach the gospel to every creature" (Mk 16:15, KJV).

As we increasingly move towards paganism in our American culture, the words of Paul in Athens become more and more relevant. Our current culture is becoming more ignorant of the Bible in each generation.

> Key Thought: We must make sure that each of us is equipped to evangelize our present culture that is ignorant of basic biblical concepts such as sin, God, and eternal life.

Paul had this desire to bring the gospel to every creature and culture. The curtain of ignorance about the one true and living God around Greece in Europe did not stop him. We have that curtain surrounding our nation more and more.

How did Paul reach the pagan Athenians? For Paul, it seems this wasn't necessarily one of his primary destinations. But in stopping through Athens on the way to Corinth, he plants a church! How did he do it? First, he began by defending the existence of the one true monotheistic almighty God to a pluralistic, polytheistic city. The crown jewel of Greece: the glorious city of Athens.

DEFENDING THE EXISTENCE OF GOD (17:16-23)

Paul arrives in Athens because he was pushed out of Berea because of persecution. He comes to a moment where he has to defend the existence of God—not that Athens denied the operations of deities, but that was it. They didn't believe in the existence of just one creator God, but of many competing gods. They were by definition, polytheistic, not monotheistic. Despite their ignorance of the one true God, they were still an incredibly accomplished city—a truly legendary city, not only in the ancient world, but until this very day.

Athens in Paul's day was in a period of decline at this time, though still recognized as a center of culture and education. The glory of its politics and commerce had long since faded. It had a famous university and numerous beautiful buildings, but it was not the influential city it once had been. The city was given over to a "cultured paganism" that was nourished by idolatry, novelty (Acts 17:21), and philosophy.[326] In

---

[326] Ibid.

the pinnacle of Greece culture they rebuilt their civilization, creating the first example of a democracy in human history at Athens: a city-state run by elected officials who were responsible to the citizens.

It was an age of democracy. In Athens they had a city-state run by elected officials who were responsible to the citizens. It was an age of amazing architecture. The Parthenon stands in Athens upon the great Acropolis in the very center of the city. It was an age of literature. The classical Greek plays were written at this time, like Prometheus Bound, Oedipus Rex, and the Cyclops. It was an age of philosophy, with Socrates and Plato. It was an age of art. They developed the classical forms of human sculpture that would one day be the chief influence Michelangelo.[327]

Paul, as a Hellenized Jew, Paul had been exposed to Greek culture with its outstanding traditions in art and philosophy. Athens was the center of that culture. In its heyday, several centuries before Christ, it had been the greatest city in the world.[328] Yet for all her greatness, Athens had no place for the true and living God.

In a culture that had no place for the one true God, Paul boldly declared and defended the existence of the monotheistic God in the midst of a fiercely polytheistic culture. He called those ignorant of any theological parameters to faith in God's Son. We are called to do the same. But where does evangelism in this post-modern world begin? For Paul, begins with a burden.

The Burden of Evangelism

> **Acts 17:16** | Now while Paul was waiting for them at Athens, his spirit was provoked within him as he saw that the city was full of idols.

Paul is launched suddenly into the center of the city of Athens. He had not intended to evangelize Athens; he was without helpers and half hoped to return to the Thessalonians, and he needed rest. But as he saw the extraordinary number of idols on every side, he became more and more exasperated.[329] But with Timothy and Silas still in Berea, he was alone in Athens. And a stroll through Athens turns into a unique evangelistic opportunity.

---

[327] Boice, *Acts: An Expositional Commentary*, 294.
[328] MacArthur, *Acts*, vol. 2, 129.
[329] Pollock, *The Apostle*, 147.

Paul saw something that moved him to tears—sights and sounds that portrayed man's fundamental idolatry and rejection of God. The city was "full of idols," and like Calvin, Paul could have said, "That man's nature, so to speak, is a perpetual factory of idols."[330]

Paul had such a heart for people that as he was in Athens, we learn that "his spirit was provoked within him" as he saw the people enslaved to idols. While Paul is in Athens, instead of gaining his co-workers right away, he sent them first to Thessalonica to establish the believers. Remember many of the persecutors that were pursuing Paul in Berea were from that beautiful port city.

> *1 Thessalonians 3:1-3* | Therefore when we could bear it no longer, we were willing to be left behind at Athens alone, ² and we sent Timothy, our brother and God's coworker in the gospel of Christ, to establish and exhort you in your faith, ³ that no one be moved by these afflictions. For you yourselves know that we are destined for this.

It was hard to be alone in Athens. During these times of our lives, we might feel like we need a rest or a break, and Paul had those times, often in the winters. But on this occasion the Spirit of God gave Paul a broken heart for these people so crushed by idols.

Do you have a burden for souls? Proverbs 11:30 tells us, "He who wins souls is wise" (NKJV). Are you wise? Are you a soul winner?

The Places of Evangelism

Paul began dialoguing with anyone who would talk, and he found three groups of hearers: the church people from the synagogue, the everyday pagans, and the sophisticated philosophers called "Epicurean and Stoic philosophers."

The Church

> **Acts 17:17a** | So he reasoned in the synagogue with the Jews and the devout persons.

There is a place for evangelism in the church. Many lost remain in the church—the wheat and the chaff abide together. There is obviously a place to evangelize in the world. This was Paul's pattern: he reasoned in the synagogue as well as in the pagan marketplace.

---

[330] John Calvin, *Institutes of the Christian Religion*, trans. Ford Lewis Battles, 2 vols., Library of Christian Classics 20–21 (Philadelphia: Westminster, 1960), 1.5.8.

The Marketplace

Acts 17:17b-18a | And in the marketplace every day with those who happened to be there. **18a** Some of the Epicurean and Stoic philosophers also conversed with him.

In the marketplace, Paul channeled his emotion into action. Because of his outrage over the Athenians' blasphemy of the Lord God by their idolatry, he was reasoning in the synagogue with the Jews and the God-fearing Gentiles, and in the market place every day with those who happened to be present. Following his normal pattern of ministry, Paul went on the Sabbath to his countrymen.[331]

There were also Epicureans and Stoics. These latter two groups represented the competing philosophies of the day. The Epicureans were the atheists. They believed that everything happens by chance, and death is the end—extinction with no afterlife. They were practical agnostics who believed pleasure is the chief end of man and that a simple lifestyle is the most pleasurable. The Stoics were pantheists, believing that everything is a god and that whatever happened to them was fate. They couldn't change it. It was their destiny.[332]

The Message of Evangelism

What was Paul preaching in the synagogue and in the marketplace? We get a glimpse of Paul in the Athenian marketplace when he meets some of the philosophers there. With all the wisdom of the Athenians, they were ignorant of the one true God, and Paul was going to make that right.

Acts 17:18 | Some of the Epicurean and Stoic philosophers also conversed with him. And some said, "What does this babbler wish to say?" Others said, "He seems to be a preacher of foreign divinities"—because he was preaching Jesus and the resurrection.

Paul's message was Jesus and the resurrection, which includes that he was crucified before he was raised from the dead. Whatever else we may say about Paul's preaching in the Areopagus, he had no qualms at all about preaching Jesus to a people who had never heard of him and who did not know the contents of the Old Testament Scriptures.[333]

---

[331] MacArthur, *Acts*, vol. 2, 130.
[332] Hughes, *Acts: The Church Afire*, 231.
[333] Thomas, *Acts*, 501.

Responses to Evangelism

There are many responses to evangelism. When I begin on a street corner, I will often ask, "Who here is a Christian, unashamed of Jesus? Raise your hand." There is always a positive response from those who love the Lord. We love evangelism! Paul was preaching the gospel of "Jesus and the resurrection" (17:18). Paul got three responses: apathy, cynicism, and curiosity.

Some are Apathetic

> **Acts 17:17a** | So he reasoned in the synagogue with the Jews and the devout persons.

When Paul unburdened himself in the synagogue, some believed, but many seem to be apathetic. Many Jews had written off their Greek neighbors and were content to treat them merely as lucrative customers, but moral and religious blindness were of no concern.

Before we judge the Jews of Paul's day, let us first judge ourselves. We are in the hotbed of materialism. This is the control center of the beast, the very world system right here in America. Satan's greatest opioid for Christians to numb them is our material prosperity. Many of you stand against the kingdom of Satan, and you see yourself as a steward of God. But some are lulled to sleep by the pleasures, fears, and cares of materialism, just like those in Athens. Are you willing to become uncomfortable for the lost? Don't be apathetic.

Some are Cynical

The Athenians may be far too sophisticated to resort to physical violence, but intellectual opposition and ridicule can be just as wearisome; and the Athenians, at least most of them, called the apostle a fool.[334]

> **Acts 17:18** | Some of the Epicurean and Stoic philosophers also conversed with him. And some said, "What does this babbler wish to say?" Others said, "He seems to be a preacher of foreign divinities"—because he was preaching Jesus and the resurrection.

Whether Paul was in the synagogue or in the marketplace, Paul's message did not change. "He was preaching Jesus and the resurrection" (17:18b).

---

[334] Ibid., *Acts*, 500.

The cynical called Paul a "babbler," literally a fool. Socrates had been sentenced to death for teaching strange doctrines, and although Paul was in no danger of hemlock, he might be expelled.

It all sounded like rubbish and possibly dangerous to the pluralistic way of life of such Athenians who troubled to listen. Though speech was free in Athens, there were limits.

Some are Curious

They decided that he must expound his views before the esteemed Court of the Areopagus, which had the right to expel unsuitable philosophers. They approached Paul good-humoredly and invited him to accompany them up the slope of the Acropolis with the great Parthenon. They would come to a small steep rock, called Mars Hill with the Acropolis as a backdrop.[335]

Acts 17:19a | And they took him and brought him to the Areopagus.

Mars Hill, Greece with a view of the Acropolis with the Parthenon

---

[335] Pollock, *The Apostle*, 149-150.

Years before, Socrates had been "brought" before this court, charged with "impiety"—a court that found him guilty of "corrupting the youth" and ordered that he be put to death by drinking the cup mixed with hemlock. They question him about his "strange" teaching, as they call it.

> **Acts 17:19-20** | And they took him and brought him to the Areopagus, saying, "May we know what this new teaching is that you are presenting? [20] For you bring some strange things to our ears. We wish to know therefore what these things mean."

What does the apostle say? It is a masterly blend of reason and rhetoric. He is addressing the intellectual elite—a bit like being asked to give a lecture before the faculty of Harvard or Yale or, in England, Oxford or Cambridge.[336] They had one thing in common: they are curious.

> **Acts 17:21** | Now all the Athenians and the foreigners who lived there would spend their time in nothing except telling or hearing something new.

The Lord in his providence will bring people together for various reasons, but it is by his sovereign grace that melt the hearts of the hearers. We need to take the opportunity to always "give an answer."

> *1 Peter 3:15* | In your hearts honor Christ the Lord as holy, always being prepared to make a defense to anyone who asks you for a reason for the hope that is in you; yet do it with gentleness and respect.

The Athenian mind-set was always in pursuit of the *nouveau*, the dazzling, the sensational, the whims of the hour. So now the crowd brought Paul before the Areopagus—the Council of Athens at Mars Hill. Immediately before him sat the most exclusive philosophical review board in the world! What a face-off! On one side stood Paul—divinely empowered, a man who had staked everything he had on his message. On the other side stood the Areopagus—sophisticated but indifferent.[337]

The Council of the Areopagus was responsible to watch over both religion and education in the city, so it was natural for them to investigate the "new doctrine" Paul was teaching. They courteously invited

---

[336] Thomas, *Acts*, 501.
[337] Hughes, *Acts: The Church Afire*, 232.

Paul to present his doctrine at what appears to have been an informal meeting of the council on Mars' Hill. Paul was not on trial; the council members only wanted him to explain what he had been telling the people.[338]

Methods of Evangelism

We reject clever marketing of the gospel or the peddling of it through tricks. We also believe you have to meet people where they are. Paul believed this and Jesus demonstrated this. Jesus used the illustration of "living water" for the woman at the well, and Paul uses the illustration of "the unknown god" to a group of mainly polytheists.

Paul was Observant

Paul was careful and observant as he went about his task of evangelism. These are precious people in God's sight. He observes that they are very religious.

> **Acts 17:22** | So Paul, standing in the midst of the Areopagus, said: "Men of Athens, I perceive that in every way you are very religious."

Paul was undoubtedly eager to protest their idolatry and point them to the truth, but he restrained himself and gave a genuine compliment first. He met them where they were.[339] He had witnessed during his time in Athens the plethora of deities carved in stone and marble.

Indeed, the Athenians were very religious. As Paul is speaking, the Parthenon is standing in the backdrop as the most famous of all the buildings of the Acropolis, the ancient fortress citadel of Athens. The Parthenon served as the treasury of Athens, but was also a temple of sorts, dedicated to the goddess Athena, whom the people of

Athena Statue Replica, Nashville, TN

---

[338] Wiersbe, *The Bible Exposition Commentary*, vol. 1, 472.
[339] Hughes, *Acts*, 232–233.

Athens considered their patroness. In fact, inside the Parthenon would have been a large statue of Athena that stood 38 feet high. There is actually an exact life-size replica of the Parthenon and the Athena statue in Nashville, Tennessee. The little god in Athena's hand is a six-foot statue of the goddess of victory, *Nike* (like the shoe company).

Paul was Missional

> **Acts 17:23a** | For as I passed along and observed the objects of your worship, I found also an altar with this inscription: 'To the unknown god.'

Why, Paul had even seen an altar bearing the inscription "The Unknown God"—just in case they may have inadvertently missed one!

Paul was so burdened by the idolatry of the Athenians, but he made his appeal God-centered and not self-centered. He did not attack the people, but like the Lord in mercy, kindness, and grace, he met the people where they were. It is so vital in evangelism that we do not have a self-righteous spirit, but realize the deep darkness people live in, and meet them there, like a compassionate fireman going into a burning building.

Paul was not a compromiser or a pragmatist. He made sure the people understood the gospel in their own context. Paul explains further in his letter to the Corinthians. He says, "to the Jew I was a Jew" and "to the Greek, I became as a Greek." Paul met the people where they were.

> *1 Corinthians 9:22* | I have become all things to all people, that by all means I might save some.

Paul was Bold

Based on his observations, Paul framed the argument for the one true living God in terms the citizens of Athens could understand. He did not hold back or withdraw because of the fear of man. He boldly proclaimed the one true God to them.

> **Acts 17:23b** | What therefore you worship as unknown, this I proclaim to you.

The Bible does not offer formal arguments for God's existence. His existence is ultimately a matter of revelation and faith (Heb 11:6; *cf* Jn

1:18; 20:29). Such faith, however, is not a blind leap in the dark but is founded on evidence.[340]

Paul was what we might call today, a presuppositionalist. That is he presupposes that everyone already knows the one true and living God in their heart, but they deny him and excuse their conscience. He lays this out in Romans 1.

> *Romans 1:19-20* | What can be known about God is plain to them, because God has shown it to them. [20] For his invisible attributes, namely, his eternal power and divine nature, have been clearly perceived, ever since the creation of the world, in the things that have been made. So they are without excuse.

Paul is using their God-given conscience to get through to them. They know God, so Paul points them to the reality that they already live in. Faith is the evidence of things not seen, and there is a lot of evidence! This is called the transcendental argument for God. There are things that are not seen that present evidence, like our conscience and creation, including the laws of science including biology and cosmology. The very cosmos points to the glory and attributes of God according to Paul.

We can all appeal to anyone, even if they have no context of Christianity because all people function under the power of a personal, transcendent God, even if they try to deny it. Paul boldly proclaimed this God. But how do you proclaim a God, when a culture has completely lost the concept of a compassionate, omnipotent God? Good question. Paul is about to answer it.

DESCRIBING THE PERSON OF GOD (17:24-29)

The Athenians were supposed to know everything, and they did, almost. But on the most important truth they came up short—they did not know God. Paul did not say this—they did ("to the unknown god"). This was the bridge God provided for Paul to share more intimately and personally with these Greek elites exactly who Jesus is, and you may be surprised that there was quite a positive response. The future pastor of the Athenian church is present. He's a judge named Dionysius who was already being drawn by God. We'll learn about him in a moment.

---

[340] MacArthur, *Acts*, vol. 2, 132.

Having established a bridge, Paul now began giving the Athenians doses of spiritual truth—first about God and then about themselves. Truth about God always helps us understand ourselves, our situation, and our eternal destiny.[341] Paul now gives them a very brief class in Christian Theology Proper 101.

God is Creator

Acts 17:24a | The God who made the world and everything in it.

There's a lot packed into this one sentence. First there is one true and living God, and he made the world and everything that is in it. You are not a god. There are not many gods. In one sentence Paul refutes polytheism and pantheism. He presents God as completely separate from his creation. He made creation. Creation is not god. God is separate from creation, and that makes him person. God, being separate from his creation is not a force. He's not some impersonal collection of laws as many people consider the concept of "God" today. No, the true God is not a detached, impersonal force. God is a caring, loving, holy and infinite Person. He is personal. He loves you, and because he is separate from creation, you can have a personal relationship with him.

The group Paul spoke with had various beliefs. They are similar to the secular humanists of today. The two groups named, as we said before were the Epicureans and Stoics. The Epicureans believed that everything happens by chance and that there is no afterlife. For them hedonism and pleasure is the chief end of man. The Stoics were pantheists, believing that everything is god—the universe is god. There were also, we assume, polytheists there who believed in the pantheon of gods. Afterall, Paul is standing in front of a building called "The Parthenon" in honor of Athena and the pantheon of gods. God exists. He is personal. He is your creator. He knows you, even though you don't know him.

God is Ruler

Paul then fortifies this point by further demonstrating the personal nature of God as ruler in heaven and earth. He distinguishes the one true God from the pantheon of false gods they worship.

---

[341] Hughes, *Acts*, 233.

Acts 17:24b | Being Lord of heaven and earth, does not live in temples made by man.

On the rocky ledges to the south of the Acropolis were countless idols. The Parthenon alone was a wonder of the world. Techniques of architecture were invented to build it. Curves were substituted for straight lines and its tapering columns leaned slightly inwards. Other subtle refinements were incorporated for strength and beauty. The greatest of all Greek sculptors, Phidias, and a number of others had been employed to adorn that temple. Everywhere he looked Paul saw the work of genius. Fifty colossal figures were in the pediment and more than 520 feet of continuous Ionic frieze including horses of the sun god, throwing up their magnificent heads and the horse of the moon goddess, which seemed poised to leap out of the very stone.

Paul dismissed it all as worthless, that is, as a sanctuary for true faith. There flashed into his mind something he had heard Stephen say years before about the Temple in Jerusalem: "The Most High does not dwell in temples made with hands" (7:48).[342]

The true God is bigger than anything you've conceived of. He is the transcendent one: omnipresent, omnipotent, Lord of heaven and earth. He's Lord of both the seen and unseen realms. He knows your heart and life. He is Lord, whether you recognize him as your Lord or not. Every knee will bow; every tongue will confess his lordship.

God is Giver

God is the source and giver of life. Every breath we take, every move we make is granted to us by God.

Acts 17:25 | Nor is he served by human hands, as though he needed anything, since he himself gives to all mankind life and breath and everything.

Men may pride themselves in serving God, but it is God who serves man. If God is God, then he is self-sufficient and needs nothing that man can supply. Not only do the temples not contain God, but the services in the temples add nothing to God! In two brief statements, Paul completely wiped out the entire religious system of Greece![343]

---

[342] Phillips, *Exploring Acts*, Ac 17:24b–25.
[343] Wiersbe, *The Bible Exposition Commentary*, vol. 1, 473.

God is Sustainer

Paul tells these Greek pagans that even though they don't worship him, he loves them and guides them. He's determined their DNA, their parents, and so much more.

> **Acts 17:26** | And he made from one man every nation of mankind to live on all the face of the earth, having determined allotted periods and the boundaries of their dwelling place.

God has determined everything about our life. There's so much we don't choose: our parents, where we are born, what language we speak, etc. As they say, "Choose your parents well." Ha! If only! Truly these are things that God chooses. He guides our lives. Theologians refer to this guidance as providence. In God alone lie his hidden counsels. We do not know the future. We do not know what God has determined to do in national affairs. Nevertheless, God is in control of what happens. He has made plans and thus also determines whatever comes to pass.[344]

We were all descended from one man. Even our genes demonstrate that. God made us all of one man, Adam (17:26), so that we bear his image as well as that of God. We each carry a genetic code that signals our descent. Paul was saying that we carry within, by the very fact of our createdness, the sense of dependence on God.[345]

God is Advocate

God is calling us to seek after him. What Paul does next is he starts to give an invitation before he even gives the gospel. He believes God's going to convert them, and God actually does convert several of them.

If God is guiding our lives, it follows that we have an obligation to seek God out and find him. God has revealed himself in creation and conscience so that we might seek him out.

> **Acts 17:27a** | That they should seek God, and perhaps feel their way toward him and find him.

Paul uses a word here for "reaching out for God and finding him." The word is used by the Greek poet Homer of the blind reaching for

---

[344] Boice, *Acts: An Expositional Commentary*, 298.
[345] Thomas, *Acts*, 504.

what he knows is there, but he cannot see it. It is as if Paul is saying: In our sin we are as blind as the blinded Cyclops in Homer's poem.[346]

Jesus is calling. He's not willing that any should perish (2 Pet 3:9). We may be blind, but he is calling out to us in the darkness to come to him.

> *John 12:32* | And I, when I am lifted up from the earth, will draw all people to myself.

Jesus calls anyone who is "weary and burdened" with care and sin to come to him (Mt 11:28). Paul says to his hearers: "In your blindness, feel after God that you might find him." Jeremiah's promise gives any lost sinner hope.

> *Jeremiah 29:13* | You will seek me and find me, when you seek me with all your heart.

Come to him now. He's right there near you.

> **Acts 17:27b** | Yet he is actually not far from each one of us.

There is a sense, even for the most hardened heart, that God is right there, next to us. God is immanent in the creation.[347]

God is Transcendent

Transcendent is a big word, but it means that God transcends time and space in his power, presence, knowledge, etc. God is bigger than anything we can fathom through idols and temples. To prove this, Paul starts where they are, not by quoting the Bible, but by quoting what these men know.

> **Acts 17:28-29** | For "'In him we live and move and have our being'; as even some of your own poets have said, "'For we are indeed his offspring.' 29 Being then God's offspring, we ought not to think that the divine being is like gold or silver or stone, an image formed by the art and imagination of man.

In particular Paul quotes the Cretan poet Epimenides noted that "in him we live and move and exist," while Aratus, from Paul's home region of Cilicia, added, "For we also are his offspring." These words, of course, were addressed to Zeus, but they nevertheless corroborate

---

[346] Boice, *Acts*, 299.
[347] Thomas, *Acts*, 504.

Paul's ideas (and testify to the breadth of Paul's education).[348] Even people with mere common grace stumble across the truth as the feel there way toward God.

These quotes illustrate the universal revelation of God as creator, ruler, and sustainer. He's the transcendent one we cannot run away from. While Paul could easily have documented those truths from the Old Testament, he chose instead illustrations familiar to his pagan audience, who were unfamiliar with Scripture.[349]

No one can run from God. You can run away, but he's still with you, talking to you through your conscience. You can try to avoid him, but everywhere you look is his masterpiece, his creation. God is transcendent. Wherever you go, he is already there.

> *Psalm 139:7-8* | Where can I go from your Spirit? Or where can I flee from your presence. ⁸ If I ascend into heaven, you are there; if I make my bed in hell, behold, you are there.

DECLARING THE MESSAGE OF GOD (17:30-34)

Now that Paul has introduced the concept of the true God who made them and reintroduced them to the one who already reveals himself to them in creation and their conscience, Paul goes from general revelation to special revelation. He turns from what all people know—that God exists—and then proclaims what you can only know by divine revelation: that Jesus died and rose for our sins. The gospel is good news to those who believe.

A Message of Repentance

All people everywhere are called to repentant faith in Christ. Repentance is a change of mind, a transformation of worldview.

> **Acts 17:30** | The times of ignorance God overlooked, but now he commands all people everywhere to repent.

Up till this point in history, Paul is saying to the Athenians, God has been unbelievably patient. He has been patient while they have built altars and temples to gods and goddesses that do not exist. He knows that they have exchanged his glory for a lie, and that every one of the statues slanders the living God. God has been putting up with

---

[348] Baker, "Acts," in *Evangelical Commentary*, 911.
[349] MacArthur, *Acts*, vol. 2, 141.

their boasting in their glorious philosophy and culture, a culture smothered in idolatry, "but now commands all men everywhere to repent" (17:30).[350]

In the Bible, whenever you see repentance, God is not just calling us to give something up, but we are to repent by trusting in the true and living God. The point of repentance is not merely the giving up of sin but giving up our idolatrous sin and trusting in and enjoying God.

A Message of Reckoning

If you repent, you will have eternal life. If you bypass God's mercy, and you reject his love, Jesus will not be your Savior but your judge. Everyone will appear before him (2 Cor 5:10).

> **Acts 17:31a** | Because he has fixed a day on which he will judge the world in righteousness by a man whom he has appointed.

The man who is also God and judge is Jesus Christ. God sent his Son to live a perfect life and die on the cross for our sins. He was buried. He was raised again from the dead. Receive him, and you'll be saved. Reject him, and you'll stand before him at the judgment.[351] Jesus Christ is not only Savior, but judge. He doesn't get pleasure out of holding your sins to an account, since he died on the cross for the world to come to him.

> *1 Timothy 2:4* | He "desires all people to be saved and to come to the knowledge of the truth."

Come to Christ today in mercy or you will one day be crushed by him in judgment. There is no escape.

> *Hebrews 9:27* | It is appointed unto men once to die, but after this the judgment.

A Message of Resurrection

How is Christ worthy of judging the human race? We learn that he conquered death, and God raised him from the dead.

> **Acts 17:31b** | And of this he has given assurance to all by raising him from the dead.

---

[350] Sproul, *Acts*, 317.
[351] Adrian Rogers, "Three Challenges to the Cross," in *Adrian Rogers Sermon Archive* (Signal Hill, CA: Rogers Family Trust, 2017), Ac 17:16–34.

We have the assurance that Jesus Christ is the judge of all since God confirmed it and gave us this assurance by raising him from the dead. He is worthy to judge since he is God, but also he is worthy because he is now a glorified man. He has permanently taken on our nature. He's been raised from the dead having tasted humanity, being tempted in every way as we are, "yet without sin."

Yet and still, the resurrection was a very difficult doctrine for any Greek to believe. Epicureans believed in no human existence after death. Stoics believed that only the immaterial spirit survived death.[352] To a Greek, the body was only a prison; and the sooner a person left his body, the happier he would be.[353] Could God work even in this crowd when the concept of resurrection had been totally rejected by every segment of society?

Our Response to the Message

Is the gospel powerful enough to save even these people?

The Curious

At first you might think, no. God will not save these ignorant people. They don't even have a right concept of God or have a category for the resurrection of Jesus Christ. Because of that, some of the great leaders began to mock Paul.

> **Acts 17:32-33** | Now when they heard of the resurrection of the dead, some mocked. But others said, "We will hear you again about this." **33** So Paul went out from their midst.

"Now Paul, you almost had me, but they you had to go to this resurrection? What is this nonsense?", they might have said.

The Converted

It is here on Mars Hill that we see so clearly that salvation is a miracle from the Holy Spirit. It's a gift of grace from God.

> **Acts 17:34** | But some men joined him and believed, among whom also were Dionysius the Areopagite and a woman named Damaris and others with them.

---

[352] Polhill, *Acts*, 378.
[353] Wiersbe, *The Bible Exposition Commentary*, vol. 1, 474.

According to church history, Dionysius was a well-respected judge in Athens. He writes that he had been in Egypt one day when the sun went completely dark, and he wrote the day and the hour down, which coincided with the crucifixion of the Lord Jesus Christ. More than twenty years later, he encounters a man on Mars Hill, the apostle Paul, telling about the crucifixion of Jesus and how the sun went out. He proclaimed the resurrection of Jesus, and Dionysius believed and was born again. It is said that Paul baptized him.[354] After his conversion, Dionysius became the first pastor of the church at Athens.[355]

Conclusion

What about you, do you believe in the power of the gospel? Do you need more than the gospel to see someone truly follow Christ? I hope not. What can we say except no person has such a hardened heart that the gospel cannot penetrate it. Preach the word with boldness and love. How? Start where you are. We have so much of the gospel, and the world has so little.

The story is told of a man who served in George Washington's cabinet. He was totally bald. The top of his head would have been the envy of a shiny billiard ball. But in contrast to that barren scalp, he had a long, flowing bushy beard. Washington pointed to him, with a touch of humor, as someone particularly reflective of the problem of "overproduction and poor distribution."

This is the problem that we, as Christians, live with every day. We have more Bible resources in this country than at any other time in world history, and yet our missions' movements are dying. Have you noticed this problem of "overproduction and poor distribution"? It starts with the same burden of heart Paul had in Athens. Are you disturbed that the most sobering reality in the world today is that people are dying and going to hell today? Will you love your neighbor by getting to know them and speaking the gospel to them?

Are your feet beautiful? As the years go on, we are all turning into raisins. We used to be grapes. We cannot stop the atrophy of our appearance. Our hair is turning grey and for some it is turning lose. But

---

[354] Nick Kampouris & G.E. Koronaios, (2022, February 20). *The History of Dionysius the Areopagite, the Patron Saint of Athens*. GreekReporter.com. Retrieved March 3, 2022, from https://greekreporter.com/2022/02/20/the-history-of-dionysius-the-areopagite-the-patron-saint-of-athens-2/

[355] Eusebius, *Historia Ecclesiae III*: iv.

you can always have beautiful feet as you go into the world and preach the gospel.

30 | ACTS 18:1-17
COURAGE AT CORINTH

The Lord said to Paul one night in a vision, "Do not be afraid, but go on speaking and do not be silent, for I am with you, and no one will attack you to harm you, for I have many in this city who are my people.
ACTS 18:9-10

A man was shoveling snow from his driveway when two boys carrying snow shovels approached him.

"Can we shovel your snow, Mister?" one of them asked. "Only two dollars!"

Puzzled, the man replied, "Can't you see that I'm doing it myself?"

"Sure," said the enterprising boy; "that's why we asked. We get most of our business from people who are half through and feel like quitting!"

So many people quit at so many things when they're only halfway through. As Christians, we need to have courage and perseverance. Charles Spurgeon reminded his London congregation, "By perseverance, the snail reached the ark."[356]

---

[356] Charles Spurgeon. "The Parable of the Ark" *The Metropolitan Tabernacle Pulpit* (London: Passmore and Alabaster, 1907), 265.

What do you do when you are completely discouraged in life? What if you've got a spiritual brick wall right in front of you? Paul had that in Corinth, and the Lord gave him four ways of gaining spiritual courage in the midst of encouragement.

Corinth, with its 200,000 people, would not be the easiest city in which to start a church, and yet that's where Paul went after leaving Athens. And he went alone! The going was tough, but the apostle did not give up. Corinth's reputation for wickedness was known all over the Roman Empire. Romans 1:18–32 which refers to how to reach a pagan culture was written in Corinth! Thanks to its location, the city was a center for both trade and travel. Money and vice, along with strange philosophies and new religions, came to Corinth and found a home there. Corinth was the capital of Achaia and one of the two most important cities of that time that Paul visited. The other was Ephesus.[357]

In the eighteenth chapter of Acts, we find Paul working for a year and a half in Corinth. Corinth was not like Athens. It was actually far more influential than the city of Athens at the time. Yet it was incredibly receptive to the gospel, and Paul spent the first long period of his missionary career in this city. Later he would spend a similarly long time in Ephesus.[358]

With the rampant paganism of Corinth, it would be so easy to give up. Dear saints, it is the same where you live. Don't lose heart. What do we need to stay strong for the Lord and reach this pagan culture?

> Key Thought: God has provided everything you need to reach this pagan culture. Instead of losing heart, we need to look up at our mighty Savior!

So how do we reach our pagan culture? We can learn a lot from the apostle Paul's ministry in Corinth. Four things we find from this passage that stem the tide of discouragement, all flowing from the gospel: gospel friendships, gospel fruit, gospel fellowship, and gospel fire.

GOSPEL FRIENDSHIPS (18:1-5A)

Paul thought he was alone in Corinth, but God sent him the fellowship and companionship of friends. He had never met these friends before, but it was like he had known them forever.

---

[357] Wiersbe, *The Bible Exposition Commentary*, vol. 1, 474.
[358] Boice, *Acts: An Expositional Commentary*, 302.

The Problem of Friendlessness

Yet when Paul left Athens and arrived in Corinth, he arrives alone.

Acts 18:1 | After this Paul left Athens and went to Corinth.

How hard is it to live the Christian life without support? It's actually impossible. We are made to be the body of Christ, not just the "eyeball" or the "finger" of Christ. We need each other. We are interconnected. The sure path to failure in the Christian life and Christian ministry is to be a loner.

What about you? Do you make an excuse because you are an introvert that it's ok for you to live the Christian life alone? Maybe you blame the body of Christ for not being "friendly." That's one of the most common excuses. Yet the Scripture tells us that if we want friends, we have to be friendly.

Proverbs 18:24 | A man that has friends must show himself friendly.

1 John 5:1 | Everyone who loves the Father loves whoever has been born of him.

1 Corinthians 12:21-22 | The eye cannot say to the hand, "I have no need of you," nor again the head to the feet, "I have no need of you." ²² On the contrary, the parts of the body that seem to be weaker are indispensable

We can't say to anyone in the body of Christ, "I have no need of you." A vital part of growing up into Christ (Eph 4:16) is being a friend to all those in the body of Christ. Be friendly! Reach out! There are no lone ranger Christians who are healthy.

The Privilege of Friendship

If you are a loner, you are not growing. Paul sought out gospel friends in Corinth. He understood the privilege of friendship. He sought out friends, and God blessed his efforts and gave him a couple who became two of Paul's best friends.

Acts 18:2 | And he found a Jew named Aquila, a native of Pontus, recently come from Italy with his wife Priscilla, because Claudius had commanded all the Jews to leave Rome. And he went to see them.

The emperor Claudius had banished all Jews from the city of Rome, and that included Aquila and his wife Priscilla. This edict, called the *"impulsore Chresto"* was associated with the Jews rioting against the preaching of Christ in Rome.[359] The edict is probably to be dated in AD 49–50, and Paul dedicates to Romans 9-11 in his epistle to settle some of the dissention that occurred in the churches as a result of this edict.

The Places of Friendship

Paul made friends at work and at worship where he preached the gospel. Work is a wonderful place for evangelism

Friends at Work

> **Acts 18:3** | And because he was of the same trade he stayed with them and worked, for they were tentmakers by trade.

Paul was a tentmaker, so this is where he met Aquila and Priscilla. Tents were made out of leather, so that the term *tentmaker* also means "leatherworker" and implies all kinds of leather goods. Allusions to this occupation of Paul's show up in several New Testament texts (Acts 20:34; 1 Cor 9:1–18; 2 Cor 11:7–12; 1 Thess 2:9; 2 Thess 3:7–10).[360] Paul worked with tents and all kinds of leather goods. This was a good place to preach the gospel. Isn't it amazing after all that Paul had seen and done, that he was willing to go to work every day to support himself? One of the early church fathers, John Chrysostom (344–407) marveled at this fact.

> *John Chrysostom* (344–407) | Paul, after countless journeys, despite such great wonders, stayed with a tentmaker and sewed skins. Angels honored him and demons trembled at him, and still he was not ashamed to say, "These same hands served my needs and those who were with me."[361]

Paul knew that work was a place to give the gospel. Now we don't get to cheat the company in order to preach the gospel. We are at work to work, where we should give our employer one hundred percent. But after work we should be making those gospel connections. Who will tell

---

[359] Marshall, *Acts*, 310.
[360] Baker, "Acts," in *Evangelical Commentary*, 912.
[361] John Chrysostom, *Homilies on the Book of Acts*, sermon 39 in Philip Schaff et al., eds. *A Select Library of the Nicene and PostNicene Fathers of the Christian Church*. 2 (Peabody, MA: Hendrickson, 1994), 1 11:241.

your co-workers the gospel? Who will go for the Lord? Who will preach his word? Who will tell your co-workers that Jesus Christ is Lord? Paul felt a great burden for the lost. Listen to him.

> *1 Corinthians 9:6, KJV* | Necessity is laid upon me. Yea, woe is unto me if I preach not the gospel!

Dear saints, you don't just work to work. Work is a place to glorify God. Work hard. Let your light shine. Make key gospel relationships. We walk in the steps of Jesus who came to heal the brokenhearted, to bind up their wounds. So many need the touch of Jesus to come into their lives through you. Christ died for the sinners you work with. Be careful about getting jaded about your co-workers. Most are lost and under the power of Satan. They will often persecute you but do good to them. Bless those who hate you and at times abuse you. Love them. Let them know that the answer to their great emptiness and misery is Jesus.

Let me mention one more thing for our men. Notice Paul is a hard worker, being both an evangelist church planter, and a tentmaker during the day. When Paul was done with work, he went to work at evangelism. So it is with you men. When you are done with work, you go back to your other ministry at home. You work with your wife and care for your children. Help with the home. Help with the kids. Shepherd your wife. When you get home from work, you need to go to minister and work at home.

For you single men and ladies, you need to be working more in the ministry. Get involved in helping the elders and deacons in their ministry tasks. Make yourself available to them. Determine to be the most faithful member of the church. Work is a dignified calling. When you are done with your daily work, don't be lazy at home. Get to work!

Friends at Worship

Paul also found the synagogue a great place to evangelize.

> **Acts 18:4** | And he reasoned in the synagogue every Sabbath, and tried to persuade Jews and Greeks.

Corinth was an important commercial center, so there was undoubtedly a large Jewish synagogue in the city. Paul entered into a dialogue with those who attended the synagogue, as was his usual custom. He was a tireless ambassador for Christ. No opportunity was wasted. Sabbath after Sabbath he held forth, making a deep impression on many.[362]

There was Paul evangelizing at a place of worship. There are many within the walls of our church who have not yet been converted. The church house is a wonderful place to bring people to faith in Christ.

The Providence of Friendship

Praise God for friendship! We cannot do it alone. We must always be connected to fellow Christians. We will shrivel up and be diseased spiritually if we do not have believers to mend our wounds and keep our eyes on Jesus.

> **Acts 18:5** | When Silas and Timothy arrived from Macedonia, Paul was occupied with the word.

The arrival of Paul's colleagues did a number of things for him. Their good report relieved him of the anxiety he felt for the churches they were ministering to. They brought with them the gift of money he received at this time from his friends at Philippi (2 Cor 11:8; Phil 4:14-20) which enabled him to give up his secular employment and devote himself full time to his missionary work. Moreover, the presence of Silas and Timothy gave him much-needed moral support.[363]

Can you imagine Lydia, the jailer, and many others taking a love offering for Paul? They likely sent it through Silas and Timothy who had stayed behind in Berea after Paul was forced to leave the city (17:14). Had they not stayed behind, who knows if Paul would have received this offering.

Friendship is providential. The people God gives you are from the Lord. Choose your friends wisely. Godly friends will bring you closer to Christ. Ungodly friends will turn you away from the Lord. Be that godly friend that those around you need!

Everyone agrees that Paul was a great Christian and a great missionary evangelist, but how much would Paul have accomplished *alone?* Friends like Aquila and Priscilla, Silas and Timothy, and the generous believers in Macedonia, made it possible for Paul to serve the

---

[362] Phillips, *Exploring Acts*, Ac 18:4-5.
[363] Ibid.

Lord effectively. His Christian friends, new and old, encouraged him at a time when he needed it the most.[364]

Listen, you might be discouraged in your Christian life. Don't give up! You have friends all around you that love you and love Jesus. You can do exactly what God wants you to do if you will stop trying to live the Christian life by yourself. Lean on your friends in Christ.

GOSPEL FRUIT (18:5B-8)

Not only are friends encouraging, but God wants to bring people to Christ through you. Paul was struggling in Corinth with loneliness, but that did not stop God from working through him to bring converts into the kingdom.

The Instrument of Conversion

Silas and Timothy arrived from the churches of Macedonia— Philippi, Thessalonica, and Berea. Paul was doing what he always did; he was holding forth the word of God.

> **Acts 18:5** | When Silas and Timothy arrived from Macedonia, Paul was occupied with the word, testifying to the Jews that the Christ was Jesus.

God's word converts the soul. The great means of the conversion of sinners is the word of God. We are born again, brought to life by grace through faith in Christ. Theologians call this miracle of God that changes the heart and nature "regeneration." We see the place of the word of God in Psalm 19.

> *Psalm 19:7* | The law of the LORD is perfect, converting the soul.

The book of Ephesians tells us more specifically how this takes place. Regeneration takes place when, as we are hearing the word of God, he opens our eyes and raises us from the dead. We come to him by grace through believing. The word must do the work.

> *Ephesians 2:4-6, 8* | But God, being rich in mercy, because of the great love with which he loved us, ⁵ even when we were dead in our trespasses, made us alive together with Christ—by grace you have been saved— ⁶ and raised us up with him and seated us with him in the heavenly places in Christ Jesus... ⁸ For by grace you have been

---

[364] Wiersbe, *The Bible Exposition Commentary*, vol. 1, 475.

saved through faith. And this is not your own doing; it is the gift of God, ⁹ not a result of works, so that no one may boast.

We know how Paul preached the churches of Macedonia, and he carried that preaching to Corinth. He said to the Macedonians in Thessalonica that it was God's word that did the converting.

> 1 Thessalonians 1:5 | Our gospel came to you not only in word, but also in power and in the Holy Spirit and with full conviction.

It wasn't just a lesson Paul was teaching, but it was the Holy Spirit teaching and converting sinners through him. Through the word of God, the Spirit brought conviction and power and conversion.

The Enemies of Conversion

And what is the result in Corinth? It was very fruitful (18:8, "many of the Corinthians hearing Paul believed"), but sadly, Paul faced fierce enemies at the synagogue. When you sincerely proclaim the gospel, you need to not be surprised at satanic attack. Look what happens when Jesus is lifted up.

> **Acts 18:6-7** | And when they opposed and reviled him, he shook out his garments and said to them, "Your blood be on your own heads! I am innocent. From now on I will go to the Gentiles." ⁷ And he left there and went to the house of a man named Titius Justus, a worshiper of God. His house was next door to the synagogue.

A major contingent of Jews in the synagogue reviled and rejected Paul's message of Jesus and the resurrection. Paul had to leave and go back to the house by the synagogue with his friend Titius. But before he did, he gave them a warning. What Paul did was reminiscent of the Old Testament prophets. Back then, the prophets communicated not only verbally but with behaviors that dramatized the message of God's judgment. Ezekiel ate a scroll. Isaiah wore only his undergarment for three years. Hosea married a prostitute.

When the Jews of the Corinthian synagogue rejected the gospel, they brought God's judgment upon themselves. Paul wanted to make sure they understood they were bring destruction on themselves. So he took off his garment and shook it to indicate that he was shaking the filth of the blasphemers off his body. Paul's conscience was clear, he had proclaimed the gospel of Jesus' death and resurrection to them, and they had rejected it. From now on, Paul said, he would give the gospel exclusively to the Gentiles there in Corinth.

Dear friend, you will be rejected, but don't weep for yourself, weep for those who are rejecting Christ. Your hands are clean, but his blood is upon their heads. Charles Spurgeon said it well:

> If sinners be damned, at least let them leap to hell over our dead bodies. And if they perish, let them perish with our arms wrapped about their knees, imploring them to stay. If hell must be filled, let it be filled in the teeth of our exertions, and let not one go unwarned and unprayed for.[365]

With Paul, we need to have a deep compassion for the lost, but after much warning, we must entrust them to the Lord, let their rejection be upon their own accounts. We can continue to pray for them, but we must move on to those the Lord is drawing. This attitude of God's sovereignty in salvation is absolutely vital. We must move on and invest in those God is saving or we will be in danger of becoming manipulative to the unresponsive.

The Fruit of Conversion

Despite the enemy, God was working mightily in the Corinthian synagogue. In fact, a very important person came to know the Lord.

Acts 18:8 | Crispus, the ruler of the synagogue, believed in the Lord, together with his entire household. And many of the Corinthians hearing Paul believed and were baptized.

Even though so many Jews were hostile to Paul, the very leader of the synagogue put his faith in Christ as well as his entire household. Many others believed, and a true church was planted in Corinth.

GOSPEL FELLOWSHIP (18:9-11)

Paul had substantial reasons to be encouraged: Priscilla and Aquila, Silas and Timothy, financial help, a full-time ministry, and encouraging results. Yet he also faced fierce and opposition. In the midst of all this, he fell prey to fear and discouragement. We know this is so because God gave him a vision to encourage him.[366]

---

[365] Charles Spurgeon. "The Wailing of Risca" *The Metropolitan Tabernacle Pulpit* (London: Passmore and Alabaster, 1861), 385.

[366] Hughes, *Acts: The Church Afire*, 239.

The Promises of Fellowship

Paul received a vision from the Lord in the night. He was getting weary, and he needed encouragement from the Lord.

Acts 18:9a | And the Lord said to Paul one night in a vision.

Paul endured excruciating spiritual warfare, not to mention the many beatings he was getting for preaching the gospel. He was losing his ability to rebound. Like Elijah, he had unbelievable victories, but was now suddenly reeling. Not to mention, there were incredible demonic strongholds in moral pollution of Corinth. Depression was starting to settle in, but the Lord Jesus gave his dear apostle a vision of encouragement.

In fellowship given a five-fold promise: God's peace, God's proclamation, God's presence, God's protection, and God's people.

A Promise of His Peace

Acts 18:9b | Do not be afraid.

Paul is called to not be afraid. Weariness can often make us fear what we shouldn't. In fellowship we are called to God's peace. If you are without peace, you've got to fellowship with God. He calls you to leave the noise of anger and anxiety. He says, "Come to me, and I will give you rest" (Mt 11:28). If you desire heavenly peace in the midst of chaos, seek the Lord. Rest in him.

A Promise of Proclamation

Acts 18:9c | But go on speaking and do not be silent.

When we are weary, we can often be quiet, keep to our self, and live in isolation. When we are tired, we live like lone ranger Christians. We make bad choices. And Satan shames us into a life of loneliness and fruitlessness. Lift up your voice. Be like Peter, who after he had fallen, preached Pentecost. Find restoration in Christ. When you find renewal, you will most certainly find your voice to proclaim Christ.

A Promise of His Presence

Acts 18:10a | For I am with you.

One of the major losses we experience with weariness is we feel alienated and distant from God. In actuality, we as believers are united to Christ. He could not be closer. We are literally "one spirit" with Christ. "He who is joined to the Lord becomes one spirit with him" (Jn 8:44). We are the very temple of the living God since the Holy Spirit dwells in us (1 Cor 6:19). We have a new heart (Eze 36:26-27). Christ said that we are one with him as he is one with his Father (Jn 17:20-23). Yet despite the reality of our union with Christ, we often feel blind and cold and far away from God. As you rest in Christ, you will know the joy of his presence once again. That's where real joy comes from. "In your presence is fullness of joy, and at your right hand there are pleasures forevermore" (Psa 16:11).

A Promise of His Protection

Acts 18:10b | And no one will attack you to harm you.

Whatever circumstance you are in that is harassing you and daring you to give up is not real or eternal. No one can touch you without God's permission. God has given you his greatest gift: the sacrifice of his Son and the indwelling presence of his Spirit. Anything bad that happens will work out for your good (Rom 8:28). Indeed, Solomon reminds us that "God makes all things beautiful in his time" (Ecc 3:11).

A Promise of His People

Acts 18:10c | For I have many in this city who are my people.

Architecturally, Corinth was a marvel, even compared to Athens. In Paul's day Corinth was a new city. No major building was more than 100 years old.[367] But morally, Corinth was the Sodom and Gomorrah of the ancient world. Yet God had a people for Paul to reach in this city. Don't let your circumstances discourage you because there are so many lost souls that God wants you to reach through you.

The Productivity of Fellowship

Paul refused to listen to his flesh. He listened to the Lord and obeyed him. As a result, he stays at Corinth a year and a half—only in Ephesus, does he stay longer: three years. He bears much fruit through the teaching ministry of the word.

---

[367] Polhill, *Acts*, 381.

Acts 18:11 | And he stayed a year and six months, teaching the word of God among them.

God's got so much fruit for you to bear so don't let the noisiness of discouragement and depression rob you of gospel fruitfulness. The more you fellowship with God, the more your heart and eyes are full of his glorious presence, setting you free to live above the circumstances of this life, and bear much fruit for the kingdom.

GOSPEL FIRE (18:12-17)

Finally, though all hell come against us, the worst our enemy can do is make us uncomfortable on this earth. He cannot keep us from fruitfulness, for Jesus said that the building of his church is unstoppable. Let us keep the fire of joy and perseverance hot deep within us by the Spirit. Christ's promise is unstoppable.

Matthew 16:18 | I will build my church, and the gates of hell shall not prevail against it.

We wrestle not against flesh and blood. Our enemy is in the spiritual realm of darkness (Eph 6:12). Our enemy can try to discourage us, but he cannot stop us.

The Enemy's Attack Can't Stop Us

Paul goes before the proconsul, Gallio. A proconsul had many hats, he had authority over the military, but he also acted as a judge. The Jews coordinate and bring a charge against Paul.

Acts 18:12 | But when Gallio was proconsul of Achaia, the Jews made a united attack on Paul and brought him before the tribunal.

Paul was brought before the tribunal or judgment seat. It would have been a large, raised stone platform that stood in the marketplace in front of the residence of the proconsul and served as the public court where he tried cases.

The Enemy's Strategy Can't Stop Us

The Jews hoped for a favorable verdict from Gallio, which could then be cited as a precedent in other places where the gospel was preached.[368] They've got Paul right where they want him. They'll get the

---

[368] MacArthur, *Acts*, vol. 2, 152.

Roman authority to convict him, and then Christianity will be outlawed! This plan surely came directly from the devil himself. Look how it went down.

> **Acts 18:13-16** | Saying, "This man is persuading people to worship God contrary to the law." **14** But when Paul was about to open his mouth, Gallio said to the Jews, "If it were a matter of wrongdoing or vicious crime, O Jews, I would have reason to accept your complaint. **15** But since it is a matter of questions about words and names and your own law, see to it yourselves. I refuse to be a judge of these things." **16** And he drove them from the tribunal.

God overruled the Jews through the governing power. God has complete control over our government. We may lose freedoms, we may be brought low as a nation, but the gospel cannot be stopped or hindered from going forth.

The Enemy is Powerless to Stop Us

I want you to see who the enemy goes after—the up-and-coming pastor of the Corinthian church, Sosthenes, who was the ruler of the synagogue. No matter: a beating never stopped the gospel from going forth.

> **Acts 18:17** | And they all seized Sosthenes, the ruler of the synagogue, and beat him in front of the tribunal, but Gallio paid no attention to any of this.

The Roman ruler "paid no attention" but God did! Even though Sosthenes, the ruler of the synagogue, was beaten, he went forward and became the pastor of the church at Corinth. We don't have to be discouraged but encouraged with the fire of the Spirit that God will do his work. Look at Paul's opening greeting from his letter to the Corinthians.

> *1 Corinthians 1:1-2* | Paul, called by the will of God to be an apostle of Christ Jesus, and our brother Sosthenes, ² To the church of God that is in Corinth, to those sanctified in Christ Jesus.

Gallio, as part of the Roman government there in Corinth, actually protected Paul. Not only was he vindicated, but the case set a new benchmark which the Christians could hardly have dared to hope for. In Achaea at least (central and southern Greece), Christianity is declared legal with the same status as the Jews![369] We have no worry in preaching the gospel anywhere because it is God who puts all rulers in their place, and they have no power except through him. What Satan means for evil, God uses for good (Gen 50:20).

Sure, Sosthenes is beaten, but it doesn't discourage him from teaching and preaching. He goes on and leads the Corinthian believers. Christ will build his church. If we try to build in any other way, but through the power of God, then we labor in vain!

Conclusion

It can be very discouraging in this cold, dark world. Don't be discouraged. Be looking for those gospel friends, that fellowship, that gospel fruit and that fire from the Holy Spirit. Stay close to Jesus, or your heart will get so cold and discouraged.

I can remember as a kid growing up on the south side of Chicago, there was this monster hill by our house. At the first good snow we all grabbed our sleds and made a b-line to divide and conquer, or at least go sledding. And if you didn't have a sled or didn't know where you put it last winter, you could always grab your cowboy boots. You could always rely on those cowboy boots to have slick enough bottoms to carry you down that slope at a neck-braking speed. Thankfully, as long as I can remember no necks were actually broken.

As much fun as sledding till we dropped was, it is true that there would come a time when we would drop. Two, three, sometimes four hours into it we would lose feeling in our toes. Our faces would finally be numb. Too much snow would get into the snowsuit. We became walking snowmen. It was time to go home.

The moment we stepped into the door, the warmth of that furnace cranked to, what 67 degrees—began to kick in. Immediately you could begin to feel your face again. You began to thaw out.

Perhaps you are discouraged. The cold world is giving you spiritual frostbite. Don't let the devil and the world freeze your heart. Get close to the fire of the Spirit. He's in you. Let him light you on fire with the persevering mindset that the gospel and the love of God are absolutely unstoppable.

---

[369] Wright, *Acts for Everyone, Part 2*, 103.

THIRD MISSIONARY JOURNEY

31 | ACTS 18:18-19:7
THIRD JOURNEY, SAME SPIRIT

He said to them, "Did you receive the Holy Spirit when you believed?" And they said, "No, we have not even heard that there is a Holy Spirit."

ACTS 19:2

The Holy Spirit is on the move. We are called to be a Spirit-filled church. Our heart's desire is to see each member of the body of Christ controlled and directed by the Holy Spirit. In Acts 18, Paul returns from his second missionary journey and then begins a third. The Spirit has to do the work of resurrecting dead sinners by the word of the gospel. But a curious thing occurs in this passage. Something is missing. There is a lack of understanding of the Holy Spirit that is holding the church back. Once they understand, the church leaps forward in fruitfulness.

It reminds me of the great John Wesley. He was the son of a clergyman, Samuel Wesley, and the unusually godly and dedicated Susanna Wesley. After a privileged upbringing John attended Oxford and became professor of both Greek and logic. He also served as his father's assistant and was even ordained by the church. Yet, something vital was missing.

While at Oxford he was a member of the "Holy Club," a group so nicknamed by the other students because they seriously attempted to cultivate their spiritual lives. Finally, he accepted an invitation to become a missionary to the American Indians in the state of Georgia, *where he utterly failed.* Forced to return to England he wrote, "I went to America to convert the Indians; but, oh, who shall convert me?"[370] The great John Wesley was missing something.

Thankfully, he had encountered some Moravians whose living faith deeply impressed him. So, upon his return to London, he sought out one of the leaders and, to use Wesley's words, he was "clearly convinced of unbelief, of the lack of that faith whereby alone we are saved." On May 24, 1738, at the age of 34, Wesley wrote in his journal:

> In the evening I went very unwillingly to a society in Aldersgate Street where one was reading Luther's preface to the Epistle to the Romans. About a quarter before nine, while he was describing the change which God works in the heart through faith in Christ, I felt my heart strangely warmed. I felt I did trust in Christ, Christ alone, for salvation; and an assurance was given me, that he had taken away my sins, even mine, and saved me from the law of sin and death.[371]

Now he knew what was missing: the indwelling presence of the Holy Spirit! John Wesley's "warming" was the regenerating work of the Holy Spirit. Amazingly, until Aldersgate, John Wesley, a man who knew more theology and was more dedicated than most believers, did not know Christ or the saving power of the Holy Spirit. He was in the church but was unconverted. Wesley was like many today. They have the form of godliness, but they do not have the life and warmth of the Holy Spirit. This is a life and death issue.[372]

In our passage, Paul finishes one missionary journey and ventures out on a third. The launch out and the people he meets highlights the one thing that the various people were missing. Some didn't have correct teaching on the Holy Spirit (Apollos) while others had never even heard of the Holy Spirit (12 disciples of John the Baptist in Ephesus). We find a pattern where Paul is utterly reliant on the Holy Spirit, and the church expands and grows beyond any human comprehension as people experience the power of God's Spirit.

---

[370] John Wesley, *The Journal of John Wesley: The Founder of the Methodist Movement,* ed. Percy Livingstone Parker (New York: F.H. Revell, 1903), journal entry from 24 January 1738.

[371] Ibid., journal entry from 24 May 1738.

[372] Hughes, *Acts: The Church Afire,* 245–246.

Key thought: As a church, we must not rely on mere Bible knowledge alone but experience the power of God's word through the Holy Spirit. Without the Spirit, all we do is vain.

Where do we begin? Paul sets sail with the wind of the Spirit. His life is a wonderful example of a humble, broken, Spirit-filled believer that would not relent until the Spirit's power had changed the face of the world he lived in. That ought to be our attitude. Let's always be setting sail, looking for the next gospel opportunity. Paul knew that without the Spirit, nothing eternal was possible. Scripture is clear about this.

Psalm 127:1 | Unless the Lord builds the house, those who build it labor in vain.

Zechariah 4:6 | Not by might, nor by power, but by my Spirit, says the Lord of hosts.

Ephesians 5:19 | Do not get drunk with wine, for that is debauchery, but be filled with the Spirit.

Paul knew that Christ would build his church, and the gates of hell could not be victorious. With that in mind, Paul got ready to sail for Ephesus. But first, he had a few more things to do in Corinth.

SET SAIL IN THE SPIRIT (18:18-22)

Paul finishes up the second missionary journey and begins a third. He leaves Corinth after a year and a half and took leave for his home church in Antioch in Syria. These four pillars here really show a mature Spirit-led life.

Anything done in the flesh is worthless. Is your life filled with the fruit of the Spirit and joy? If hard times come and you find yourself filled with fear and bitterness, you are living a miserable life. Be done with your self-life and surrender fully and completely to the Spirit. Walk in the light. We can't do it alone. God gave Paul a special team: Pricilla and Aquila.

His Team

Paul was mature enough to know he could not live the Christian life or do Christian ministry alone. Paul always journeyed with a team, and this one was very special to Paul.

Acts 18:18a | After this, Paul stayed many days longer and then took leave of the brothers and set sail for Syria, and with him Priscilla and Aquila.

Who are Aquila and Pricilla? They are originally from Rome, but are kicked out when Claudius became emperor, and Jews were outlawed until he died in A.D. 54. They make their temporary home in Corinth and take their leather business on the road. It's in the leather business they meet Paul who needs leather to make tents.

Priscilla and Aquila were working people, though Pricilla is from a more upper-class family. Her name is originally Prisca, which is a name for the wealthy at that time. Nonetheless, they were humble tentmakers, which probably means that they worked in leather since tents were usually made of skins. They were not from the upper classes certainly. They were probably not particularly well educated. They were Jews. They had been living in Rome. But when the emperor Claudius issued his well-known edict banishing the Jews from Rome, Priscilla and Aquila left the capital of the empire and went to Corinth, where Paul met them.[373] They were free to help Paul in Corinth, and as Paul leaves for Antioch, Pricilla and Aquila depart with Paul since their trade did not tie them to one spot.

It's interesting that most of the time Pricilla is named first, as it seems she might have been more grounded in teaching the Scripture. She, with her husband Aquila, will later help Apollo get grounded. This tells us that in the home a wife may have stronger gifts than her husband, but we see that Aquila is still doing the leading and protecting of his beloved wife.

His Thankfulness

Paul was so grateful for all God had done while he was in Corinth, we can see that the vision he received from the Lord did so much to encourage him (18:9-11). He wanted to do something to express his joy: he took a vow of gratitude while in Corinth.

Acts 18:18b | At Cenchreae he had cut his hair, for he was under a vow.

---

[373] Boice, *Acts: An Expositional Commentary*, 313.

Before setting sail for the great city of Ephesus, Paul had his hair cut: he had allowed it to grow long for the duration of a vow which he had undertaken.[374]

At Cenchreae, Paul had his hair cut because of a vow. When a Jew particularly wanted to thank God for some blessing, he would take a vow. This was not a Nazarite vow, since he would have to go to Jerusalem for that (Num 6:1–21). But it was similar to the Nazarite vow in that it was a vow of gratitude. Normally when a vow like this is carried out in full, it would mean that for thirty days he neither ate meat nor drank wine; and he allowed his hair to grow. For this vow, all we know is that Paul grew his hair out, as a way of showing gratitude. At the conclusion of the vow, Paul's hair would be cut and burned as an offering to God. No doubt Paul was thinking of all God's goodness to him in Corinth and took this vow to show his gratitude.[375] This vow was also characteristic of Paul's ministry. "To the Jews I became a Jew" (1 Cor 9:20), and there were many Jews in Corinth as well as those he would be returning home to in Antioch soon (18:22).

As Paul concluded his time at Corinth and "stayed many days longer" he must have been so grateful to God and took the vow. He did not go to the temple and offer sacrifice, but merely cut his hair that had grown out during the Nazarite vow. He was so grateful! To the Jews he would often live as a Jew in order to win them to Christ. This vow was a way to model Christlike love to the Jews in the Corinthian church as well as those he was returning to at Antioch.

His Target

Paul was mature in the word and was willing to trust God for fruit. He had Pricilla and Aquila set up their leather/tentmaking business up in Ephesus, and then Paul made a beeline for the synagogue to proclaim the gospel from the Scriptures.

> **Acts 18:19** | And they came to Ephesus, and he left them there, but he himself went into the synagogue and reasoned with the Jews.

At that time Ephesus was the most important commercial city in all of Asia Minor. It stood between two mountain ranges near the mouth of a lovely river. Major highways radiated out from Ephesus. Just as all

---

[374] F. F. Bruce, F. F. *The Book of Acts*, Ac 18:18.
[375] Barclay, *The Acts of the Apostles*, 161–162.

roads in the ancient world led to Rome, so all roads in Asia Minor led to Ephesus.[376]

Because of the great city's strategic location, Ephesus was a place of great political importance—the capital of Asia Minor. If the gospel spread in Ephesus, it would spread across the world. In Paul's day, it was a free Greek city, with its own senate and duly elected civic government. It was also a magisterial seat with its house of justice.

Its chief pride, however, was the temple of Diana (Artemis)—a goddess of prosperity and fertility—which was famed as one of the seven wonders of the world. Many traders made a great living there, making money of the pilgrims that would journey to the great temple of Diana. The Jews in Ephesus were protected by religious liberties afforded to them by the emperor Augustus.

Nonetheless, Paul would shortly return to Ephesus and start a church that would destroy the idolatry industry in Ephesus. We'll learn much about that in Acts 19. Suffice it to say Paul thought he was just dropping off friends in Ephesus, but it became one the most important church plants of his entire ministry. The list of pastors that would one day pastor in Ephesus is like a sanctified hall of fame. Paul, Apollos, Timothy, and the apostle John all pastored the church in different seasons. Later on, the John likely wrote his gospel while pastoring in Ephesus around 90 A.D. Paul's little stop over at Ephesus will turn out to be a major advance for Christianity for all of history.

His Tenderness

Paul had a very soft heart for the Ephesians. They begged him to stay, but he had to get back to Antioch, so he declined, but he promised to come back if God allowed him.

> **Acts 18:20-21** | When they asked him to stay for a longer period, he declined. ²¹ But on taking leave of them he said, "I will return to you if God wills," and he set sail from Ephesus.

We are not told why Paul was in such a hurry to go to Jerusalem at this time, nor indeed why he felt the need to go at all. His vow might have had something to do with it. Surely, he wanted to get back to Jerusalem by Passover.

---

[376] Phillips, *Exploring Acts*, Ac 18:19a.

Ephesus promised to be another fruitful field but a very demanding one. Paul had every intention of returning, and he will return and spend the most time at any church that he's planted (three years). In the meantime, Aquila and Priscilla could be trusted to prepare the ground there in Ephesus.

Paul is not under a legalistic pressure to save the world. He really trusts in God's sovereignty to return to Ephesus, but he is not overwrought. He is not overwhelmed. He's at peace in the will of God. Paul was at the same time broken for lost souls and at peace in the will of God.

His Tribe

Paul's tribe, his forever family, is that wonderful church at Antioch in Syria. Paul had deep relationships of love, encouragement, and accountability there with his home church.

> **Acts 18:22** | When he had landed at Caesarea, he went up and greeted the church, and then went down to Antioch.

Home sweet home—Antioch of Syria. This was the church that sent Paul and Barnabas off for their first missionary journey to Galatia. They then sent Paul and Silas on a second missionary journey to Europe. Now Paul rests in Antioch, and then he launches out for a third missionary journey.

How vital it is to always have a home church where you can have people who have known you for decades at a time. Families can put their roots down and have lifetime relationships. Though Paul was a single man, he had plenty of family at his beloved home church of Antioch.

STRENGTHEN LEADERS FOR THE SPIRIT (18:23-28)

Here we're going to see how the mature apostle finds those who need some growing in their lives and how we too are to help solidify leaders for our ministry. Paul here begins his third missionary journey. How does Paul multiply his ministry? How do we advance the kingdom of God?

We Need Healthy Churches

In order to see God's kingdom multiply and advance, we have to make sure we have healthy churches. Paul gets refreshed at his home church at Antioch, and then launches out on his third and final missionary journey.

> **Acts 18:23** | After spending some time there, he departed and went from one place to the next through the region of Galatia and Phrygia, strengthening all the disciples.

Paul begins this third missionary journey by strengthening the churches he had planted in the quad-cities Galatia (Antioch of Pisidia, Iconium, Lystra and Derbe) and the tri-cities of Phrygia (Colossae, Laodicea, and Hierapolis). Everywhere Paul had the same message: "Be strong!" He knew well of the instability of the Galatian believers. We can fill in the substance of his sermons in those cities by glancing at his epistle to the Galatians. "Don't go back to law! You are saved by grace and sanctified by grace, not by the law. Enjoy your freedom in Christ. Walk in the Spirit. Keep in step, moment by moment with the Spirit. There's no power in the flesh." Paul preached the Spirit-filled life. That's what strengthens churches.

Paul lifted up Christ in Colossae and the other cities of Phrygia. We can hear him preaching, because we have his letter to the Colossians of Phrygia—which contains some of the most exalted language in the New Testament. To have healthy churches there must be an exalted focus on Christ.

> *Colossians 1:15-17* | He is the image of the invisible God, the firstborn of all creation. [16] For by him all things were created, in heaven and on earth, visible and invisible, whether thrones or dominions or rulers or authorities—all things were created through him and for him. [17] And he is before all things, and in him all things hold together.

Paul solidified the leaders in the churches of Galatia and Phrygia by preaching the gospel by grace alone through faith alone in Christ alone to the glory of God alone. This kind of Christ-centered, God-exalting preaching is what strengthens the churches. Paul was setting an example of preaching for the pastors and elders shepherding these churches. Do you want to grow a church? Lift up Jesus Christ!

We Need Healthy Discipleship

While Paul was busy strengthening the churches in Galatia, Pricilla and Aquila are holding down the fort in Ephesus, and there they find a wonderful disciple named Apollos.

A Cultured Disciple

Acts 18:24 | Now a Jew named Apollos, a native of Alexandria, came to Ephesus. He was an eloquent man, competent in the Scriptures.

Apollos had come from Alexandria, Egypt—a place of incredible scholarship. Alexandria was the second most important city in the Roman Empire. A center for education and philosophy, the city was founded by (and named after) Alexander the Great, and it boasted a university with a library of almost 700,000 volumes of papyri scrolls.[377] The Septuagint was compiled there. Apollos represented an amazing synthesis of Greek and Hebrew learning.[378]

This was Apollos' home where he had acquired the advanced learning of his day. He had gone through what we would call university and graduate school. His credentials were impressive. Apollos was one of those scholarly, eloquent men, extremely cultured and precise in his language. Most of all, he was "competent" in the Scriptures, a man of great learning. Since Apollos knew the Scriptures well, it is probable that he had been in touch with and perhaps even have studied under the great Jewish historian from Alexandria, Philo, who was also very learned in the Scriptures.[379]

A Converted Disciple

Acts 18:25 | He had been instructed in the way of the Lord. And being fervent in spirit, he spoke and taught accurately the things concerning Jesus, though he knew only the baptism of John.

Apollos was passionate—"he spoke with great fervor." Literally the word means "burning" or "boiling hot." He exemplified Lloyd-Jones's definition of preaching: "logic on fire."[380] But he was missing something. Apollos had been converted, but not yet given Christian baptism, only knowing the baptism of John. For all his scholarship, there was something lacking in his training. He knew only the baptism of John. When we come to deal with the next passage, we shall see more clearly what that means. Apollos had seen his need for repentance and have recognized Jesus as the Messiah, but he needed a fuller understanding

---

[377] Wiersbe, *The Bible Exposition Commentary*, vol. 1, 479.
[378] Hughes, *Acts: The Church Afire*, 247.
[379] Boice, *Acts: An Expositional Commentary*, 314.
[380] Hughes, *Acts*, 247.

of the ministry of the Spirit and of Christian baptism.[381] That fuller commitment to the church community through baptism and filling of the Spirit did not take very long once he met Paul's good friends Priscilla and Aquila.

A Committed Disciple

> **Acts 18:26** | He began to speak boldly in the synagogue, but when Priscilla and Aquila heard him, they took him aside and explained to him the way of God more accurately.

Apollos could speak clearly of the prophecies of Jesus right from the Scriptures, and he boldly spoke the gospel in the synagogue there in Ephesus, but he had only known the baptism of John. So, Priscilla and Aquila "explained the way of God" more fully.

I can almost hear Pricilla and Aquilla discussing it. "This man is a very able man," they must have said to one another, "but there's something missing in what he's saying. It's not that he's saying anything that is untrue; it is just that he doesn't seem to possess the assurance that comes from knowing Jesus in all his fullness and the baptism that is a sign and seal of a relationship with Jesus. We need to invite him back for dinner and talk with him."[382]

What exactly did Apollos need to understand more fully? It likely means that he has been baptized with John's baptism and is well informed of Jesus' deeds and words to a certain point. What he lacks is both instruction in and experience of the rest of the story, notably Acts 1 and 2, including baptism in the Holy Spirit.[383] He was very likely indwelt by the Holy Spirit, but had no clear understanding of what happened to him when he believed. He spoke about everything so clearly, but he needed to speak more clearly about the new birth and the Holy Spirit. So Pricilla and Aquilla discipled Apollos and helped educate him in the Pauline theology of the Bible (at which time the New Testament was still being written).

Look how powerful it is to disciple each other. There are those who have all the gifts, calling, and conversion to bring others to Christ, but they need encouragement and doctrinal clarity. They also need to understand the fullness of the Spirit as Pricilla and Aquila explained to

---

[381] Barclay, *The Acts of the Apostles*, 163.
[382] Thomas, *Acts*, 533.
[383] Faw, *Acts*, 213.

Apollos. Who's your Apollos? Who are you helping to grow in the Spirit-filled life?

We Need Healthy Duplication

Once Apollos is thoroughly instructed, he goes to Achaia with the blessing of the churches there, the primary of which was in Corinth.

> **Acts 18:27-28** | And when he wished to cross to Achaia, the brothers encouraged him and wrote to the disciples to welcome him. When he arrived, he greatly helped those who through grace had believed, [28] for he powerfully refuted the Jews in public, showing by the Scriptures that the Christ was Jesus.

Luke tells us that Apollos was in the province of Achaia, most likely in Corinth where we understand he was also useful in "watering" the spiritual seed which Paul had planted.

> *1 Corinthians 3:5-6* | What then is Apollos? What is Paul? Servants through whom you believed, as the Lord assigned to each. [6] I planted, Apollos watered, but God gave the growth.

In essence, Paul had for all intents and purposes duplicated his ministry. Paul heads out to Ephesus while Apollos works at Corinth. Apollos' role in the early stages of that church is that he got to see the true harvest at Corinth, where God gives an amazing influx of souls into the kingdom. As the Spirit of God works in you personally, you will see his work duplicated in others, drawing the lost to Christ, and strengthening other believers.

SOLIDIFY THE SPIRIT'S WORK (19:1-7)

Paul departs for Ephesus and begins a concentrated effort there that will last the most of any other church: three years.

The Place of the Spirit's Work

> **Acts 19:1a** | And it happened that while Apollos was at Corinth, Paul passed through the inland country and came to Ephesus.

In Paul's time, Ephesus was the commercial center of the region and the fourth-largest city in the empire. Estimations of its population range from two hundred thousand to four hundred thousand during

New Testament times.[384] It boasted the twenty-five-thousand-seat amphitheater, but the greatest attraction was the temple of Diana, goddess of fertility and prosperity. The temple was also a bank where people from all over the world deposited money. It was considered one of the seven wonders of the ancient world. The temple was one of the main sources of revenue. We are going to see that with the Spirit's power and the preaching of the gospel, this center of idolatry would be shut down!

The Spirit had already been working in Ephesus. There were people who had seen the ministry of Jesus and had been baptized with John's baptism but were not yet baptized in the Holy Spirit.

There is something we need to realize when we pray for a local or a person. If we have a burden on our heart for a place or a person, that is because God is already at work there. Whoever you are praying for, God is already there working ahead of you. The Spirit draws, we preach, and God gives the increase!

The People of the Spirit's Work

God is moving among all people at all times. Some people are stuck, and the people that Paul meets in Ephesus are quite stuck. Not only do they lack understanding of baptism, but they have never even heard of the Holy Spirit.

> **Acts 19:1b-3** | Paul passed through the inland country and came to Ephesus. There he found some disciples. **2** And he said to them, "Did you receive the Holy Spirit when you believed?" And they said, "No, we have not even heard that there is a Holy Spirit." **3** And he said, "Into what then were you baptized?" They said, "Into John's baptism."

During the latter part of the eighteenth century many colonists left Virginia and started through the mountains to settle the valleys that lay far to the west. Fear of Indians, the death of a horse, or the breaking down of a wagon forced many to stay in the mountains. For over twenty years these settlers hid in the mountains, until a group of travelers straggled into the neighborhood. Naturally there was much conversation about the outside world. The travelers asked the mountaineers what they thought of the new republic and the policies of the

---

[384] P. R. Treblico, "Asia," in *The Book of Acts in Its Graeco-Roman Setting*, ed. David W. J. Gill and Conrad H. Gempf (Grand Rapids: Eerdmans; Carlisle, UK: Paternoster, 1994), 302–59.

Continental Congress. The others answered, "We have not so much as heard of a Continental Congress or a Republic." They thought of themselves as loyal subjects of the British king and had not even heard of George Washington or the Revolutionary War.[385]

That's kind of what's happened in Ephesus. We have a group of Jews, twelve in all, according to verse 7, and they do not understand baptism, either water baptism or the baptism of the Holy Spirit.

After coming into contact with the teaching of John the Baptist, these men in Ephesus had become spiritual Rip Van Winkles. Their reply, "No, we have not even heard that there is a Holy Spirit," does not mean they knew nothing about the Holy Spirit, for the Holy Spirit came on Jesus when he was baptized, and John taught that the Messiah would baptize believers with the Spirit and with fire. These men simply did not know that the promised Spirit had come. The prophecy of Joel had been fulfilled. Paul knew just what to do—he preached Christ![386]

The Proof of the Spirit's Work

Paul preaches Christ, and the disciples give a Pentecost-like evidence of the Holy Spirit.

> **Acts 19:4-7** | And Paul said, "John baptized with the baptism of repentance, telling the people to believe in the one who was to come after him, that is, Jesus." ⁵ On hearing this, they were baptized in the name of the Lord Jesus. ⁶ And when Paul had laid his hands on them, the Holy Spirit came on them, and they began speaking in tongues and prophesying. ⁷ There were about twelve men in all.

This was a mini-Pentecost. We see the Pentecost experience four times in the book of Acts: to *Jewish* believers in Jerusalem, to the *Samaritans* through Philip, to the *Gentiles* by Peter, and here to *dispersed Jews* through Paul. This was a time of ecstasy and emotional release. They praised God in other languages. Tears flowed freely. Some cried aloud for joy. They "prophesied." The word *prophecy* comes from two words—*pro*, "before," and *phaino*, "to shine." They were shining forth the power of Jesus.

---

[385] Donald Grey Barnhouse, *Let Me Illustrate* (Old Tappan, NJ: Revell, 1967), 159-160.

[386] Hughes, *Acts: The Church Afire*, 250-251.

Today, the gift of tongues is not an evidence for most people of the baptism of the Spirit or the fullness of the Spirit. Paul asked, "Do all speak with tongues?" (1 Cor 12:30) and the Greek construction demands no as an answer. When Paul wrote to his Ephesian friends about the filling of the Holy Spirit, he said nothing about tongues (Eph 5:18ff).[387] But each time the gospel expands, this time to dispersed Jews, there is this mini-Pentecost.

Ephesus, the city with everything, had never seen anything like this. This was springtime in the church. These men praised God, which is always a sign that the Holy Spirit is at work. They exalted Jesus Christ. These men could not stop talking about Jesus. Like Apollos, they made a difference in their world.

Ultimately the presence of these Spirit-energized believers in Ephesus so destroyed the idol industry in Ephesus that the idol makers started rioting.[388] The idol industry is gutted by the power of these Spirit-filled believers. Let us be encouraged by this. The power of the Spirit is unstoppable. As a church, let us covenant together to have soft hearts, sensitive to the Holy Spirit.

Conclusion

The old hymn is right on when it comes to the power of the Spirit. "All is vain unless the Spirit of the holy one comes down."[389]

It reminds me of a story about a parade on New Year's day. One New Years, in the Tournament of Roses parade, a beautiful float suddenly sputtered and quit. It was out of gas. The whole parade was held up until someone could get a can of gas. The amusing thing was this float represented the Standard Oil Company. With its vast oil resources, its truck was out of gas.

Even though Christians have access to God's omnipotence, if we do not avail ourselves of his Spirit we will run out of power.

---

[387] Wiersbe, *The Bible Exposition Commentary*, vol. 1, 481.
[388] Ibid.
[389] William Moore, *Columbian Harmony*, "Brethren, We Have Met to Worship: (New York: George Atkins Publishing, 1819), Hymn 107.

32 | ACTS 19:8-41
RIOTING AND REJOICING IN EPHESUS

Many of those who were now believers came, confessing and divulging their practices. And a number of those who had practiced magic arts brought their books together and burned them in the sight of all. And they counted the value of them and found it came to fifty thousand pieces of silver. So the word of the Lord continued to increase and prevail mightily.
ACTS 19:18-20

Virtual reality is now being used to treat soldiers and burn victims with PTSD to reduce pain through distraction and alternative focus. It has been found to reduce pain and trauma almost by 50% for most patients.[390] By changing focus, they are able to drastically reduce discomfort.

For the Christian, we are called to change our focus and "set our affections on things above, not on things on the earth" (Col 3:1ff). We don't need "virtual reality" because the heavenly realm is ultimate reality. We as Christians are called to do God's will "on earth as it is in

---

[390] Maani, C. V., Hoffman, H. G., Morrow, M., Maiers, A., Gaylord, K., McGhee, L. L., &; DeSocio, P. A. (2011, July). "Virtual Reality Pain Control During Burn Wound Debridement of Combat-Related Burn Injuries Using Robot-Like Arm Mounted VR Goggles," *The Journal of Trauma*. Retrieved April 25, 2022, from https://www.ncbi.nlm.nih.gov/pmc/articles/PMC4460976/

heaven" (Mt 6:10). We ought not be afraid of anything but turn our focus on our all loving, and all sovereign God.

In our text today we have an overview of Paul's ministry among the Ephesian church. He spends the longest time of his ministry—three years—there in Ephesus. After all his ministry there, he almost loses it all when everything looks like it's going to end in a riot. Yet Paul trust in the Lord, and the Lord cares for the ministry. Nonetheless, as believers, we are sometimes we are afraid to really draw near to God because we know that he conforms us to the image of Christ through suffering. My desire is to demonstrate from Paul's church plant at Ephesus that the misery of worldliness is far more damaging and difficult and dangerous than the suffering we have in sanctification.

The Christian can maintain a deep and satisfying joy in Christ, despite the most impossible suffering. Do not be afraid of any kind of suffering or trials in the Christian life. Suffering in the world bring far worse misery. Dare to trust in your Abba, Father. He will always see you through if you trust in him.

God uses us the most when we suffer for Christ. He's trying the dross out of our lives, that we might come forth as gold. That's exactly what Job testified.

> *Job 23:10* | When he has tried me, I shall come out as gold.

Choose to live the Christian life, all for Christ, no matter what the suffering. It is the suffering that draws us near to God and makes us the most productive for his kingdom.

THE PREPARATION FOR SUFFERING (19:8-12)

Don't be afraid to preach God's word and share the gospel. Let any suffering you endure drive you deeper into the riches of Christ's love. Abide in him. Drink deeply of his love. In this way we can agree with Paul.

> *2 Timothy 3:12* | All who desire to live godly in Christ Jesus will suffer persecution.

> *Romans 8:18* | The sufferings of this present time are not worth comparing with the glory that is to be revealed to us.

Whatever the sufferings of the Christian life bring, they are far more merciful than anything in the world. When we suffer as

Christians, we have the love, joy, peace, and patience to endure because Christ is with us. We can dive deeper into his love. But when we choose sin, we choose suffering in the world, and it is attended with fear and anger and despair. We are eaten up with bitterness and gall, terror, dread, and even illness. Stress and demonic harassment can cause so much suffering that leads to more feelings of rejection, abandonment, and deep insecurities.

Dear saints, let us be done with this kind of worldly suffering, and let us tend to the miracles of the Spirit that come for every saint as we resist the devil. He must leave. He can no longer harass us. Don't open the door of your heart to him even an inch.

Working in the Word

Acts 19:8a | And he entered the synagogue and for three months spoke boldly.

Don't be afraid to lay the foundation of the gospel even though it will be accompanied by suffering. Paul went to the synagogue as was his custom. His method was "reasoning" or literally "dialoguing"—exchange, question and answer, give and take. Some were persuaded by Paul's reasoning, and "some of them became obstinate."[391]

The Message of the Word

Acts 19:8 | And he entered the synagogue and for three months spoke boldly, reasoning and persuading them about the kingdom of God.

Paul persuaded them about the kingdom of God. The kingdom of God is the rule of Christ in the hearts of his people. It was portrayed in a picture in the Old Testament and for Israel, but then in the New Testament, Jesus said, "The kingdom of God is at hand!" (Mk 1:15). The King has come!" The Messianic kingdom has arrived. It comes first in the hearts of his people and then he will rule and reign on the earth. He will dash the unbelieving people into pieces like the shards of a potter's vessel. He will comfort and protect his people from any harm.

Paul was preaching the kingdom of God. The kingdom is centered in the King—the one who was crucified at Calvary and risen on the third day. He came to restore true freedom and victory for man under

---

[391] Hughes, *Acts: The Church Afire*, 254.

submission to God, a life that glorifies God. It is the kingdom of which the Lord spoke to Nicodemus when he said: "Unless one is born again he cannot see the kingdom of God" (Jn 3:3), the kingdom that today is inward rather than outward—"the kingdom of God is within you" (Lk 17:21).[392]

The Persecution of the Word

Acts 19:9-10 | But when some became stubborn and continued in unbelief, speaking evil of the Way before the congregation, he withdrew from them and took the disciples with him, reasoning daily in the hall of Tyrannus. **10** This continued for two years, so that all the residents of Asia heard the word of the Lord, both Jews and Greeks.

When persecution set in, Paul and his followers made arrangements to continue the dialogue in a rented hall belonging to a local philosopher named Tyrannus, which literally means "tyrant." Certainly this must have been a nickname given by the philosopher's students.[393]

What was Paul's reward for faithful teaching? The enemy stirred several in the congregation and slandered Paul, twisting the word of God. This was such a satanic attack, that Paul had to withdraw. He goes from the synagogue to the hall of Tyrannus. It turns out to be a fantastic move, and Paul teaches there for two years. It's one of the most popular lecture halls in all of Asia Minor.

Paul put preaching the word first. Above all, people come to faith in Christ and grow in him through receiving and applying the word. Don't be afraid for any persecution both internal or external that may come to you. It is far easier to suffer with Christ than to suffer in the world.

Working in the World

Paul of course was not paid to lecture in the word at the hall of Tyrannus. Likely he had to pay rent. He also took care of his own support. Therefore, he had to work. Remember Paul is a leather worker and a tent maker.

---

[392] Phillips, *Exploring Acts*, Ac 19:8.
[393] Richard N. Longenecker, *The Expositor's Bible Commentary*, Volume 9, *John-Acts* (Grand Rapids, MI: Zondervan, 1981), 495.

Acts 20:34 | You yourselves know that these hands of mine have supplied my own needs.

On the surface, this move to the halls of Tyrannus does not seem very significant. The synagogue authorities in Ephesus tolerated Paul's preaching for three months—but at last they decided that enough was enough. When opposition reached a point which made it impossible for him to use the synagogue any longer, Paul found another auditorium in the lecture hall of Tyrannus. Tyrannus vacated his lecture hall during the hottest part of the day, and it was then (11 am to 4 pm, according to the western text) that it was at Paul's disposal.[394]

This change shows Paul's aggressiveness and determination in assaulting the powers of darkness. The Western text says Paul rented Tyrannus' quarters "from the fifth hour to the tenth"—that is, from 11 A.M. to 4 P.M. That was when the people of Ephesus took their midday siesta. The workday began at 7, broke at 11, and continued from 4 until about 9:30 at night, as it is in Spain and other parts of the European world today. Evidently Paul made tents during the morning hours, taught between 11 and 4, and then went back to work. Paul used his siesta to teach, but still had a fulltime job. Paul kept a killer schedule![395]

There is a strength and perseverance when it comes to the Christian life. We will face difficulty. At times we will be exhausted. But there is a joy to working hard. Paul was willing to work with his own hands for the Ephesian believers. This was a sweetheart church for him. He stayed there longer than anywhere else. Hard work is worth it. God is our employer. We work for him and do all for his glory.

Working Wonders

When we faithfully teach the word, ministering the presence of Jesus through the Spirit, extraordinary miracles will occur, namely healing of demonic symptoms and the departure of evil spirits.

> **Acts 19:11-12** | And God was doing extraordinary miracles by the hands of Paul, **12** so that even handkerchiefs or aprons that had touched his skin were carried away to the sick, and their diseases left them and the evil spirits came out of them.

---

[394] Bruce, *Acts: Bible Study Commentary*, Ac 19:8–20.
[395] Hughes, *Acts: The Church Afire*, 255.

God uses faith. In working wonders, it is faith alone that saves, not the props of the rags Paul used to wipe his sweat in tent making nor the aprons he wore. What exactly does this mean for Paul then and for us today? Certainly, in Paul's day as it is today, sickness caused by demons was cured. Handkerchiefs or aprons Paul had from tent making were brought to the sick and demonized. This was not some kind of superstition, but a sign of faith in Jesus. This reminds me of the woman who touch just the hem of Jesus' garment who was healed (Lk 8:43–48). Or how Peter's shadow would fall on people, and they would be healed (5:15). What is certain is that it is faith—not in any apostle, but in Jesus Christ alone—that brings healing and the resistance of Satan and the demonic. "Submit yourselves therefore to God. Resist the devil, and he will flee from you" (Jas 4:7).

Faith protects us from demonic harassment. Do demons still harass Christians? Are some sicknesses caused by demons? The answer is yes. Christians are harassed only if they allow it. This can lead to terrible sickness. Lost people are demonized constantly. Much of the sickness we have is due to the atrophy of our bodies and minds due to the curse of sin. Ten out of ten people die, and it is due to the curse. The second law of thermodynamics is that all things are falling apart. God can heal that kind of sickness. We deal a majority of the time with physical ailments due to the atrophy that old age and the broken world we live in brings.

But there are many illnesses as well that are demonically induced. For several years as a child, I lived with a kind of fear and PTSD due to abuse that was mostly due to demonic harassment. The more I gave into fear, the more irrational controlling thoughts paralyzed me. I would sweat through my clothes at night because of the deep fear within me. I could hardly eat. I could hardly speak at times. When I resisted the devil through saving faith, coming to a full salvation in Jesus one night in September 1989, that PTSD left me, and I was as light as a feather. I was free. I experienced overwhelming peace. The harassment of the wicked one left me. When I submitted myself to God through the word of truth, believing the gospel that Jesus died for me, the signs of the Spirit manifested to me. No longer was I filled with fear. Now I was filled with hope and peace and protected by trust in the almighty God. He holds me in his hand.

God uses sickness for the Christian's sanctification. You may be harassed by the devil to the point of sickness even if you are living a righteous life. But God's purpose for the child of God is sanctification. He destroyed Job's body, even though he was a righteous man. Sickness often has nothing to do with disobedience, but is a test and trial for the righteous, that they might "come forth as gold" and not please themselves, but please God.

Be careful to avoid sickness due to demonization. There is sickness due to demonic harassment and demonization. And the only protection from that harassment is a total surrender to Jesus. This is what the apostles preached. And when we preach the gospel and we lift up Jesus, and people surrender, sickness caused by demonic harassment will depart. What about you? Are you dabbling with demons, dear saint of God? Do you think you can be double minded and remain protected by God? Don't you know that whom the Lord loves he chastises? There is a point when you could be "given over to Satan for the destruction of the body" so that your soul might be saved in the day of Christ?

When you open the door to fear and anger, worldliness, drink or lust, or any sin, and you decide not to repent, not to deal with it, don't you understand that the devil comes immediately to harass you? Shut the door through repentant faith. Confess your sins to one another. Abide in Christ and enjoy his perfect peace (Isa 26:3). Rejoice in fellowship, walking in the light, despising even the spot of sin in your life. Humble yourself in God's sight and receive the empowerment of grace. Surrender to the Spirit. Be controlled by the Spirit, not drunk with wine or substance. When you suffer, don't open the door worldliness and satanic harassment. Go to the Spirit and be filled and satisfied with Christ. Drink deeply of the wells of living water. Eat to the full of the Bread of life. He is all you need.

Paul was working wonders, preaching the word, and he was working this whole time, leading people to Christ. Did that bring suffering, yes! But the suffering we have in Christ is a thousand times better than suffering in sin.

THE POWER OF SUFFERING (19:13-20)

One thing this next story illustrates is that we are all going to suffer, and we have to make a choice. Are we going to suffer for the gospel like

Paul, or will we suffer with the oppression of the wicked one? What's your choice? Everyone is under supernatural power, either under the power of Christ and his Holy Spirit, or under the power of the one who is utterly depraved, the wicked one. Each choice we make, we are choosing sides. We find a curious story about seven Jewish exorcists.

The Power of Oppression

Acts 19:13-14 | Then some of the itinerant Jewish exorcists undertook to invoke the name of the Lord Jesus over those who had evil spirits, saying, "I adjure you by the Jesus whom Paul proclaims." ¹⁴ Seven sons of a Jewish high priest named Sceva were doing this.

The story told by Luke demonstrates the power of demonic oppression. There is no high priest named Sceva, though he was likely distantly related to a high priestly family. We may compare Sceva's title to the way in which modern hucksters take on such titles as 'Doctor' or 'Professor' without earning the degrees, like donated dignity.[396] These Jewish peddlers were casting out demons with the name of Jesus, like those tricksters on television today. They have an air of religion, but their real motive is they love money. They are using an incantation—using Jesus' name as some kind of magic word. They are fleecing the people with false promises. The interesting thing is they are exposed by the demons they are attempting to exorcise.

The Devil Leaves You Harassed

Acts 19:15 | But the evil spirit answered them, "Jesus I know, and Paul I recognize, but who are you?"

The devil could care less about those he harasses. The seven sons of Sceva had used an incantation with Jesus' name. Jesus' name is not a magic word. That's dangerous. the evil spirit in the man whom they were trying to cure confessed to knowing about Jesus and about Paul but challenged their right to use the name. [397] Luke must have enjoyed writing this episode. It is filled with humor. Upon their abjuration, the demon responded: "Jesus I *know*, and Paul I *respect*, but who are you?" Remember how James told us: "Even the demons believe and shudder"

---

[396] Marshall, *Acts*, 329.
[397] Ibid., 329–330.

(Jas 2:19). As so often with the exorcisms performed by Jesus, the demon *confessed* Jesus and even respected that Jesus' power was working through Paul. However, the evil spirit was not about to yield any turf to these seven sons of Sceva. They had no power over him whatever. He turned on them with a vengeance.[398] You ought to be afraid to use the name of Jesus you are not on the side of Jesus. You are just asking for demonic harassment.

The Devil Leaves You Humiliated

The seven sons of Sceva thought they would have another quick exorcism and an easy buck—until they intoned the name Jesus. Then the demoniac rolled his frenzied eyes and said, "I know who Jesus is, and I know who Paul is, but who do you think you are?" After that, all they remembered were some rights and lefts, the door opening, and streaking madly for cover![399] The demon came after these hucksters with a vengeance. He overpowered them and sent them running naked from the house.

> **Acts 19:16** | And the man in whom was the evil spirit leaped on them, mastered all of them and overpowered them, so that they fled out of that house naked and wounded.

The hucksters lived, but they fled the house naked and wounded. You can't make this stuff up. It's a fitting understanding of what Satan wants to do. He has no care for you. He uses the pleasure of sin to bankrupt you and leave you broken, bruised, hardened, and abandoned. Remember the warning of Jesus.

> *John 10:10* | The thief comes only to steal and kill and destroy. I came that they may have life and have it abundantly.

Which power will you submit to? Are you under the power of the Holy Spirit day in and day out, or have you given yourself to the power of the devil? If you continue in sin, you should be very afraid. The devil has no mercy.

The Power of Revival

As people heard of the devastating power of Satan, and the mercy of the Lord, and they said, "Enough is enough!" That's what we need to

---

[398] Polhill, *Acts*, 404.
[399] Hughes, *Acts: The Church Afire*, 258.

say. And they turned to Christ. They no longer wanted to be under the power of the wicked one. He is utterly depraved with no mercy. Many citizens of Ephesus were moved to resist the devil because they experienced the fear of the Lord. They worshipped and lifted up the name of Jesus in a powerful way. The devil had to flee.

> **Acts 19:17-18** | And this became known to all the residents of Ephesus, both Jews and Greeks. And fear fell upon them all, and the name of the Lord Jesus was extolled. **18** Also many of those who were now believers came, confessing and divulging their practices.

People were awed at what was happening. There was power—soul-saving, demon-conquering, life-transforming power—in the name of Jesus. But it was no name to take lightly on one's lips.[400] There was deep awe and reverence at the name of Jesus. People were extolling and worshipping the risen Christ.

The Price of Revival

The power of the gospel at Ephesus broke the shackles Satan had fastened on the people. Many confessed their involvement in the black arts and showed their repentance by publicly burning their books on magic and their curios covered with charms and spells. They had previously treasured these things, whose commercial value was enormous.

> **Acts 19:19-20** | And a number of those who had practiced magic arts brought their books together and burned them in the sight of all. And they counted the value of them and found it came to fifty thousand pieces of silver. **20** So the word of the Lord continued to increase and prevail mightily.

Notice when Christ visits a people through his Holy Spirit, the people open up the sewers. They expose the works of darkness by dragging them out into the light. And they repent no matter what the cost.

A piece of silver for the average person was quite small, valued around twenty dollars. Yet for these Ephesian residents, they rid themselves of what amounted to at least a million to a million and a half dollars' worth of items from their old life.

When people are truly born again, they are willing to pay any price. When we repent and are willing to pay any price to follow Jesus, there is revival and joy and freedom from demonic harassment. You want

---

[400] Phillips, *Exploring Acts*, Ac 19:17.

revival? At what price? Are you willing to be done completely with the old life? Or will you just live a life half in the world and half in the church, being harassed like the seven sons of Sceva? Won't you be like those citizens of Ephesus, who came to know Christ, and were willing to pay the price and get rid of anything that kept them chained to the world? Won't you surrender everything? Isn't Jesus worth it?

GOD'S PROTECTION DURING SUFFERING (19:21-41)

Don't be afraid to follow the Lord wholeheartedly. He's got you, and no one can pluck you out of his hand (Jn 10:28). Satan cannot harm you if you follow the Lord. That's not to say you won't suffer difficulty and persecution. But you'll understand as you grow in Christ, that even this is part of your sanctification. Every difficulty brings you more into conformity with the loving, peaceful heart of Christ. All hades can be breaking lose, and you can have perfect peace (cf Isa 26:3).

Trust God's Providence

Despite all the persecution and suffering, Paul's steps were guided by God. Paul decides it's time to depart from Ephesus, but he's not allowed. So he sends two of his co-workers ahead to Macedonia.

> **Acts 19:21-22** | Now after these events Paul resolved in the Spirit to pass through Macedonia and Achaia and go to Jerusalem, saying, "After I have been there, I must also see Rome." ²² And having sent into Macedonia two of his helpers, Timothy and Erastus, he himself stayed in Asia for a while.

Almost three years had now passed since Paul arrived in Ephesus on this, his third missionary journey. Paul began to feel that his work in Ephesus was about over. Why would Paul have such a strange itinerary if he wanted to go to Jerusalem? Because Jerusalem had endured a deadly famine. As a result, many in the church at Jerusalem were poor and in need of sustained financial assistance. To meet that need, Paul wanted to take to Jerusalem with him a love offering from the largely Gentile churches he had founded. Before returning to Jerusalem, he revisited Macedonia and Achaia (i.e., Philippi and Corinth) to collect that offering (Rom 15:25–27; 1 Cor 16:1–4; 2 Cor 8–9).[401]

---

[401] MacArthur, *Acts*, vol. 2, 181.

Paul also desperately wanted to have "Rome" on his itinerary. How he wanted to preach the gospel in the imperial city so that he might be a help and blessing to the church there, too.[402]

Prior to leaving Ephesus, however, a climactic event of the gospel confronting pagan idolatry takes place in this beloved city of Diana's temple, and a riot ensues.[403]

What does it mean for you to trust the providence of God? You have to realize that all the difficulty, all the trials, all the upside-down events in your life are actually pushing you to Christ, to be conformed to his image. What is ugly today will one day be beautiful.

Ecclesiastes 3:11 | He has made everything beautiful in its time.

Isaiah 61:1, 3 | He has sent me to bind up the brokenhearted; ... he will give a crown of beauty for ashes.

Trusting God's providence means believing God will redeem everything in his time. Paul had his Jerusalem, where famine was destroying their livelihood, but it was also bringing the Jewish and Gentile churches together into one. Remember "all things work together for good" for God's people to conform us to Christ (Rom 8:28-30).

Ephesians 1:10-11 | God has a "a plan for the fullness of time, to unite all things in him [Christ], things in heaven and things on earth. ¹¹ In him we have obtained an inheritance, having been predestined according to the purpose of him who works all things according to the counsel of his will."

God restores the years the locusts have eaten. We have to believe this. Satan may mean all the suffering you are enduring for evil, but God means it all for your good (Gen 50:20). This is what it means to trust in God's providence.

Trust God's Power

"Greater is he who is in you than he who is in the world" (1 Jn 4:4). Before Paul was able to leave Ephesus, a man named Demetrius, who was a silversmith and an idol maker, tries to cause a riot. People may rebel against the gospel, but they can do nothing against the power of God. God's power is working in the hearts of people. Try as they may to

---

[402] Phillips, *Exploring Acts: An Expository Commentary*, Ac 19:21–22.
[403] Hamilton, *John–Acts*, 519.

defeat God's people, God's enemies will not prevail, since the battle and the power is the Lord's.

> **Acts 19:23-28** | About that time there arose no little disturbance concerning the Way. ²⁴ For a man named Demetrius, a silversmith, who made silver shrines of Artemis, brought no little business to the craftsmen. ²⁵ These he gathered together, with the workmen in similar trades, and said, "Men, you know that from this business we have our wealth. ²⁶ And you see and hear that not only in Ephesus but in almost all of Asia this Paul has persuaded and turned away a great many people, saying that gods made with hands are not gods. ²⁷ And there is danger not only that this trade of ours may come into disrepute but also that the temple of the great goddess Artemis may be counted as nothing, and that she may even be deposed from her magnificence, she whom all Asia and the world worship."

Demetrius the silver smith is frightened about what "the Way" will do to his idol making business. The Way was an early title for the Christian faith (*cf* Acts 9:2; 19:9; 22:4; 24:14, 22), probably deriving from Jesus' description of himself as "the way, and the truth, and the life" (Jn 14:6).[404]

Prior to the fresh growth of the church, the local artisans had a good thing going—big business! The epicenter of Artemis worship was a black meteorite that either resembled or had been fashioned into a grotesque image of a woman. The lower part was wrapped like a mummy, and the upper image was covered with round objects resembled a woman's body (breasts) symbolizing fertility.[405]

Wherever the church boldly and faithfully proclaims the gospel it faces Satanic opposition. It comes as no surprise, then, that persecution also arose in Ephesus, stemming from a pseudo-religious materialism. Hardened hearts, hypocrisy, and hatred energized the opposition to the gospel.[406] Don't be afraid of what man can do. Look to the power of God.

---

[404] MacArthur, *Acts*, vol. 2, 183.
[405] Hughes, *Acts: The Church Afire*, 263.
[406] MacArthur, *Acts*, vol. 2, 181.

Trust God's Plan

God's ways are not our ways. His plans are higher than our plans (Isa 55:8-9)! Paul sees the riot coming, and he wants to address the crowd, but God has a different plan. Often when things seem to be unravelling, it's actually just Satan's smoke and mirrors. He can harass and try to cause havoc, but he has no real power to destroy the plan of God. When Paul told the Ephesians that "all things work after the counsel of his own will" (Eph 1:11) They had learned about God's plan and providence by many treacherous experiences, one of which we read about in our passage. A riot was almost started.

> **Acts 19:28-34** | When they heard this they were enraged and were crying out, "Great is Artemis of the Ephesians!" [29] So the city was filled with the confusion, and they rushed together into the theater, dragging with them Gaius and Aristarchus, Macedonians who were Paul's companions in travel. [30] But when Paul wished to go in among the crowd, the disciples would not let him. [31] And even some of the Asiarchs, who were friends of his, sent to him and were urging him not to venture into the theater. [32] Now some cried out one thing, some another, for the assembly was in confusion, and most of them did not know why they had come together. [33] Some of the crowd prompted Alexander, whom the Jews had put forward. And Alexander, motioning with his hand, wanted to make a defense to the crowd. [34] But when they recognized that he was a Jew, for about two hours they all cried out with one voice, "Great is Artemis of the Ephesians!"

Here it looks like a defeat for Paul. After three years of successful ministry, his time in Ephesus, it seems, will end in a riot with the church in ruins. But don't believe it. God's plans include both rioting and rejoicing, but God's plan always ends with a victory for the child of God!

During Napoleon's Battle of Waterloo, England waited silently for news of the outcome. Would Napoleon win? If England's General Wellington could not defeat Napoleon, England had a frightening future. Finally, from the top of Winchester Cathedral, trained eyes read the symbols for morse code. The message read:

W-E-L-L-I-N-G-T-O-N-D-E-F-E-A-T-E-D

Just then fog set in, and no further transmission was possible. "Wellington Defeated" was relayed throughout England. Despair reigned as people prepared for the worst. What would the treacherous Napoleon do to their beloved land? But later the fog lifted, and the full message was revealed:

W-E-L-L-I-N-G-T-O-N-D-E-F-E-A-T-E-D-T-H-E-E-N-E-M-Y

How different history would be without those final two words.[407] Listen, there are times when you may feel defeated in the plan of God, but defeat is impossible for the Christian. The Christian is predestined to be conformed to Christ. Paul told us that we cannot fail. God will complete his plan for us.

> *Philippians 1:6* | He who began a good work in you will bring it to completion at the day of Jesus Christ.

You can bank on it. God is not finished with you yet. No matter how sorrowful your circumstances, God promises to turn you mourning into laughter.

> *Jeremiah 31:13* | I will turn their mourning into joy; I will comfort them, and give them gladness for sorrow.

> *Psalm 126:3* | Those who sow in tears shall reap with shouts of joy!

Dear saints, the enemy is already a defeated foe. Don't act like he's in charge, even if he tries to pretend that he has the victory. We have our victory in Jesus! God's plan is unstoppable. "We are more than conquerors through him who loved us" (Rom 8:37).

Trust God's Position

In this final section, we see God's position over the magistrates of Ephesus. God has ordained the powers that be (Rom 13:1-7). He put them there, so we can trust God even if we can't trust our magistrates. "He removes kings and sets up kings" (Dan 2:21).

In Psalm 2, the Bible says that God "sits in the heavens and laughs" at man's attempts at derailing the gospel. It's impossible. We have nothing to fear because God is in absolute control. Jesus said, "I will build my church, and the gates of hell will not prevail against it" (Mt 16:18). We see God's power exercised through the magistrates in Ephesus.

---

[407] Hughes, *Acts*, 253.

Acts 19:35-41 | And when the town clerk had quieted the crowd, he said, "Men of Ephesus, who is there who does not know that the city of the Ephesians is temple keeper of the great Artemis, and of the sacred stone that fell from the sky? ³⁶ Seeing then that these things cannot be denied, you ought to be quiet and do nothing rash. ³⁷ For you have brought these men here who are neither sacrilegious nor blasphemers of our goddess. ³⁸ If therefore Demetrius and the craftsmen with him have a complaint against anyone, the courts are open, and there are proconsuls. Let them bring charges against one another. ³⁹ But if you seek anything further, it shall be settled in the regular assembly. ⁴⁰ For we really are in danger of being charged with rioting today, since there is no cause that we can give to justify this commotion." ⁴¹ And when he had said these things, he dismissed the assembly.

At the end of this attempted riot, nothing significant happened. As in so many other cities where Paul was, the fury of the people only worked to increase the spread of the gospel. Henry Martyn, Anglican missionary to India and Persia summed up what our attitude should be.

> I am immortal until God's work for me is finished. —Henry Martyn[408]

When Isaiah got a vision of the great position of our Lord and King, he said, "I saw the Lord sitting upon a throne, high and lifted up; and the train of his robe filled the temple" (Isa 6:1). How exalted is our Lord! He rules and reigns in the kingdoms of men. We have nothing to fear. Listen to the words of King David.

Psalm 118:6 | The LORD is on my side; I will not fear. What can man do to me?

What are you afraid of dear saint? All magistrates and kings, governors and presidents are put there by the living God. What can the enemy do to you without God's permission?

---

[408] Henry Martyn in John Piper, *Future Grace: The Purifying Power of the Promises of God*, revised edition (Colorado Springs, CO: Multnomah Books, 2012), 287.

Conclusion

Someone asked C.S. Lewis, "Why do the righteous suffer?" "Why not?" he replied. "They're the only ones who can take it."[409]

We are told at the Nicene Council, an important church meeting in the 4th century A.D., of the 318 delegates attending, fewer than 12 had not lost an eye or lost a hand or did not limp on a leg lamed because of the persecution they endured for their faith in Christ.[410]

We are going to suffer dear saints. The question is: will you suffer for Christ or for this world? There is glory and honor and joy in suffering for Christ. There is misery and bitterness and despair in suffering for worldliness. Stop turning to the wicked one and turn to Christ anew and afresh. Paul told us that our suffering would lead us to the glory of Christlikeness.

An artist in Florence, Italy once asked the great Renaissance sculptor Michelangelo what he saw when he approached a huge block of marble. The famous sculptor stood back and looked at that big square block of white marble, rubbed his chin thoughtfully, and replied, "I see a beautiful form trapped inside and it is my responsibility to take my mallet and chisel and chip away until the figure is set free." I love that illustration because you can relate to it. It is "Christ in you, the hope of glory" (Col 1:27).

God uses affliction like a hammer and trouble just like a chisel, and he chips and cuts away at us through trials to reveal Jesus' image in you and me. God chooses as his model his Son, Jesus Christ. We are predestined to Christlikeness.

Romans 8:29 | For those God foreknew he also predestined to be conformed to the likeness of his Son.

The chisel of God in your life may hurt, but it is meant to draw you nearer to the abounding joy, the perfect peace and the glorious blessedness that is found living a life of surrender to the living God. Any suffering we endure on the road to glory is far easier than the misery that comes from sin.

---

[409] C.S. Lewis, *Surprised by Joy: The Shape of My Early Life* (Orlando, FL: Harcourt Brace & Company, 1955), 229.

[410] John M. Perkins, Karen Waddles, *Count It All Joy: The Ridiculous Paradox of Suffering*. (Chicago: Moody Publishers, 2021), 96.

33 | ACTS 20:1-12
FALLING ASLEEP IN CHURCH

A young man named Eutychus, sitting at the window, sank into a deep sleep as Paul talked still longer. And being overcome by sleep, he fell down from the third story and was taken up dead. But Paul went down and bent over him, and taking him in his arms, said, "Do not be alarmed, for his life is in him."

ACTS 20:9-10

The passage before us introduces us to a young man named Eutychus whose name means "fortunate" or "lucky." He is known throughout history as the young man who fell asleep in church and fell from a window while Paul was preaching. Paul had to perform a resurrection.

We all have trouble staying awake at times. For me a movie is a $12 nap session. I still haven't seen the end of Frozen II! For those of you in school or college, after lunch is a terrible time to have a class because you are likely to travel to "La La" land.

Race car driver Dale Earnhardt was known for being so calm before races that occasionally he would take a catnap just before the start. While other drivers would have a pulse rate of 100 to 120 before a race, his would be less than 60.

But on August 31, 1997, at the Southern 500 race, Earnhardt unintentionally took catnapping to a dangerous new level. At the start of the race, Earnhardt fell asleep at the wheel-he went into a semiconscious state but kept on driving. When he reached the first turn, he hit the wall but kept on going. At the second turn he again hit the wall, harder this time. He continued slowly around the track for two laps, looking for his pit but unable to find it. Finally, he pulled off the track. Later he would say he remembered nothing of this.

Sixteen doctors examined Earnhardt to find out what had happened. They found nothing definite. The doctors didn't think the problem would recur, and they cleared Earnhardt to continue racing.[411]

Frightening but true, it is possible, for a while, to drive over one hundred miles an hour and yet be asleep. In the same way, we can be busily racing through life-our eyes seemingly open, our hands on the wheel, our foot to the floor-yet spiritually asleep. Sooner or later, though, the trouble begins.

When someone in the congregation falls asleep during the sermon, the preacher may see it, though most often I hardly notice. It is understandable when the ill or the elderly fall asleep during the service. However, if you are healthy and young, there are two things you should know. First, if you fall off your chair and break your neck and die, the best the preacher can do for you is call the undertaker. Preachers today do not have the apostolic powers that Paul had.

Second, and more serious, is the danger of nodding off when God's word is being proclaimed. Why does the mind begin to engage in day dreaming? That rarely happens when we attend football games or other events attended with great excitement.[412] I once nodded off during the exposition of Daniel and Revelation when I was in college. The professor was very kind, and he knew I had a 3 a.m. paper route. There is real physical exhaustion that we all deal with, especially mothers of young children.

What is most concerning is the spiritual sleepiness that leaves love for one another behind and hardens the heart. It's dangerous. Paul told the Corinthians that some of them were spiritually sleepy.

---

[411] Associated Press, "Earnhardt Blacked out in '97 Southern 500." ESPN Internet Ventures, June 2, 2005. https://www.espn.com/racing/news/story?series-wc&id=2074527.

[412] Sproul, *Acts*, 339–340.

Ephesians 5:14 | Awake, O sleeper, and arise from the dead, and Christ will shine on you.

Wake up Christian! Don't be lulled to sleep by the spiritual opioids of anger and bitterness. Don't be paralyzed by worldly fear. Flee from worldly carnality, drunkenness, and foolishness that numbs you. Be done with lust and pornography. Wake up!

It may be that you have allowed the busyness of life and the cares of this world to harden your heart. Perhaps it's been a long time since you've really enjoyed the presence of Jesus. Oh, how dangerous is the state of your soul. All who know Christ will be chastened when they become spiritually sleepy. If chastening doesn't come, it means there's no life of the Spirit in you. Some may not be merely asleep, but dead in your trespasses and sins.

> Key thought: The sign of the Spirit's life in your soul is your alertness and sensitivity to spiritual light in the word of God. We must be extremely careful to keep our hearts tender to the Spirit's work.

Paul's ministry was so effective because he stayed awake and alert. He was always on guard, always fitted with the full armor of God. What can we do to remain spiritually sensitive and tender to the Spirit?

STAY AWAKE (20:1-2)

To stay tender to the Spirit, we must stay awake. Paul wanted all the churches to remain awake and alert, so he was constantly doing follow up. This was a sort of farewell tour for Paul before he takes his last trip to Jerusalem. He'll eventually make his way to Rome, not as a missionary, but as a prisoner. But it was vital that he keep his heart, and the hearts of his hearers tender to the Spirit.

Be Awake to God's Plan

After the potential riot was quelled at Ephesus, Paul concludes his three-year ministry.

Acts 20:1 | After the uproar ceased, Paul sent for the disciples, and after encouraging them, he said farewell and departed for Macedonia.

Wherever Paul was ministering, God had to give the increase. If God didn't do the work, the world would never be transformed. Paul knew he was expendable. He could go from one place to another trusting in the almighty God to save the souls of those Paul loved and ministered to.

A Plan of Expansion

Why did Paul spend three years in Ephesus but sometimes only a few months in other places? Paul was awake and alert to the spiritual progress and expansion in each church. Paul may have spent a bit more time in Ephesus and Corinth because they were leading cities where he could set up training centers for pastors and missionaries. He was always alert to God's plans. God's plan is one of constant expansion, yet the timetable is God's.

Expansion for the kingdom for Paul meant relatively short stints in each city. For most pastors it means 20 to 40 or 50 years in one place. Charles Spurgeon preached for 39 years in London all at the same church. I would love to follow in those steps. Others are meant to minister for shorter periods. Adoniram Judson and William Carrey were often on the move. After three years, Paul was ready to depart to Jerusalem, but first he must go through the poor, but generous churches of Macedonia.

A Plan of Generosity

Paul encouraged the Ephesian believers, and knowing they were established with officers and well shepherded, he departed for Macedonia, i.e., Philippi and Thessalonica where he had received such generous gifts for the saints in Jerusalem before. He knew the Lord would build his church. Alert, and awake, Paul was able to leave the church at Ephesus in the Lord's hands as he made his way to the churches of Macedonia.

A Plan of Expendability

How hard it must have been to say goodbye. Paul loved this sweetheart church. Yet God's plan is much bigger than one minister or even an apostle. Paul was clear about his own expendability.

> *1 Corinthians 3:5-7* | What then is Apollos? What is Paul? Servants through whom you believed, as the Lord assigned to each. [6] I planted, Apollos watered, but God gave the growth. [7] So neither he who plants nor he who waters is anything, but only God who gives the growth.

Paul could leave because he was expendable. This was the final leg of his missionary journeys before being incarcerated in Rome. Paul wouldn't live forever on this broken planet, and neither will you. Your life will be cut short by death or the second coming. If the Lord tarries his coming, who are you investing the gospel in?

Be Awake to God's Power

The power to stay awake is found precisely in the exposition and application of God's word through the ministry of his Spirit. Now Paul gives "encouragement" or literally, "exhortation" to the saints in Macedonia. He wanted them to be awake to the word of God. We are helpless without the word of God (Jn 15:5).

> **Acts 20:2** | When he had gone through those regions and had given them much encouragement, he came to Greece.

From Macedonia Paul went on to Greece, and especially, to Corinth. While there he wrote his theological masterpiece, his epistle to the Romans. Paul, who had long planned to go to Rome, now seemed to be sensing the Holy Spirit's approval for that move.[413] Paul speaks of this discouragement in 2 Corinthians, that he has a thorn in his side.

> *2 Corinthians 12:7-9* | So to keep me from becoming conceited because of the surpassing greatness of the revelations, a thorn was given me in the flesh, a messenger of Satan to harass me, to keep me from becoming conceited. ⁸ Three times I pleaded with the Lord about this, that it should leave me. ⁹ But he said to me, "My grace is sufficient for you, for my power is made perfect in weakness." Therefore I will boast all the more gladly of my weaknesses, so that the power of Christ may rest upon me.

We know Paul was no great preacher or articulate philosopher, but he understood the power of the word of God. The messages he gave wouldn't have impressed any homiletician, but he was filled with the Spirit and the power of God. He taught the brothers and sisters in the churches to receive his word as he preached as the Spirit-led message for their life.

A key to spiritual growth and awakening is knowing how growth works in the Christian life. We can try to grow mechanically or organically. Mechanical growth is like a pile of bricks. If you want it to grow

---

[413] Phillips, *Exploring Acts*, Ac 20:2–3.

you have to add more bricks. Some Christians lack the love, joy, peace, and patience in their life because they are forcing themselves into a mold externally, but not growing internally. Organic growth on the other hand is primarily internal growth that results in external growth. It is like a dead seed put into the ground, and that little acorn goes in and a sprout comes up. It's watered and nurtured by sunlight. Suddenly there's a root system and a truck and branches. Leaves and fruit follow. It continues to grow for hundreds of years organically. That's how the Christian is to grow.

STAY ALERT (20:3-6)

We must be alert for satanic attack. There is always a serious onslaught that is against us. But we must remember that the battle is the Lord's. We put on the whole armor of God and walk in the Spirit, giving no stronghold or occasion for the flesh. Paul had to be on constant alert. Don't be distracted by the plots and pressures and pain of the enemy. Stay alert!

> *1 Peter 5:8* | Be sober-minded; be watchful. Your adversary the devil prowls around like a roaring lion, seeking someone to devour.

There is a spiritual sleepiness that comes from the weariness of satanic attack. It may come from your workplace or your own family. It may even come from someone in the body of Christ. Satan wants to catch us off guard and introduce bitterness and hopelessness into our lives. Of all people on earth, we should reject bitterness. We should be the most optimistic people in the world. The only way to not allow ourselves to become battle warn, weary, jaded, and cynical, is to stay alert with a tender heart to the Lord. We need to develop thick skin and a big heart.

The Plot

A plot for Paul's life could derail his ministry and discourage him greatly. But Paul is alert and doesn't allow this awful trial to overtake him.

Being alert includes realizing the enemy is always on the prowl. So it was for Paul. Paul was there in Greece for three months, likely in Corinth a plot for his life came to his attention.

> **Acts 20:3a** | There he spent three months, and when a plot was made against him by the Jews as he was about to set sail for Syria.

Sometimes we read about these plots against Paul and other Christian leaders as if the great men of God are emotionless and made of Teflon. Not so. We learn from 2 Corinthians, a letter he wrote at this time from Philippi (2 Cor 1:8; 2:13; 7:5), certainly the most autobiographical of all his epistles, that Paul arrived in Macedonia in a state of spiritual depression, but he turns to the word for his joy (Phil 4:4-7). Depression did not keep Paul from the great task of winning souls to Christ. So often depression is Satan's tool to keep our mind on ourselves and off the need of a perishing world. That device of Satan did not work with Paul.[414]

Paul foils the plans of his enemies and goes back the way he came through Macedonia.[415] It seems churches were planted during this time, specifically in Illyricum (Rom 15:29). The plots of God's enemies resulted in church plants and powerful church growth. Don't be afraid of the plots of the enemy. God will use what Satan means for evil for your good.

If you are going to stay spiritually awake, you have to be aware of the plotting of the enemy. Don't give up when the enemy stands against you. Persevere, and you will bear fruit.

The Pressure

Because of the pressure of the death threats, Paul's plans to go to Jerusalem were put on hold, but God's plans continued. Pressure can be very good. Pressure can make us alert to new plans God has for us that we were not previously aware of.

Acts 20:3b | He decided to return through Macedonia.

What occurs as a result of the plot and the pressure, is that more funds are raised for the church at Jerusalem. We must not be upset when our plans are diverted.

Proverbs 16:9 | The heart of man plans his way, but the LORD establishes his steps.

Paul entrusted the pressure of his life to the Lord who directed his steps. We need to do the same. Sometimes the enemy's pressure can bring us to new places with fresh spiritual fruit.

---

[414] J. Phillips, *Exploring Acts*, Ac 20:2–3.
[415] Baker, "Acts," in *Evangelical Commentary*, 914.

The People

Paul knew that with all the pressure of persecution and plots for his life, he needed a strong support system to help him keep alert in the Christian life. God has designed in the local church. Because of the plot against Paul, his plans to bless the Jerusalem church were placed on hold. He gathers a diverse team and returns through Macedonia (20:3b). His group of travel companions are seven representatives of the various congregations mentioned with their names, entrusted with the relief money for the saints in Jerusalem (24:17; cf 11:29–30).[416] What a special team is mentioned in the following verses! Seven men from all the major areas Paul had evangelized.

> **Acts 20:4-6** | Sopater the Berean, son of Pyrrhus, accompanied him; and of the Thessalonians, Aristarchus and Secundus; and Gaius of Derbe, and Timothy; and the Asians, Tychicus and Trophimus. **5** These went on ahead and were waiting for us at Troas, **6** but we sailed away from Philippi after the days of Unleavened Bread, and in five days we came to them at Troas, where we stayed for seven days.

Luke's reference to this group of men (20:4) represents almost all the areas where the gospel had gone as accompanying Paul.[417] They are together gathering the funds for Jerusalem.

After this journey through Macedonia the plan was to pass through Troas where an interesting meeting takes place in which a young man falls asleep and dies and then Paul raises him from the dead.

Be alert! Don't be afraid of the plots of the enemy. Don't be distracted by fear or bitterness because of the evil of the enemy. The Lord is your shelter and your Shepherd.

Paul didn't have time for a lot of discouragement. What a team of supporters God had given him. What kind of support do you have in your life? Do you have someone you trust in your life to talk to about deep and difficult things in your life? Don't bottle up your pressure and struggles. Find a gospel support system in the local church.

---

[416] Paw, *Acts*, 231.
[417] Baker, "Acts," in *Evangelical Commentary*, 914.

STAY ALIVE (20:7-12)

Now we get to the part of the story where the miracle of raising Eutychus from the dead occurs. His name is quite humorous to me, since Eutychus means "Lucky" and he surely did not live up to his name! He has trouble staying alive. I suppose we could say he was blessed and fortunate to have an apostle nearby who could raise this very lucky boy from the dead!

I love this passage of Scripture because it teaches us that there is a vitality in the Christian life. The life of the Spirit comes from the Scriptures and fellowship and the joy of worship. Paul makes a stop in Troas on his way to Jerusalem, and it's the first day of the week, and he teaches into the evening and eventually through the night.

We see the life of the church meeting here in Troas. We see how the means of grace, as primitive as they may be, actually keep us alive and healthy spiritually. So it's important to stay awake in church, though Eutychus didn't think that was so important.

The Midnight Message

Paul preaches until midnight. His stop in Troas included worship on the Lord's day, the Lord's supper, and a very long sermon.

The Lord's Day

Acts 20:7a | On the first day of the week.

The Christians of Paul's day took their day of rest on the Lord's Day (*cf* 1 Cor 16:1–2). The first day came to be called "the Lord's Day" because on that day the Lord Jesus Christ arose from the dead (Rev 1:10). We should also remember that the church was born on the first day of the week when the Spirit came at Pentecost.

The church met in the evening because Sunday was not a holiday during which people were free from daily employment. Some of the believers would no doubt be slaves, unable to come to the assembly until their work was done. The believers met in an upper room because they had no church buildings in which to gather. This room may have been in the private home of one of the believers. The assembly would have been a very diverse group, but their social and national distinctions made no difference: they were "all one in Christ Jesus" (Gal 3:28).[418]

---

[418] Wiersbe, *The Bible Exposition Commentary*, vol. 1, 484.

If we are going to "stay alive" in the power of the Spirit, we have to make sure we make the Lord's Day priority, just as the early church did. When I worked in the world, I made sure my employer knew I was not available on Sunday mornings. The law of Illinois and most states is on our side since by law you have the right to have one time a week when you can worship, and they have to accommodate you unless you are in some kind of emergency work. If you want to "stay alive" spiritually, you've got to be continually meeting with the saints.

> *Hebrews 10:24-25* | Let us consider how to stir up one another to love and good works, ²⁵ not neglecting to meet together, as is the habit of some, but encouraging one another, and all the more as you see the Day drawing near.

Fellowship is a kind of spiritual food. If you starve yourself of fellowship, you will begin to die spiritually.

The Lord's Supper

The Lord's supper was a way to remember the death of Christ, because we are so prone to forget it. A key reason for meeting together is celebrating this family meal for all Christians everywhere.

> **Acts 20:7b** | On the first day of the week, when we were gathered together to break bread.

The Lord's supper meal is designed to bring us back to our first love, when we first came to know the efficacy of the blood of Jesus. We renew our first love and look forward to the time when we will celebrate this feast with Jesus at the marriage supper of the Lamb. I can't wait for that, what about you?!

The early church would share a "potluck" meal called the "agape feast" after which they would observe the Lord's supper (2:42; 1 Cor 11:17–34). The "breaking of bread" in Acts 20:7, 11 refers to the agape feast with the Lord's supper. By sharing and eating with one another, the church enjoyed fellowship and also gave witness of their oneness in Christ. Slaves would actually eat at the same table with their masters, something unheard of in that day.

It is likely that the church observed the Lord's supper each Lord's Day when they met for fellowship and worship. While Scripture does not give us specific instructions in the matter ("as often," 1 Cor 11:26), the example of the early church would encourage us to meet at the

Lord's table often. However, the communion must not become routine, causing us to fail to receive the blessings involved.[419]

An important reason for the Lord's table is to rid ourselves of self-righteousness. Our flesh often pushes us toward the performance mindset, but we have to confess that our only glory is in the cross of Jesus! Let's have this meal often and celebrate what our Lord has done for us!

A Long Sermon

Acts 20:7c | Paul talked with them, intending to depart on the next day, and he prolonged his speech until midnight.

Paul's common practice was to exposit the word of God, but since he didn't have much time on his way to Jerusalem, he availed himself in the word even until midnight.

The word of God was always preached and taught in the Christian gatherings, and this included the public reading of the Old Testament Scriptures (1 Tim 4:13) as well as whatever apostolic letters had been received (Col 4:16). It is sad to see how the word is neglected in church services today. Knowing that this would probably be his last meeting with the saints at Troas, Paul preached a long sermon, after which he ate and conversed with the people until morning. It's doubtful that anybody complained. How we today wish we could have been there to hear the Apostle Paul preach!

The word of God is important to the people of God, and the ministry of the word is vital to our Christian growth. Watching videos or listening to audio is good, but only gathering in person has that human touch with real life-on-life discipleship. If God's people are going to have the life-giving power of the Spirit, we must attend to the public ministry of the word of God.

The Mishap

Now we come to the young man Eutychus who just couldn't stay awake during the preaching. There were torches lighting up the room, but the fire was stealing the oxygen. Perhaps Eutychus had a condition where he felt lightheaded and sat by the window where he could get some fresh air. Ultimately this window seat was a bad choice.

---

[419] Ibid.

As Paul's preaching approaches midnight, this young man in attendance named Eutychus ("Lucky") accidentally falls to his death from an upper window. Mr. Lucky wasn't so lucky! Some people die in their sleep. Others through disease. Eutychus' death was unique. His obituary could have read: *death by sermon!* The incident is so unusual.

> **Acts 20:8-9** | There were many lamps in the upper room where we were gathered. ⁹ And a young man named Eutychus, sitting at the window, sank into a deep sleep as Paul talked still longer. And being overcome by sleep, he fell down from the third story and was taken up dead.

The tenses of the Greek verbs portray poor Eutychus as being gradually overcome despite his struggle to remain awake.[420] The word translated "sleep" is the word from which we derive the English word *hypnosis*. The lamps in the room were torches, and the lack or oxygen and hypnotic flickering of the flames did their work. Eutychus' eyes shut, he relaxed, and out he went—headlong to the pavement three floors below. The congregation must have given a horrified gasp and immediately rushed down the outside stairs to the broken form. Some of them began to shriek a Middle Eastern death wail.[421]

Let's not be too hard on Eutychus. At least he was there for the service, and he did try to keep awake. He sat near ventilation, and he must have tried to fight off the sleep that finally conquered him. The tense of the Greek verb indicates that he was gradually overcome, not suddenly. Also, let's not be too hard on Paul. After all, he was preaching his farewell sermon to this assembly, and he had a great deal to tell them for their own good.

Perhaps each of us should ask ourselves, "What really keeps me awake?" Christians who slumber during one hour in church somehow manage to stay awake during early-morning fishing trips, lengthy sporting events and concerts, late-night TV specials, or dinner with a special someone. We need to prepare ourselves physically for public worship to make sure we are at our best. More than that, we need to have live awakened in the Spirit. "Remember," said Spurgeon, "if we go

---

[420] Thomas Walker, *The Acts of the Apostles* (Chicago: Moody, 1965), 438.
[421] Hughes, *Acts: The Church Afire*, 270.

to sleep during the sermon and die, there are no apostles to restore us!"[422]

The Miracle
Paul raises him from the dead.

> **Acts 20:10** | But Paul went down and bent over him, and taking him in his arms, said, "Do not be alarmed, for his life is in him."

Paul prostrated himself across the boy's lifeless form much as did the prophets Elijah and Elisha—and the young man was revived! It was a miracle! [423] What occurs when Paul says, "He's alive!" is a bona fide resurrection, one of a few of its kind in the New Testament. No one was sleepy now. Back up to church they went.

> **Acts 20:11-12** | And when Paul had gone up and had broken bread and eaten, he conversed with them a long while, until daybreak, and so departed. ¹²And they took the youth away alive, and were not a little comforted.

Perhaps equally significant is the spiritual appetite of these believers which keeps them listening to Paul all night long (20:11), another reason for not criticizing Paul for long-windedness.[424]

I feel sorry for Eutychus, first, because he fell asleep on the Apostle Paul, second, because his sleepiness had such unhappy results, and third, because Luke was there to record the whole thing! This is the first record ever of someone falling asleep in church. There have been thousands of successors, but Eutychus is the one everyone remembers.

Conclusion
How vital it is that we stay awake spiritually, but I am afraid some are asleep in the Body of Christ. I've never been a sleepwalker, but the Mayo Clinic describes how people can act when sleepwalking. They may get out of bed and walk around. I heard of one guy who had the vacuum in hand, vacuuming the floor with no power. People have eaten whole meals while sleepwalking. I've even heard of sleep driving—people waking up and they sleepwalked to the car. Some sleepwalkers may even have their eyes open and appear to be awake. They may not

---

[422] Wiersbe, *The Bible Exposition Commentary*, vol. 1, 485.
[423] Hughes, *Acts*, 271.
[424] Baker, "Acts," in *Evangelical Commentary*, 914.

remember later what they've done while asleep. How much more dangerous is it to sleep in the Christian life.

Martin Luther had a parable or a dream about how on one occasion the devil sat upon his throne listening to his agents report on the progress they had made in opposing the truth of Christ and destroying the souls of men. One spirit said there was a company of Christians crossing the desert. "I loosed the lions upon them, and soon the sands of the desert were strewn with their mangled corpses."

"What of that?" answered Satan. "The lions destroyed their bodies, but their souls were saved. It is their souls that I am after."

Another reported, "There was a company of Christian pilgrims sailing through the sea on a vessel. I sent a great wind against the ship that drove the ship on the rocks, and every Christian aboard the ship was drowned."

"What of that?" said Satan. "Their bodies were drowned in the sea, but their souls were saved. It is their souls that I am after."

The third came forward to give his report, and he said, "For ten years I have been trying to cast a Christian into a deep sleep, and at last I have succeeded." And with that the corridors of Hell rang with shouts of malignant triumph. If we are asleep, let us hear God's call today![425]

How dangerous is it to sleepwalk in the Christian life! Let us live life awake to God and intentionally surrendered to the Spirit. Satan rejoices that you are asleep. Are you not afraid of the living God? Let the light and love of Christ awaken you.

---

[425] Clarence E. Macartney, *Chariots of Fire* (Nashville: Abingdon, 1951), 50-51.

34 | ACTS 20:13-24
A MODEL OF SUPERNATURAL MINISTRY

You yourselves know how I lived among you the whole time from the first day that I set foot in Asia, serving the Lord with all humility and with tears and with trials that happened to me through the plots of the Jews.
ACTS 20:18-19

It is Mother's Day, and I was thinking of things I would never hear my mother say. "Let me smell that shirt—Yeah, it's good for another week."

"Please just leave all the lights on…it makes the house feel more cheery."

"Go ahead and keep that stray dog, honey. I'll be glad to feed him and walk him every day. You don't need to worry about anything."

"Don't worry; you don't have to brush your teeth today."

I heard about two children who ordered their mother to sleep in on Mother's Day. She woke up at her usual time nonetheless and looked forward to breakfast in bed as the smell of bacon and eggs floated into the bedroom.

She waited for a while, but then her curiosity got the better of her, and she went downstairs to check what was going on. Once in the kitchen, she saw them sitting at the kitchen table, eating breakfast.

When they saw her, smiles spread across their faces as her son said, "As a surprise for Mother's Day, we decided to cook our own breakfast."

Seriously though, I think of John Wesley who said,

> I learned more about Christianity from my mother than from all the theologians in England. [426]

One of the biggest and most significant tasks facing the church today is to raise the next generation of strong believers. Is there a more pressing task than for us to leave behind an army of theologians—our own daughters and sons—stronger than we proved to be? It is a task to which every woman and man in the church is called and which demands the best from us. Some of the toughest theological questions are asked between supper and bedtime.[427]

One of the things that bothers me the most is that parents think that if you send kids to church, they are going to go in a sinner and pop out born again. The church is not a toaster oven. I don't think anyone would actually articulate it that way, but it is seen in how little mothers and fathers spend in family worship. Can we all agree that we need the Lord to build our homes?

> *Psalm 127:1* | Unless the Lord builds the house, those who build it labor in vain.

My heart today as we consider what Paul says to the Ephesian elders, is to realize that the greatest pastoral ministry happens in the home, and the greatest missionaries are missionary mom and missionary dad. The following is from the 'Farewell Sermon' of Jonathan Edwards, the leader of the Great Awakening in New England.

> Every Christian family ought to be as it were a little church, consecrated to Christ, and wholly influenced and governed by his rules. And family education and order are some of the chief means of grace. If these fail, all other means are likely to prove ineffectual.[428]

---

[426] John Wesley in Carolyn Custis James, "The Dreaded T-Word and Why Women Avoid It," ed. David A. Powlison, *The Journal of Biblical Counseling, Number 3, Spring 2003* 21 (2003): 77.

[427] Ibid, 78.

[428] Jonathan Edwards, *The Works of Jonathan Edwards, Vol. 1* (London: F. Westley & A.H. Davis, 1835), 418.

Did you hear what he said? He said if you fail at family worship, "all other means are likely to prove ineffectual." Edwards said, you've got to lead your children personally to God, or all the other stuff you do for them—Sunday school, children's church, Bible memory—it's all vain. Sounds like

Now let me give you some encouragement. You cannot do what only God can do, but you can lead your children to God. We can't just bring our children to church or have them memorize a Bible verse and they be saved. They need to learn from you what it is to worship God.

The Ephesian elders learned from Paul's daily example. He led them in worship, and he led them in life. Let's consider Paul's understanding of ministry. For him anything divine that happened in the life of another was a miracle. We can't give our sons and daughters new hearts. God has to do that.

The church of the living God is a living organism created by the Spirit of God. The congregation of the saints is a miracle group of people that have been touched and built up by the Spirit of God. We are the army of dry bones that God told to live (*cf* Eze 37).

The Lord must build his church. Man cannot reproduce what is supernaturally birthed. What can we do? We can follow Paul as he follows Christ. We are not talking about methodology, but his dependence on God to birth the church. Consider the words of Charles Haddon Spurgeon.

> Without the Spirit of God, we can do nothing. We are as ships without the wind, branches without sap, and like coals without fire, we are useless.[429]

We see in Acts 20 how the birth and growth of the church looked in Paul's life and ministry. What was his view of ministry? How does this kind of Spirit-enabled, supernatural ministry take place?

SERVICE TO GOD (20:13-19)

When it came to serving God, Paul counted himself as a living sacrifice (Rom 12:1-2). Paul was totally committed to serving God.

---

[429] Charles Spurgeon. "A Revival Promise" *The Metropolitan Tabernacle Pulpit*, volume 20 (London: Passmore and Alabaster, 1874), 18.

Commitment means different things to different people. Consider the young man who waxed eloquent in a love letter to the girl of his dreams, saying,

> My dear, I would climb the highest mountain, swim the widest stream, cross the burning desert, die at the stake for you!
>
> P.S. *I will see you on Saturday if it doesn't rain.*

Paul was not like that! Paul had a total surrender in his service to God.[430] How do we daily, consistently, have that heart of surrender to God.

Serve with a Heavenly Mindset

Paul's highest desire was to "serve the Lord with gladness" (Psa 100:1). He could have said, "the joy of the Lord is my strength" (Neh 8:10). He said he had worked harder than all the other apostles, and I do not doubt him, especially since the Holy Spirit inspired his statement (cf 1 Cor 15:10). But what drove Paul to have such power and energy and perseverance in his service to God? He made sure his heart set on heaven.

Paul decided to travel separately from his team. It seems, more than anything, he needed time with the Lord, time to reflect and pray. Paul said, "I fought with beasts at Ephesus" (1 Cor 15:32). He had just raised the body of a slave boy in Troas. He needed some time with the Lord. So, Paul went separate from his team going by foot instead of by ship like the rest of the team.

> **Acts 20:13** | But going ahead to the ship, we set sail for Assos, intending to take Paul aboard there, for so he had arranged, intending himself to go by land.

The distance between Troas and Assos was about twenty miles, about a day's journey on foot. Paul determined to walk that distance. It seems he wanted to be alone. The others agreed to meet Paul at Assos, boarded a coasting vessel, and sailed away.[431]

Imagine Paul walking that day as he climbed from the coastal plain into the low hills and walked on the common highway. By midday, from the mountaintop road, he had one of the superb panoramas of Asia

---

[430] Hughes, *Acts: The Church Afire*, 276–277.
[431] J. Phillips, *Exploring Acts*, Ac 20:13.

Minor: On his right hand across the narrow strip of sapphire water of the Aegean Sea. From the heights of the mountains, he could see several of the cities of the seven churches of Asia Minor. His heart went out to them. [432] Most of all, he had some solitude with the Lord. As he walked, he reached the final crisis of his life: whether to turn back or to press forward. Undisturbed except by sheep with their bells, guard dogs to bark at him, and donkeys and a camel or two, he was able to learn his Master's will and reach the conclusion that he "nothing can separate us from the love of Christ." I can just hear him praying alone that road on the mountaintop along the Aegean Sea. Maybe he spoke the words he had written to the Romans.

> *Romans 8:35, 37-39* | Who shall separate us from the love of Christ? Shall tribulation, or distress, or persecution, or famine, or nakedness, or danger, or sword?... [37] No, in all these things we are more than conquerors through him who loved us. [38] For I am sure that neither death nor life, nor angels nor rulers, nor things present nor things to come, nor powers, [39] nor height nor depth, nor anything else in all creation, will be able to separate us from the love of God in Christ Jesus our Lord.

Paul needed to get alone so he could maintain his heavenly mindset. One of the problems of a busy life is the lack of time to be alone with God. Paul evidently felt the need for spiritual renewal. This third missionary journey had been extensive and strenuous. Do you have a heavenly mindset?

> *Colossians 3:2-3* | Set your minds on things that are above, not on things that are on earth. [3] For you have died, and your life is hidden with Christ in God.

You cannot be effective in supernatural ministry unless you have your heart and mind set on the supernatural. We have died to this life, and we need to be living not in this age, but in the eternal age that has already begun. You are here on earth, but your heart should be always with Christ. Indeed, God has "seated us with him in the heavenly places in Christ Jesus" (Eph 2:6).

Some struggle with being more concerned about job and money than meeting with God's people on the Lord's Day or about daily helping each other grow and change. This is a fleshly mindset that grieves

---

[432] Pollock, *The Apostle*, 232-33.

the Spirit. Many of God's people are living without the daily joy and encouragement of the Spirit's ministry. A lot of our problems in life will be solved when we fully surrender and submit to the new life and the Spirit's ministry of joy and love and fullness will overcome us.

Serve with a Heart for People

Paul had God's heart for people. How did Paul do so much in so little time? He did not stress about many things. Instead, it seems he was very orderly in his planning. He boarded the ship with Luke and Timothy and others and took time to reflect and to consider his plans and priorities. He let God guide his heart to kingdom priorities. Paul travelled through five port cities in about five days and landed at Miletus.

> **Acts 20:14-17** | And when he met us at Assos, we took him on board and went to Mitylene. **15** And sailing from there we came the following day opposite Chios; the next day we touched at Samos; and the day after that we went to Miletus. **16** For Paul had decided to sail past Ephesus, so that he might not have to spend time in Asia, for he was hastening to be at Jerusalem, if possible, on the day of Pentecost. **17** Now from Miletus he sent to Ephesus and called the elders of the church to come to him.

Paul knew Ephesus was not safe to return to at this time. Yet he was able to rest and plan for the next steps. The coasting vessel Paul boarded at Assos would have traveled along the inner sea lanes so that Paul could see the shoreline. Paul was a veteran traveler, but the peace and beauty of the voyage must have been balm to his soul. We can see him sitting on the deck in the shade of the great mainsail, enjoying the breeze and the sun, drinking in the scenery, thinking about what would be doing next.[433]

He wanted to return to Jerusalem and bless the saints with the offering from the churches, but there was something he needed to tend to first. The holy land had been going through a famine, and the believers there were in dire straits.

But something perhaps worse was happening at Ephesus. There were false teachers starting to enter into the Ephesian church. He called for the Ephesian elders to meet him in Miletus, about 30 miles from

---

[433] J. Phillips, *Exploring Acts.*, Ac 20:14–15.

Ephesus. Paul could be safe and still address and instruct these elders. God loved these elders, and so did Paul.

How vital it is that we truly learn to love the body of Christ, and to care for one another. Paul cared for the church at Ephesus and made it a priority to meet with them. It takes a heart of love and commitment to people to be intentional and responsible to encourage others in the body of Christ. So he arranged a meeting with the Ephesian elders, to bid them a final farewell. Paul served with a heart for people, but he went a step further. He trained godly men to shepherd God's flock.

Serve with Honorable Men

Acts 20:17 | Now from Miletus he sent to Ephesus and called the elders of the church to come to him.

Paul always had a team with him, if possible. He was careful to find the faithful, honorable men and train them for leadership. He did this for three years at Ephesus. His audience is variously described in the passage as elders, pastors, overseers, or shepherds. The word "elder" is *presbutos* in the Greek ("presbyter") and refers to a mature person who has been selected to serve in office (14:23). These same people are called "overseers" in Acts 20:28, which is *episkopos* or "bishop." They were chosen to "feed the church" (20:28; *cf* 1 Pet 5:2), which means "to shepherd." Paul called the local church "a flock, (20:28–29), so these men were also pastors. (The word *pastor* means "shepherd.") Thus, in the New Testament churches, the three titles *elder, bishop,* and *pastor* were synonymous. The qualifications for this office are given in 1 Timothy 3:1–7 and Titus 1:5–9.[434]

Paul had ensured that a plurality of elders had been appointed in the churches he planted (see Acts 14:23), men who would look after the people as shepherds look after sheep. [435] Speaking of these leaders in the church, the writer to Hebrews calls on Christians to follow the ministry of their elders.

Hebrews 13:17 | Obey your leaders and submit to them, for they are keeping watch over your souls, as those who will have to give an account. Let them do this with joy and not with groaning, for that would be of no advantage to you.

---

[434] Wiersbe, *The Bible Exposition Commentary*, vol. 1, 486.
[435] Thomas, *Acts*, 576.

Paul told the Ephesian elders that he was leaving Asia Minor. He had completed his missionary activity there and was entrusting the future of the church at Ephesus to the bishops and elders, the pastors and shepherds of the people there, and he gave them various instructions. At this time, Paul's heart was heavy, as were the hearts of all assembled, because they recognized this as Paul's farewell address.[436] Paul was telling them that they had a heavenly responsibility placed upon them for the lives of the saints. If God saves people, and he does, and he appoints men to oversee the souls of the saints, and he does, then there should be a mutual accountability for all believers in Christ's local churches.

God builds the church, and he commands all true believers to be a part of a local church. It's not an option. It's not just a "nice thing" to do. It's a command. We are called never to neglect the assembling of ourselves together. We are called to live life as a body, being equipped by the teachers and pastors (*cf* Eph 4:11-12; Heb 10:25). Because of this, elders have a very high and holy responsibility. Consider the words of John Calvin, one of the reformers of the sixteenth century.

> So highly does the Lord esteem the communion of his church that he considers everyone a traitor and apostate from religion who perversely withdraws himself from any Christian society which preserves the true ministry of the word and sacraments.[437]

We are all called to do the work of the ministry. We cannot live the Christian life as lone rangers. We need the entire body to function (Eph 5:11-16; 1 Cor 12). God called Paul to raise up godly men to oversee the growth of the Lord's church.

Serve with Humility

We say, "To God be the glory, great things he hath done." Truly, there is no room for boasting except in our great and compassionate God who gave his Son for us. When Paul addressed the Ephesian elders, he was clear about how lived among them with humility, not taking any credit for what was done among them. God deserved all the honor and glory, for he had done great things.

---

[436] Polhill, *Acts*, 424.
[437] John Calvin, *Institutes of the Christian Religion*, 2:1012.

Acts 20:18-19a | And when they came to him, he said to them: "You yourselves know how I lived among you the whole time from the first day that I set foot in Asia, **19** serving the Lord with all humility.

The proper demeanor of a servant is *humility*, and Paul frequently pointed to that quality as a major hallmark of the Christian life (Phil 2:3; Col 3:12; Eph 4:2). Humility is important, of course, because the opposite of humility is pride, and pride is a great danger for those who are in prominent positions of church leadership.[438]

The man of God must understand that the church of God is built by the Lord. There is no room for pride in skills or eloquence. Paul insisted on boasting in his weakness.

> *2 Corinthians 12:9* | He [Jesus] said to me, "My grace is sufficient for you, for my power is made perfect in weakness." Therefore I will boast all the more gladly of my weaknesses, so that the power of Christ may rest upon me.

"Isn't it amazing," Paul might have said, "that God could do such great things through people like me who are so weak, barely making it because of suffering and persecution?" Paul gloried in his weakness. Most of all, Paul gloried in the cross of Christ, which, by the ministry of the Spirit, is what did the work to build the congregation of the saints across the world.

> *Galatians 6:14* | As for me, may I never boast about anything except the cross of our Lord Jesus Christ.

Humility is a complete God-dependence and a self-forgetfulness where you are fully aware of the transcendent presence of God. It's not thinking less of yourself, but it is not thinking of yourself at all. It is a magnification of the Lord in all things, so that there is no room for self.

Serve with Hardship

Our ministry takes place in enemy occupied territory. Christ builds his church in the territory where Satan prowls, seeking to destroy every effort.[439] Paul reminded the Ephesian elders of his trials through the plots of the Jews and how he never gave up on them despite the intense suffering he endured.

---

[438] Boice, *Acts: An Expositional Commentary*, 344.
[439] Thomas, *Acts*, 580.

Acts 20:19 | Serving the Lord with all humility and with tears and with trials that happened to me through the plots of the Jews.

You cannot serve the Lord effectively without great suffering.

2 Timothy 3:12 | All who live godly in Christ Jesus will suffer persecution.

Paul, as a good and qualified shepherd, was willing to suffer in order to rescue and protect the sheep. He served with many tears and stood firm against the wicked one's distractions and discouragements. He didn't let the pain of ministry harden his heart.

1 Thessalonians 2:7-8 | We were gentle among you, like a nursing mother taking care of her own children. ⁸ So, being affectionately desirous of you, we were ready to share with you not only the gospel of God but also our own selves, because you had become very dear to us.

We are going to have to persevere in hardship as the saints. We are all ministers of the gospel, and that requires thick skin and a big heart. Don't let the discouragements of the wicked one make you jaded or bitter or cynical. Keep a soft heart toward the saints despite the suffering you have to endure. How else does supernatural ministry occur?

Paul served the Lord with joy and gladness. He never slowed down. Supernatural ministry comes when we realize that we serve God, but God must give the increase.

1 Corinthians 3:6 | I planted, Apollos watered, but God gave the increase.

We do serve. We do plant. We do water. But God has to do the miracle of growth. Paul's first way of supernatural ministry was service to God.

TEACHING FOR THE CHURCH (20:20)

Another way supernatural ministry occurs is through the teaching of the word of God. As we preach the word with the Spirit's power, we will God's power to transform resting in the hearts of God's people. This is why Paul would not shrink back from teaching the word.

Acts 20:20 | How I did not shrink from declaring to you anything that was profitable, and teaching you in public and from house to house.

The word is profitable. It conforms us into the image of Christ. Paul held nothing back of the word of God in his teaching. He saw clearly that his obligation toward the church was to teach. As he wrote in Ephesians 4:12, the primary task of leaders in the church is "to equip the saints for the work of ministry, for building up the body of Christ"—a goal that can only be accomplished through the consistent, thorough teaching of God's word.

Our Attitude Toward Teaching

> **Acts 20:20a** | How I did not shrink from declaring to you anything that was profitable.

Paul reminds the Ephesian leaders that he did not shrink from declaring to them anything that was profitable. Shrink means "to draw back" or "to withhold." Paul held back nothing of the wise counsel and holy, sovereign purpose of God; he withheld no doctrine, exhortation, or admonition that was profitable.[440] Remember Paul's charge to Timothy.

> *2 Timothy 4:1-5* | I charge you in the presence of God and of Christ Jesus, who is to judge the living and the dead, and by his appearing and his kingdom: ² preach the word; be ready in season and out of season; reprove, rebuke, and exhort, with complete patience and teaching. ³ For the time is coming when people will not endure sound teaching, but having itching ears they will accumulate for themselves teachers to suit their own passions, ⁴ and will turn away from listening to the truth and wander off into myths. ⁵ As for you, always be sober-minded, endure suffering, do the work of an evangelist, fulfill your ministry.

We are not to fear man, but God and to preach the whole counsel of God's word.

> *Acts 20:27* | I did not shrink from declaring to you the whole counsel of God.

We are not called to edit the word. We are called to declare it. We are called to "guard the deposit" of the word (2 Tim 1:14). We are to lead with the word, not the culture or the constantly shifting values and morals of this age. It is the Spirit through the ministry of the word that

---

[440] MacArthur, *Acts*, vol. 2, 213.

transforms people. If we want a supernatural ministry, we have to be committed to the supernatural word which is able to transform us (*cf* Jas 1:18).

I don't have a choice in declaring the whole counsel of God. God requires it of me. God's going to ask of us as pastors and elders,

"What did you keep back? What were you afraid to preach? How much of my counsel did you declare to the people under your care? It was your task when I consecrated you to hold nothing back, to proclaim the whole counsel of God."[441] The prophet Ezekiel gives a message that contains a sobering warning of the consequences of failing to declare God's truth.

> *Ezekiel 33:7-9* | So you, son of man, I have made a watchman for the house of Israel. Whenever you hear a word from my mouth, you shall give them warning from me. ⁸ If I say to the wicked, O wicked one, you shall surely die, and you do not speak to warn the wicked to turn from his way, that wicked person shall die in his iniquity, but his blood I will require at your hand. ⁹ But if you warn the wicked to turn from his way, and he does not turn from his way, that person shall die in his iniquity, but you will have delivered your soul.

Pray for your shepherds. We don't want to hold anything back.

The Application of Teaching

Acts 20:20b | How I did not shrink from declaring to you anything that was profitable.

Paul wasn't concerned that the people just have a better life, or great Bible knowledge. Paul was concerned that the people knew how to walk profitably in the word of God. We are called not to be "hearers only" but "doers" of the word, walking in the word and applying it to our lives (Jas 1:22). The word of God is sufficient and powerful to change your life and transform your heart (*cf* Heb 4:12).

> *2 Timothy 3:16-17* | All Scripture is breathed out by God and profitable for teaching, for reproof, for correction, and for training in righteousness, ¹⁷ that the man of God may be complete, equipped for every good work.

---

[441] Sproul, *Acts*, 346.

We believe the Bible is sufficient. While understanding science and psychology and personality types can be fun and helpful, we don't rely on any of that to achieve the Lord's purpose for our lives. We are called to be conformed to the image of Jesus Christ in our hearts and character, and only the word of God by the supernatural ministry of the Holy Spirit can bring that about.

> *Psalm 119:105* | Your word is a lamp to my feet and a light to my path.

We believe that the heart change God wants for us can only be experienced through applying the word of God through faith, believing God and knowing him in a personal way as he reveals himself in his word. You cannot know the true and living God outside of his revelations of himself. The whole purpose of your life is to know God and to be changed into his image as you love and worship him. That occurs when we look deeply into the mirror of God's word and are transformed into Christ's likeness.

> *2 Corinthians 3:18* | We all, with unveiled face, beholding the glory of the Lord, are being transformed into the same image from one degree of glory to another. For this comes from the Lord who is the Spirit.

Everything we experience in life—every trial, tribulation, and test—every victory and joy—they are all meant to conform us to the image of Christ as we gaze on his glory through the word of God (Rom 8:28-29).

The Arenas of Teaching

God's word is not just to be taught *publicly* on the Lord's Day, but also *privately* from house to house.

> **Acts 20:20c** | And teaching you in public and from house to house.

Paul did not just teach the word to people in public. He was concerned with the saints' everyday lives in private. Paul did not go to people simply as a scholar instructing them in theology; his heart was with them. He wept and prayed with them and endured all manner of attacks and suffering from hostile hands for their sakes.[442] He taught them both publicly and personally. He had "refrigerator rights" at their homes. Whether in public or in private, the servant of Jesus Christ does

---

[442] Ibid.

not fail to declare the profitable truths of God's word. How else does supernatural ministry occur?

EVANGELISM FOR THE LOST (20:21)

Acts 20:21 | Testifying both to Jews and to Greeks of repentance toward God and of faith in our Lord Jesus Christ.

No view of the ministry is complete that fails to have a proper perspective on reaching the lost. Paul saw himself as an evangelist, having a mandate to reach sinners with the truth of the gospel. So intense was Paul's concern for the lost that he cried out, "Woe is me if I do not preach the gospel" (1 Cor 9:16).[443]

The Recipients of Evangelism

Acts 20:21a | Testifying both to Jews and to Greeks.

No one is excluded from the gospel. Pagans are welcome. The religious need Christ too. Christ's body is made up of every culture. God wants his churches to look like heaven.

> *Revelation 7:9* | I looked, and behold, a great multitude that no one could number, from every nation, from all tribes and peoples and languages, standing before the throne and before the Lamb, clothed in white robes.

Our King's marching orders were:

> *Mark 16:15* | Go into all the world and preach the gospel to every creature.

> *Acts 4:12* | There is salvation in no one else, for there is no other name under heaven given among men by which we must be saved.

God's "commands all people everywhere to repent" (Acts 17:30). He's "not wishing that any should perish, but that all should reach repentance" (2 Pet 3:9). Every nation under heaven is called to come to Christ. Remember the striking words of Ezekiel to Israel.

> *Ezekiel 33:11* | As I live, declares the Lord God, I have no pleasure in the death of the wicked, but that the wicked turn from his way and

---

[443] MacArthur, *Acts*, vol. 2, 215.

live; turn back, turn back from your evil ways, for why will you die, O house of Israel?

If you don't know him, turn to him. He has no pleasure in you perishing apart from his favor forever. He wants his heaven full! He says,

> Luke 14:23, NLT | Go out to the roads and country lanes and compel them to come in, so that my house will be full.

The Response to Evangelism

Acts 20:21b | Testifying... of repentance toward God and of faith in our Lord Jesus Christ.

Paul's method of visitation was not just to leave a cheery greeting and an invitation to church. His purpose was to confront people with the claims of Christ, with the need for repentance and regeneration. It did not matter to Paul if it was a Jewish home or a Gentile home, a pious home or a pagan home. His message was to the point: repent and put your faith in the Lord Jesus Christ.[444]

A biblically sound gospel presentation must contain two components repentance and faith. First, it must include repentance toward God. *Metanoia* (repentance) is a rich and important New Testament word, meaning "to change one's mind or purpose." It describes a change of mind that results in a change of behavior; it is the conscious act of a sinner turning from his sins to God.[445] Repentance means to have a complete and radical change of your worldview, how you see everything. This is not possible through human means but is a gift from God.

Faith means to entrust your soul to Christ, believing he substituted himself for us, to satisfy the wrath of God, and that he rose again and gives us his Spirit. We now live the life of faith since our heart is God's abode.

The Reward of Evangelism

Acts 20:21b | Testifying... of repentance toward God and of faith in our Lord Jesus Christ.

---

[444] J. Phillips, *Exploring Acts*, Ac 20:21b.
[445] MacArthur, *Acts.*, 216.

Our reward is that the lost can know the Lord Jesus Christ. What is it that we preach? Redemption in Christ. Cross-shaped, Christ-centered preaching is vital. Listen to J.I. Packer.

> The preachers' commission is to declare the whole counsel of God; but the cross is the center of that counsel, and the Puritans knew that the traveler through the Bible landscape misses his way as soon as he loses sight of the hill called Calvary.[446]

Paul had a cross-shaped ministry. What does that mean? It's not my works that gain me heaven. It's Christ. It's not my church attendance. It's not my perfect life. No, it's Christ alone. Jesus said,

> *John 14:6* | I am the way, and the truth, and the life. No one comes to the Father except through me.

> *Ephesians 2:8-9* | For by grace you have been saved through faith. And this is not your own doing; it is the gift of God, ⁹ not a result of works, so that no one may boast.

The way through the narrow gate is to come through the righteousness of Jesus Christ. He takes our robe of shame and sin, and we get his perfect record. Isn't that amazing! Put your faith in Christ and his work! He said, "It is finished." There's nothing left for you to do except to hate your old life and receive Christ and his eternal life. How else does supernatural ministry occur?

SACRIFICE OF SELF (20:22-24)

Supernatural ministry comes as we give all of our selves in sacrifice for the Lord and his church. Paul was all about the supernatural ministry of God. He knew nothing depended on him, but it all depended on the Lord. He was willing to give all he had for the Lord to use him, but the Lord had to do the work. All believers are called to give our lives away for Christ.

A Spirit-led Sacrifice

The world is all about take, take, take. But Paul wanted to give everything for the Lord, even if it meant his own death. When the Spirit is leading, you have God's power to do the hard things. You can do whatever he calls you to do!

---

[446] J. I. Packer, *A Quest for Godliness* (Wheaton, IL: Crossway, 1990), 286.

Acts 20:22-23 | And now, behold, I am going to Jerusalem, constrained by the Spirit, not knowing what will happen to me there, ²³ except that the Holy Spirit testifies to me in every city that imprisonment and afflictions await me.

Paul was constrained, or literally "bound," by the Spirit to go to Jerusalem. The prophecies were clear: great suffering and imprisonment would await, but the Spirit was leading Paul to anyway.

How was it possible that Paul could go to Jerusalem, which would lead to his death in Rome in 67 A.D., not to mention close to ten years of imprisonment in various locations? It's the Spirit of God that led him to give all. Let the Spirit lead you, for when the Spirit leads, he also empowers!

A Selfless Sacrifice

Paul sacrificed all for Christ, even his comfort and eventually his own life.

Acts 20:24a | But I do not account my life of any value nor as precious to myself.

What happened to him was of no consequence (*cf* 21:13) when compared to the high and holy call on his life. John the Baptist said it well, "He must increase, but I must decrease" (Jn 3:30). My life is worth anything only as I reflect Jesus Christ and am conformed to his image.

A Satisfying Sacrifice

Paul was constrained by the Spirit to finish his ministry.

Acts 20:24b | If only I may finish my course and the ministry that I received from the Lord Jesus, to testify to the gospel of the grace of God.

Dear saints, one day it's all going to be over. The race will be done. Only one thing mattered to Paul: to finish the work God had given him to do. And what was the product of Paul's life? He wrote thirteen books in the New Testament, and seven of them were written from prison. He makes his testimony clear to Timothy.

2 Timothy 4:7 | I have fought the good fight, I have finished the race, I have kept the faith.

Whatever your pain or sacrifice for Christ is, it will not be wasted. He will use your persecution, your trials, and your difficulties to expand the kingdom. Paul's legacy of pain was seven letters to the churches. He didn't give up or give in when he went to jail for preaching the gospel. He made it the most fruitful time of his ministry. What about you? Do you realize that whatever pain and suffering you go through, it's worth it to be a part of this supernatural ministry? Jesus says,

> John 15:5 | Without me, you can do nothing.

That you is a "ye." It's plural. It means the church can do nothing without Christ. I appreciate the words of A.C. Dixon.

> When we depend upon organizations, we get what organizations can do; when we depend upon education, we get what education can do; when we depend upon man, we get what man can do; but when we depend upon God, we get what God can do.[447]

Conclusion

Oh, mothers (and fathers), we want you to see the work of supernatural ministry in your home. If you will surrender to the Lord, you can't even imagine what influence you will have on your child. And by the way, children grow up don't they?

First Lady Laura Bush recalls one overnight visit with her husband in the home of his parents, the former President and Mrs. Bush.

George W. Bush woke up at 6 A.M. as usual and went downstairs to get a cup of coffee. He sists down on the sofa with his parents and put his feet up. And suddenly, his mother Barbara Bush yelled, "George, put your feet down!"

George's dad replied, "Give him a break, Barbara, he's the President of the United States."

And Barbara said, "I don't care. I don't want his feet on my table."

The president promptly did as he was told. What's the point of that story? Mothers have a profound influence on their children, and even Presidents must listen to their mothers.

Dear mom, lead your children to Christ. You don't have to be an Ephesian elder or an apostle to do so. You have all the means of grace at your fingertips in your well-worn Bible.

---

[447] Amzi Clarence Dixon, *Evangelism Old and New: God's Search for Man in All Ages* (New York: American Tract Society, 1905), 18.

35 | ACTS 20:25-38
A CHARGE TO THE EPHESIAN ELDERS

> *Pay careful attention to yourselves and to all the flock, in which the Holy Spirit has made you overseers, to care for the church of God, which he obtained with his own blood.*
> ACTS 20:28

A man has written a book talking about how to be successful by managing your life and your time. It has a really helpful story in it. It's the story of a teacher who stood before his class, and he had a wide-mouthed jar.

In that jar he'd put some large stones, and he filled it up to the brim with these large stones. And then, he asked his class, "Is the jar full?" And some of the students carelessly said, "Yes, the jar is full." It was up to the very top with those large stones. He said, "No, the jar is not full."

Then, he took some scoops of gravel and put them in the jar and shook it 'til the gravel filled all the crevices there. Then he asked the question: "Now is the jar full?" Of course, the students were a bit wary. They didn't want to answer. But, one or two said, "Yes, now it's full." He said, "No, it's not yet full."

Then, he took some sand, and poured the sand in over the gravel, and shook it, and compacted it, and smoothed the sand off up at the top. "Now," he said, "is the jar full?" No one wanted to lift their hand anymore, but maybe one said, "Well, it looks full." He said, as you can guess, "No, it's not full."

And then, he took some water and poured the water in over the sand 'til it came up to the brim. And then, he said, "Now is the jar full?" And, they had to admit it certainly looked full. Then he asked this question to this class: he said, "Now, what is the truth, the lesson, in what I have just done?" He said, "Here is the lesson: if I had not put the big rocks in first, there would have been no room for them later on." And so it is for us: if we don't put in the "big rocks"—the most important things—first in our lives, there won't be room for them later. Remember the words of Jesus.

> Matthew 6:33 | Seek first the kingdom of God and his righteousness, and all these things will be added to you.

What are the big rocks? What are the things that really matter, things that you may be leaving out of your life—a lot of smaller things that have filled the capacity of your life, and you have left out the things that really matter, the big rocks? That's what we're going to be talking about—things that really, really, really matter.

In our text in Acts 20, the Apostle Paul is giving his farewell address to the elders at the church of Ephesus. They met him in Miletus because it was too dangerous for Paul to go back to Ephesus. He's had taught them, discipled them, and mentored them. Now, he's saying goodbye to them for the last time. This is Paul's final farewell. They know that perhaps the next time they meet it'll be on the shore of eternity.[448] Paul gives them the five "big rocks," or the five foundations of a fruitful, supernatural ministry for the Lord.

> Key thought: Lay the foundations of your life on Christ, and he will give the increase of supernatural influence and legacy, long after you are gone.

COUNSEL YOURSELF (20:25-28A)

The first thing he tells them to prepare for when he is gone is that they need to care for their own spiritual walk. They have to be in the habit of counseling themselves and living according to the word in faithfulness. Paul had done that for them.

---

[448] Adrian Rogers, "Things That Really Matter," in *Adrian Rogers Sermon Archive* (Signal Hill, CA: Rogers Family Trust, 2017), Ac 20:17–38.

A Faithful Ministry

When Paul says, "Pay careful attention to yourselves" in verse 28, he is preaching what he practices. Paul has faithfully cared for his own spiritual walk with God that he could "proclaim the kingdom" with power and conviction.

> **Acts 20:25** | And now, behold, I know that none of you among whom I have gone about proclaiming the kingdom will see my face again.

Paul has faithfully preached the kingdom, and now he will never see them again. He has given them an example of faithful ministry to follow. He preached the kingdom to himself first, and then to others. I love the words of Martyn Lloyd Jones.

> Have you realized that most of your unhappiness in life is due to the fact that you are listening to yourself instead of talking to yourself?... Talk to yourself, and though the devil will suggest that because you do not feel, you are not a Christian, say: ... 'Whether I feel or not, I believe the Scriptures. I believe God's word is true and I will stay my soul on it, I will believe in it come what may.[449]

We must be constantly teaching the word of God to each other, but first we must counsel ourselves. That's where faithful ministry comes from.

Choosing to walk in the word on a personal level, counseling yourself on a daily basis, is going to result in a life of fruitful and faithful ministry like Paul. He was constantly proclaiming the message of the kingdom because it had changed his life so much.

What about you? Have you tapped into the word in such a way that it is personal and enriching to you so that others can follow your counsel? Are you able to read the Bible on a constant basis so that you are growing and changing into the image of Jesus Christ? This is one of those "big rock" foundations in your life. Daily walking with Christ, proclaiming the kingdom, will result in a faithful ministry.

A Divine Direction

Another way Paul counseled himself was in the word of God. He got his direction from God's word. This is the last time Paul will see the

---

[449] D. Martyn Lloyd-Jones, *Spiritual Depression: Its Causes and Cures* (Grand Rapids, MI: Zondervan, 2016), 20-21.

Ephesian elders. Paul knows by prophecy that he's on his way to Jerusalem to get arrested. God's going to have him write his prison epistles.

Acts 20:25b | I know that none of you... will see my face again.

Now Paul's face and physical appearance wasn't much to look at. One early record gives us a description of the great apostle.

> A man small of stature, thin-haired upon the head and crooked legs, in a good state of body, with eyebrows meeting and nose somewhat hooked, his face, full of grace: for sometimes he appeared like a man, and sometimes he had the face of an angel. [450]

Regardless, it wasn't Paul appearance they would miss. It was his love and devotion to God and his care for their souls. But now Paul was on a journey to Jerusalem. He had received this direction from God through some of the New Testament prophets.

Now I don't know of any prophets today that can tell you God's will for your life, but I do know that New Testament prophets today are pastors and elders of local churches who teach the word of God. They lift up the word of God which is sufficient to direct your life.

Perhaps you lack discernment for direction. I believe every Christian can have discernment. There is no "gift of discernment" just like there is no "gift of love" or "gift of patience." There are certain number of virtues that all Christians are called to have and have access to, and discernment is on the top of the list. We are all called to be discerning by studying and applying the word of God. If you lack discernment, you need to get vitally connected to the word and to mature saints in your local church. Being around wise people will make you wise. You cannot live the Christian life alone. You need to be vitally connected to the saints if you are going to have God's divine direction.

A Clean Conscience

The reason Paul could counsel himself so well, was that he had a clean conscience. Listen to his amazing testimony.

Acts 20:26 | Therefore I testify to you this day that I am innocent of the blood of all.

---

[450] Jeremy W. Barrier. *The Acts of Paul and Thecla: A Critical Introduction and Commentary* (Tübingen, Germany: Gulde Druck Publishing, 2009), 73.

Paul believed the gospel that he counseled himself with. He knew the peace of God that passes understanding, and he did everything he could to protect that peace. The direct result was that he wanted others to know this peace. In fact, he thought it would be criminal, like worse than murder, to not tell people about the threat of eternal death in the lake of fire. That's why he says, "I'm innocent of the blood of all." What's he saying? He was concerned for the lost.

He's referring back to Ezekiel 33:8, where God says, as the watchman of Israel, if you don't warn the wicked that God is going to judge their sin, then their blood is on your hands. But if you warn them him and they still don't repent, you are free from their blood. Paul said, "As a watchman, I'm innocent because I've given the warning. I've given the gospel. I'm called people to repentant faith in Jesus. That's all I can do."

Young person, you are walking with Jesus, but you have a friend who is lost. You need to warn them. Let them know about Christ. It might be a friend at church. They need you to tell them. My brother, you might have a co-worker at your place of employment, and you care about them. But do you care about them enough to warn them about the wrath of the Lamb that is coming. Right now they can escape that judgment through faith in Christ. Will you tell them? Tell them of Christ's sacrifice. Dear sister, you live in a neighborhood with somebody who's not saved—you are the watchman on the wall. It's fine to talk about your kids, but are you praying for an opportunity to tell them about Jesus?

Brothers and sisters, do you have clean hands when it comes to evangelism? God calls you to be his instrument. You are the watchman. If you don't tell them about Christ, then who will? Where you have failed confess it and be cleansed. But Paul didn't have to confess. Every opportunity God gave him, he took and lifted up Christ.

God is calling every mother's child in this building to be a soul winner. You say, "Well, God didn't call me to be a soul winner. God called me to be a mother or father," or, "God called me to be a musician," or, "God called me to be in business." God calls all of us to seek his business and his kingdom first. He says to go into all the world and evangelize. That's not a spiritual gift, but it's a command for every Christian. If you're not interested in bringing souls to Jesus Christ, you are guilty of high treason against heaven's King. Listen to Spurgeon's conviction about soul winning.

> "Oh!" says one, I am not my brother's keeper." No, I will tell you your name; it is Cain. You are your brother's murderer; for every professing Christian, who is not his brother's keeper, is his brother's killer; and be you sure that it is so; for you may kill by neglect quite as surely as you may kill by the bow or by the dagger. [451]

May the Lord give us grace to see souls as Paul saw them, as those under the attack of the enemy. He saw himself as the watchman to warn the people that the enemy was about to destroy them. Are you sounding the alarm to your family, friends, and neighbors?

A Noble Legacy

One major way the pastor counsels himself and the entire congregation is considering the entire counsel of God's word.

> **Acts 20:27** | For I did not shrink from declaring to you the whole counsel of God.

Paul preached to himself the whole counsel of God, so he could teach it to others. We are not called to preach our own pet doctrines or new psychological insights. The whole counsel of the word is sufficient for life and godliness. In the time that I have ministered among you (in the last fifteen years), there have been around 2000 sermons preached from all but six books of the Bible from your pastors and elders. I know you are wondering which books we have not preached from. According to my records the books are 2 John, and five of the minor prophets (Amos, Micah, Nahum, Habakkuk, Zephaniah). Many of the series have gone through entire books of the Bible. It is my desire to preach through the entire Bible with one congregation. Please pray that I will be able to do that.

Why do we preach expositorily— "line upon line, precept upon precept," chapter by chapter, and book by book in the Bible (Isa 28:10)? Because it is the safest way to preach the whole counsel of God. Spurgeon did not preach book by book, but in his ministry, he preached

---

[451] Charles Haddon Spurgeon, *We Endeavor: Helpful Words for Members of the Young People's Society of Christian Endeavor* (London: Passmore and Alabaster, 1897), 67.

most of the contents of every book of the Bible over a span of 3600 messages during thirty-eight years of ministry at one congregation.

A Personal Care

Are you counseling yourself with an attention to personal care? This is something Paul exhorted the Ephesian elders to do, but every Christian should participate in the means of grace with the direct intention of applying the word to our own hearts.

> **Acts 20:28a** | Pay careful attention to yourselves.

Sound doctrine is vital, but alone it is not enough, because according to Scripture, the fundamental qualification for pastoral ministry is godly character. This is what Paul is getting at when he tells the pastors and elders at Ephesus to "pay careful attention" to their personal walk. The elders are to keep a watch on their own lives lest they set a bad example to those they shepherd. It is a fact that the saints of a particular congregation will hardly ever rise to greater expressions of holiness than that of their elders.[452] Oh, that we as your elders would have a heart for Christ above all else. Neither skill, nor knowledge, nor wisdom, nor reputation, nor personality, nor apparent fruitfulness of public ministry is enough. Look carefully at the qualifications for the elder in 1 Timothy 3 and Titus 1, and you will encounter a profile of personal holiness. Listen to Paul's admonition later to Timothy.

> *1 Timothy 4:16* | Keep a close watch on yourself and on the teaching. Persist in this, for by so doing you will save both yourself and your hearers.

Ah, but one task is easier than the other, is it not? Don't you find it far more appealing and enjoyable to study doctrine than to study your own heart? Isn't it much more pleasant to examine our books than to examine our motives? Aren't we far quicker to apply ourselves to a specific text in preparation for a sermon than to apply that same text to our own heart and life? Listen to what Puritan Richard Baxter wrote.

---

[452] Thomas, *Acts*, 582.

> It is a palpable error of some ministers... who study hard to preach exactly, yet study little or not at all to live exactly.[453] —Richard Baxter

He goes on to speak of the damage done by inconstant elders and pastors.

> Take heed to yourself, lest your example contradict your doctrine, and lest you lay such stumbling blocks from your own life before poor blind sinners, as may be the occasion of their ruin; lest you unsay with your life, what you have proclaimed with your tongue.[454] —Richard Baxter

The saints need a consistent walk from their elders just as much as the sound teaching. They need to see that sound teaching results in holiness of life. We cannot be content with merely understanding robust theology if we don't worship Christ from our hearts and in our walk. Bad living almost always reveals bad theology on the heart level. See a minister start to morally compromise in his life, and you will find a minister who does not believe what he is teaching or is beginning to teach falsely.

There ought to be the fruit of the Spirit that emanates from our attitudes and life. Indeed, no matter how extensive one's scriptural knowledge, how amazing one's memory, it is self-deception if that is all there is. Sound doctrine is the foundation for godly living, and it is not mere proclamation, but obedience to the word that demonstrates genuine faith.[455] Spurgeon said it well to his pastor's college.

> Our characters must be more persuasive than our speech.[456]

Pray for your elders that each of us would persevere in the power of the Holy Spirit and live a life of holiness and joy as we endeavor to preach the word and live a humble example before the flock.

---

[453] Richard Baxter, *The Reformed Pastor* (Carlisle: Banner of Truth, 1974), 63-64.

[454] Ibid., 33.

[455] Peter H. Davids, *New International Biblical Commentary: James* (Peabody: Hendrickson Publishers, 1983), 41.

[456] Charles Haddon Spurgeon, *Lectures to My Students*, (Pasadena, TX: Pilgrim Publications, 1881), 13.

SHEPHERD THE FLOCK (20:28B)

Acts 20:28b | And to all the flock, in which the Holy Spirit has made you overseers, to care for the church of God, which he obtained with his own blood.

If we are going to have lasting fruit as a congregation, we have to shepherd the flock. Elders shepherd, and then we need to shepherd each other. What shepherds display is that out of personal watch care over themselves, they are able, through example, model what the entire church of God should be doing. We are only as useful as we are devoted to Christ.[457]

A Word about Membership

Acts 20:28b | And to all the flock.

Notice first, there is a word about membership. Notice that the church is compared to a flock of sheep. A flock is not a random collection of lambs. Sheep belong to specific flocks. Ultimately all Christians are part of Jesus's flock (universal church). Christ is the chief Shepherd. Elders are under-shepherds who care for Christ's church and give his lambs spiritual protection and direction. There are many metaphors for the church. We are called a flock, a temple (Eph 2:21), a family (Eph 2:19), and a body (1 Cor 12:27). All share the characteristic of being joined together and led. The sheep are to be shepherded like a flock, cared for. Looked out for. Are you being shepherded? Are you committed to a local church?

A Word about Eldership

Acts 20:28c | In which the Holy Spirit has made you overseers.

Second there is a word about eldership. The Holy Spirit made the Ephesian elders, and all the rightly called men of the church to be overseers or literally guardians of the church. Paul speaks to the Ephesian elders as a father to his dear sons in the faith. The apostle is intimately acquainted with their frailties and the perils of pastoral ministry in a sinful world. Yet he knows the sufficient grace of God. they can do it. How can weak and frail elders shepherd the flock? Shepherds lead the

---

[457] Thomas, *Acts*, 582.

flock by the Holy Spirit who made us overseers. We do not rely on man's wisdom or man's organization. We rely on the Holy Spirit's power that raised Jesus from the dead.

A Word about Discipleship

Acts 20:28d | To care for the church of God, which he obtained with his own blood.

Finally, there is a word about discipleship. A disciple is literally a "learner." Elders are to teach and help disciple God's flock. As God's shepherds, we are "to care for the church of God, which he obtained with his own blood." The price God paid was the blood of his own Son.

Elders are to care for the church in the same way Christ did: we are to give our life and our time and all that we are to the sheep. Elders will get their hearts broken many times over because we care. We care and are willing to have thick skin and a big heart. We are not to be jaded by the problems of the sheep in a broken, sinful world. We are to keep a tender, caring heart. And who is our example for that? Our Lord Jesus Christ is our model, who laid down his life for the sheep. He obtained his flock by giving his own blood. We keep going after the sheep, laying our lives down for them, as Christ did for his church.

Dear saints, pray for your elders and pastors. We are called to shepherd you. We ask that you think the best and realize the many obstacles we have against us. Just as with Christ, he had spiritual, evil enemies in the realm of darkness. Satan would have shepherds to be discouraged, but the Spirit of God is our comforter. Walk together with us as elders. If you feel you are being left behind or neglected, call us. Talk to us. Let us know.

If you really want the Lord to bless our congregation, we have to see the elders training the saints for the work of ministry (Eph 4:11-12). The shepherds equip the saints with the word, and also give them an example with their lives, but it is the saints who do the work of the ministry. Every saint is a minister. Let's lay down those big foundational rocks in our lives.

This is the chief way the elders care for the flock. The more this happens, the more the health of the church increases. The more people we can reach. This is the work of discipleship.

A Word about Headship

Acts 20:28e | Which he obtained with his own blood.

Jesus is the head of the church. Jesus doesn't need Paul. He purchased all believers with his own blood. Christ is the ultimate Shepherd of the church, not Paul, and not the elders. That is a relief in some ways. It is also an incredible motivation to make sure the saints are living under the lordship of Jesus.

PROTECT GOD'S PEOPLE (20:29-31)

Paul calls the elders to guard and protect God's people. False doctrine brings wrong living, which will bring dishonor to God and misery to the saints. How vital it is to look out for the dangers that harass the sheep. Paul provides a threefold incentive for this watch-care ministry.

There, as it were, a threefold attack against the church.

Dangers Around Us

First, Paul says there are dangers around us.

Acts 20:29 | I know that after my departure fierce wolves will come in among you, not sparing the flock.

There are dangers *around us*, "wolves" that want to surround the flock and ravage her (20:29). Paul was referring to false teachers, the counterfeits who exploit the church for personal gain (Mt 7:15–23; 10:16; Lk 10:3; 2 Pet 2:1–3). [458] How important it is that believers know the word of God and be able to live above the world, exposing false teaching, and living a life of holiness in the light of God's word.

Fierce wolves will attack the church, "which he obtained with his own blood" (20:28). There are some who will be drawn away by their enticing words to believe lies shrouded in plausible ideas. Lives will be compromised, marriages ruined, testimonies in disarray. The church is in the midst of hostile territory—wolves may appear charming from a distance, but they have teeth and intend to use them for wicked and evil purposes. Elders need to surround the weak and bruised and protect them from the pack of wolves that encircles, being ready to lay down their lives, if necessary, in order that the flock be spared.

---

[458] Wiersbe, *The Bible Exposition Commentary*, vol. 1, 487.

The only way to resist the dangers around you is to resist the devil by knowing Christ and trusting his word. You have to be filled with the Spirit, with a heart filled with holiness, and the devil cannot harass you as he wants. Sure we can be tested by the devil like Job, but being filled with the Spirit, we won't give in. We'll bow down and worship like Job when all is stripped from us. Stay close to the Shepherd because the wolves are coming! Expect satanic attack!

Dangers Among Us

Then, Paul says there are dangers among us. Some false teachers will arise from outside, but alarmingly, some will arise "from among your own selves."

> **Acts 20:30** | And from among your own selves will arise men speaking twisted things, to draw away the disciples after them.

Savage wolves will arise from within the ranks of the Ephesian eldership itself. Some among them would become intoxicated with the power and control the office brings. Instead of being servant leaders, they would become tyrants, forcing their errant views on the weak and impressionable. Paul urges them to be on the alert! [459]

It's your responsibility to make sure the elders continue in humility. Love and support them. Support that kind of elder ministry. Don't allow yourself to be a distraction from what God is doing. Stay filled with the Spirit and busy in the means of grace, or you may fall away.

Make sure the elders are not teaching anything new. If it's new, it's not true. There's nothing novel about the gospel. It was preached to Abraham. It's preached to us today, "we come to God by grace through faith." Christ alone! There's no other gospel. At our church, we will not allow the word of God to be twisted! We don't rest on psychology or self-help or self-promotion. Kick out those wolves who would ever do that!

Dangers Within Us

Then, Paul says there are dangers within us.

> **Acts 20:31** | Therefore be alert, remembering that for three years I did not cease night or day to admonish every one with tears.

---

[459] Thomas, *Acts*, 585-586.

Be alert. Paul didn't even trust himself, but admonished everyone from the Scriptures day and night, with tears. We are called to be alert to the move of the Spirit, that the Lord moves by the Scriptures, which Paul preached for three years, day and night. I can just hear Paul reading from Isaiah 53, "By his stripes we are healed," tears rolling down his face. "I'm healed. He healed me of my self-righteousness and all my sin." Let's believe it and live it to the point of tears and deep emotions. If we are not gripped by the Scriptures, we are in danger from our own hearts!

STUDY THE WORD (20:32)

Paul was going away. He could not stay to chase away the wolves. The flock would not be left defenseless, however; they had God, and they had their elders, whom the Holy Spirit had appointed to that flock. The elders had to teach the flock, as Paul did, that the greatest defense they had was God's word. If they would cultivate a relationship with God through his word, they would be unstoppable.

> **Acts 20:32** | And now I commend you to God and to the word of his grace, which is able to build you up and to give you the inheritance among all those who are sanctified.

Here we see another great foundation stone of the Christian life that elders are to lead in is the study of the word of God. It is therefore, vital that we read and study the Bible.

The Bible Saves Us

> **Acts 20:32a** | And now I commend you to God and to the word of his grace.

It is by the preaching of the word of grace, the gospel that we are saved. By the word we were drawn to God and regenerated. The word saves us and brings us into a vital relationship with God as adopted children of God.

We cannot build the church unless God is building our lives daily. There is a connection here between a personal walk with God ("I commend you to God") and the word of God ("the word of his grace"). God reveals himself to us through his word. We cannot know him otherwise. The word of God alone is able to open up the way to a relationship with the Lord, and the spiritual leader must spend time daily in the word of

God and prayer, living out this relationship with God, in a vital, personal walk with him.[460]

The elders are protected by God's word, and they protect the flock with it. Remember the Bible is called the "sword of the Spirit" (Eph 6:17). How exactly are we protected by God's word?

The Bible Strengthens Us

> **Acts 20:32b** | The word of his grace... is able to build you up.

The Bible has *strengthening* power to build up our faith. We get spiritual faith muscles as we obey and apply the word of God to our lives. The word is the only standard for truth and faith. We must put away the lies of the wicked one through God's gracious word. There is no other way to grow. As we put away the lies and see God in his glory, we grow into the image of Christ. We also enjoy life a whole lot more. The joy of the Lord is our strength. We become God-dependent, not man-dependent. The only way to grow in this way is through the word of God.

The Bible Secures Us

> **Acts 20:32c** | I commend you to ... the word of his grace, which is able ... to give you the inheritance among all those who are sanctified.

The Bible has *securing* power to guarantee our inheritance, which is God himself. Under the new covenant, the "inheritance" of God's people is not the land of Israel but the final inheritance of the kingdom of God, which is God himself. This inheritance is certain, obtained and held by those God has sanctified; it is possessed already through faith and the Spirit, the guarantee of that inheritance (Eph 1:14).[461]

As we put away the lies, we see that this world that we live in is about to collapse on all the lies. It breathes deceit, promising happiness in sin for a season, but it is followed by a lifetime of misery. The Christian on the other hand lives for the world and the age to come. We have eternal life. We are seated in the heavenly realm already with Christ. We are to be living in the age to come, now. Don't wait saint! Set your affections on things above, not on things of the earth. Your inheritance is the presence of Christ. Enjoy that inheritance now!

---

[460] Wiersbe, *The Bible Exposition Commentary*, vol. 1, 487.
[461] Hamilton, *John–Acts*, 528.

The Bible Sanctifies Us

Acts 20:32d | Among all those who are sanctified.

The Bible has *sanctifying* power to conform us into the image of Jesus Christ.[462] The evangelist Dwight L. Moody once said it well.

> Sin will keep you from the Bible, or the Bible will keep you from sin. Here search, and great shall be your store. Here drink, and you shall thirst no more.[463]

God's word has the power to protect us. Remember Jesus prayed, "Sanctify them by your truth. Your word is truth" (Jn 17:17). The whole purpose and goal of our lives is to enjoy God and to love him, being conformed to the image of Jesus Christ (Rom 8:28-29).

SPURN THE WORLD (20:33-38)

Jesus told us that we are "in the world" but we are not "of the world" (Jn 17:16). We are actually living for another world. We exist, spiritually, in another age. We are united with Christ in the heavens, and our heart is to be there, with Christ, in his kingdom. And we pray and live that Christ's "will would be done on earth as it is in heaven" (Mt 6:10). Like Paul, we spurn the world. We are crucified to it. We live for a better world, one which will fully be revealed at Christ's coming, but one that, nonetheless, exists now, in his people. We are his temple, and we live according to the new world that Christ will bring with him. That's how Paul lived. He expressed this to the Ephesians elders.

Our Christ-centered Hope

Paul was not looking for this world's goods. Paul's hope was in Christ alone. Though he was biblically allowed to have support from the church at Ephesus and other churches (1 Thess 2:6), since "the laborer is worthy of his hire" (1 Tim 5:18), he chose not to take support to exemplify a heavenly hope.

Acts 20:33 | I coveted no one's silver or gold or apparel.

---

[462] J. Phillips, *Exploring Acts*, Ac 20:32.
[463] Dwight Lyman Moody, *Notes from My Bible: From Genesis to Revelation* (New York: Fleming H. Revell Company, 1895), 8.

Paul said, "For me to live is Christ and to die is gain." His hope was Christ alone. He was content in any circumstance. What more can any of us want than the Redeemer who loved us and died for us?

When Paul wrote to Timothy about the qualifications for an elder, he is expressly stated that he must not be guilty of the sin of covetousness (1 Tim 3:3), and Paul lived this out.[464] The Lord Jesus Christ put it simply and directly when he warned us of the danger of trying to have two masters.

> *Matthew 6:24* | No one can serve two masters... You cannot serve God and mammon.

Those who care for the flock of God must not do so for material gain, but for Christ alone. Paul has just talked about his "inheritance" that he had in Christ. Anything compared to knowing Christ, to Paul, was refuse.

> *Philippians 3:8* | Yea doubtless, and I count all things but loss for the excellency of the knowledge of Christ Jesus my Lord: for whom I have suffered the loss of all things, and do count them but dung, that I may win Christ.

You cannot be an effective Christian if your hope is in the security of this world. If we are to grow and change in Christ, our relationship with money needs to be one of stewardship, not mastery. For any servant of God, money must never be a motivation.

Have you ever gone to take a drink of milk, and it was sour? That's what idolatry does to our relationship with Christ. If money and earthly security is your motivation in life, or if you are afraid to lose your earthly security, your growth will be stifled by your covetousness. You are going to be at a standstill. Put your all on the altar, seek first the kingdom of Jesus, and be sure everything else will be added unto you (Mt 6:33).

Our Christ-centered Hands

Paul was not worldly in what he worked for. Everything he did was for the kingdom. Paul's hands were holding onto heavenly treasure. He invested in the kingdom not in his own earthly security.

---

[464] Wiersbe, *The Bible Exposition Commentary*, vol. 1, 488.

Acts 20:34-35 | You yourselves know that these hands ministered to my necessities and to those who were with me. ³⁵ In all things I have shown you that by working hard in this way we must help the weak and remember the words of the Lord Jesus, how he himself said, 'It is more blessed to give than to receive.'"

Paul was a man of great sacrifice, like his Lord. He was up early and, most probably, late to bed, with his settled hours of prayer and devotion to God. Then he had his long stretches of physical work with Aquila and Priscilla in the shop, snatching hours here and there to go and teach in the lecture-room, hurrying round to someone's house where there was suffering or sorrow. He loved to disciple the saints, and the best times were not merely in the lecture hall, but in their times of greatest need.[465]

That a great apostle, filled with the Holy Spirit, uniquely gifted, gloriously blessed in the ministry, should find it necessary at times to labor with his hands in order to support himself in the ministry speaks volumes. His example is so different from the false teachers today who preach a prosperity gospel. They don't know the people they shepherd, because as wolves they don't care about shepherding, but fleecing the sheep.

Paul was never a burden on the saints but provided for himself when necessary. Paul is not issuing a command for pastors to be bi-vocational, but to underscore that he displayed his genuine concern for them the whole time he was with them by taking care of his own needs rather than asking for support.[466]

Our Christ-centered Heart

Paul did not love this world. He loved the true and living God. He loved and sacrificed for God's people. He demonstrated his relationship with God not merely through teaching, but through walking with the Ephesians themselves in prayer and in life-on-life discipleship. At his final goodbye, he broke down weeping and fell down on his knees, asking God to sustain him and the flock of dear sheep at Ephesus.

---

[465] Wright, *Acts for Everyone, Part 2*, 136.
[466] Hamilton, *John–Acts*, 528.

Acts 20:36-37 | And when he had said these things, he knelt down and prayed with them all. **37**And there was much weeping on the part of all; they embraced Paul and kissed him.

Oh, the tears! And today, it seems there is little connection in churches between believers. The elders had a deep and loving relationship with Paul. The warmth of hearts on fire for God and filled with love for one another begins with the elders. The ministry of prayer must have reflected hundreds of prayer times the elders had together.

This is how I feel about the elders at our church. Continually we are praying together, fellowshipping together, even at times with sweet tears of joy for what God is doing in our congregation. We can spurn the world by keeping our hearts warm for God and for each other.

Our Christ-centered Harvest

When Paul said goodbye, it was incredibly emotional for the Ephesian elders.

Acts 20:37-38 | And there was much weeping on the part of all; they embraced Paul and kissed him, **38** being sorrowful most of all because of the word he had spoken, that they would not see his face again. And they accompanied him to the ship.

The Ephesian church led by these dear elders was God's harvest. Paul said that some plant and some water, but "God gives the increase." They may not see each other again, but it is not Paul that builds the church of Jesus Christ. Jesus said, "I will build my church, and the gates of hell will not prevail against it" (Mt 16:18). Yet there are still strong and deep emotions. There is loss when we say goodbye on earth. There will be a time when God calls you or me somewhere else. That's not my desire. My goal is to spend a lifetime at one church. I don't know if that is possible, but it is my deep desire and hope. But there will be a day when we say goodbye either through God calling us to heaven or calling us to another ministry. If that day comes, I will weep. I love you all more than any treasure you could dream of on this earth. You are eternal treasures to me. You are God's letters written with the Spirit's own words on your heart. You are unspeakably precious to me. And this deep love I have for the congregation begins with the elders. I love you all. It is my highest honor in life to serve God with you. I have always been unworthy to serve with such distinguished me. I will never deserve it, but it is my deepest joy to walk side by side together with you and the Holy Spirit. Isn't God good?

Paul knew that death was coming. This is why his goodbye is accompanied by much *weeping* since they will never see him again (20:37–38, *cf* 20:25). They show their deep affection for him by hugging and kissing (20:36), a practice in harmony with the apostle's own teaching on holding others deep in the heart and showing mutual affection (Phil 1:7–8; Rom 12:10). In deep sorrow and love, the Ephesian elders reluctantly escort Paul to the ship and see him on board for his long journey to Jerusalem (20:38b).[467]

The address to the Ephesian elders at Miletus marks the end of Paul's missionary work according to the account in Acts. From there he journeyed to Jerusalem where he was to be arrested and imprisoned, subjected to various trials, and finally sent off to Rome to appear before the Emperor.[468] This is how it should be. We plant, we water, but God must give the increase. We leave the ultimate results up to God.

Conclusion

Do these things and you will have a fruitful ministry. We are all leaving behind a legacy. What will your legacy be? I pray that you will have a legacy of following Jesus and helping others to follow Jesus. That's a legacy of discipleship.

Admiral James Stockdale is well known for being the Vice-Presidential Candidate for the third party with Ross Perot in 1992. His opening words to the Vice-Presidential debate were, "Who am I, and why am I here?" So many are living the Christian life aimlessly, just barely surviving.

Today we asked, who are the elders and why are they here? They are shepherds who set the example for the flock. They do what all Christians should be doing. They lay the foundation for an abundant Christian life as they counsel themselves in the word, as they shepherd the flock, as they protect God's people, study the word, and spurn the world. This is what we all should be doing.

For my first job after college, I was an iron worker and National Bullet Proof in Hickory Hills, Illinois. I'm completely shocked to this day that I got the job! I had never worked in iron working, so why would

---

[467] Faw, *Acts*, 235.
[468] Marshall, *Acts*, 356.

they hire me? The application basically tested my math and fractions skills. Could I read instructions! I could follow directions. I could divide and subdivide fractions. After that, I feel that I became a success at National Bullet Proof. I certainly wasn't their most valuable worker—but I knew how to follow the blueprints, how to read the tape measure, and to how follow the boss.

The boss, whose name was Fred, was the owner, and he was beloved by all, even though he was a pretty inflexible person. We were not union, so he had trained every work on the floor how to do what they were doing. He taught the welders. He taught the shearers. He taught the polishers. He taught those who formed the steel and punched the steel. He might have even taught the painters and shippers. He could train anyone to do anything. That was Fred's reputation. If you didn't want to do the job right, he would only half-jokingly threaten to hire then next guy walking in front of the plant to do your job.

In following Christ, you will counsel yourself, shepherd the flock, protect God's people, study the word, and spurn the world. And you will bear fruit. He can use anyone, but he chooses to use you!

36 | ACTS 21:1-16
BOLD STEPS FOR CHRIST

Paul answered, "What are you doing, weeping and breaking my heart? For I am ready not only to be imprisoned but even to die in Jerusalem for the name of the Lord Jesus." And since he would not be persuaded, we ceased and said, "Let the will of the Lord be done."

ACTS 21:14-15

Sometimes in life we need to take some very bold steps. It's always done in humility and brokenness. We walk by faith, and the moment we surrender to God is the moment is sovereign hand begins to move the mountains.

Centuries ago, when map makers ran out of known world before they ran out of parchment, they would sketch a dragon at the edge of the scroll. This was a sign to the explorer that he would be entering uncharted territory at his own risk. Unfortunately, some explorers took this symbol literally and were afraid to push on to new worlds. Other more adventuresome explorers saw the dragons as a sign of opportunity, a door to new territory.[469]

---

[469] Roger von Oech, *A Kick in the Seat of the Pants* (New York: William Marrow Paperbacks, 1986), 39.

Today, God is calling our congregation to bold, new steps of faith, to higher ground in holiness, but it's going to cost, and for us it is all uncharted territory, though the Lord has planned it from the foundation of the world.

> Key thought: As believers we are not to be afraid of the unknown but take bold steps to follow Christ no matter what the cost, as long as Christ is at the center, leading us by his word.

In Acts 21, Paul travels to Jerusalem despite prophecies that he will be imprisoned and despite his friends' pleading with him not to endanger his life by going. Yet God is leading him, so he is unafraid. Sure enough, in Jerusalem Paul is arrested and brought before the city's Roman commander.[470] He's not afraid. He is willing to follow Jesus no matter what.

We see there are three things Paul did that left a legacy. He followed the Lord unconditionally. He fellowshipped with the saints as a priority. And he forsook the world unreservedly.

DETERMINE TO FOLLOW THE LORD (21:1-3)

We take steps every day. Some forward, some backwards, some steps of fear, some steps into the unknown. God calls us to take bold steps of faith. Big things don't happen in our life without taking bold steps in faith. As we take bold steps for Christ, we cannot be afraid to follow the Lord and his word, no matter what the price.

Sometimes in order to bear fruit there is much pain. Some of you are entering a time of trial precisely because you are choosing to do what is right. The message today is, don't be afraid of the pain because there's going to be so much joy. Jesus said that when trial and persecution come, we should rejoice and be exceedingly glad. We need to "count it all joy" when our faith is tried (Jas 1:2-3). Don't be afraid of the pain dear saints. God has to prune the vine before much fruit can come.

The Price of Following God

Paul pays a huge price for following God, which means he eventually loses his life. Nero is in power. It's 57 A.D., but Paul will die the year Nero infamously sets fire to Rome, in 64 A.D.

---

[470] H. L. Willmington, *The Outline Bible* (Wheaton, IL: Tyndale House Publishers, 1999), Ac 21.

Paul leaves the Ephesian elders in Miletus and sets sail for Tyre, on his way to Jerusalem. Paul knew the prophecies about his arrest in Jerusalem and eventual death in Rome 7 years later under the tyrannical Roman emperor. Yet a lot of good fruit will come out of Paul's willingness to be imprisoned and suffer. It all starts with a journey toward Jerusalem.

> **Acts 21:1-3** | And when we had parted from them and set sail, we came by a straight course to Cos, and the next day to Rhodes, and from there to Patara. ²And having found a ship crossing to Phoenicia, we went aboard and set sail. ³When we had come in sight of Cyprus, leaving it on the left we sailed to Syria and landed at Tyre, for there the ship was to unload its cargo.

The cost of following the Lord will be high. Usually, it means humbling our ego in total surrender. It means dragging our sin out into the light, confessing our sin one to another, so that we can hate it and forsake it. It means submitting to discipleship and learning how to walk with stability. All these things Paul did early on in his life. But then there is a time to launch out, to count the cost, to suffer for the cause of Christ. Paul was willing to go anywhere, do anything, pay any cost, as long as Christ was exalted in his life.

Paul lands at Tyre, north of Jerusalem, but his destination is the holy city. Paul was going to have two fairly long imprisonments as a result of his journey to Jerusalem, but during those imprisonments, he would write seven of his thirteen New Testament epistles to the churches. During his first imprisonment, under house arrest in Rome (60-62 A.D.) he would write Ephesians, Philippians, Colossians, and Philemon. He was likely free for a year when he established a church in Crete and wrote 1 Timothy and Titus. Then, during his second and final imprisonment in Rome around 64 A.D., Paul wrote 2 Timothy. Satan meant Paul to suffer but God meant Paul to study and write and prepare his legacy!

The Providence of God

I love all the seemingly random things mentioned in this text. They passed through various cities, and then they "found" a ship crossing to another city. They had various travels that would land Paul in Jerusalem at a specific time for a specific event. God's providence is his overarching sovereign guidance that weaves all things together for your good and his glory. Solomon speaks of this very comforting doctrine in Proverbs.

Proverbs 16:9 | A man's heart plans his way, but the Lord directs his steps.

Or here's another.

Proverbs 19:21 | Many are the plans in the mind of a man, but it is the purpose of the LORD that will stand.

As children of God, we are to be comforted by the providence of God. He's guiding your life. He is getting you to where he wants you to be.

The Promises of God

Paul wasn't going blindly to Jerusalem. He knows something bad is going to happen. But what is bad in this realm of brokenness and sin can work together for good in the realm of the kingdom. In fact, God can make bad things work together for good.

Paul's going to get arrested (*cf* 21:27-37). But God's leading him right to where he wants him to go. We can't understand how the difficulties can work together for good, but we need to trust God. Listen to Solomon again.

Ecclesiastes 3:11 | He has made everything beautiful in its time. Also, he has put eternity into man's heart, yet so that he cannot find out what God has done from the beginning to the end.

We are called to trust that because we are predestined to be conformed to Christ (Rom 8:29), that the Lord will make all things beautiful in his time. Get your eyes on the Lord, like Paul did. He knew he was called to go to Jerusalem to suffer. But there was an incredible plan that God had for the church through Paul's suffering. Paul is not afraid of suffering because he wants to follow Christ no matter what.

DETERMINE TO FELLOWSHIP WITH THE SAINTS (21:4-7)

Paul arrives in Tyre, and he fellowships there for seven days and gets encouragement from fellow believers. What we find, is that if we are going to take bold steps, we have to have support from our fellow believers.

Fellowship is Essential

Notice that the first thing Paul does in Tyre is seek out disciples to fellowship with. And he stays there for a week. The disciples have received a message from the Spirit for Paul.

> **Acts 21:4** | And having sought out the disciples, we stayed there for seven days. And through the Spirit they were telling Paul not to go on to Jerusalem.

These unnamed believers, led by a prophet speaking through the Spirit, urge Paul not to go on to Jerusalem. It seems clear that the Spirit is telling both Paul and the other believers, that Paul was headed for a lot of suffering at Jerusalem. But Paul and his brothers in Tyre had different opinions as to what God's will was.

Nonetheless, we see that fellowship is essential. His friends didn't want Paul to suffer, but it seems Paul had great leading from the Spirit that it was ok to go and suffer in Jerusalem. God had great plans for Paul, though they included suffering. The Holy Spirit had never before prohibited Paul from going to Jerusalem. According to Acts 20:22–23, He warned Paul repeatedly of what would happen to him when he got there but did not tell him not to go. The Spirit's message to Paul in Tyre, as elsewhere, was a warning, not a prohibition.[471]

Notice that fellowship does not replace a relationship with God. Paul was also hearing from the Spirit that he would have to suffer, but he had a different understanding what God's leading was. That's ok. There was a clear leading from the Spirit confirmed by his fellowship with the brothers, that Paul would suffer.

This reminds me of our Lord when he told his disciples that he would have to go to Jerusalem and suffer, and Peter rebuked him. Despite the disagreement, Paul's heart was joined with his brothers in Christ. We are not meant to live the Christian life alone. We need each other.

Fellowship is Encouraging

It is touching to see how the believers had come to love Paul, though they had known him only a week.[472]

---

[471] MacArthur, *Acts*, vol. 2, 237-238.
[472] Wiersbe, *The Bible Exposition Commentary*, vol. 1, 489.

Acts 21:5-6a | When our days there were ended, we departed and went on our journey, and they all, with wives and children, accompanied us until we were outside the city. And kneeling down on the beach, we prayed ⁶ and said farewell to one another.

The Spirit predicted persecution against the apostle, and the people's love for Paul caused them to beg him not to go. This was rough on Paul! He was in Tyre for only seven days, and yet when he left, they "all," along with "their wives and children," escorted him out of the city and knelt with him on the beach for prayer! They loved him![473] As much as it hurt for them to say goodbye, it must have been an incredible encouragement for Paul to know how much the brothers loved him so much, though he's only been there a week.

Fellowship is such a cure for our depression, despair, and discouragement. It helps us shut the doors that allow Satan in to harass us. It's like "taking up the shield of faith" together, and it "quenches all the fiery arrows of the wicked one" (Eph 6:16). We need to constantly be seeking out fellowship with believers.

Fellowship is Everywhere

Paul boards a ship again to journey further to his destination in Jerusalem. There he finds even more believers.

Acts 21:6b-7 | Then we went on board the ship, and they returned home. ⁷ When we had finished the voyage from Tyre, we arrived at Ptolemais, and we greeted the brothers and stayed with them for one day.

Our fellowship with God brings us fullness of joy, but sometimes we can be discouraged and not feel the presence of God. This is why we need other believers. They can be "Jesus with skin on." They are temples of the Holy Spirit, ministering the presence of Jesus.

The depth of camaraderie among the first Christians is portrayed in the early chapters of Acts. The believers met together in house groups for teaching, fellowship, the Lord's Supper, and prayer (Acts 2:42, 46). So profound was their sense of togetherness that the Christians pooled their possessions and distributed them to brothers and sisters in need (2:44–45; 4:32–35). Perhaps the dominant characteristic of this early Christian fellowship was the love among the believers

---

[473] Hughes, *Acts: The Church Afire*, 286.

(1 Thess 4:9; 1 Pet 1:22).[474] Paul made this fellowship a priority in his life.

Dear saint, we need to make fellowship with the saints a priority. If all you do is meet with the saints on the Lord's day, that's good, but it is not enough. You need to share the presence of God with other believers during the week. You need your family, but as a man, you need another man. As a woman you need another woman. You need their encouragement, and they need yours. Seek out fellowship continually.

DETERMINE TO FORSAKE THE WORLD (21:8-16)

On Paul's way to Jerusalem, his final stopover is Caesarea. Now what we find out next is that the world is constantly trying to divert our walk with Christ. Christ followers do not love the world (1 Jn 2:15-16). We live lives separate from the world, not given to the counsel of the ungodly but to the word of God (Psa 1:1-3).

Through Godly Friendships

Paul visits with Philip the evangelist, one of the seven deacons. Remember he led the Ethiopian eunuch who was a high-level statesman, to the Lord there in Caesarea. It was there that Philip settled with his wife and four daughters.

> **Acts 21:8** | On the next day we departed and came to Caesarea, and we entered the house of Philip the evangelist, who was one of the seven, and stayed with him.

One amazing way to stay away from the paths of the world is to have good, godly friends. Someone said, "Show me your friends and I will show you your future." Do you count the warriors of God as your friends? Do you have those around you who are fighting for your holiness and your joy in God? Paul had this.

Through Godly Family

Philip has four unmarried daughters who have the gift of prophecy.

> **Acts 21:9** | He had four unmarried daughters, who prophesied.

We see here that Philip's daughters have the gift of prophecy. It's interesting to think of this since the New Testaments has no place for

---

[474] Walter A. Elwell and Philip Wesley Comfort, *Tyndale Bible Dictionary*, Tyndale Reference Library (Wheaton, IL: Tyndale House Publishers, 2001), 484.

women in the eldership of the church. Yet some indeed have the prophetic gift to apply the word of God and study the word of God and give guidance. This guidance is not to be on the level of an elder but in a robust ministry to other women, or as we consider in Pricilla and Aquila's case, Pricilla was able to teach Apollos more fully under the headship of her husband. The main thrust of the ministry of Philip's was the reiteration or exposition of existing divine revelation, much like today's preachers and teachers of the word.[475] Paul described the gift in 1 Corinthians.

> *1 Corinthians 14:3* | The one who prophesies speaks to people for their upbuilding and encouragement and consolation

What about you? If you are a parent, are you seeing your children follow Christ? Are you encouraging them in their spiritual gifts? Philip had obviously fanned into flame the gifts in his daughters. They knew their way around the word of God and could prophesy.

What does the gift of prophecy look like today? For some men, it means the ministry of elder and pastor and shepherd. For most it means a biblical counseling ministry, helping people walk in the word, growing and changing into the image of Christ from their hearts.

Through Godly Fellowship

Paul now has fellowship with a dear prophet and elder from the church in Jerusalem, named Agabus. Now we get to the place where Paul's willingness to suffer is tested. We find that he wants to do the will of God no matter what, following his Lord and ours. This beloved prophet Agabus enters the scene.

God speaks though Agabus, warning Paul of his arrest and imprisonment in Jerusalem.

> **Acts 21:10-11** | While we were staying for many days, a prophet named Agabus came down from Judea. ¹¹And coming to us, he took Paul's belt and bound his own feet and hands and said, "Thus says the Holy Spirit, 'This is how the Jews at Jerusalem will bind the man who owns this belt and deliver him into the hands of the Gentiles.'"

---

[475] MacArthur, *Acts*, vol. 2, 240.

Agabus at that moment was following a rich tradition in Old Testament history. Even in the New Testament, prophets not only delivered the oracles of God with their lips but with object lessons, dramatizing the word God had given to them.

In the Old Testament one prophet (Ahijah) tore his garments, symbolizing that the united kingdom of Israel would be torn asunder after the death of Solomon (1 Kgs 11:30). Isaiah shocked everybody when he stripped to his undergarments, and walked down the street barefoot, giving the message of how God was going to deal with the Egyptians. He would humiliate them and drive them away (Isa 20:2-3). Ezekiel built a replica of Jerusalem and used it to show the people what God was going to do when he destroyed the city (Eze 4:1-17).[476]

So Agabus takes Paul's belt and binds his own hands and feet and says, this is what is awaiting you. You will be delivered to the Gentiles. Paul had always wanted to go to Rome and preach the gospel. This, I'm sure, was quite different than what Paul imagined.

Of course, we know that within seven years of his arrest in Jerusalem (57 A.D), Paul would be put to death in Rome (64 A.D.). He would have two years of house arrest in Rome, be set free briefly, but then after his second arrest die by beheading under Nero's rule.

Through Godly Forethought

Paul's traveling companions and the believers at Caesarea beg him not to go to Jerusalem. They know by the Spirit what is going to happen.

> **Acts 21:12** | When we heard this, we and the people there urged him not to go up to Jerusalem.

There is a genuine plea not to go to Jerusalem, because they knew Paul would suffer, and eventually, we know, he would die there. Paul appreciated his fellowship with Agabus, and the prophecy he received that he would be bound and sent to the Gentiles. Though the news was discouraging, the prophecy was helpful for Paul. He didn't want to take the easy way out. He wanted to do God's will no matter what the cost.

---

[476] Sproul, *Acts*, 353.

Through a God-Honoring Future

Realizing Paul is determined to visit Jerusalem, the believers declare: "The will of the Lord be done!" The believers saw Paul's motive was to honor God, and they recognized this sacrifice as God's will.

> **Acts 21:13-16** | Then Paul answered, "What are you doing, weeping and breaking my heart? For I am ready not only to be imprisoned but even to die in Jerusalem for the name of the Lord Jesus." **14** And since he would not be persuaded, we ceased and said, "Let the will of the Lord be done." **15** After these days we got ready and went up to Jerusalem. **16** And some of the disciples from Caesarea went with us, bringing us to the house of Mnason of Cyprus, an early disciple, with whom we should lodge.

"Your will be done!" What a profound theological insight! Of course, the will of the Lord was going to be done, and Paul knew that. Jesus knew the will of God when he wrestled in the garden and prayed.[477] Consider Jesus' prayer!

> *Luke 22:42* | Father, if you are willing, remove this cup from me. Nevertheless, not my will, but yours, be done.

So it was with Paul. You can almost hear him saying, "I want to follow my Lord. As he went to Jerusalem, I follow him." Wherever the Lord leads us, we should follow.

Conclusion

We are called to follow the Lord, wherever he leads, no matter what the cost. The Civil War battle of Antietam was one of the bloodiest days in American military history. On that September day in 1862 nearly 6,000 Union and Confederate soldiers were killed, and 17,000 others wounded. To put that in perspective, one historian writes:

> The casualties at Antietam numbered four times the total suffered by American soldiers at the Normandy beaches on June 6, 1944. More than twice as many Americans lost their lives in one day at Sharpsburg [Antietam] as fell in combat in the War of 1812, the Mexican War, and the Spanish-American war *combined*.[478]

---

[477] Ibid., 355.
[478] James McPherson, *Battle Cry of Freedom* (New York: Oxford, 1988), 544.

Some of the fiercest fighting on that awful day took place in a part of the battlefield known as the Cornfield. Some Union soldiers, their ranks decimated by heavy Confederate fire, fled toward the rear in wild panic—only to be stopped by the contagious courage of one young man. Historian Bruce Catton describes the scene:

> The Pennsylvanians broke and ran again—to be stopped, incomprehensibly, a few yards in the rear by a boyish private who stood on a little hillock and kept swinging his hat, shouting: "Rally, boys, rally! Die like men, don't run like dogs!" Strangely, on that desperate field where men were madly heroic and full of abject panic by turns, this lone private stopped the retreat. [479]

Like that nameless soldier, Paul had the courage not only to face the enemy himself but also to inspire others to do likewise.[480] Dear saint, do you understand that Christ laid down his life? He is calling you to make some bold steps of faith toward holiness. Drag your sin in to the light. Choose to reach out to another brother or sister for life-on-life discipleship. If your marriage is in need of revitalization, get some of our marriage enrichment discipleship.

God may be calling someone here into full time ministry. He may be calling you to start serving at this church. He may be calling you to give the gospel to a loved one. He may be calling you to love your spouse in a way that is radical. Search yourself. Open your heart. What is the next step that God is calling you to take? Don't retreat. Don't run from the fight. Boldly lay your life down for Christ.

---

[479] Bruce Catton, *Mr. Lincoln's Army* (New York: Fairfax Press, 1984), 162.
[480] MacArthur, *Acts*, vol. 2, 242–243.

37 | ACTS 21:17-36
PAUL'S ARREST: MAGNIFYING GOD ALONE

You see, brother, how many thousands there are among the Jews of those who have believed.
ACTS 21:20

Do you ever fear bad news? The email from work. The message from the doctor. The text message from a hurting relative. Maybe it's the conversation you need to have with a spouse or family member. David says it

> *Psalm 112:1, 7-8* | Blessed is the man who fears the LORD ... ⁷He is not afraid of bad news; his heart is firm, trusting in the LORD. ⁸His heart is steady; he will not be afraid.

We don't have to live in fear of a difficult trial we might go through, or a trying season of our marriage, or someone's words against us. We don't have to fear what's going to happen in our state or country? What about my health? Lots of things confront us that may bring suffering into our lives. But here's the truth: we as believers don't need to be afraid if we have a big view of God. Instead of magnifying our fear or our circumstances, we need to magnify our great, infinite, loving God. I think of David's motto when difficulties overwhelmed him.

> *Psalm 34:3* | Oh, magnify the LORD with me, and let us exalt his name together!

It reminds me of a story of a famous college coach. Luigi Piccolo, or better known as "Lou Little" was football coach at Georgetown University from 1924-1929. Back then, he had on his squad a player of average ability who rarely got into the game. But Coach Little was fond of him. He especially liked the way he walked arm-in-arm with his father on campus. One day, shortly before a big game with Fordham, the boy's mother called with the news that his father had died that morning of a heart attack.

The student went home with a heavy heart but was back three days later. "Coach," he pleaded, "will you start me in the game against Fordham? I think that is what my father would have enjoyed most." After a moment's hesitation, Little said, "Okay, but only for a play or two."

True to his word, he put the boy in—but he never took him out. For sixty action-packed minutes that inspired young man ran and blocked like an All-American. After the game the coach praised him. "Son, you have never played like that before. What got into you?"

"Remember how my father and I used to go arm-in-arm?" answered the boy. "Well, he was totally blind, and today was the first time he ever saw me play!" The young football player's desire to please someone he loved—someone not visibly present—made all the difference. His love for his father was magnified!

The Apostle Paul magnified the Lord! He lived, fought, and died with the abiding consciousness that he was doing it all for God. Because he served the risen Christ, he did not allow the well-meaning pleadings of his loving friends—arguments that appealed to his desire for self-comfort, even self-preservation—to sidetrack him from obeying God by going on to Jerusalem.[481]

Paul's arrival in Jerusalem marked the end of his missionary journeys. He would soon be arrested and remain an "ambassador in chains" (Eph 6:20) for the remainder of the period covered by Acts.[482] Paul was eager to do God's will no matter what the cost. He refused to be controlled by fear. Instead he magnified the greatness and glory of God.

> Key Thought: Instead of magnifying our fear or our circumstances, we need to magnify our great and glorious, infinite and loving God.

---

[481] Hughes, *Acts: The Church Afire*, 291.
[482] MacArthur, *Acts*, vol. 2, 247.

How do we do that? Paul did it by getting encouragement from the church, having empathy for the seekers, understanding the spiritual warfare with the enemy, and having a heart to evangelize the lost.

MAGNIFY GOD WITH COMMUNITY (21:17-20A)

We need to magnify the Lord by looking to his community, our forever family, his church. Despite all the foreboding about his arrival to Jerusalem, Paul was actually delighted to get there. You need the help of your local church, your forever family, if you are going to magnify the Lord. This is clear from Paul's practice. The first thing he did when he came to Jerusalem is to seek out the brothers in the local congregation.

The most foundational truth about God's covenant people, his church, is that Jesus is the architect. He will build his church and the gates of hell will not prevail (Mt 16:18).

Support Fellowship

Acts 21:17 | When we had come to Jerusalem, the brothers received us gladly.

Paul no doubt arrived in Jerusalem by the Day of Pentecost as he had planned (20:16). What sweet fellowship Paul and his team must have had. The church received Paul and his team gladly.

How vital fellowship is when you are in a warzone. Likeminded brothers and sisters who can encourage and support you is a big part of living an abundant Christian life (1 Jn 1:7). We can't live the Christian life alone. Love must rule and reign among us.

Paul would have been deeply encouraged, but he must have wondered whether the Gentiles' gift would be acceptable to the Jerusalem church as a whole. Much would hang on his meeting with James and the other elders (21:18).[483] He met with the pastor and elders in Jerusalem the next day.

Submit to Leadership

Acts 21:18 | On the following day Paul went in with us to James, and all the elders were present.

---

[483] Bruce, *Acts: Bible Study Commentary*, Ac 21:15–26.

James is the half-brother of our Lord Jesus Christ. What a joy for James to hear of Paul's great expeditions for the church of Jesus Christ. Certainly, the leadership of Jerusalem church were pleased and grateful for the generous expression of love from the Gentile churches in the much needed offering Paul and the others brought (2 Cor 8:20).[484]

Paul's collection for the Jerusalem church occupies significant portions of his letters (1 Cor 16:1–4; 2 Cor 8:1–9:15; Rom 15:14–32). What compelled Paul to raise funds among his Gentile converts for the poor in Jerusalem? First, he's helping those who have been affected financially among the Jews. A very severe famine occurred in Judea around 46-47 A.D. and support was needed for the [485] Paul's reasoning is found in Romans 15. Listen to his appeal to the Gentiles at the church at Rome.

> *Romans 15:26-27* | For Macedonia and Achaia have been pleased to make some contribution for the poor among the saints at Jerusalem. ²⁷ For they were pleased to do it, and indeed they owe it to them. For if the Gentiles have come to share in their spiritual blessings, they ought also to be of service to them in material blessings.

Another reason for the offering for the Jerusalem church was to bring solidarity with the churches in Gentile lands. Paul was accompanied by the representatives of the Gentile churches who had come up to Jerusalem with him. We may assume that the presence of the latter was connected with the presentation of the collection to the Jerusalem church (Acts 24:17). From Luke's point of view the Gentile brothers were present to confirm Paul's account of his successful missionary campaign.[486]

Celebrate Partnership

Gospel partnership is not something that can happen merely by human plans and programs. The Holy Spirit connected the apostle Paul with countless Gentile peoples in various cities around the ancient world. When Jesus said, "I will build my church" there were no churches in Rome, Corinth, Philippi, and Ephesus, etc. The Spirit of

---

[484] MacArthur, *Acts*, vol. 2, 247.
[485] Bruce W. Winter, "Acts and Food Shortages," in *The Book of Acts in its Graeco-Roman Setting*, ed. David W. J. Gill and Conrad Gempf, (Grand Rapids: Eerdmans, 1994), 59-78.
[486] Marshall, *Acts*, 362.

God raised these churches up through Paul's and others' preaching. Paul had the great honor of giving a first-hand account of all that God had done to build his church.

> **Acts 21:19-20a** | After greeting them, he related one by one the things that God had done among the Gentiles through his ministry. ²⁰ª And when they heard it, they glorified God.

Happily, all seemed to go well. The Jerusalem elders glorified God when they heard Paul's report of his Gentile evangelism and church planting. The Jerusalem leaders had agreed years before that Paul should minister to the Gentiles (Gal 2:7–10), and the elders rejoiced at what they heard. One by one, Paul related the incredible events that had occurred. He gave a full and accurate account, not of what he had done, but of what the Lord had done through his ministry (*cf* 1 Cor 15:10).[487]

How amazing it must have been to have the Gentile converts there as a visual representation of God's goodness to the Jerusalem elders (*cf* 20:4-6).[488] It's also appropriate that all this happened at the Feast of Pentecost. Remember what the Lord said before he had ascended?

> *Acts 1:8* | You will receive power when the Holy Spirit has come upon you, and you will be my witnesses in Jerusalem and in all Judea and Samaria, and to the end of the earth.

God had fulfilled what he had promised! God builds the community of the saints. We are his workmanship, his masterpiece, his new creation (Eph 2:10). And now Paul is in Jerusalem at the Feast of Pentecost where it had all begun so many years before. It's around 57 A.D. and the Holy Spirit was poured out at Jerusalem around 33 A.D. It's been a bit over twenty years, and here are the Gentile converts standing in their midst.

Plans and programs are fine but they alone are not enough to create the Gospel partnerships that the Holy Spirit intends. All human plans come to nothing. As the old hymn says, "All is vain unless the Spirit of the Holy one comes down." Open your heart to what God can do.

---

[487] Wiersbe, *The Bible Exposition Commentary*, vol. 1, 490.
[488] Bruce, *Acts: Bible Study Commentary*, Ac 21:15–26.

MAGNIFY GOD WITH EXPANSION (21:20B-26)

We need to magnify the Lord by looking to his expansion of God's kingdom. Paul enjoyed fellowship with the community of saints at Jerusalem, and he's reaching so many Gentiles for Christ. Of course, new church members means a new culture, and there seemed to be some misunderstanding by some of the Jewish believers as to what Paul was teaching.

Expect Hostility

In their delight of Paul's ministry, the elders bring a concern to Paul. So many Gentiles are coming to Christ, and rumors are spreading that Paul doesn't care about the Old Testament law of Moses.

> **Acts 21:20b-22** | And they said to him, "You see, brother, how many thousands there are among the Jews of those who have believed. They are all zealous for the law, [21] and they have been told about you that you teach all the Jews who are among the Gentiles to forsake Moses, telling them not to circumcise their children or walk according to our customs. [22] What then is to be done? They will certainly hear that you have come."

Though the elders rejoiced with Paul's ministry, there were still people around who were intensely suspicious of Paul. The rumors were false, but you could see how they could misunderstand Paul. They were saying that Paul was telling Jewish Christians to basically stop being Jewish. Indeed, Paul proclaimed that Christ was the end of the law (Rom 10:4), but there is no evidence that he actively persuaded Jewish Christians to forego circumcising their children or to give up Jewish customs.[489]

Paul was dealing with misinformation and slander. The Bible is clear that spreading rumors in the church without any discussion with the person you are talking about was a problem in the early church, and it's a problem in our church from time to time. We are called to go privately and gather information instead of gossiping and spreading rumors.

That reminds me of a story about a lady in an eastern land who repeated a bit of gossip about a neighbor, and within a short time the whole town knew the story. The slandered person was deeply hurt and

---

[489] Marshall, *Acts*, 362-363.

most unhappy. But then the lady responsible for spreading the rumor learned that it was completely untrue, so she went to a wise old sage to find out what she could do to repair the damage. After listening to her problem, he said, "Go to the marketplace, purchase a fowl, and have it killed. Then on your way home pluck its feathers one by one and drop them along the path!" Though surprised by this unusual advice, the woman did as she was told.

The next day she informed the man that she had done as instructed. "Now go and collect all those feathers and bring them back to me," the sage said. The lady followed the same path, but to her dismay the wind had blown all the feathers away. After searching all day long, she returned with only two or three in hand. "You see," said the old wise man, "it is easy to drop them, but impossible to bring them all back. Likewise, it does not take much to spread a false rumor, but you can never completely undo the wrong." We Christians must take this to heart![490]

Just when we think all is going well, Satan has his schemes to try and disrupt the unity of the saints and our fellowship with the Lord.

When God is doing great things, especially when new cultures are being reached with the gospel, the devil brings many challenges and much confusion. A challenge is made to the heart of Paul's ministry.

What about you? Are you open to God reaching new cultures with the gospel no matter what opposition you might face? We seem to be happy if God is reaching people that are just like us. But heaven will not be filled with people mostly like you. He is saving people from every nation under heaven. Satan hates the expansion of the church, but we are called to lay down our lives no matter what the opposition.

Work for Unity

Paul had come to the elders and told them: God is working mightily, and they glorified God, but they let Paul know, "There is some misinformation among the people going on." They didn't have email where they could email everyone, so they decided to make a public demonstration of Paul's love for the Jewish people. The elders at Jerusalem had an idea for Paul to pay for a Thanksgiving offering at the temple.

Acts 21:23-25 | "Do therefore what we tell you. We have four men who are under a vow; ²⁴ take these men and purify yourself along with them and pay their expenses, so that they may shave their heads.

---

[490] Hughes, *Acts: The Church Afire*, 293.

Thus all will know that there is nothing in what they have been told about you, but that you yourself also live in observance of the law. **25** But as for the Gentiles who have believed, we have sent a letter with our judgment that they should abstain from what has been sacrificed to idols, and from blood, and from what has been strangled, and from sexual immorality."

In order to clarify that in Paul's ministry of evangelism to Gentiles, that he is not telling Jews to stop being Jewish, the elders present an idea to Paul. James, it appears, recommended that Paul should openly endorse and support something very Jewish, the Nazarite vows of several men. Paul had taken a similar vow himself (see on 18:18 and Nu. 6:1–21), so he would not be supporting something merely for political reasons. James hoped that by such participation, everyone would *know there is no truth in these reports* about Paul.[491] James, in the letter from the Jerusalem council, was clear that Gentiles did not have to live like Jews, as the letter at the counsel of Jerusalem stated. But it would now be clear that Paul is not forbidding the Jews from being Jewish.

Was this the wisest advice? It's not that important. Their motives were good, but Paul's life is not in the hands of the elders of Jerusalem. All of us children of God are in the Lord's hands. It had already been prophesied by multiple people that Paul would be arrested and bound in Jerusalem and be on his way to Rome.

Sacrifice for the Community

Paul was willing to give up his Jewish culture for the Gentiles or celebrate his Jewish culture for his countrymen, as long as Christ was exalted. His true culture and citizenship was in heaven (Phil 1:20).

Since one of Paul's desires is the unity of the church, of which the offering from Macedonia, Achaia, and Asia is also a token, he agrees to do carry out the elders' wishes.[492] He is empathetic to the believing Gentiles who are grafted into Israel. Paul was willing to do whatever it took to build up and edify the church, both Jew and Gentile. He was never against Jewish culture and customs since he himself was also a Jew!

---

[491] Conrad Gempf, "Acts," in *New Bible Commentary: 21st Century Edition*, ed. D. A. Carson et al., 4th ed. (Leicester, England; Downers Grove, IL: Inter-Varsity Press, 1994), 1100.

[492] Baker, "Acts," in *Evangelical Commentary*, 915–916.

Acts 21:26 | Then Paul took the men, and the next day he purified himself along with them and went into the temple, giving notice when the days of purification would be fulfilled and the offering presented for each one of them.

Paul was always ready to be a Jew to the Jews.[493] This was a vow taken in gratitude for some special blessing from the hand of God. It involved abstention from meat and wine for thirty days, during which the hair had to be allowed to grow. It seems that in most cases at least the last seven days had to be spent entirely in the temple courts.

At the end of the seven days, certain offerings had to be brought— a year-old lamb for a sin offering, a ram for a peace offering, a basket of unleavened bread, cakes of fine flour mixed with oil and a meat offering and a drink offering. Finally, the hair had to be cut and burned on the altar with the sacrifice.[494] This was an expensive ritual, and Paul was willing to cover the expenses. Paul gave notice that he would be providing the resources and the sacrifices for all four men. By doing this, he could live out the reality of his faith.

1 Corinthians 9:20 | To the Jews I became as a Jew, in order to win Jews.

For Paul the various cultures of the world, including his own culture, was something he was willing to give up or use to the advantage of the gospel. For us as western Christians, we need to also at times be willing to give up our culture for the gospel's sake.

I think of Hudson Taylor who gave up his western culture to win the Chinese, and today there more than a hundred million believers there today. We adapt in many different ways to each other's various cultures in our own congregation, as we should. Today we have eastern brothers and sisters in with us as western brothers and sisters. Eastern worship is very different than western worship, and that's ok. We need to be a church of many different cultures. We want our church to match the culture of heaven, with people from every tribe and language and nation.

---

[493] Polhill, *Acts*, 450.
[494] Barclay, *The Acts of the Apostles*, 183.

MAGNIFY GOD AMIDST OPPOSITION (21:27-32)

Despite Paul's best efforts in following the elders' advice, the attack of the enemy follows Paul from Asia. We understand that the enemy is already defeated.

1 John 4:4 | Greater is he that is in you than he that is in the world.

Look to God in the Face of Defamation

Some of the Jewish zealots in Ephesus had followed Paul to Jerusalem to stir up strife. They hated Paul and created a conspiracy to bring him down, but Paul is unafraid. He walks in his integrity since he did nothing wrong.

> **Acts 21:27-29** | When the seven days were almost completed, the Jews from Asia, seeing him in the temple, stirred up the whole crowd and laid hands on him, **28** crying out, "Men of Israel, help! This is the man who is teaching everyone everywhere against the people and the law and this place. Moreover, he even brought Greeks into the temple and has defiled this holy place." **29** For they had previously seen Trophimus the Ephesian with him in the city, and they supposed that Paul had brought him into the temple.

It so happened that Paul's effort toward unity instead led to disaster. It was the time of Pentecost. Jews were present in Jerusalem once again from all over the world, and certain Jews from Asia were there, who no doubt knew how effective Paul's work in Asia had been. They had seen Paul in the city with Trophimus, whom they most probably knew. The business of the vow had taken Paul frequently into the temple courts, and these Asian Jews assumed that Paul had taken Trophimus into the temple along with him.[495] When the devil comes to attack, he is the accuser of the brothers, and he always assumes the worst.

The accusation against Paul was that he brought a Gentile into the court of Israel, in the temple complex, which was a death penalty offense. In the temple, separating the court of the Gentiles from the other courts, stood a wall beyond which no Gentile was allowed to go (*cf* Eph 2:14). On the wall was this solemn inscription:

---

[495] Barclay, *The Acts of the Apostles*, 184–185.

No foreigner may enter within the barricade which surrounds the sanctuary and enclosure. Anyone who is caught so doing will have himself to blame for his ensuing death.

The Romans had granted the Jewish religious leaders authority to deal with anybody who broke this law, and this included the right of execution. This law plays an important role in what happened to Paul a week after he and the four Nazarites began their purification ceremonies.[496]

Look to God in the Face of Death

A small riot begins at the temple mount over these accusations, so much that they have to close the entire temple compound down and shut the gates for a time.

> **Acts 21:30-31** | Then all the city was stirred up, and the people ran together. They seized Paul and dragged him out of the temple, and at once the gates were shut. [31] And as they were seeking to kill him, word came to the tribune of the cohort that all Jerusalem was in confusion.

The Jews from Asia had stirred up the whole city, so that they started beating Paul (21:32), and they were going to put him to death. They told the officer in charge of the centurions, called a "tribune." He was one of the highest-ranking officers in the Roman military, and he, by God's grace, stepped in and saved Paul's life.

Look to God for Deliverance

When word reached the Roman tribune in charge of keeping peace in the city, he ordered soldiers and centurions to protect Paul. The crowd was beating Paul to a pulp. They believed he had committed a crime worthy of death, and they were glad to help him to it.

> **Acts 21:32-33** | He at once took soldiers and centurions and ran down to them. And when they saw the tribune and the soldiers, they stopped beating Paul. [33] Then the tribune came up and arrested him and ordered him to be bound with two chains. He inquired who he was and what he had done.

Only with the presence of Roman soldiers did the zealous Jews stop beating Paul. The soldiers arrived and arrested Paul, binding him with

---

[496] Wiersbe, *The Bible Exposition Commentary*, vol. 1, 491.

chains that would become the familiar jewelry of the apostle for most of the rest of his life. They carried him out of the temple courts to the steps of the Fortress Antonia where our Lord was mocked with a purple robe and crown of thorns.

Remember the Lord had warned Paul when the Lord Jesus first appeared to him how much he would have to suffer.

> *Acts 21:32* | I will show him how much he must suffer for the sake of my name.

Dear saint, when we are called to be joined with Christ through faith, we become members of his family and of his army. We can never rest. We must be willing to suffer for the Lord. Thankfully, God used a Roman platoon of soldiers to rescue the apostle, because he's got a lot more work to be done. The first order of business: he tries to address the crowd.

MAGNIFY GOD WITH EVANGELISM (21:34-36)

Whatever riots are rumbling on earth, God is bringing sinners to himself, and all heaven is rejoicing. Don't be so concerned about the spiritual opposition and satanic harassment on earth. Through the fog of war, God is bringing the lost to himself. Don't magnify the obstacles. Magnify God's omnipotence to build his church. The gates of hell will never prevail!

God can turn a mob into a miracle. He can turn a beating into a testimony time, and that's just what the Lord does.

> **Acts 21:34-36** | Some in the crowd were shouting one thing, some another. And as he could not learn the facts because of the uproar, he ordered him to be brought into the barracks. [35] And when he came to the steps, he was actually carried by the soldiers because of the violence of the crowd, [36] for the mob of the people followed, crying out, "Away with him!"

As Paul is bound with chains and being taken away to the Antonia Fortress. He's mobbed by the crowd. Paul asks to speak to the crowd (21:37), and he's able to give his testimony. We will cover that in our next lesson. But understand that Paul had signed up for suffering as long as that suffering resulted in the expansion of the kingdom of God.

The rest of the chapter is taken up with Paul giving his testimony in detail to the crowd there. He's able to evangelize the great crowd gathered for the Feast of Pentecost there in 57 A.D., about 24 years after the Holy Spirit was poured out when Peter preached. He's also going to be sent off to various imprisonments, including two at Rome, where the great apostle will write out seven of his thirteen New Testament letters to the churches.

The point is, whatever you are going through, learn to suffer well. God will use it to evangelize the lost. You may feel like such a failure, but if the Spirit of God is in you, he is communicating his love to a dying world through you. The crowd cried out "Away with him" or as some translations say, "Kill him!" They wanted Paul dead. Yet Paul gave life to those wanting his death. He just kept testifying knowing he is immortal until God is finished. He magnified the Lord, not his circumstances.

Conclusion

The missionary journeys are completed. Paul had visited Jerusalem for the last. He is arrested and though he is released for a short time, for the most part, he never again finds freedom.[497] Yet, where is his freedom? Though Paul is in chains, he is indeed free—free to testify to kings and the Pretorian guard of the gospel of Jesus Christ, and some in Caesar's own household will come to Christ as a result. He would never have had that opportunity if he had not been incarcerated for preaching Christ. Paul was arrested, but he didn't magnify his problems. He magnified the Lord.

In his book, William Hendricks, *Revealing Stories of Why People are Leaving the Church*, he took a survey asking folks why they no longer attended church. Surprisingly, the most common complaint was not the music, or the facility, or that church was dull. The most common reason given for leaving the church was that the church did not provide them an opportunity to meet with God. E.g., it was not 'worshipful' enough! They came hoping to experience something of God, to be spiritually fed, but many left empty. Hendricks wrote:

> Apparently, it doesn't matter if the service is entertaining. When interaction with God is absent, eventually the church loses its appeal.[498]

---

[497] Boice, *Acts: An Expositional Commentary*, 355.
[498] William D. Hendricks, *Exit Interviews: Revealing Stories of Why People Are Leaving Church* (Chicago: Moody Publishers, 1993).

Dear saints, let's make sure when we come to church, we come to magnify the Lord. We need to see and experience God every moment we are together and when we are not together. That's the key. Magnify the Lord! He's bigger than any problem we are going through.

38 | ACTS 21:37-22:29
WITNESSING FOR JESUS IN JERUSALEM

As I was on my way and drew near to Damascus, about noon a great light from heaven suddenly shone around me. And I fell to the ground and heard a voice saying to me, 'Saul, Saul, why are you persecuting me?' And I answered, 'Who are you, Lord?' And he said to me, 'I am Jesus of Nazareth, whom you are persecuting.'

ACTS 22:6-8

You never know when you are going to have the opportunity to preach the gospel. My youth pastor used to tell me, "Always be ready to preach, pray, or die." That's a good rule for any Christian. We are each called to "go into all the world and preach the gospel" to all people. And you never know who you're talking to when you evangelize. Every Christian needs to feel the weight of souls that Jesus felt. He died for his church. We need to go and rescue the lost!

Years ago, as a child, I lived in the deep woods in the bayou of Louisiana. Many youth groups, burdened for souls, came to my door when I lived in the swamp country, near the Natalbany River. Various youth groups from different churches would journey a mile into the bayou to visit to our home and evangelize us. They didn't know that one day I would follow Christ. They faithfully gave the word, not knowing that one day I would plant churches in Spain and lead a church in northwest

Chicago. From the least to the greatest, we just don't know who we are witnessing to.

I think of Charles Spurgeon. Spurgeon was converted as a youth in a snowstorm. Because of a snowstorm, the 15-year-old's path to church was diverted down a side street. For shelter, he ducked into the Primitive Methodist Chapel on Artillery Street in London. The blizzard was so bad, the pastor couldn't even attend, so a deacon preached a simple message. He stepped into the pulpit and read his text—Isaiah 45:22 (KJV)—"Look unto me, and be ye saved, all the ends of the earth; for I am God, and there is none else." Spurgeon's Autobiography records his reaction:

> He had not much to say, thank God, for that compelled him to keep on repeating his text, and there was nothing needed—by me, at any rate except his text. Then, stopping, he pointed to where I was sitting under the gallery, and he said, "That young man there looks very miserable," and he shouted, as I think only a Primitive Methodist can, "Look! Look! Look, young man! Look now!" Then I had this vision—not a vision to my eyes, but to my heart. I saw what a Savior Christ was. Now I can never tell you how it was, but I no sooner saw whom I was to believe than I also understood what it was to believe, and I did believe in one moment.[499]

Who knew that this young man would be the "prince of preachers" in how he pointed people to Christ! Similarly, Dwight Lyman Moody was just an ordinary shoe salesman in Boston when he was reached for Christ. Moody tells the story of his conversion this way:

> When I was in Boston as a young man, I used to attend a Sunday school class, and one day I recollect my teacher came around behind the counter of the shop I was at work in, and put his hand upon my shoulder, and talked to me about Christ and my soul. I had not felt that I had a soul till then. I said to myself, "This is a very strange thing. Here is a man who never saw me till lately, and he is weeping over my sins, and I never shed a tear about them." But I understand it now and know what it is to have a passion for men's souls and weep over their sins. I don't remember what he said, but I can still feel the power of that man's hand on my shoulder tonight.[500]

---

[499] Charles Haddon Spurgeon, *C.H. Spurgeon's Autobiography: 1834-1854* (London: Passmore and Alabaster, 1899), 106.

[500] Frank Grenville Beardsley, *A History of American Revivals* (New York: American Tract Society, 1912), 257.

The concern and tears of a godly Bible teacher resulted in the conversion of a man who saw a million souls saved in his evangelistic campaigns. How we need to have a deep concern for souls. Our testimony is a vital way to introduce the gospel to people. Here with Paul under arrest in Jerusalem, he's unexpectedly able to give his testimony to the crowds gathered for the Feast of Pentecost.

After the accusation that Paul had violated the temple code by bringing a Gentile into the inner court of Israel in the temple, the crowd seized Paul and would have killed him had the Roman guards not intervened in the nick of time. At least 1,000 soldiers were stationed in the Antonia Fortress at the northwest corner of the temple area. The temple crowd was in an uproar, beating him, ready to put Paul to death.[501]

> Key thought: We need to go into the whole world and preach the gospel and leave the results to God.

GOD'S PROTECTION (21:37-22:1)

Paul had spent his entire Christian life witnessing for Jesus. He believed the command to "go into all the world and preach the gospel." It wasn't an option. He was often in and out of trouble with the authorities in various towns. Sometimes he went to jail. Once he was even given the death penalty by stoning. This time in Jerusalem looked like one of those more dangerous times. Paul knew the words of the Psalmist.

> *Psalm 118:6* | The LORD is on my side; I will not fear. What can man do to me?

Paul wasn't reckless, but he trusted in the Lord, and in the midst of a riot, God protected him, and Paul had been pulled into the barracks, into the citadel there, where our Lord had also stood before Pontius Pilate.

Protected by an Unlikely Ally

Paul had a question and began to speak to the tribune, who we later come to know as "Claudius Lysias." He was kind of a one-star general of sorts. Paul speaks in Greek, which gets Lysias' attention. Before him

---

[501] Wiersbe, *The Bible Exposition Commentary*, vol. 1, 491.

stood Paul, his hair matted from the blood and gashes on his face, bruised and beaten.[502]

> **Acts 21:37** | As Paul was about to be brought into the barracks, he said to the tribune, "May I say something to you?" And he [*the tribune*] said, "Do you know Greek?"

By this time the tribune (possibly the same "Lysias the tribune" from 24:22) was convinced that Paul was a dangerous troublemaker, and already he had an opinion as to who Paul was. When Paul spoke to him politely, however, in cultured Greek, the tribune's opinion changed. Paul's language was in polite, polished Greek, and the tribune was amazed that he would speak Greek in the first place.[503] Here was no wild-eyed radical, no fanatical religious firebrand; here was an educated individual speaking the language of the cultured and educated world with obvious fluency. He expressed his astonishment. "Do you know *Greek*?" The implication was that he was no back woods Judean, but a cultured and educated Greek speaker.

This seemingly insignificant incident, but it is not. Due to Paul's good education and cultured manner, we have one of the turning points of history. From this moment on, the tribune took more than a passing interest in Paul and protected him from his enemies.[504] Paul might have been put to death that day, but God did not allow it. Instead, Paul would be under the protective custody of Rome, and able to complete his mission, which with seven more books of the Bible to write.

Protected with a Unique Heritage

Paul was from the province of Cilicia, but he was mistaken for an Egyptian who had started a riot in Jerusalem. Thousands of rioters were executed, many by crucifixion in Rome, but the Egyptian had escaped. Lysias the tribune thought Paul was the Egyptian revolutionary.[505]

> **Acts 21:38-39** | "Are you not the Egyptian, then, who recently stirred up a revolt and led the four thousand men of the Assassins out into the wilderness?" **39** Paul replied, "I am a Jew, from Tarsus

---

[502] Sproul, *Acts*, 361.
[503] Polhill, *Acts*, 455.
[504] J. Phillips, *Exploring Acts*, Ac 21:37.
[505] Flavius Josephus, *War of the Jews*, 2:261–263.

in Cilicia, a citizen of no obscure city. I beg you, permit me to speak to the people."

Paul immediately relates to the crowd. He's in chains due to a Roman, but he's addressing the Jews in Jerusalem. Paul was a Jew, and that was something he never forgot (*cf* 2 Cor 11:22; Phil 3:4–5). He was a man of Tarsus, which hosted one of the greatest universities of the ancient world. What is more, Paul was a Rabbi, trained at the feet of Gamaliel, who had been 'the glory of the law' and who had died only about five years before.[506]

Protected with an Uncanny Permission

Shockingly, the Roman tribune is the one to give Paul permission to preach the gospel one last time to the crowd at Jerusalem, here at the Feast of Pentecost in 57 A.D.

Acts 21:40a | And when he had given him permission, Paul, standing on the steps, motioned with his hand to the people.

Paul turned and raised one bruised, chained hand. Lysias, the tribune, was yet more astonished: Paul's gesture quieted the crowd. The yells died to murmurs.[507] And he gets permission from this Roman officer, like a one star general. He hears Paul speak in beautiful, eloquent Greek. I find that God opens doors in the most unusual and unexpected ways.

Protected with an Unbelievable Opportunity

Paul is about to address the crowd in the language of the Hebrews, in Aramaic, and the people were eager to listen. It's the Day of Pentecost. He had been carried from the temple courts by the soldiers who had bound him in chains. They brought him to the steps of the Antonia Fortress where Jesus had once been mocked with purple robe and crown of thorns. He was able to address the crowd. Understand that Paul has been beaten. Imagine what he must have looked like. Blood running down his face. His hands bound with Roman chains. Roman soldiers and centurions surrounding him. There he is at the top of the steps of the Antonia Fortress where the Lord Jesus had been. He's

---

[506] Barclay, *The Acts of the Apostles*, 188.
[507] Pollock, *The Apostle*, 243.

about to address the crowd, and they are so curious what he's going to say, there is a great hush.

> **Acts 21:40b-22:1** | And when there was a great hush, he addressed them in the Hebrew language, saying: **22:1** "Brothers and fathers, hear the defense that I now make before you."

Paul was able to look down on the crowd from the top of the steps of the Fortress, motion for silence, and then address them in their own vernacular. Hebrew was often used to speak of the language of the Hebrews which was 'Aramaic" at the time. [508] This seems to have a desired effect. They keep listening! Paul is about to give a defense, not of himself primarily, but of the gospel. The word for "defense" is "apologia" like Peter used when defending the gospel.

> *1 Peter 3:15* | Always being prepared to make a defense to anyone who asks you for a reason for the hope that is in you; yet do it with gentleness and respect.

He knew this was not about anything earthly. The charges that he had brought a Gentile into the temple courts were false. This was his opportunity to give the gospel! The crowd wants to hear this former student of Gamaliel gone rogue. They didn't have Netflix or social media. This was something riveting to them.

GOD'S POWER (22:2-21)

Paul is surrounded by Roman soldiers. The distinguished Roman tribune in charge of overseeing the Festival of the Jews at Pentecost, is shockingly giving Paul the opportunity to address the crowd, probably to get more information out of Paul and to understand his situation. Of course, since Paul is addressing the crowd in the language of the Hebrews, Aramaic, the tribune won't get much out of it. He's going to tell this Jerusalem crowd the good news, just as Peter had done almost thirty years earlier on the feast of Pentecost.

God's Power to a Lost Sinner

The first thing he tells the crowd, is that despite having the best religious education with the best person (Gamaliel), and with a sincere zeal for God, Paul himself had actually been a lost sinner. He had been lost and in need of the Savior.

---

[508] Marshall, *Acts*, 372.

Acts 22:2-5 | And when they heard that he was addressing them in the Hebrew language, they became even more quiet. And he said: **3** "I am a Jew, born in Tarsus in Cilicia, but brought up in this city, educated at the feet of Gamaliel according to the strict manner of the law of our fathers, being zealous for God as all of you are this day. **4** I persecuted this Way to the death, binding and delivering to prison both men and women, **5** as the high priest and the whole council of elders can bear me witness. From them I received letters to the brothers, and I journeyed toward Damascus to take those also who were there and bring them in bonds to Jerusalem to be punished.

Lost in religion. Paul was ultra-religious but completely lost. He was an expert in the word, but he didn't know the God of the word. What an amazing pedigree Paul had—born in Tarsus, the great university city in the beautiful Taurus mountain range. Paul was indeed committed to Judaism more than anyone in his audience. He was taught by the great Rabbi Gamaliel. He had been carefully and thoroughly instructed in the Old Testament law and the rabbinic traditions, and he was once a Pharisee who was blameless under the law (*cf* Phil 3:5–6). Considering that, the charge that he opposed the law (21:28) was ridiculous. His personal conviction was that the law was "holy ... and righteous and good" (Rom 7:12).[509]

Lost in zeal. Paul had been zealous, persecuting Christians. Though it had been almost 30 years, Paul knew many of the seventy elders on the Sanhedrin, the council that ruled Israel, with the high priest as well. And of course, they knew him. The charge against Paul that he didn't respect Judaism is false on its face. Paul loved the law of the Lord.

The problem with Paul is that he was religious but lost. All people, whether born in a pagan home or Christian home, are born lost. Our religion does not save us. The children that are in the church, for the most part, are from loving Christian homes. But no one is saved just because their parents are committed Christians. Each child has to come to Christ on their own accord. Each of us has to come to Jesus for our own sins, seeing him as Savior and Redeemer.

---

[509] MacArthur, *Acts*, vol. 2, 265.

God's Power through a Loving Savior

Even though Paul had known God's word so well, as an expert, he did not know the Savior. He was actually persecuting the Savior and his people (21:8). In fact, he was on his way to Damascus to continue his unrelenting persecution and punishment of God's people. But something or *Someone* interrupted him.

> **Acts 22:6-11** | As I was on my way and drew near to Damascus, about noon a great light from heaven suddenly shone around me. **7** And I fell to the ground and heard a voice saying to me, 'Saul, Saul, why are you persecuting me?' **8** And I answered, 'Who are you, Lord?' And he said to me, 'I am Jesus of Nazareth, whom you are persecuting.' **9** Now those who were with me saw the light but did not understand the voice of the one who was speaking to me. **10** And I said, 'What shall I do, Lord?' And the Lord said to me, 'Rise, and go into Damascus, and there you will be told all that is appointed for you to do.' **11** And since I could not see because of the brightness of that light, I was led by the hand by those who were with me, and came into Damascus.

The Savior's Revelation

> **Acts 22:6** | As I was on my way and drew near to Damascus, about noon a great light from heaven suddenly shone around me.

After Paul showed his commitment to the law of God, explaining how zealous he was, he then demonstrated how the God of Israel himself had sought Paul out personally. The first thing that made Paul aware of God's presence was the "great light from heaven" shining all around him. This would be immediately recognizable as the glory cloud from the Old Testament that led the children of Israel. The Lord Jesus had sought Paul out, by revealing his glory from heaven. Instantly Paul knew he had been wrong. He'd been saying that Jesus had been a liar and a charlatan—a false Messiah. Now he knew that Jesus truly is the God of glory, the Lord of heaven and earth. In a moment, Paul knew Jesus was Yahweh in human flesh. And it was Yahweh that Paul was persecuting.

Paul's Repentance

> **Acts 22:7-9** | And I fell to the ground and heard a voice saying to me, 'Saul, Saul, why are you persecuting me?' **8** And I answered,

'Who are you, Lord?' And he said to me, 'I am Jesus of Nazareth, whom you are persecuting.' [9] Now those who were with me saw the light but did not understand the voice of the one who was speaking to me.

As the Lord Jesus called Paul to salvation, Paul asked the Lord to identify himself. He said he was "Jesus the Nazarene who you have been persecuting." This was said to bring Paul to repentance. When we repent, we bring our sin into the light and see it in all its ugliness.

Paul's Response

Acts 22:10-11 | And I said, 'What shall I do, Lord?' And the Lord said to me, 'Rise, and go into Damascus, and there you will be told all that is appointed for you to do.' [11] And since I could not see because of the brightness of that light, I was led by the hand by those who were with me, and came into Damascus.

Paul responded by asking what to do! He's to go to Damascus and meet a man named Ananias. Paul obeyed. Theologians call this "irresistible grace." Paul, who was once unwilling and opposed to Christ became "willing in the day of God's power" (Psa 110:3). Not all of us get a Damascus Road experience, but we all are drawn to the Father and given eyes to see. Though Paul was blinded by the light, he had surrendered by faith to Jesus. After all Paul's persecution of Christians, Jesus pursued Paul and softened his heart.

God's Power for a Life-Changing Salvation

Ananias, a faithful brother in Damascus, met Paul and restored his sight. At that moment Paul was given a commission to evangelize and a command to be baptized.

Paul's New Friend

Acts 22:12 | And one Ananias, a devout man according to the law, well spoken of by all the Jews who lived there.

Ananias was a devout disciple of Christ from Damascus, but he was known by the Jews as someone who was faithful to the law. Even the Jews in Jerusalem seem to know that Ananias is a good and blameless man.

Paul's New Sight

Acts 22:13-15 | And one Ananias … came to me, and standing by me said to me, 'Brother Saul, receive your sight.' And at that very hour I received my sight and saw him. ¹⁴ And he said, 'The God of our fathers appointed you to know his will, to see the Righteous One and to hear a voice from his mouth; ¹⁵ for you will be a witness for him to everyone of what you have seen and heard.

It is touching that this godly man Ananias had a gift of healing of sorts. He says, "Brother Saul, receive your sight." He was able to restore Saul of Tarsus' sight back to him. This is a true, physical healing, but it is also representative of what was happening in Paul's life. With John Newton, Paul could say, "I once was lost but not I'm found, was blind but now I see." This a beautiful picture of repentant faith, which is a brand-new worldview. Paul is seeing through new eyes. It's also an appropriate picture of regeneration, for Paul could see because he had a new heart and a new nature by the Holy Spirit, now indwelling him.

Paul's New Family

Acts 22:16 | And now why do you wait? Rise and be baptized and wash away your sins, calling on his name.'

Paul had been circumcised on the eighth day to be assimilated into the people of Israel, but now he was told to seek a new induction and assimilate into the church of the living God through baptism. Baptism is a way to testify to the world and God and to angels that you are not ashamed of the gospel. It is an outward sign of the inward reality that God has "washed away all your sins." Paul was indeed baptized, calling on the name of the Lord for salvation. Let's give glory to God for giving us a true salvation. Listen to Jesus' call to each of us:

John 3:3 | Ye must be born again in order to enter the kingdom of heaven.

Let us be patient and look for our children, our friends, and neighbors to truly come to Christ and see with new eyes and a new wonder. So many make false professions because they have not been born again.

God's Power for a Lifelong Calling

Paul now turns to the reality of what God has done. The majority of the Jews had rejected the gospel. Paul had fallen into a trance while he was in the temple. There God gave him a vision that the Jews had rejected the Messiah, and that Paul's ministry was to be far away from the Jews in the distant lands of the Gentiles.

> **Acts 22:17-21** | "When I had returned to Jerusalem and was praying in the temple, I fell into a trance [18] and saw him saying to me, 'Make haste and get out of Jerusalem quickly, because they will not accept your testimony about me.' [19] And I said, 'Lord, they themselves know that in one synagogue after another I imprisoned and beat those who believed in you. [20] And when the blood of Stephen your witness was being shed, I myself was standing by and approving and watching over the garments of those who killed him.' [21] And he said to me, 'Go, for I will send you far away to the Gentiles.'"

At Paul's conversion, he was told by the Lord to go far away to the Gentiles. Paul becomes the apostle to the Gentiles. There is a certain sense of disappointed longing here. Paul has an incredible love for his kinsmen according to the flesh, so much that he could wish to be accursed if that would save them (cf Rom 9:1-3). As with the Lord Jesus, Paul's own people would not receive him (Jn 1:11). He is literally saying: 'I had a priceless gift for you, but you would not take it; so it was offered to the Gentiles.'[510]

Paul at first does flee away from Jerusalem and is launched out on three missionary journeys. Now he is back in Jerusalem but will again go "far away to the Gentiles" with an escort of Roman soldiers. He'll be witnessing to them all along the way. He will indeed make his way to Rome eventually, and then he will be free for a time and possibly even preach in Spain before he is imprisoned again, this time at the Mamertine prison in Rome, being cellmates with the apostle Peter. Church tradition states that they died on the same day around October 67 A.D.

Paul's calling was to expand the gospel outside of Israel, to the ends of the earth! We too cannot be content with just going to church and evangelizing our own families. That's vital, but we must have the calling and vision of Paul in our own lives. It reminds me of a sad story I read recently in an Ethics book about a tragedy here in Chicago.

Christopher Sercye was playing basketball with his friends on May 16, 1998, when he was shot in the chest, and a stray bullet perforated

---

[510] Barclay, *The Acts of the Apostles*, 190.

his aorta. His friends helped him get to within forty feet of the entrance to Ravenswood Hospital and then went inside and asked for help. The hospital staff refused to help Christopher saying that it was against the hospital's policies to administer aid to those outside the hospital. Eventually a policeman was able to get a wheelchair and wheeled Christopher into the hospital where he was helped by the hospital staff. It was too late, however, and Christopher died about an hour later.[511]

Many times, it seems that churches are surrounded by people that desperately need to hear the gospel, yet Christians are content to share it only with those that manage to come inside their church. Let's never forget the gospel's power! Bring your loved ones to Christ!

> *Romans 1:16* | I am not ashamed of the gospel, for it is the power of God for salvation to everyone who believes.

I think of John Paton, who was willing to give his life to the gospel no matter what the cost. He was headed to the Hebrides Islands off the Northwest coast of Scotland where there had been those who had already lost their lives due to the people who were cannibals. When Paton said he was headed there, a Mr. Dickson exploded, "The cannibals! You will be eaten by cannibals!" But to this Paton responded:

> Mr. Dickson, you are advanced in years now, and your own prospect is soon to be laid in the grave, there to be eaten by worms; I confess to you, that if I can but live and die serving and honoring the Lord Jesus, it will make no difference to me whether I am eaten by Cannibals or by worms; and in the Great Day my Resurrection body will rise as fair as yours in the likeness of our risen Redeemer.[512]

God protected John Paton, and he claimed the little island of Aniwa for Christ, and the entire island of several hundred formerly cannibal islanders came to Christ and stopped practicing cannibalism. Paton said:

> I claimed Aniwa for Jesus, and by the grace of God, Aniwa now worships at the Savior's feet. [513]

---

[511] Robert T. Hall, *An Introduction to Healthcare Organizational Ethics* (Oxford, England: Oxford University Press, 2000, 151.

[512] Ralph Bell, *John G. Paton: Missionary to the New Hebrides* (Butler, IN: The Highley Press, 1957), 56.

[513] Ibid., 312.

God rewards our courage to witness to our loved ones. Paul loved his own people and was willing to be accursed for them. What a joy for Paul to give his testimony to the great crowd on the day of Pentecost.

But God's plan was to remove Paul from Jerusalem and set him on his way to Rome. In order to get there, he's thrust into a dangerous situation when the crowd rejects his message.

GOD'S PLAN (22:22-29)

God's Plan Sometimes Includes Danger

Paul's just tells his story to the people of Israel gathered for Pentecost, but they are not happy. A riot was brewing over Paul announcing to the crowd of Jews at Pentecost that they had rejected their Messiah, and now Paul was commanded by the Lord to go "far away to the Gentiles." This was an insult to the Jews, and Paul was saying that it came from the Lord himself. They now want to kill Paul.

> **Acts 22:22-24** | Up to this word they listened to him. Then they raised their voices and said, "Away with such a fellow from the earth! For he should not be allowed to live." 23 And as they were shouting and throwing off their cloaks and flinging dust into the air, 24 the tribune ordered him to be brought into the barracks, saying that he should be examined by flogging, to find out why they were shouting against him like this.

This was nothing like that first Pentecost of the church when the Holy Spirit was poured out. This time the people were under the control of the wicked one. They believed he was guilty of the death penalty. If a person brought a Gentile into the inner court of Israel at the temple, that was considered a capital crime. They showed their disapproval in the traditional way by shouting and waving their garments and throwing up dust in the air.[514]

The Jews may have removed their cloaks in preparation to stone Paul, torn them in an expression of horror at his "blasphemy," or thrown them and the dust into the air as an expression of outrage.[515] Sometimes when we do what is right, bad things happen. But the Lord is with us. He will never leave us nor forsake us.

---

[514] Barclay, *The Acts of the Apostles*, 191.
[515] MacArthur, *Acts*, vol. 2, 271.

A riot begins to brew. The tribune must act swiftly. Paul is removed from the crowd and brought to the tribune. He is about to get the flogging and most brutal beating of his life. He is brought before the Gentiles and now before the Sanhedrin council of the Jews. A riot nearly starts again, but this time it is among the Sanhedrin, Israel's Supreme Court (seventy men of Israel plus the high priest). Finally, Paul is brought before the Lord where he is comforted. What we learn in this chapter is this.

The Roman officer decided to interrogate Paul and ordered him into the barracks of the Antonia Fortress to be flogged with the dreaded flagellum, a cat-o-nine tails, as our Lord was. This was to extract information from him. I've been in the Antonia Fortress, in the torture chamber where they flogged people.

The sunlight faded, and the noise died as they marched Paul to the lower floor of the Antonia Fortress, into vaulted cellars lit by flickering torches, and into the torture chamber. They removed his chains, stripped him, then bound his ankles to a bar and secured his wrists above him. His arms were stretched high above his head and his whole body was hung taut and tight. The position was painful in itself and every blow would fall on tightened nerves and muscles. By now Paul knew what was intended. He was to be given the dreaded flagellum, a murderous whip of heavy rawhide loaded with jagged bits of zinc, iron, and bone.[516] It could turn the body into hamburger meat, leaving muscles hanging and bones exposed. Paul may live through this, but he would be handicapped after this and may never preach again.

Paul knew he would live since he had been given a vision that he would make his way to Rome to preach the gospel. But he needed wisdom to know what to do. He could be permanently injured from such a flogging. Yet, Paul *trusted God's plan*. Do you trust God's plan in fearful situations? God calls us to trust him in the most fearful situations, believing in his plan, that he will use all things to conform us to Christ's image.

> *Romans 8:28-29* | We know that for those who love God all things work together for good, for those who are called according to his purpose. [29] ... predestined to be conformed to the image of his Son.

---

[516] Pollock, *The Apostle*, 247.

Trust the plan of God for your life, even if pain and danger are looming! He's conforming you to Christ through your hard circumstances.

God's Plan Often Brings Deliverance

Paul was stretched out to be tortured. The centurion attending Paul had made sure this would be the most painful experience for the apostle. Before the beating began Paul had a question for the centurion. God gave Paul great wisdom in his moment of trial.

> **Acts 22:25-26** | But when they had stretched him out for the whips, Paul said to the centurion who was standing by, "Is it lawful for you to flog a man who is a Roman citizen and uncondemned?" [26] When the centurion heard this, he went to the tribune and said to him, "What are you about to do? For this man is a Roman citizen."

The centurion, discovering that Paul is a Roman citizen goes directly to his general, the Roman tribune and lets him know of Paul's Roman citizenship. This changed everything. They could not lawfully torture a Roman citizen. It was not that Paul feared the pain. He had suffered without protest at Philippi (16:22). The kind of scourging he was facing was probably with an instrument that could cripple a person for life.

God's Plan Always Has a Sovereign Purpose

The Roman tribune, who was a very high commander interviews Paul.

> **Acts 22:27-29** | So the tribune came and said to him, "Tell me, are you a Roman citizen?" And he said, "Yes." [28] The tribune answered, "I bought this citizenship for a large sum." Paul said, "But I am a citizen by birth." [29] So those who were about to examine him withdrew from him immediately, and the tribune also was afraid, for he realized that Paul was a Roman citizen and that he had bound him.

The tribune, one of the highest Roman officers, was afraid. Alarmed at how close he had come to scourging a Roman citizen, Lysias the tribune immediately ordered his subordinates to release Paul. He was also afraid because he was guilty of putting a Roman citizen in chains without a preliminary hearing which was illegal.[517] Commander Lysias did not want to be reprimanded or even be demoted from his high post for something like this.

Paul's Roman citizenship forces Lysias to take an entirely different approach, so he decides to have Paul appear before the Jewish Supreme Court, the Sanhedrin (22:30), in hopes of getting at the root of the matter.[518] Paul was not just trying to save his own life. He knew he would be on his way to Rome to preach the gospel. God's sovereign purpose is often far beyond what the present circumstances seem to indicate. Though it looked like Paul's life and well-being were in danger, God had greater purposes. He had just been able to witness to a great crowd at the Feast of Pentecost. Now he was on his way to appear before the Jewish Supreme Court, the Sanhedrin.

God's Plan is the Only One that Matters

When you have to stand alone, trust God's plan. Paul's captors had just been informed by the apostle that he was a Roman citizen. This changed matters instantaneously. Commander Lysias (24:22) wanted to know what Paul's real story was, so he unbound him and released him for a hearing before the great Jewish council of seventy, the Sanhedrin.

> **Acts 22:30** | But on the next day, desiring to know the real reason why he was being accused by the Jews, he unbound him and commanded the chief priests and all the council [*the Jewish Sanhedrin*] to meet, and he brought Paul down and set him before them.

The Romans' Plan. Paul had been a free ambassador of Jesus Christ for nearly twenty years, but in Acts 22 he passes from being a free man to being a prisoner of the Roman state. We would think that being in Roman hands would be worse than being in Jewish hands. But we soon discover that Paul was better off in the hands of the secular authorities than he would have been in the hands of his own people.

The Jews' Plan. The Jews were trying to kill Paul.[519] The Romans, on the other hand, were willing to give him a fair trial, after which they would eventually set him free for a time. Paul had been arrested in Jerusalem and was now in chains. Standing on the steps that led to the

---

[517] MacArthur, *Acts*, vol. 2, 272.
[518] Baker, "Acts," in *Evangelical Commentary,* 916-917.
[519] Boice, *Acts: An Expositional Commentary*, 371.

Roman barracks at the Antonia Fortress where Jesus had been tried, he gave an impromptu defense of his actions there during the Feast of Pentecost. When the Roman commander Lysias had ordered that Paul be flogged, the apostle told a centurion standing near him that he was a Roman citizen. Roman citizens were not to be flogged.[520] The Jews were the ones who wanted Paul executed. They trumped up a false charge of bringing a Gentile into the inner court of the temple. Paul had testified in Aramaic before the crowd, that he was devoted to the law, and would never do such a thing. Now he's brought to the Jewish Supreme Court, but this does not fare well either.

The Lord's Plan. What was the Lord's plan for Paul? We find out in verse 11 of the next chapter. The Lord later tells Paul, "Take courage, for as you have testified to the facts about me in Jerusalem, so you must testify also in Rome" (23:11). God's ways are greater than our ways!

> *Isaiah 55:8-9* | For my thoughts are not your thoughts, neither are your ways my ways, declares the Lord. ⁹ For as the heavens are higher than the earth, so are my ways higher than your ways and my thoughts than your thoughts.

Paul had no control over his circumstances, but he was trusting the Lord with all his heart.

Conclusion

We are called to be "fishers of men." I'm not much of a fisherman, but at different times of the year, if you go to the Wabash River in Indiana, there are these massive flying silver carp that will literally jump out of the water and into your boat. Hundreds of carp can be seen jumping five feet out of the water and often landing in someone's boat. But that's not how evangelism works most of the time. The lost fish don't come to you normally. They're not just going to jump in your boat like the flying carp in the Wabash River. You have to go to them. "How are they to believe in him of whom they have never heard? And how are they to hear without someone preaching?" (Rom 10:14).

Our country desperately needs us to go to them with the gospel and rescue them! Like Paul standing in Jerusalem, we need to stand in our own community and point people to Christ. Are you willing to suffer and to be uncomfortable in evangelizing others for the gospel? How many around you are not yet ready for heaven? Point them to Christ.

---

[520] Thomas, *Acts*, 637.

Dare to care enough to lead them to Jesus. Paul didn't worry about the consequences of sharing Jesus with others, and neither should we.

39 | ACTS 22:30-23:11
STANDING ALONE: PAUL BEFORE THE SANHEDRIN

The following night the Lord stood by him and said, "Take courage, for as you have testified to the facts about me in Jerusalem, so you must testify also in Rome."
ACTS 23:11

We are all called to stand alone as Christians. We are crucified with Christ. We must put aside our reputation, what people think of us—and freely testify of Christ no matter what the consequences.

The night I came to know Christ, the preacher said, "If you don't stand for something, you'll fall for anything," and I was falling for everything. I was willing to stand for Christ that night, even if it meant losing my friends. I did end up losing my friends, but everything and everyone I lost, God gave me a hundred-fold more friends and forever family.

Paul in Acts 22 has to stand alone, but he's never really alone because the Lord is standing with him. We can stand alone because we believe God is omnipotent and sovereign over all events, lovingly guiding our life to be conformed to the image of Christ. We have nothing to fear.

Paul gives his testimony, and as a result, experiences maltreatment. He becomes a prisoner. In the Christian life, there is always spiritual attack, and there is not always a clear way out. While we can always escape temptation to sin, we cannot always escape persecution and maltreatment. Yet Paul is serving God and never feels alone because God is with him, baptizing him with his Spirit continually. He can stand alone because he is never alone.

> Key Thought: We cannot be growing in the Christian life, unless we are serving Christ daily, filled with the fullness of God's presence. The moment we stop experiencing his presence, we stop standing, and we can compromise. Let us be active, serving the Lord, knowing that even when we stand alone, we are never alone, for the Lord is standing with us!

Paul was constantly growing, and because he wouldn't compromise. He was willing to stand alone. Paul was an evangelist, as we all ought to be, ready to give his testimony and the way to Christ at any time. This costs him. It seems like he's alone, but he's never alone. The Lord is with him.

Paul the apostle becomes "Paul the prisoner" (Acts 23:18). This was the name the Roman soldiers used for the apostle, a designation he himself often used (Eph 3:1; 4:1; 2 Tim 1:8; Phm 1, 9). Paul was under "military custody," which meant he was bound to a Roman soldier who was responsible for him. Prisoners under "public custody" were put in the common jail, a horrible place for any human being to suffer (Acts 16:19–24). This was Paul's new home for now.

Paul's friends could visit him and help meet his personal needs. It is sad that we don't read, "And prayer was made fervently by the church for Paul" (cf Acts 12:5). There is no record that the Jerusalem church took any steps to assist him, either in Jerusalem or during his two years in Caesarea. Of course, Paul often asked for prayer for himself as a "prisoner in chains." It seems that Paul was entering a phase in his ministry where he was utterly alone at times.

So how is one to act when the whole world is against you? Paul has the Gentiles against him. The Jews against him. We find out in this chapter that only the Lord is for him. And when the Lord is for you, that is enough.

TRUST GOD'S PLAN (22:30)

Paul is willing to stand alone and give his testimony, calling the people of Israel once again to repentance on the Day of Pentecost. He's on the steps of the Antonia Fortress where the Lord Jesus was mocked with purple robe and crown of thorns. He's protected by a thousand Roman soldiers. The people really did not like what Paul had to say, and they tried to kill him.

When you have to stand alone, trust God's plan. Paul's captors had just been informed by the apostle that he was a Roman citizen. This changed matters instantaneously. Commander Lysias (24:22) wanted to know what Paul's real story was, so he unbound him and released him for a hearing before the great Jewish council of seventy, the Sanhedrin.

> **Acts 22:30** | But on the next day, desiring to know the real reason why he was being accused by the Jews, he unbound him and commanded the chief priests and all the council to meet, and he brought Paul down and set him before them.

The Plan of the Romans

Paul had been a free ambassador of Jesus Christ for nearly twenty years, but in Acts 22 he passes from being a free man to being a prisoner of the Roman state. We would think that being in Roman hands would be worse than being in Jewish hands. But we soon discover that Paul was better off in the hands of the secular authorities than he would have been in the hands of his own people.

The Plan of the Jews

The Jews were trying to kill Paul.[521] The Romans, on the other hand, were willing to give him a fair trial, after which they would eventually set him free for a time.

Paul had been arrested in Jerusalem and was now in chains. Standing on the steps that led to the Roman barracks at the Antonia Fortress where Jesus had been tried, he gave an impromptu defense of his actions there during the Feast of Pentecost. When the Roman commander Lysias had ordered that Paul be flogged, the apostle told a

---

[521] Boice, *Acts: An Expositional Commentary*, 371.

centurion standing near him that he was a Roman citizen. Roman citizens were not to be flogged.[522]

The Jews were the ones who wanted Paul executed. They trumped up a false charge of bringing a Gentile into the inner court of the temple. Paul had testified in Aramaic before the crowd, that he was devoted to the law, and would never do such a thing. Now he's brought to the Jewish Supreme Court, but this does not fare well either.

The Plan of God

The Lord is later going to tell Paul, "Take courage, for as you have testified to the facts about me in Jerusalem, so you must testify also in Rome" (23:11). God's ways are greater than our ways!

> *Isaiah 55:8-9* | For my thoughts are not your thoughts, neither are your ways my ways, declares the Lord. ⁹ For as the heavens are higher than the earth, so are my ways higher than your ways and my thoughts than your thoughts.

Paul had no control over his circumstances, but he was trusting the Lord with all his heart.

WALK IN GOD'S WISDOM (23:1-10)

When you have to stand alone, you need to remember to walk in God's wisdom.

Wisdom in the Word

Paul did not choose to see the world through his own physical eyes, but through the eyes of his heart where he treasured God's word. When bad things happened, he reached in to where he had treasured God's word. He was not a slave to his circumstances, but a slave of Jesus.

What we find out with Paul is that he's interrogated and slapped by command of the high priest, and what comes out of him is God's word. Paul testifies that he has a clean conscience and has not lived in violation of God's law.

> **Acts 23:1-5** | And looking intently at the council, Paul said, "Brothers, I have lived my life before God in all good conscience up to this day." ² And the high priest Ananias commanded those who stood by him to strike him on the mouth. ³ Then Paul said to him, "God is going to strike you, you whitewashed wall! Are you sitting to

---

[522] Thomas, *Acts*, 637.

judge me according to the law, and yet contrary to the law you order me to be struck?" **⁴** Those who stood by said, "Would you revile God's high priest?" **⁵** And Paul said, "I did not know, brothers, that he was the high priest, for it is written, 'You shall not speak evil of a ruler of your people.'"

Paul responds in righteous anger toward the high priest, but he didn't know he was the high priest. Yet the high priest himself was indeed in violation of God's law. Paul could see he, like his Savior, was in a kangaroo court. Like our Lord, he called out God's enemies as "whitewashed walls." Remember the Lord had called the Pharisees "whitewashed tombs."

Despite the wrong of the high priest, Paul knew the word of God and realized he also was wrong to speak out against the high priest. Paul apologized, quoting from Exodus 22:28 as his reason for doing so. The man was despicable, but the office was venerable.[523] When pressed, and even when mistaken, Paul was always guided by the word of God.

Saints, we must prepare ourselves with the word of God. Not everything we learn is for this moment, but we treasure God's word in our heart that at the right moment, the Lord will bring it to mind.

Wisdom in the Situation

Now that Paul had apologized to the high priest, he made a move that was brilliant. Remember Jesus told us to be "wise as serpents and harmless as doves" (Mt 10:16). He knew the Sanhedrin was divided between Pharisees, who believed in a resurrection at the Last Day and in the existence of angels and spiritual beings, and the party of the Sadducees, who held rationalist, materialist views. They denied the supernatural. Paul was sure that many of the Pharisees would believe in Jesus if only they saw him as he, a Pharisee, had seen him on the Damascus Road. Belief in the risen Jesus was the only honest conclusion for a true Pharisee. Perhaps if he awakened the Pharisees to the resurrection of Jesus, they would believe.

> **Acts 23:6-9** | Now when Paul perceived that one part were Sadducees and the other Pharisees, he cried out in the council, "Brothers, I am a Pharisee, a son of Pharisees. It is with respect to the hope and the resurrection of the dead that I am on trial." **⁷** And when he had said this, a dissension arose between the Pharisees and

---

[523] J. Phillips, *Exploring Acts*, Ac 23:4–5.

the Sadducees, and the assembly was divided. **⁸** For the Sadducees say that there is no resurrection, nor angel, nor spirit, but the Pharisees acknowledge them all. **⁹** Then a great clamor arose, and some of the scribes of the Pharisees' party stood up and contended sharply, "We find nothing wrong in this man. What if a spirit or an angel spoke to him?"

Instead of the Pharisees inquiring more into the resurrection of Jesus, they started a riot with the Sadducees. Paul was in the midst of them, and it was judged that he was about to be "torn to pieces" (23:10).

Wisdom in the Will of God

Theologians call the way God directs our lives "providence." God is all wise, and we have to trust that he directs all events in our lives. If we fuss and fret over everything, we will be no good for God. Paul trusted the wisdom of God's guidance in his life. God certainly came through.

> **Acts 23:10** | And when the dissension became violent, the tribune, afraid that Paul would be torn to pieces by them, commanded the soldiers to go down and take him away from among them by force and bring him into the barracks.

How interesting it is that such a distinguished leadership group would become so stirred up by Paul's words that they "became violent"? When the Sadducees on the Sanhedrin decided Paul was worthy of death, they about tore Paul "to pieces." So again, the Roman soldiers had to rescue Paul and brought him back to the barracks of the Antonia Fortress in Jerusalem.

We need to remember that God is watching over us as his children, just as he was Paul. He can even use worldly entities to rescue us from harm. I recall when the office of homeland security wanted to ship my dear friend Ahmed Joktan back to Saudi Arabia, God used a United States Senator, Dick Durbin, a Democrat from Chicago, to step in and sponsor Dr. Ahmed for asylum. God can use the most unlikely people for our protection![524] Don't be so concerned about your own wisdom or how you can get yourself out of a situation. Trust in God's wisdom and his will for your life.

---

[524] To read the entire story, see Ahmed Joktan, *From Mecca to Christ: The True Story of the Son of the Meccan Mufti* (Wenatchee, WA: Proclaim Publishers, 2020), 171-173.

Proverbs 16:9 | The heart of man plans his way, but the Lord determines his steps.

You are God's workmanship, and your steps are predetermined to walk in each day (Eph 2:10).

EXPERIENCE GOD'S COMFORT (23:11)

When you have to stand alone, experience God's comfort.

Acts 23:11 | The following night the Lord stood by him and said, "Take courage, for as you have testified to the facts about me in Jerusalem, so you must testify also in Rome."

Notice that the Christian life is not one where we grow in relationship with pages in a book, but through the word, we grow in relation with the living Lord. This is the Lord who stood by Paul.

Comfort in God's Presence

Acts 23:11a | The following night the Lord stood by him.

Wherever you are, and whatever you are doing, the Lord is with you. This realization of God's presence is a concept in the Bible called "the fear of the Lord." We become wise through what the Puritans called "practicing the presence of God." Remember the words of King Solomon.

Proverbs 9:10 | The fear of the LORD is the beginning of wisdom, and the knowledge of the Holy One is insight.

The Lord stood by Paul after his encounter with the Sanhedrin. This was a group of men that at one time he loved and had deep relationships with. When a person comes to know Christ, it changes our earthly relationships. Sometimes we can feel so alone. But when we feel forsaken, we must always avail ourselves of the Lord's presence. Instead of being controlled by worries and what ifs, we have to cast our care on Jesus, who abides in us by the Holy Spirit. We are his temple. Our hearts are his home!

1 Peter 5:7 | Casting all your anxieties on him, because he cares for you.

You may not often find great joy in your circumstances, but you must always find joy in the presence of Jesus!

Psalm 16:11 | In your presence there is fullness of joy; at your right hand are pleasures forevermore.

Comfort in God's Praise

Paul also must have been deeply encouraged by what the Lord told him. He had given a good testimony in Jerusalem.

Acts 23:11b | And said, "Take courage, for as you have testified to the facts about me in Jerusalem, so you must testify also in Rome."

We cannot assess our success just by looking at the earthly circumstances. God's ways are higher than our ways. God is pleased with what Paul has said and done and praises him for it. "Good job in Jerusalem! Now let's get you to Rome!"

Comfort in God's Plan

Acts 23:11c | "So you must testify also in Rome."

Paul has sincerely spoken for Christ and tried to be as wise as possible. At the end of the day, though it looks like a total disaster, with the Jews and the Sanhedrin rejecting him, Paul's faithfulness sets him up to preach the gospel to kings and to soldiers and officers of Caesar's household.

Conclusion

Ignacy Jan Paderewski (1860-1941), the famous Polish composer-pianist, was scheduled to perform at a great concert hall in America. He once famously said, "The mere fact of knowing that a great audience waits on your labor is enough to shake all your nerves to pieces."[525]

It would be an evening to remember—a black-tux-long-evening-dress, high-society extravaganza. In the audience that evening sat a mother with her fidgety nine-year-old son. Weary of waiting for the concert to begin, the lad squirmed constantly in his seat. His mother hoped her boy would be encouraged to practice the piano once he heard the immortal Paderewski. That is why, against his wishes, he was there.

When the little boy's mother turned to talk with some friends, the impatient boy could stay seated no longer. He slipped away from her side, strangely drawn to the ebony concert grand Steinway and its

---

[525] Paderewski in Charles Phillips, *The Story of a Modern Immortal* (New York: Macmillan, 1934), 130.

leather-tufted stool on the huge stage flooded with brilliant lights. Largely ignored by the sophisticated audience, the boy sat down at the stool, staring wide-eyed at the black and white keys. He placed his small, trembling fingers in the right location and began to play "Chopsticks." The roar of the crowd quickly ceased as hundreds of frowning faces turned in his direction. Irritated and embarrassed, they began to shout at the bold youngster.

Backstage the master, overhearing the sounds, hurriedly grabbed his coat and rushed toward the stage, where he stood behind the boy and began to improvise a countermelody to harmonize with and enhance "Chopsticks." As the two of them played together, Paderewski kept whispering in the boy's ears, "Keep going. Don't quit, son. Keep on playing. Do not stop. Do not quit." What a gracious genius!

In the kingdom of God, we have been called to play a spiritual tune for Christ.[526] And though we may at times be flooded with difficult and confusing circumstances in life, God tells us, "Don't quit! Keep going! I'm with you! I'll never leave you or forsake you!"

---

[526] Hughes, *Acts: The Church Afire*, 308.

40 | ACTS 23:12-35
GOD'S PROTECTION: PAUL AND HIS 40 ASSASSINS

When it was day, the Jews made a plot and bound themselves by an oath neither to eat nor drink till they had killed Paul. There were more than forty who made this conspiracy.
ACTS 23:12-13

Sometimes, we feel quite helpless in life. We feel abandoned. If you've not felt that way, you will. But the Lord will never abandon you. He says, "I will never leave you or forsake you" (Heb 13:5). If everyone else has left you behind, the Lord will carry you through the flood and through the fire.

> *Isaiah 43:1-3* | Fear not, for I have redeemed you; I have called you by name, you are mine. ²When you pass through the waters, I will be with you; and through the rivers, they shall not overwhelm you; when you walk through fire you shall not be burned, and the flame shall not consume you. ³For I am the Lord your God, the Holy One of Israel, your Savior.

Sometimes as believers, we feel forgotten and abandoned. We are kind of like a special rock a little boy found that started the first gold rush. It was a precious, large gold nugget. In 1799, twelve-year-old Conrad Reed, skipped his Sunday School class to go fishing, and he found a massive gold nugget in Little Meadow Creek in Barrier Mills, North Carolina. His discovery triggered America's first gold rush. Not knowing what it was made of his family used it as a doorstop for three years. In 1802, his father, John Reed, took it to a jeweler who identified it as a lump of gold and offered him $3.50. John took it, not knowing it's actual worth, which was $3,600 in the 1800s or $400K in today's money! That lump of gold, which was used as a doorstop for three years in North Carolina, is one of the biggest gold nuggets ever found east of the Rockies.[527]

We are kind of like that forgotten gold nugget, unappreciated by the world, but treasured by our heavenly Father. When you are maltreated on this earth, the Lord loves you. We learn this from the life of the apostle Paul.

> Key Thought: When you feel most abandoned, it is then that God carries you and protects you. He treasures you as his child, guiding your every step toward Christlikeness.

At times we feel like that rock, forgotten, unvalued, and unprotected. But the Lord does protect us at all times. There is always a hedge of protection around the child of God.

THE DESIGN OF THE ENEMY (23:12-15)

The enemy's design is to make you feel abandoned by God. Paul might have felt that way. He was under severe attack by the wicked one. He had testified of Christ before the riotous crowd on the day of Pentecost in Jerusalem. He had appeared before the Sanhedrin. Now he had been taken into Roman custody. While he is waiting, trusting in God, little does he know there are 40 assassins plotting to kill him. Yet Paul is perfectly safe. We can say with missionary John Paton:

> I am immortal till my Master's work with me is done.[528]

Don't be afraid of the design of the enemy. Your steps are predestined by God (Prov 16:9; Eph 2:10). Your life is predestined to be conformed to the image of Christ (Rom 8:29).

---

[527] John Hairr and Joey Powell, *Gold Mines in North Carolina* (Charleston, SC: Arcadia Publishing, 2004), 8-9.

[528] John Paton, *Missionary to the New Hebrides: An Autobiography* (Carlisle, PA: Banner of Truth, 2018), 207.

The Pledge

These forty assassins pledged not to eat or drink until they had killed Paul. Notice that even if forty people have pledged themselves to execute the apostle, he is immortal until God is finished with him.

> **Acts 23:12-13** | When it was day, the Jews made a plot and bound themselves by an oath neither to eat nor drink till they had killed Paul. ¹³ There were more than forty who made this conspiracy.

Paul was untouchable, despite those who wanted to kill him because he had God's hedge of protection around him. The assassins had their pledge, but Paul had God's hedge. It's like he said of Job.

> *Job 1:10* | Have you not put a hedge around him and his house and all that he has, on every side?

So it is with us. We have God's hedge of protection around us. Who knows how many members of God's angel armies are escorting you right now? The only way you breach that hedge is through sin. Remember that Satan is the enemy of your soul. He hates you, and he wants God's plans for you to be defeated. This story reminds us that the safest place for the Christian is the center of God's will. Despite the oath of the forty assassins, Paul was safe in the will of God, as you are.

The Priests

It is frightening to know that Satan has his pawns in high places, even in religious circles. Here there is an agreement with the chief priests and elders with this posse of forty assassins.

> **Acts 23:14** | They went to the chief priests and elders and said, "We have strictly bound ourselves by an oath to taste no food till we have killed Paul."

No matter how high the enemies are that plot against God's people, they are not higher than God himself who watches over his children.

The Plot

Shockingly, the chief priests are in with the Sanhedrin to deceive the Roman commander Lysias who was tribune for Paul.

> **Acts 23:15** | "Now therefore you, along with the council, give notice to the tribune to bring him down to you, as though you were going

to determine his case more exactly. And we are ready to kill him before he comes near."

Careless of their own lives, thinking to do God a service, these sophisticated assassins would rid Judaism of Paul once and for all. The Jewish leaders, however, had to play their part with the Roman military commander. For these religious leaders, following God was just a cover. They were controlled by the wicked one. How sad that these leaders should disgrace themselves with dark plots, lies, and violence. Their ideas were spawned by the father of lies, he who was a murderer from the beginning.[529] Paul's enemy was in the unseen realm.

> *Ephesians 6:12* | We are not fighting against flesh-and-blood enemies, but against evil rulers and authorities of the unseen world, against mighty powers in this dark world, and against evil spirits in the heavenly places.

Paul's greatest enemy was not the Sanhedrin or his posse of forty assassins. His chief enemy and yours is the devil. But remember, Satan cannot touch you without God's permission. All the highest-ranking leaders in Israel want Paul dead, but they cannot make it happen since Paul is immortal until God is finished with him. The same could be said of every one of God's children. Your enemy is already a defeated foe.

> *1 John 4:4 (KJV)* | Greater is he that is in you, than he that is in the world.

Satan knows his time is short (Rev 12:12). He's soon going to be put away forever, never to harass the saints again!

> *Revelation 20:10* | The devil who had deceived them was thrown into the lake of fire and sulfur where the beast and the false prophet were, and they will be tormented day and night forever and ever.

Don't give an opportunity for the devil through sin on your part (Eph 4:27). Walk in holiness and humility. Resist the devil, and he will flee from you (Jas 4:7).

THE DELIVERANCE OF GOD (23:16-30)

God uses the most unlikely people to protect his servants. He uses little David to defeat a giant. He uses young Josiah to turn a nation from

---

[529] J. Phillips, *Exploring Acts*, Ac 23:15.

idolatry. He uses a little boy to feed a multitude with his lunch. He preserved three Hebrew children from perishing in a fiery furnace, and there was a fourth man in the fire: the Son of God! God uses the most weak and unlikely people to deliver us. For Paul, God uses his own nephew, a young boy who found courage and protected his Uncle Paul.

God's Agent

It is Paul's little nephew that God uses to protect the great apostle. Who knew Paul had a sister or a nephew? We don't know his name or age, but he seems to be just a boy who is at the right place at the right time.

> **Acts 23:16-22** | Now the son of Paul's sister heard of their ambush, so he went and entered the barracks and told Paul. [17] Paul called one of the centurions and said, "Take this young man to the tribune, for he has something to tell him." [18] So he took him and brought him to the tribune and said, "Paul the prisoner called me and asked me to bring this young man to you, as he has something to say to you." [19] The tribune took him by the hand, and going aside asked him privately, "What is it that you have to tell me?" [20] And he said, "The Jews have agreed to ask you to bring Paul down to the council tomorrow, as though they were going to inquire somewhat more closely about him. [21] But do not be persuaded by them, for more than forty of their men are lying in ambush for him, who have bound themselves by an oath neither to eat nor drink till they have killed him. And now they are ready, waiting for your consent." [22] So the tribune dismissed the young man, charging him, "Tell no one that you have informed me of these things."

First of all, Paul's 40 assassins must have either starved to death or broken their vow, because God wasn't going to let them touch Paul, no matter how intriguing their plot against Paul was. God is going to use a little boy to protect the great apostle.

The boy must have been quite young, since the tribune, Commander Lysias, "took him by the hand" (23:19) to hear the plot against Paul. The tribune received Paul's nephew graciously, taking him to a quiet spot where he could listen to his story.

How had the boy gained access to the Antonia Fortress? It's likely that Paul welcomed his sister and nephew there since he was free to have any guests he liked. Paul's status as a Roman citizen stood him in good stead. Although in custody, he was able to receive visitors, and his requests were handled by the centurions.[530]

We don't know how the boy heard about the murder plot against Paul, but it may have been a rumor that had gotten out. The boy brought the plot to the Roman commander Lysias, and he insisted he tell no one. His own life would not be worth much if the conspirators found out he had betrayed them to the Romans. The commander dismissed the young man, for he had done his job well!

It's vital that young people serve the Lord at the earliest of ages. Learn from Paul's young nephew that God can do great and mighty things through the youngest of his children. Remember the words of Jesus.

> *Matthew 19:14* | Let the little children come to me and do not hinder them, for to such belongs the kingdom of heaven.

Let me urge the children and young people of our church to come to Christ now. Don't wait until you are older. It will be harder to come the longer you wait. Come now and trust him so that you have your whole life to serve him. Don't waste your life in sin. Give your heart to Christ and have your sins forgiven! Be a member of God's dear family. Don't ever think you are too young to be saved or to be used mightily by the living God.

God's Army

So after our unlikely agent, this little nephew of Paul's, we have an unlikely army. The Roman soldiers are now recruited to protect Paul from this plot of forty assassins. How unusual is the life of a Christian! God can utilize anyone on earth to protect his people. Commander Lysias, the Roman tribune calls his centurions and forms a little army for the apostle Paul.

> **Acts 23:23-24** | Then he called two of the centurions and said, "Get ready two hundred soldiers, with seventy horsemen and two hundred spearmen to go as far as Caesarea at the third hour of the night. ²⁴ Also provide mounts for Paul to ride and bring him safely to Felix the governor."

---

[530] Phillips, *Exploring Acts*, Ac 23:17–18.

Two hundred soldiers, 70 horsemen and 200 spearmen are gathered! That's 470 Roman soldiers in all! They go in "the third hour of the night" which is nine o'clock at night. Paul was even given a horse to ride. Surrounded by a great army, Paul rode through the night on his way to Caesarea.

There was no way Commander Lysias could risk having Paul remain in Jerusalem another night, and he must therefore be escorted to a more secure location—and the jurisdiction of the governor (procurator) of the province of Judea, Tiberius Antonius Felix. As Roman procurator, Felix resided in Caesarea, visiting Jerusalem only for the feasts (to ensure order).[531] So Paul was on his way with the Roman army conscripted by God for his humble apostle!

God's Ambassador

Who does God use to deliver Paul to Caesarea, but his faithful Commander, General-like leader—a Roman tribune named Claudius Lysias. He writes a letter to the governor of Palestine at the time, named Felix.

> **Acts 23:25-30** | And he wrote a letter to this effect: [26] "Claudius Lysias, to his Excellency the governor Felix, greetings. [27] This man was seized by the Jews and was about to be killed by them when I came upon them with the soldiers and rescued him, having learned that he was a Roman citizen. [28] And desiring to know the charge for which they were accusing him, I brought him down to their council. [29] I found that he was being accused about questions of their law, but charged with nothing deserving death or imprisonment. [30] And when it was disclosed to me that there would be a plot against the man, I sent him to you at once, ordering his accusers also to state before you what they have against him."

The only way Luke would have direct access to this letter would be through the trials that the apostle would go through with various dignitaries and kings. Luke, it seems was present when this letter would have been presented. What is clear in the letter, is the way the Roman tribune Claudius Lysias is actually acting as God's ambassador and lawyer for Paul.

Isn't it amazing how God can protect his children? He can use the most unlikely people to open doors and guide our way. When Abraham

---

[531] Thomas, *Acts*, 654–655.

gave his wife to Pharaoh's harem, God protected Sarah and spoke directly to Pharaoh in a dream. It was Pharaoh himself that protected Sarah, not Abraham. God is bigger than whatever you can see with your eyes. He can utilize Pharaohs and donkeys and angels to protect his people. You are not alone. You have God's hedge of protection around you.

THE DESTINATION OF THE APOSTLE (23:31-35)

Perhaps Paul thought that due to seeming exoneration he would be set free. But instead, he's going to start a very long journey of incarceration and eventually imprisonment. God's destination for the child of God is never what the world offers. Sometimes we are given difficult circumstances so that we can be fruitful.

Safe Passage

Paul's life is in danger, but quickly the tribune sends him away to Caesarea. The soldiers ride with Paul as far as Antipatris, the halfway point to Caesarea from Jerusalem. Then the soldiers return back to the barracks of the Antonia Fortress in Jerusalem and Paul continues on with the horsemen to Caesarea Maritima by the Mediterranean Sea.

> **Acts 23:31-33** | So the soldiers, according to their instructions, took Paul and brought him by night to Antipatris. **32** And on the next day they returned to the barracks, letting the horsemen go on with him. **33** When they had come to Caesarea and delivered the letter to the governor [Felix], they presented Paul also before him.

The two hundred soldiers went back to Jerusalem, and the 200 spearman and 70 horsemen guarded Paul and delivered him to Governor Felix. Two-hundred seventy is still an incredible security detail! Despite all the plots and schemes to kill Paul, note here that Paul is immortal until God is finished with him. How is that?

> *Psalm 4:8* | In peace I will lie down and sleep, for you alone, LORD, make me dwell in safety.

> *Nahum 1:7* | The LORD is good, a refuge in times of trouble. He cares for those who trust in him.

Can you testify that the safest place for any of us is in the center of God's will? Are you living in the peace of God, or is fear eating at you?

There is legitimate fear that God gives. If you see a lion you should run. But truly, most of our fear is not legitimate. Most of our fear is a sinful anxiety that is a lack of trust in God. Dear saint, don't spend one more second in sinful fear. Ask God, where am I not trusting you? God's peace will come as you conquer fear. The Scripture tells us we are not to be sinfully anxious about anything.

> *Philippians 4:6-7* | Do not be anxious about anything, but in everything by prayer and supplication with thanksgiving let your requests be made known to God. [7] And the peace of God, which surpasses all understanding, will guard your hearts and your minds in Christ Jesus.

Jesus says it's the Gentile unbelievers that worry. They are atheists. They don't trust in God. Worry makes people into practical atheists. You forget that God loves you, that he's in control, and that he's guiding all events to a glorious conclusion for your good and his glory. Don't be worrying about anything. The Gentiles worry about all these things.

> *Matthew 6:32-33* | Your heavenly Father knows that you need them all. [33] But seek first the kingdom of God and his righteousness, and all these things will be added to you.

You never have to worry if you constantly entrust your soul to God (Pro 3:5-6). Worry is a toxin of the soul. It can paralyze you. Don't get comfortable.

Sound Preaching

Governor Felix decides to accept the case, promising to hear from Paul when his accusers arrived from Jerusalem. Paul was a Roman citizen and had not yet been charged with a crime.[532]

> **Acts 23:34-35a** | On reading the letter, he [Governor Felix] asked what province he was from. And when he learned that he was from Cilicia, [35] he said, "I will give you a hearing when your accusers arrive."

Paul was going to be able to preach the gospel to Governor Felix on many occasions over the course of two years (24:27). Paul would have to wait a long time, but during this time, he would preach Christ to many dignitaries. Jesus had said this would happen.

---

[532] Charles R. Swindoll, *Acts*, Swindoll's Living Insights New Testament Commentary (Carol Stream, IL: Tyndale House Publishers, Inc., 2016), 459.

> *Matthew 10:17-19* | Beware of men, for they will deliver you over to courts and flog you in their synagogues, ¹⁸ and you will be **dragged before governors and kings for my sake**, to bear witness before them and the Gentiles. ¹⁹ When they deliver you over, do not be anxious how you are to speak or what you are to say, for what you are to say will be given to you in that hour.

This is basically the story of the apostle Paul's life! The Lord had said of Paul that he was a chosen instrument for the Gentiles.

> *Acts 9:15* | The Lord said to him, "Go, for he is a chosen instrument of mine to carry my name before the Gentiles and kings and the children of Israel."

Now Paul was going to have plenty of opportunities to preach the gospel to Gentiles and kings, and even those of Caesar's household (Phil 1:13; *cf* 4:22).

Secure Prison

Paul would remain under guard in Herod's beautiful palace in Caesarea in relative comfort.[533]

> **Acts 23:35b** | And he commanded him to be guarded in Herod's praetorium.

Herod's praetorium was a beautiful palace built by Herod the Great on the coast of the Mediterranean Sea in Caesarea. It's a massive palace, and Paul would have been kept with a Roman soldier in one of the rooms day and night. Every six hours, Paul would get a new Roman soldier to preach to![534] That's what I call a jail ministry!

Sometimes God's protection is very different than what we would have planned. Paul's desire was to go to Rome and testify there, but this was a very different pathway than anyone would have desired.

It seemed like Paul's ministry was over. Have you ever felt that way? The truth is often our ministry is just beginning after our legacy is completed. We read Paul's letters of inspired Scripture even to this very day. We are studying his life. Just when perhaps he thought his ministry was ending, it had really hardly begun at all.

---

[533] Ibid.

[534] Kathryn L. Gleason, et al. "The Promontory Palace at Caesarea Maritima: Preliminary Evidence for Herod's praetorium." JRA 11 (1998): 23–52.

I think of Jonathan Edwards, who after many years of faithful service to his congregation in Northampton, was fired on the basis of false reports and slander and exiled from the town. As a result, he went to work among the Indians. He then was asked to be president of Princeton University. A week after his installation, he gave himself the smallpox vaccine, and died. Of course today Edwards is regarded as the foremost theologian of the American continent.[535]

Or what about C.H. Spurgeon? He was run out of his church during the downgrade controversy when his church joined a compromised denomination. It is said that Spurgeon died at a fairly young age of 57 of a broken heart. His wife, Susannah, wrote following his death that "his fight for the faith ... cost him his life."[536] Yet we read his sermons and enjoy his books to this very day.

Paul was under the watch of a Roman soldier day and night as he waited for what would be two years there in Caesarea near the Mediterranean Sea. Pointless? Not at all. He'd be busy evangelizing kings and governors and the Roman soldiers. Paul was given a new "jailhouse" ministry. What was God doing? He was refining Paul by reinventing his mission field. No longer was he to go to the synagogue or the marketplace. Now it was to the governor's court, the king's palace, and the soldier's jail cell.

Conclusion

Paul may have at times felt abandoned, put on the shelf, but he was not. God never puts his saints on the shelf. We will suffer. We will be tried by fire through tests and tribulations. He refines us to make us more useful, conformed to the image of Christ. All of our suffering is pushing us toward Christlikeness.

In the 1800s, a group of women met to study the Bible in Dublin, Ireland. They were puzzled by the words of Malachi 3.

Malachi 3:3 | And he shall sit as a refiner and purifier of silver.

Why would a refiner sit and watch the silver? One of the ladies promised to call on a silversmith and report to the group, and she did

---

[535] Sproul, *Acts*, 376–377.
[536] Charles Haddon Spurgeon, Susannah Spurgeon, Joseph Harrald, *C.H. Spurgeon's Autobiography: 1878-1892, vol 4* (London: Passmore and Alabaster, 1900), 255.

just that. "Is it true," asked the lady to the silversmith, "that you must sit while the silver is being refined?"

"Oh yes, Madam," replied the silversmith, "I must sit with my eye steadily fixed on the furnace. For if the time necessary for refining be exceeded in the slightest degree, the silver will be ruined." The silversmith then noted that the way he knew the process of purifying was complete was by seeing his own image reflected in the silver. So it is with the Christian. When Christ's image is reflected in us his work of purifying is accomplished.[537]

So Paul was in the fire. It seemed he was done for. But actually, God was refining him for even greater use. What about you? You're in the fire right now. You can't understand it. You feel put on the shelf. But learn the lessons God is teaching you. Surrender to him, and you will see that he is preparing you for an even greater legacy with greater fruit.

---

[537] A.G. Whittelsey. *Magazine for Mothers and Daughters, Volume 3* (New York: Whittelsey Press, 1852), 33.

41 | ACTS 24:1-27
WAITING ON GOD (FELIX)

After some days Felix came with his wife Drusilla, who was Jewish, and he sent for Paul and heard him speak about faith in Christ Jesus.
ACTS 24:24

The Chinese bamboo tree is one of the most remarkable plants on earth. Once the gardener plants the seed, he will see nothing but a single shoot coming out of the bulb — for five full years! That tiny shoot, however, must have daily food and water. During all the time the gardener is caring for the plant, the exterior shoot will grow less than an inch.

At the end of five years, however, the Chinese bamboo will perform an incredible feat. It will grow an amazing ninety feet tall in only ninety days! Now ask yourself this: When did the tree actually grow? During the first five years, or during those last ninety days?

The answer lies in the unseen part of the tree, the underground root system. During the first five years, the fibrous root structure spreads deep and wide in the earth, preparing to support the incredible heights the tree will eventually reach.[538]

---

[538] James H. Wandersee, Joel J. Mintzes, and Joseph D. Novak, *Assessing Science Understanding A Human Constructivist View* (San Diego, CA: Elsevier Academic Press, 2005), 145.

An oak or a mushroom? It's been said that when God wants to grow mushrooms, he can do it overnight, but when he wants to grow a mighty oak, it takes a few years. What do we want to be, a mushroom or an oak? If we want to be an oak, it is well worth the wait.

Paul is willing to go through the long haul for the gospel. He spent a year and a half in Corinth (18:11-12) and over three years in Ephesus (20:31). Now for the last seven years of his life, most of his time is going to be spent in incarceration. His jewelry will be the shackles on his hands and feet. Like the bamboo tree, Paul doesn't see much growth in his jail ministry at first, but he faithfully gives the gospel as he presents his case as an incarcerated man, even though no formal charges have been filed against him.

In Paul's younger years, when Paul and Silas had found themselves in a Philippian jail, they began singing, and God sent an earthquake to release them. No such earthquake was given with Paul incarcerated in Caesarea. Instead, God wanted him to give a good testimony to all around him. But first he had to confront his accusers from Jerusalem.

> Key thought: It's vital to never give up, and never faint in your circumstances. We are to wait on God, because he promises to make all things beautiful in his time. Wait on him, and he will bring his perfect will to pass!

What do you do when you are waiting? Waiting is hard! And do you know what makes it harder? Distractions!

DISTRACTIONS WITH WAITING OF GOD (24:1-9)

Distractions from your walk with God come in many forms, but normally they are an attack on you from the enemy in various forms.

Flattery

There are those in our lives that live for themselves. They "do not serve our Lord Jesus Christ, but their own belly, and by smooth words and flattering speech deceive" (Rom 16:18). Flattery is a form of lying that uses flattering falsehoods to manipulate and get their way.

The Jews confronted Paul and brought a lawyer, or more of a professional speaker, Tertullus to flatter and lie and to Governor Felix.

> **Acts 24:1-4** | And after five days the high priest Ananias came down with some elders and a spokesman, one Tertullus. They laid before the governor their case against Paul. ² And when he had been

summoned, Tertullus began to accuse him, saying: "Since through you we enjoy much peace, and since by your foresight, most excellent Felix, reforms are being made for this nation, ³ in every way and everywhere we accept this with all gratitude. ⁴ But, to detain you no further, I beg you in your kindness to hear us briefly."

While we are waiting on God, we will have to endure the enemy's attack. The enemy will manipulate to try to get our attention off the Lord. Tertullus was evidently a Hellenistic Jew competent in both Jewish and Roman law. Tertullus uses flattery to gain favor with Governor Felix in order to hurt Paul. God tells us that the flatterer will be exposed by God.

Proverbs 29:5 | A man who flatters his neighbor spreads a net for his feet.

God will vindicate us when we are attacked by the wicked one through manipulation and flattery. When you are waiting on God, keep the focus of your heart on the Lord, and he will give you perfect peace even in the midst of distracting attacks.

Isaiah 26:3 | You keep him in perfect peace whose mind is stayed on you, because he trusts in you.

Falsehoods

Tertullus accused Paul of being guilty of two capital crimes.

Acts 24:5-8 | For we have found this man a plague, one who stirs up riots among all the Jews throughout the world and is a ringleader of the sect of the Nazarenes. ⁶ He even tried to profane the temple, but we seized him. ⁸ By examining him yourself you will be able to find out from him about everything of which we accuse him."

The first capital crime charged against Paul are that he was a rioter who threatened the Pax Romana (Roman peace). Starting riots was a capital offense, and Felix had executed others charged with the same crime. The second capital and that he "tried to profane the temple" by bringing a Gentile into the inner court of the temple.[539]

---

[539] Baker, "Acts," in *Evangelical Commentary*, 918.

False Witnesses

Many false witnesses came forward against Paul, likely most of them Sadducees, since the Pharisees defended Paul in previous proceedings.

> **Acts 24:9** | The Jews also joined in the charge, affirming that all these things were so.

Don't be afraid of accusations. The Christian life is one of full surrender. Paul had constant accusations thrown at him. In following Christ, we must first and foremost surrender our reputation.

> *Proverbs 29:25* | The fear of man lays a snare, but whoever trusts in the LORD is safe.

Jesus said when we follow him, people will accuse us and say "all manner of evil against us falsely" (Mt 5:11-12). In response, we are to rejoice that we are counted worthy to suffer for Christ.

Don't be distracted by the enemy's attack when you are waiting on God.

HELPS FOR WAITING ON GOD (24:10-21)

No one likes to wait. But we wait in traffic, in holding patterns, in grocery stores, for parking lots, for the doctor, for a spouse, for a baby, for retirement, and most importantly, for Jesus to return!

Waiting is not just something we have to do while we get what we want. Waiting is the process of becoming what God wants us to be. What God does in us while we wait is as important as what it is we are waiting for. Waiting, biblical waiting, is not a passive waiting around, but a sure expectation that God is making us what we ought to be. Since Paul was being accused of two capital crimes, let's consider what he was guilty of. He was guilty of cheerfulness, of integrity, of faith, and of generosity. Other than that, he was blameless!

An Attitude of Cheerfulness

Paul's missionary activity has been halted, but he is actually cheerful, and not bitter, to make his defense. He knows God is in control.

> **Acts 24:10** | And when the governor had nodded to him to speak, Paul replied: "Knowing that for many years you have been a judge over this nation, I cheerfully make my defense."

As a human being, I don't like to wait, but instead I want to fix things immediately. We want to fix our problems, our relationships, our conflicts, our career, and our church. Fixing and controlling situations and people is like trying to expedite the rising of the sun. From time to time I have to be reminded that I am not God, and therefore I am not in control. But I can trust the one who is in control. This is why Paul could have an attitude of cheerfulness.

A Walk of Integrity

Another thing Paul is guilty of—a walk of integrity. Paul is cheerful in making his defense because he is walking with a blameless life and a clean conscience.

> **Acts 24:11-13** | "You can verify that it is not more than twelve days since I went up to worship in Jerusalem, ¹² and they did not find me disputing with anyone or stirring up a crowd, either in the temple or in the synagogues or in the city. ¹³ Neither can they prove to you what they now bring up against me."

Paul is able to retrace his steps in the last twelve days since he'd come to Jerusalem. He could account for everything he had done, and his story hadn't changed, because Paul was a man of integrity. He wasn't guilty of defiling the temple or stirring up any crowds. They had no proof because Paul was there. He could walk in his own integrity.

In our nation—and in the church—there has been a falling away, a breakdown, and a compromise in integrity. It starts in the home with you and with me. We have to be the same people in private as we are in public. All too often we find a moral laxity in our private lives, and it ought not to be. You don't have to be afraid of anything if you have your integrity.

> *Proverbs 10:9* | He who walks with integrity walks securely, but he who perverts his ways will become known.

When you walk in your integrity you have nothing to hide. When your conscience is not clean, you are alarmed and worried you will get caught. You always have to be changing your story. Someone said, "The test of your character is what it takes to stop you." Nothing could stop Paul, not even threats of torture or prison. He was a man who walked in his intregrity.

Integrity means the absence of duplicity and is the opposite of putting on a mask. If you are a person of integrity, your life is consistent. You cannot have integrity without inviting a lot of accountability. This means other people know your heart and the details of your life. Integrity demands financial accountability, personal reliability, and private purity.

Integrity does not mean perfection, but it does mean confession. Are you regularly confessing your sins to God and others? You cannot be a lone ranger Christian and have integrity. That would be impossible.

Can you walk in your integrity, or do you have to hide parts of your life? There's no freedom like being blameless. Do you have a clean conscience? If not, confess your sins, and the Lord is faithful and just to forgive you. Drag your sins out into the sunlight and learn to hate them instead of hide them. Paul had learned that lesson well, and he could walk in integrity.

Integrity demands great courage. It means you have to admit that you are not perfect, that you need to grow. It means you have to be brave in confessing your sins to godly saints in the church. The words of Louis Adamic seem fitting.

> There is a certain blend of courage, integrity, character and principle which has no satisfactory dictionary name but has been called different things at different times in different countries. Our American name for it is "guts."[540]

You want to shock the world? Start here. Demonstrate the guts to do what's right when no one is looking. It takes real guts to stand strong with integrity in a culture weakened Integrity is essential in the church, in the marketplace, and especially in the home. When you walk in integrity, you leave it as a legacy for your children to follow.

Proverbs 20:7 | The godly walk with integrity; blessed are their children who follow them.

It's what you might call the parent's thumbprint. Blessed are you if you had a mother or father with integrity and a mother with guts to live out your Christian life. Praise God even if you don't have parents that

---

[540] Louis Adamic, *A Study in Courage*, as quoted by John Bartlett in Familiar Quotations, 13th ed. (Boston: Little, Brown & Co., 1956), 981.

point the way to Christ, in the church you have dozens of godly fathers and mothers.

Paul had his integrity, and it helped him not to be afraid when he was falsely accused. Nothing alarmed his conscience. He could simply walk in his integrity.

A Life of Faith

Paul is guilty of having a life of faith that is in harmony with the law and the prophets. They charged him of being sectarian, but he was a man of faith. He affirms that faith in Jesus Christ is in full accordance with the Old Testament Scriptures and that he had the same hope of resurrection as his accusers.

> **Acts 24:14-16** | "But this I confess to you, that according to the Way, which they call a sect, I worship the God of our fathers, believing everything laid down by the Law and written in the Prophets, [15] having a hope in God, which these men themselves accept, that there will be a resurrection of both the just and the unjust. [16] So I always take pains to have a clear conscience toward both God and man."

Although the Jewish leaders denounced Christianity as a dangerous sect, Paul emphatically declared, "I do serve the God of our fathers" which was the historic title for expressing the true faith (Gen 48:15; Exo 3:15; Deut. 26:7; 1 Chr 12:17; 29:18; 2 Chr 20:6; Ezra 7:27; Dan 2:23; Acts 3:13; 5:30). To be a Christian, Paul insisted, was not to worship the true God, the God of Abraham, Isaac, and Jacob.[541] This was Paul's consistent testimony in the New Testament. Consider what he says about the Christian faith. It is true fulfilled Judaism, the fulfillment of the Old Testament worship.

> *Romans 2:29* | But a Jew is one inwardly, and circumcision is a matter of the heart, by the Spirit, not by the letter.

> *Galatians 3:29* | If you are Christ's, then you are Abraham's offspring, heirs according to promise.

> *Philippians 3:3* | We are the circumcision, who worship by the Spirit of God and glory in Christ Jesus and put no confidence in the flesh.

---

[541] MacArthur, *Acts*, vol. 2, 307.

Galatians 3:8 | The Scripture, foreseeing that God would justify the Gentiles by faith, preached the gospel beforehand to Abraham, saying, "In you shall all the nations be blessed."

Paul's testimony in all the churches is that Christianity is indeed the faith of Abraham. What a life of faith Paul had. He promoted the faith of our father Abraham!

A Heart of Generosity

What was Paul guilty of? A heart of generosity. He had come to his home to bring alms—a love offering for the churches of Jerusalem and to present offerings at the temple, the sponsoring of the four men with the Nazarite vow, which he did.

> **Acts 24:17-21** | "Now after several years I came to bring alms to my nation and to present offerings. [18] While I was doing this, they found me purified in the temple, without any crowd or tumult. But some Jews from Asia— [19] they ought to be here before you and to make an accusation, should they have anything against me. [20] Or else let these men themselves say what wrongdoing they found when I stood before the council, [21] other than this one thing that I cried out while standing among them: 'It is with respect to the resurrection of the dead that I am on trial before you this day.'"

From Paul's own account of his activities in his letters (1 Cor 16:1–4; 2 Cor 8–9; Rom 15:25–33) we know that on this visit to Jerusalem Paul had brought with him a substantial sum of money collected from his churches "for the poor among the saints at Jerusalem" (Rom. 15:26). It was a gift from the Gentile Christians to their Jewish brothers, a material gift as a sign of gratitude for the spiritual blessing of the gospel which ultimately stemmed from the church at Jerusalem. [542]

Paul had not defiled the temple but was fully purified. He also did not start any tumult. He had done nothing worthy of death but was guilty of generosity and love for his own people, having risked his life for the offering and alms for the churches. He was generous.

Paul also was "guilty" of pleading his case for the resurrection and final before the Sanhedrin, which many of the Pharisees already believed. Here Paul placed himself, in contrast to the skeptical Sadducees,

---

[542] Marshall, *Acts*, 398–399.

firmly within mainstream Jewish theology.[543] He wanted them to believe in the resurrection of Christ as well. He wanted them to all partake in Christ's free gift of salvation.

OPPORTUNITIES WHILE WAITING ON GOD (24:22-26)

Waiting is hard. Have you ever gotten behind someone on the highway that was going way below the speed limit? I heard of one lady who was going 22 mph in a 45. The officer pulled this lady over. Approaching the car, he notices that there are five older ladies, two in the front seat and three in the back, wide eyed and pale as ghosts. She insisted she was doing exactly the speed limit, 22 miles an hour. The officer, trying to contain a chuckle, explains to her that "22" was the route number, not the speed limit. A bit embarrassed, the woman grinned and thanked the officer for pointing out her error.

"But before I let you go, Ma'am," the officer said, "I have to ask, is everyone in this car okay? These women seem awfully shaken and they haven't muttered a single peep this whole time."

The lady replied, "Oh, they'll be all right in a minute officer. We just got off Route 119."

Yes, waiting can be hard, but listen, when we are waiting on God, he gives us so many opportunities to grow and expand his kingdom. A lot of times when we are waiting on the next thing, we miss the most important thing that God wants to accomplish.

An Opportunity to Enjoy God

Paul's heart was settled that whatever the verdict of his case, he was innocent of the charges.

> **Acts 24:22** | But Felix, having a rather accurate knowledge of the Way, put them off, saying, "When Lysias the tribune comes down, I will decide your case."

Felix says, "Paul, you'll have to wait until another day!" But waiting for the Christian means walking another day with God. To us waiting is wasting. But to God waiting is him working!

Felix did indeed understand some of the facts of Christianity, then called "the Way" since Jesus said he is "the way" to the Father (Jn 14:6). His knowledge likely came from his young wife Drusilla who was

---

[543] MacArthur, *Acts*, vol. 2, 307.

granddaughter of King Agrippa II. She was even at a young age a great sinner but seems to have been drawn with curiosity to learn about Jesus. More on that in a bit.

Paul didn't have his hope in any man, and that included Felix. He didn't have to trust Felix or even the Roman Commander Lysias who had been so kind and loyal to him. No, the great apostle Paul trusted God in God alone. He was waiting on what God wanted him to do. Felix was a unpredictable and fickle human governor. Paul wasn't concerned with the opinions of men and monarchs, but of the one true Monarch of heaven. Paul was not waiting on what Felix or even Lysias, Roman general who had been so loyal to Paul. Human opinions can be manipulated and change. But God never changes. So Paul waited for the Lord's commands and verdicts.

Paul trusted and enjoyed God while he waited because he knew God was working. Circumstances are constantly changing, but we need to be founded on the one who is immoveable. G. Campbell Morgan was a London preacher of a hundred years ago. His words are helpful.

> The concept of "waiting" in Hebrew means "to entrench." God works for him who entrenches himself in him. The idea of waiting on God is that of digging ourselves in to God. When circumstances are chaotic, when it is impossible to understand outcomes, that is the hour we are to wait on God. God is certain, everything else crumbles.... Waiting on God is not laziness. Waiting on God is the ability to do nothing until the command is given.[544]

Are you ready "to do nothing until the command is given"? Morgan went on to say that waiting on God has the idea of "entrenching ourselves into God" and not moving until he moves. Are you willing to entrench yourself into God, and not move until he moves? Waiting on God then is a full surrender to him, no matter what the circumstances. The Psalmist said it this way:

Psalm 46:10 | Be still and know that I am God.

That's the best statement of waiting on God that can be given. That's what Paul was committed to. Your situation may seem out of control. Don't do anything rash. Be under God's control. Be still and

---

[544] G. Campbell Morgan, *The Westminster Pulpit: The Preaching of G. Campbell Morgan, Volume 9*, "Waiting for God" (Eugene, OR: Wipf & Stock Publishers, 2012), 320.

know that he is God; he is good; he is gentle; he'll make all of this beautiful in his time. It's ok. Trust him! Surrender fully to him. Andrew Murray goes even further in his description of a life that is waiting on God.

> Waiting becomes then the only way to the experience of a full salvation, the only way, truly, to know God as the God of our salvation. All the difficulties that are brought forward as keeping us back from full salvation, have their cause in this one thing: the defective knowledge and practice of waiting upon God and surrendering to him entirely.[545]

We can enjoy God in the waiting, because in our waiting God is working great and mighty things!

An Opportunity to Edify Saints

We don't start out wanting to wait. Our natural response to waiting is often anger or doubt. Fortunately, God is gracious and merciful, understanding of our tendencies. But we can't let those feelings of uncertainty carry us. We will miss what God wants us to do in the waiting. What did Paul do while he was waiting? He edified the saints! Governor Felix gave Paul a little freedom, and he used it to edify his brothers in Christ.

> **Acts 24:23** | Then he gave orders to the centurion that he should be kept in custody but have some liberty, and that none of his friends should be prevented from attending to his needs.

Paul's friends would come in and bring him a meal and probably a scroll of one of the Old Testament prophets or the law of Moses, and they would look for Christ in all of Scripture.

Sometimes in your hardest times, you are the most fruitful. It doesn't seem like it, but it's true. When we are hurting, we are often more prone to call out to God. It is then when God has humbled us that we are most useful.

> *2 Corinthians 1:3-5* | Blessed be the God and Father of our Lord Jesus Christ, the Father of mercies and God of all comfort, ⁴ who comforts us in all our affliction, so that we may be able to comfort those who are in any affliction, with the comfort with which we ourselves are

---

[545] Andrew Murray, *Waiting on God* (New York: Fleming H. Revell Company, 1894), 18.

comforted by God. ⁵ For as we share abundantly in Christ's sufferings, so through Christ we share abundantly in comfort too.

Don't waste your pain and sorrow. Find comfort in the Scriptures and edify the saints. This was Paul's practice.

An Opportunity to Evangelize Sinners

I can just imagine Paul having Bible study after Bible study with the saints, and there was always a Roman soldier shackled to Paul's arm. So the Roman guard, one by one, was able to hear the way of Christ. But Paul was also called upon by the governor himself to converse about Jesus.

His Audience

Felix arrives at the prison with his wife Drusilla. Felix was the governor of Palestine and his wife, a daughter of Herod Agrippa I, had a very bad reputation as a great sinner. Drusilla, being Jewish, it seems is curious about Paul's message of grace and faith, and so they hear the great apostle give a clear gospel presentation.

> **Acts 24:24** | After some days Felix came with his wife Drusilla, who was Jewish, and he sent for Paul and heard him speak about faith in Christ Jesus.

There is a note in one of the early texts (the Harclean Syriac and a Bohairic manuscript) that Drusilla was the one who instigated the meeting and who likely was the one who gave Felix "a rather accurate knowledge of the Way" (24:22). The Western text, adds to verse 24 that Drusilla "asked to see Paul and hear him speak" and that Felix consequently summoned Paul "wishing to satisfy her."[546] At any rate, it seems that Drusilla was we might call a "seeker."

Paul spoke to them about "faith in Christ." Regardless of their status, there is no difference with God. Great and small, rich and poor will appear before him. The only way to know God is stop trusting in this world for success and comfort, and repent and trust in God through Jesus Christ. Only by believing in him can we receive his gift of eternal life.

---

[546] Polhill, *Acts*, 489.

His Message

Paul did not hold back from preaching a message of repentant faith. Paul was a holiness preacher. Grace never means that we deviate from God's holiness. God doesn't lower the standard, and neither did Paul.

> **Acts 24:25** | And as he reasoned about righteousness and self-control and the coming judgment, Felix was alarmed and said, "Go away for the present. When I get an opportunity I will summon you."

This is shorthand for the entire gospel. "Righteousness" is the same word as "justification," or what it means to be saved, which undoubtedly includes the death and resurrection of Jesus. Christ took our robe of sin and gave us his robe of righteousness.

"Self-control" refers to holiness in the Christian life. We are called to repent and live a life controlled by the Spirit.

"The coming judgment" is referring to the second coming, when Jesus will judge the living and the dead. Here Paul warns Felix of judgment for those who refuse, but also with hope for those who believe.[547]

Governor Felix was alarmed by Paul's gospel. Paul had preached a Christ-centered, pertinent message to Governor Felix. The conviction of the Holy Spirit was so strong that Felix trembled with alarm. We might say he was right at the door of salvation. He was right in front of the narrow gate, but he decided to wait until another day to go through.

He said, "Now, Paul, go your way for a time. When I have a convenient season, then I'm going to call for you." That is, "Paul, I know you're right. I'm under conviction. I do need this Christ that you speak about. But I'm not going to do it now. I'm going to wait for a better time." And so the devil trapped him. And so today, as far as we know, Governor is in hell.

How dangerous it is to put off the conviction of the Holy Spirit. As those who believe in the sovereign election of God, we can sometimes be tempted to brush moments like this aside, but Jesus didn't do such a horrible thing. We do believe in the sovereignty of God in salvation, but that does not dismiss God's love for sinners. When he saw that the people of Jerusalem were to reject his salvation, he wept over it.

> *Luke 19:41* | When he drew near and saw the city, he wept over it.

---

[547] Hamilton, *John–Acts*, 552.

Are you one who takes the state of sinners around you lightly? Can you look on the state of your loved ones, your neighbors and you nation, and simply move on? Paul couldn't. Jesus didn't. We must take every opportunity to bring the Holy Spirit's conviction on sinners.

Romans 10:14 | How are they to hear without someone preaching?

We must press not only tell sinners about God's love, but we must call them to repentance, as Jesus did. They cannot understand the weight of Jesus' sacrifice until they know the eternal weight of their own sin, that is dragging them down to the depths of hell for all eternity. Let us be sure to preach a true gospel message, one of justification, holiness, and the judgment to come!

His Pattern

Acts 24:26 | At the same time he hoped that money would be given him by Paul. So he sent for him often and conversed with him.

Despite the governor's wrong motives and lust for money, Paul was able to freely preach and "speak about faith in Christ Jesus" (24:23). As Jesus promised, Paul would give the gospel to kings and governors and high officials.

Jesus loves all the world. He loves the small and the great. He doesn't just love your little son or daughter; he also loves the presidents and the kings and the soldiers and the generals. He loves the lost religious people and the lost prostitutes and lost thugs. He loves the meth addict and the homosexual. He loves the one committing adultery on his wife and offers him salvation. He loves the schoolboy who is a straight A student but still needs Jesus. Jesus loves all mankind, and all mankind is corrupt. All mankind needs Jesus. Anyone who comes to Jesus will never be turned away. Even the most vile may come, and Jesus will save them. Paul was willing to preach the gospel to every creature, even if that meant he started a jailhouse ministry where there was no exit.

THE LEGACY OF WAITING ON GOD (24:27)

Friends, we find that Paul is to wait there on God under incarceration for two years there in Caesarea.

A Time to Wait on God

Not only do I not like waiting, but I want to speed up his process. I understand that the father of the modern missionary movement, William Carey, waited seven years before his first convert in India, as did Adoniram Judson in Burma. As a pastor, I want to speed up the growth process of my church and its ministries. We all want to speed up what God is doing. For Paul, it seemed like the Lord was slowing things down. He waited two years, rotting away in chains there in Caesarea until Felix was replaced by a new governor named Porcius Festus.

> **Acts 24:27a** | When two years had elapsed, Felix was succeeded by Porcius Festus.

There is something beautiful about waiting on God when we are completely helpless. When God moves in those circumstances, he gets all the glory. We may not know during this lifetime all the fruit that Paul was given while waiting on God these two years. Surely only heaven will provide that record.

The key to waiting on God is to trust that God is doing what he promises he will do. He's predestined you to be conformed to the image of Christ. When you are waiting, you need to yield and surrender to Christ, trusting God's timing and God's heart. Don't worry so much about temporal things. It's all about eternity.

A Purpose for Waiting on God

Felix had a purpose for Paul's waiting. He wanted to gain favor with the Jews. So he left him there to rot in chains for two years.

> **Acts 24:27b** | And desiring to do the Jews a favor, Felix left Paul in prison.

Felix had a self-centered purpose for leaving Paul incarcerated, but God had an entirely different purpose. God's purpose for every second of your life is to conform you to Christ (Rom 8:29), and it was no different with God's purpose for Paul. In Ecclesiastes 3, Solomon reminds us that there is a time for everything under heaven. God has specific purposes for all things that happen in his children's lives. There are eternal purposes in our waiting times.

> *Ecclesiastes 3:11* | He has made everything beautiful in its time. Also, he has put eternity into man's heart.

Moses waited and worked for forty years as a shepherd before God called him to go and rescue his people from Egypt. Joseph was sold into slavery and falsely accused, sitting in a prison cell before God made him the Prince of Egypt. It was nearly 15 years between the time little David was anointed and when he became the king of Israel. The point is, God has a purpose for you waiting. Like that bamboo plant, God is preparing your root system so that when he uses you, you are humble and ready.

Conclusion

Those who study birds say these glorious, winged creatures have three methods of flight. Flapping is keeping their wings in constant motion, like a hummingbird, to counteract gravity. Flapping keeps them in the air, but it is a lot of work.

Second is gliding. Here the bird builds up enough speed, then coasts downward a while. It is much more graceful than flapping, but unfortunately it does not get the bird very far. Gravity sets in quickly. Gliding is nice, but it does not last.

The third way is soaring. Only a few birds, such as eagles, are capable of soaring. Eagles' wings are so strong that they are capable of catching rising currents of warm air — thermal winds that go straight up from the earth - and without moving a feather can soar up to great heights. Eagles have been clocked at up to 80 m.p.h. without flapping at all. They just soar on invisible columns of air.[548]

As believers, we don't want to be flapping, trying to change our circumstances while we wait. We surely don't want to be gliding, hoping bad things will just go away. We want to be soaring, and that's what the Lord promises us as Christians.

> *Isaiah 40:31* | They who wait for the Lord shall renew their strength; they shall mount up with wings like eagles; they shall run and not be weary; they shall walk and not faint.

Dear saints, we have nothing to be afraid of. It's ok to wait. Let us soar to the highest heights as we wait on the Lord. When we are waiting on him is often when the Lord does his best work!

---

[548] Michael L. Morrison, Amanda D. Rodewald, and Gary Voelker, *Ornithology: Foundation, Analysis, and Application* (Baltimore: Johns Hopkins University Press, 2018), 283.

42 | ACTS 25:1-12
FROM BITTERNESS TO BLESSING (FESTUS)

If then I am a wrongdoer and have committed anything for which I deserve to die, I do not seek to escape death. But if there is nothing to their charges against me, no one can give me up to them. I appeal to Caesar.
ACTS 25:11

Someone once wisely said, "Bitterness is like drinking poison hoping the other person will die." What exactly is bitterness, and why is it so dangerous? It seems so innocuous, but it's deadly.

Bitterness is anger under wraps. It's testy, irritable, rude, and critical. It's a disagreeable attitude swimming in biting, snarky comments, an attitude dripping self-righteousness and self-pity. It grows like black mold in the heart.[549]

Someone else described it this way:

Bitterness is the result of not forgiving others. If you are bitter at someone, it means that you haven't truly forgiven that person. To put

---

[549] Lucy Ann Moll, "Bitterness: Turn It into Better-ness!," Biblical Counseling Center, May 24, 2017, https://biblicalcounselingcenter.org/how-to-kill-bitterness/.

it another way, bitterness is the result of responding improperly (unbiblically) to an offense. [550]

If bitterness in your heart saint, you've got to get rid of it, or it will kill your walk with God. Bitterness and unforgiveness can hurt your Christian walk almost more than any other weapon Satan has in his arsenal. It's so deadly, bitterness can derail your faith. Most of those who have forsaken their faith, forsaken their family and who have lost their happiness altogether can trace it to the hardness of heart that comes from an offense that eats at them. I've found for those who fall away from the faith, bitterness in some form was their pathway. Bitterness is the fastest way to atheism. You can't follow a God who you don't believe is just and fair. And let me tell you, he is. Yet there are many tragedies on earth we are tempted to be bitter about.

On the early morning hours of October 4, 1980, a young nursing student was brutally murdered in the Chicago suburb of Oak Park. Following the advice of well-meaning friends, Steve Linscott, a student at Emmaus Bible College, told police about a dream he'd had the night of the crime. Oak Park police later arrested him, interpreting his dream account as the roundabout confession of a psychopathic killer. Later a jury found Linscott guilty, and he was sentenced to forty years in prison. There was just one problem—Linscott was innocent! Only after time in prison and numerous legal appeals—a process that lasted twelve years—was Linscott free and vindicated!

Those years undoubtedly brought the most difficult challenges Linscott will ever face—separated from his wife and children for three and a half years except for brief visits, wondering if he had somehow brought all this on himself and why God had allowed it to happen, surviving prison violence. Those were tough years, and yet years of growth and a growing awareness of the goodness of God.[551] In Linscott's words:

> I have come to realize that we cannot judge God's purposes, nor where he places us, nor why he chooses one path for our lives as opposed to another. The Bible itself is replete with accounts of divine action (or inaction) that does not seem fair, that does not make sense except when viewed in light of God's perfect plan. Thousands of Egyptian children were massacred while a baby named Moses was

---

[550] Lou Priolo, *Bitterness: The Root That Pollutes* (Phillipsburg, NJ: P&R Publishing, 2008), 2-3.

[551] Hughes, *Acts: The Church Afire*, 315–318.

spared. Jacob was a liar and a thief, and yet it was he, not the favored son Esau, who received the blessing of their father Isaac and of God. On one level it makes no sense that God would allow his Son to die for the sins of humankind. But God has a plan—a perfect plan.[552]

It is an awful thing to be falsely accused. It is even more horrific to be falsely incarcerated. Many in our prison systems can relate with Paul. Slander and betrayal hurts. Yet Paul is not bitter.

When bitterness sinks in, it can be seen in your attitude, your negative spirit, sharp words, and irritability. Bitterness robs a Christian of their joy and peace and love. It leads them to a place of forsaking their faith. Paul tells us what to do with bitterness.

> *Hebrews 12:15* | See to it that no one fails to obtain the grace of God; that no 'root of bitterness' springs up and causes trouble, and by it many become defiled.

"What you don't forgive, you pass on and spread to others," a counselor wisely pointed out to a woman whose husband lived a double life for twenty-five years. Only when her husband was dying of AIDS did she realize that the man she had tried so hard to trust had deceived her and potentially could have passed the disease on to her. Now, a few years after his death, she was faced with a decision: Should she keep her anger and desire for vengeance alive, or would she give it up for her own benefit and in obedience to the Lord she had come to love?[553] Her conclusion was that bitterness must be rigorously avoided.

Bitterness and offense can overcome a soul and make them build up high walls of resistance. Solomon says as much.

> *Proverbs 18:19* | An offended brother is more unyielding than a fortified city, and disputes are like the barred gates of a citadel.

Solomon says you can more easily conquer a castle than reconcile an offended brother or friend. Just as you can't remove the barred gates of a castle, you sometimes cannot peaceably enter the life of a wounded brother or sister. Scaling a stone wall is one thing; winning over a stony heart is another.[554]

---

[552] Steven Linscott with Randall L. Frame, *Maximum Security* (Wheaton, IL: Crossway Books, 1994), 189.

[553] Erwin W. Lutzer, *When You've Been Wronged: Moving from Bitterness to Forgiveness* (Chicago, IL: Moody Publishers, 2007).

[554] Lutzer, ibid.

Paul had been falsely accused and could have allowed himself to be bitter, but instead he was able to live in the freedom of forgiveness. He was fruitful and not barren. Are you living a life of freedom, or are you paralyzed by bitterness?

> Key Thought: We need to put away bitterness and live in the love and freedom of forgiveness if we are going to have a fruitful Christian life.

Felix, Governor of Judea, was now gone. There had been an uprising in Caesarea and Nero recalled him from the position that Pontius Pilate once held. Felix was a great procrastinator, but the new provincial governor of Judea, the great Festus, is in office a mere three days before he journeys to Jerusalem to meet with Paul's accusers. He's far more invested at the start than Felix ever was.

THE PAIN OF INJUSTICE (25:1-5)

Paul had waited for two years, while Felix had just wanted bribes. This was a great injustice to Paul. Injustice and wrong against us is very difficult to deal with. It's easy to get sidetracked with bitterness and unforgiveness. Instead, we need to realize that we are going to be harassed with injustice from time to time, and we as followers of Christ have no place to hold on to bitterness. Sinners are going to sin, and often their irresponsible decisions are going to affect you. But our sovereign God is guiding even the injustices of the world for your good and his glory. We must trust God's plan, as Joseph did. When his brothers injured him, he did not hold it against them, but he forgave them, and trusted in the God who overrules people's plans for evil against us. God doesn't stop men from sinning, but he uses it for good. We can say to those who have hurt us what Joseph said to his brothers.

> *Genesis 50:20* | You intended to harm me, but God intended it for good to accomplish what is now being done, the saving of many lives.

Wow, if you can do that, you will live a very happy life. I really don't believe that level of forgiveness is possible without the grace of Jesus Christ. So how can we get good at that? We need to realize that God's plans to do you good are much greater than anything man can plan for your harm. You are God's child, and even the harm that man plans will end up in your favor. God will use it to shape you into the image of Christ. Remember Christ was injured and killed, and he was innocent.

"By his stripes we are healed" (Isa 53:5). Listen, bitterness will slowly kill you, but forgiveness will heal you. Let's see this in the life of Paul.

A Plan to Injure

Paul had plenty of reasons to be bitter, but instead he was fruitful and joyful even though he was in chains. Let's read about the plans of his enemies to injure him. They actually have another murder plot against him. Yet Festus was not at all like Antonius Felix. Felix was known to be a cruel, but weak man, a slick character, wanting bribes from Paul. But Festus was a noble man, who hardly waited three days into his place as procurator (the same office as Pontius Pilate) to see Paul.

> **Acts 25:1-3** | Now three days after Festus had arrived in the province, he went up to Jerusalem from Caesarea. ² And the chief priests and the principal men of the Jews laid out their case against Paul, and they urged him, ³ asking as a favor against Paul that he summon him to Jerusalem—because they were planning an ambush to kill him on the way.

The Jews have no real case against Paul, and they know it, so they want to coax Festus into getting Paul to Jerusalem so they can kill him as they had planned. Festus encouraged a trial in Jerusalem, not knowing that they wanted to murder Paul.

Consider what Paul had already endured. He had been arrested in Jerusalem though he had done nothing wrong, had spoken to an angry mob, had addressed the Sanhedrin, had been transferred to Caesarea to avoid assassination, had been tried before Felix, and now was about to appear before Festus, the new governor. He had not committed any crime, and yet he was a prisoner of the Roman Empire and on the receiving end of spurious accusations of hateful Jews.

To fully appreciate this passage, we need to catch a whiff of the cell that had been the apostle's home for two years, to feel the burden of his iron manacles, to share his heart's burden for the spiritual bankruptcy of Rome. I've stood above the cell beneath the ground where Paul would have been held before his trials. It's basically a broken cistern that was turned into a jail cell. He would have been lowered there into this holding cell before his trials.

How the apostle's soul must have longed to minister the gospel freely wherever and to whomever he wished.[555] Instead he's "stuck" here in the jail, having to answer spurious questions curious monarch after curious monarch.

The Jewish leaders, likely a great deal of Sadducees from the Sanhedrin and their chief priests meet with Governor Festus and bring their charges against Paul. They had brought these accusations before. They said Paul was guilty of two capital crimes: desecrating the temple and inciting a riot, both of which were made up. But the real reason the Jews appeared before Festus in Caesarea was to bring Paul to Jerusalem to murder him.

How easy it would be for Paul to be given to worry or bitterness. Yet Paul had faced much worse before. Fear and bitterness are idol indicators. They are sure signs that your heart is not trusting in God. He could live in peace because he knew God was in control and had delivered him from death countless times. He may have even come back from the dead himself in Lystra when he was executed by stoning (*cf* 14:19-20). Paul's enemies wanted to murder him, but Paul was not moved. His trust was in God.

A Plan Interrupted

Festus sees through their plan and invites the delegation of the Sanhedrin to come to Caesarea where Paul's case can be tried without any danger to him.

> **Acts 25:4-5** | Festus replied that Paul was being kept at Caesarea and that he himself intended to go there [*to Jerusalem*] shortly. **5** "So," said he, "let the men of authority among you go down with me, and if there is anything wrong about the man, let them bring charges against him."

Paul would be tried in Caesarea. Remember he had been transported there from Jerusalem two years earlier with the help of 470 soldiers, since 40 assassins had covenanted to kill Paul. The Sanhedrin would have to bring their charges to Paul.

What was Paul's crime? Preaching the one true God and his Son Jesus Christ. How dare he! Why, Paul must have been as villainous as William Tyndale, who actually dared to translate the Bible into English,

---

[555] Hughes, *Acts: The Church Afire*, 318.

or the ten Boom family, who dared to hide Jews rather than let the Nazis take them away to concentration camps! When men forbid what God requires, we must side with the apostles who said,

> Acts 5:29 | We must obey God rather than men.

Imagine the pain Paul could have suffered. He had dodged one murder plot, and now his enemies were planning another. For Paul, there was no need for bitterness or drama. His trust was in the Lord. When trust and hope is in the Lord, peace replaces pain. We know God has a good plan that will overrule the worst our enemies can do. Let us keep our eyes on the prize of knowing Christ. Those who hurt us or falsely accuse us need the love of Christ.

Don't give into the pain of injustice. Don't go down the path of bitterness. If you do give in, bitterness will eat you away. Instead, find God's peace through forgiveness and trusting God's plan. Lou Priolo in *Keeping Your Cool* that if you don't deal with bitterness, it will paralyze you.

> If you do not respond biblically to the hurt (this would involve forgiving the sin, overlooking the sin, or realizing the 'offense' was not wrong in God's eyes) — you may begin to rehearse the offense in your mind, reviewing it over and over again. The practice of continually reviewing and imputing (charging your offender with the fault or the responsibility for) the offense violates 1 Corinthians 13:5 ("love does not keep a running account of evil"). It also cultivates the seed of hurt that matures into a "root of bitterness." [556]

Bitterness has no place in the Christian's life. Bitterness is really the chief characteristic of a fool. The fool says in his own heart "there is no God," and that's how a fool lives, as a practical atheist (14:1). A fool may say with his mouth, "I love Jesus" but in his heart, he lives as if God doesn't exist. Consider how a fool is described in Proverbs, and you'll see that the fool of Proverbs is a proud, bitter, self-righteous person.

- He despises wisdom and instruction (1:7)
- He hates knowledge—doesn't listen (1:22)
- He hurts his mother (7:25)
- He grieves his father (17:25)

---

[556] Lou Priolo, *Keeping Your Cool* (Phillipsburg, NJ: P&R Publishing, 2014), 14.

- He rejects his father's instruction (15:5)
- He grieves his mother (10:1)
- He despises his mother (15:20)
- He is right in his own eyes (12:15)
- He is quick to anger (12:16)
- He is deceitful (14:8)
- He is arrogant and careless (14:16)
- He does not respond well to discipline (17:10)
- He does not understand wisdom (17:16)
- He has a worldly focus (17:24)
- He does not consider discussing any other viewpoint but his own (18:2)
- He provokes others to anger by the things he says (18:6)
- He has a smart mouth that usually gets him into trouble (18:7)
- He is quarrelsome (20:3)
- He is a spendthrift (21:20)
- He repeats his folly and won't change (26:11)
- He trusts in his own heart (28:26)
- He cannot resolve conflicts (29:9)
- He gives full vent to his anger (29:11)

The fool is controlled by the pain of injustice. He blames injustice on God, not realizing that Jesus is coming again to judge the world and make all things right. There is coming a day when...

> 2 Thessalonians 1:7-9 | The Lord Jesus is revealed from heaven with his mighty angels [8] in flaming fire, inflicting vengeance on those who do not know God and on those who do not obey the gospel of our Lord Jesus. [9] They will suffer the punishment of eternal destruction, away from the presence of the Lord and from the glory of his might.

You should rest in the justice of the Lord. A bitter person is not awaiting the justice of the second coming, but furious that things haven't gone his or her way, or that justice hasn't come sooner. They are bitter because they don't want justice on God's terms and in God's perfect timing, but they've taken the place of God, and want a kind of self-centered human vengeance (*cf* Heb 12:19).

A PLAN FOR INJUSTICE (25:6-10)

Often people who injure or slander us do not have a lot of information. Their intent is not to gain justice, but to hurt and discourage us. What are you as a Christian supposed to do when you are slandered or maligned?

Trust Not in Man

This was a kangaroo court. How hard it is that Paul has to endure slanders against him when he is blameless. He refused to put his trust in any man but trusted the sovereign hand of God in all things. The words of Jeremiah must have often rang in his heart.

> *Jeremiah 17:6-8* | Cursed is the man who trusts in man and makes flesh his strength, whose heart turns away from the Lord. He is like a shrub in the desert, and shall not see any good come.... ⁷Blessed is the man who trusts in the Lord, whose trust is the Lord. ⁸He is like a tree planted by water.

Consider Your Enemies

Paul's enemies are in God's hands. The same goes for us. No one can harm you without God's permission. If you have been harmed in a violent way, call the police. If you've been hurt or abused, you should get the authorities involved. Godly leaders will always help the victim of abuse. Paul had nothing to fear, even though he may have felt helpless. God is greater than some of the chief priests who brought slanderous accusations against Paul before the new procurator, Festus.

> **Acts 25:6-7** | After he [Festus] stayed among them not more than eight or ten days, he went down to Caesarea. And the next day he took his seat on the tribunal and ordered Paul to be brought. ⁷When he had arrived, the Jews who had come down from Jerusalem stood around him, bringing many and serious charges against him that they could not prove.

Paul's enemies had no power and were there by God's permission. They couldn't hurt Paul, even though they wanted to kill him.

Immediately after Festus had returned to Caesarea he held his court and the case of Paul was taken up. Luke does not go into details about the charges brought against Paul. They were doubtless similar to those already made by Tertullus, but it is probable that the Jews did their best to increase and strengthen them. Yet Luke comments that they could not prove them. Since the case was now two years old, it would have been difficult in any case to secure eyewitnesses to specific accusations.557

Dear saints, often when wrong is done to us God is in control. It might be an unbeliever that slanders us. It could be an immature Christian. It can also be a fully mature Christian who has lost sight of the Lord. Remember Peter himself, who had spent three years with our Lord, betrayed him and denied him three times at his hour of need. Never trust in man. Trust in the Lord!

Our ultimate enemy is a defeated foe. The Bible says that God "disarmed the rulers and authorities" of hell and darkness "and put them to open shame, by triumphing over them" in Christ (Col 2:15). Consider that the plan of the enemy is already defeated. There is no condemnation for anyone who is in Christ Jesus (Rom 8:1).

Consider Yourself

When injustice comes, you need to consider yourself. You are a sinner. You have lied and perhaps slandered others. Paul was not too proud to admit that he was once a persecutor of Christians, so he should not be too hurt or too proud as he hears these slanders. This is what he himself did before the Lord saved him. Before you judge others, consider yourself. Paul said:

> 1 Timothy 1:15 | The saying is trustworthy and deserving of full acceptance, that Christ Jesus came into the world to save sinners, of whom I am the foremost.

Paul says, "I am the chief of sinners." You have hurt others. Show mercy to your slanderers. Be good and kind to them. That doesn't mean you don't hold them accountable, but there is no need for hatred, demonization, and bitterness. Each person is made in the image of God, and our Lord taught us to treat even our enemies with utmost kindness (Lk 6:27-36). God showed kindness to you when you hated him. Can you love your enemies as God has loved you?

Consider Christ's Example

It was a kangaroo court that crucified our Lord. He entrusted himself completely to the Father (1 Pet 2:23). He cried out to all:

---

557 Marshall, *Acts*, 403–404.

Luke 23:34 | Father, forgive them for they know not what they do.

If Jesus was treated unjustly by all around him, so will you. Even his own disciples forsook him. Yet God is in perfect control, and you can forgive like Jesus.

Follow Christ's Example

Paul's mission and yours is the same as it's always been. It's not personal comfort or earthly security. It's not to guard our reputation or live our best life now. Your mission is to preach the gospel and bring people to Christ from every nation (Mt 28:18-20). Your mission is not to build your kingdom, but Christ's. Don't get sidetracked. Get on that cross. You can only follow Christ from the view of the cross. Remember his words.

Matthew 16:24 | If anyone would come after me, let him deny himself and take up his cross and follow me.

Be willing to be maligned. In fact, rejoice when you are maligned and slandered. This is the way Christ was treated as well as all the faithful prophets.

Walk in Your Integrity

Paul was not brought down by false charges and slander, but he walked with a pure heart in the presence of God. With David, he could say:

Psalm 26:11-12 | As for me, I shall walk in my integrity; redeem me, and be gracious to me. [12] My foot stands on level ground; in the great assembly I will bless the Lord.

Tell the Truth

In times of injustice, you never have to hide anything if you walk in your integrity. That's what Paul did. He always told the truth. He had nothing to hide.

Acts 25:8 | Paul argued in his defense, "Neither against the law of the Jews, nor against the temple, nor against Caesar have I committed any offense."

I love how brief Paul is. He's been asked about this over and over. No trustworthy evidence has been produced. He's done nothing at the temple to desecrate the faith that he loves, and now since he's appealed to Caesar, he makes it clear, he's done nothing against the Emperor Nero. All he can do is tell the truth and leave the results up to the Lord.

Trust in the Lord

We can see from Paul's attitude that he's not moved by the Jews accusations. Festus then plays in the Jews hands and tries to get Paul to go to Jerusalem, but Paul stands his ground and trusts in the Lord.

> **Acts 25:9-10** | But Festus, wishing to do the Jews a favor, said to Paul, "Do you wish to go up to Jerusalem and there be tried on these charges before me?" [10] But Paul said, "I am standing before Caesar's tribunal, where I ought to be tried. To the Jews I have done no wrong, as you yourself know very well."

Men will fail you, but the Lord will never fail. Paul knew that he could trust God's plan for him. God manifested himself in love through his Son. Even in your pain, God's love for you is something you can trust! I think of the words of David Livingstone, the great missionary to Africa speaks of the deep love of God toward the most wretched sinners.

> What is the atonement of Christ? It is himself: it is the inherent and everlasting mercy of God made apparent to human eyes and ears. The everlasting love was disclosed by our Lord's life and death. It showed that God forgives, because he loves to forgive. He works by smiles, if possible, if not by frowns; pain is only a means of enforcing love.[558]

Dare to trust in the most benevolent being in the universe. He's holy, but he's good. He's terrifying in his justice, but he's welcoming in his mercy. Releasing yourself to his care is the beginning of wisdom. Forgiving those who hurt you is the wisest action you can take.

THE PROVIDENCE OF INJUSTICE (25:11-12)

Remember the most sinful act in the history of the world (the crucifixion of the Son of God), was guided by the providence of God. God is also guiding your life, and you can trust his providence to bring about what he wants. This guidance over all your suffering and injustices that you experience is called the providence of God.

---

[558] David Livingstone in Horace Waller. *The Last Journals of David Livingstone, in Central Africa* (New York: Harper & Brothers Publishers, 1875), 453.

Providence is the benevolent and purposeful ordering of all events of history. Nothing happens by chance. Though not always perceptible to human understanding, there is a divine or cosmic plan to the universe, a reason for everything.[559]

There is no room for bitterness when you give yourself to the one who promises to "make all things beautiful in his time" (Ecc 3:11) and who "works all things together for good" for those who love him (Rom 8:28).

Paul understood God's providence. Many prophets had told Paul that he must testify in Rome, and the Lord himself had said the same to Paul in visions given to the apostle (cf 23:11). So Paul's eyes are on God's mission, not his own. He's not looking for freedom. He's looking to go where the Lord wants him to go, and that is Rome.

Paul appeals to Caesar, but he knows there's no real justice there. He calls the government of Rome, "the beast." There's no real justice in Rome, but there are plenty of ministry opportunities. So Paul makes his plea to go to Rome and appear before Caesar's courts in the city of Rome.

Acts 25:11-12 | "If then I am a wrongdoer and have committed anything for which I deserve to die, I do not seek to escape death. But if there is nothing to their charges against me, no one can give me up to them. I appeal to Caesar." **12** Then Festus, when he had conferred with his council, answered, "To Caesar you have appealed; to Caesar you shall go."

The truth is human government maintains a lot of injustice. Only temporary and hugely imperfect justice can be maintained on earth. There is so much corruption. Only at the second coming with the playing field be leveled. Paul did not trust human government, but he trusted God who controls human government.

Daniel 2:21 | He removes kings and sets up kings.

Romans 13:1 | Let every person be subject to the governing authorities. For there is no authority except from God.

---

[559] Paul J. Achtemeier, Harper & Row and Society of Biblical Literature, *Harper's Bible Dictionary* (San Francisco: Harper & Row, 1985), 832.

Be Free from Fear

When we trust in God's providence, we can be free from fear. Paul was clearly not afraid to die.

> **Acts 25:11a** | "If then I am a wrongdoer and have committed anything for which I deserve to die, I do not seek to escape death."

Paul was very wise. He was not reckless. But he was also not afraid of death. Even if death comes, we know that it is by the sovereign hand of God. The child of God longs to see Jesus face to face. Every tear wiped away. No more pain. No more sin. Death, who is our greatest enemy, is already defeated!

Be Full of Faith

Paul wasn't bitter for all the wrongs done to him. He's willing to allow the wrongs of man to carry him to Rome where he could preach the gospel. He's full of hope and faith.

Bitterness can only harm you. It's like a rattlesnake. If a rattlesnake is cornered, it will sometimes become so angry it will bite itself. That is exactly what the harboring of hate and resentment against others is—a biting of oneself. We think that we are harming others in holding grudges and playing the hurts over and over, but the deeper harm is to ourselves. God wants us to be rid of bitterness and filled with faith and hope!

When we trust in God's providence, we can be free from bitterness—that's what Paul did. Knowing that God has a much larger plan beyond the hurts and betrayals in our lives allows us to live in the love and peace of Jesus.

Paul is focused on something more important than his own personal injustices. He knows God's plans are much bigger than the hurts and betrayals he's enduring. He loves the souls of men and wants to preach the gospel at Rome. So makes a surprising appeal. He asks that his trial be moved to Rome under the authority of the Caesar, who is Nero at the time.

> **Acts 25:11a-12** | "But if there is nothing to their charges against me, no one can give me up to them. I appeal to Caesar." **12** Then Festus, when he had conferred with his council, answered, "To Caesar you have appealed; to Caesar you shall go."

Appealing to Caesar is Paul's ticket to Rome. No more waiting around in Caesarea. He's been there for over two years. He's ready to make his way to preach the gospel not to the citizens of Rome, but to the soldiers of Rome and to Caesar's household. By the way, Paul has an incredibly successful ministry there. He evangelizes Caesar's household and writes seven more books of our New Testament.

Did you notice Paul's defense earlier? It's extremely brief. He's not bitter. Bitter people can go on and on and on about their hurt. They are so focused on it. But Paul is not focused on bitterness. Paul is not worried about his own personal hurts, because he's given them to Christ. He doesn't carry around injuries from how people have hurt him. He's too busy praying for souls to be concerned for his own reputation or comfort.

Applications

Paul was dismissed, at least temporarily, from the jurisdiction of Festus. Though Festus would subject Paul to one more hearing before a neighboring king, Agrippa, he delivered Paul to the hands of Caesar, and Paul had to wait again for his case to be decided.[560] This didn't move Paul. His eyes were on the Lord. Consider these applications: (1) have the right focus, (2) exercise plentiful forgiveness, (3) practice unrelenting kindness, and (4) get busy and blessed serving God.

Have the right focus. Paul's focus was on the Lord, not on his enemies or himself. Paul knew his enemies weren't the Jews. They were slaves of Satan. He wanted them released from that satanic slavery. He knew that his battle wasn't against flesh and blood, but against Satanic forces from the unseen realm (Eph 6:12-13). His focus was on the Lord, since "the battle is the Lord's" Paul wanted his enemies to come to know the joy and peace in Christ. His focus was not on his small hurt on this earth, but on his persecutors' eternal salvation. He said, "my heart's desire and prayer to God for them is that they may be saved" (Rom 10:1). Paul was once a persecutor of Christians. Paul's focus was on the gospel and the glory of God. He wanted to be conformed to the image of Christ.

Exercise plentiful forgiveness. The way to get rid of bitterness, anger, and hatred is to forgive as the Lord forgives. You have to cover that slander or that injustice with the blood of Jesus. If you are in danger,

---

[560] Sproul, *Acts*, 396.

call the police. If someone is hurting you, run! Get out of there. But you should still pray for the repentance of your enemies. Pray for them to be converted, or if they are a child of God, pray for them to live a surrendered, Spirit-filled life.

Practice unrelenting kindness. Another way to get rid of bitterness is to be kind to the person who hurt you. Do good to them. Pray for them. Until there is real repentance you may not be able to reconcile. That may not happen until heaven. But you can do good to them. You can pray for them. You can hope the best for them. Be bigger than the offense. "Don't be overcome by evil but overcome evil with good" (Rom 12:21).

Get busy and blessed in serving God. Stop sulking and get busy serving the Lord. Trust God's hand in all your suffering and injustice. Get out of the casket of self-focus that is bent inward and enjoy the power of the resurrection. Start praising the Lord in all things. Start evangelizing. Invest your life in the Lord's church with discipleship and worship and service. When you are so busy and blessed, you'll forget to be bitter!

Conclusion

Let me close by telling you the tragic story of a young man named Bruce Goodrich. He was being initiated into the cadet corps at Texas A & M University. One night, Bruce was forced to run until he dropped—but he never got up. His initiation led to his death. Bruce Goodrich died before he even entered college. A short time after the tragedy, Bruce's father wrote this letter to the administration, faculty, student body, and the corps of cadets to explain the peace he had from God's plan and providence. He was not bitter at all but trusted in the sovereign God in the death of his son.

> I would like to take this opportunity to express the appreciation of my family for the great outpouring of concern and sympathy from Texas A & M University and the college community over the loss of our son Bruce. We were deeply touched by the tribute paid to him in the battalion. We were particularly pleased to note that his Christian witness did not go unnoticed during his brief time on campus.

Mr. Goodrich went on:

> I hope it will be some comfort to know that we harbor no ill will in the matter. We know our God makes no mistakes. Bruce had an appointment with his Lord and is now secure in his celestial home.

When the question is asked, "Why did this happen?" perhaps one answer will be, "So that many will consider where they will spend eternity."[561]

Every evil thing that went against our Lord ended up being used for our redemption. We are the extension of Jesus on this earth, his very body. Let us not be bitter about the injustices we face. Let us endure and use them for the expansion of his kingdom.

---

[561] Michael Youssef, *God, Just Tell Me What to Do* (Eugene, OR: Harvest House Publishers, 2014), 105-106.

43 | ACTS 25:13-26:32
ALMOST PERSUADED (AGRIPPA)

Agrippa said to Paul, "In a short time would you persuade me to be a Christian?" And Paul said, "Whether short or long, I would to God that not only you but also all who hear me this day might become such as I am—except for these chains."
ACTS 25:28-29

In this passage, Paul the apostle is accused of being out of his mind for believing and teaching the gospel. It seems like such a far-fetched thing that the God of the universe would take on human flesh, live and die on behalf of broken sinners, and then rise again, bidding them to come into his kingdom and serve him. This is love and mercy, but it seemed too good to be true to King Agrippa II whom, Paul appeared before. Paul was so sincere, forthright, and believable that the great King was almost persuaded in such a short time to be a Christian.

Almost is the difference between heaven and hell. To know Christ is all or nothing. You can't serve two masters. You've got to choose Christ, and choose him now. I think of the story of D.L. Moody, who, by his own admission, made a mistake on October 8, 1871. It was a mistake he determined never to repeat. He had been preaching in the city of Chicago. That particular night drew his largest audience yet. His message was "What will you do with Jesus?" By the end of the service, he was tired. He concluded his message, and once again presented the true gospel with a concluding statement: "Now i give you a week to think that over ... and when we come together again, you will have an opportunity to respond."

A soloist began to sing. But before the final note, the music was drowned out by clanging bells and wailing sirens screaming through the streets. The great Chicago fire was blazing. In the ashen aftermath, hundreds were dead and over a hundred thousand were homeless. There was no meeting a week later. Without a doubt, some who heard Moody's message had died in the fire. He reflected remorsefully that he would have given his right arm before he would ever give an audience another week to think over the message of the gospel.

When I read that story, I thought about the Scripture that is in front of us. There are some here in this service that are at the very door of salvation. God has been drawing you, but you have not been surrendering. You've been putting it off. To be almost persuaded is to be entirely lost. There's coming a day when the harvest will be past. Death comes for all of us. No longer will you hear the gospel call because it will be too late. You will find yourself in the lake of fire, in a place where there are no exits. If Christ is calling you today young person or older person, turn to him today. Let your heart soften and feel the conviction of the Holy Spirit. Give in to the Lord's loving hand and plan for you.

> Key thought: To be almost persuaded is to be entirely lost. If you are lost, don't put off turning to Christ for another day. Turn now and receive eternal life.

A good knowledge of the gospel is not enough for eternal life. There must be a total and complete surrender to Christ. To be almost persuaded is still completely unregenerate, headed for hell, and still under the wrath and condemnation of God's holy justice. Total surrender, by grace through faith in Christ is the only way to gain the mercy of God.

THOSE NEEDING GOSPEL PERSUASION (25:13-27)

Festus didn't know it, but he had in his prison in Caesarea the greatest evangelist perhaps that had ever lived. Paul was all about giving sinners hope for eternal life in Christ. How Festus needed Christ. But he was far more focused on his legal case, and he didn't have expertise in the laws of the Jews. And as far as Roman law was concerned, he had already proclaimed that Paul had done nothing worthy of death or imprisonment. Festus needed expert help in the Jewish law if he was going to write an appeal to Nero, who was the emperor at the time. From a civil perspective, there would be none greater to help him than Herod Agrippa II, the king over Palestine.

Governor Festus was hoping King Agrippa could help him write to emperor Nero something about what the charges really were. It would look extremely odd for a prisoner to arrive under heavy guard in Rome but with no statement of the accusation against him.[562] In Festus' view, Paul was completely innocent. So in comes the great King Agrippa.

The Prince, Agrippa

> **Acts 25:13** | Now when some days had passed, Agrippa the king and Bernice arrived at Caesarea and greeted Festus.

Here is the great King Agrippa II, who had almost the same land mass as his great grandfather to rule over in Israel, the infamous King Herod the Great. Agrippa has a long life and stays on the scene in Israel until the end of the century, dying in 100 A.D. Agrippa II was king of the land of Palestine, appointed by the Romans. In the earthly realm, he is great, but in the heavenly realm, he is condemned by his own sins before a just and holy God. He needs to be persuaded of the gospel.

Agrippa was the grandson of Herod the Great. Agrippa's father, Herod Agrippa I, had arrested Peter and beheaded James, the brother of John, son of Zebedee. Agrippa II was a pretty civilized king compared to his father and grandfather. Except one thing: he was living in an incestuous relationship with his sister, Bernice, which hardly commends him as a model of virtue. Bernice was the sort of figure whose photograph, had she lived in our times, would seldom have been out of the glossy magazines. Bernice was her generation's Marilyn Monroe.

Bernice and Agrippa had another sister as well, Drusilla, who was the wife of the former governor, Felix.[563] So scandalous was Bernice's act of marrying her own full-blooded brother, that when she later became the Emperor Titus' mistress, he had to send her away because of the moral outcry of pagan Rome.[564] Though Luke mentions none of this, the fact that he just says 'and Bernice' in verse 13 may tell its own story; most of his first hearers or readers would raise at least one

---

[562] Wright, *Acts for Everyone, Part 2*, 202.
[563] MacArthur, *Acts*, vol. 2, 327.
[564] Earnest Cary, trans., *Dio's Roman History* (Cambridge, MA: Harvard University Press, 1961), 56:18.

eyebrow at the thought of this fashionable and powerful woman coming into contact with Paul.[565] King Agrippa and Queen Bernice were a sick, sin-infested couple. So this was quite the family affair. Oh, how they needed to hear the gospel, and from an apostle no less!

Because of his relation to his grandfather (Herod the Great), Herod Agrippa II was considered an expert in the Jewish religion. The Romans granted him the custody of the ceremonial vestments worn by the high priest on the Day of Atonement. He also held the authority to appoint the high priest. In this respect he could be considered "king of the Jews."[566] Despite his paganism and immoral life, he was well educated in the Jewish religion and culture, likely more as a curiosity than anything else. There was at least this in his favor: he would be able to understand Paul's situation, which is how he got involved in his trial.[567]

How King Agrippa II needed to hear the good news! When he hears it, he is "almost persuaded" to become a Christian (26:28). And how often does anyone on earth get to hear the gospel message from an actual apostle of Jesus Christ? The scene is set now for Agrippa's evangelization. Enter Paul.

The Prisoner, Paul

Festus brought Paul's case to Agrippa II toward the end of his state visit to welcome Festus the new proconsul. Agrippa expressed a wish to hear Paul in Caesarea. Paul prepared his speech with great care, for he looked on it less as a defense than an opportunity of preaching the gospel before an exalted influential audience.[568] Paul could remember his own commission from the Lord Jesus. "You are 'a chosen instrument of mine to carry my name before the Gentiles and kings,'" Paul could hear the Lord say (*cf* Acts 9:15).

> **Acts 25:14-22** | And as they stayed there many days, Festus laid Paul's case before the king, saying, "There is a man left prisoner by Felix, **15** and when I was at Jerusalem, the chief priests and the elders of the Jews laid out their case against him, asking for a sentence of condemnation against him. **16** I answered them that it was not the custom of the Romans to give up anyone before the accused

---

[565] Wright, *Acts for Everyone, Part 2*, 202.
[566] Polhill, *Acts*, 492–493. See also Bruce, *Acts:* NIC, 481f.
[567] Boice, *Acts: An Expositional Commentary*, 401–402.
[568] Pollock, *The Apostle*, 260.

met the accusers face to face and had opportunity to make his defense concerning the charge laid against him. **17** So when they came together here, I made no delay, but on the next day took my seat on the tribunal and ordered the man to be brought. **18** When the accusers stood up, they brought no charge in his case of such evils as I supposed. **19** Rather they had certain points of dispute with him about their own religion and about a certain Jesus, who was dead, but whom Paul asserted to be alive. **20** Being at a loss how to investigate these questions, I asked whether he wanted to go to Jerusalem and be tried there regarding them. **21** But when Paul had appealed to be kept in custody for the decision of the emperor, I ordered him to be held until I could send him to Caesar." **22** Then Agrippa said to Festus, "I would like to hear the man myself." "Tomorrow," said he, "you will hear him."

Festus tells Agrippa all about Paul, who here is called a "prisoner." Felix and Agrippa have all the earthly power. In the earthly realm, Paul is a poor prisoner. He was a leftover of Governor Felix. Paul had rotted in the Caesarean jail now for two years. Festus lays out the history of the case, careful to show both that he has done everything by the book.[569] The Jews had brought their case against Paul, but his only charge was "about a certain Jesus, who was dead, but whom Paul asserted to be alive" (25:19). Paul wanted to get to Rome, so he appealed to the emperor. Agrippa was curious to hear Paul, so a time was arranged for the next day. You see, Paul the poor prisoner is the mighty apostle with the good news that can give eternal life to all the kings of the earth if they will just repent.

Paul had been a glorious recipient of the good news. He's going to give his testimony of salvation to Agrippa the next day, but he had been a high-ranking Pharisee, possibly a former member of the Sanhedrin, and most importantly, before his conversion, he was the chief persecutor of Christians. He put them to death if he could, and the rest he jailed. By hating the Christians, he thought he was doing God service. As he will tell us later (26:1-23), Paul was converted to Christ through a vision from the Lord. Jesus revealed himself to Paul as the Son of God, creator of the world. And he commissioned Paul to reach the Gentiles, which is why Paul was in this jail. Paul was imprisoned so much

---

[569] Hamilton, *John–Acts*, 558.

that he was glad to take on that identity. Paul wore his Roman chains as a symbol of what God can do through the weakest of people.

Ephesians 6:20 | I am an ambassador in chains, that I may declare it boldly, as I ought to speak.

Ephesians 3:1 | Paul, a prisoner of Christ Jesus on behalf of you Gentiles.

Philippians 1:12 | What has happened to me has really served to advance the gospel.

On a human level, one would expect that Paul's imprisonment would slow or perhaps even stop the progress of the gospel.[570] After all, Paul cannot plant churches while in Roman custody. Yet God does his best work with the weakest of people. But we must remember what Paul states elsewhere.

1 Corinthians 1:25 | The foolishness of God is wiser than men, and the weakness of God is stronger than men.

The irony is that while Rome has imprisoned Paul in an effort to prevent his message from spreading, that very imprisonment has become the means by which the gospel advances. Paul may be in chains, but the gospel runs free. That is the surprising but true state of affairs.

Just as Joseph saw that what his brothers meant for evil God meant for good (Gen 50:20), so too Paul sees the sovereign hand of a good God behind the evil intentions of his Jewish accusers and Roman captors.

What about you? What are the chains in your life? Do you see them as mere limitations, or can you see with the eyes of faith how God has given you those limitations for the advancement of the gospel? It may be a health problem. You may be a bit bitter at how the pain or paralysis has limited you. Perhaps it's a difficult marriage or a crushing job situation. Maybe it is a wayward child, or it could be an unmet expectation or severe disappointment in life. These circumstances can feel like chains. I challenge you to look deeper and see the hand of God in your limitations. Through our limitations, God humbles us. We need to embrace our weakness that the power of Christ would rest upon us. Your

---

[570] Jerry L. Sumney, *Philippians: A Greek Student's Intermediate Reader* (Peabody: Hendrickson, 2007), 19.

limitations are often the very things God uses to advance the gospel. Paul was a weak, limited man, but that's exactly who God uses.

The Proconsul, Festus

Festus is the governor of Judea, like Pontius Pilate many years before. He welcomes King Agrippa and his Queen Bernice to Judea. In the eyes of the world, Festus looks regal with his sister/queen Bernice. He is esteemed in the world but condemned before God for his sins. Roles are quite reversed in the heavenly realm. Yet and still, Festus calls a fancy meeting to introduce Paul and King Agrippa.

The Fancy Meeting

Acts 25:23a | So on the next day Agrippa and Bernice came with great pomp, and they entered the audience hall with the military tribunes and the prominent men of the city.

Governor Festus is a man under the authority of King Agrippa II. Agrippa has brought Bernice, his wife and full-blooded sister. Agrippa arrives with full military honors and "great pomp." Incredible details are given by Luke, who some believe may have been granted permission to be there with Paul. King Agrippa and Queen Bernice would have been escorted to their thrones, with blare of trumpets, waving of peacock feather fans, and rigid salutes of the generals. Agrippa and Bernice would be arrayed in purple, Festus in red. Agrippa apparently has the same flair for pomp and circumstance that his father had (and died over). Dignitaries and military personnel assemble—the most powerful and influential people in that region of the empire—and Paul is ushered in (25:23).[571] Luke notes that they entered into the "audience hall" or the courtroom of Festus' palace there at Caesarea where Agrippa would act as judge and hear Paul's case.

The Frail Apostle

Acts 25:23b | At the command of Festus, Paul was brought in.

Paul was brought in before Agrippa and Festus and the whole ensemble. Here stood the apostle, small, almost stooping with his "bald head and crooked legs."[572] Yet he was alert and energetic in manner,

---

[571] Hamilton, *John–Acts*, 558.
[572] Barrier. *The Acts of Paul and* Thecla, 73.

gray-bearded now. Perhaps he was a little less thin and wiry after years in moderate comfort, safe from stoning, or beatings or long treks from city to city, yet with a frailty and a scarred face in sharp contrast to the hearty young soldier who led him, politely enough, by a chain.[573] Imagine, Paul was likely better taken care of in the prison of a palace than with all the persecutions he had been through.

The Facts from Festus

Acts 25:23-27 | And Festus said, "King Agrippa and all who are present with us, you see this man about whom the whole Jewish people petitioned me, both in Jerusalem and here, shouting that he ought not to live any longer. **25** But I found that he had done nothing deserving death. And as he himself appealed to the emperor, I decided to go ahead and send him. **26** But I have nothing definite to write to my lord about him. Therefore I have brought him before you all, and especially before you, King Agrippa, so that, after we have examined him, I may have something to write. **27** For it seems to me unreasonable, in sending a prisoner, not to indicate the charges against him."

Festus summarizes the case before King Agrippa, giving only the bare details, but leaving the full report to be given by Paul the apostle. He says that Paul is innocent of the charges, but further than that, he needs Agrippa's help so that when he gives a letter to Nero the emperor, he will have "something to write."

But what do we actually know about Governor Porcius Festus? According to the historical annals at the time, Festus was appointed in "Nero's fifth year in A.D. 59." We know this to be a fact since each time a new governor was appointed there would be "change in the provincial coinage of Judaea" with the new governor's symbol on it (a palm branch), and the year he began.[574] There are many of these coins available today. In fact, you can purchase an original Festus coin for as little as $60 online. Josephus wrote that Festus ruled wisely and justly, in contrast to his predecessor Felix.[575] The bandits armed with swords who had terrorized the Palestinian countryside were eliminated under Festus's rule. In spite of this, he could not reverse the damage incurred

---

[573] Pollock, *The Apostle*, 260.
[574] F.F. Bruce, *New Testament History* (New York: Doubleday, 1983), 345f.
[575] Flavius Josephus, *Antiquities of the Jews*, XX, viii, 9; XX, ix, 1.

by his predecessor, Felix, who had aggravated the conflict between Rome and the Jews.[576] The Jewish Wars came shortly after Felix died, resulting in the destruction of the Jerusalem temple in 70 A.D.

Festus availed himself of the aid of Agrippa II, an able and popular ruler among both Jews and Greeks, and a person with a close acquaintance with both Judaism and Christianity. Festus wanted to honor the old Herodian family in calling upon the great Herod Agrippa II.[577]

The Fatal Suspicion

Festus' great claim to fame is regarding Paul to be insane. At the conclusion of Paul's giving of the gospel, Festus would shout at Paul.

> Acts 26:24 | Paul, you are out of your mind; your great learning is driving you to madness!

Festus outright rejects the gospel, which we will speak of more in a moment. But with all their riches and power, what advantage did these kings and governors have over Paul or any child of God? What good do earthly power and riches do for the eternal state?

> Mark 8:36 | What does it profit a man to gain the whole world and forfeit his soul?

Oh, how these kings on earth desperately needed the good news. Their positions on earth would not give them eternal life. We can gain the highest places with the greatest wealth on earth, but we will lose our soul if we don't know Christ.

THE POWER OF GOSPEL PERSUASION (26:1-23)

Now it was time for Paul to present his case to the Roman appointed "King of the Jews," Agrippa II. Paul himself, a most unlikely candidate, had been persuaded by the gospel.

Paul's Case

Paul is not merely going to make a case for his own innocence. That has already been expressed on several occasions. Paul's case is for the gospel. It saved him, and he wants it to save Festus and Agrippa.

---

[576] Walter A. Elwell and Philip Wesley Comfort, *Tyndale Bible Dictionary*, Tyndale Reference Library (Wheaton, IL: Tyndale House Publishers, 2001), 485.

[577] E. M. Blaiklock, *The Century of the New Testament* (Downers Grove, IL: InterVarsity Press, 1962), ch. 6.

Indeed, he does all he can to persuade them to trust in the Lord for salvation. The gospel that had saved Paul can save anyone—it's the power of God for salvation!

> Romans 1:16 | For I am not ashamed of the gospel, for it is the power of God for salvation to everyone who believes, to the Jew first and also to the Greek.

The Magistrate of Paul's Case

Presiding over Paul's case is Agrippa II, an expert in Jewish law as far as a civil magistrate.

> **Acts 26:1-3a** | So Agrippa said to Paul, "You have permission to speak for yourself." Then Paul stretched out his hand and made his defense: ² "I consider myself fortunate that it is before you, King Agrippa, I am going to make my defense today against all the accusations of the Jews, ³ especially because you are familiar with all the customs and controversies of the Jews.

Paul is glad to speak before Agrippa, since the Herodian king is "familiar with all the customs and controversies of the Jews" (Acts 26:3). This chapter contains the most extensive testimony from Paul in Acts. As in his defense at Jerusalem, Paul mentions his personal background and presents himself—and, by extension, the Christian faith—as the proper expression of the Jewish religion.[578] Paul stretched out his hand to make his defense. He asks for Agrippa's patience.

Paul was grateful that he could present his case before someone eminently familiar with Judaism, the grandson of the infamous Herod the Great, who had constructed the Jerusalem temple and launched it to a place of incredible prominence in the ancient world. Agrippa II was familiar with the Old Testament Scriptures, so for the first time in over two years, Paul can finally give a full presentation of the real reason he is imprisoned. Agrippa has enough background to understand that Paul is innocent of insurrection at Jerusalem and desecration of the temple. What he is guilty of? Preaching the good news that the Messiah has come to fulfill all that is written in the Old Testament Scriptures.

The Motive of Paul's Case

> **Acts 26:1b-3** | Therefore I beg you to listen to me patiently.

---

[578] Hamilton, *John–Acts*, 560.

Paul asks the king for patience as he begins his defense. This is just what Paul had longed for during his bleak two years in prison—a knowledgeable judge and a non-antagonistic audience before whom he could make his case. Speaking with remarkable optimism and fervor, Paul's speech was not so much a personal defense as a positive presentation of the gospel and an evangelistic appeal.[579]

Paul's Character

Paul now uses himself as an example for faithful Judaism. He claims that Christianity is nothing new—it's actually the faith of the fathers, Abraham, Isaac, and Jacob. Agrippa would have appreciated this since he was well versed in the religion of the Jews. Paul uses his own life to say that he is merely living faithfully according to the Jewish Scriptures.

The Apostle's Faithfulness

Paul's conversion story is so shocking because he would have been the most faithful Pharisee in all of Israel. No one could doubt the apostle's faithfulness. At a young age, he left his home in Tarsus and moved to the holy city of Jerusalem to learn under a great rabbi.

> **Acts 26:4-5** | "My manner of life from my youth, spent from the beginning among my own nation and in Jerusalem, is known by all the Jews. **⁵** They have known for a long time, if they are willing to testify, that according to the strictest party of our religion I have lived as a Pharisee."

When Paul moved to Jerusalem, he trained under the rabbi Gamaliel (cf 22:3). Very few boys would be allowed to move to Jerusalem to be trained by the grandson of the great Hillel, but Saul of Tarsus was one of a handful. He would have begun around age 15. It was more than just classroom learning, but the small group of students would imitate whatever the rabbi did. Paul exceeded his fellow students and became the most faithful Jew of his day, from the strictest group: the Pharisees. He describes himself in Philippians 3:5-6, "Circumcised on the eighth day, of the people of Israel, of the tribe of Benjamin, a Hebrew of Hebrews; as to the law, a Pharisee; 6 as to zeal, a persecutor of the church; as to righteousness under the law, blameless." He's imprisoned

---

[579] Hughes, *Acts: The Church Afire*, 326.

presently because he's trying to continue to be faithful. The true Messiah called him. He speaks of the depth of his character and knowledge of the Jewish religion, presenting his own life as a follower of Christ as the fulfillment of the faith of Abraham.

The Ancient Faith

Paul has not invented something new but is living out the ancient faith of Abraham. Paul speaks directly to the real charge against him. He's living out the true faith of a child of Abraham. Paul is guilty of being committed to the ancient faith. The hope of Israel is not in this life, but the promise of the resurrection. This is why he's being held in prison.

> **Acts 26:6-7** | "And now I stand here on trial because of my hope in the promise made by God to our fathers, **7** to which our twelve tribes hope to attain, as they earnestly worship night and day. And for this hope I am accused by Jews, O king!"

Paul describes his faith in Christ as "my hope in the promise made by God to our fathers" (26:6). Paul claimed, it was for his adherence to the hope of fulfilment of God's promises to the ancestors of the Jews that he now stood on trial. [580] It was that promise that was made by God throughout the Old Testament: Messiah would come to take away sin and establish his kingdom of righteousness. And it was that very promise to which the twelve tribes of Israel hoped to attain as they earnestly served God night and day. [581]

Paul was about to present a case that Jesus had come according to the Old Testament prophecies and promises. Faithful Judaism always looked forward to the Messiah. Now he had come! Jesus had fulfilled the law. Paul hadn't invented anything new. The ultimate true expression of Judaism now that the Messiah had come had to be exclusively through God's ultimate Son and King whom he'd promised since the opening chapters of Genesis (cf Gen 3:15). Paul's speech before Agrippa is parallel with what he says in numerous passages in his writings. He wasn't rejecting something he didn't really know. He wasn't teaching odd things because he'd only picked up a garbled version of Judaism.[582]

---

[580] Marshall, *Acts*, 412.
[581] MacArthur, *Acts*, vol. 2, 333.
[582] Wright, *Acts for Everyone, Part 2*, 206.

Paul is an expert in the law by anyone's standard (Gal 1:13–14, Phil 3:5–6, Rom 10:2), and he is presenting a case that Jesus Christ is the fulfillment of all the promises of God from the Old Testament. Paul is going to argue that his faith is the faith of the Old Testament prophets (26:27). His point is that he's not made something up or created something new. Jesus is the Messiah that all the prophets spoke of.

Paul mentions his personal background and presents himself—and, by extension, the Christian faith—as the proper expression of the Jewish religion.[583] Paul had been born a true Jew, reared a true Jew, trained in the strictest Pharisaic viewpoint of Judaism, and still remained a true Jew. It was precisely his faith in the resurrection of Jesus that most pointed to his fidelity to Judaism because in the resurrection Israel's hope in God's promises had been fulfilled.[584] How vital it is that we not only believe the faith of Abraham but live it out!

The Amazing Fact

Paul presents to Agrippa the one fact for which he's incarcerated: that God raises the dead. He raised Jesus from the dead. This is the central claim of the Christian faith.

Acts 26:8 | "Why is it thought incredible by any of you that God raises the dead?"

Since Agrippa has a deep respect for the Jewish religion, Paul knows it shouldn't be a stretch for Agrippa to believe that God raises the dead. In fact, Paul extends it to "any of you." If God really is the Almighty, then why would it be incredible for him to do anything?

Paul makes it clear that it is for the hope of the gospel, specifically that God raises the dead, that he is incarcerated. This is short for the gospel, which Paul likely explained. Christ died for the ungodly. The death of Jesus of Nazareth was well-known throughout Judea. Paul lets the king know that God can indeed raise the dead! Jesus didn't stay dead but rose from the grave on the third day!

Paul's Commitment

Yet, Paul realizes what an incredible claim this sounds like on the surface to these Roman rulers who were so focused on the power and

---

[583] Hamilton, *John–Acts*, 560.
[584] Polhill, *Acts*, 500.

glory and materialism. And even though the king knows the Jewish religion well, as you can see from his life (he married his sister), Agrippa doesn't believe it whatsoever. It's just a family and cultural thing for him. Really? God raises the dead? How in the world did you come up with this Paul? They must have already thought he was out of his mind, but remember Paul had asked for patience, and it seems Agrippa and Festus were surely doing their best to hear Paul out. Paul lets them know that he was a notorious persecutor of the church.

Saul of Tarsus was an enemy of Christ and a fierce persecutor of the church. It would take something "out of this world" to convince the great Saul of Tarsus that Jesus of Nazareth was the Messiah.

> **Acts 26:9-11** | "I myself was convinced that I ought to do many things in opposing the name of Jesus of Nazareth. [10] And I did so in Jerusalem. I not only locked up many of the saints in prison after receiving authority from the chief priests, but when they were put to death I cast my vote against them. [11] And I punished them often in all the synagogues and tried to make them blaspheme, and in raging fury against them I persecuted them even to foreign cities.

We have Stephen's martyrdom recorded in sacred Scripture. Paul was there approving and holding the garments of those who stoned him.

> *Acts 7:58* | They cast him out of the city and stoned him. And the witnesses laid down their garments at the feet of a young man named Saul.

Saul of Tarsus had no mercy on the Christians. He locked them up and put them to death, but now he was one, standing there before Agrippa, on trial for his faith.

Paul's Conversion

"How in the world," Agrippa must have thought, "could one who opposed Christians now be one?" Paul was about to answer the question Agrippa must have been thinking. It all happened one day when he was on his way to Damascus in Syria, just outside of Dan in Israel, the northern most point. I've stood on the hill overlooking that Damascus Road in Israel. Paul was on a mission to persecute and discourage Christians, but the Lord was about to change Paul's mission. He was about to be converted from Christ hater to Christ follower. Here for the third time in Acts, Paul gives his testimony of conversion (*cf* 9:1–30; 22:5–21).

> **Acts 26:12-15** | "In this connection I journeyed to Damascus with the authority and commission of the chief priests. [13] At midday, O king, I saw on the way a light from heaven, brighter than the sun, that shone around me and those who journeyed with me. [14] And when we had all fallen to the ground, I heard a voice saying to me in the Hebrew language, 'Saul, Saul, why are you persecuting me? It is hard for you to kick against the goads.' [15] And I said, 'Who are you, Lord?' And the Lord said, 'I am Jesus whom you are persecuting."

This is what it takes to convert the great Saul of Tarsus: seeing the resurrected Christ! Paul now gets extremely personal. He shares his vision of the risen Christ. How could a man so committed to persecuting Christians suddenly and dramatically change his mind? Paul let's Agrippa know. "I met a man who was raised from the dead, and he's the Jewish Messiah."

Paul tells the king that when he was persecuting Christ's followers, that the Lord Jesus Christ took it personally. When Paul persecuted Christians, he was actually persecuting Jesus the Messiah.

Jesus said to him, "It's hard for you to kick against the goads." A goad is a sharp stick, about six to eight feet long, with a sharp end on it to keep the cattle going in a straight line when you are plowing on a farm. It's a prod of sorts. The more the cattle kicked against the prod or goad, it would stick in them more. The farmer would prick the animal to steer it in the right direction. In essence, the more an ox rebelled, the more it suffered. Paul had to learn the hard way that resistance to Jesus was a losing battle — hopeless. God is sovereign. He can convert and subdue even the most stubborn ox, like a Saul of Tarsus. Jesus was going to goad and direct and sovereignly steer Paul in the right direction. It was futile for him to kick against the prod that God was using. What else could Paul do be give in and surrender to the goad of God? The goad was an instrument of submission and training.

Conversion is like that goad. We have to face the pain of our own sin and our own choices. Paul thought he was righteous, but he was painfully wrong. His self-righteousness was stripped away so much that he called himself the "chief of sinners" because he "persecuted the church of God." Who would want to persecute God's own forever family? Paul thought he was so right, but he was so wrong.

What about you? What is your testimony of salvation? When did you come to know Christ? Has there been a time when you've turned from your sin to Christ? It doesn't have to be as dramatic as Paul's testimony. The greatest conversion stories are those of little children putting their faith in Christ. But no matter what your age, conversion is a new way of living, turning from sin and turning to Jesus Christ.

One more thing—if you have a testimony, share it! Everywhere Paul was, he shared what God had done for him. That was always a powerful way to introduce the gospel. Are you sharing your testimony everywhere you go? Do you serve the living God? Is he alive and active in your life?

Paul's Commission

Paul was immediately commissioned to preach the gospel. And he's going to suffer a lot, but it will be worth it. God is going to turn whole groups of people from darkness to light and from Satan to God. Paul had just undergone conversion, and now he was being commissioned to convert others.

> **Acts 26:16-18** | 'But rise and stand upon your feet, for I have appeared to you for this purpose, to appoint you as a servant and witness to the things in which you have seen me and to those in which I will appear to you, [17] delivering you from your people and from the Gentiles—to whom I am sending you [18] to open their eyes, so that they may turn from darkness to light and from the power of Satan to God, that they may receive forgiveness of sins and a place among those who are sanctified by faith in me.'

Paul was to bring true deliverance to both Jews and Gentiles, but he had a specific and special commission to the Gentiles. We are not saved to sit and soak but commissioned to serve. Jesus said to "go into all the world and preaching the gospel to every creature" (Mk 16:15, NKJV).

If we obey his commission God promises to do for us what he did for Paul. God will "open their eyes, so that they may turn from darkness to light and from the power of Satan to God" (26:18). People are in slavery to Satan. Paul tells the Corinthians that unbelievers are blinded by the devil. Only God can open their eyes!

> *2 Corinthians 4:4* | The god of this world has blinded the minds of the unbelievers, to keep them from seeing the light of the gospel of the glory of Christ, who is the image of God.

God will open their eyes as you give the gospel. That's why we need to be giving the gospel everywhere we go. When blind eyes can see, they will put receive complete forgiveness of their sins. Judgment day is canceled for the believer. Sinners become saints. They are "sanctified by faith" in Jesus. Those once robed in the rags of sin are now robed in Jesus' righteousness. Hallelujah! What a Savior!

Paul's Calling

Paul tells King Agrippa, "I obeyed my calling." Imagine the surprise of the Jews in Damascus, that instead of bringing Christians to them for arrest and execution or imprisonment, he tells them to turn to Jesus in faith!

> **Acts 26:19-20** | "Therefore, O King Agrippa, I was not disobedient to the heavenly vision, [20] but declared first to those in Damascus, then in Jerusalem and throughout all the region of Judea, and also to the Gentiles, that they should repent and turn to God, performing deeds in keeping with their repentance.

Paul's call was not just to the Jews. The good news was never just for one group of people. God's love and mercy is for the entire world. So Paul was obedient and told everyone, both Jews and Gentiles that they needed to open their eyes to the truth. Repentance means "a change of mind." It's like being given new eyes and the ability to hear. You see God in all his beauty and his grace becomes irresistible. Whenever a person truly repents, they produce a life "in keeping with repentance." They live as if they see life differently, in submission to Christ, because they see everything through his eyes.

Paul's Charges

Paul says, "The real charges are against me because of the gospel. I've been faithful to the faith of my ancestors and to the Scriptures I've read and loved all my life."

> **Acts 26:21-23** | For this reason the Jews seized me in the temple and tried to kill me. [22] To this day I have had the help that comes from God, and so I stand here testifying both to small and great, saying nothing but what the prophets and Moses said would come to

pass: **²³** that the Christ must suffer and that, by being the first to rise from the dead, he would proclaim light both to our people and to the Gentiles."

What is Paul guilty of? Preaching the Old Testament Scriptures in a faithful manner. "Moses and the prophets" point to one thing: the Redeemer that would come into the world and suffer, just like Isaiah said, and that he would be "the first to rise from the dead" just as Hosea said. He's the light of the world, "the way, the truth, and the life" not just for Paul's people, the Jews, but for the whole world. Paul was guilty of being a faithful son of Abraham and preaching the faith of Abraham and Moses in the coming King who is both Savior and Lord of all, who will judge the living and the dead.

What about you? Would you be found guilty of being a Christian? Are you faithful to the faith of Abraham? Are you faithful to the message of Moses, entrusting your life to the God who is "merciful and gracious, slow to anger, and abounding in unrelenting love and faithfulness" (Exo 34:6)?

THE TRAGEDY OF BEING "ALMOST" PERSUADED (26:24-32)

What was the response to the good news that Paul preached? Not good.

Gospel Foolishness

Festus interrupts Paul and lets him know that for such a learned man, he sounds like he is out of his mind.

> **Acts 26:24** | And as he was saying these things in his defense, Festus said with a loud voice, "Paul, you are out of your mind; your great learning is driving you out of your mind."

Despite conventional references to Roman gods, the typical Roman worshiped imperial fortune—the prominence and success of the Empire. [585] Festus, being first and last a politician, worshiped power and was a practical materialist.[586] Saying Paul was out of his mind was not an insult from the great Governor Festus. Festus was genuinely amazed—not that Paul would think there is something greater than

---

[585] Charles Cochrane, *Christianity and Classical Culture* (London: Oxford University Press, 1944), 113.

[586] Hughes, *Acts: The Church Afire*, 327.

power and glory and material wealth, the Jews held to that—but that Paul actually lived by it. Most of the Jewish leaders, at least the Pharisees, had similar theology to Paul's but they didn't live by it. They sought the power and influence and wealth of this world. Paul forsook this world for the pleasures of Christ.

Festus must have been amazed at Paul's response to the vision he received from Jesus. He left everything and was willing to suffer for the Lord. This stretched Festus' rationality to the limit. It made no sense to him for Paul to choose a path that not only brought the apostle less pleasure but more suffering![587]

Paul could have lived a very pampered life with all his connections and respect within Judaism. Now he looked "out of his mind." Paul was accused of insanity, just like his Lord. Jesus enemies and his own family thought our Lord had lost his mind (cf Mk 3:20; Jn 10:20).

I think of the great Tevye in the theatre production, "Fiddler on the Roof." He says, "Oh, dear Lord, you made many, many poor people I realize, of course, it's no shame to be poor, but it's no great honor either! So, what would have been so terrible if I had a small fortune?"[588] Even Tevye had visions of wealth, and he dreams of what could be possible if he were a wealthy man. Paul's mind was so fixed on heaven, that Festus thought Paul had lost his mind. Truly the things of the Spirit are foolishness to the natural, lost person.

> *1 Corinthians 2:14, NIV* | The person without the Spirit does not accept the things that come from the Spirit of God but considers them foolishness, and cannot understand them because they are discerned only through the Spirit.

The good news of Jesus is foolishness to those who are lost. They are "dead in their trespasses and sins" (Eph 1:1-3). They are "blinded by the god of this world" (2 Cor 4:4). They see the gospel as ridiculous, and nonsense. They cannot and will not endure it. They need the Spirit of God to open their eyes. They need the Father to draw them.

---

[587] Ibid.

[588] Jerry Bock, Joseph Stein, Sheldon Harnick, and Sholem Aleichem, *Fiddler on the Roof* (New York: Limelight Editions, 1990—first performance September 22, 1964), 21.

Gospel Boldness

Paul hadn't lost his mind. He knew the king understood the Scriptures. Paul was bold because that's what mercy and love does to the heart of a Christian. Our love for sinners makes us bold.

> **Acts 26:25-27** | But Paul said, "I am not out of my mind, most excellent Festus, but I am speaking true and rational words. [26] For the king knows about these things, and to him I speak boldly. For I am persuaded that none of these things has escaped his notice, for this has not been done in a corner. [27] King Agrippa, do you believe the prophets? I know that you believe."

Paul gives an invitation to King Agrippa to believe the gospel. Remember Agrippa's father had beheaded the apostle James and would have done the same to Peter had an angel not rescued him. Look how far the gospel has reached. Now the great Agrippa II is giving a fair hearing to the gospel.

Neither Paul or any Christian is out of our minds! Our minds are set on things above where true reality lies (Col 3:1). We who are heavenly minded know that God's ways are so much higher and beyond comprehension of mere human ways, that they seem insane (Isa 55:8-9). What Paul was speaking may sound outrageous, since the natural mind cannot comprehend or appreciate the things of God.

> *Romans 8:7* | The mind that is set on the flesh is hostile to God, for it does not submit to God's law; indeed, it cannot.

Agrippa was around when Jesus was raised from the dead. "None of these things" escaped the notice of the king. They weren't "done in a corner." People by the score had been healed by Jesus. Thousands had feasted on loaves and fish miraculously multiplied from a little boy's lunch. Demons recognized the Lord and fled before his command. The very dead had been raised. Moreover, our Lord had a lived a life of perfect holiness combined with all-embracing compassion and love.

Agrippa would have known about his illegal trial and crucifixion, his burial in the tomb of one of the wealthiest and most influential Jews in the country, and his subsequent resurrection. All these things had rocked the country. The futile attempts of the Jewish authorities to cover up their crimes by making the resulting Christianity illegal (including Paul's persecution of the church) were also public knowledge.

Nobody could factually deny the resurrection of Christ. Christ had appeared again and again—on one occasion to more than five hundred credible witnesses. Nothing but deliberate refusal to face the facts could account for unbelief. "This thing was not done in a corner." The facts were public knowledge, and all attempts to repress them had failed.[589] All these things had been done according to the prophets. Carried away by the marvelous truth of the gospel, Paul ceased to be the advocate in his own defense and became God's advocate to the conscience of the king. Paul asks a bold question, "King Agrippa, do you believe the prophets? I know that you believe."

Gospel Persuasion

Agrippa is a bit surprised by Paul's boldness and seeming expectation that King Agrippa would turn to Christ right then and repent.

> **Acts 26:28** | And Agrippa said to Paul, "In a short time would you [almost] persuade me to be a Christian?"

These were the most tragic words Agrippa uttered in his life. The Apostle of Christ was standing before him, preaching Christ to him, and Agrippa said that he was almost persuaded, but not quite.[590] All his life Agrippa had learned to ride both horses, as it were: to be a good Roman and to give honor the Jews, but now Paul is asking him to choose sides. Agrippa is essentially saying, "Do you think you can convince me to give up my power and my honor to follow Christ, in such a short time? I'll pass for now. Maybe another day."

> **Acts 26:29** | And Paul said, "Whether short or long, I would to God that not only you but also all who hear me this day might become such as I am—except for these chains."

And Paul, picking up Agrippa's clever if embarrassed response, turns it neatly round and sends it back with a joke. "Actually, yes, I'd like everyone here to be just like me"—and then, glancing down in mock surprise at the clunky shackles round his ankles—"except for these chains, of course."[591] Clearly Paul was attempting to persuade the great king to follow Christ!

---

[589] J. Phillips, *Exploring Acts*, Ac 26:25c–26.
[590] Sproul, *Acts*, 408.
[591] Wright, *Acts for Everyone, Part 2*, 218.

Gospel Exoneration

As Agrippa, Bernice, and Festus dismissed themselves, they conversed with one another about Paul's innocence.

> **Acts 26:30-31** | Then the king rose, and the governor and Bernice and those who were sitting with them. **31** And when they had withdrawn, they said to one another, "This man is doing nothing to deserve death or imprisonment."

Paul was acquitted on all charges. What every Gentile authority in the book of Acts recognizes is that whatever the charges, Paul is innocent of anything deserving of death or imprisonment. Kings, rulers, and authorities at various levels see this all as a dispute between a few Jews, but in reality, it is a dispute over loyalty to the true King, Jesus of Nazareth.[592] Paul was completely innocent but had appealed to have a court date in Rome.

Gospel Direction

Agrippa makes a point that would have affected most people, but not Paul.

> **Acts 26:32** | And Agrippa said to Festus, "This man could have been set free if he had not appealed to Caesar."

Paul could have been set free, but he wasn't at all concerned about his personal freedom. Paul's heart was to go to Rome and preach the gospel there. Paul's goal in life was not personal comfort but gospel expansion.

The Roman soldiers would escort him to Rome. This meant he was safe from potential Jewish assassins, and he didn't even have to organize his own passage. He was going to Rome at last.[593] Festus and Agrippa indeed thought Paul had lost his mind. But truly those with the mind of Christ will often look like they have gone mad to this world.

Conclusion

I'm getting ready for my high school's 30-year class reunion in the fall. I've been trying to get in shape for a while. But at a class reunion everyone wants to shape up to fit in.

---

[592] Hamilton, *John–Acts*, 558.
[593] Wright, *Acts for Everyone, Part 2*, 219.

My daughter, and other ladies who got married recently—they made sure they could fit into that wedding dress.

This year, I was so excited for Easter because I had the perfect suit that one of the brothers at our church gave me, but when I went to get in it, I forgot to get the waist fitted, so I did not fit in at all. It was way too small.

I don't fit into this world anymore, but where I do fit in is God's forever family. That's the place where we fit. In the world's eyes, we are the crazy ones. We truly are crazy for Jesus. We will never again fit into this world. We don't belong here. But we fit in among God's people. Praise his name that though we look "out of our minds" when it comes to this world, we are right at home among those with hearts and minds made new by the Holy Spirit.

I'll tell you what though – for anyone who is on the fence, you understand that all this comfort will be ripped away from you at the judgement of God. All people will live forever somewhere. All the comfort and ease we have on earth will not matter if you are thrown into the lake of fire. Don't be "almost persuaded." Follow Christ today!

44 | ACTS 27:1-44
GOD'S PROVIDENCE IN OUR SHIPWRECKS

> *This very night there stood before me an angel of the God to whom I belong and whom I worship, and he said, 'Do not be afraid, Paul; you must stand before Caesar.*
>
> ACTS 27:23-24

Sometimes there are such trials, traumas, tragedies, and evils, that we can't make sense of them in this life. How do we come to grips with pain in the Christian life? Charles Spurgeon, the most popular preacher of nineteenth-century London, battled depression throughout his life. He said,

> If God is in control, if his name is hallowed, then that means he is in control of my depression. Fate is blind; providence has eyes. [594]

God in his providence was using Spurgeon's depression to humble him and make him like Christ. John Flavel says it even more clearly and poetically.

> The providence of God is like a Hebrew word – it can only be read backwards. [595]

---

[594] Charles Haddon Spurgeon. "Providence" *New Park Street Pulpit, vol 4* (London: Passemore & Alabaster, 1858), preached April 11, 1858.

[595] John Flavel in Sinclair B. Ferguson, *A Heart for God* (Carol Stream, IL: Nav Press: 1985), 145.

That means that God works all things, the good, the bad, and the ugly, for our good and his glory. But we can only see how it works out on the other side. It's backwards. Only when we see Jesus face to face will we understand. This is why Paul can say that our future glory outweighs our present suffering!

> Romans 8:18 | I consider that the sufferings of this present time are not worth comparing with the glory that is to be revealed to us.

Consider this child of God, God's providence means that nothing truly eternally bad can happen to us. All the bad on this earth is temporary, and it works to our eternal good to conform us to Jesus Christ. Do you believe that? You ought to. Your entire happiness depends on it. No matter what your eyes see, or what your heart feels, you must believe that God is working it out for your good.

I think of an unusual story of Joan Murray. When her plane leveled off at 14,500 feet, she took a deep breath and jumped out the door. The bank executive from Charlotte, North Carolina, was enjoying her free fall through the air until she pulled the ripcord for her parachute, and nothing happened. Just about then she had an extreme rush of adrenaline.

But she didn't panic – she knew she had a backup parachute. She was falling 120 miles per hour when she released the reserve chute. It opened just fine, but she lost her bearings and, in her struggle to right herself, she deflated the chute. While the chute briefly slowed her descent, she continued to fall at 80 miles per hour.

She struck the earth with a violent blow shattering her right side and jarring the fillings from her teeth. She was barely conscious, and her heart was failing. Just when it seemed things could not get much worse, she realized she had fallen into a mound of fire ants that didn't appreciate her disturbing their solitude. All told they stung her about 200 times before the paramedics arrived.[596]

But things are not always as they seem. The doctors that treated Joan believe that the ants actually saved her life. They credit the stings of the ants that shocked her heart enough to keep it beating!

The apostle Paul had many opportunities to learn about God's providence himself. Satan means it for evil but God uses all things for

---

[596] Editors of People Magazine, *Amazing Stories of Survival*. New York: Liberty Street Publishing House, 2006), 15.

his glory and our good (Gen 50:20). Our great God makes "all things beautiful in its time" (Ecc 3:11).

Acts 27 is the tale of one of the most famous shipwrecks in history—that of the Apostle Paul on his way to Rome, and how God used it for good. It is also one of the best-told, most-detailed shipwreck accounts in ancient history—and certainly the most profitable to the hearer.[597]

What we learn from Paul's shipwreck, and all the shipwrecks in the Christian life is that God is in control. Whatever happens is for our good and for God's glory. We call that God's providence.

This doctrine of God's providence helps us trust the Lord in every circumstance. It may not answer every question, but at least it provides the only possible foundation for understanding: God is bigger than your problems. He's working it out for his glorious purposes.

In English the word "providence" has two parts. It's "pro" (before) and "video" (to see). Put them together, and you have: "to see before." God is outside of time, sees all things at once, and works them for good.

Though the word providence is not found in most modern translations of the Bible, the concept is certainly biblical. It refers to "God's gracious oversight of the universe." Oversight means that he directs the course of affairs. "He works all things after the counsel of his own will" (Eph 1:11). The word universe tells us that God not only knows the big picture, he created it and also concerns himself with the tiniest details. Here are five statements that unfold the meaning of God's providence in more detail. God's providence means: He upholds all things. He governs all events. He directs everything to its appointed end. He does this all the time and in every circumstance. He does it always for his own glory and for your good. The doctrine of God's providence magnifies his compassion toward his people.

First, God cares about the tiniest details of life. Nothing escapes his notice for he is concerned about the small as well as the big. In fact, with God there is no big or small. He knows when a sparrow falls, and he numbers the hairs on your head. He keeps track of the stars in the skies and the rivers that flow to the oceans. He sets the day of your birth, the day of your death, and he ordains everything that comes to pass in between.

---

[597] Hughes, *Acts: The Church Afire*, 331.

Second, he uses everything and wastes nothing. There are no accidents with God, only incidents. This includes events that seem to us to be senseless tragedies.

Third, God's ultimate purpose is to shape his children into the image of Jesus Christ (Rom 8:29). He often uses difficult moments and human tragedies to accomplish that purpose.[598]

The Bible teaches us that God is the creator of heaven and earth, and that all that occurs in the universe takes place under his divine providence — that is, under his sovereign guidance and control. God governs creation as our loving Father, working all things for good (Rom 8:28, Ecc 3:11, Gen 50:20). Moreover, God is an absolutely perfect being. He is omniscient or all-knowing, not only aware of the future, but active in shaping every event for his glory and our good (Eph 1:10, 2:10, Pro 16:9).

> Key Thought: Because of God's loving guidance and providence over our lives, we do not need to fear the day of adversity. God is in control of the storms of our lives for our good and his glory.

It's one thing to believe in God's providence theoretically, or to learn about it for an exam, but what if you are called on to trust God in the hardest of circumstances? That's where believing in God's good plan and omnipotent power to guide our lives is essential. Without a firm belief in God's providence, you will enter into the unbelief of bitterness and anger. Paul wasn't like that. He knew it was all working toward a larger plan.

THE PLAN OF GOD'S PROVIDENCE (27:1-8)

How difficult it is to be under the control or authority of another, yet God is the one in ultimate control of our steps. How can we trust God in his plan for our lives? Let's look at how Paul trusted God.

The Wonder of God's Plan

Paul was truly amazed at the wonder of God's plan. Everything God said, he was faithful to do for Paul. God said Paul would preach in Rome, and finally, Paul got on a ship that set sail for Rome, Italy.

---

[598] Ray Pritchard, "The Invisible Hand: Coming to Grips With God's Providence" (Keep on Believing Ministries, Sermon from February 2, 1997), Genesis 50:20.

Acts 27:1 | And when it was decided that we should sail for Italy, they delivered Paul and some other prisoners to a centurion of the Augustan Cohort named Julius.

Festus handed Paul to a centurion named Julius serving with the imperial guard (Augustan cohort), whose officers and men traveled throughout the empire escorting people where they needed to go. Julius commanded a detail of likely about a dozen soldiers: Paul was the only prisoner of rank, permitted to take two friends who were listed as his personal attendants: Aristarchus and Luke the physician (vs 2-3). The other prisoners would be convicts on their grim way to "make a Roman holiday," either as lion fodder at the games or, if burly enough, for training as gladiators. These would all be chained to timbers below decks. Paul, a Roman citizen, and his attendants could move about freely, though he must always wear a loose chain as a symbol of his status.[599]

Paul wasn't so concerned about the chains he was wearing. He was on his way to a new mission field that he had long prayed for. How he had dreamed of preaching. He had long ago given up any specific expectations. He was God's slave. But God had called him to preach in Rome, so he knew, however he got there, he would most certainly get there. The wonder of God's plan is that it's predetermined before the foundation of the world.

> *Ephesians 2:10* | We are his workmanship, created in Christ Jesus for good works, which God prepared beforehand, that we should walk in them.

We as God's workmanship, his masterpiece, are in awe that he would prepare all the good plans he has for us beforehand, guiding our lives, that we should walk in them. God said he'd give grace, and Paul said, "His grace is sufficient" (2 Cor 12:9). God said, "I'll never leave you nor forsake you" (Heb 13:5), and Paul could testify, "Nothing can separate me from the love of Christ" (Rom 8:39). God was working everything according to plan.

The Welfare of God's Plan

Even though Paul was gifted as a great apostle with the power to do miracles, who had visions of the Lord directly and wrote thirteen

---

[599] Pollock, *The Apostle*, 265.

inspired books of the Bible, he still needed to be attached to the body of Christ. Even Paul could not live the Christian life alone. All who come to Christ in faith become intensely aware of our need for the fellowship and encouragement of other believers. For Paul he had his physician Luke and Aristarchus from the church at Thessalonica. Even Julius, the high-ranking officer in charge of Paul was a great encouragement.

> **Acts 27:2-3** | And embarking in a ship of Adramyttium, which was about to sail to the ports along the coast of Asia, we put to sea, accompanied by Aristarchus, a Macedonian from Thessalonica. ³ The next day we put in at Sidon. And Julius treated Paul kindly and gave him leave to go to his friends and be cared for.

Being a Roman citizen and an obvious gentleman, Paul was allowed to take along his companions Dr. Luke and Aristarchus, a devoted Christian brother from Thessalonica. Paul was treated so well that the next day, when they landed at Sidon, he was allowed to disembark and visit his friends there.[600]

It wouldn't be at all surprising if Paul had pointed Julius to saving faith in Christ. The point is, we must be connected to the body of Christ to grow up into the headship and lordship of Jesus Christ. The Lord requires Holy Spirit empowered obedience, with a life of grace infused good works. It is not possible to grow up into maturity without being connected to the body. Paul makes this clear in his letter to the Ephesians.

> *Ephesians 4:15-16* | We are to grow up in every way into him who is the head, into Christ, ¹⁶ from whom the whole body, joined and held together by every joint with which it is equipped, when each part is working properly, makes the body grow so that it builds itself up in love.

Even at a time when Paul has no control over his life for the most part, God ensures that Paul has sufficient support, fellowship, and encouragement from fellow believers. God will also provide for the absolute necessity of fellowship in your life. Choosing to be unaccountable will cause you to go astray in your life. Stop abusing the grace of God and yield to the relationships in Christ he has for you. Our salvation and relationship with God is a covenant. We are no different than

---

[600] Hughes, *Acts: The Church Afire*, 331–332.

Abraham or those in Deuteronomy heading into the promised land from the plains of Moab. We have a covenant with God like marriage. He says, "I will be your God, and you will be my people" Exo 29:45; Zech 8:8; 2 Cor 6:16; Heb 8:10; Jer 32:38; Eze 11:20; Rev 21:3; Psa 81:19; Isa 41:10). That means we remain intimately connected to him and to his people.

Perhaps you are afraid of deep friendship because of your sin. You've broken covenant with God. Don't be afraid. You may break your covenant, but God will never break his. He'll never leave you or forsake you. We have to drag our sin into the light together and hate it so we can walk in the light and have fellowship together (cf 1 Jn 1:7-9). What a comfort to know that even when we are at our weakest, God has encouragers for us. In that sense, we might way Christians are "Jesus with skin on."

The Winds of God's Plan

Paul was on a ship that was forced to hug the coast of Cyprus because the winds were bad. They finally made it to the open sea and then to the coast of Asia

> **Acts 27:4-8** | And putting out to sea from there we sailed under the lee of Cyprus, because the winds were against us. ⁵ And when we had sailed across the open sea along the coast of Cilicia and Pamphylia, we came to Myra in Lycia. ⁶ There the centurion found a ship of Alexandria sailing for Italy and put us on board. ⁷ We sailed slowly for a number of days and arrived with difficulty off Cnidus, and as the wind did not allow us to go farther, we sailed under the lee of Crete off Salmone. ⁸ Coasting along it with difficulty, we came to a place called Fair Havens, near which was the city of Lasea.

In this passage, there is a lot of talk of how hard and heavy the winds of the sea are. They have to hug the coasts of Cyprus and then Crete, but they are finally on their way to Italy—the focus of his ministry dreams. The centurion "finds" a ship for Paul and the other prisoners. Understand that all of this is the hand of God.

Sometimes the winds of life can be tempestuous. It can feel like you are about to go off course. Remember that God is in charge of the winds and waves, not only of the sea, but he's got you when you are in the storms of life. God had a destination for Paul: to preach the word in

Italy. But even that destination was secondary. Paul was very clear that his ultimate destination was to be conformed into the image of Jesus Christ (Rom 8:29) and then to be able to know him and one day see him face to face.

Perhaps you are facing some heavy winds of change in your life. Things seem unsettled or uncertain. What good does it do to worry? Will it add another second to your life span? Will worry make you an inch taller? The opposite of worry is worship. Instead of worrying, embrace the winds of change in your life. Your earthly dreams may at times be shattered, but "laying up treasure on earth" has never been a wise endeavor. Paul's treasures could not be affected by earthly storms.

OUR PERSEVERANCE IN GOD'S PROVIDENCE (27:9-12)

Apparently, there is a meeting at Fair Havens, and Paul, of all people is consulted. He relays an important warning. We are going to see that during all of this, Paul is at peace. He's persevering under God's mighty hand. Fear or frustration do not take hold of the apostle.

An Important Warning

> **Acts 27:9-10** | Since much time had passed, and the voyage was now dangerous because even the Fast was already over, Paul advised them, ¹⁰ saying, "Sirs, I perceive that the voyage will be with injury and much loss, not only of the cargo and the ship, but also of our lives."

Sailing season was coming to a close. For the Jews, that meant they stopped sailing abound the time of the Fast, or the Day of Atonement (fall season).

Subsequent events proved that Paul's advice was sound: they should have remained at Fair Havens. The season for sea travel was coming to a close. Calculated by the phases of the moon, the Day of Atonement fell always in late September or early October. For ancient travel on the Mediterranean, mid-September to early November was considered a dangerous time for traveling the open sea. After early November such travel ceased altogether and generally was not resumed until the beginning of February at the earliest. Paul's advice was based on this well-known fact. It was well into the dangerous season. Any travel now would be risky business. They had already encountered bad winds. Paul had been in peril at sea before. He knew the danger. Paul himself says, "Three times I was shipwrecked; a night and a day I was adrift at sea" (2 Cor 11:25). Whether his advice was truly prophetic or merely based on his opinion is at this point unclear. He warned that there could be loss both of cargo and of life. As it turned out, the ship and cargo would indeed be lost, but there was no loss of life. The important thing is that his apprehensions proved true. When he later gave his opinion, it was taken seriously by Julius (vs 31). At this point it was not, and that proved nearly disastrous.[601]

An Ignored Warning

Julius the centurion ignores Paul's warning and heads into what will soon become the tempestuous sea.

> **Acts 27:11-12** | But the centurion paid more attention to the pilot and to the owner of the ship than to what Paul said. [12] And because the harbor was not suitable to spend the winter in, the majority decided to put out to sea from there, on the chance that somehow they could reach Phoenix, a harbor of Crete, facing both southwest and northwest, and spend the winter there.

As

As fair as Fair Havens might have been, the majority out ruled Paul, with the centurion Julius likely being in charge. How difficult is it to submit to those in authority over us. We are going to see that while Julius makes a very dangerous decision, God uses it for Paul's good and his own divine glory.

We can read between the lines here and see that Paul is not panicked or angry when his sound advice is not taken. He knows his life is in the hands of God. Neither should any of God's children panic but be at peace in the control of the one who controls the winds and the waves. Paul persevered in peace even when he could see disaster coming!

What do you do when you are ignored? Are you able to persevere in peace? What do you do when you see disaster coming and you have no control? Are you able to yield to the control of God who has you? Trust his good heart and his mighty hand!

I think of the story of Corrie Ten Boom. She and her sister were imprisoned for hiding Jewish people from the Nazis in World War II. The concentration camp building they were in was crawling with fleas,

---

[601] Polhill, *Acts*, 518–519.

and they prayed that they could endure. They didn't know why after all the inhumane things they endured, they had to endure the fleas too. They did have one Bible, and they would take a page of the Bible at a time and distribute it to each of the inmate ladies so they could learn the word of God. But the fleas were just unbearable at times! Yet, later, when Corrie was free, she found out that the fleas were what kept the guards away from their building. This is why they were so free to read the Bible in that Nazi concentration camp! God's gracious providence he was using the fleas to protect them!

GOD'S PRESENCE IN HIS PROVIDENCE (27:13-24)

Now as Paul, trusting God, enters the ship, knowing he could die, we are taught by Paul's example that God will deliver us out of danger and despair. God is with us and will never leave us, but we desperately need to experience God's manifest presence by the Holy Spirit in all circumstances. Let him speak his word into your heart. Listen to his still, small voice, and don't be distracted by the noise of the storm!

God is Present in Danger

No one likes to consider the possibilities of danger and difficulty in the Christian life, yet the Lord calls us to be prepared for trials and dangers on our journey to Christlike maturity. We are not only to expect trials, but to "count it all joy" when we fall into "trials of various kinds" (Jas 1:2). Why? Because our perseverance in difficulties and dangers grows us to a place of "perfection and maturity" where we are "lacking in nothing" (Jas 1:3). Paul boards the ship, and things start out as well as could be expected, but things quickly turn for the worst. And that's ok, because God is in control.

> **Acts 27:13-19** | Now when the south wind blew gently, supposing that they had obtained their purpose, they weighed anchor and sailed along Crete, close to the shore. **14** But soon a tempestuous wind, called the northeaster, struck down from the land. **15** And when the ship was caught and could not face the wind, we gave way to it and were driven along. **16** Running under the lee of a small island called Cauda, we managed with difficulty to secure the ship's boat. **17** After hoisting it up, they used supports to undergird the ship. Then, fearing that they would run aground on the Syrtis, they lowered the gear, and thus they were driven along. **18** Since we were violently storm-tossed, they began the next day to

jettison the cargo. ¹⁹ And on the third day they threw the ship's tackle overboard with their own hands.

Things were going from bad to worse. First, they girded the ship with supports, then they were violently tossed by the storm, and on the second day they had to change their mission from sales to survival. The ship had to be lightened as much as possible. First the bulk of the grain cargo was thrown overboard and then the movable baggage and all the spare gear.[602] Luke's details of the ancient way of ship faring are remarkably accurate, albeit in laymen's terms.

Now if the apostles were put into storms and difficulties beyond their control and certainly far beyond their comfort zone, it is clear all Christians must be ready for danger to at times envelop our lives. We have no control over so much that happens in life, but we know the one who does. Listen to what God told Isaiah.

> *Isaiah 45:7* | I form light and create darkness; I make well-being and create calamity; I am the LORD, who does all these things.

God is never in heaven wringing his hands. He is working "all things together for good" for your predestined conformity to Christ (Rom 8:29; Ecc 3:11).

God is Present in Despair

Sometimes a situation can be so bleak that you can despair even of your life. The storm was so fierce on Paul's journey to Rome that they did not see the sun or the moon for many days.

> **Acts 27:20** | When neither sun nor stars appeared for many days, and no small tempest lay on us, all hope of our being saved was at last abandoned.

This ship had various parties on board: prisoners, merchants, and sailors. The merchants had already lost their cargo, and now all on board were wondering if they'd even make it to Italy with their lives intact.

Dear saints, even in the most intense and difficult circumstances we may out of pain long for heaven, but we must never be faithless or hopeless. The Christian life is not at all absent from sorrow and grief.

---

[602] Bruce, *Acts: Bible Study Commentary*, Ac 27:13–32.

Jesus was "a man of sorrow and acquainted with grief" (Isa 53:3). Hebrews tells us our Lord wept many tears with "loud cries."

> *Hebrews 5:7* | In the days of his flesh, Jesus offered up prayers and supplications, with loud cries and tears, to him who was able to save him from death, and he was heard because of his reverence.

There are times of deep grief, but depression and self-focused despair are sinful. We are always to remember the deep roots of our faith and joy and hope must never come from our circumstances, but from the promises of God. Even in our grief we can say, "Blessed are the poor in spirit... blessed are those who mourn for they shall be comforted" (Mt 5:3-4).

Perhaps you are struggling with despair. Despair is caused by doubt. "God could change my situation, but he won't." There is some truth in this, but in despair we charge God with negligence and even hardness of heart to us, and it couldn't be farther from the truth. He's loved you with an everlasting love (Jer 31:3). His main goal is not your comfort and earthly happiness but your eternal holiness and conformity to Jesus Christ. He cannot ever forget or neglect you since he's "graven you" on the palms of his hands (Isa 49:16). Most of all, God's given you his one and only Son.

> *Romans 8:32* | He who did not spare his own Son but gave him up for us all, how will he not also with him graciously give us all things?

God wants to bless you with perfect peace in all your storms. In all of our anguish, God anguishes, dear child of God. When a dear mother or father sees their child suffer, the parent suffers too. So it is with God. When he sees his children suffer in Jeremiah he says:

> *Jeremiah 4:19* | My anguish, my anguish! I writhe in pain! Oh the walls of my heart!

God's people are on their way to captivity, and God has not forsaken them. They need discipline, and it inflicts the heart of God with pain to see his children suffer!

God is Present to Deliver

Yet even in the storm, Paul knew he wasn't abandoned.

> **Acts 27:21-24** | Since they had been without food for a long time, Paul stood up among them and said, "Men, you should have listened

> to me and not have set sail from Crete and incurred this injury and loss. **22** Yet now I urge you to take heart, for there will be no loss of life among you, but only of the ship. **23** For this very night there stood before me an angel of the God to whom I belong and whom I worship, **24** and he said, 'Do not be afraid, Paul; you must stand before Caesar. And behold, God has granted you all those who sail with you.'

Paul was not being petty and saying, "I told you so." Rather, he wanted to make sure they would hear him when he gives glory to God for their rescue. He has a prophecy that's he's received from the Lord. The Lord says, "You'll lose the ship but not your lives." Paul wants to introduce them to "the God to whom I belong and whom I worship" (27:23).

God himself had sent an angel to Paul to let him know that Paul need not be afraid. All will survive since Paul has an appointment to preach the gospel in Rome.

Remember God directs all things for your good and his glory. He is not the author of sin, nor does he force men to do anything. Yet his plan is not at all hindered by the evil choices of man. He raises up kings and puts them down. He creates tempests and calms the storms. He causes wars to cease. He's the almighty God and "all things happen after the counsel and decree of his own will" (Eph 1:11).

God goes one giant leap further for the Christian in all our troubles. He works "all things for good" for his own family (Rom 8:28). You belong to him dear saint! What's the worst that could happen? You could die and go directly into the presence of the Lord. This earth is the most hell the child of God will ever experience.

THE PARADOX OF GOD'S PROVIDENCE (27:25-44)

Sometimes the ways of the Lord can be mysterious. This life is like a tapestry—we only see the dangling and knotted ends of the yarns going in every direction, but God sees the perfect tapestry of the other side.

His providence is most often a paradox to us mainly because we are creatures addicted to ease. We think if we do good for God, then the Lord promises to always prosper us. There is truth to that. Live life the way God designed, and most often you will indeed prosper. But this does not mean your life is absolved and protected from shipwrecks and trials. God stretches our faith and grows our heart through hardship and trials.

Grace means no matter how bad my circumstances are, I'm experiencing infinitely less than I deserve. My hardest, most brutal day is heaven compared to what I ought to get, which is eternity in hell, experiencing the Lord's everlasting judgment. Nonetheless, when we do what is right and we receive hardship and harshness in life, there can be a feeling of paradox, even tempting us to doubt the goodness of God.

The Faithfulness of God

Despite the storms and shipwrecks, God is faithful! Paul was not tossed about the storm like the others. His faith in the Lord was his anchor. He was able to encourage the sailors, merchants, and prisoners. "Take heart!"

> **Acts 27:25-26** | So take heart, men, for I have faith in God that it will be exactly as I have been told. ²⁶ But we must run aground on some island."

Is your anchor in the faithfulness of God or in the constantly changing circumstances in life? The key to peace is not to stop the shipwrecks, but to put your focus on God and "take heart" in him and in his salvation (*cf* Psa 13, e.g.).

The Fickleness of Man

Don't depend on yourself or on other human beings for peace. Our hearts are fickle. "Cursed is the man who trusts in man and makes flesh his strength, whose heart turns away from the Lord" (Jer 17:5). Get your eyes off of self and others and turn your eyes on Jesus!

> **Acts 27:27-32** | When the fourteenth night had come, as we were being driven across the Adriatic Sea, about midnight the sailors suspected that they were nearing land. ²⁸ So they took a sounding and found twenty fathoms. A little farther on they took a sounding again and found fifteen fathoms. ²⁹ And fearing that we might run on the rocks, they let down four anchors from the stern and prayed for day to come. ³⁰ And as the sailors were seeking to escape from the ship, and had lowered the ship's boat into the sea under pretense of laying out anchors from the bow, ³¹ Paul said to the centurion and the soldiers, "Unless these men stay in

the ship, you cannot be saved." **32** Then the soldiers cut away the ropes of the ship's boat and let it go.

Paul warned that the passengers risked death if they got on the spare boats. They had to stay on the sinking ship to be saved.

Paul had just told the crew of sailors to "take heart" and trust in the Lord with him, but faith in the Lord had not yet taken hold of them. They lowered the smaller boat on the pretext of using it to drop anchors, but Paul knew their plan. He had been through three previous shipwrecks, so he knew all the tricks and how people would behave. They couldn't afford to let any of the crew abandon ship; the other passengers didn't have the sailing experience required to guide the vessel close to land without crashing.[603]

Don't be so dishearten that sinners act like sinners. Don't take it personally. You can warn them as Paul did, and sometimes they will respond. But don't take it personally. Keep your eyes on Christ, not on the fickleness of lost sinners or confused saints.

The Fortitude of Leaders

Paul was never a dominating, demanding leader. He was truly gentle and respectful. He waited on God. When his advice wasn't headed, he let God vindicate him. As a leader he didn't have to demand or fuss or pout. That's the sign of an abusive leader. If that's you dear brother, you need to stop it and repent and treat those under your care with gentleness. Notice when Paul's advice was clearly demonstrating great wisdom, the crew started listening to him.

> **Acts 27:33-38** | As day was about to dawn, Paul urged them all to take some food, saying, "Today is the fourteenth day that you have continued in suspense and without food, having taken nothing. **34** Therefore I urge you to take some food. For it will give you strength, for not a hair is to perish from the head of any of you." **35** And when he had said these things, he took bread, and giving thanks to God in the presence of all he broke it and began to eat. **36** Then they all were encouraged and ate some food themselves. **37** (We were in all 276 persons in the ship.) **38** And when they had eaten enough, they lightened the ship, throwing out the wheat into the sea.

---

[603] Swindoll, *Acts*, 502.

Paul says, "Not one hair on any of our heads will be harmed. This is our last day at sea, so get something to eat! Celebrate!" After all they had endured, Paul emerged as the clear leader of the group. The sound of surf and the soundings confirmed they were close to land, so the next few hours would be physically demanding for everyone, especially the crew. Paul spoke with divine authority to reassure each person he or she would survive the grounding. Because most of the people aboard had not eaten in the past several days, Paul led them in a meal (27:33–36). He used the opportunity to thank God for their continued safety.[604]

Everyone followed Paul's lead. After a really good meal, they got to work. They wouldn't need the wheat anymore. They used it as a ballast during the storm but as they neared land, they knew they wouldn't need it, so they threw that overboard.

The Fortification of the Lord

After saving everyone on board and securing the ships, all looked way better than could be expected. Suddenly, the ship got stuck on the reef and the strong waters ripped the stern to pieces. Julius, the centurion heard of the soldiers' plan to kill all the prisoners. Julius might at this time have become a believer, and he valiantly saves everyone on board.

> **Acts 27:39-44** | Now when it was day, they did not recognize the land, but they noticed a bay with a beach, on which they planned if possible to run the ship ashore. **40** So they cast off the anchors and left them in the sea, at the same time loosening the ropes that tied the rudders. Then hoisting the foresail to the wind they made for the beach. **41** But striking a reef, they ran the vessel aground. The bow stuck and remained immovable, and the stern was being broken up by the surf. **42** The soldiers' plan was to kill the prisoners, lest any should swim away and escape. **43** But the centurion, wishing to save Paul, kept them from carrying out their plan. He ordered those who could swim to jump overboard first and make for the land, **44** and the rest on planks or on pieces of the ship. And so it was that all were brought safely to land.

Those who could swim made their way to the land, and those who couldn't were afforded planks and pieces of the ship that was now torn

---

[604] Charles R. Swindoll, *Acts*, Swindoll's Living Insights New Testament Commentary (Carol Stream, IL: Tyndale House Publishers, Inc., 2016), 502.

and unsailable. Regardless of the shipwreck, God was moving his plan to bring the gospel to Rome. God was moving the gospel around the world, so that this shipwreck has an impact on us here today for the glory of God.

Whatever you are going through, as a child of God, the Lord is using it for his magnificent purposes in Christ. Your life is crowning Christ as King of kings. You are in covenant with God, and for better or worse, you are bringing glory to God. Through obedient suffering or suffering by chastening, you are going to bring glory to God as a child of God. Your shipwrecks are moving toward the enthronement of Jesus Christ over the cosmos.

Conclusion

What do we learn from this story? As my dear wife says, "Boring is good." We enjoy life when it's peaceful and calm. But often we have no control over the intense trials we are called to walk through. God promises his children that he will walk with us through the fire and through the flood. Indeed, he will carry us!

When 276 people boarded the grain ship to leave Fair Havens, they expected to sail no more than 40 miles down the coast of Crete to Phoenix, a more suitable harbor for spending the winter. But, as often happens, nature turned their simple plan into a terrifying ordeal. A half-day jaunt became two weeks at sea, forcing them to fight for survival through a long series of life-threatening events. As their situation worsened, each leader aboard grew silent and faded from the narrative, leaving Paul as the standout leader. While the crew threw out anchors to regain control of the ship, Paul cast the spiritual anchor of faith in God's presence and plan to help the people cling to hope.[605]

When I was in Israel, I had the privilege of sailing on a boat over the Sea of Galilee. I'm told that waves there can get up to 20 feet high and overtake the ships during certain seasons. Once a storm came and almost swallowed the boat with the disciples. Though they were alone in the boat, someone was with them in the storm. They could see through the mist of the storm and the terror of the waves that Jesus was there. Peter said, "Lord, if it's you, bid me to walk on the water with you." He did that. People are sometimes down on Peter, but he was the only one who had the faith to even walk on water in the entire Bible.

---

[605] Ibid., 503.

Jesus says, "Peace! Be still!" And the wind and waves obeyed him. Can you imagine Peter and Jesus going back to the boat after Peter had fallen under the water? I can imagine them walking arm and arm on the water. Dear saint, God says to you in your storm: "Be still and know that I am God."

Whatever way the storm is blowing, God knows it has a certain outcome. It's like the Mississippi River. Ask any school aged child, "Which way does the Mississippi River flow?" He will say, "From north to south." If you have flown over the Mississippi, there are times and places where the Mississippi River will flow north. There are times and places where the Mississippi River will flow due west, but it ultimately and finally flows south. This is what we learn from Paul—that the elective purpose of God in Christ Jesus may seem to be frustrated, turned, and twisted, but it is God's purpose of the ages that the reign and kingdom shall belong to his dear Son, King of kings and Lord of lords. Whatever is happening in your life, it is leading to the enthronement of Jesus over all creation.[606] Hallelujah!

---

[606] W.A. Criswell, "The Eternal Purpose of God," sermon, First Baptist Church of Dallas, Texas, September 27, 1970.

45 | ACTS 28:1-16
MINISTRY ON CASTAWAY ISLAND

It happened that the father of Publius lay sick with fever and dysentery. And Paul visited him and prayed, and putting his hands on him, healed him. And when this had taken place, the rest of the people on the island who had diseases also came and were cured.

ACTS 28:8-9

Trauma and difficulty can be paralyzing. In our story, Paul is shipwrecked and snake-bitten, but instead of becoming paralyzed, he receives the healing and the presence of the Lord and turns his shipwrecks and snakebites into ministry.

In 1967, seventeen-year-old Joni Eareckson Tada took a dive that would change her life. One afternoon, she headed out for a dip in the Chesapeake Bay with her sister. Spying a wooden raft anchored nearby, Joni took a headlong dive from the raft into very shallow water. That moment changed the rest of her life. She became a quadriplegic, destined to spend the remainder of her days in a wheelchair, without any feeling in her hands or legs. It was an emotional blow that nearly drove her to suicide. But Joni couldn't hold a razor or push pills, so she thought of ways to end her life mentally, emotionally, spiritually.

Even in that dark season of Joni's life, a glimmer of hope still shone. She knew Jesus Christ as her personal Savior, and the promises of his word spoke to her suffering heart. She remembered 1 Thessalonians 5:18, which says, "In everything give thanks," and she resolved to be thankful. At first, she could only think of little things. But over time her perspective widened, and she identified bigger blessings. As her faith grew, her life was transformed, and she began to embrace it.

Armed with moral support and a daily dependence on God, Joni began the complicated and physically exhausting process of learning how to function in a wheelchair without the use of her hands or feet.

Joni didn't just learn how to function—she learned how to thrive. During her two years in rehabilitation, she spent long hours learning how to paint with a brush between her teeth. More than that, Joni learned that God can turn a mess into a ministry. She's learned to share her story internationally and inspire others. God turned her paralysis into a praise! God can turn your trauma into a triumph. That's what we are going to learn today.

Paul and the crew of criminals, businessmen and maybe even a few tourists are put into a very dangerous situation. They are sailing the Mediterranean when the winds and waves are dangerous. The Fall-Winter season has arrived, and the capitan is insistent on sailing when Paul voiced that it was not a good idea at all. The results: they lose their entire cargo of merchandise and goods, they lose the ship, and they almost lose their lives. They crash by the Island of Malta. They are now castaways on an unfamiliar island. Does anyone even live on this island?

Paul has his own "Castaway Island" that he's on. His ship has been torn to pieces, so he and the other passengers find themselves ashore on the Island of Malta.

After a long ordeal in Caesarea and this two-week crisis at sea, Paul undoubtedly enjoyed this three-month rest on the Island of Malta before pushing on to Rome. But more than his personal rest and health would be affected in Malta—God would bear witness through the apostle by healing many on the island. Times of trauma in our lives can also bring times of great healing: physical, mental, and emotional healing. Trauma and difficulty can form us for the better and open us to the pain others are going through as well. [607]

---

[607] Swindoll, *Acts*, 506.

We all have invented ways to cover our trauma and put a band aid on it. God doesn't just want you to ignore your pain or cover it. He wants to heal you, Remember the words of wise Solomon.

> *Ecclesiastes 3:1, 3* | There is an appointed time for everything. And there is a time for every event under heaven... a time to heal.

I find it strange that in our modern, "enlightened" era, when medicine has advanced light-years beyond the knowledge of Luke and Hippocrates, we have so little room in our theology for rest or the biblical concept of "time to heal." We want people to "get over it." If you have spent much time trying to recover from an ailment that cannot be explained by an X-ray, if you have been trapped in the dregs of depression, if you have grieved deeply the loss of a loved one and you can't seem to recover, you've undoubtedly heard from someone "Snap out of it!" or "Get with it!" Instead, we need to say: run to the Lord. Give the Lord time to heal you. It's going to take time, but God can and will do it.

When that healing comes, it blossoms into ministry. Paul's shipwreck turns into a time of deep and powerful ministry. In this passage we discover the secret to satisfying ministry for God. Paul gets stranded on an island, gets bit by a viper, and after he is healed by the Lord, he begins a healing ministry himself. Have you ever thought that the most painful part of your life might turn into your greatest ministry to others?

> Key Thought: Trust the Lord in your most painful moments. God knows what he's doing. He's allowing you to experience his deepest healing so that you can minister that same healing to others.

THE MESS OF MINISTRY (28:1-6)

Trials can be very difficult, but we must realize God is doing something in the mess. God's goal is not for you to have a perfect marriage or an uninterrupted life. His plan for you is to be conformed to Jesus Christ in humility, like a humble child. But in being conformed to Jesus, it may surprise you that the Lord wants you to minister to others out of the things you have learned from your trials and suffering. We see the pattern in 2 Corinthians 1.

> *2 Corinthians 1:3-4* | Blessed be the God and Father of our Lord Jesus Christ, the Father of mercies and God of all comfort, [4] who comforts

us in all our affliction, so that we may be able to comfort those who are in any affliction, with the comfort with which we ourselves are comforted by God.

How did Paul's healing ministry begin? It began with the kind gestures of the islanders.

The Kindness

The People's Kindness. The people of Malta at this time were regarded as barbarians, but that's likely because of the unknown. Sometimes we inflate our fears of the unknown, and this was an unknown people group. But Paul and the rest of the passengers were glad to find out that people of Malta are quite friendly.

> **Acts 28:1-2** | After we were brought safely through, we then learned that the island was called Malta. ² The native people showed us unusual kindness, for they kindled a fire and welcomed us all, because it had begun to rain and was cold.

I love the observation of the islanders: they showed "unusual kindness" to Paul, the sailors, and washed-up passengers. God had brought them to the Isle of Malta (which means "refuge"), where the native people welcomed all 276 shivering passengers and did their best to make them comfortable.[608] They kindled a nice fire was an incredible blessing since it was so rainy and cold. Winter had arrived, and though the island didn't have all the amenities of the mainland, Paul was able to roam freely, no longer confined to a soldier or a jail cell.

Paul's Kindness. Paul showed kindness to his hosts and gathered sticks for the fire. Wood needed to be added continually to the bonfire to keep it from going out. It is a measure of Paul's character that he humbly stooped to perform such a menial task. Humility is essential to true leadership.[609]

It reminds me of the story of a very special coach driver at Moody Bible Institute in Northfield, Massachusetts. One rainy day, a man accompanied by two women arrived at Northfield, hoping to enroll his daughter in D.L. Moody's Bible Institute. The three needed help in getting their luggage from the railway depot to the hotel, so the visitor "drafted" a rather common-looking man with a horse and wagon,

---

[608] Wiersbe, *The Bible Exposition Commentary*, vol. 1, 510.
[609] MacArthur, *Acts*, vol. 2, 361.

assuming he was a local cabby. The "cabby" said he was waiting for students, but the visitor ordered him to take them to the hotel. The visitor was shocked when the "cabby" did not charge him and was even more shocked to discover that the "cabby" was D.L. Moody himself! Moody was a leader because he knew how to be a servant.[610]

Paul as a servant leader wants to be the first to be aware of people's needs and to make himself available. But something terrible happens. We sometimes jokingly say "no good deed goes unpunished." It seems like Paul experiences this when he grabs a stick that is not a stick at all.

The Creature

Suddenly the narrative changes. In bundling sticks for the fire, Paul is attacked by a viper. His good efforts are rewarded with a viper bite. As he was gathering the bundles of sticks, one of the sticks was alive and attacked him! It looks like the end of the story, but it's really just the beginning.

> **Acts 28:3-5** | When Paul had gathered a bundle of sticks and put them on the fire, a viper came out because of the heat and fastened on his hand. **4** When the native people saw the creature hanging from his hand, they said to one another, "No doubt this man is a murderer. Though he has escaped from the sea, Justice has not allowed him to live." **5** He, however, shook off the creature into the fire and suffered no harm.

The people at that time were very superstitious. They assumed that if something bad happened to a person, it was the reward for bad behavior. They conclude in their superstition that Paul was a murderer. As believers, we should never be assuming or superstitious. Often horrible things can happen to God's people. God's plan is not our comfort but our conformity to Jesus Christ. It can often be confusing because we are serving the Lord, and we know God promises to protect us. But God will often allow his saints to be tested so they can grow in their faith. Think of Job and Joseph.

It's important to recognize both aspects of suffering. On a personal level, God promises to bring chastening to us if our lives are out of order. But often suffering is not a result of chastening, but God wants to keep us humble and moldable. Remember Paul who had asked for the

---

[610] Wiersbe, *The Bible Exposition Commentary*, vol. 1, 510.

thorn in his flesh to be removed, all the while the messenger of Satan who was pummeling him. Remember what Jesus said?

> *2 Corinthians 12:9* | My grace is sufficient for you, for my power is made perfect in weakness.

Paul's response was, "Now that I know his power is perfected when I am weak, I will glory in all my weaknesses, in insults, in persecutions and tribulations."

What is that which makes you weak in your life? Paul had a snake that could have hurt him badly. Do you see how God takes all circumstances in our lives and makes them beautiful in his time (Ecc 3:11)? What is it that is humbling you right now? Can you trust the Lord to use your weakness for his kingdom?

The Confusion

The viper's venom had no effect on Paul, and this was quite a surprise to the islanders of Malta. At first, they thought he was a murderer, but now that he seems immune from death, their view of Paul became hyperbolic.

> **Acts 28:6** | They were waiting for him to swell up or suddenly fall down dead. But when they had waited a long time and saw no misfortune come to him, they changed their minds and said that he was a god.

The apostle's calmness was conspicuous; most people bitten by poisonous snake's panic. But Paul had absolute faith in God's repeated promises that he would see Rome (Acts 23:11; 27:24). Therefore, he knew he would not die on Malta. As always in Acts, God used this miracle to authenticate is message and his messenger.[611]

The people seeing the apostle is immune from a poisonous snake bite wrongly conclude that Paul is a god. Readers of Acts should have no doubt that Paul denies personal divine power or identity.[612] By now the apostle had seen a lot and had been worshiped as a god before (14:11). Luke doesn't conclude the story to show Paul's response. By now his readers could guess. Instead, he transitions to another incident the apostle used for evangelism.[613]

---

[611] MacArthur, *Acts*, vol. 2, 362.
[612] Hamilton, *John–Acts*, 576.
[613] Swindoll, *Acts*, 507.

Without God, you can see the fickleness of the people. Suffering does not mean we are the scum of the earth, abandoned by God. Neither does a lack of suffering or even a miracle mean that we are good or that we are gods. Suffering and blessing are merely tools God uses to conform us to Christ.

One more application is vital. In our service to Jesus, we may be hated at one moment and heralded at another moment. We must never, never get our identity from people's opinion of us. There are haters and flatterers, but the only opinion that matters is the opinion of the Lord. God alone knows who we are in our heart. We as sincere believers constantly walk in the face of God with prayers like David in Psalm 139.

> *Psalm 139:23-24* | Search me, O God, and know my heart! Try me and know my thoughts! ²⁴ And see if there be any grievous way in me, and lead me in the way everlasting!

We need a focus like Paul who wasn't distracted by shipwrecks and snakebites. He wanted to show the mercy of God to these dear people of Malta.

THE MIRACLES OF MINISTRY (28:7-10)

With Paul's new fame, he was introduced to the leading people of the island. He turns the mess of shipwrecks and snakebites into a new ministry of miracles! It begins with the wonderful hospitality of the islanders.

The Hospitality

Whatever the people's reaction, Paul didn't waste his opportunity. Their honoring of Paul shows God's work in their hearts. They have a divine openness to the gospel and seem to accept the good news of Jesus' love.

> **Acts 28:7** | Now in the neighborhood of that place were lands belonging to the chief man of the island, named Publius, who received us and entertained us hospitably for three days.

Publius, the Roman governor of the island, spoke with the apostle for three days, and we can imagine what they talked about. Paul surely explained how we all have been created by the one living God of heaven and earth, and how God sent his Son to die for our sins. Publius showed Paul sweet hospitality, giving him food and drink and a soft place to rest his head. Publius had his family with him as governor of the island, and we find out that this also included his own father, perhaps quite elderly.

The Healings

It wasn't long that the sweet hospitality they were enjoying turned sad, and they had a shadow cast upon them. Publius' father became terribly ill.

> **Acts 28:8** | It happened that the father of Publius lay sick with fever and dysentery. And Paul visited him and prayed, and putting his hands on him, healed him.

Dysentery is the leading cause of death in the developing world especially among the very young and very old. Publius' father gets quite ill. What was the sickness? It is often thought to have been a local affliction caused by contamination of goat's milk (known widely as 'Malta fever'). It's a horrible disease—the symptoms include dysentery, profuse sweating and joint and muscle pain, and there is no cure. It almost always lasts for a lifetime.

God now affirms Paul's message and office as an apostle through the healing of Publius' father. Healing came about through *prayer* and the laying on of hands.

The Hand of God

What happens next? The prominence of the person healed led to much publicity, and God moved mightily. We may assume that Paul and the other Christians in the group preached the good news.[614]

> **Acts 28:9** | And when this had taken place, the rest of the people on the island who had diseases also came and were cured.

Luke seems to describe Paul's stay in Malta as a time of extraordinary blessing and a welcome change from the two years of incarceration that he had previously known, not to mention what lay ahead of him upon arrival in Rome. It was a time of revival that must have reminded the apostle to some degree of previous days of missionary labor. God drew near and blessed his ministry during a deeply difficult time. Despite the shipwreck and the fact that Paul was still a prisoner, God refreshed Paul's spirit, preparing him for what lay ahead in Rome.

---

[614] Gempf, "Acts," in *New Bible Commentary*, 1106.

The three months in Malta were a welcome hiatus in what had otherwise been a time of enormous frustration.

The Honor

It is almost an incidental point, but we are told that such was the honor in which Paul and his companions (Luke and Aristarchus) were held that when it came time to leave the island, the weather more favorable for journeying west, the islanders loaded the ship with whatever was needed. [615]

> **Acts 28:10** | They also honored us greatly, and when we were about to sail, they put on board whatever we needed.

Once more, the Lord provided for all that was needed to ensure that Paul was brought safely to Rome. By the grace of God, a shipwreck turns into a three-month time of fruitful ministry on the island of Malta.

God will provide for you in your time of difficulty. You are not abandoned! I wonder what do you expect when life goes wrong? Do you trust God wants to bless you through humbling times?

THE MEANING OF MINISTRY (28:11-16)

If God wanted Paul in Rome to preach the gospel, why did he have to wait and wander? Why the imprisonment, the snakebite, the shipwreck? What about you? What is the meaning of your trials, your hurts, your suffering, and your tribulation?

Waiting Matures Us

Paul had waited two years in a Caesarean prison. God had told him he would preach in Rome, but instead what he experienced was waiting, waiting, and more waiting. When he finally makes his way to Rome there is a shipwreck!

> **Acts 28:11** | After three months we set sail in a ship that had wintered in the island, a ship of Alexandria, with the twin gods as a figurehead.

Paul finally set sail to Rome! Whether all 276 people boarded the Alexandrian ship, or just Julius and his guard and prisoners, we do not know. Luke notes that the ship that takes them from Malta sports on

---

[615] Thomas, *Acts*, 724.

its "figurehead" the twin gods Castor and Pollux, Greek gods believed to protect sailing ships, provide good winds, and help shipwrecked sailors.[616]

The truth is, Paul didn't need some mystical superstition. Christians ought never to need a rabbit's foot or be afraid to stay on the 13th floor. We have the presence of the Lord. Why would we lower ourselves to serve an image or need a trinket? God is transcendent, and he is with us wherever we go.

Nonetheless, the transcendent God had Paul wait before he was finally on his way to Rome. Why the waiting? I think I've often had the wrong idea of waiting. I've had great ambitions for the kingdom of the Lord, but I've found that God does a lot of his greatest work during the waiting times. Some of the most important times of growing occur during the times we are suffering, hurting, or waiting for that one thing we've been working toward.

I think of Moses who fled from Egypt after slaying an Egyptian and found himself tending sheep from age 40 to 80. It wasn't until he was 80 years old that he heard the voice of the Lord from the burning bush. As an octogenarian, he got his first placement in ministry! It was the waiting time that prepared him. It was during the times of confusion and uncertainty that he must have humbled himself and learned how to depend on the Lord.

In the same way we could talk about Joseph who was betrayed by his brothers and was trapped in a pit, and sold to Potiphar, then put in prison and finally after a lot of long an painful waiting, he was exalted to become Prime Minister of Egypt.

Don't overburden yourself with the working out of your ambitions. Let the Lord direct your steps. The Lord told us not to be anxious, but to seek him first.

> Matthew 6:33 | But seek first the kingdom of God and his righteousness, and all these things will be added to you.

Dear saint, trust the Lord for what he has for you in your time of suffering. He's got you. You are predestined to be conformed to the image of Jesus Christ. Through your humbling circumstances, God wants you to reach your highest potential: to be like Jesus! Be like Jesus and invest your life in others. That's your highest potential.

---

[616] Hamilton, *John–Acts*, 577–578.

God Uses Wandering

Now we have the record of Paul's journey from port to port. It seems arbitrary that a "south wind sprang up" and brought them to a specific port where there was a group of believers. Even "wandering" is under the control of God.

> **Acts 28:12-15** | Putting in at Syracuse, we stayed there for three days. ¹³ And from there we made a circuit and arrived at Rhegium. And after one day a south wind sprang up, and on the second day we came to Puteoli. ¹⁴ There we found brothers and were invited to stay with them for seven days. And so we came to Rome. ¹⁵ And the brothers there, when they heard about us, came as far as the Forum of Appius and Three Taverns to meet us. On seeing them, Paul thanked God and took courage.

There were various ports in Rome, but this one was accessible to a precious group of believers that encouraged Paul. When it says "brothers," as in many languages, it often means "brothers and sisters" as in this context. This was Paul's forever family. Though Paul was there to evangelize, he took courage the church already established at Rome.

What are the south winds in your life that you might be worried about? Perhaps you are suffering an accident or a tragedy. God's in control. Perhaps it's a new job, a new child, or a hard patch in your marriage. God knows and is guiding you. It feels like "wandering," but it's under God's control. He's leading you to greater humility, vulnerability and richer fellowship. For Paul, that wandering brought him to a time of encouragement and fellowship in his life that he wouldn't have had otherwise. The point is, there is no real "wandering" in the Christian life. Paul says, "all things work after the counsel of his own will" (Eph 1:11). King Solomon, many years before, said something similar.

> *Proverbs 16:9* | Man plans his ways, but the Lord directs his steps.

God Uses Witnessing

Finally, Paul arrives in Rome! Instead of cities full of Gentiles seeking the Lord, the Lord has another plan for Paul. He wants him in Rome to speak to what Paul will refer to as "Caesar's household."

> **Acts 28:16** | And when we came into Rome, Paul was allowed to stay by himself, with the soldier who guarded him.

Paul was under house arrest in Rome, and he shared his testimony of Jesus "throughout the whole imperial guard" (Phil 1:13). The imperial guard, known as the Praetorians, were the elite of the Roman army and were paid double a normal soldier's wage for their service. There were 10,000 specifically to guard the emperor of Rome. Paul's testimony spread throughout the Praetorian Guard, and even saints deep in "Caesar's household," i.e., those in and about the emperor's palace and among his family (Phil 4:22).

Paul would be held under house arrest for another two years (28:30) with some of the imperial guard, very elite. Paul was a Roman citizen and received great treatment. Non-Roman citizens, even of high status, were often harshly treated. In contrast, house arrest was typically more comfortable for the prisoner, who was usually physically chained to a guard but could still host visitors.

Paul is twice referred to as having been "bound in chains" (Acts 28:20; Eph 6:20). The *chains* referred to were a short length of chain by which the wrist of a prisoner was bound to the wrist of a soldier who was guarding him, so that escape was impossible, both for Paul, *and* the guard! So who was the real prisoner? This was amazing for Paul. It's not like the soldier could shut the door in Paul's face!

Conclusion

How we need to accept God's sovereign plan for our lives. Difficult things happen. We are called on to suffer. We get seemingly sidetracked from our goals and hopes and dreams, waiting for what feels like forever. We need to realize that our times of greatest difficulty and suffering will create the platform for our greatest blessing.

46 | ACTS 28:17-31
WORTH IT ALL

He lived there [in Rome] two whole years at his own expense, and welcomed all who came to him, proclaiming the kingdom of God and teaching about the Lord Jesus Christ with all boldness and without hindrance.
ACTS 28:30-31

Would you say that you are truly happy in your walk with God at this moment in your life? God wants to give you real joy in your life, but there is a price to pay for it, and it is so incredibly worth it! This is the last message in the book of Acts, and we see Paul having lost everything, but gaining Christ, and it is worth it all. Whatever loss you incur to follow Christ, it is worth it. We see this lived out in our story from Paul's life. The book of Acts ends with Paul chained to a Roman soldier for two years preaching the kingdom of God. Paul was single minded. He had one hope and one happiness: Jesus Christ.

All of us know what it is like to give up in order to gain. Athletes give up free time and foods they like to gain strength and speed to play football. Young couples give up sleep, extra income, freedoms in order to gain children. Students give up hang-out time in order to gain the required grade on the test. Fathers give up unwind time in order to gain investment into their children. Many give up cookies and desserts in order to gain weight loss. Christians give up day off options in order to gain opportunities to serve Christ. As faithful stewards, we all lose a generous portion of our income in order to invest in heavenly riches. We are called to lose our lives for Christ. We hear this in Jesus' own words.

> Matthew 10:39 | Whoever finds his life will lose it, and whoever loses his life for my sake will find it.

Jesus also says that knowing him is like finding a buried treasure in a plot of land. You would sell everything just to buy that land.

> Matthew 13:44 | The kingdom of heaven is like treasure hidden in a field, which a man found and covered up. Then in his joy he goes and sells all that he has and buys that field.

What am I saying? If you lose everything in pursuit of knowing Christ. It's worth it all. Paul says as much to the Philippians.

> Philippians 3:8, KJV | Yea doubtless, and I count all things but loss for the excellency of the knowledge of Christ Jesus my Lord: for whom I have suffered the loss of all things, and do count them but dung, that I may win Christ.

Paul finds himself in a very uncomfortable situation of great loss. It looks like he lost his church planting ministry. He lost his earthly comfort and freedom and is now chained to a Roman soldier.

Perhaps you find yourself suffering loss today. You've lost a spouse or a child or both. And you never dreamed life would be this way. You're not where you thought you'd be in your life or your walk with Jesus Christ. Perhaps you have failed too often in marriage or singleness. You feel like a failure.

I want to help you see that God is working to make you his glorious workmanship and masterpiece (Eph 2:10). He is the potter, and you are the clay. You are God's child, and every loss you experience is an invitation to depend totally on Christ. Your total surrender to him means your total happiness and a harvest for the kingdom.

> Key Thought: Whatever you have to lose to know Christ better is worth it all.

Paul lives this out in this conclusion to the book of Acts. You might wonder, "If I'm stuck in a place of loss, how do I get to a place where I count all as loss and find my contentment in Christ? How can I become content in Christ in all circumstances?" There is one answer: focus on hope that is everlasting.

The temporal things will crumble. We must focus on what is eternal. Hebrews tells us that God is going to shake the heavens and the earth, so that that which cannot be shaken may remain (Heb 12:26-27). The reason we get stuck is because of the nearsightedness and blindness that a focus on earthly things creates. Your hurt, your pain, your injustice needs to be left behind through a focus on eternal things. Circumstances are not guaranteed. The life of anyone around you is not guaranteed. Your health is not guaranteed. Your earthly financial security is not guaranteed. Worship God, not the demon god of mammon. You can't worship both. You cannot serve two masters (*cf* Mt 6:24).

Paul's focus was cosmic, not myopic. How do we focus our affections on things above (Col 3:1-3)? Paul focused first on "the hope of Israel"—Jesus the Messiah had come! He had conquered death and risen from the dead for the redemption of his people.

THE HOPE OF ISRAEL (28:17-23)

It looks like everything is crashing down for Paul, but for Paul of course the story was only just beginning. Everything he had done in his life was a preparation for this moment ... when he was going to stand before Caesar.[617] He's going to preach what he calls "the hope of Israel." God's people through the ages have had a hope, that Messiah would come. When Jesus comes, he dies, and then he rises again. Paul preached his glorious resurrection.

It was this very preaching of Jesus as the resurrected King that irritated the Jewish authorities.[618] The kingdom of Messiah, the hope of Israel, had finally arrived.

Jesus is Presented

Paul takes three days to get settled into a rented lodging, and then calls the local leaders of the Jews to him. He cannot make it to them, so he calls them to come to him where he is under house arrest by the Romans, waiting to appear before Caesar who is Nero at the time.

> **Acts 28:17-20** | After three days he called together the local leaders of the Jews, and when they had gathered, he said to them,

---

[617] Wright, *Acts for Everyone, Part 2*. 239.
[618] MacArthur, *Acts*, vol. 2, 370.

"Brothers, though I had done nothing against our people or the customs of our fathers, yet I was delivered as a prisoner from Jerusalem into the hands of the Romans. [18] When they had examined me, they wished to set me at liberty, because there was no reason for the death penalty in my case. [19] But because the Jews objected, I was compelled to appeal to Caesar—though I had no charge to bring against my nation. [20] For this reason, therefore, I have asked to see you and speak with you, since it is because of the hope of Israel that I am wearing this chain."

The Jews had several plots against Paul's life, so he had to appeal to Caesar, or else he would have already been set free. It worked out for the best since Paul was able to declare the true reason he was imprisoned: for "the hope of Israel" he says that he has to be shackled in chains.

Jesus is Pondered

This group of Jews from Rome had not yet heard about Jesus, and so they are curious.

Acts 28:21-22 | And they said to him, "We have received no letters from Judea about you, and none of the brothers coming here has reported or spoken any evil about you. [22] But we desire to hear from you what your views are, for with regard to this sect we know that everywhere it is spoken against."

It's a wonderful invitation to preach the gospel when these Jews had already heard bad things about "this sect" of believers. By this time, they had heard that it is "everywhere spoken against," but they didn't know why. They desired to hear Paul out. What a great opportunity for Paul to go "to the Jew first," and then to the Gentiles.

Jesus is Preached

Paul upholds Jesus as the fulfillment of all of the Scriptures. We read in verse 23.

Acts 28:23 | When they had appointed a day for him, they came to him at his lodging in greater numbers. From morning till evening he expounded to them, testifying to the kingdom of God and trying to convince them about Jesus both from the Law of Moses and from the Prophets.

Jesus' teaching on the road to Emmaus (Luke 24), profoundly influenced and shaped all of the apostles in Acts, and this is the driving focus to the end of the narrative.[619] Paul was under attack for simply being a loyal, Jew who is faithful to the Messiah. He was following the hope of Abraham, the hope of all Israel, from Adam until now. The Seed of the woman would be born as a Jew, under the law. This was Israel's hope. Paul showed how Christ is seen in the great messianic prophecies found in Isaiah, the Psalms, and elsewhere. He confronted them with the need for personally accepting Jesus as Messiah and personal Savior and thus to enter the kingdom of God.[620]

Israel's hope, Jesus, would be born of a "virgin" (Isa 7:14), born in Bethlehem (Mic 5:2). He would be the true word of God, a prophet greater than Moses (Deut 18:15). The Messiah would be rejected by his people, betrayed by his own (Psa 41:9), and "pierced for our transgressions" (Isa 53:5). He himself says, "They have pierced my hands and feet" (Psa 22:16). And then according to the Scriptures, he would rise again on the third day (Hos 6:2). These are just a few of the prophecies Paul would have considered.

Paul took an entire day "from morning till evening" telling them about Jesus of Nazareth, God in human flesh, testifying that Jesus is the King over the kingdom of God. Every knee must bow to him. Every tongue must confess. The hope is for Messiah to come into the world and redeem a people, so that he would take our sin upon himself, and he would give us his righteousness (2 Cor 5:21).

As Messiah, Jesus is not only Savior of the world, but he is the Judge of all the earth. If you don't bow to him now, you will be judged for all your sins on the Last Day. Each believer is called to evangelize and present the gospel to sinners. The response is not our responsibility. We are called to present the hope of salvation to all people. Jesus said,

John 12:32 | When I am lifted up from the earth, will draw all people to myself.

Are you in the word, hiding the Scriptures in your heart, so that when the time comes, you can present the gospel to your loved ones, friends, and neighbors?

---

[619] Hamilton, *Acts*, 579.
[620] J. Phillips, *Exploring Acts*, Ac 28:23.

THE HOPE OF SALVATION (28:24-29)

Our hope for salvation is Jesus alone. What we find here is that the hope of salvation is the kingdom of a certain king. He is the King of all kings and Lord of all lords. Paul turns his prison cell into an evangelism center and testifies to "the kingdom of God" where Jesus is king.

The Peril of Rejecting Christ

Paul did not sugarcoat salvation. Jesus alone is King of kings. When many of the others disbelieved, Paul warned them. There are eternal consequences. Some of Paul's hearers were gloriously convinced and converted, while others rejected the Messiah.

> **Acts 28:24-27** | And some were convinced by what he said, but others disbelieved. **25** And disagreeing among themselves, they departed after Paul had made one statement: "The Holy Spirit was right in saying to your fathers through Isaiah the prophet: **26** "'Go to this people, and say, "You will indeed hear but never understand, and you will indeed see but never perceive." **27** For this people's heart has grown dull, and with their ears they can barely hear, and their eyes they have closed; lest they should see with their eyes and hear with their ears and understand with their heart and turn, and I would heal them.'

Paul quoted from Isaiah 6:9–10 to warn them of judgment, and to again call for their repentance so that they would hear and understand with their heart, and turn, and the Lord says, "I would heal them." Yet there were those there who didn't want the Messiah's healing.

> *John 1:11* | He came to his own, and his own people did not receive him.

For those Jews who rejected Paul, giving this passage to them is a moment of final judicial warning. That passage was also quoted by the Lord Jesus Christ as a rebuke of Israel's hardhearted rejection of the gospel (*cf* Mt 13:14–15; Jn 12:39–40). Israel's willful act of rejection was sovereignly confirmed by God; because of continual unbelief, she became unable to believe (*cf* Jn 12:37, 39–40).[621]

This is a divine judgment upon them because they hardened their hearts to the word of God. God's word brings the diagnosis of sin, which

---

[621] MacArthur, *Acts*, vol. 2,F.374–375.

is painful to hear and accept, but at the same time it wounds in order to heal. Once a person deliberately refuses the word, there comes a point when he is deprived of the capacity to receive it. It is a stern warning to those who trifle with the gospel.[622]

The point is, if you feel a tenderness to God's word, don't put it off. Respond immediately and wholeheartedly no matter what the cost. You are not guaranteed a second chance. God may give you over to a hard heart. Ponder the claims of Christ and respond in tenderness. Don't delay!

The Prize of Receiving Christ

Paul now attempts to make the Jews jealous. He says that the Gentiles will receive what they have rejected.

> **Acts 28:28-29** | Therefore let it be known to you that this salvation of God has been sent to the Gentiles; they will listen." [29] (NKJV) And when he had said these words, the Jews departed and had a great dispute among themselves.

The Jews disputed over this great gift that was given to them. Paul gives more understanding in Romans as to what the Jews rejection of the gospel means. In Romans 11, he says that the Gentiles are called to salvation in order to make the Jews jealous.

> Romans 11:11-12 | Through their trespass salvation has come to the Gentiles, so as to make Israel jealous. [12] Now if their trespass means riches for the world, and if their failure means riches for the Gentiles, how much more will their full inclusion mean!

Though the Jews rejected Christ, God's desire for them was for them to be saved (Rom 11:26). Paul's desire them to be saved so much that he was willing to be accursed, damned to hell.

> Romans 9:1-3 | I am speaking the truth in Christ—I am not lying; my conscience bears me witness in the Holy Spirit— [2] that I have great sorrow and unceasing anguish in my heart. [3] For I could wish that I myself were accursed and cut off from Christ for the sake of my brothers, my kinsmen according to the flesh.

The hope of salvation for Israel and the Gentiles is Jesus Christ alone. Now is not a time for dispute or argumentation. It is a time to

---

[622] Marshall, *Acts*, 445.

surrender to the kingdom of God that Paul preached where Jesus is King of kings. Yield your life to him today.

Christ is worth the loss of all things! Paul was teaching these things while he was without home and chained to a Roman soldier. What have you lost for Christ? Take heart! He has given you something of an infinite worth: salvation in Christ!

THE HOPE OF THE WORLD (28:30-31)

Regardless of the Jews disputing among themselves, this salvation and hope was not just for Israel, but for the whole world.

> *Galatians 3:6-9, NLT* | "Abraham believed God, and God counted him as righteous because of his faith." [7] The real children of Abraham, then, are those who put their faith in God. [8] What's more, the Scriptures looked forward to this time when God would make the Gentiles right in his sight because of their faith. God proclaimed this good news to Abraham long ago when he said, "All nations will be blessed through you." [9] So all who put their faith in Christ share the same blessing Abraham received because of his faith.

Israel's hope is your hope. And Paul tells us that we as believing Gentiles are "grafted in" to Israel (Rom 11:17).

> Now, if you have faith in Jesus, "then you are Abraham's offspring, heirs according to promise" (Gal 3:29).

When I was first saved, I thought, "If this is really true, then the whole world needs to know." I still believe that today. Paul believed it too. Wherever he was, even when he's incarcerated, he's preaching Jesus.

Paul is in his own rented home, which was his jail cell. He wasn't free to travel and plant churches, but he couldn't have known the worldwide impact him ministry would have from that moment until now. For now Paul had a new ministry.

A New Ministry

Paul' entire ministry was now confined to a rented room that served as his prison cell. The situation remained with Paul under house arrest but free to witness to anyone who came within earshot.

> **Acts 28:30** | He lived there two whole years at his own expense, and welcomed all who came to him.

Paul was chained to a soldier day and night, so he at least had one Roman soldier in his audience at all times. He was not at liberty to go where he wished, but he was at liberty to receive all who cared to come to him.

Why did Paul have to be confined? We ponder the mystery of God's plans and ways for us. God, through Isaiah, reminds us that he has all the cards. He knows how your rugged, discouraging pathway will lead you closer to Christ.

> *Isaiah 55:8-9* | My thoughts are not your thoughts, neither are your ways my ways, declares the Lord. ⁹ For as the heavens are higher than the earth, so are my ways higher than your ways and my thoughts than your thoughts.

We do not know all the reasons, though indeed we are indebted to Paul's imprisonment for his epistles to the Philippians, Ephesians, Colossians, and Philemon, not to mention 1 and 2nd Timothy and Titus. Paul's prolonged captivity is part of the Lord unsearchable ways. We can be sure, however, that the Lord of the harvest, who is in charge of the entire mission program of the church, makes no mistakes.[623]

An Old Message

Paul's message never changed. It wasn't just forgiveness of sins, although that was the foundation. What did Paul preach?

> **Acts 28:31a** | Proclaiming the kingdom of God and teaching about the Lord Jesus Christ.

Paul taught about Christ as King over our lives and over the world. That's the pathway to true joy. Be willing to lose everything for Christ. How sweet he is when he's all you have! Surrender to him. Walk with him. He's coming soon! Very soon the nature of this world will change with all things under the headship of Jesus Christ. Heaven and earth will become one. Our greatest joys on earth will seem like misery compared to the glorified joy that awaits us.

A Glorious Freedom

Paul's hired house in Rome became the headquarters of world evangelism. He could not go, but others could. People flocked to him.

---

[623] J. Phillips, *Exploring Acts*, Ac 28:30a.

Acts 28:31b | Teaching about the Lord Jesus Christ with all boldness and without hindrance.

Paul taught and led people to Christ, won many of the Roman soldiers who were guarding him (Phil 1:13–18), and led several within "Caesar's household" (Phil 4:22) to Christ. Do you see that the loss of everything means nothing to the surrendered Christian? You can be happy and fruitful right where you are.

And that is where Luke puts down his pen. He gives us this final glimpse of Paul, living victoriously despite his captivity in Rome. What better place could there be to end the inspired written history of the Christian church—not just looking back but looking ahead! [624]

PAUL'S HOPE AND OURS

Paul is in Rome for two whole years, and then he is set free for a time. During this time, it seems he meets Titus and establishes a church in Crete.

The Outpost of Paul's Hope

The outpost of Paul's hope was a jailcell of the worst kind. Sometime after the fire in Rome, Nero starts an awful persecution against Christians, and Paul is arrested for a final time, probably around the year 67. This time his situation was changed drastically. He did not live in a house but was chained in the dreaded Mamertine prison and treated like a convicted criminal (2 Tim 1:16; 2:9). According to church history, Peter and Paul were imprisoned at the same time at the Mamertine prison. It consists of two chambers, one above the other. Sallust describes the lower chamber, as a horrible dungeon, "repulsive and terrible on account of neglect, dampness, and smell."[625] It has now been turned into a church since the middle ages. The cells they were held in were made available for those who were V.I.P.s who were a threat to the state.[626]

The Mamertine Prison was nothing more than a glorified hole in the ground, yet it was the holding tank where Paul and Peter—as part

---

[624] J. Phillips, *Exploring Acts*, Ac 28:30b–31.

[625] Sallust. *Jugurthine War and Conspiracy of Catiline With an English Commentary, and Geographical and Historical Indexes*, "Chapter 55" (Cambridge, Massachusetts: Harvard University Press, 11841), 286.

[626] Maurice Hassett, "Mamertine Prison" in The Catholic Encyclopedia (New York: Robert Appleton Company, 1910), vol. 9, New Advent edition online.

of Nero's crackdown on Christians—spent the last days of their lives on earth. While there Paul wrote some of his most important letters, including the two to young Timothy. The conditions were deplorable. The author's feet were bound. The damp, cold musty air was barely breathable. The iron grate covering the lone entry allowed dust-filled light as well as rain and cold to pour in. And though Paul never complained about his inhumane conditions, the prison was the perfect setting to write to young Timothy about perseverance and endurance, since Paul was living it!

Look at Paul. He's truly suffering at the end. He's lost everything. Everything! Yet he has everything he needs in Christ. When he is weak, he's strong, and the power of Christ rests upon him.

Winter was coming, and he asked Timothy to bring him his cloak (2 Tim 4:13). But the saddest thing about this second imprisonment was his being forsaken by the believers in Rome (2 Tim 4:16–17). The great apostle to the Gentiles was abandoned by the very people he came to assist.[627] What could Paul do in that prison cell? He did what he'd always done. He preached and he wrote.

It reminds me of the story of John Bunyan. At age thirty, Bunyan started preaching. But, as any seasoned pastor knows, preaching is never easy. And, because Bunyan lacked governmental approval to preach, he was picked up by the police, hauled off to jail, and tossed into a prison cell for the disgraceful act of preaching without a license. The nerve!

Finally, after three months of confinement, he was brought before the local magistrate and offered a full pardon on one condition: "Stop preaching the gospel!" But that was something John Bunyan couldn't do. So back into the slammer he went—twelve more years of incarceration in the Bedford city jail. He waived his chance at freedom because, more than freedom, preaching was an even greater gift. No conditional pardon could satisfy the heart that must proclaim God's Word. But our God is never hemmed in by seemingly impenetrable walls. In fact, it was from that cell that Bunyan wrote The Pilgrim's Progress—next to the Bible the most widely read book in the world, serving as the No. 2 bestseller for centuries.

Paul had lost everything but chose to stay focused on his only joy: Christ! Paul didn't have a pity party but was joyful! He was the chief of

---

[627] Wiersbe, *The Bible Exposition Commentary*, vol. 1, 512.

sinners, and he had been given the gift of eternal life. Paul offered that gift to all, even from the hole in the ground, the Mamertine prison.

The Outcome of Paul's Hope

The outcome of Paul's hope was to be glorified in Christ. He left this life behind. He was sentenced to death by beheading under the reign of Nero. In Paul's last letter to Timothy, he speaks of his firm hope in Christ. He's sentenced to death but is unafraid.

> *2 Timothy 4:6-8* | The time of my departure has come. [7] I have fought the good fight, I have finished the race, I have kept the faith. [8] Henceforth there is laid up for me the crown of righteousness, which the Lord, the righteous judge, will award to me on that day, and not only to me but also to all who have loved his appearing.

Paul is said to have died in October of 67 A.D., the fourteenth year of Nero's reign (*cf* Jerome, Eusebius). Clement of Rome in his *First Epistle to the Corinthians*, 5:5–6, written around 96 A.D., almost thirty years after Paul's death says this of great apostle.

> By reason of jealousy and strife Paul by his example displayed the prize of patient endurance. After he had been imprisoned seven times, had been driven into exile, had been stoned, had preached in the East and in the West, he won the noble renown which was the reward of his faith, having taught righteousness unto the whole world and having reached the farthest reaches of the West; and when he had borne his testimony before the rulers, so he departed from the world and went unto the holy place, having been found a notable pattern of patient endurance.[628]

Jerome later says that Paul and Peter were martyred the same day, Peter through crucifixion and Paul through beheading.

> Paul, then, in the fourteenth year of Nero on the same day with Peter, was beheaded at Rome for Christ's sake and was buried in the Ostian way, the twenty-seventh year after our Lord's passion.[629]

Paul lost everything, even his head! Think about that. What a seemingly short ministry Paul had. Less than twenty-seven years. His secret

---

[628] Clement of Rome, *The First Epistle of Clement to the Corinthians*, 5:5–6 in Joseph Barber Lightfoot, *The Apostolic Fathers: A Revised Text with Introductions, Notes, Dissertations, and Translations* (New York: Macmillan, 1890), 274.

[629] Jerome, De Viris Illustribus (On Illustrious Men), 5. See also Eusebius, History of the Church, 2.25.

was his joy in Jesus Christ alone. He didn't put his joy in anything else. All else was dung to Paul. For Paul, losing everything was worth it all! Remember what he said to the Philippians? May this be our theme too!

Philippians 1:21 | For to me to live is Christ, and to die is gain.

Conclusion

During the gymnastics portion of the 1976 Olympics a Japanese athlete named Shun Fujimoto broke his leg during one of his floor routines, and he tried to hide it. As the competition turned out, the last day's performances on the rings would determine whether the championship went to the Japanese or the Russians.

Despite his leg being broken, the injured athlete mounted the rings for a final performance on the rings, swinging so high above the ground. The look of pride on his face was magnificent. But there was also obvious anguish as from ten feet above the ground he came hurtling to the floor for his dismount, landing on his broken leg. His fighting spirit made him invincible. With his goal firmly in mind, he refused to quit, no matter how severe the pain. He kept his balance, earning the best score of his life despite his broken leg. It was literally the best he'd ever done. He was willing to lose everything just to win a temporary Olympic medal. [630]

Paul lost everything, but he had one thing that changed the world: his love for Jesus Christ. What about you? Are you willing to be that vessel that God can use?

Where Acts 28 ends, you story begins. Don't let anything hold you back. Be willing to lose everything for Christ. Christ is the lamb who was slain, and he deserves the reward for his suffering. Lift him up! Lift him high. Proclaim his name, and he will draw all men to him. Whatever you have to lose for knowing Christ and making him know is worth it all!

---

[630] Paul Jones, "Olympics: How Japanese Gymnast Shun Fujimoto Hid His Broken Knee to Lead His Country to Gold" (London: Radio Times, August 8, 2016).

SELECTED BIBLIOGRAPHY

In order of appearance in the commentary

COMMENTARIES

Tom Wright, *Acts for Everyone, Parts 1 and 2* (London: Society for Promoting Christian Knowledge, 2008).

R. Kent Hughes, *Acts: The Church Afire*, Preaching the Word (Wheaton, IL: Crossway Books, 1996).

James Montgomery Boice, *Acts: An Expositional Commentary* (Grand Rapids, MI: Baker Books, 1997).

William H. Baker, "Acts," in *Evangelical Commentary on the Bible*, vol. 3, Baker Reference Library (Grand Rapids, MI: Baker Book House, 1995).

Peter Williams, *Acts: Church on the Move: An Expositional Commentary on the Acts of the Apostles*, Exploring the Bible Commentary (Leominster: DayOne, 2004).

Simon J. Kistemaker, *Exposition of the Acts of the Apostles*, vol. 17, New Testament Commentary (Grand Rapids: Baker Book House, 1953–2001).

Chalmer Ernest Faw, *Acts*, Believers Church Bible Commentary (Scottdale, PA: Herald Press, 1993).

Derek W. H. Thomas, *Acts*, ed. Richard D. Phillips, Philip Graham Ryken, and Daniel M. Doriani, Reformed Expository Commentary (Phillipsburg, NJ: P&R Publishing, 2011).

G. Campbell Morgan. *The Acts of the Apostles* (New York: Fleming H. Revell Company, 1924).

R. C. Sproul, *Acts*, St. Andrew's Expositional Commentary (Wheaton, IL: Crossway, 2010).

F. F. Bruce, *Acts: Bible Study Commentary* (Nashville, TN; Bath, England: Kingsley Books, 2017).

James M. Hamilton Jr. and Brian J. Vickers, *John–Acts*, ed. Iain M. Duguid, James M. Hamilton Jr., and Jay Sklar, vol. IX, ESV Expository Commentary (Wheaton, IL: Crossway, 2019).

Tony Merida. *Exalting Jesus in Acts* (Christ-Centered Exposition Commentary) (Nashville: B&H Publishing Group, 2017).

John B. Polhill, *Acts*, vol. 26, The New American Commentary (Nashville: Broadman & Holman Publishers, 1992).

I. Howard Marshall, *Acts: An Introduction and Commentary*, vol. 5, Tyndale New Testament Commentaries (Downers Grove, IL: InterVarsity Press, 1980).

John F. MacArthur Jr., *Acts*, vols. 1 & 2, MacArthur New Testament Commentary (Chicago: Moody Press, 1994).

Everett Harrison, *Interpreting Acts: The Expanding Church* (Grand Rapids: Zondervan, 1986).

Richard N. Longenecker, *The Expositor's Bible Commentary*, Volume 9, *John-Acts* (Grand Rapids, MI: Zondervan, 1981).

Peter H. Davids, *New International Biblical Commentary: James* (Peabody: Hendrickson Publishers, 1983).

Charles R. Swindoll, *Acts*, Swindoll's Living Insights New Testament Commentary (Carol Stream, IL: Tyndale House Publishers, Inc., 2016).

Conrad Gempf, "Acts," in *New Bible Commentary: 21st Century Edition*, ed. D. A. Carson et al., 4th ed. (Leicester, England; Downers Grove, IL: Inter-Varsity Press, 1994).

Warren W. Wiersbe, *The Bible Exposition Commentary*, vol. 1 (Wheaton, IL: Victor Books, 1996).

John Phillips. *Exploring Acts: An Expository Commentary*, The John Phillips Commentary Series (Grand Rapids, MI: Kregel Publications, 2009).

Lawrence O. Richards, *The Teacher's Commentary* (Wheaton, IL: Victor Books, 1987).

SERMONS

D.L. Moody, *The Overcoming Life and Other Sermons* (Chicago: Bible Institute Colportage Association, 1896).

Dwight Lyman Moody, *Notes from My Bible: From Genesis to Revelation* (New York: Fleming H. Revell Company, 1895).

John Piper, "You Will Be Baptized with the Holy Spirit" Sermon from Acts 1:4-5. (Minneapolis, MN: Bethlehem Baptist Church, September 23, 1990) Accessed 23 January 2021. https://desiringgod.org/messages/you-will-be-baptized-with-the-holy-spirit

Charles Haddon Spurgeon, "Christ in You" Metropolitan Tabernacle Pulpit Volume 29 (London: Passemore & Alabaster, 1873), preached May 13, 1883.

Jonathan Edwards, "A History of Redemption", *Works*, vol. 1 (Carlisle, PA: Banner of Truth Trust, 1974).

G. Campbell Morgan, *The Westminster Pulpit: The Preaching of G. Campbell Morgan, Volume 9*, "Waiting for God" (Eugene, OR: Wipf & Stock Publishers, 2012).

W.A. Criswell, "The Eternal Purpose of God," sermon, First Baptist Church of Dallas, Texas, September 27, 1970.

ANCIENT SOURCES

Jeremy W. Barrier, *The Acts of Paul and Thecla: A Critical Introduction and Commentary* (Tübingen, Germany: Gulde Druck Publishing, 2009).

Flavius Josephus, *Wars of the Jews*

Westminster Assembly, *The Westminster Confession of Faith: Edinburgh Edition* (Philadelphia: William S. Young).

Eusebius, *Historia Ecclesiae* (History of the Church).

John Chrysostom, *Homilies on the Book of Acts,* in Philip Schaff et al., eds. *A Select Library of the Nicene and PostNicene Fathers of the Christian Church.* 2 (Peabody, MA: Hendrickson, 1994).

Clement of Rome, *The First Epistle of Clement to the Corinthians*, 5:5–6 in Joseph Barber Lightfoot, *The Apostolic Fathers: A Revised Text with Introductions, Notes, Dissertations, and Translations* (New York: Macmillan, 1890).

Jerome, De Viris Illustribus (On Illustrious Men).

Martin Luther, *Luther's Works. Volume 27: Lectures on Galatians, 1535,* (Saint Louis: Concordia Publishing House, 1964).
John Calvin, *Institutes of the Christian Religion,* trans. Ford Lewis Battles, 2 vols., Library of Christian Classics 20–21 (Philadelphia: Westminster, 1960).
Richard Sibbes, *The Bruised Reed and Smoking Flax* (London: Gooch Booksellers, 1630).
John Wesley, *The Journal of John Wesley: The Founder of the Methodist Movement,* ed. Percy Livingstone Parker (New York: F.H. Revell, 1903).
Jonathan Edwards, *The Works of Jonathan Edwards, Vol. 1* (London: F. Westley & A.H. Davis, 1835).

BIOGRAPHICAL

John Pollock, *The Apostle: The Life of Paul* (John Pollock Series) (Colorado Springs, CO: David C Cook, 2012).
Elijah P. Brown, *The Real Billy Sunday: The Life and Work of Rev. William Ashley Sunday, The Baseball Evangelist* (Dayton, OH: Otterbein Press, 1914).
D.L. Moody in Roberts Liardon, *God's Generals Dwight L. Moody* (New Kensington, PA: Whitaker House, 2008).
Rev. Richard Green, *John Wesley—Evangelist* (London: Religious Tract Society, 1905; Nampa, ID: Northwest Nazarene University, 1999), http://wesley.nnu.edu/john_wesley/methodist/ch12.htm
Roland H. Bainton, *Here I Stand* (Nashville: Pierce and Smith, 1950).
Ahmed Joktan, *From Mecca to Christ: The True Story of the Son of the Meccan Mufti* (Wenatchee, WA: Proclaim Publishers, 2020).
David Livingstone in Horace Waller, *The Last Journals of David Livingstone, in Central Africa* (New York: Harper & Brothers Publishers, 1875).
Charles Haddon Spurgeon, Susannah Spurgeon, Joseph Harrald, *C.H. Spurgeon's Autobiography: 1878-1892, vol 4* (London: Passmore and Alabaster, 1900).

DICTIONARIES

Walter A. Elwell and Barry J. Beitzel, "Eschatology," *Baker Encyclopedia of the Bible* (Grand Rapids, MI: Baker Book House, 1988).

Grant R. Osborne, "Baptism," *Baker Encyclopedia of the Bible* (Grand Rapids, MI: Baker Book House, 1988).

Paul J. Achtemeier, "Providence", Harper & Row and Society of Biblical Literature, *Harper's Bible Dictionary* (San Francisco: Harper & Row, 1985).

NEW TESTAMENT

Howard Clark Kee & Franklin W. Young, *Understanding The New Testament* (Englewood Cliffs, New Jersey: Prentice Hall, Inc. 1958).

F.F. Bruce, *New Testament History* (New York: Doubleday, 1983).

E. M. Blaiklock, *The Century of the New Testament* (Downers Grove, IL: InterVarsity Press, 1962).

BACKGROUNDS

Rabbi Maurice Lamm, "The Mikveh's Significance in Traditional Conversion." My Jewish Learning. Accessed 20 February 2021. https://www.myjewishlearning.com/article/why-immerse-in-the-mikveh/

Eduard Verhoef, *Philippi: How Christianity Began in Europe: The Epistle to the Philippians and the Excavations at Philippi* (New York: T&T Clark, 2013).

Pieter W. van der Horst, *Japheth in the Tents of Shem: Studies on Jewish Hellenism in Antiquity* (Peeters: Leuven, 2002).

Nick Kampouris & G.E. Koronaios, (2022, February 20). *The History of Dionysius the Areopagite, the Patron Saint of Athens.* GreekReporter.com. Retrieved March 3, 2022, from https://greekreporter.com/2022/02/20/the-history-of-dionysius-the-areopagite-the-patron-saint-of-athens-2/

P. R. Treblico, "Asia," in *The Book of Acts in Its Graeco-Roman Setting*, ed. David W. J. Gill and Conrad H. Gempf (Grand Rapids: Eerdmans; Carlisle, UK: Paternoster, 1994).

Bruce W. Winter, "Acts and Food Shortages," in *The Book of Acts in its Graeco-Roman Setting*, ed. David W. J. Gill and Conrad Gempf, (Grand Rapids: Eerdmans, 1994).

Frank Grenville Beardsley, *A History of American Revivals* (New York: American Tract Society, 1912).

Kathryn L. Gleason, et al. "The Promontory Palace at Caesarea Maritima: Preliminary Evidence for Herod's praetorium." JRA 11 (1998).

Maurice Hassett, "Mamertine Prison" in The Catholic Encyclopedia (New York: Robert Appleton Company, 1910), vol. 9, New Advent edition online.

Charles Cochrane, *Christianity and Classical Culture* (London: Oxford University Press, 1944).

THEOLOGY

Timothy George, *Theology of the Reformers* (Nashville, TN: B&H Publishing Group, 2013).

TOPICAL

Robert Kellemen, *Gospel-Centered Counseling* (Equipping Biblical Counselors) (Grand Rapids, MI: Zondervan, 2014).

C. H. Spurgeon, *Morning and Evening* (Fearn, Ross-shire, UK: Christian Focus, 1994).

John Stott, *Through the Bible: Through the Year* (Grand Rapids: Baker, 2006).

Lou Priolo, *Keeping Your Cool* (Phillipsburg, NJ: P&R Publishing, 2014).

C. S. Lewis, *The Problem of Pain* (New York: Simon & Schuster, 1996).

John Piper, *Future Grace: The Purifying Power of the Promises of God,* revised edition (Colorado Springs, CO: Multnomah Books, 2012).

C.S. Lewis, *Surprised by Joy: The Shape of My Early Life* (Orlando, FL: Harcourt Brace & Company, 1955).

John M. Perkins, Karen Waddles, *Count It All Joy: The Ridiculous Paradox of Suffering.* (Chicago: Moody Publishers, 2021).

Amzi Clarence Dixon, *Evangelism Old and New: God's Search for Man in All Ages* (New York: American Tract Society, 1905).

D. Martyn Lloyd-Jones, *Spiritual Depression: Its Causes and Cures* (Grand Rapids, MI: Zondervan, 2016).

Charles Haddon Spurgeon, *We Endeavor: Helpful Words for Members of the Young People's Society of Christian Endeavor* (London: Passmore and Alabaster, 1897).

Charles Haddon Spurgeon, *Lectures to My Students*, (Pasadena, TX: Pilgrim Publications, 1881.

William D. Hendricks, *Exit Interviews: Revealing Stories of Why People Are Leaving Church* (Chicago: Moody Publishers, 1993).

Andrew Murray, *Waiting on God* (New York: Fleming H. Revell Company, 1894).

Lucy Ann Moll, "Bitterness: Turn It into Better-ness!" Biblical Counseling Center, May 24, 2017, https://biblicalcounselingcenter.org/how-to-kill-bitterness/.

Steven Linscott with Randall L. Frame, *Maximum Security* (Wheaton, IL: Crossway Books, 1994).

Michael Youssef, *God, Just Tell Me What to Do* (Eugene, OR: Harvest House Publishers, 2014).

Erwin W. Lutzer, *When You've Been Wronged: Moving from Bitterness to Forgiveness* (Chicago, IL: Moody Publishers, 2007).

WENATCHEE, WASHINGTON

You may obtain this, and many other fine resources made available by Proclaim Publishers by contacting us:

Web:
proclaimpublishers.com

Email:
contact@proclaimpublishers.com

Postal Mail:
Proclaim Publishers
PO Box 2082
Wenatchee, WA 98807

Soli Deo Gloria

www.ingramcontent.com/pod-product-compliance
Lightning Source LLC
Chambersburg PA
CBHW022101290426
44112CB00008B/507